DICTIONARY OF BANKING AND FINANCE

Bc

DICTIONARY
OF
BANKING
AND
FINANCE

Jerry M. Rosenberg, Ph.D.

Professor, Graduate School of Management
Chairman, Department of Business Administration
Newark College of Arts and Sciences
Rutgers University

JOHN WILEY & SONS

New York • Chichester • Brisbane • Toronto • Singapore

Library of Congress Cataloging in Publication Data:

Rosenberg, Jerry Martin.
    Dictionary of banking and finance.

    Includes index.
    1. Banks and banking—Dictionaries.   2. Finance
—Dictionaries.   I. Title.

HG151.R67   332′.03′21   81-21961
ISBN 0-471-08096-9   AACR2

Printed in the United States of America

10 9 8 7 6 5 4 3 2 1

To Lauren

with love

FOREWORD

David Rockefeller
Chase Manhattan Bank,
N.A.
Chairman and Chief
Executive Officer (retired)

As I look back over nearly 35 years as a banker, I cannot help noting how much more complex banking is now than when I began my career. It has indeed been a business of change, with the rate of change itself continually increasing.

From all indications, this rapid change in the banking business is not likely to abate. Rather, all indicators suggest that it is likely to increase geometrically in the days ahead. Increasingly responsive communications and increasingly diverse and demanding market forces have led to more complex arrangements for lending, funding, money transfers, and other bank services. At the same time, increased competition has made it necessary for financial institutions to market their products and services more vigorously and effectively.

New international financial structures which have emerged in past decades have themselves induced other changes in banking—and it is likely that more structural changes will be created in the future to serve international financial needs and markets.

Meanwhile, on the domestic scene, crumbling statutory and regulatory barriers between banks and other kinds of financial institutions, in conjunction with long overdue trends toward reduced regulation, have added new competition for commercial banks. New and more innovative competitive responses will no doubt be required.

New markets, new products, new regulatory constraints, new participants, and new competitors in the financial marketplace—all these represent challenges to clear understanding and communications in an increasingly complex and evolving business.

In this challenging atmosphere of transition and turmoil in the financial industry, effective communication—clear understanding among people and financial institutions—is absolutely fundamental to business effectiveness. Simply put, we must know how to express precisely what we mean, and we must be able to discern correctly the intended meaning of what is being said to us. The changes in our financial community, domestically and internationally, and the need to communicate more clearly make it essential that we use terminology accurately, and that we agree on the full meaning of the terms we use in our business affairs. This clarity of meaning is as important in our letters to associates and statements to the public as it is in our highly structured financial communications, letters of credit, and loan agreements.

Thus, as we face a changing business and financial environment and recognize the need to communicate more clearly, I am confident that Professor Rosenberg's dictionary of terms in banking and finance will be welcomed by the community it seeks to serve. I am particularly pleased that it reaches to the periphery of banking and financial services so that relevant terms in such areas as computer systems, organization, and manpower can be understood in their banking and financial contexts.

August, 1980

PREFACE

A revolution among financial institutions is under way. Differences between them are fading, arbitrary barriers to nationwide retail banking are threatened, and the dividing line between banking and securities is challenged.

Sweeping legislation passed in 1980—the Depository Institutions Deregulation and Monetary Control Act—ratified and extended innovation and price competition in the financial marketplace, and over the course of the next few years these changes will bring about a rationalization of the industry via interstate banking.

As the shape of financial institutions is transformed, savings and loan associations are going to take on more qualities usually attributed to commercial banks, and they will have to manage their assets and liabilities more like commercial banks.

In sum, with deregulation in banking and finance, change is bound to create a combination of threats and challenges, requiring a better awareness of the full range of strategies, options, and meanings open to all.

This dictionary is a practical guide and reference tool for proper handling of the many banking and financial problems and questions that arise in business every day. It provides a deeper understanding of operations, methods, and practices in the rapidly changing fields of banking and finance.

This work of approximately 10,000 entries has been prepared with the hope that awareness of the accepted meanings of terms may enhance the process of sharing information and ideas. Though it cannot eliminate the need for the user to determine how a writer or speaker treats a word, such a dictionary shows what usages exist. It should reduce arguments about words and assist in stabilizing terminology. Most important, it should aid people in saying and writing just what they intend with greater clarity.

A word can take on different meanings in different contexts. There may be as many meanings as there are areas of specialty. A goal of this dictionary is to be broad and to establish core definitions that represent the variety of individual meanings. My purpose is to enhance parsimony and clearness in the communication process within the banking and financial fields.

Many terms are used in different ways. I have tried to unite them without bias of giving one advantage or dominance over another. Whenever possible (without creating a controversy), I have stated the connection among multiple usages.

Commonly used symbols, acronyms, and abbreviations are given. Foreign words and phrases are included only if they have become an integral part of our English vocabulary.

Other dictionaries that deal with a similar subject tend to define their task rather narrowly, whereas this work purports to reach throughout all departments within banks and financial institutions by acknowledging that the sum of an organization is greater than any of its individual parts—the result, an all-inclusive dictionary of banking and financial terms.

The broad base in the banking and financial fields necessitated inclusion of terms within this dictionary from accounting, banking, brokerage, capital structure, capitalization, collections, commercial banking, commodities markets, computer systems, credit, credit unions, financial institutions, financial law, financial management, financial planning, financial reports, foreign trade, funding, government regulations and agencies, import-export, insurance, investments, lending, methods of financing, manpower and human resources, money concepts, mortgages, organization, personal finance, public finance, savings and loan associations, savings banks, securities markets, services, sources of bank and financial information, systems, transfers, and trusts.

ORGANIZATION

This is a defining work rather than a compilation of facts. The line is not easy to draw because in the final analysis meanings are based on facts. Consequently, factual information is used where necessary to make a term more easily understood.

All terms are presented in the language of those who use them. Obviously, the level of complexity needed for a definition will vary with the user; one person's complexity is another's precise and parsimonious statement. Several meanings are sometimes given—relatively simple for the layman, more developed and technical for the specialist.

I have organized the dictionary to provide information easily and rapidly. Keeping in mind two categories of user—the experienced person who demands precise information about a particular word, and the newcomer, support member, teacher, or student who seeks general explanations—I have in most cases supplied both general and specialized entries. This combination of "umbrella" entries and specialized definitions should make this dictionary an unusually useful reference source.

FORMAT

Alphabetization. Words are presented alphabetically. Compound terms are placed where the reader is most likely to look for them. They are entered under their most distinctive component, usually nouns, which tend to be more distinctive than are adjectives. Should you fail to locate a word where you initially look for it, turn to a variant spelling, a synonym, or another, differing word of the compound term.

Entries containing mutual concepts are usually grouped for comparison. They are then given in inverted order; that is, the expected order of words is reversed to allow the major word of the phrase to appear at the beginning of the term. These entries precede those that are given in the expected order. The terms are alphabetized up to the first comma and then by words following the comma, thus establishing clusters of related terms.

Headings. The currently popular term is usually given as the principal entry, with other terms cross-referenced to it. Some terms have been included for historical significance, even though they are not presently in common usage.

Cross-References. The rule followed for cross-references calls for going from the general to the specific. Occasionally, "see" references from the specific to the general are used to inform the user of words related to particular entries. "See" references to presently accepted terminology are made wherever possible. The use of "Cf." suggests words to be compared with the original entry.

Synonyms. The word "synonymous" following a definition does not imply that the term is exactly equivalent to the principal entry under which it appears. Usually the term only approximates the primary sense of the original entry.

Disciplines. Many words are given multiple definitions based on their utilization in various fields of activity. The definition with the widest application is then given first, with the remaining definitions listed by area of specialty (iden-

tified in boldface italic type). Since the areas may overlap, the reader should examine all multiple definitions of a term.

ACKNOWLEDGMENTS

No dictionary can be the exclusive product of one person's effort. Even when written by one individual, such a work requires the tapping of many sources, which is especially true of this book. By the very nature of the fields included, I have had to rely on the able and extensive efforts of others, especially the members of the Advisory Board.

When I have quoted a definition from another copyrighted source, a number in brackets appears at the end of the definition. This number indicates the primary reference used in defining the term which is identified in Appendix K of the dictionary. When no reference source is shown following a term, this suggests that I have not deliberately quoted the definition from any copyrighted source. Any apparent similarity to existing, unreleased definitions in these cases is purely accidental and the result of the limitations of language.

Much assistance has come indirectly from authors of books, journal articles, and reference materials. They are too numerous to be named here. Various organizations have aided me directly by providing informative source materials. Some government agencies and not-for-profit associations have provided a considerable amount of usable information.

On a more personal level, I thank the various individuals whom I used as a sounding board to clarify my ideas and approach; they offered valuable suggestions and encouraged me to go on with the project. Stephen Kippur, my editor, of John Wiley & Sons, had the foresight to initiate this book, and with sensitivity and creativity followed it through to publication. And I thank, once again, my wife Ellen and my daughters Lauren and Elizabeth, who showed understanding and offered full support during the preparation of this book.

FEEDBACK

The definitions given here have been reviewed by bank and finance specialists, and educators. However, I am solely responsible for choosing the terms to be included. The vast range of material makes it inevitable that definitions may vary based on perspective, background, and connotation. I welcome critical comments bringing errors to my attention, to make it possible to correct them in later editions, thus evolving a greater conformity of meaning for all.

JERRY M. ROSENBERG, PH.D.

New York
January, 1982

CONTENTS

DICTIONARY OF BANKING AND FINANCE

A:
  (1) see *account.*
  (2) Class "A" or Series "A."
  (3) the total average dollar inventory.
A1: the highest class rating.
AA:
  (1) see *active account.*
  (2) see *active assets.*
AAD: at a discount.
AB: see *bond adjustment.*
ABA:
  (1) see *American Bankers Association.*
  (2) see *American Bankers Association number.*
abandonment
  (1) *general:* giving up a facility without the intention of regaining possession at some later time.
  (2) *finance:* the elimination from use of a fixed asset. The total retirement of a fixed asset from service, following salvage or other reclaiming of removable parts.
  (3) *law:* with a patent, trademark, or copyright, the cession of rights by the owner, wherein his invention, design, or name falls into the public domain.
abandt: see *abandonment.*
abatement
  (1) *finance:* the cancellation of part or all of an expenditure.
  (2) *finance:* the cancellation or reduction of an assessed tax.

  (3) *law:* a reduction or pulling down, as with a nuisance.
abator: one who gains illegal possession of an estate, thus preventing the rightful heirs from obtaining possession.
ABA Transit Code: see *American Bankers Association number.*
ABC Agreement: when buying a New York Stock Exchange seat, the applicant's membership can be bought by a member firm for his use with monies advanced by the member firm.
Abe's cabe: slang, a $5 bill.
abeyance
  (1) *banking:* a temporary suspension of title to property before the correct owner is determined. See *cloud on title.*
  (2) *law:* the state of not having been settled.
ability: skill, aptitude, and other factors essential in job performance. It is measured by work records, performance measures, and other ratings designed to identify an employee's day-to-day handling of his work.
ability test: a test of performance, prepared to reveal a level of present ability (e.g., a bank teller test or a typing test).
ability to pay
  (1) *general:* the ability of the bank or financial organization's management to meet the financial demands

of a union. This capacity depends on the financial condition of the institution and is often disputed.

(2) *general:* also used regarding a borrower—that is, capacity to pay back.

(3) *finance:* a criterion used to ascertain who shall bear the cost of government programs; the rationale for taxing individuals in the form of a progressive income tax.

ab initio: "from the beginning" (Latin). For example, an individual who enters the land of another person by permission and thereafter abuses that right becomes a trespasser ab initio—that is, becomes a trespasser from the first time he walked on the property.

above par (value): the price of a stock or bond, higher than its face amount.

abrasion: weight loss in coins that results from wear in circulation.

abrogation of agreement: the cancellation or setting aside of a contract or any portion of it.

absence: an employee's temporary unavailability for work lasting for one or more days or shifts.

absenteeism: being absent from work, especially when deliberate or habitual.

absenteeism, chronic: the constant recurrence of absences.

absolute address

(1) *computers:* the actual address of a location described in terms of a machine code numbering system.

(2) synonymous with "specific address" and *machine address.*

absolute advantage: an advantage of one nation or area over another in the costs of manufacturing an item in terms of used resources.

absolute code

(1) *computers:* coding designed so that all instructions are described in basic machine language.

(2) synonymous with "specific coding".

absolute error

(1) *computers:* a form of error in which the magnitude of error is determined without regard for the algebraic sign or direction.

(2) *statistics:* the amount of error expressed in the same units as the quantity holding the error.

absolute ownership: where the interest or exclusive right of possession of the insured is so free from limitations, restrictions, or qualifications that it cannot be taken from him without his consent. [56]

absolute priority rule: the concept that creditors' rights must be satisfied prior to stockholders' equities following liquidations or corporate reorganizations.

absolute title: a title without any conditions. An absolute title is usually critical to the granting of a mortage by a bank.

absorb

(1) *general:* to merge by transfer all or portions of an account with another account, resulting in the loss of identity of the first account.

(2) *finance:* to include pertinent actual costs in determining a price or standard cost.

(3) *investments:* to assimilate sell orders of stock with offsetting requests to buy.

absorbed: designates a security, no longer in the hands of an underwriter, and now with a shareholder.

absorbtion account: see *adjunct account.*

absorption point: the point at which the securities market rejects further offerings unaccompanied by price concessions. see *digested securities, undigested securities.*

abstinence concept: a theory according to which a postponement in the use of an item involves a cost that should be reimbursed by a payment such as interest.

abstract: a brief summary of a potential employee's background, interests, and other relevant information.

abstraction of bank funds: laws dealing with criminal offenses in the banking field. For example, embezzlement, abstraction, or willful misapplication of bank funds are misdemeanors and punishable by fine up to $5,000 and/or imprisonment for five years.

abstract of title: an attorney's prepared statement tracing the history of the ownership of real property to determine the present title. see *deed, encumbrance, search, title deed, title insurance.*

abutting: joining or adjacent; contiguous to another property. This variable is clearly identified in the granting of a bank mortgage.

AC
(1) see *account current.*
(2) see *active capital.*

A/C: see *account.*

ACB: see *Associated Credit Bureaus of America, Inc.*

Acc.
(1) accept.
(2) accepted.
(3) see *account.*

accelerated depreciation: deprecia-

tion at a larger than expected rate; makes the depreciation allowance, therefore the tax allowance, available sooner, resulting in a benefit to the owner.

accelerating premium pay: a wage incentive system under which the bonus or premium is progressively higher as the production standard is exceeded.

acceleration: by law, when an installment obligation goes into default, all remaining installments become immediately due and payable; thus suit can be brought for the entire unpaid balance. see *recomputation.* [55]

acceleration clause
(1) *banking:* the statement that a debt must be paid in total in the event of default of any of its covenants.
(2) *law:* a clause included in the body of a contract, stipulating that the entire balance shall become due immediately and payable in the event of a breach of certain other conditions of the contract, such as insolvency or the debtor's failure to pay taxes on the mortgaged property.

accelerator: see *marginal propensity to invest.*

acceptability: an attitude toward money resulting in its acceptance as a medium of exchange in the marketplace. see *eligible paper, rediscount.*

acceptance: a time draft (bill of exchange) on the face of which the drawee has written "accepted" over his signature. The date and place payable are also indicated. The person accepting the draft is known as the acceptor. A "bank acceptance" is a draft drawn on and accepted by a bank. see *bank acceptance, draft, trade acceptance.*

acceptance credit: commercial banks and foreign banking institutions are able to participate in the acceptance practice to assist in financing import-export and domestic transactions by establishing an acceptance credit with a bank. see *bank acceptance, letter of credit.*

acceptance for honor: the receiving of a draft or bill of exchange by another party when collection has been rejected by the drawee and protest for nonacceptance has been claimed. cf. *notice of dishonor.*

acceptance house: an organization that specializes in lending funds on the security of bills of exchange or offers its name as an endorser to a bill drawn on another party.

acceptance liability: a bank's full liability that has been accepted in handling bills drawn on it by customers for financing domestic, import, or export business. Banks are required by law to keep a record of the total of the liability by such acceptances in an account called liability on account of acceptances. see *acceptance credit, acceptance line, letter of credit.*

acceptance liability ledger: a ledger listing the bills accepted for each bank customer entered under an account containing his name, including name and address of customer, line, date, letter of credit number, acceptance number, expiration date, bill amount, total amount accepted or expired, and payment date. see *acceptance liability.*

acceptance line: the maximum limit in monies that a bank commits itself to accept for a single client.

acceptance maturity tickler: an accounting where acceptances are listed in order of maturity dates so that the amount of daily maturities can be grasped quickly. One page is usually given to the maturities for each day. see *tickler.*

acceptance register: a record containing details on all bills accepted by a bank for its depositors. Listed by date, these entries include date of acceptance, bank's acceptance number, name of bank representative giving authorization, signature of representative, customer's number of bill, date, tenor, maturity, drawee, payee, amount, list of document collected, affixed original or duplicates, number, and credit date.

acceptance supra protest: following a protest, the payment of a bill to preserve the reputation or credit of the drawer or endorser.

acceptor: the drawee of a note for acceptance, who upon signing the form, agrees to pay a draft or bill when due.

access: the process or act of putting financial data into computer storage or retrieving data from the computer.

accession
(1) *general:* the hiring of a new employee or the rehiring of a former worker.
(2) *banking:* elevation to a higher office within the bank.
(3) *law:* the doctrine that the property owner is entitled to all that is added or affixed to the property.

accession rates: the average number of persons added to a payroll in a given period per 100 employees. see *turnover.*

access right: the right of an owner of property or another person with the owner's approval to enter, enjoy, or leave the property without obstruction. If the property abuts on a public way, this is called a direct access right. If there is other property intervening between the owned property and the public way, the right is known as an easement right.

access time

(1) *computers:* the time interval between the instant at which data are requested from a storage device and the moment delivery begins.

(2) *computers:* the time interval between the moment data become ready for storage and the instant storage is terminated.

accidental death benefit: a benefit in addition to the face amount of a life insurance policy, payable if the insured dies as the result of an accident. Sometimes referred to as *double indemnity.* [58]

accident severity: a measure of the amount of time lost as the result of an accident.

accommodation: historically, the lending of currency by a person who has it to another who has need of it, without collateral. More popularly, the lending of a person's honor or credit, without any consideration, to enable another to obtain borrowed money.

accommodation bill (of lading): a bill of lading issued by a common carrier before receipt of items for shipment. see *bill of lading.*

accommodation charge: a single purchase when credit is arranged on a temporary basis without the need to open a regular credit account. synonymous with "this transaction only."

accommodation check: a check drawn by an association on its account with a bank, payable to a third party named by the saver making the withdrawal. [59]

accommodation endorsement: the signature or endorsement of a note or draft solely for the purpose of inducing a bank to lend money to a borrower whose personal credit is not substantial enough to warrant a loan.

accommodation endorser: a person who endorses a negotiable instrument for the accommodation of another person or parties, having no ownership right but simply guaranteeing the fulfillment of the contract to subsequent holders of the instrument. see *endorsement; endorser.*

accommodation note: any note that has received an accommodation endorsement.

accommodation paper: a promissory note, endorsed by an individual(s), allowing the original signer of the note to receive bank credit; thus the second or other signer(s) accept the guarantee of credit.

accommodation party: one who signs a note as maker, drawer, acceptor, or endorser without receiving value, although remaining totally liable for the purpose of lending the credit worthiness of his or her name to another person. see *accommodation paper.*

accord and satisfaction: an agreement between two people, one of whom has a right of action against the other, that the latter should do or give, and that the former accepts, something in satisfaction of the right of action that is different from, and often less than, what might be enforced by law.

account: a record of all the transactions and the date of each, affecting a particular phase of a bank or financial institution, expressed in debits and credits, evaluated in money, and showing the current balance, if any. see *bank account.*

accountabilities: assets, liabilities, items held in trust, and the like, for which an individual, organization, or other legal entity renders an accounting. For example, when bank officials give an accounting of the disbursed funds entrusted to their care, the items are referred to as accountabilities.

accountability: the management process by which a person is evaluated on the basis of end results.

account activity: all transactions on individual or group accounts, including, for example, debts, credits, and status changes.

account analysis: the process of determining and explaining the profit or loss on any account by means of systematic procedures.

account and risk: based on a relationship between a customer and his broker. Serving as the customer's agent, the broker will execute, buy, and sell orders at the risk of the customer.

accountant: an individual engaged in accounting work. cf. *certified public accountant.*

accountant's certificate: a report prepared by an independent accountant or auditor addressed to stockholders, directors, or owners of the firm that has been audited. The form and scope of the audit is stated and an expression of the fairness of the appended financial statement is given.

account balance: the net debit or net credit amount in a specific account in the ledger. An excess of total debits over total credits results in a debit balance, whereas an excess of total credits over total debits results in a credit balance.

account current: a statement posting the debits and credits of a depositor and the balance at the end of the accounting period or cycle billing time.

account day: the day identified by stock and commodity exchanges for the settlement of accounts between members. synonymous with *settlement day.*

account debtor: an individual who is obligated on an account, contract right, or general intangible.

account executive: see *registered representative.*

account hold: a warning placed on a savings, loan, or other account to indicate the need for special handling. [59]

account in balance: an account where the debit and credit footings are equal.

accounting: the art, science, interpretation, and organized method of recording all transactions affecting the financial condition of a given business or organization.

accounting cycle: the series of accounting activities that occur from the commencement of an accounting period to the end of that period. The cycle begins with the determination of the account balance at the beginning of the period; then the effects of transactions occurring during the period are recorded, the records are closed, and financial statements for the period are prepared.

accounting period: the 12-month period used for keeping a taxpayer's records. When the accounting period ends other than in the month of December, a fiscal year is established. For income tax purposes a special 52–53–week accounting period is also acknowledged. cf. *fiscal year.*

accounting processes: the classification of accounts, accounting records, forms, procedures and controls through which changes in asset, liability, reserves, capital, income, and expense account transactions are generally recorded and controlled. [59]

accounting rate of return: income for a period divided by the average investment that has occurred during that period.

accounting system: the total structure of records and procedures that discover, record, classify, and report information on the financial position and operations of a governmental unit or any of its funds, balanced account groups, and organizational components. [49]

account in trust: an account opened by an individual to be held in trust and maintained for the benefit of another. In the absence of a legally constituted trust fund, withdrawals from the account are subject to the approval of the individual who has established the account. see *Totten trust.*

account number: the numerical identification given to an account in a given institution or business, such numerical identification being a part of and in direct harmony with the whole system of numerical descrip-

tion given to the accounts as a whole that exist in that institution or business. cf. *American Bankers Association number.*

account reconciliation plan (ARP): a program using the auxiliary On-Us field on MICR checks to give high–volume accounts a list and the sum of paid and/or outstanding checks in numerical serial sequence and to assist in the balance of the bank's statement to the customer's check register.

account sales: a record prepared by a broker, consignee, or other agent, indicating the proceeds of goods or securities purchased for the account of the owner.

accounts payable: a current liability representing the amount owed by an individual or a business to a creditor for merchandise or services purchased on an open account or short-term credit. see *accounts payable account.*

accounts payable account: an account in the general ledger showing the full amount owed to creditors for items bought on account; the title of the general ledger controlling account that affects the accounts payable ledger and that indicates the sum owed to creditors on account.

accounts receivable: money owed a business enterprise for merchandise bought on open account. see *accounts receivable account.*

accounts receivable account: the title of the general ledger controlling account that affects the accounts receivable ledger and indicates the sum to be collected on account from all of the firm's customers.

accounts receivable financing: the

securing of working capital by borrowing with accounts receivable as collateral, or by selling accounts receivable outright. The latter is referred to as factoring.

accounts receivable turnover: used in determining credit risks; the determination of how rapidly accounts receivables are turned over—that is, when credit conditions are met as indicated by collections.

account stated: the understanding and liability of a debtor that an account or bill presented is valid if it has not been questioned by the debtor within a reasonable time period.

Accrd. Int.: see *accrued interest.*

Accred.: accredited.

accretion account: a record of the increase between the acquisition value and the face value of bonds purchased at a discount.

accrual basis: the basis of accounting under which revenues are recorded when earned and expenditures are recorded as soon as they result in liabilities for benefits received, notwithstanding that the receipt of the revenue or the payment of the expenditure may take place, in whole or in part, in another accounting period. see *accrue(d), levy.* [49]

accrual of discount: the yearly addition to book value of bonds that have been bought below par. see *amortization.*

accrual system: a method of recording and apportioning expense and income for the period in which each is involved, regardless of the date of payment or collection.

accrue(d)
(1) *general:* to gain or profit by.
(2) *finance:* to accumulate, grow,

or add in an orderly fashion (e.g., interest accrues on invested funds).
(3) *law:* to become eligible for a right or claim.

accrued assets: interest, commission, services offered, and items of revenue neither received nor past due but earned (e.g., accrued dividends).

accrued charges: as contrasted with payment in advance, charges that though known are not yet due (e.g., margin payment).

accrued depreciation: depreciation, or loss in value, that has occurred during a specified period. [59]

accrued dividend: the customary, regular dividend considered to be earned but not declared or payable on legally issued stock or other instruments of part ownership of a legally organized business or financial institution.

accrued expenses: expenses that are recognized by a firm prior to that firm's disbursement of cash. Accrued expenses arise when a company has used goods or services before it has paid for them.

accrued income: income earned (e.g., commissions or interest on notes receivable) but not received.

accrued interest: a bond's accumulated interest made since the last interest payment. The purchaser of the bond pays the market price plus accrued interest. Bonds that are in default and income bonds are exceptions. see *flat.*

accrued interest payable: interest accumulated on an indebtedness (e.g., time deposits or borrowed money) but not yet paid.

accrued interest receivable: interest

earned by a bank but not yet collected.

accrued liabilities: liabilities arising from expenses that have been incurred but have not yet been paid. Accrued liabilities are the counterpart of *prepaid expenses*.

accumulate: a purchase by traders who hope to retain the contracts for a more or less extended period.

accumulated: added onto what had previously been in existence.

accumulated dividend: a dividend not paid when due. The dividend is expected to be paid at a later time, but it becomes a business liability until payment.

accumulated earnings tax: a tax on earnings accumulated beyond the business requirement of the frm. By design, it attempts to tax corporations on earnings that have been kept for no apparent business purpose.

accumulated interest: unpaid interest payments that are past due.

accumulated profit tax: a tax penalty directed at corporations that avoid announcing dividends to reduce stockholders' declarations of additional income.

accumulated surplus: a corporation's excess of profits that are either reinvested or held.

accumulation
(1) *banking:* the opposite of amortization: a percentage added to life insurance benefits as a form of reward for continuous renewal.
(2) *finance:* adding income from dividends, interest, and other sources to the principal amount of a fund, and the treatment of such additions as capital.
(3) *investments:* the deliberate,

well-controlled assembling of blocks of stock without necessarily bidding up prices.
(4) *investments:* profits that are not distributed to stockholders as dividends but instead are transferred to a capital account.

accumulation plan: a schedule that permits an investor to buy mutual fund shares on a regular basis in differing amounts, with provisions for the investment of income dividends and the acceptance of capital gains distribution in additional shares. Such plans can be either voluntary or contractual.

accumulative: see *cumulative.*

accumulative dividend: see *cumulative dividends.*

accumulator
(1) *computers:* a device in which the result of an arithmetic or logic operation is determined.
(2) *computers:* a register that stores a quantity. When a second quantity is entered, it arithmetically combines the quantity and stores the result in the location of the register.

ACE
(1) see *Amex Commodities Exchange.*
(2) slang, a one-dollar bill.

ACH: see *automated clearinghouse.*

achievement battery: a collection of tests designed to measure a level of skill or knowledge attained in several areas.

achievement test: a measure of proficiency level determined by testing performance displayed in a particular field. It is designed to determine the relative excellence of an individual's past learning.

acid test ratio: a credit barometer

used by lending institutions; indicates the ability of a business enterprise to meet its current obligations. The formula used to determine the ratio is

$$\frac{\text{cash + receivables} + \text{marketable securities}}{\text{current liabilities}}$$

Usually a 1 : 1 ratio is considered to be satisfactory.

Ack.

(1)   acknowledge.

(2)   see *acknowledgment.*

acknowledgment

(1)   *general:* on a document, a signature that has received certification from an authorized person.

(2)   *banking:* a written notification that an item, now received, is available for its immediate payment.

(3)   *law:* a statement that a proper document has been submitted.

Ac. Pay.: see *accounts payable.*

Acpt.

(1)   accept.

(2)   see *acceptance.*

Acq.: see *exchange acquisition.*

acquired surplus

(1)   the surplus of an enterprise existing at the date of its acquisition by another enterprise.

(2)   the initial surplus of a successor enterprise where there has been a pooling of interests and no full capitalization of surplus. The initial surplus may be paid-in surplus or retained earnings or both, depending on the nature of the predecessor. [43]

acquisition: a general term for the taking over of one company by another. see *amalgamation, merger.*

acquisition cost

(1)   *banking:* monies paid in order to obtain property title prior to the granting of a mortgage.

(2)   *finance:* the cost to a company of securing business; primarily commissions to agents and brokers.

acquittance: a document giving written evidence of the discharge of, or freedom from, a debt or financial obligation.

Acrd.: see *accrue(d).*

Ac. Rec.: see *accounts receivable.*

acronym: a word formed from the first letter or letters of words in a term, title, or proper name (e.g., COBOL for common business-oriented language).

across the board

(1)   *general:* applying to all, in a uniform fashion.

(2)   *investments:* referring to the unified price activity of the daily securities market, as when described as being weak, slow, strong, or active across the board.

across-the-board increase: a general pay increase affecting equally all or most of the employees covered by a contract. May be expressed as a percentage or in cents per hour.

Acs. Pay.: see *accounts payable.*

Acs. Rec.: see *accounts receivable.*

action

(1)   *investments:* the performance by a stock with respect to trading volume and price trend.

(2)   *investments:* in France, a share of stock.

(3)   *law:* the legal demand for rights as asked of a court.

action ex contractu: an action at law to receive damages for breach of a responsibility specified in a contract. The action can arise out of contract (ex contractu) or out of tort (ex delicto). cf. *action ex delicto.*

action ex delicto: an action at law to receive damages arising out of an infraction of a civil or criminal law (e.g., receiving damages for personal injury created by negligent use of a car). Tort, or wrong, is the reason for the action. cf. *action ex contractu.*

active account
(1) *banking:* an account in which bank deposits or withdrawals are frequent.
(2) *investments:* an account handled by one broker who makes frequent purchases and sales.

active assets: company assets that are used for daily operations of the firm.

active bad debt account: an account charged off but judged to be collectible at a later date. see *inactive bad debt account.* [55]

active capital: capital that is continuously used in profit-making activities.

active corporation: an organization that maintains a system for operating property or administering its financial affairs.

active crowd: the New York Stock Exchange's Bond Department for the trading of active bonds. These bonds are usually convertible bonds and are only a small percentage of the total bonds traded. see *cabinet crowd.* synonymous with *free crowd.*

active market: characterized by numerous transactions in securities trading. see *New York Stock Exchange.*

active money: currency in circulation.

active partner: a partner of an organization who participates actively in the firm's operations for the benefit of all

associates.

active securities: stocks and bonds that are actively traded each day and where quotations on these transactions are available to the public.

active stock: a specific stock issue that has a continuous broad market and is sold and purchased with ease.

active trade balance: a balance of trade that is favorable.

active trust: a trust where the trustee has a specific role to perform, as contrasted with a passive, bare, dry, or naked trust. see *trust.*

activity
(1) *banking:* a sign that a record in a bank's file has moved or has been referred to.
(2) *banking:* any data resulting in use or modification of the data in a bank or financial institution's master file.
(3) *computers:* indicating the percentage of records in a file that are processed.

activity charge: a service charge imposed on checking account depositors by banks for check or deposit activity, where the average balances maintained are not enough to compensate for the cost of handling the items. see *checking account.*

acts of bankruptcy: any act listed under Section 3 of the National Bankruptcy Act, the most common being the inability to settle debts of not less than $1000 as they mature and voluntarily appearing in a bankruptcy court or undergoing involuntary bankruptcy where unpaid creditors petition the bankruptcy court. see *bankruptcy.*

Act to Regulate Commerce of 1887: federal legislation regulating the practices, rates, and rules of firms engaged in transportation in interstate commerce. Known in its current amended state as the Interstate Commerce Act.

actual: any physical commodity.

actual cash value: the cost of repairing or replacing damaged property with other of like kind and quality in the same physical condition; commonly defined as replacement cost less depreciation.

actually outstanding: applied to securities that have actually been issued and not reacquired by or for the issuing corporation.

actuals: an actual physical commodity; as distinguished from *futures*.

actual value: the price that property commands when sold on the open market.

actuarial: related to a bank's insurance mathematics and the application of statistics.

actuary: an individual, often holding a professional degree, whose primary functions include determining rates and rating systems, determining reserves against future liabilities for corporate and rate-making purposes, and designing and interpreting experience systems. see *insurance*.

Act. Val.:   see *actual value*.

ACUs: see *Asian Currency Units*.

ACV: see *actual cash value*.

AD

(1)   see *accrued dividend*.

(2)   see *after date*.

(3)   anno Domini (in the year of our Lord).

(4)   ante diem (before the day).

(5)   see *availability date*.

ADA: see *Airlines Deregulation Act*.

ad damnum clause: a clause in a plaintiff's complaint or statement that makes the demand for damages and declares the monies involved.

added-value tax: see *value-added tax*.

addendum: "thing added" (Latin). An addition to an agreement, contract, or written statement.

additional insured: a person, other than the one identified as the insured in a policy, who is also protected, either by being listed as an additional insured, or by definition, according to the terms of the policy.

additions: any supplemental fixed asset that yields greater capacity without replacing existing capacity. The addition of a wing to an existing structure is an example of an addition.

add-on charge: a method, no longer permissible, of advertising an interest rate on installment loans that understates the true interest rate. [78]

add-on clause: a provision allowing additional purchases on an existing installment credit agreement, normally stating that default in making payments on the additional purchases constitutes default on all purchases. [78]

add-on purchase: combining a new purchase with an older one, adding it to an existing installment contract. [28]

add-on rate: an installment finance technique where the rate is computed on the advance. The factor for each maturity is pro rata per annum of the rate. Five percent add-on means $5 per $100 for one year, $10 per $100 for two years, etc., on monthly and seasonal contracts.

add-ons: additional cash or remittance letters prepared to be included with letters previously sent on the same business day. Each add-on contains the total of its letter and the grand total of all items sent. Preparing and sending several letters during the day reduces the work load at the end of the day. see *cash letter, remittance letter.* [10]

address
(1) *general:* the location of a customer.
(2) *banking:* the location of a mortgaged structure or property.
(3) *computers:* an identification, as represented by a name, label, or number for a location or any other data source.

address of record: the official or primary location for an individual, company, or other organization.

address register: a register in which an address is stored in a computer.

ad hoc: "for this" (Latin). Refers to a specific situation; for one purpose only.

ad idem: "to the same point or effect" (Latin).

Adj.: see *adjustment.*

adjacent property: property near to or in the immediate vicinity of the insured property which may increase the hazard of loss. [56]

adjoining property: property that touches in some part the insured property. As distinguished from *adjacent property.* [56]

adjudicate: to carry out judicial authority by hearing, trying, and identifying the claims of litigants at court.

adjudication: the resolution of a dispute by a court or tribunal. Specifically, the act of a court's declaring a person bankrupt.

adjunct account: an account that

adds to another existing account, represented by transfers from another account (e.g., the balances of related accounts are combined when preparing a financial statement). synonymous with *absorption account.*

adjustable life insurance: a type of insurance that allows the insured to switch the type of protection, raise or lower the face amount of the policy, increase or decrease the premium, and lengthen or shorten the protection period. [58]

adjustable mortgage rate: see *variable-rate mortgages.*

adjustable peg: a system permitting changes in the par rate of foreign exchange after a country has had long-run disequilibrium in its balance of payments. It also allows for short-run variations within a narrow range of a few percentage points around the par value.

adjusted capital funds: used in determining a bank's capital adequacy ratios—the change in book total of capital funds indicating more precise availability of capital cushion to risk assets—for establishing the risk asset ratio.

adjusted gross estate: the value of an estate after all allowable deductions have reduced the gross estate, but before federal estate taxes. [34]

adjusted gross income: an individual's gross income minus business expenses, deductions for income-producing property, some property losses, self-employment expenses, and moving expenses. Used primarily in federal income tax returns.

adjusted monetary base (AMB): a measure that is intended to isolate the effects of Federal Reserve actions that affect the money stock in a single summary measure. see *reserve adjustment magnitude.* [79]

adjuster: an individual who reviews a bank customer's complaint concerning service or accuracy, with the authority to find an appropriate remedy.

adjustment: a change in an account to correct an incorrect entry or for some other sound reason.

adjustment bond: see *bond, adjustment.*

adjustment mortgage: any mortgage that has been released out of a reorganization.

adjustment preferred securities: preferred stock that has resulted from an adjustment of claims in a restructuring of the company.

adjustments: deductions made to charge off losses, as with bad debts or the sale of commodities.

ad litem: for purposes of a suit; for a suit's duration. see *guardian ad litem.*

administered price: the price established under situations of imbalanced competition wherein one business has some degree of control.

administration
(1) *general:* designates those who determine purpose and policy in an organization.
(2) *law:* the management and settling of the estate of an intestate person, under a commission from a proper authority.

administration board: a retirement board or retirement committee charged with the policy direction of a retirement system. The board may consist of representatives of the employer and employees, and sometimes pensioners. An administrative board is also frequently referred to as the pension board or retirement board. [2]

administrative expenses: expenses chargeable to the managerial and policy-making phases of a business. cf. *cost.*

administrative law: laws emanating from regulations of a government agency that is responsible for carrying out statute law. Administrative law is distinguished from common law or statute law.

administrative provisions: provisions in a will or trust agreement setting forth the duties and powers of the executor or the trustee regarding the care and management of the property; to be distinguished from *dispositive provisions.* [37]

administrator:
(1) *general:* a key executive in an organization.
(2) *banking:* a qualified individual or bank appointed by a court of law to manage and distribute the estate of a person who died intestate (without leaving a will) or leaving a will that fails to name an executor. see *executor, letter of administration.*

administrator ad colligendum: an administrator appointed to collect foreign assets. [37]

administrator ad litem: an administrator appointed by the court to supply a party to an action at law or in equity in which the decedent or his representative was, or is, a necessary party. [37]

administrator cum testamento annexo (administrator with the will annexed): An individual or a trust institution appointed by a court to settle the estate of a deceased person in accordance with the terms of his or her will when no executor has been named in the will or when the one named has failed to qualify. [37]

administrator cum testamento annexo de bonis non (administrator with the will annexed as to property not yet distributed): an individual or a trust institution appointed by a court to complete the settlement of the estate of a deceased person in accordance with the terms of his or her will when the executor or the administrator with the will annexed has failed to continue in office. [37]

administrator de bonis non (administrator as to property not yet distributed): an individual or a trust institution appointed by a court to complete the settlement of the estate of a person who has died without leaving a valid will when the administrator originally appointed has failed to continue in office. [37]

administrator de son tort: an individual or corporation charged with the duties and liabilities of an administrator, although not appointed one, because of his or its own wrongdoing with respect to assets in his or its possession. [37]

administrator durante absentia: an administrator appointed by the court to serve during the absence of the executor or administrator. [37]

administrator pendente lite: an individual or a trust institution appointed by a court to take over and safeguard an estate during a suit over an alleged will, or over the right of appointment of an executor or administrator. [37]

administrator's deed: see *deed, administrator's.*

administrator with the will annexed: an individual or a trust institution appointed by a court to settle the estate of a deceased person in accordance with the terms of his or her will when no executor has been named in the will or when the one named has failed to qualify. [37]

administratrix: the feminine form of "administrator."

admission by investment: the addition to a partnership of a new partner who contributes more cash to the business, thus increasing the assets and the number of owners of the firm.

admission temporaire: the free entry of goods normally dutiable for the purpose of processing items for export.

admitted assets: used when reporting claims with the state's insurance departments, those assets that can be identified under the rules and regulations of the state's insurance laws.

admitted to dealings: following approval by the SEC, a security can be officially listed and traded on an exchange.

ADP
(1) *computers:* automatic data processing; used to describe equipment.
(2) *computers:* processing of information by a system of electromechanical interacting to minimize the intervention of human beings.
(3) also referred to as integrated data processing.

ADR: see *American depositary receipt.*

ad referendum: indicating that even though a contract has been signed, specific issues remain to be considered.

Ad. Val.: see *ad valorem.*

ad valorem: according to value. Rates or duty on a percentage of the invoice value, not on weight or quantity. see *tariff.*

ad valorem taxes: real-estate taxes determined by the value of the property. see *land tax.*

advance

(1) *general:* a price increase.

(2) *banking:* a loan.

(3) *finance:* a payment on account made prior to the due date.

(4) *finance:* a rise in value or cost.

(5) *investments:* an increase in the price of stocks.

advance bill: a bill of exchange drawn prior to the shipment of goods.

advanced optical character reader (AOCR): a new generation of optical character readers capable of storing approximately 90 fonts of typewritten addresses.

advance funding: a method for making contributions to a pension plan in advance of the date when the funds are actually required to meet payments for benefits. Actuarial reserve financed pension plans imply advance funding. [52]

advancement

(1) *general:* a promotion.

(2) *finance:* money paid in advance.

(3) *law:* a gift made to a child of a portion of what will ultimately be that individual's share of an intestate's estate.

advance premium: payment made at the beginning of the period covered by an insurance policy. [56]

advance refunding: used in public debt refinancing. Possessors of a government security maturing soon are able to exchange their securities ahead of the due date for others that mature at a later time. By this process, the national debt is extended.

advantage: favorable state or circumstances; superiority over a competitor.

adventure

(1) *finance:* a speculative undertaking involving the sale of goods overseas at the best available price.

(2) *investments:* a security flotation by a syndicate; a joint venture.

(3) see entries under *venture.*

adverse action

(1) the refusal to grant credit in the amount or under the terms requested.

(2) the termination of an account.

(3) the refusal to increase the amount of an existing credit line when the applicant requested it in accordance with the creditor's procedures.

(4) an unfavorable change in terms that affects only some of the debtors. [78]

adverse claim: as applied to a bank account, a claim to ownership by a person other than the one in whose name the account has been entered. [39]

adverse possession: acquiring of property by a person who does not have title, or who has a defective title to it.

advice book: a statement of incoming and outgoing advices. see *advices.*

advice department: a department within the bank that processes advices. see *advices.*

advice fate item: see *wire fate item.*

advices: the term "advices" connotes several types of forms used in the banking field. Generally speaking, an advice is a form of letter that relates or acknowledges a certain activity or result with regard to a depositor's relations with a bank. Examples include credit advice, debit advice, advice of payment, and advice of execution. In commercial transactions, information on a business transaction such as a shipment of goods. [10]

adviser: the organization employed by a mutual fund to give professional advice on its investments and management of its assets. [23]

AE: see *accommodation endorsement.*

A&F: August and February (semiannual interest payments).

affairs, statement of: a declaration indicating the estimated results of liquidating a financially depressed firm, frequently prepared for creditors or for a receiver or court of bankruptcy.

affiant: one who makes an affidavit.

affidavit: a written, notarized, dated, and sworn statement of the facts pertaining to a financial transaction or civil event. Such a statement must show the name and address of the affiant, be signed by that person, and bear the signature of the attesting official (e.g., a notary).

affidavit of claim: the form required when filing a claim. In general, it contains the information on which the claim is based.

Affil.: see *affiliate.*

affiliate: a legal term described in the Banking Act of 1933, pertaining to any organization which a bank owns or controls by stock holdings, or which the bank's shareholders possess, or whose officers are also directors of the bank. see *subsidiary.*

affiliated company: under the Investment Company Act, a company in which there is any direct or indirect ownership of 5 percent or more of the outstanding voting securities. [30]

affiliation

(1) *general:* adoption as a member or branch.

(2) *labor relations:* the association of a local or international union with a larger group (e.g., of a state, national, or international labor union federation).

affinity: relationship by marriage; to be distinguished from consanguinity, which is relationship by blood. [37]

affirmative action: positive steps taken by banks and other financial organizations to remedy imbalances in their employment of members of minority groups. see *Federal Contract Compliance Office.*

affluent society: term popularized by John Kenneth Galbraith to describe a wealthy nation, most of whose citizens enjoy an abundance of material items.

affreightment: an agreement for chartering a carrier for the movement of goods.

afghani: monetary unit of Afghanistan.

AFH: see *acceptance for honor.*

AFL: see *American Federation of Labor.*

AFL-CIO: see *American Federation of Labor–Congress of Industrial Organizations.*

a fortiori: "by a stronger reason" (Latin). Since conclusions are made from stated and accepted facts, there are other facts that logically follow to make the conclusion even stronger.

AFT: see *automatic fund transfers.*

after-acquired clause: a section of the mortgage stating that any additional property which the mortgagor acquires after the mortgage is drawn will also be used as security for the loan.

after-acquired property: property acquired by a corporation subsequent to the execution of a mortgage or by a testator subsequent to the making of his or her will. [37]

after-born child: a child born after the execution of the parent's will; to be distinguished from "posthumous child." [37]

after date: used in bills of exchange and notes; the stated maturity of the instrument.

after market: the market that automatically exists once a corporation's securities have been offered for sale to the public. see *go public.*

after sight: used in a bill to determine the due date of payment and meaning "after the bill is given to the drawee for acceptance."

AG: silver (from *argentum*).

against actuals: see *exchange of spot.*

against the box: in a short sale of stock, a person selling against the box actually owns the security sold short but prefers not to or cannot deliver the stock to the buyer. The result is that, through a broker, he or she borrows the stock in order to make delivery. see *short sale.*

age change: the date halfway between natural birthdays when the age of an individual, for the purposes of life insurance rating, changes to the next higher age.

Age Discrimination in Employment Act of 1967: federal legislation that bans employers of 20 or more workers from firing or refusing to hire an individual 40 to 65 years of age simply because of age—unless age is a bona fide qualification; forbids employment agencies to refuse to refer a job applicant because of age and to indulge in other discriminatory practices. Violators of the law face penalties. Amended in 1978, it raised from 65 to 70 the age at which an employer can require workers to retire involuntarily.

agency: a term used to describe certain types of accounts in trust institutions. The main distinguishing characteristic of an agency is that the title to the property does not pass to the trust institution but remains in the name of the owner of the property, who is known as the principal. [32]

agency bond: see *bond, agency.*

agency coupled with an interest: an agency in which the agent has a legal interest in the subject matter. Such an agency is not terminated, as are other agencies, by the death of the principal but continues in effect until the agent can realize upon his legal interest. [37]

Agency for International Development (AID): agency in the U.S. Department of State charged with coordinating overseas economic assistance.

agency shop: the result of a provision of collective agreement stating that nonunion employees in the bargaining unit must pay the union a sum equal to union fees and dues as a condition of continuing employment. Nonunion workers are not required to join the union, however. The agency shop is the most commonly encountered union security measure in the public sector.

agenda: a listing of activities to be carried out during a meeting.

agent: an individual authorized by a bank or financial institution to act in behalf of another person, the principal. Banks are also appointed by individuals to act as their agents.

agent de change: a member of the Paris Bourse (stock exchange).

aggregate: any total (e.g., the gross national product; the sum of monthly sales).

aggregate balance: the calculated accumulation of account balances during the statement period. Used to determine the *average daily balance.* [31]

aggregate contractual liability: the total amount of money which an insurance company will pay under the terms of liability policy for claims that arise as a result of liability assumed by the insured under contracts. [56]

aggregate corporation: an incorporated venture having more than one stockholder.

aggregate demand: the total of personal consumption expenditures, business investments, and government spending.

aggregate economics: see *macroeconomics.*

aggregate supply: the capacity of a country's total resources to produce real goods and services.

aggressive growth fund: a mutual fund whose investment objective is capital appreciation. Most investments are in common stocks of higher growth potential and risk.

AGI: see *adjusted gross income.*

aging of receivables: an accounting check that analyzes the time interval between the date of sale and the current date; used to evaluate the adequacy of a firm's allowance for uncollectable accounts. see *accounts receivable turnover.*

agio
(1) *finance:* a premium paid for the exchange of one nation's currency for that of another's. cf. *disagio.*
(2) *finance:* the sum given above a nominal value, as in "the agio of exchange."
(3) *finance:* the rate of exchange among differing countries.

agreement: a mutual understanding between two or more persons, requiring a consideration.

agreement, collective bargaining: a written agreement (contract) arrived at as the result of negotiation between an employer or a group of employers and a union, which sets the conditions of employment and the procedure to be used in settling disputes that may arise during the term of the contract.

agreement for deed: a contract describing additional property payments and conditions; the deed will be delivered and title will pass after fulfillment of these terms.

agribusiness: the activity of farming as a major force of the economy. California has the largest agribusiness in the United States.

Agricultural Adjustment Act of 1933: federal legislation originally intended to provide emergency assistance to agriculture during the Depression years; also contains "omnibus" provisions regarding farm mortgage aid and price stimulation. Also referred to as *AAA Farm Relief Act.*

agricultural loans: loans to farmers not secured by real estate. [40]

agricultural paper: notes and acceptances resulting from transactions dealing with farming and ranching, as distinguished from traditional commercial or industrial activities. see *Federal Intermediate Credit Banks, Federal Loan Bank.*

Agt.:
(1) see *agent.*
(2) see *agreement.*

Agy.: agency.

AI:
(1) see *accrued interest.*
(2) see *accumulated interest.*

AID: see *Agency for International Development.*

Airlines Deregulation Act: federal legislation signed on October 28, 1978. Designed as an anti-inflation tool, the act enabled many new carriers to enter new routes and permitted operators to change flight schedules and their fares.

air pocket: noticeably extreme weakness in a specific stock.

air rights: the right to use open space above a property, or conversely, the right to control the air space by not constructing to ensure that light and air will not be blocked out.

Aj.: see *adjustment.*

AJOJ: April, July, October, January, (quarterly interest payments or dividends).

a/k/a: "also known as" (e.g., John Doe a/k/a J. Doe).

AL: see *accrued liabilities.*

Aldrich-Vreeland Act: a forerunner of the Federal Reserve Act. Congress in 1908 passed legislation as a temporary relief measure until such time as new banking rules could be formulated.

ALGOL: algorithmic language. Primarily a means of expressing computer programs by algorithms or problem-solving formulas for machine analysis. see *general purpose computer, linear programming, program.*

alienation: the transfer of interest and property title to another person or organization. see *involuntary alienation, voluntary alienation.*

alien company: an incorporated company formed and operating under the regulations of a foreign nation.

all-commodity index: a measure of changes in the averages of the wholesale prices of commodities. The U.S. Bureau of Labor Statistics releases such an index.

Alliance for Progress: a cooperative effort begun in 1961 by 20 countries to improve the economic and social conditions in Latin America. see *Inter-American Development Bank.*

allied members: voting shareholders or partners in a stock exchange member organization who are permitted to carry out business on the trading floor of the exchange.

all-inclusive concept: a form of income statement presentation incorporating all items of revenue and expense in the computation of net income for an accounting period. This concept makes no distinction between items related to the current operations of the entity and those that are unusual and infrequent.

allocated expense: proportioned expense, usually by company or function. [12]

allocation: assigning one or more items of cost or revenue to one or more segments of an organization according to benefits received, responsibilities, or other logical measure of use.

allonge: a paper affixed to a bill on which further endorsements are written.

all or any part: used in discretionary accounts by brokers when representing their clients. It authorizes the securities broker to execute all or any part of an order as he or she deems appropriate, but only at the customer's specified price limit.

all or none order

(1) *investments:* a stipulation that a request to purchase or sell a security must be achieved in total or not at all.

(2) *investments:* all securities sold by a broker or underwriter of a new issue become final only when the entire issue is purchased within a stated time period.

allot: to divide an appropriation into amounts for certain periods or for specific purposes. [49]

allotment

(1) *general:* an assignment of pay for the benefit of dependents.

(2) *finance:* the separation of anticipated revenues among specific classes of expenditures.

(3) *investments:* the part of a stock issue apportioned or assigned by an investment firm to a purchaser or subscriber.

allotment ledger: a subsidiary ledger that contains an account for each allotment, showing the amount allotted, expenditures, encumbrances, the net balance, and other related information. see *appropriation ledger.* [49]

allotment notice: a document completed by an investment banker or syndicate manager which states the amount and related information or price and time of payment for securities and which is transmitted to the subscriber. It can be for the full amount of securities asked for by the subscriber, or less.

allottee: the firm or person that has subscribed to buy securities and has been assigned a share or allotment.

allowance: a reserve, or money set aside, for bad debts or for depreciation.

alloy: base metal or metals combined with gold or silver to create a coin with superior durability. Today most coins are base-metal coins.

all-purpose computer: a computer combining the benefits previously assigned solely to general-purpose or special-purpose computers. synonymous with *general-purpose computer.*

All-Savers certificates: a tax break under the Economic Recovery Tax Act of 1981 to encourage savings, the law created this instrument designed basically to benefit savings and loan associations rather than investors. Under the act, thrift institutions will be able to offer a new, one-year Treasury note yield for a little more than 10 percent at current interest rates. What makes the new certificate attractive is that interest income up to $1000 ($2000 on a joint return) is exempt from federal income tax. see also *Economic Recovery Tax Act of 1981.*

Alot: see *allotment.*

Alotm.: see *allotment.*

alphameric: see *alphanumeric.*

alphanumeric

(1) **computers:** describes characters that may be letters of the alphabet, numerals, or symbols.

(2) **computers:** pertains to a character set that contains letters, digits, and other characters (e.g., punctuation marks).

(3) synonymous with *alphameric.*

alteration: any change involving an erasure or rewriting in the date, amount, or payee of a check or other negotiable instrument. In accounting records, necessary alterations are best made by crossing out the unwanted figure, leaving it legible, and writing the correct one above or below the original.

altered check: check on which the date, payee, or amount has been changed or erased. A bank is responsible for paying a check only as it is originally drawn; consequently, it may refuse to pay a check that has been altered.

alternate account: an account in the name of two or more persons, any of whom may draw against the account without further authority from the others. see *joint account; survivorship account. [50]*

alternate depositors: holders of a joint account; a deposit account made out in the names of husband and wife or of two partners which is payable to either or to the survivor is a joint account.

alternative mortgage instruments (AMIs): one of three alternatives to the traditional fixed-rate mortgage. see *graduated-payment mortgages, reverse-annuity mortgage, variable-rate mortgage.*

alternative mortgages: see *flexible loan insurance plan, graduated-payment mortgages, shared-appreciation mortgage.*

alternative payee: one of two parties to whom an account or negotiable instrument, other bill, or draft is payable. Payment to either removes the payor of that extent of obligation to both or either. In a joint account in the name of a spouse, the financial organization may pay either as holder of the draft, passbook, or other financial instrument.

AM:

(1) see *active market.*

(2) see *after market.*

(3) ante meridiem (before noon).

amalgamation

(1) **general:** the joining together of businesses for the mutual advantage of all.

(2) **finance:** a combination under a single title of all or a portion of the assets and liabilities of two or more business units by either merger or consolidation. It may take the form of a merger, where one company absorbs another, or a consolidation, in which the original companies form a new one. see *consolidation, merger.*

AMB: see *adjusted monetary base.*

amendment: an addition, deletion, or change in a legal document. *[37]*

American Arbitration Association: a private not-for-profit organization formed in 1926 to encourage the use of arbitration in the settlement of disputes.

American Bankers Association (ABA): the national organization of banking formed in 1875 to ''promote the general welfare and usefulness of banks and financial institutions.'' The association consists of 35 working groups, 4 divisions, 7 commissions, and a number of councils and committees.

American Bankers Association (ABA) number: a unit in the numerical coding system originated by the American Bankers Association for the easy identification of banks and to aid in sorting checks for their proper and ultimate destinations. Used principally on checks, the ABA number is usually placed in the upper right-hand corner of the check after the drawee bank's name.

American depository receipt: a form similar to a stock certificate which is registered in the holder's name. The certificate represents a certain number of shares in an alien corporation. Such shares are held by an alien bank that serves as the agent for a domestic commercial bank which has released the depository receipt.

American Federation of Labor (AFL): organized in 1881 as a federation of craft unions. Originally called the Federation of Organized Trade and Labor Unions of the United States and Canada, the name ''American Federation of Labor'' was adopted in 1886. In 1955 the AFL merged with the Congress of Industrial Organizations (CIO), which had been expelled from the AFL in 1937, to form the AFL-CIO.

American Federation of Labor– Congress of Industrial Organizations (AFL-CIO): a federation of craft and industrial unions, as well as unions of mixed structure. Created in 1955 by the merger of the AFL and the CIO,

the AFL-CIO is not itself a bargaining agent. Its primary functions are education, lobbying, and furnishing organizational aid to constituent unions.

American Institute of Banking: the educational section of the American Bankers Association, organized in 1900 to provide educational opportunity in banking for bank people. The institute's activities are carried on through numerous chapters and study groups in many cities and towns. In addition to its regular classes, the institute conducts correspondence courses. Membership is open only to employees and officers of ABA member institutions. [10]

American parity: Used in foreign exchange, showing the equivalent in U.S. funds of the foreign price of securities traded overseas.

Americans: the expression used on the London Stock Exchange for U.S. securities.

American selling price: the price charged by U.S. producers for goods, used to determine the duty to be paid on a similar item brought into the United States, rather than determining the duty on the actual cost of the item to an importer.

American Stock Exchange (Amex): the second largest securities exchange in the country; called the Little Board or the Curb Exchange, from the market's origin on a a street in downtown Manhattan. Amex began listing stock options in 1975. see *Commodity Exchange, MC.*; cf. *Big Board.*

Amex: see *American Stock Exchange.*

Amex Commodities Exchange (ACE):

a commodity exchange launched by the American Stock Exchange in 1977 to offer its member firms a broader range of products. ACE functions as an independent exchange, sharing facilities and services with the Amex by contract. Merged in 1980 with the New York Futures Exchange. see *New Your Futures Exchange.*

AMIs: see *alternative mortgage instruments.*

amortisement: synonymous with *amortization.*

amortization

(1) *banking:* the gradual reduction of a debt by means of equal periodic payments sufficient to meet current interest and to liquidate the debt at maturity. When the debt involves real property, the periodic payments often include a sum sufficient to pay taxes and insurance on the property.

(2) *finance:* an attempt to liquidate a future obligation slowly by making charges against a capital account or by adding monies to cover the debt.

amortization loan: long-term loan permitted by the Federal Farm Loan Act where the principal is eliminated or amortized during the time the loan is made. see *amortized mortgage loan.*

amortization of discount on funded debt: a charge to income each fiscal period for a proportion of the discount and expense on funded debt obligations applicable to that period. The proportion is determined according to a rule, the uniform application of which through the interval between the date of sale and date of maturity will extinguish the discount and expense on funded debt. However, the accounting company may, at its option, charge to profit and loss all or any portion of discount and expense remaining unextinguished at any time. [18]

amortization reserve: a balance sheet account in which are recorded the net accumulated provisions for the extinguishment of an asset at the end of a predetermined period. [3]

amortize

(1) *general:* to write off a portion or all of the cost of an asset; to retire debt over a period of time.

(2) *banking:* to discharge a debt in periodic payments until the total, including the interest, has been paid.

amortized mortgage loan: a mortgage loan that provides for repayment within a specified time by means of regular payments at stated intervals (usually monthly, quarterly, or semiannually) to reduce the principal amount of the loan and to cover interest as it is due. [44]

amortized value: the investment value of a security determined by the process of amortization. This value is appropriate for use in connection with bonds that are fully secured, and are not in default as to either principal or interest. see *amortization.* [12]

amount at interest: principal sum deposited for the purpose of earning interest. [12]

amount financed: the amount lent or financed exclusive of finance charges; total of payments less the finance charge. [55]

Amt.: amount.

AMW: see *average monthly wage.*

AN: see *account number.*

analog(ue) computer: a machine that performs arithmetical functions upon numbers where the numbers are represented by a physical quantity. An analog computer accepts data continuously and performs operations of addition, subtraction, multiplication, division, integration, and so on. The result may be a graph, a marking on a electron tube, or a signal to be used as a control of some machine or process. Analog computers, unlike digital computers, cannot store large quantities of financial data.

analysis, multivariate: any of a number of methods or techniques used to identify, or show the effect of, many variables when interacting. cf. *MAPS.*

analysis, sequential: a procedure in which a certain set of calculations is performed after each observation, and on the basis of that calculation it is decided whether the hypothesis is acceptable or, the alternative, to withhold judgment until more data are found.

analysis department: the statistical unit of a financial institution dealing with the interpretation and preparation of operating data and cost accounting.

analysis history record: a statement that contains the profits or losses and other historical conditions concerning the account over a period of time, usually month by month. [31]

analysis of covariance: an extension of methods used in the analysis of variance to include two or more related variables.

analysis of variance: a method for determining whether the differences found in a dependent variable, when it is exposed to the influence of one or more experimental variables, exceed what may be expected by chance.

analyst: a specialist in a brokerage firm or other investment organization who is primarily responsible for determing the assets and liabilities of a new or existing corporation for purposes of making a recommendation to the sales representatives of his organization. Analysts are also found in banks.

analyst, program: a person who creates sets of instructions for computers in addition to analyzing problems, systems, and specific specialties as requested. The instructions are used by the computer as numerical codes for analysis of financial data. see *programming.*

anarchism

(1) *general:* the concept that formal government is unnecessary and wrong in purpose. Elimination of the government is often intended to be achieved by riot or revolt.

(2) *finance:* the elimination of ownership or private property by coercive government.

ancestor: one who precedes another in the line of descent. In common law the term "ancestor" is applied only to a person in direct line of ascent (father, grandfather, or other forebear), but by statute it has been broadened to apply also to a person of collateral relationship (uncle or aunt, for example) from whom property has been acquired. [32]

ancillary: designating or pertaining to a document, proceeding, officer, office, etc., that is subordinate to, or in aid of, another primary or principal one; that is, an ancillary attachment, bill, or suit presupposes the existence of another principal proceeding. [62]

ancillary letters testamentary: letters subordinate or auxiliary to letters testamentary, as, for example, those issued in one jurisdiction for probate of property owned by a nonresident decedent. [37]

ancillary receiver: a person appointed to assist a receiver. Usually, the receiver is handling a foreign corporation (one located outside the state) and the ancillary receiver aids in the liquidation and handles the claims within his own domestic state reporting to and taking guidance from the receiver who is in the foreign state. see *receiver, receivership.*

and interest: a bond quotation term to show that accrued interest is to be added to the price; that is, the price quoted is exclusive of interest. see *accrued interest.*

ANFM: August, November, February, May (quarterly interest payments or dividends).

Ann.
   (1) annual.
   (2) see *annuity.*

annual balanced budget: a concept holding that total revenues and expenditures in a government's budget should be balanced or brought into equality each year.

annual basis: statistical shifting of data that are for a period less than 12 months in order to estimate the full results for an entire year. To be accurate, the processing should consider the effect of the seasonal variation.

annual earnings: the total of all monies received during a year; income less expenses during a year.

annual percentage rate (APR): the cost of credit on a yearly basis expressed as a percentage. [1]

annual report: a report of financial and organizational conditions prepared by corporate management at yearly intervals. In most cases, the Securities Exchange Commission requires an annual report for publicly held firms. see *annual statement.*

annual return: see *yield.*

annual statement: the annual report made by a company at the close of the fiscal year, stating the company's receipts and disbursements, assets and liabilities. Such a statement usually includes an account of the progress made by the company during the year. see *annual report.* [54]

annual wage: a guaranteed minimum income for total number of hours of employment during a year. see *guaranteed annual wage.*

annual yield: the percentage of return or income in dividends or interest that an investment yields each year.

annuitant: an individual to whom an annuity is payable, the person usually to receive the annuity during his or her lifetime. see *variable annuity.*

annuity
   (1) *general:* a scheduled payment to a retired person.
   (2) *finance:* a series of equal payments at fixed intervals.

annuity, installment refund: a life annuity with an agreement that the insurer will, on the death of the annuitant, continue payments to a beneficiary until the total of the payments to annuitant and beneficiary equals the consideration paid to the insurer. [53]

annuity, joint and survivor: an annuity payable as long as any one of two or more persons survives. [53]

annuity, life: an annuity payable as long as the annuitant or annuitants live. [53]

annuity, retirement: a deferred annuity for which the premiums, less loading, are accumulated at interest and are used to purchase an annuity at a specified age. Prior to that age, the annuitant is entitled to a cash surrender value. In case of death, the surrender value is paid to his beneficiary. [53]

annuity, survivorship: an annuity payable to the annuitant for the period during which he survives the insured. [53]

annuity bond: see *bond, perpetual.*

annuity reserve: a monetary sum equal to the actuarial value of future payments to be made on account of an annuity. [52]

annuity reserve fund: an amount or sum set aside in a reserve to provide for the payment of annuities. Usually derived from the members' accumulated contributions, or contributions by the members and the employer. [52]

annuity table: a listing of the present values of $1.00 per year or month payable for life, or for a term of years at specified ages for each sex, computed on the basis of assumed rates or mortality and interest. [52]

annulment: a judicial decree that a marriage was void from the beginning. [76]

antecedents: used in making credit inquiries to determine if the corpora-tion has been controlled by the existing employer(s) for a short or long time period and how often the firm has changed ownership.

antedate: to place on a check a date prior to the current one.

anticipated acceptance: an acceptance that has been paid prior to the specified terms of payment.

anticipated balance: the bank account balance projected through the end of the interest or dividend period, assuming that no additional deposit or withdrawal transactions occur.

anticipated interest: the amount of interest projected as earnings on bank accounts, assuming that no deposits or withdrawals occur before the end of the current interest period. This figure is updated after each deposit or withdrawal activity.

anticipation
(1) *banking:* payment of an account before the actual due date, thus permitting a discount.
(2) *finance:* assigning or making charges against income or profit before such gain is actually realized.
(3) *law:* describing a situation in which a claimed invention is known to others regardless of whether the anticipating invention has been patented.

anticipation, right of: the privilege given the mortgagor, by a provision in the mortgage instruments, to pay all or any portion of the outstanding balance of the obligation prior to its due date without penalty. [44]

anticipation and intentions data: provide information on the plans of businessmen and consumers regarding their economic activities in the near future. These plans are considered valuable aids to economic forecasting, either directly or as an indication of the state of confidence concerning the economic outlook. [73]

anticipatory breach: the informing of the seller by a buyer before the closing of title that the buyer plans to terminate any involvement in the transaction.

Antidumping Act of 1974: legislation designed to prevent the sale of goods at a lower price than exists in the goods' country or origin. The Treasury Department determines whether imported products are being sold at "less than fair value" in this country. Should it be determined that the domestic industry is harmed by the imports, extra duties can be imposed.

Antikickback Law: see *Copeland Act of 1934.*

Antiracketeering Law: the Hobbs Act of 1934, making it a felony to interfere with commerce by robbery or extortion, by conspiracy, or by threat of violence.

antitrust: describing an action of the courts taken to curb monopolistic tendencies or to limit power stemming from monopolies.

antitrust acts: see *Celler Antimerger Act, Clayton Antitrust Act of 1914, Robinson-Patman Act of 1936, Sherman Antitrust Act of 1890.*

A&O: April and October (semiannual interest payments).

AO
(1) account of.
(2) see *average out.*

AOCR: see *advanced optical character reader.*

AP: see *authority to purchase.*

appellant: the party who makes a motion for an appeal from one jurisdiction or court to another.

appellee: the individual or stated party in a cause against whom an appeal is made.

application
(1) *computers:* the problem or business situation in relation to which a computer is used.
(2) *law:* any offer to purchase something or to enter into some form of contract.

application-for-loan form: a printed form used by most financial institutions which contains a prospective borrower's request for a loan. [51]

application of funds statement: constructed from balance sheets to two periods, the statement allows an analysis of the changes that have evolved during the period that was chosen.

apportion: to assign a cost factor to a person, unit, product, or order.

apportionment
(1) *general:* dividing a unit into proportionate parts; the proper allocation of receipts and expenses between income and principal.
(2) *banking:* involves the question of how much each of two or more insurance policies will contribute to the loss sustained by a covered risk. The decision of distribution is the apportionment.

appraisal: the setting of a value or evaluation of a specific piece of personal or real property, or the property of another as a whole. see *Baltimore method, Bernard rule, cost approach to value.*

appraisal fee: a charge for estimating the value of collateral being offered as security. [78]

appraisal of business: an examination to decide how much a business is worth. [61]

appraisal report: a written report of the factors considered in arriving at a valuation of a particular piece of property. [61]

appraisal rights of minority stockholders: the statutory rights for the protection of dissenting minority stockholders during a shift in shares at the time of a merger or consolidation.

appraisal surplus: the excess of appraised values over book values. [62]

appraise: to determine the cost, quality, or value of an item (e.g., to appraise the value of one's house). Also used to appraise the adequacy and effectiveness of systems and procedures.

appraiser: a person who makes appraisals.

appraising: see *valuation.*

appreciation: the increase in the value of an asset in excess of its depreciable cost which is due to economic and other conditions; the increase of present value over the listed book value. see *capital gain.*

appreciation rate: the index figure used against the actual or estimated cost of property in computing its cost of reproduction, new as of a different date or under different conditions of a higher price level. [62]

appropriation: an authorized sum of money set aside to pay certain known or anticipated costs of a given item or service.

appropriation ledger: a subsidiary ledger containing an account with each appropriation. Each account usually shows the amount originally appropriated, transfers to or from the appropriation charged against the appropriation, the net balance, and other related information. If allotments are made and a separate ledger is maintained for them, each account in the appropriation ledger usually shows the amount appropriated, transfers to or from the appropriation, the amount allotted, and the unallotted balance. see also *allotment ledger.* [49]

approved bond: see *bond, approved.*

approved list: a list, statutory or otherwise, which contains the authorized investments that a fiduciary may acquire. [37]

approved plan: the term used to denote a plan that has been accepted by the U.S. Internal Revenue Service for tax deduction of contributions thereunder. [52]

appurtenances: rights and interest that attach to and pass with the land.

APR: see *annual percentage rate.*

a priori: a general, first-impression statement based on presuppositions, not facts.

Aprx.: approximately.

A&R: see *account and risk.*

AR:
(1) see *accounts receivable.*
(2) see *annual report.*
(3) see *annual return.*

arbitrage
(1) *finance:* simultaneous purchasing and selling of the identical item in different markets in order to yield profits. The result is that the price of an item becomes equal in all markets.
(2) *finance:* the purchase of foreign exchange, stocks, bonds, silver, gold, or other commodities in one market for sale in another market at a profit.

arbitrage house: a financial institution, such as a foreign exchange dealer or private banker, conducting business in arbitrage. see *arbitrage.*

arbitrager (arbitrageur): an individual who engages in the activity of arbitrage. see *arbitrage.*

arbitragist: synonymous with *arbitrager.*

arbitration of exchange: the prices of bills of exchange payable in foreign currency will vary throughout financial centers in the world. Consequently, an individual from country A may find it profitable to purchase a bill of exchange from country B for payment in still another country. This is "arbitration of exchange."

archmonetarist: a supporter of Milton Friedman's monetary theory that changes in growth of money supply operate on the economy with such a long time lag that it is impossible for the authorities to know at any one moment what policy should be. cf. *balanced budget exercises, compensatory fiscal policy, and New Economics.*

Area Redevelopment Program: a federal program under the Area Redevelopment Act of 1961 to stimulate employment and business growth in depressed locales.

arguendo: Latin, referring to the case by way of argument or within an argument.

arithmetic mean: the sum of all items divided by the number of items added.

ARQ: answer-return query.

array: an arrangement of single observations or times in ranked order, from the least to the most, or the reverse.

arrearages on preferred securities: the accumulation of unpaid dividends. A statement that such dividends for cumulative preferred stock must be paid prior to payment on the firm's common stock.

arrears

(1) a real or contingent obligation remaining unpaid at the date of maturity. Frequently used in connection with installment notes, mortgages, rent, and other obligations due and payable on a certain specified date.

(2) monies due but unpaid.

arrival draft: a draft accompanying shipping documents that is payable when the goods arrive as described in the papers. The arrival draft is presented upon receipt to the drawee as a means of preparing him to pay when the goods have arrived. see *draft.*

articles of agreement: any contract between two or more people that is reduced to a written instrument.

articles of association: any instrument that is similar to a corporate certificate; usually used with non-stock corporations (e.g., charitable organizations).

articles of incorporation: a document filed with an appropriate state agency by persons establishing a corporation. Upon return accompanied by a certificate of incorporation, the document becomes the firm's charter.

AS:

(1) see *accumulated surplus.*
(2) see *active securities.*
(3) see *assented securities.*
(4) see *assessable stock.*

ASAP: as soon as possible.

Asd.: assented.

ASE: see *American Stock Exchange.*

as earned: describes the basis of income of a customer who is not paid on a regular basis—that is, business-for-self. [55]

Asian Currency Units (ACUs): the separate accounting entities by which the Asiadollar deposit market was created. The market emerged from a Bank of America proposal. ACUs totaled over $42 billion in early 1980.

ask: an offer to sell at a designated price.

asked: see *bid and asked.*

asked (asking) price

(1) *general:* the price that is officially offered in a sale.

(2) *investments:* the price at which a stock is offered for sale. In open-end shares, the price at which the purchaser may buy stock from the investment firm. In closed-end shares, the lowest price at which the stock is then offered for sale in the public market.

ASP: see *American selling price.*

as per advice: words on a bill of exchange showing that the drawee has been notified that the bill has been drawn on him or her.

assay: a test of content, composition, and purity, often carried out in an assayer's office, on metals, usually gold and silver.

assay office: a location designated for the testing of ore, commodities, and bullion in addition to foreign coin.

assay office bar: assayed by an assay office and made at a mint, a bar of pure or near pure gold or silver.

assemblage: the act of bringing two or more individuals or things to form an aggregate whole; specifically, the cost or estimated cost of assembling two or more parcels of land under a single ownership and unit of utility over the normal cost or current market prices of the parcels held individually. [62]

assembling: the activities involved in concentrating supplies or assortments of goods or services to facilitate sale or purchase. [48]

assembling land: the combining of nearby or contiguous properties to form one tract.

assented securities: securities whose owners agree to some change in status, usually in case of corporate restructuring, when an assessment is made or the amount of securities is reduced according to some logical plan.

assess: to determine the value of something, or to fix its value for tax purposes.

assessable stock: security that is subject to an assessment order resulting from a corporation's reorganization or insolvency.

assessed value: the official record of a tax assessed and collected; the tax roll value assigned to property.

assessment

(1) *banking:* a charge made against property for the purpose of levying a tax. see *nonassessable stock.*

(2) *finance:* any levy on members of a corporation for purposes of raising capital.

assessment roll

(1) in the case of real property the official list containing the legal description of each parcel of property and its assessed valuation. The name and address of the last known owner are also usually shown.

(2)   in the case of personal property, the assessment roll is the official list containing the name and address of the owner, a description of the personal property, and its assessed value. [49]

asset: anything owned by an individual or business that has commercial or exchange value. Assets may consist of specific property or claims against others, in contract to obligations due others.   see *balance sheet, current assets to current debt, fixed assets, intangible asset, tangible assets.*

asset, capital: see *capital assets.*

asset, contingent: see *contingent asset.*

asset, current: see *current assets to current debt.*

asset, dead: see *dead asset.*

asset, deferred: see *deferred asset.*

asset, fixed: see *fixed assets.*

asset, fixed register: see *fixed register asset.*

asset, fixed test: see *fixed test asset.*

asset, fixed to tangible net worth: see *fixed-to-tangible-net-worth asset.*

asset, floating: see *floating assets.*

asset, fluid: see *current assets.*

asset, frozen: see *frozen asset.*

asset, gross: see *gross asset.*

asset, hypothecated: see *hypothecated asset.*

asset, inactive: see *inactive asset.*

asset, intangible: see *intangible asset.*

asset, ledger: see *ledger asset.*

asset, liquid: see *liquid assets.*

asset, minus: see *minus asset.*

asset, net: see *net assets.*

asset, net value: see *net asset value.*

asset, nominal: see *nominal asset.*

asset, nonaccrual: see *nonaccrual asset.*

asset, nonledger: see *nonledger asset.*

asset, ordinary: see *ordinary asset.*

asset, original: see *original asset.*

asset, permanent: see *permanent asset.*

asset, personal: see *personal asset.*

asset, physical: see *tangible assets.*

asset, pledged: see *pledged assets.*

asset, quick: see *quick assets.*

asset, tangible: see *tangible assets.*

asset, value: see *value asset.*

asset, wasting: see *wasting assets.*

asset, working: see *working asset.*

asset coverage: *direct*—the extent to which net assets (after all prior claims) cover a specific senior obligation, whether bank loans, debentures, or preferred stock. It may be expressed in either dollar, percentage, or ratio terms. *Overall*—the ratio of total assets to the sum of all prior obligations including that of the specific issue under consideration taken at liquidating value. [30]

asset currency: bank notes that are not secured by any particular assets but by the general assets of the issuing bank. Some countries have such characteristics. Today, more popularly referred to as *general asset currency.*   see also *Baltimore method.*

assets, total: see *total assets.*

assign: to transfer to another. A person to whom property is assigned. [76]

assignability: the capacity of property to be transferred to another person or organization.

assignat: paper currency issue during the French Revolution backed by land that was confiscated from the church and aristocracy. The money was later repudiated.

assigned account: an account, usually receivable, which has been assigned to a bank as security for a loan by a borrower. In theory, the bank takes possession of the account pledged. In actual practice, however, so as not to jeopardize the relationship between the borrower and his customer (whose account has been pledged), the bank will allow the account to be paid by the customer in the normal manner, and will rely upon the integrity of the borrower to apply this payment against the loan balance. [31]

assigned book account: see *assigned account.*

assigned expense: expense incurred by a particular function. [12]

assigned in blank: the space on a transfer-of-ownership document for placing the new owner's name. Often street certificates are assigned in blank where no name appears on the certificate.

assignee
(1) *general:* one to whom an assignment is granted.
(2) *law:* an individual to whom property or rights have been transferred for the benefit of self or others. see *assignment, assignment in blank, assignor.*

assignment
(1) *banking:* the transfer in writing by one individual to another of title of property.
(2) *investments:* the transfer of title of stocks.
(3) *law:* a transfer in writing of the legal right in a policy to another party. see *assignment in blank, good delivery, stop order.*

assignment, lease: transferring a leasehold interest to another person or group.

assignment, mortgage: transferring a mortgage to another person or group.

assignment for the benefit of creditors: a person or firm's action to transfer legal title to property to a trustee who has been authorized to administer and liquidate the property and make a distribution to creditors. see also *National Bankruptcy Act of 1898.*

assignment in blank: see *assigned in blank.*

assignment of leases: additional security often taken in connection with mortgages of commercial properties. [22]

assignment of mortgage: the written instrument evidencing an association's transfer of a loan obligation from the original borrower to a third person. [59]

assignment of rents: a written document that transfers to a mortgagee on default the owner's right to collect rents. [59]

assignment to creditors: the transfer of property in trust or for the benefit of creditors. [76]

assignor: an individual who assigns or transfers a claim, right, or property. see *assignment, assignment in blank, assignment for the benefit of creditors.*

assimilation: the completed distribution of new shares of securities to the public by the issue's underwriters and syndicate members.

assistance and subsidies: cash contributions and subsidies to persons and foreign governments, not in payment for goods or services or for claims against the government. Includes direct cash assistance to public welfare recipients; veterans bonuses; direct cash grants for tuition, scholarship, and aid to nonpublic educational institutions; and payments for agricultural support programs and foreign aid.

Assmt.: see *assessment.*

Assn.: see *association.*

associated banks: banks that are associated through membership in a clearinghouse association.

Associated Credit Bureaus of America, Inc.: membership organization of credit bureaus and collection service departments throughout the nation. Facilitates interbureau credit reporting by means of a "coupon" system. [41]

association: a grouping of people for mutually beneficial purposes or for the furtherance of some goal. An unincorporated group, not formed for profit. see *voluntary association.*

Asst. Cash.: assistant cashier.

assumed bond: see *bond, assumed.*

assumed liability: an obligation for payment accepted by another person.

assumpsit
(1) a common law action alleging that damages have been incurred.
(2) a common law action to recover damages for breach of contract.

assumption: bank loan payments accepted by a party other than the original maker.

assumption of debt: taking on another's debt. [61]

assumption of mortgage: accepting a property title that has an existing mortgage with personal liability for all payments by another.

assurance: commonly used in England. Similar to "insurance," but differs in that assurance does not depend on a possibility: it is a payment of a premium at regular periods for a stated sum that becomes payable at a given time.

Astd.: assented.

AT: see *absolute title.*

ATB: see *across the board.*

at call: any transaction occurring in the call money market. see *call money, call money market.*

Atlanta Payments Project: An extensive research program sponsored jointly by commercial banks and the Federal Reserve Bank in Atlanta, Georgia. The project concluded in 1974 after publishing major research results and included the planning and implementation effort for the Georgia Automated Clearing House Association. The participating commercial banks were formed into the Committee on Paperless Entries (COPE). [36]

ATM:
(1) see *at the market.*
(2) see *automated teller machine.*

at market: see *at the market.*

ATO: see *at the opening.*

at or better: when placing a purchase order for securities, to buy at the price specified or under; in a selling request, to sell at the price given or above.

ATP: see *authority to purchase.*

at par: designating a bond or share of preferred stock issued or selling at its face amount.

ATS: see *automatic transfer service accounts.*

at seller's option: see *seller's option.*

at sight: a term used in the body of negotiable instruments indicating that payment is due upon presentation or demand.

attached account: an account against which a court order has been issued, permitting disbursement of the balance only with the consent of the court. see *frozen account*.

attached ledger: the book or ledger in which records of attached accounts are segregated and kept.

attachment: the legal proceeding following a court's action whereby a plaintiff acquires a lien on a defendant's property as security for payment of a judgment that the plaintiff can recover.

attachment ledger: see *attached ledger*.

attest: to bear witness to; as, to attest a will or other document. [32]

attestation: the act of bearing witness or giving authenticity to a document by signing as a witness to the signature of another. see *notary public*.

attested wills: prepared in writing or typewritten and signed by the testator or by someone for him and acknowledged by him. His signature has to be witnessed by two or more adults at the time of execution. Attested wills are the most popular form of will.

attesting witness: one who testifies to the authenticity of a document, as the attesting witness to a will; to be distinguished from *subscribing witness*. [37]

at the market: an order that the broker has executed at the best price available after it was received by the broker on the floor of the exchange. synonymous with *market order*. see *limit order*.

at the opening: referring to a securities order that is either executed immediately following the opening of the exchange or canceled entirely. see *odd lot*.

attorney-at-law: an person who has a state license giving the privilege to practice law.

attorney-in-fact: an person who has the written authorization of another to carry out business for his or her principal out of court.

attorney of record: the lawyer whose name is entered in the records of the court as the representative of a party in a legal action or suit.

Atty.: attorney.

AU: gold (from *arum*).

auction: a unique trading market in which there is one seller and many potential buyers. see also *Dutch auction*.

auction market: the system of trading securities through brokers or agents on an exchange such as the New York Stock Exchange. Buyers compete with other sellers for the most advantageous price. Most transactions are executed with public customers on both sides since the specialist buys or sells for his own account primarily to offset imbalances in public supply and demand. see *dealer, quotation, specialist*. [20]

Aud.

(1) see *audit*.

(2) see *auditor*.

audit

(1) *general:* inspection of a firm's books; a final statement of account.

(2) *finance:* periodic or continuous verification of the stated assets and liabilities of a company or other organization. see *bank examination*.

audited voucher: a voucher that has been examined and approved for payment. see *accounts payable*. [49]

audit function: periodic or continuous verification of the bank's assets and liabilities. This function is performed by the auditor. The auditor is appointed by the board of directors and is responsible for the carrying out of this verification. Among the assets and liabilities more regularly verified are cash, loans, collateral for loans, and savings and checking accounts. Verification may consist of a physical count of the assets as reflected by the general ledger or a listing of the balances, as shown on each savings or checking account, with a proof of the total as shown on the general ledger. Direct verification may also be made with borrowers or depositors. [10]

auditing department: a unit within a bank or other financial organization, responsible for bookkeeping, accounting and auditing activities. Daily control of all transactions is the primary goal of this department, usually headed by an auditor.

auditor: a person qualified to conduct an audit. Qualification is defined by each state. see *audit, auditing department, bank examiner, certified public accountant.*

auditor's certificate: a statement signed by an auditor in which he states that he has examined the financial statements, the system of internal control, the accounting records, and supporting evidence in accordance with generally accepted auditing standards and in which he expresses his opinion, based on such examination, regarding the fi-

nancial condition of a unit or any of its enterprises, the results from operations, and any facts that he has investigated in his professional capacity.

audit program: a detailed outline of work to be done and the procedure to be followed in any given audit. [49]

audit report: the report prepared by an auditor covering the audit or investigation made by him. As a rule, the report should include a statement of the scope of the audit, a summary of findings, recommendations, a certificate, financial statements, and, sometimes, statistical tables. [49]

audit trial: a printed record of transaction listings created as a by-product of data-processing runs or manual or mechanized accounting operations.

autarky: an attempt to minimize a nation's dependence on other countries by substituting national manufacturing imports of goods.

Auth.: authority.

authenticated copy: a copy of an instrument on which an attestation is made in the manner required by law by an official authorized to make such certification, as by the certification and seal of a specified public official. [37]

authentication

(1) *investments:* the signing of a certificate on a bond by a trustee in order to identify it as having been issued under a specific indenture, thereby validating the bond.

(2) *law:* the verification of a document as truthful, genuine, or valid.

authority bond: see *bond, authority.*

authority to purchase: used in Far Eastern trade, a substitute for a commercial "letter of credit"; this instrument permits the bank to which it is directed to purchase drafts drawn on an importer rather than on a bank. see *letter of credit.*

authorization center: a credit-card centralized office that has records of the cardholder's account with an issuer bank. If sufficient credit is there, the purchase is authorized.

authorization index: listing of credit customers by name and address, credit limits, and other instructions or restrictions. Can be arranged alphabetically or geographically. In the latter case the street number is the primary key to the index. [41]

authorized investment: an investment that is authorized by the trust instrument; to be distinguished from legal investment. [37]

authorized stock: the maximum number of all classes of securities that can be issued by a corporation. see *capital stock.*

authorizor: the person in a credit office designated to approve or disapprove requests for purchases to be charged to credit accounts. [41]

automated clearinghouse (ACH): a computerized facility used by member depository institutions to process (i.e., combine, sort, and distribute) payment orders in machine-readable form (computer tapes or punched cards).

automated teller machine (ATM): a machine capable of processing a variety of transactions between a depository institution and its customers. These functions might include accepting deposits, providing withdrawals, transferring funds between accounts, and accepting instructions to pay third parties in the transaction.

An ATM may or may not be on-line to a computer system and may be located on or off the premises of a depository institution. Placement in certain locations may permit customer access 7 days a week, 24 hours a day. see *Bellevue Project, cash dispenser, debit card; Customer-Bank Communication Terminal.*

automated transit: the basic transit functions are reading, calculating, accumulating, printing, and sorting of all out-of-city MCR-encoded items. When automated, these functions are performed on MICR sorters/readers, high-speed check listers, and computers. [10]

automatic currency: see *elasticity.*

automatic data processing: see *ADP.*

automatic deposit plan: a savings account deposit plan whereby the customer arranges for checks, such as Social Security payments and stock dividends, to be sent directly to his association for deposit to his savings account. [59]

automatic fiscal stabilizers: nondiscretionary approaches that automatically cushion recession by assisting in creating a budget deficit and curb inflation by helping to create a budget surplus.

automatic fund transfer: a regulation by the Federal Reserve Board and the Federal Deposit Insurance Corporation permitting a financial institution to move funds from a depositor's savings account to his checking account upon specific request.

automatic guarantee: a provision of the Veterans Administration under which it will guarantee with prior approval a mortgage loan made by a supervised lender. [59]

automatic reinvestment: a service, often associated with mutual funds, enabling the investor to automatically put income dividends or capital gains distributions back into the fund to buy new shares and thereby build up new holdings.

automatic stabilizer: a tool of economics and finance used to compensate for shifts in the business cycle without the involvement of a government official.

automatic transfer service (ATS) accounts: effective November 1, 1978, commercial banks began offering interest-paying checking accounts. Automatic transfer service accounts allow a bank saver to keep funds in a 5 percent passbook account, allowing the bank to shift a predetermined amount into a checking account periodically. see *negotiable order of withdrawal.*

automation: conversion to the use of automatic machines or devices designed to control various processes. Originally coined in 1935 by D. S. Harder of the Ford Motor Company and popularized by John Diebold. In banks and financial institutions, this term usually refers to the use of electronic equipment and computers.

autonomous transactions: transactions among nations that arise from factors unrelated to the balance of payments as such. The primary classes are merchandise trade and services and long-term capital movements as well as and unilateral transfers.

auxiliary account: a contra, offset, or adjunct account that is related to the principal account.

auxiliary operation: an operation performed by equipment off-line or not under continuous control of the central processor. A supplemental function to be combined with others to complete a major transaction. [10]

auxiliary storage: a storage device used to supplement the main internal storage of a computer (e.g., magnetic tape, disc, or drum). Such devices are used to store software; master files, such as savings and demand deposit accounts and records; and so on. see *software.* [10]

Av.: see *average.*

AV

(1) see *actual value.*

(2) see *ad valorem.*

avail: the amount remaining following a discount or expense deduction.

availability date: the date on which checks payable at out-of-town banks are considered to be collected and available for customers withdrawal; determined by the geographical location of the drawee bank, in relation to time and distance from the sending bank. Recently, local banks were included, and volume is replacing distance.

available assets: a person's or firm's assets that may be readily sold to meet a need. Such assets would usually not be mortgaged or pledged.

available balance: the book balance less any hold, uncollected funds, and restrictions against an account. [31]

available fund: the amount of cash or demand deposits obtainable by a person or organization to fulfill a need. Such assets would usually not be pledged. Also, the collected balance less the reserve requirement available for investment.

available time

(1) *general:* time other than maintenance time.

(2) *computers:* time when the computer's power is turned on and the device is ready for use.

avails: the proceeds from a discounted note. see *net avails.*

average

(1) *general:* a measure of central tendency.

(2) *investments:* to buy or sell more shares, items, or whatever with the goal of receiving a better average price.

average adjustor: the person who prepares claims made under the average clause in insurance contracts.

average annual bill per customer: annual revenue (exclusive of discounts and penalties) from a class of service divided by the average annual number of customers for that class of service. [3]

average balance

(1) *general:* the sum of the daily balances in an account during a month divided by the number of days in that month.

(2) *banking:* a high average balance for an account, indicating a more profitable account than another with a lower average balance.

average bond: see *bond, average.*

average book: lender's record, as in a bank, showing differing averages, such as the average balance or average loan, by each customer, which are posted and often entered into the computer to aid management in future planning.

average collected balance: the average collected balance of a depositor's account is usually determined on a monthly basis. It is arrived at by adding the daily balances of the account, and deducting the sum of the float, or uncollected items, from the formal total, and dividing the remainder by the number of days in the month. [10]

average cost: the sum of all output costs divided by the quantity of production.

average daily balance: the average amount of money that a customer keeps on deposit; determined by adding the daily balances of an account for a given length of time and dividing the total by the number of days covered.

average due date: the average date when several payments, coming due at differing times, can be paid.

average hourly earnings: the amount of money actually received by an employee per hour of work during a pay period.

average loan file: see *average book.*

average monthly wage: the average rate of remuneration per month, computed as prescribed by law.

average number of customers: the average of the number of customers counted regularly once in each of 12 consecutive months. [3]

average out: to conclude a buy or sell transaction without any loss, and hopefully with a profit, by the process of averaging. see *averaging.*

average revenue: the amount received from all sales divided by the number of items that have been sold.

average straight-time hourly earnings: the actual earnings per straight-time hour, excluding shift differentials and overtime pay but including incentive and merit payments.

averages: various ways of measuring the trend of securities prices; one of the most popular is the Dow Jones average of 30 industrial stocks listed on the New York Stock Exchange. Formulas—some very elaborate—have been devised to compensate for stock splits and stock dividends and thus given continuity to the average. In the case of the Dow Jones industrial average, the prices of the 30 stocks are totaled and then divided by a divisor which is intended to compensate for past stock splits and stock dividends and which is changed from time to time. As a result, point changes in the average have only the vaguest relationship to dollar price changes in stocks included in the average. see *NYSE Common Stock Index, points, split.* [20]

average weekly benefit: as prescribed by law, the amount payable per week to compensate for disability or death. It is usually a percentage of the average weekly wage, subject to a minimum and a maximum amount. In workmen's compensation insurance, this is referred to as weekly compensation. The benefit is paid by an insurance carrier of the institution.

average weekly wage: the average rate of remuneration per week, computed as prescribed by law.

averaging
(1) *federal income taxes:* a benefit allowing individuals to average taxable income for four preceding years over a five-year period.
(2) *investments:* the methods used in an attempt to improve the average price paid or received for securities.

Avg.: see *average.*

avoirdupois
(1) *general:* French, having weight.
(2) *finance:* commodities sold by weight.

AVT:
(1) see *ad valorem taxes.*
(2) see *value-added tax.*

avulsion: any shift of land from one property to another caused by forces of nature without change in ownership.

award
(1) *finance:* the acceptance of a bid or the assigning of a project on the basis of a made offer. see *competitive bid.*
(2) *investments:* the acceptance by a borrower of a competitive bid for a security issue in the form of notification to the high-bidder investment banker or syndicate.
(3) *labor relations:* the final decision of an arbitrator, binding on both parties to the dispute.
(4) *law:* the findings of a competent court or board on a matter to be settled by such a body in favor of one of the parties to the case.

AY: see *annual yield.*

B: see *bid.*

B&A: see *bid and asked.*

BA: see *bank acceptance.*

baby bond: see *bond, baby.*

Baby Wagner Acts: state and territorial labor laws based on the Wagner-Connery Act which deal with representation procedures and unfair labor and management practices.

back: to finance, sponsor, or endorse (e.g., to back a plan to add a wing to the plant).

Back.: see *backwardation.*

backdating: placing on a statement a date prior to the date on which it was drawn up.

back door: another name for the U.S. Treasury.

backdoor financing

(1) the practice enabling a government agency to borrow from the U.S. Treasury instead of relying on congressional appropriations.

(2) synonymous with *public debt transaction.*

backer: an individual who supports with money a project or person.

back freight: freight payable when delivery is not taken within a reasonable period at the discharge point; the executive in charge deals with the items at the owner's expense.

back office crunch (crush)

(1) *general:* a delay in daily operations, often resulting from a pileup of unprocessed work.

(2) *investments:* an operational failure, where brokerage houses are deficient in processing a heavier than normal volume of transactions.

back order: part of an original order that was not filled in the first shipment, to be sent when ready, without obliging the customer to reorder the item(s).

back pay: wages due an employee because of employer violation of minimum wage laws, layoff or discharge in violation of a collective agreement, or adjustment of piece rate following the settlement of a grievance.

back spread: exists when the price for identical items in two markets is less than the normal difference (e.g., a stock is selling for $50 on a New York stock exchange and for the equivalent of $55 on the London Stock Exchange, the difference being due to shipping costs, insurance, and other factors).

backtracking: using seniority rights to displace junior workers when business conditions warrant layoffs. see *bump.*

backwardation: a basic pricing system in commodity futures trading. A price structure in which the nearer deliveries of a commodity cost more than contracts that are due to mature many months in the future. A backwardation price pattern occurs mainly because the demand for supplies in the near future is greater than the demand for supplies at some more distant time.

bad debt: amount due on an open account that has been proved to be uncollectible; any uncollectible receivable.

bad debt expense: the cost of uncollectible accounts receivable. In most companies, bad debt expense is debited for the estimated amount uncollectible, and allowance for uncollectible accounts is credited.

bad debt recovery: money collected on a bad debt account. [55]

bad debt writeoff: a customer's account that is removed from the books when payment appears unlikely.

bad delivery
(1) *general:* a delivered item not conforming to the original terms of agreement.
(2) *investments:* an improperly prepared or transferred security or certificate.

bad faith: the intent to mislead or deceive (mala fides). It does not include misleading by an honest, inadvertent, or uncalled-for misstatement. see *fraud.*

bad news: slang, any bill for money owed.

baht: monetary unit of Thailand.

bail
(1) *as a noun:* a bond given by another in his or her behalf, for the payment of money in the event that the accused fails to appear in court on a specific day. see *bond, penal.*
(2) *as a verb:* to release an arrested or imprisoned individual.

bail bond: see *bond, bail.*

bailee: a person who acts as a receiver for personal property.

bailee receipt: the receipt presented to a bank holding title to goods by a bailee, a customer of the bank who is allowed to sell them for the amount of the owning bank.

bailment
(1) *general:* the providing of bail for an arrested person.
(2) *law:* delivery of personal property to another person for a specific purpose.

bailor: an individual who delivers personal property for possession to another.

bailout: the use of corporate monies to provide to shareholders payments that are taxable at desirable capital gains rates. The Securities Exchange Commission has ruled the bailout illegal.

Bal.: see *balance.*

balance: the amount standing to the credit of a customer's account, representing the amount he is entitled to withdraw. The difference between total debits and credits, whether against or in favor of a bank at the clearinghouse. [31]

balance as a whole: a form of proof method employed in banks, usually in the bookkeeping department. A control total is established for several books or ledgers. Each bookkeeper processes his work by posting to his accounts. At the end of the posting run, several bookkeepers will add their combined totals, and will "balance as a whole" to the control total for their group of ledgers. [10]

balanced budget: a budget in which forward expenditures for a set period are matched by expected revenues for the same period.

balanced budget exercises: government spending that keeps the size of the budget deficit the same by simultaneously increasing and decreasing various taxes. cf. *archmonetarist.*

balanced economy: a condition of national finances in which imports and exports are equal.

balanced fund: a mutual fund which has an investment policy of "balancing" its portfolio, generally by including bonds, preferred stocks, and common stocks. [23]

balance due: the total amount needed to equalize the debit and credit sum of an account; the amount you owe.

balance of account: the net amount of the total debits and total credits posted to a given account. Balances are of three types: *zero balance,* indicating that total debits and total credits are equal; *debit balance,* indicating an excess of total debits over total credits; and *credit balance,* indicating an excess of total credits over debits, at a given time.

balance of payments (b.o.p.): a statement identifying all financial transaction of a country and its population with the other nations of the world. cf. *dollar shortage.*

balance of trade: the difference between a country's imports and exports over a set period.

balance on goods and services: the algebraic sum of exports and imports of goods and services. It includes merchandise trade (exports and imports of goods) and the so-called invisible items: shipping charges, income on investments, rents, royalties, payments for insurance, donations, and travel. A surplus balance on goods and services is compatible with an export of capital or an ac-

cumulation of foreign exchange reserves. On the other hand, a deficit balance on goods and services must be financed by an import of capital or a drawing down of foreign exchange reserves. [73]

balance on goods, services, and unilateral transfer: the balance on goods, services, and unilateral transfers represents the balance on current account which—except for errors and omissions—must be counterbalanced by capital movements, a change in official reserves, or both. All transactions involving transfers of goods and services are included in the current account, with the exception of monetary gold transactions, which are recorded as a component part of U.S. official reserve assets. The balance on goods, services, and unilateral transfers is net foreign investment by the United States. [73]

balance sheet: an itemized statement listing the total assets and the total liabilities of a given business to portray its net worth at a given moment in time.

balance sheet audit: an examination of a statement of financial condition as of a given date, usually at the end of the normal accounting period. [49]

balances with domestic banks: the total amounts that reporting member banks have on deposit in other commercial banks. [40]

balance transfer: the process of forwarding the balance from an old to a new ledger sheet. All or part of the old ledger becomes a statement of account which will be sent to a customer. [31]

balancing: the ultimate act of bringing

two sets of related figures into agreement. As in proof work—the total of deposits being in agreement with the totals of all items making up the deposits—this is "balance" in banking parlance. All work in banks must be in balance, all debits equaling all credits. Minor errors that develop from large volumes are carried into "difference" or "suspense" accounts until uncovered by audits or until customers' discrepancies are reported and located. Adjustments are then made, and the difference account properly adjusted. [10]

balboa: monetary unit of Panama.

balloon: a lump-sum payment a home borrower owes after expiration of a home loan payable to the loaning bank. see *buy down, roll over.*

ballooning: price manipulation used to send prices beyond safe or real values.

balloon loan: a loan on which small payments are made during the term of the obligation.

balloon mortgage: a mortgage that allows for payments that do not completely amortize the loan at the time of termination. As a result, the final payment is larger than any single payment made previously.

balloon note: a promissory note requiring only a small payment during the initial loan period, which is then offset by larger payments made before the date of maturity.

balloon payment: a large extra payment that may be charged at the end of a loan or lease. [1]

Baltimore method: a formula for appraising corner lots in which the lot is determined to be worth the value of the inside lots on each of its sides.

Baltimore Stock Exchange: see *Philadelphia-Baltimore-Washington Stock Exchange.*

banded currency: paper money that has been sorted, counted, and banded in separate denominations. [59]

bank: an organization, normally a corporation, chartered by the state or federal government, the principal functions of which are: (a) to receive demand and time deposits, honor instruments drawn against them, and pay interest on them as permitted by law; (b) to discount notes, make loans, and invest in government or other securities; (c) to collect checks, drafts, notes, etc.; (d) to issue drafts and cashier's checks; (e) to certify depositor's checks; and (f) when authorized by a chartering government, to act in a fiduciary capacity. see *branch banking, commercial bank, correspondent bank, country bank, drive-in banking, Federal Reserve Bank, group banking, independent bank, industrial bank, insured bank, investment banking, member bank, mortgage banker, multiple banking, mutual savings bank, national bank, private bank, savings bank, state bank, trust company*

bankable bill: a document that can be discounted at a bank.

bankable paper: paper that meets the credit standards for acceptance or endorsement by a bank. This paper is called bank paper. see also *bankable bill.*

bank acceptance: signed by a bank, any accepted bill of exchange or draft.

bank accommodation: a short-term bank loan to a customer, either on the individual's own note or on the endorsement of another's note owed to him or her.

bank account: a financial relationship created in the name of a business or individual. There are a variety of such accounts, including time accounts; demand accounts; and single name, multiname, joint, or trustee accounts. Minimum balance and payment of interest will vary. see specific types of accounts.

Bank Act, Canada: passed in December, 1980 in Toronto, Canada, the size of any foreign-owned banking operation was limited to 8 percent of the domestic assets of all banks. The act automatically terminates in 10 years unless revised or extended.

BankAmericard Service Exchange: see *BASE.*

bank balance: the funds in a depositor's account after all deposits have been added to the previous balance and the depositor's checks and services charges have been subtracted.

bank bill: see *bank note.*

bank book: a passbook used by banks to list entries such as interest, deposits, and withdrawals for a customer. In ordinary situations, the customer retains the book as a permanent record.

bankbooks: a bank's records of the status of other banks' deposits with it and vice versa. The term "bankbook" is sometimes used in lieu of "passbook." [31]

bank call: a request for a bank's balance sheet for a specified date, made by government statement.

bank card: see *bank credit card.*

bank charge plans: a relatively new and important development in the general field of consumer credit. Usually a copyrighted plan brought to a community by a bank or private organization under charter or franchise for providing a complete credit service, including credit authorization, billing, and collection of 30-day accounts for representative stores. Most banks charge 5 percent or less of total credit sales for their service. [41]

bank check: a check drawn by a bank on itself and signed by an authorized officer. Savings banks do not usually draw such checks. synonymous with *cashier's check, officer's check, treasurer's check.* [39]

bank clearing

(1) *banking:* bank items sent by member banks to a local clearinghouse for collection.

(2) *finance:* the total volume of dollars on all items that are exchanged among members of a local clearinghouse(s).

bank clubs: to cope with possible bankruptcies and near-failures, lending institutions are attempting, through the formation of a group of creditors, to administer the orderly liquidation or rehabilitation of their shakiest borrowers.

bank credit: credit created by commercial banks through the media of loans and discounts granted with or without collateral. The amount of credit so extended is controlled in part by the rediscount rates established by the Federal Reserve Board.

bank credit card: a credit card issued by a bank, enabling the borrower to buy goods and services or obtain a cash loan from banks honoring that card. [78]

bank currency: see *bank note.*

bank debits: the sum total of all debits drawn against deposited funds of individuals, partnerships, corporations, and other legal entities during a given period—usually reported by banks daily.

bank deposit: the placing of valuables, including money, in a bank for safekeeping.

Bank Deposit Insurance Act of 1934: federal legislation, to protect depositors, extended to June 1935 for bank deposit insurance originally established by the Banking Act of 1933. This act eventually led to the creation of a permanent deposit insurance program in 1935.

bank deregulation: see *Depository Institutions Deregulation Committee*

bank directors: selected by the stockholders of a bank from among their own number, directors are responsible to the stockholders for profitable management and to government supervisory authority for operation of the bank according to law and sound banking principles. [50]

bank discount: a charge, often expressed as a percent of the face amount of the commercial paper or personal note, which is imposed by a bank for payment prior to the note's maturity.

bank draft: a check drawn by one bank against funds deposited to its account in another bank.

bank-eligible issues: issues of U.S. Treasury obligations eligible for immediate purchase by commercial banks—mainly those due or callable within 10 years. [67]

bank endorsement: an endorsement stamped on the back of items passing through the bank. This endorsement is stamped either by a hand stamp or by endorsing machines. Banks either endorse or identify all items taken in through the teller's window or deposited through the mail, except "on us" checks cashed or items coming into the bank from clearinghouse exchanges or in cash letters. Banks in larger cities may use endorsing equipment whereby they can delete a portion of the bank endorsement, and show only the date and ABA transit number of the bank sending in the item. In this way, these banks can identify any item as to the bank which sent it to them. Bank endorsements contain the following legend: "Pay to the order of any bank, banker, or trust company. All prior endorsements guaranteed." The endorsement will show the date, the bank's name in full, and the bank's transit number, usually in two places. Bank endorsements are very important to all bankers, in that they provide a means of tracing items through the collection channels of the banking system. see *examine for bank endorsement, return item.* [10]

banker's acceptance: bill of exchange drawn on or accepted by a bank to pay specific bills for one of its customers when the bills become due.

banker's bank: a central bank. In the United States, one of the 12 Federal Reserve District Banks. They are:

1st District	Boston
2nd District	New York
3rd District	Philadelphia
4th District	Cleveland
5th District	Richmond

6th District	Atlanta
7th District	Chicago
8th District	St. Louis
9th District	Minneapolis
10th District	Kansas City
11th District	Dallas
12th District	San Francisco

bank examination: an examination made by representatives of a federal or state bank supervisory authority to make certain that a bank is solvent and is operating in conformity with banking laws and sound banking principles. [50]

bank examiner: a person who, as the representative of a federal or state bank supervisory authority, examines the banks under its jurisdiction with respect to their financial condition, management, and policies. [31]

bank exchanges: checks, notes, drafts, and so on, that are collected through a clearinghouse system.

bank failure: the closing of a bank, either temporarily or permanently, resulting from financial difficulties.

bank for cooperatives: see *Farm Credit Administration.*

Bank for International Settlements (BIS): established in 1930, this organization was designed to foster cooperation among world central banks, to seek opportunities for development of financial activity among governments, and to serve as an agent involving the transfer of payments. BIS is located in Basel, Switzerland.

bank holding company: in general usage, any company that owns or controls one or more banks. However, a bank holding company as defined in the Bank Holding Company Act of 1956 is one that controls two or more banks. Such companies must register with the Board of Governors of the Federal Reserve System and are commonly referred to as registered bank holding companies. see entries under *Bank Holding Company Act.*

Bank Holding Company Act of 1956: applied to any corporation controlling 25 percent or more of the voting shares of at least two banks, or otherwise controlling the election of a majority of the directors of two or more banks. The law formulated standards for the formation of bank holding companies. These companies were strictly limited to the business of banking, managing banks, and providing services to affiliated banks. see *Bank Holding Company Act Amendments of 1966, 1970.* [64]

Bank Holding Company Act Amendments of 1966: established uniform standards for bank agencies and the court in evaluating the legality of bank holding company acquisitions. see *Bank Holding Company Act of 1956, Bank Holding Company Act Amendments of 1970.* [64]

Bank Holding Company Act Amendments of 1970: ended the exemption from the Bank Holding Company Act that one-bank holding companies had enjoyed since 1956. This last amendment clearly regulated the ownership of bank shares and limited bank holding company entries into activities related only to the business of banking. see *Bank Holding Company Act of 1956, Bank Holding Company Act Amendments of 1966.* [64]

bank holiday: a day on which banks are closed.

Banking Act of 1933: the first major

piece of banking legislation during the Roosevelt administration; it led to significant changes in banking laws (see, e.g., *bank credit, branch banking, insurance*). see also *Federal Deposit Insurance Corporation.*

Banking Act of 1935: federal legislation amending the Banking Act of 1933, the Federal Reserve Act, and other banking regulations, to make these laws more specific.

banking business: primarily the business of receiving funds on deposit and making loans. [10]

banking power: the strength of investing possessed by a bank as determined by the bank's excess reserves.

banking syndicate: a group of banks created for the purpose of underwriting and selling of an issue of securities.

bank insolvency: where a bank's capital is impaired and the appropriate authorities decide to close and/or liquidate the bank.

bank loan: any money borrowed from a bank for the purposes of business investment.

Bank Merger Act: federal legislation of 1960, amended in 1966, identifying the legal responsibilities resulting from bank mergers. see also entries under *Bank Holding Company Act.*

bank money order: see *money order.*

bank note

(1) a promissory note released by an authorized bank that is payable on demand to the bearer and can be used as cash. Such notes, as established by law, are redeemable as money and are considered to be full legal tender.

(2) synonymous with *bank bill* or *bank currency.*

bank number: see *American Bankers Association number.*

bank of deposit: usually associated with commercial banks that accept deposits subject to demand check withdrawal.

bank of discount: banks, usually commercial, that offer credit on acceptances, bills of exchange, and notes. When Federal Reserve Banks engage in discounting, it is properly called "rediscounting" because the notes have already been discounted by the borrowing commercial bank.

bank of issue: any bank that is legally permitted to issue money (e.g., bank notes).

bank overdraft: an amount owed to a bank by a customer on his or her account, resulting from payment of checks for an amount in excess of the drawer's balance. The bank levies a charge based on the amount overdrawn and calculated on a day-to-day basis, establishing a fixed limit that the customer may withdraw.

bank paper: paper showing acceptance or endorsement by a bank; paper that meets the credit standards for acceptance or bank endorsement.

bank passbook: a small book given to the customer by a bank to record deposits and withdrawals.

bank post remittance: the conversion into cash or a money form of a foreign bill of exchange, and subsequent mailing of the latter to the payee.

bank premises: book value of building and equipment. [40]

bank rate

(1) the rate of discount established by the national bank of a country for

rediscounting of eligible paper.

(2) the rate charged by the national bank of a country on advances on specific collateral to banks.

bank reconcilliation: see *reconciliation.*

bank reference: the name of the bank with which a firm has an account, presented to another firm as a reference so that its credit position can be assessed.

bank reserves: commercial banks that are members of the Federal Reserve System are required to hold a proportion of their deposit liabilities in the form of reserves with the Federal Reserve District Bank or till cash. Nonmember state banks only have to fulfill the requirements of their state's banking laws.

bank return: a statement of a check clearinghouse.

bankroll: slang, to support with money any project managed by others.

bank run: a series of unusually large withdrawals made on a bank out of fear that the bank may run out of funds.

bankrupt: a person, corporation, or other legal entity which, being unable to meet its financial obligations, has been declared by a decree of the court to be insolvent, and whose property becomes liable to administration under the Bankruptcy Reform Act of 1978. see *insolvent.*

bankruptcy: the conditions under which the financial position of an individual, corporation, or other legal entity are such as to cause actual or legal insolvency. Two types are: (a) *involuntary bankruptcy*—one or more creditors of an insolvent debtor file a petition having the debtor declared a bankrupt; and (b) *voluntary bankruptcy*—the debtor files a petition claiming inability to meet debts and willingness to be declared a bankrupt. A court adjudges and declares a debtor a bankrupt. see *Bankruptcy Reform Act of 1978. insolvency, National Bankruptcy Act of 1898.*

Bankruptcy Reform Act of 1978: taking effect on October 1, 1978, the first complete overhaul of bankruptcy statutes in 75 years. Some major provisions are: (a) a consolidation of the three sections of the old law that dealt with business reorganizations—in effect, a restructuring to permit a company to return to fiscal soundness—into a new, streamlined Chapter 11; (b) various new tactical weapons for business creditors, one of which may allow them, in certain instances, to file their own reorganization plans for a company; (c) new federal exemptions for consumers that may allow them to keep more property after bankruptcy than they could under state laws unless the states take contrary action; and (d) a new procedure that will allow small businesses to pay off their debts gradually under a proceeding similar to a reorganization. see *bankruptcy.*

Bankruptcy Tax Act of 1980: federal legislation that went into effect on January 1, 1981. In part, the law says that a company that buys back its own bonds at a discount price must pay income tax on the spread between the face value of the bonds, or the original sales price, and the discount repurchase price. see also *solvent debtor section.*

Bank Secrecy Act of 1970: federal

legislation compelling banks to keep records of all customer transactions and to report any financial dealings involving more than $10,000 to the U.S. Treasury Department. The government contends that the records are the bank's business records and are not owned by the depositor.

bank securities: commercial bank offerings include convertible or nonconvertible capital debentures, convertible or nonconvertible preferred stock, and common stock.

bank stamp: a bank's endorsement placed on the back side of a check, note, or other negotiable instrument with an endorsement machine or rubber stamp.

bank statement

(1) **banking:** a statement of a customer's account periodically rendered by the bank. It shows all deposits made and all checks paid and other debits posted during the period, usually one month, as well as the current balance; the customer's canceled checks may or may not be enclosed.

(2) **banking:** a bank's financial statement.

Bank Wire System: a private, computerized message system administered for and by participating banks, through the facilities of Western Union. The system links about 250 banks in about 75 cities. Like the Fedwire, the Bank Wire transmits funds and transfers information, but also relays data concerning loan participations, bond closings, payment for securities, borrowing of federal funds, and balances in company accounts.

banque d'affaires: a French bank in-volved in long-term financing and in the ownership of companies, usually industrial firms. synonymous with *merchant bank.*

Banque de France: the central bank of France, created by Napoleon Bonaparte in 1800.

Ban Ser Corp: formed in 1974 to service insurance plans offered by savings banks to their employees, depositors, and/or mortgagors. Ban Ser does not handle general lines of insurance or service claims. Rather, it acts as liaison between savings banking and the insurance industry in developing new insurance plans to meet savings banks' changing needs and in monitoring existing plans for pricing, service, and standards of coverage. Ban Ser offers a complete insurance consulting service for thrift institutions. [8]

bargain counter: describing stocks offered for sale at prices below their intrinsic value.

bargain hunter

(1) **general:** an individual who seeks out the store selling items at the lowest possible price.

(2) **investments:** a speculator or investor who waits until stocks are on the bargain counter.

bargaining agent: the formally designated agency, usually a labor union, that represents employees seeking or having a collective bargaining agreement (contract). Its rights and obligations are defined by federal law (e.g., National Labor Relations Act).

bargaining creep: progress made in collective bargaining that is slow, with minimal compromise.

bargaining rights

(1) **general:** the legal rights of

workers to bargain collectively with their employers.

(2) **labor relations:** the right of a specific union to represent its members in collective bargaining.

bargaining unit: the group of employees, usually defined by the National Labor Relations Board after a hearing, which a union may seek to represent as bargaining agent on wages, hours, and working conditions. see *collective bargaining.*

"barometers": business measurements used to determine the condition of a market or economy (e.g., Consumer Price Index, housing starts, gross national product, new plant expenditures).

barometer securities: stocks that move in the same direction as the market and are considered to be representative of the market.

barren money: currency that does not earn interest or other forms of income.

Barron's: a weekly publication of financial and investment matters by Dow Jones & Company.

barter: the direct exchange of one item for another without the transfer of money.

BAS: see *block automation system.*

BASE (BankAmericard Service Exchange): the national authorization and electronic draft interchange network used to process BankAmericard credit transactions. [36]

base

(1) **general:** a reference value.

(2) **computers:** the number of characters of use in the digital positions of a numbering system.

(3) **finance:** metal, coin, or bullion that is adulterated, containing inferi-

or of less valuable metal. They have little value when compared to precious metals of gold and silver.

(4) **statistics:** a number that is multiplied by itself.

Basel Agreement: signed in 1967 between Great Britian and the major nations of the West, this agreement determined the repayment of advances for funds given to the United Kingdom during its sterling crisis. The agreement is important since it represents the first time that a nation agreed to a dollar guarantee on its debt to other nations.

base pay: the regular rate of pay for an identified time period, excluding overtime, bonuses, and other premiums. see *basic wages.*

base period

(1) **finance:** a chosen date from the past used in measuring the price index.

(2) **personnel:** the period during which an employee fulfills the length of employment required to receive state unemployment insurance benefits.

base time: the established time for the normal performance of work by an average employee, excluding time allowed for rest, mechanical failures, and other delays.

basic crops: clearly identified farm items subject to government price support, including wheat, corn, cotton, rice, and peanuts.

basic piece rate: part of a wage incentive plan allowing for payment to be made as a direct proportion to the production yield.

basic rating: standard classification under the numerical system for selection of risks. [12]

basic wages: payment received by employees for work performed, based on time or output. see *base pay.*

basis

(1) *finance:* the yield to maturity of bonds at a given price, as shown by bond tables.

(2) *taxation:* in calculating capital gains or losses, the value employed as the original property cost, which may or may not be the true cost.

(3) *investments:* the difference between the cash price of a money market instrument that is hedged and a futures contract.

basis point: $\frac{1}{100}$ of 1 percent, a minimal measure in finance and trade.

basis quote: the sale or offer of a cash commodity measured as the difference less than or more than a futures price.

basis value: the value of a security considered as an investment, and, with bonds, as bearing interest, if held to maturity.

basket purchase: the purchase of a group of assets for one price. So that the items can be recorded individually in the accounts, however, a cost is assigned to each asset.

batch: a group of deposits, or a group of other items, which are proved in one operation. synonymous with *block.* [39]

batch processing

(1) *computers:* the technique of executing a set of computer programs such that each is completed before the next program of the set is begun.

(2) *systems:* a sequential processing procedure that uses an accumulation or set of units.

batch proof: a system for proving deposits, usually performed in the following sequence: (a) deposits are assembled in groups of various sizes; (b) deposit tickets are sorted into one group; (c) checks are sorted into several classifications, such as clearings, transit, and bookkeeping; (d) cash release tickets are sorted according to teller; (e) deposit tickets, checks, and cash release tickets are listed on a "batch" or "block" sheet in their respective columns; and (f) the total of the deposit and other credits should equal the recapitulation of the checks and debits. [10]

batch sheet: a proof sheet used in the batch proof system. The batch sheet is arranged in columns for deposits, various classifications of checks and other debits, and cash release tickets. After sorting, all items in the batch are listed in their respective columns, the totals recapped and proved. The batch sheet then becomes a permanent record of the bank, and is used by bank auditors to check any errors arising from transactions. [10]

batch system: see *batch proof.*

batch ticket: when used in an MICR system, the batch ticket is a control document encoded with the total amount of a batch and identified by a special transaction code. The batch ticket can also contain such encoded information as batch number, source number, and/or proof machine number. This ticket accompanies the items from the proof department to the document processing center. [31]

bath, to take a: slang, to go into bankruptcy.

batten: to grow wealthy at another's expense.

bay: space on a selling floor between four columns; a recess or opening in walls. [63]

BB

(1) see *Big Board.*

(2) see *bond, baby.*

(3) see *bond, bearer.*

(4) see *buy back.*

BC: see *blue chip.*

BD

(1) see *bad delivery.*

(2) see *bill discounted.*

Bd.

(1) see *board.*

(2) see *bond.*

BDO: see *bottom dropped out.*

B/E: see *bill of exchange.*

bear: a person who thinks security prices will fall. A bear market is one that goes down over a period of time. see *bears.* [68]

bear account: any short account.

bear clique: a group of people or organizations that attempt to depress the price of stocks and commodities by selling short. The formation of a bear clique for this manipulative objective is outlawed. see *bear raid, short sale.*

bearer: any person holding a negotiable instrument.

bearer bond: see *bond, bearer.*

bearer certificate: a certificate that is not filled out in the name of a particular person. Since these certificates are negotiable without endorsement, they should always be kept in a safe place.

bearer check: a check payable to cash or to the bearer rather than to a specific party. [59]

bearer form: in a form payable to bearer, the security having no registered owner. [67]

bearer instrument: a negotiable instrument payable on demand to the individual who holds the instrument. Title passes by delivery without endorsement.

bear hug: an unnegotiated corporate takeover proposal, made privately or publicly to directors. The major goal is to force a board into a decision.

bearish and bullish: when conditions suggest lower prices, a bearish situation is said to exist. If higher prices appear warranted, the situation is said to be bullish. [2]

bear market: a declining stock market. [20]

bear position: stance taken by a person who expects the market to fall. As a consequence, he or she sells securities short, hoping that the market will move downward.

bear raid: attempts to depress the price of a security or item by heavy selling.

bears: speculators who anticipate that prices are going to drop. see *bear, hammering the market.*

beat down: slang, to bargain to lower the cost of an item.

beating the gun: prohibited by the SEC, the practice of accepting customer orders for a new stock, and/or releasing significant data on a new offering, prior to the registration statement of the security's becoming effective.

beewy: slang, money, especially coins.

beggar-my-neighbor policy: an attempt to discourage imports by increasing tariffs or using other effective means.

Bellevue Project: a banking program of study and implementation leading to the Bellevue Exchange, an automated teller facility in Bellevue, Washington, available to the customers of a group of cooperating thrift institutions on a shared basis and has become a model for other banks.

bellweather stock: any security used as a measure of the stock market's movement. In most cases, these are stocks that indicate the direction of the general market about two or three weeks before other securities follow a similar pattern.

below par: at a discount; less than face amount.

benchmark reserves: reserve funds, representing a specified percentage of savings deposits, that all savings association members of the Federal Savings and Loan Insurance Corporation must hold. [59]

Benef.: see *beneficiary*.

beneficial interest (owner): an individual, not the true owner of property, who enjoys all or part of the benefits to it, by reason of a trust or private arrangement.

beneficiary
(1) *general:* a person beneficially interested in a trust or estate.
(2) *banking:* the person(s) to whom the proceeds of a life insurance contract are payable at the death of the insured.
(3) *law:* the person for whose benefit a trust, policy, will, or contract promise is made. synonymous with *cestui que trust.*

beneficiary, change of: process of altering the beneficiary endorsement to provide for payment to one other than originally named, or to provide for payment in a different manner. [12]

beneficiary, contingent: a beneficiary who is entitled to benefits only after the death of a primary beneficiary. [53]

beneficiary, endorsement: an endorsement placed on (or attached to in rider form) the policy setting forth the names of the beneficiaries, relationship to the insured, manner in which policy proceeds are to be paid, and conditions upon which each beneficiary's right to receive such payment is based. [12]

beneficiary, irrevocable: a benficiary for whom another may not be substituted by the insured. [53]

beneficiary, primary: the first beneficiary entitled to benefits upon the death of an insured. [53]

benefit
(1) *general:* a gain or advantage received by an individual; that which fulfills a need.
(2) *banking:* the amount of indemnity to be regularly paid.

benefit formula: a formula for computing the amount of annuity, pension, or other benefit payable under a retirement plan, usually based upon salary, or wages, length of service, and age. [52]

benefit principle of taxation: the rationale for taxation based on the benefits received from the government by the taxpayer.

Benelux: a cooperative organization formed by Belgium, The Netherlands, and Luxembourg to encourage economic activity among the three nations.

bequeath: to offer personal property in a will.

bequest: a gift of personal property made by a testator. see *legacy.*

Bernard rule: a rule for appraising a corner lot. First, the property is appraised as if it were an inside lot fronting on a side street; it is then taken as an inside lot on the main street. The value placed on the corner lot is the total of the two appraisals.

Beta: a measure of a stock's sensitivity to the movement of the general market (S&P 500), in either direction over the last five years. A Beta of 1.6 means that over the past five years, the stock has moved 60 percent greater than the S&P 500, both up and down. [68]

Better Business Bureau: a voluntary agency of business executives created to improve business practices and to define fair standards and ethics in the conduct of business activity. The movement to better conditions began in 1921, when Vigilance Committees for Truth in Advertising first appeared in local advertising clubs.

betterment: an improvement made to property that increases its value more than would ordinary repair or maintence work.

BF: see *backdoor financing.*

Bfcy.: see *beneficiary.*

Bgt.: bought.

BH: see *bank holiday.*

biannual: occurring twice a year [61]

bid: an offering of money in exchange for property (items, goods, etc.) put up for sale. Types of bids are: *best bid*—not necessarily the lowest or highest, but good for the organization seeking a bid; *competitive bid*—a bid secured from a public announce-

ment of the competition; and *sealed bid*—a bid that is not disclosed until a specified time, when all other bids are revealed and compared. (This approach purports to guarantee the independence of bidders.)

bid and asked: a "bid" is the quotation of a prospective buyer for a purchase; "asked" is the quotation of a seller for the sale of a trading unit or other specified amount of security. Often referred to as a quotation or quote. The bid is the highest price offered by anyone for a security at a given time.

bid bond: see *bond, bid.*

bidding

(1) *general:* the application by an employee for consideration for a job open in a plant or office. In most contracts, assuming all qualifications to be equal, first preference is given to the applicant with the most seniority. see *posting.*

(2) *finance:* the act of offering money as an exchange for an item or service.

bidding up: the activity of raising the price bid for a security, for fear of failing to have an order executed before an upswing begins.

bid price: in the case of open-end shares, the price at which the holder may redeem his shares; in most cases, it is the current net asset value per share. In the case of closed-end shares, the highest price then offered for stock in the public market. [30]

bids and offers: a "bid" is the quotation of a prospective buyer for the purchase; and an "offer" is the quotation of a seller for the sale of a trading unit or other specified amount of a security. Some of the established methods of trading in securities are: *for cash*—delivery and payment must be made on the same day; *regular way delivery*—securities must be delivered and paid for on the third full business day after sale; and *seller's option*—the seller has the right to deliver the securities within a period of not less than 4 nor more than 60 days. [10]

bid wanted: a request by the seller of a stock or commodity who wishes to locate a purchaser for it.

big bath accounting: the practice not only of writing off segments of a business that are obviously doing poorly, but of getting rid of marginal operations as well. The value of the item being written down is reduced by a one-time subtraction from the asset side of the balance sheet, and income is reduced accordingly. But lowering the values of plant and equipment also means lower depreciation costs in the future; and a smaller depreciation expense—which is subtracted from gross sales—means higher earnings.

Big Board: the New York Stock Exchange, Inc. cf. *Little Board.*

Big Eight: the eight largest public accounting firms; in alphabetical order: Arthur Andersen and Co.; Coopers and Lybrand; Ernst and Ernst; Haskins and Sells; Peat, Marwick, Mitchell and Co.; Price Waterhouse and Co.; Touche Ross and Co.; and Arthur Young and Company.

Big Five

(1) the five largest credit card companies: American Express, Carte Blanche, Diners Club, Master Card, and Visa (BankAmericard).

(2) the five largest commercial banks of the United Kingdom: Midland Bank Ltd., Barclay's Bank Ltd., Lloyd's Bank Ltd., National Provincial Bank Ltd., and Westminster Bank Ltd.

big George: slang, a quarter (25 cents).

big one: slang, $1000, usually a $1000 bill.

Big Steel: referring to the United States Steel Corporation. Sometimes the term is used to include the other large manufacturers of steel: Bethlehem, Republic, National, Armco, Jones Laughlin, Inland Steel, and Youngstown Sheet and Tube. see *Little Steel.*

Big Three: the three largest automobile manufacturers in the United States: General Motors Corporation, the Ford Motor Company, and the Chrysler Corporation.

big ticket: slang, the selling of an expensive item to a customer.

bilateral agreement: an agreement made between two persons or two groups.

bilateral contract: an agreement containing promises, with each party serving as a promisor or promisee.

bilateral monopoly: exists when there is only one purchaser for an item or service and the creation of the supply is controlled by one seller.

bilateral payments agreement: an agreement between two countries or their central banks to channel all or specified settlements between themselves through special accounts, normally subject to a reciprocal credit margin (swing). Arrangements of this nature usually imply that the use of convertible foreign currencies or gold between the partner countries is avoided except when the credit margin is exceeded or net balances are settled. [42]

bill

(1) *general:* an invoice of charges for services or a product.

(2) *finance:* paper currency.

(3) *law:* the instrument of formal issuance of a complaint before a court; a court's formal statement reporting its findings.

bill adjuster: a person employed in a credit office. Receives and investigates complaints made by customers of errors on bills. [41]

bill book: synonymous with *liability ledger.* see *liability ledger.*

bill broker: any financial dealer in bills of exchange.

bill check: a payment system in which a debtor, on receipt of an invoice or statement, authorizes the creditor to obtain payment directly from the debtor's deposit account.

bill discounted: a promissory note or bill of exchange from which a bank deducts its interest in advance.

billed escrow: the amount of escrow payment that represents a total of the regular escrow payment plus arrears or minus prepaid escrow amounts.

billed principal: the amount of principal payment that represents a total of the normal principal amount plus any arrears.

biller: a person trained in operation of bookkeeping or billing machines and responsible for posting all debit and credit transactions to a group of individual customers' accounts. [41]

billing: the process of submitting invoices or bills.

billing cycle: time interval, often a month, between regular periodic billing statement dates. [78]

billing error: a mistake in a periodic statement due to a charge made by someone not authorized by the cardholder, an error in arithmetic, failure to reflect a credit, a charge for which the cardholder requests clarification, or other instances defined by the Fair Credit Billing Act and Regulation Z. [78]

bill of credit

(1) *banking:* an individual's written request to a bank asking for the delivery of money to the bearer on the credit or account of the writer.

(2) *finance:* used as if it were a state's currency. Article 1 of the U.S. Constitution forbids the states to issue their own currency.

bill of exchange: instructions from one party to another party to pay a third party following completion of an assignment. see *commercial set.*

bill of lading: a statement whereby the carrier acknowledges receipt of freight, identifies the freight, and sets forth a contract of carriage. see *commercial set;* cf. *accommodation, clean, straight, through, bill of lading.*

bill of materials: a specification of the quantities of direct materials allowed for manufacturing a given quantity of output.

bill of sale

(1) *general:* a written agreement by whose terms the ownership of goods is transferred or assigned to another person.

(2) *banking:* a formal written agreement by which one person transfers to another his or her rights, interest, and title in specified property. It is considered to be sufficient warranty of the seller's title to the property and his or her right to sell; it

need not be recorded as a deed for real property.

bill of sight: a temporary entry permit, authorized by a customs official, for imported items, allowing the goods to be unloaded from a carrier to permit examination by a customs agent to identify their true character.

bills discounted: bills of exchange, notes, and acceptances that a bank has discounted for its customers.

bills of credit: an obsolete term found in the U.S. Constitution for paper money issued by the government.

bills payable
(1) *general:* a comprehensive term that includes all notes and trade acceptances that are owed by a business to trade creditors and must be paid by the business at maturity.
(2) *banking:* refers to the sum of money that a member bank has borrowed, on its own collateral note, from a Federal Reserve Bank.

bills receivable: a comprehensive term that includes the total of all notes and trade acceptances given by customers, usually in payment of merchandise, which the debtors must pay at maturity.

bimetallism: a double standard of metals used in coins. The ratio of content and weight must be specified in terms of, for example, gold and silver. cf. *monometallism, parallel standard, real money.*

binary
(1) *general:* pertaining to a characteristic or property involving a selection, choice, or condition in which there are two possibilities.
(2) *computers:* a numbering system based on 2's rather than 10's that

uses only the digits 0 and 1 when written.

binary card: a standard data-processing card on which information is punched in binary form.

binder
(1) *banking:* a legal agreement issued either by an agent or by a company, to provide temporary insurance until a policy can be written. It usually contains a definite time limit, is in writing, and clearly designates the company in which the risk is bound the amount, the perils insured against, and the type of insurance.
(2) *banking:* an initially written agreement, with a valuable consideration given as evidence of good faith by the offerer to purchase property.
(3) *law:* any temporary agreement obligating the several parties to the contract.

binding signature: a legally acceptable signature. One which when affixed to a legal document makes that document valid and enforceable. [55]

bird-dog: to seek data to assist in studying a firm's position and potential earnings.

BIS: see *Bank for International Settlements.*

bit
(1) *computers:* a binary digit (acronym).
(2) *computers:* a single character in a binary number.

Bk.: see *bank.*

Bkg.: banking.

Bkr.: see *broker.*

Bks.: see *book(s).*

B&L ASSN: see *building and loan association.*

B/L: see *bill of lading.*

blackboard trading: the practice of selling commodities from a blackboard on a wall of a commodity exchange.

black box: a projected working model of a wholly electronic stock exchange that some predict will eventually replace the traditional stock exchanges.

black capitalism: an attempt to increase business ownership among the blacks.

Black Friday: September 24, 1869: the day of a business panic resulting from an attempt by financiers to corner the gold market. A depression followed. Coincidentally, the financial panics of 1873 and 1929 also first became serious on Fridays, hence the term, indicating a day of evil or calamity.

black market: buying or selling of products and commodities, or engaging in exchange of foreign currencies in violation of government restrictions. cf. *gray market.*

black money: slang, for income that is not reported for tax purposes because of its illegal origin.

black work: slang, for tax-evading labor that people do outside their regular jobs. Black work induces some workers to demand cuts in normal working hours so that they will have more time for outside jobs, where they attempt to escape mandatory Social Security contributions. see *moonlight.*

Bland-Allison Act: federal legislation of 1878 authorizing limited governmental purchase and coinage of silver; also permitted the issuance of silver certificates secured by silver in amounts equal to the face value of the certificates.

blank check: a bank form that has been signed, although the amount payable or the name of the payee has been left out.

blank endorsement: the signature or endorsement of a person or firm on an instrument such as a note or check making it payable to the bearer and therefore negotiable without restrictions.

blanket agreement: a collective bargaining agreement based on an industrywide negotiation or large geographic areas within an industry, as established by the Norris-LaGuardia Act (the Anti-Injunction Act). see *Anti-Injunction Act of 1932; also injunction.*

blanket bond: see *bond, blanket.*

blanket loan: a loan made to a developer or contractor for a number of individual properties. [59]

blanket mortgage: a mortgage covering all the property of a corporation and given to secure a single debt.

blanket order: a preseason order to meet expected buyer demand.

blasted: slang, a person without money.

blighted area: an area in a community or neighborhood that is about to become a slum.

blind entry: a bookkeeping entry stating only the accounts and the amounts debited and credited, but not giving other data or accounting factors essential to an accurate record.

blip: slang, a nickel (5 cents).

block

(1) *banking:* a bundle of checks deposited for credit with a bank, along with their relative deposit slips.

(2) **computers:** a group of words or characters considered or transported as a unit, particularly with reference to input and output.

(3) **investments:** a large holding or transaction of stock popularly considered to be 10,000 shares or more. [20]

blockade: the act of preventing commercial exchange with a country or port, usually during wartime, by physically preventing carriers from entering a specific port or nation. see *embargo, navicert;* cf. *preclusive purchasing.*

blockage: designating the administration of an account as subject to U.S. Treasury control because of enemy or suspected enemy interest. A discount from the established market for which a large block of stock of a single corporation would have to be sold if the entire holding were placed on the market at a given date (a term used in connection with federal estate tax). [37]

block automation system: initiated in 1970 by the New York Stock Exchange, a computerized communications network to aid in large-block transactions by institutional investors. This approach enables such investors to identify buyers and sellers rapidly when they are considering a trade.

block busting: the unethical real estate practice of creating fear by renting or selling units in a neighborhood to families of a religion or race different from that of the current residents, thus exploiting the prejudices and emotions of property owners so that they will sell their homes at reduced prices.

blocked accounts: in time of war the president of the United States issues directives to financial institutions to suspend payment of the accounts of enemy nationals of or individuals inhabiting occupied countries in the sphere of enemy influence. These funds may be released only by executive order, or by license under certain conditions. This action was taken in 1979 during the Iranian crisis.

block sale: the sale of a significant number of shares, with a buying price of usually more than $100,000.

block system: see *batch proof.*

blood bath: slang, a tremendous loss suffered by investors when the stock market declines sharply.

blotter: a book of accounts or a journal used for entering the first or temporary list of transactions or occurrences. cf. *daily reports.*

blowing off: a temporary purchasing peak, often along with heavy trading volume and occurring after an extended advance.

BLS: see *Bureau of Labor Statistics.*

blue chip: stock market term used to describe a corporation maintaining a good dividend return and having sound management and good growth potential. see also *gilt-edged bond, seasoned issues, seasoned security.*

blue-collar workers: production and maintenance workers, as contrasted with office and professional personnel. The force of blue-collar workers is declining numerically, and by 1980 there were more white-collar workers.

blue law: any state or local law restricting business activity on Sunday. Blue laws have been contested as an infringement of individual and free enterprise rights.

blue list: the trade offering sheets of bond dealers, listing dealers' offerings of municipal bonds for sale all over the country. A composite list published five days a week by The Blue List Publishing Company, New York City, showing current municipal bond offerings by banks and municipal bond houses all over the country. [67]

blue sky law: name given to certain laws enacted by the various states to regulate the sale and issuance of securities, specifically, attempting to prevent fraud in their sale and disposition. cf. *SEC.*

BM

(1) see *bear market.*

(2) see *buyers' market.*

BN: see *bank note.*

BO

(1) see *back order.*

(2) see *buy order.*

board: a standing committee of high rank or importance (e.g., a board of directors).

board lot: the unit of trading for stocks on an exchange; the unit of trading in stocks on the New York Stock Exchange is 100 shares. see *even lots.*

board of directors: people chosen by stockholders of a corporation to manage the enterprise.

Board of Governors: the seven-member governing body of the Federal Reserve System.

board of managers: a term given in some states to the board of trustees of a mutual savings bank. [39]

board of trade: business executives who operate a local commodities ex-

change or a member of commerce.

board of trustees: the body in a mutual savings bank which manages the institution, establishes the policies under which it is to be operated, appoints the officers, and the like. [39]

boardroom

(1) *finance:* a room set aside for use by the board of directors of a business.

(2) *investments:* a room for registered representatives and customers in a broker's office, where opening, high, low, and last prices of leading stocks used to be posted on a board throughout the market day. Today such price displays are normally electronically controlled, although most board rooms have replaced the board with the ticker and/or individual quotation machines. [20]

BOC

(1) see *back office crunch.*

(2) see *breach of contract.*

BOD: see *board of directors.*

Boerse: Dutch and German, for stock exchange.

boffo: slang, $1.

boff out: slang, to lose one's money.

BOG: see *Board of Governors.*

bogey: efforts by employees to restrict output by setting up an informal standard (bogey), which the employees do exceed.

bogus: false, counterfeit, nonexistent, or fraudulent: bogus money is counterfeit currency; a bogus check is written on nonexistent account or bank.

boilerplate: slang, standard legal language used in motions, wills, closings, and so on.

boiler room tactic: selling of very speculative and often worthless securities through the use of high-pressured and misleading literature. see also *dynamiter.*

bolivar: monetary unit of Venezuela.

bolsa: Spanish, for stock exchange.

BOM: see *buying on margin.*

bona fide: "in good faith" (Latin); with honest intent. cf. *mala fides.*

bonanza

(1) *general:* an enormously successful business venture.

(2) *investments:* a highly profitable investment resulting in sudden wealth for the owner.

bona vacentia: describing property of which there is no apparent owner nor claimant (e.g., property in the hands of a liquidator after a firm has been dissolved).

bond

(1) *general:* an interest-bearing certificate of debt, usually issued in series, by which the issuer obligates itself to pay the principal amount at a specified time, usually five years or more after date of issue, and to pay interest periodically, usually semiannually. Bonds may be distinguished from promissory notes or other evidences of debt because of their formal execution under seal, and because a bank has certified that their issue has been authorized by the board of directors of a corporation or other governing body. Corporate bonds are usually secured by a lien against certain specified property. Bonds may be issued in "bearer" or "registered" form.

(2) *banking:* an instrument used as proof of a debt, usually secured by a mortgage. see other entries under *bond.* [5]

(3) *finance:* a promise, under seal

(i.e., closed from view by the public) to pay money.

(4) *finance:* the obligation to answer for the debt of another person.

bond, adjustment: an income bond issued for a firm's reorganization.

bond, agency: a bond issued by U.S. agencies and corporations to cover their own debt—for example, the Federal National Mortgage Association, the Tennessee Valley Authority, and the Federal Financing Bank. Maturities are up to 30 years, and these agency securities rank just below Treasury paper.

bond, annuity: see *bond, perpetual.*

bond, approved: in the preparation for fiduciaries, "legal lists" are determined in some states. The bonds named in the legal list are approved bonds. see *legal list.*

bond, assumed: a bond of one corporation whose liability is taken on by another corporation. see *bond, guaranteed.*

bond, authority: a bond payable from the revenues of a specific authority. Since such authorities usually have no revenue other than charges for services, their bonds are ordinarily revenue bonds. [49]

bond, average: a bond given by an individual in receipt of freight, stating that the recipient will contribute to any standard claim.

bond, baby: a bond with a face value usually of $100 or less.

bond, bail: a bond guaranteeing the appearance in court of the principal named in the bond. [53]

bond, bearer: a bond payable to the holder that does not have the owner's name registered on the books of the issuing company.

bond, bid: a guarantee that the contractor will enter into a contract, if it is awarded to him, and will furnish such contract bond (sometimes called performance bond) as is required by the terms of the bond. [54]

bond, blanket: a form of broad-coverage protection carried by financial institutions to cover losses from robbery, burglary, or employee dishonesty.

bond, borrowed: to meet specific requirements, banks and other financial institutions borrow bonds. Banks borrow bonds to comply with collateral requirements of governmental agencies, whereas brokers borrow bonds to make delivery on short sales.

bond, callable: a bond issue, all of part of which may be redeemed by the issuing corporation under definite conditions, before the issue reaches maturity.

bond, called: a bond that the debtor has declared to be due and payable on a certain date, prior to maturity, in accordance with the provisions of an issue to be redeemed; the bonds to be retired are usually drawn by loss. [37]

bond, city: see *bond, municipal.*

bond, civil: a bond circulated by any governmental agency.

bond, classified: a debt security that receives a designation such as "Series A" or "Series B" to differentiate it from another bond of the same debtor. The series differ as to maturity date and interest.

bond, clean: a bond of the coupon type that has not been changed by any endorsement or rephrasing of the original contract such as the words "assented" or "extended." see *stamped security.*

bond, collateral: further security for a loan.

bond, collateral trust: an issue of bonds for which collateral has been pledged to guarantee repayment of the principal. This type of bond usually arises out of intercompany transactions in which the parent company issues bonds with securities of a subsidiary as the underlying collateral.

bond, combination: a bond issued by a governmental unit which is payable from the revenues of a governmental enterprise but which is also backed by the full faith and credit of the governmental unit. [49]

bond, consolidated: a debt instrument issued to replace two or more bonds issued earlier, often done to simplify a debt structure or to benefit from a lower prevailing rate of interest.

bond, continued: a debt instrument that need not be redeemed at maturity but can continue to earn interest.

bond, contract: a guarantee of the faithful performance of a construction contract and the payment of all labor and materials bills incident thereto. In those situations where two bonds are required—one to cover performance and the other to cover payment of labor and material—the former is known as a performance bond and the latter as a payment bond. [54]

bond, convertible: a bond that gives to its owner the privilege of exchanging it for other securities of the issuing corporation on a preferred basis at some future date or under certain conditions.

bond, corporate: an obligation of a corporation. see *bond, long-term corporate.*

bond, coupon: a bond with interest coupons attached. The coupons are clipped as they come due and are presented by the holder for payment of interest. see *talon.* [20]

bond, court: all bonds and mortgages required of litigants to enable them to pursue certain remedies of the courts. [54]

bond, currency: in 1934 the U.S. Supreme Court decided that all bonds, even those with gold clauses, were henceforth to be paid in lawful currency.

bond, cushion: a high-interest-rate bond of top quality that sells at a premium level above par and that usually results in a higher yield to maturity.

bond, customhouse: a bond required by the federal government in connection with the payment of duties or to produce bills of lading.

bond, debenture: a bond for which there is no specific security set aside or allocated for repayment of the principal.

bond, deferred: see *bond, extended.*

bond, deferred serial: a serial bond in which the first installment does not fall due for two or more years from the date of issue. [49]

bond, definitive: any bond issued in final form; used particularly with reference to permanent bonds for which temporary bonds or interim certificates were issued.

bond, depository: a bond guaranteeing payment of funds to depositors in accordance with the terms of a deposit in a bank. [53]

bond, drawn: a bond that has been called for redemption by lot. see *bond, called.*

bond, endorsed: a bond that has been extraneously signed permitting it to be considered for normal delivery according to the regulations of the exchange and which therefore must be sold.

bond, escrow: bond held in escrow. see *escrow.*

bond, estate tax: a certain designated government bond redeemable at par less accrued interest for federal estate taxes to the extent that the entire proceeds are applied to such taxes due, providing the securities were owned by the decedent at the time of death. [52]

bond, extended: a bond that has matured and on which the debtor has not yet paid the principal but has agreed to extend or continue to pay the principal at a later time. Upon the creditor's accepting the extension, the bonds are stamped to show such agreement. synonymous with *"deferred bond."*

bond, external: a bond issued by a country or firm for purchase outside that nation, usually denominated in the currency of the purchaser.

bond, federal: the promissory note of a central government. [28]

bond, fidelity: insurance for an employer (the insured) for loss sustained by him or her because of any dishonest act by an employee covered by the insurance. Blanket fidelity bonds cover groups of employees. see *fidelity insurance.*

bond, fiduciary: a bond, in behalf of a person appointed by a court to a position of trust, as executor of an estate. [12]

bond, flat income: this term means that the price at which a bond is traded includes consideration for all unpaid accruals of interest. Bonds that are in default of interest or principal are traded flat. Income bonds, which pay interest only to the extent earned, are usually traded flat. All other bonds are usually dealt in "and interest," which means that the buyer pays to the seller the market price plus interest accrued since the last payment date. [20]

bond, flower: a U.S. government bond. Until the Tax Reform Act of 1976, flower bonds sold at a substantial premium in relation to other bonds issued at similarly low interest rates because the Treasury accepted them for estate tax payments at 100 cents on the dollar, whatever their cost at the time of purchase. Now this benefit is in part taxable as a capital gain.

bond, forgery: insurance against loss due to forgery or alteration of, on, or in checks or other instruments. [53]

bond, free: an unpledged bond; any bond immediately disposable.

bond, funding: a bond issued to retire outstanding floating debt and to eliminate deficits. [49]

bond, gilt-edged: a high-grade bond issued by a company that has demonstrated its ability to earn a comfortable profit over a period of years and to pay its bondholders their interest without interruption. see also *blue chip.*

bond, government: an obligation of the U.S. government, regarded as the highest-grade issues in existence. see *Treasury bills; Treasury notes.* [20]

bond, guaranteed: a bond on which the principal or income or both are guaranteed by another corporation or parent company in case of default by the issuing corporation.

bond, honor: a consumer-size certificate of deposit with denominations as low as $5.00, many banks promoted these bonds and told purchasers that they were merely honor-bound to report the interest on their tax returns. The Internal Revenue Service moved swiftly to eliminate this irregularity.

bond, improvement: any bond issued by a municipality to finance a public improvement.

bond, improvement mortgage: a bond issued for financing improvements of the debtor business that are secured by a general mortgage.

bond, inactive: see *inactive stock (bond).*

bond, income: a type of bond on which interest is paid when and only when earned by the issuing corporation.

bond, indemnity: a bond that protects the obligee (the party for whom the applicant for bond, the "principal," has undertaken to perform specified duties) against losses resulting from the principal's failure to fulfill his obligations. Examples of miscellaneous indemnity bonds are warehouse, lost instrument, and lien.

bond, indenture: a written agreement under which bonds are issued, setting forth maturity date, interest rate, and other terms.

bond, installment: synonymous with the term "serial bond." see *bond, serial.*

bond, insular: a bond issued by a unit

of the United States (e.g., Alaska, New York). synonymous with "territoral bond."

bond, interchangeable: a bond in either a registered or coupon form that can be converted to the other form or its original form at the request of the holder. A service charge is often made for such a conversion.

bond, interim: sometimes used before the issuance of permanent bonds to raise funds needed only temporarily. synonymous with *temporary bond.* see *bond, temporary.*

bond, intermediate: a callable bond bearing no date of maturity. The call aspect usually is not effective until some stated time period has passed.

bond, internal: a bond issued by a country payable in its own currency; to be distinguished from an external bond, which is a bond issued by one country and sold in another country and payable in the currency of that other country. [37]

bond, internal revenue: a bond required by the U.S. government which guarantees payment of federal taxes and compliance with government regulations. [54]

bond, irredeemable: a bond issued which contains no provisions for being "called" or redeemed prior to maturity date. [10]

bond, joint and several: any debt instrument where the holder seeks payment from more than one corporation up to the full face amount of the security.

bond, joint control: a bond needed prior to transfer of the assets of an estate to the custody of the principal.

bond, judgment: bond issued to fund judgments. see *funding.* [49]

bond, junior: those bonds that are not senior; they are subordinate or secondary to another issue which in the event of liquidation, would have prior claim to the junior bond.

bond, legal: a bond that federal and state laws identify as an acceptable and legal investment for fiduciary institutions.

bond, limited tax: a bond that is secured by a tax that is limited as to amount and rate.

bond, long-term corporate: a debt of industrial corporations, finance companies, utilities, and telephone companies. Maturities range from 10 to 40 years, with intermediates running from 4 to 10 years. They are rated AAA and AA for high quality, A and BBB for medium quality. The face denomination for corporate bonds is $1000, but new issues are often marketed above or below par to adjust to current yields. Older bonds with lower interest coupons sell at discounts.

bond, maintenance: a bond guaranteeing against defects in workmanship or materials for a stated time after the acceptance of work.

bond, mortgage: a bond that has as an underlying security a mortgage on all properties of the issuing corporation.

bond, municipal: a bond issued by a state or a political subdivision (county, city, town, village, etc.). Also, a bond issued by a state agency or authority. In general, interest paid on municipal bonds is exempt from federal income taxes and state and local taxes in the state of issue.

bond, municipal revenue: banks now

may underwrite a few kinds of revenue bonds, which are obligations backed not by city or state tax revenues, but by revenue produced by the facilities that are financed—for example, a housing project. Banks want to be permitted to underwrite more kinds of revenue bonds. In addition, the Comptroller of the Currency is seeking to determine the legality of municipal revenue bonds underwriting, under which banks offer, in effect, to repurchase the bonds at par within five years. This recent activity in banking is testing the Glass-Steagall Act. see *Glass-Steagall Act.*

bond, noncallable: a bond that cannot, under the terms of the issue, be called by the obligor (the corporation) for redemption or conversion. [37]

bond, obligation: a bond authorized by a mortgagor that is larger than the original mortgage amount. A personal obligation is created to safeguard the lender against any costs that may develop over the amount of the mortgage.

bond, open-end: a mortgage bond of an issue that has no limit on the number or quantity of bonds that can be issued under the mortgage. However, some relationship is often required of the number and quantity of bonds to the value of the property that has been mortgaged.

bond, optional: see *bond, callable.*

bond, optional payment: a bond that gives the holder the choice to receive payment of interest or principal or both in the currency of one or more foreign countries, as well as in domestic funds. [37]

bond, overlying: a junior bond, subject to the claim of a senior underlying bond having priority of claim.

bond, participating: a bond which, following the receipt of a fixed rate of periodic interest, also receives some of the profit held by the issuing business. A form of profit sharing, this bond is rarely used today.

bond, passive: a bond that does not carry any interest. Often these bonds are issued following a reorganization.

bond, penal: a bond given by an accused, or by another in his or her behalf, for the repayment of money in the event that the accused fails to appear in court on a specific day. see also *bond, surety.*

bond, performance: a bond supplied by one party to another protecting the second party against loss in the event of improper performance or completion of the terms of an existing contract.

bond, permit: a bond guaranteeing that the person to whom a permit is, or is to be, issued will comply with the law or ordinance regulating the privilege for which the permit is issued. [53]

bond, perpetual: any bond having no maturity date; rarely issued in the United States.

bond, plain: any debenture. see *certificates of debt.*

bond, preference: any income or adjustment bond.

bond, premium: in the United States, a bond that is selling above its face value. In Europe, a bond having a lottery feature. When called, as distinguished from regular maturity, a premium bond generally pays substantially more than the face amount. Also, the excess of the price at which a bond is acquired or sold, over its face value. The price does not include accrued interest at the date of acquisition or sale. [49]

bond, prior-lien: a bond holding precedence over other bonds issued by the same corporation.

bond, privileged: a convertible bond that has attached warrants.

bond, public: any bond issued by a governmental agency, domestic or foreign.

bond, purchase-money: a bond having as security a purchase-money mortgage. *see purchase-money mortgage.*

bond, real estate: a bond secured by a mortgage or trust conveyance of real estate.

bond, redeemable: any callable bond. see *bond, callable; callable.*

bond, redemption: a refunding bond. see *redemption.*

bond, redemption value: guaranteed face amount of a bond payable at maturity. [12]

bond, refunding: a bond issued to retire a bond already outstanding. Refunding bonds may be sold for cash and outstanding bonds redeemed in cash, or they may be exchanged with holders of outstanding bonds. [49]

bond, registered: a bond in which the name of the owner is designated, and the proceeds are payable only to him or her. Bonds may be registered as to principal and interest, or principal only. Interest on a bond registered as to both principal and interest is paid to the owner by check as it becomes due. Bonds registered as to principal only have coupons at-

tached which are detached and collected as the interest becomes due. [10]

bond, regular serial: serial bond in which all periodic instalments of principal repayment are equal in amount. [49].

bond, reorganization: a debt security issued in the recapitalization of a firm in financial difficulty; an adjustment bond.

bond, revenue: a bond whose principal and interest are to be paid solely from earnings; such bonds are usually issued by a municipally owned utility or other public service enterprise the revenues and possibly the properties of which are pledged for this purpose. [49]

Bond, Savings (U.S.): Series EE, introduced at the start of 1980, replaced the highly popular Series E bonds. These new bonds are available in face-value denominations of $50, $75, up to $10,000, and are sold at one-half their face value. EE bonds pay varying interest rates—as much as one percent at six-month intervals if market conditions warrant. Presently, the maturity on Series EE bonds is eight years, down from nine years, effectively boosting the rate on those bonds to 9 percent. The rate on HH bonds is 8.5 percent. HH bonds are bought at face value, pay interest semiannually, and mature in 10 years.

bond, schedule: a bond listing the names and positions of employees included as principals. see *bond, fidelity.* [12]

bond, second-mortgage: a bond issued on property that already has a first mortgage outstanding on it.

bond, secured: a bond secured by the pledge of assets (plant or equipment), the title to which is transferred to bondholders in case of foreclosure.

bond, senior: those bonds having prior claim to the assets of the debtor upon liquidation.

bond, serial: an issue of bonds in which a certain proportion of the bonds is retired at regular intervals, issued when the security depreciates through use or obsolescence. These issues usually provide that the bonds outstanding shall not exceed the vaue of the security.

bond, serial annuity: a serial bond in which the annual installments of the bond prinicpal are so arranged that the payments for principal and interest combined are approximaely the same each year. [49]

bond, sinking fund: a bond secured by the deposit of specified amounts. The issuing corporation makes these deposits to secure the principal of the bonds, and it is sometimes required that the funds be invested in other securities.

bond, special assessment: a bond payable from the proceeds of special assessments. The bond is payable only from the proceeds of special asessments levied against the properties presumed to be benefited by such improvements or services. [49]

bond, special district: a bond issue of a local taxing district which has been organized for a special purpose, such as road, sewer, fire, drainage, irrigation, and levee districts. [49]

bond, special lien: a special assessment bond that acts as a lien against a particular piece (or pieces) of property. [49]

bond, stamped: when a debtor fears default on a bond, should he receive approval from the holder, the maturity date and/or rate of interest can be altered and a stamp affixed to the bond to signify the holder's acceptance of the terms.

bond, state: a division of municipal bonds, or the promissóry note of a state. [28]

bond, straight serial: a serial bond in which the annual installments of bond principal are approximately equal. [49]

bond, surety: an agreement providing for monetary compensation in the event of failure to perform specified acts within a stated period. The firm that is the surety company, for example, becomes responsible for fulfillment of a contract if the contractor defaults. see also *bond, penal.*

bond, tax anticipation: any short-term, interest-bearing bond created to be bought by businesses with money assembled as a reserve in order to pay taxes.

bond, tax-exempt: any security of a state, city, or other public authority specified under federal law, the interest on which is either wholy or partly exempt from federal income taxes. see *bond, municipal.* [20]

bond, temporary: similar to a definitive bond except that it has been printed rather than engraved. see *bond, definitive.*

bond, term: bonds of the same issue usually maturing all at one time and ordinarily to be retired from sinking funds. Sometimes a term bond has more than one maturity date—for example, a serial issue having postponed maturities in only a few late years of its term. [49].

bond, terminable: any bond having a stated maturity.

bond, territorial: see *bond, insular.*

bond, treasury: a U.S. government long-term security, sold to the public and having a maturity longer than five years.

bond, underlying: a bond that has a senior lien where subsequently claims exist.

bond, unified: see *bond, consolidated.*

bond, unlimited tax: a bond secured by pledge of taxes which may be levied by the issuer in unlimited rate or amount. [52]

bond, unsecured: a bond backed up by the faith and credit of the issuer instead of the pledge of assets.

Bond, U.S. Savings: see *Bond, Savings (U.S.)*

bond, warehouse customs: bonds given only on statements prescribed by the U.S. Treasury Department that are required by federal regulations in connection with the importation of items that carry a duty.

bond, zero-coupon: a security sold at a deep discount from its face value and redeemed at the full amount at maturity. The difference between the cost of the bond and its value when redeemed is the investor's return. These notes provide no interest payments to holders.

bond amortization: indicating the premium over par that has been paid for a bond.

bond anticipation notes: short-term notes of a municipality sold in anticipation of bond issuance which are full faith and credit obligations of the governmental unit and are to be retired from the proceeds of the bonds to be issued. see *interim borrowing.* *[49].*

bond buy-backs: as prices for corporate bonds drop, often a result of soaring interest rates, the buying up of a firm's outstanding bonds at discounts creates yields of 15 to 20 percent, thus exceeding those on most other short-term investments. In addition, corporate buyers save interest while they get ahead of their required sinking fund payments and clean up their balance sheets. see *buy back, sinking fund.*

bond circular: a full description of a bond offering used to communicate the major facts of the issue. The circular is prepared by the underwriters and distributed to interested persons and firms.

bond crowd: brokers working in the securities markets who specialize in the trading of bonds.

bond discount: the amount below the face or par amount of a bond at which the bond is purchased.

bonded

(1) *general:* protected or secured by a pledge of property or by a bond.

(2) *finance:* describing a messenger who delivers valuables.

(3) *finance:* a bond posted as security that a tax or tariff will be paid on time.

(4) *government:* describing goods in a government-supervised storage facility, where items are stored without the payment of duties or taxes until they are removed.

bonded debt: that amount of the debt of a company or government which is represented by bonds. If there are sinking fund bonds, this term should be replaced by "gross bonded debt" and "net bonded debt." [49]

bonded indebtedness: see *bonded debt.* [49]

bonded items: items stored in a bonded warehouse to guarantee the government that the tax or duty on the merchandise will be paid upon withdrawal of the items.

bonded (state) warehouse: see *warehouse, state bonded; warehouse, U.S. Customs bonded.*

bond fund

(1) A fund established to receive and disburse the proceeds of a governmental bond issue. [49]

(2) An investment company, the portfolio of which consists primarily of bonds. [23]

bondholder: one who owns bonds and therefore is a creditor of the issuer. [50]

bond house: a financial organization whose major activity is the selling of bonds.

bonding company: an organization whose business is the forming of contracts of surety and the providing of bonds.

bond interest: interest on bonds, often paid twice a year, as determined by the conditions of the bonds. Should the bond be registered, it might take the form of a check. If it is a bearer bond, the interest may be paid with a coupon.

bond market

(1) the place where bonds are sold. Most are sold over the counter; others, in large amounts, are sold on an exchange.

(2) financial institutions that buy bonds (e.g., trust funds, banks, insurance firms).

bond of indemnity: an indemnity agreement used in filing a claim when the claimant, unable to show the freight bill or bill of lading, is given relief from liability for any action for which a carrier would have otherwise been liable.

bond ordinance or resolution: an ordinance or resolution authorizing a bond issue. [49]

bond power: a form of assignment executed by the owner of registered bonds which contains an irrevocable appointment of an attorney-in-fact to make the actual transfer on the books of the corporation. see *power of attorney, stock power.* [37]

bond premium: the excess of the price at which a bond is acquired or sold over its face value. [49]

bond rating: appraising and rating, by a recognized financial organization (e.g., Woody's Investors Service) of the worth of a bond as a sound investment. Ratings are based on the reputation of the organization, its record of interest payments, its profitability, and the like. A triple A (AAA) bond is the most secure, followed by AA, A, B, and so on.

bond register: a book of original entry, in bound or loose-leaf form, in which are recorded the details relative to the purchase and sale of bonds for the firm's own investment account. [10]

bonds authorized and unissued: bonds that have been legally authorized but have not been issued and which can be issued and sold without further authorization. [49]

bonds issued: bonds sold. [49]

bonds payable, matured: bonds that have reached or passed their maturity date but remain unpaid. [49]

bond swap: the simultaneous sale of one issue and the purchase of another. Ideally, a swap should consist of, in effect, trading a shorter maturity for a longer one because longer maturities tend to sell for less than shorter ones in today's market and have a greater potential for appreciation should interest rates drop.

bond value tables: tables of bond yields to bond values used to compute bond yields to maturity or to determine the price of a bond necessary to afford a given yield to a given maturity.

bond yield: the rate of return on bonds. [37]

bonification

(1) *general:* rendering of an advantage or benefit.

(2) *finance:* said to be achieved when certain items that are made for export relieve the manufacturer of paying an excise tax on such items.

(3) *taxation:* the return or exclusion of a tax.

bonus account: a savings account that earns interest at a bonus rate if the customer makes regular deposits to the account, leaves a specified amount on deposit for a specified term, or fulfills other conditons of the account contract. [59]

bonus futures: a recently uncovered means for increasing executive bonuses. For example, an executive hedges his expectations of a substandard year-end bonus from the company by selling a future to a colleague. The purchaser agrees to guarantee the seller an amount equivalent to, say, 10 percent of the seller's annual salary. If the company at year-end grants a bonus of more than 10 percent, the futures buyer gets the excess and makes a nice profit. On the other hand, if the company gives out a disappointing bonus of 9 percent, the futures speculator suffers a loss.

bonus stock: securities given most often to top management and other employees as a bonus.

boodle

(1) money received through corruption in public activities.

(2) counterfeit money.

book: a notebook the specialist in a stock exchange uses to keep a record of the buy and sell orders at specified prices, in strict sequence of receipt, which are left with him by other brokers. [20]

book, close: the date the transfer agent closes the transfer books of a firm and reviews the stockholder list to identify those who are eligible to receive dividends and vote.

book, open: the date the transfer agent opens the transfer books of a firm to continue the activity of transferring stocks after they have been closed to determine the stockholder list.

book crowd: see *cabinet crowd.*

book depreciation: the amount that can be deducted for depreciation purposes from the cost of an asset of the property owner.

bookkeeper: a person who makes entries on the general ledger of a business.

bookkeeping: the art, practice, or labor involved in the systematic recording of the transactions affecting a business.

bookkeeping department: a department of a bank where the records of all depositors' checking accounts are posted and kept. In the larger banks, there may be found several bookkeeping departments, such as commercial, corporation accounts, special checking, general ledger, bank ledger, foreign accounts, stock transfer, and trust bookkeeping. [10]

book liability: the amount at which securities issued or assumed by the carrier and other liability items are recorded in the accounts of the carrier. [18]

book of final entry: a book to which information is transferred from a book of original entry.

book of original entry: the record in which transactions are formally recorded for the first time, such as the cash journal, check register, or general journal. Where machine bookkeeping is used, it may happen that one transaction is recorded simultaneously in several records, one of which may be regarded as the book of original entry. [49]

book of secondary entry: ledger; not books of original entry (i.e., journals).

book profit: the increase in the value of a stock that has not been sold; for example, a stock is bought at $50 and its price climbs to $60, but it is not sold, leading to a book profit of $10. cf. *realized profit.*

bookshares: a modern share-recording system which eliminates the need for mutual fund share certificates but gives the fund shareowner a record of his holdings. [23]

book value
(1) *general:* the amount of an asset found in the company's records, not necessarily that which it could bring in the open market. see *depreciated cost.*
(2) *investments:* determined from a company's records by adding all assets, then deducting all debts and other liabilities, plus the liquidation price of any preferred issues. The sum arrived at is divided by the number of common shares outstanding, and the result is "book value per common share." [20]

boom
(1) *general:* a period of rapidly rising prices and an increased demand for goods and services, usually accompanied by full employment.
(2) *investments:* when business expands and the value of commodities and securities increases.

boomerang: an international program to minimize the practice of goods dumping, by returning such items duty free and exempt of quantity restrictions.

boot: payments by or to the U.S. Treasury that may be necessary in an advance refunding in order to align more closely the respective values of the eligible issues and the issues offered. [71]

boot money: money used as an additional compensation by one of the parties to a bargain.

bootstrap
(1) *general:* a technique designed to bring about a desired state by internally generated means.
(2) *computers:* a method for getting the first few instructions into memory when a routine is loaded.

bop: see *balance of payments*.

borax: slang, cheap or low-grade items.

borrow: to receive something from another, with the understanding that the item is to be returned.

borrowed bond: see *bond, borrowed*.

borrowed reserves: discounts and advances from Federal Reserve Banks; mainly advances secured by U.S. government securities or eligible paper. [72]

borrowed stock: the security a broker borrows to complete the obligation of a short selling contract held by his client. see *loan stock*.

borrower: one who borrows cash or buys something on time.

borrowings: the amount borrowed by reporting member banks; the breakdown shows the amounts borrowed from the Federal Reserve Banks, and from others—mostly other commercial banks. [40]

Boston Stock Exchange: organized on October 13, 1834, this stock exchange has but once failed to perform its operations, when it closed from July 30, 1913 to December 10, 1914 during the frantic period at the beginning of World War I.

BOT: see *board of trustees*.

Bot.: bought.

bottom dropped out: a situation of sharply falling prices occurring when the market is well liquidated, thus establishing a panic atmosphere.

bottom-fishing: buying stocks in countries whose currencies are lowest against the U.S. dollar.

bottom price: the lowest price for a stock or commodity for a period of time, such as a day, week, year, or cyclical period.

bottomry: a loan secured by a lien on a vessel. The contract of bottomry is in the nature of a mortgage. If the carrier is lost, the debt is canceled.

bounce: slang, the failure of a check to fulfill payment for an item or service.

bounty: added payments offered by a government as an incentive for a specific industry or the export of certain items.

bourse: French, for stock exchange.

boxcar discovery: slang, request for every remotely relevant document.

boycott

(1) *finance:* an attempt to prevent the carrying on of a business by urging people not to buy from the firm being boycotted. Frequently used on the international scene for political or economic reasons; illustrated by appeals, threats, and so on, to secure redress of a grievance.

(2) *labor relations:* collective pressure against an employer to discourage public acceptance of his products or services. A primary boycott involves one employer and his employees only; a secondary boycott involves a third party, and in many cases is forbidden by law.

BP

(1) see *bills payable*.

(2) see *book profit*.

BQ: see *basis quote*.

BR

(1) see *bills receivable*.

(2) see *bond rating*.

Br.: see *branch*.

BRA: see *Bankruptcy Reform Act of 1978*.

bracket creep: a reaction when taxpayers receive raises to offset the ravages of inflation. In this situation, they are taxed more heavily on some or all of their added income under a system that levies at a progressively higher rate. see *Economic Recovery Tax Act of 1981.*

brain storm: slang, a rapidly arrived-at solution to a problem; a good, spontaneous idea.

branch

(1) *computers:* a set of instructions in a program consisting of a series of changes from the normal sequence of steps.

(2) *systems:* a point in a routine at which one of two or more alternatives is selected, under control of the routine.

branch banking: any banking system where there are few parent institutions, each having branches operating over a large geographic area. Some states have authorized the concept of branch banking under strict regulation. Federal control is maintained by the Board of Governors of the Federal Reserve System and the Office of Comptroller of the Currency. In the United States, there is no nationwide branch banking, whereas in some countries (e.g., Canada, England, France, and Germany), the branch system of banking dominates.

brand: a name, term, sign, symbol, or design, or a combination of these which is intended to identify the goods or services of one seller or group of sellers and to differentiate them from those of its competitors. [48]

Brannan plan: a proposal made in 1949 by U.S. Secretary of Agriculture Charles F. Brannan to eliminate parity payments to farmers and give

them direct payments instead. cf. *price support.*

brassage: the charge made by a government for producing coins from bullion. see *seignorage.*

brazen law of wages: see *iron law of wages.*

breach of contract: not fulfilling one's part in an agreement; breaking a promise to carry out one's contractual responsibility.

breach of trust: violation of a duty of a trustee to a beneficiary. [37]

breach of warranty: when a warranty made by a seller is found to be false, the warranty is said to be breached.

bread: slang, money.

break

(1) *general:* as with "giving a break," a second chance or another opportunity.

(2) *finance:* a discount.

(3) *investments:* an unexpected drop in the price of stocks and commodities.

breakage

(1) *general:* an allowance for losses resulting from breakage of merchandise.

(2) *finance:* the fractional pennies due either party resulting from percentage calculations (e.g., when the decimal shows itself to be 0.5 or more, an added point is entered).

break-even point: the point of activity at which the company earns zero profit. It is reached when total revenue equals total expense. see *margin of safety.*

breaking bulk: the practice of some middlemen to take the large, economical shipment from a manufacturer and divide it into smaller units for sale for greater profit.

breakout: when a specific security climbs above a level where strong selling resistance exists, or drops below a level of strong purchasing support.

breakup value: in an investment fund or an issue of a holding firm, the value of the assets available for the issue, taking all marketable securities at their market price.

B. Rec.: see *bills receivable.*

Bretton Woods Agreement of 1944: articles of agreement adopted by the international monetary conference of 44 nations which met at Bretton Woods, New Hampshire. The International Monetary Fund and the International Bank for Reconstruction and Development were created. The fund's major responsibility is to maintain orderly currency practices in international trade, while the bank's function is to facilitate extension of long-term investments for productive purposes. Periodic meetings are held at Bretton Woods to amend the original agreement.

bribe: a payment resulting in the payer's receiving some right, benefit, or preference to which he has no legal right and which he would not have obtained except with the payment of the money. A bribe is a criminal offense.

brick: a term used in banks to describe a package of new currency which is banded with steel straps, the straps being sealed at the joining points. New currency is shipped from the Federal Reserve Bank by this method of packaging. [10]

bring out: the offering to the public of a new security issue by one or more underwriters.

broad market: describing a time of considerable volume in the buying and selling of stocks and bonds.

broad tape: slang, the Dow Jones news ticker displayed in brokerage houses as a large rectangular screen on which lines of copy roll upward.

Brok.: see *broker, brokerage.*

broke: slang, without funds.

broken lot: an odd lot, usually less than 100 shares of a stock.

broken time: work schedule or shift where the employee works for a certain length of time, then is off duty, then returns for another period of work.

broker

(1) *general:* a person who prepares contracts with third parties on behalf of the broker's principal.

(2) *banking:* a specialist who represents buyers of property and liability insurance and deals with either agents or companies in arranging for the coverage required by the customer. The broker is licensed by the state or states in which he or she conducts business.

(3) *banking:* a state-licensed individual who acts as middleman in property transactions between a buyer and seller.

(4) *investments:* a member of a stock exchange firm or any exchange member who handles orders to buy and sell securities and commodities for a commission. cf. *street broker;* see also *floor broker.*

brokerage: the business of a broker. [62]

broker-dealer: a firm that retails mutual fund shares and other securities to the public. [23]

brokering: slang, when an attorney gives a case to another lawyer for a forwarding fee. It is considered by the legal profession as an unethical way of making money.

broker's loan: a loan made to a stockbroker and secured by stock exchange collateral.

broker's market: exists when the investing public is generally inactive at the same time that brokers are trading quite heavily with their own accounts.

broker's ticket: a written statement of all buy and sell orders executed by a broker, giving the date, name, and amount of the security traded, the price, the customer's name, the broker's name, and so on.

brown Abe: slang, a penny.

BS

(1) see *back spread.*
(2) see *balance sheet.*
(3) see *bellweather stock.*
(4) see *bill of sale.*
(5) see *block sale.*
(6) see *butterfly spread.*

Bs.L.: see *bill of lading.*

Bt.: bought.

BTG: see *beating the gun.*

BTM: see *bulling the market.*

bubble: an unwise business venture in which the price of the item has little or no relationship to the value of the asset.

bubble company: a firm that never had any true business or did not intend to be honest, or a firm created to defraud the public.

buck: slang, one dollar.

bucketing: activity of a broker who executes a customer's order for his or her own account instead of on the market, with the expectation of profit-

ing from a balancing transaction at a future time. This activity is forbidden by the SEC.

bucket shop

(1) *general:* slang, an institution engaged in securities dealings of doubtful legality.

(2) *investments:* an unlicensed, dishonest business; customers place bets on the increase or decrease of stock prices on the regular exchange. No orders are filled, but profits and losses are based on the actual price movement on the exchange, with a commission going to the broker. The SEC has declared the maintenance of a bucket shop illegal.

budget

(1) *general:* an itemized listing, and frequently the allotment, of the amount of all estimated revenue a given business anticipates receiving; and the listing, and frequently the segregation, of the amount of all estimated costs and expenses that will be incurred in obtaining the revenue during a stated period of time. see also *cash, flexible budget.*

(2) *government:* an annual statement of the probable revenues (see estimated revenues) and expenditures of a nation for the following year. see *federal budget expenditures, federal budget receipts, general control expenditures, planning-programming-budgeting, zero-base budgeting.*

budget, cash: see *cash budget.*

budget, flexible: see *flexible budget.*

budget account: see *charge account.*

budgetary accounts: those accounts necessary to reflect budget operations and conditions, such as estimated revenues, appropriations, and encumbrances, as distinguished from *proprietary accounts.* [49]

budgetary control: a plan to control all operations in order to secure maximum profit from a minimum capital investment. This is accomplished by setting standards against which actual performance can be measured. An efficient budgetary control program not only detects inefficiencies but also definitely fixes responsibility upon the proper person or persons. [38]

budget deficit: excess of expenditures over revenues.

budget document: the instrument used by the budget-making authority to present a comprehensive financial program to the appropriate body. [49]

budget loan: a mortgage loan that requires a proportionate amount of tax, insurance, and assessment to be held in escrow, in addition to interest and principal payments.

budget plan: a system of buying or making expenditures in divided equal payments over a period of time. [28]

budget surplus: excess of revenues over expenditures.

bug
(1) *computers:* a mistake or malfunction. cf. *debug.*
(2) *computers:* any electrical or mechanical defect that interferes with the operation of the computer.

building and loan association: a cooperative or stock society for the saving, accumulation, and lending of money. Deposits in an institution of this kind may be represented by shares issued in the name of the depositor. [31]

building loan: a mortgage loan made to finance the construction of a building. It is advanced in stages as the construction work progresses. see *construction loan.* [39]

building societies: a British term for public deposits where a high interest rate is given to attract funds to finance home loans and property purchases. Similar to savings and loan associations in the United States.

bulge: a temporary, though sudden climb in the price of a stock or commodity.

bulk cargo: cargo that consists entirely of one commodity.

bulk discount: a reduced charge for quantity or multiple purchases.

bulk transfer: the transfer of more than 50 accounts from one branch office to one or more other branch offices in a one-week period. [55]

bulk zoning: division of an area by the size and number of buildings, their shape, and other characteristics.

bull: a person who believes security prices will rise. [68]

bulletproof: slang, any document with no loopholes.

bulling the market: speculator trading purporting to force the level of prices upward. Techniques include spreading rumors and entering price orders at levels somewhat above the prevailing price.

bullion: usually gold or silver, formed in ingots or bars, for use as a coin.

bull market: an advancing stock market. [20]

bulls: speculators who anticipate that prices will rise.

bump
(1) *general:* to dismiss a worker.

(2) *labor relations:* slang, to reassign work from an employee of lower seniority to another of higher seniority to retain the older worker and fire the younger one.

bunched securities: referring to repeated sales of the same stock at similar or identical prices as shown repeatedly on the ticker tape of an exchange.

bunco game: one of a variety of methods of swindling.

Bundesbank: established in 1875, the central bank of West Germany, located in Frankfurt.

bundle: slang, a large amount of money.

bundle of rights: the legal rights that go with property ownership: the rights to sell, lease, build, mortgage, improve, and so on.

buoyant: advancing stock; securities that continue to climb in value.

burden: cost of manufacture or production not directly identifiable with specific products; factory overhead or service cost; indirect costs; and apportionable costs. [43]

burden of proof: the duty of proving a position taken in a court of law. Failure in the performance of that duty calls for judgment against the person on whom the duty rests. Thus, the burden of proof that the paper written is not the valid will of the testator is upon the person who contests the will. [37]

Bureau of Customs: an agency of the U.S. Treasury Department established in its present form in 1927, responsible for the collection of customs tariffs, vessel licensing and regulation, and other functions. It maintains offices in all ports of entry.

Bureau of Employment Security: a part of the U.S. Department of Labor; it is responsible for the U.S. Employment Service, providing a nationwide job placement service, training programs, and developing resolutions of manpower problems; and the Unemployment Insurance Service, providing assistance to state agencies in unemployment insurance programs and making available to the states information on job opportunities.

Bureau of Labor Standards: formerly the Division of Labor Standards; as a part of the U.S. Department of Labor, it is concerned with developing and establishing better working standards, primarily in the field of labor legislation.

Bureau of Labor Statistics (BLS): a research agency of the U.S. Department of Labor; it compiles statistics on hours of work, average hourly earnings, employment and unemployment, consumer prices, and many other variables.

Bureau of the Budget: originally part of the U.S. Treasury Department, this federal agency was responsible for the presentation of the federal budget. Now under the Executive Office of the President, the bureau is called the Office of Management and Budget. see *Office of Management and Budget.*

Bureau of the Census: a federal unit in the U.S. Department of Commerce, responsible for conducting various censuses of population, housing, business, and so on. It assists other government groups in collecting pertinent data.

burn: slang, cheating a business partner out of his profits.

business

(1) *general:* the buying and selling of goods and services.

(2) *finance:* the activity of an individual, partnership, or organization involving production, commerce, and/or service.

(3) *personnel:* one's occupation or employment.

business agent: an elected or appointed representative of one or more local unions, with responsibility for negotiating contracts, administering existing contracts, and adjusting grievances. The agent is usually a full-time unionist, as contrasted with the shop steward or committeeman. The business agent may also have organizing duties.

business credit: the privilege of deferring payment for purchases, extended to customers by the vendors of items and services.

business cycle: any interval embracing alternating periods of economic prosperity and depression. see *compensatory fiscal policy, contraction, expansion, inflation, recession, recovery, reflation.*

business data processing: use of automatic data processing for a wide variety of commercial operations.

business ethics: socially accepted rules of behavior that place pressure on business executives to maintain a high sense of values and to be honest and fair in their dealings with the public.

business insurance trust: a trust of life insurance policy contracts created in connection with a business enterprise. The term is applied both to a trust created for the liquidation of business interests and to a trust cre-

ated for credit purposes or otherwise for the benefit of a business enterprise. [32]

business life insurance: life insurance purchased by a business enterprise on the life of a member of the firm. It is often bought by partnerships to protect the surviving partners against loss caused by the death of a partner, or by a corporation to reimburse it for loss caused by the death of a key employee. [58]

business manager

(1) *general:* the individual responsible for overseeing a firm, department, or other unit, to ensure smooth operations.

(2) *labor relations:* a business agent. see *business agent.*

business paper: see *commercial paper.*

business transfer payments: transfers from business to persons which are charges against business products but for which no services are rendered currently. Major items of this type are corporate gifts to nonprofit institutions and allowance for consumer bad debts.

business trust: an unincorporated business organization in which title to the property is given to trustees to hold, manage, or sell. This structure is sometimes employed when a parcel of land is divided, improved, or sold. Has been referred to as a Massachusetts trust or common law trust.

bust: a severe decrease in business activity leading to high unemployment, low incomes, and low profits.

butterfly spread: the simultaneous purchase or sale of three futures contracts in the same or different markets. For example, buying 10 soybean futures contracts in January, and other 10 for an April delivery, and at the same moment selling (going short) 20 soybean contracts for May of the same year. Borrowing power and profits may result. In addition, any profits are held until after the tax year ends. see also *spread, straddle.*

buttonwood tree: on May 17, 1792, 24 men (the original founders of the New York Stock Exchange) declared themselves "brokers for the purchase and sale of public stocks." A buttonwood tree (sycamore) once stood at that location.

buy

(1) *general:* the quality of a purchase (e.g., a good buy).

(2) *finance:* to acquire ownership of something in exchange for a monetary consideration.

"Buy American" statutes: regulations, some dating back four decades, establishing standards for government procurement worldwide. Provisionally written into multilateral trade agreements, they typically add 6 to 12 percent to the bids of foreign suppliers in order to give domestic companies an advantage.

buy back: buying an identical amount of the same stock that had been sold short in order to satisfy the agreement within the seller's contract and complete the sale. synonymous with *short covering;* see *bond buy-backs, short sale.*

buy down: a builder pays the bank a lump sum of money in advance to reduce the monthly interest charges on the mortgage. see *balloon, roll over.*

buyers' market: a market characterized by low or falling prices, occurring when supply is greater than demand. The buyers tend to set the prices and terms of sale.

buyer's monopoly: a characteristic of the market of many sellers and one purchaser.

buyers over: a situation of more buyers than sellers. cf. *overbought.*

buyer's right to route: the purchaser's privilege to determine the route of the shipment when the seller does not pay the freight charges. If the seller proceeds to alter the buyer's wishes, the seller is liable for any loss incurred.

buying basis: the difference between the cost of a cash commodity and a future sold to hedge it.

buying hedge: a hedge that is initiated by taking a long position in the futures market equal to the amount of the cash commodity that is eventually needed. see also *hedge.*

buying in: when a seller does not hand over his securities at the expected time, the purchaser obtains shares wherever he can find them, and the seller becomes responsible for all added expenses.

buying on a shoestring: acquiring stocks or commodities with the minimum margin.

buying on balance: occurs when a stockbroker's orders to buy exceed his or her cumulative orders to sell.

buying on margin: purchasing securities without paying the full price immediately. Margin regulations are closely controlled by the SEC. see *margin, marginal trading, margin call.*

buying on scale: a procedure for purchasing securities where the broker is told to purchase a given number of shares at given intervals of a price decline. Since the buyer does not know how low the price can drop, by buying on scale as the price declines, his average cost per share also declines.

buying outright: paying with cash only; buying an item with 100 percent cash. In securities, the opposite of margin.

buying power: money available for spending and consumption. A combination of liquid assets plus available credit.

buying rate: the publicized quotation for buying such things as foreign exchange, commodities, and bills of exchange which a bank or other buyer employs to inform the trader of his desire to buy.

buy on close (or opening): to buy at the end (or beginning) of the session at a price within the closing or (opening range). [2]

buy order: order to a broker, investment representative, bank, or manufacturer, to purchase a specified quantity of security or item.

buy out: to purchase all the assets, stock, and so on, of an ongoing organization; to purchase the interest in a firm that is owned by another.

buy-sell agreement: an agreement wherein owners of a business arrange to transfer their respective ownership interests upon the death of one, or upon some other event, to provide continued control of the business or other desired end. [37]

buy ticket: a form prepared in multiple copies, used by the investment department to instruct the order department to purchase a security.[37]

BV: see *book value.*

BW: see *bid wanted.*

by-bidder: a person who makes fictitious bids at an auction, on behalf of the owner or seller of the items, to obtain a higher price or to encourage further bidding.

by-laws: rules accepted by board members of a firm or other organization for governance. Such rules cannot be in opposition to laws imposed by government.

byte: a sequence of adjacent binary digits operated on as a unit and usually shorter than a computer word.

C
- (1) see *cash.*
- (2) see *cent.*

CA
- (1) see *capital account.*
- (2) see *capital appreciation.*
- (3) see *capital assets.*
- (4) see *cash account.*
- (5) see *chartered accountant.*
- (6) see *current account.*
- (7) see *current assets.*
- (8) see *custodian account.*

cabbage: slang, paper money, banknotes, or other funds.

cabinet crowd: the section of the bond trading unit of the New York Stock exchanges that handles trading in active bonds. synonymous with "book crowd" and "inactive crowd."

cable rate: the charge for a cable transfer, contrasted with the check (demand draft) rate, and the rate for 30-, 60-, and 90-day bills of exchange. The cable rate is at all times higher than the check rate. see *check rate.*

cable transfer: use of a cablegram to place funds in the hands of an individual in a foreign country. Funds are deposited with a local (i.e., domestic) bank, which cables instructions to a correspondent bank abroad to make the funds available to the payee.

CAD: see *cash against documents.*

cadastre: the official inventory of the real property in a community, the cadastre is used for determining taxes and its appraised value.

CAF: see *C&F.*

calculating machine: a machine designed to make mathematical calculations in addition to straightforward addition and subtraction.

calculator: a device that performs arithmetic operations based on data and instructions placed manually or on punched cards.

calendar spreading: the simultaneous purchase and sale of options within the same class having different expiration dates.

calendar year experience: experience developed on premium and loss transactions occurring during the 12 calendar months beginning January 1, irrespective of the effective dates of the policies on which these transactions took place.

call
- (1) *banking:* to demand payment of a loan secured by collateral because of failure by a borrower to comply with the terms of the loan.
- (2) *computers:* the branching or transferring of control to a specified closed subroutine.
- (3) *finance:* to demand payment of an installment of the price of bonds or stocks that have been subscribed.
- (4) *investments:* see *calls.*

callable

(1) *banking:* that which must be paid on request, as a loan.

(2) *finance:* a bond issue or preferred stock, all or part of which may be redeemed by the issuing corporation under definite conditions, before maturity.

callable bond: see *bond, callable.*

call-back: the act of reading back posting media to the postings, or checks making up a list to the listing of the items. One person reads the amounts to another person, who is checking the "run" for accuracy. Call-backs are often made when a balance or settlement is not accomplished, the call back being one form of proving the accuracy of a run of items. [10]

call date: the date on which a bond may be redeemed before maturity at the option of the issuer. [52]

called bond: see *bond, called.*

called preferred stock: preferred stock, containing call provisions, which is redeemed by a corporation. [37]

call loan: a loan payable on request. cf. *day loan.*

call money: currency lent by banks, usually to stock exchange brokers, for which payment can be demanded at any time.

call money market: an activity of brokers and dealers having call funds secured by stock exchange collateral and government securities to meet their money needs to cover customers' margin accounts and their own securities inventory.

call of more: the right to call again for the same amount of goods previously bought. Used primarily in the purchase of options.

call option: giving the option buyer the right to buy 100 shares of stock at a stated price at any time before a deadline, at which point the option expires.

call premium

(1) the premium payable by the issuer if he or she redeems a callable bond before maturity. It will be fixed in the indenture and normally decreases as maturity approaches.

(2) the premium payable by an issuer when he or she redeems, if appropriate, preferred stock at an amount in excess of par or stated value. [43]

call price: the price at which a callable bond is redeemable; used in connection with preferred stocks and debt securities having a fixed claim. It is the price that an issuer must pay to voluntarily retire such securities. Often the call price exceeds the par or liquidating price in order to compensate the holder of the called security for his or her loss of income and investment position resulting from the call. [30]

call provision: the call provision describes the terms under which a bond may be redeemed by the issuer in whole or in part prior to maturity. [52]

call purchase: the buying of commodities when the seller has some option of pricing at a later date within a given range of the existing price. cf. *call sale.*

call report: agencies such as the Comptroller of the Currency and Federal Reserve Banks require periodic status reports from banks under their jurisdiction. The precise date is not given in advance so as to minimize manipulation of the information.

calls

(1) an option contract that entitles the holder to buy a number of shares of the underlying security at a stated price on or before a fixed expiration date. [5]

(2) see *puts and calls.*

call sale: an agreement for the sale of a commodity where the price is set by the purchaser in the future. The setting of the price is at the "call" of the purchaser and is within a few points above or below the price of a stated future on the day of fixing the price of the contract. Opposite of *call purchase.*

cambism: engaging in the sale of foreign monies.

cambist

(1) *finance:* an individual who buys and sells foreign currencies.

(2) *international:* a handbook in which foreign country funds are converted into currency tables of the country for which the handbook is issued.

cambistry: the study of exchange of foreign currencies, with emphasis on identifying the least expensive procedure for remitting to a foreign nation.

cameralism: see *kameralism.*

Can.: see *cancellation.*

Canadian Bank Act: see *Bank Act, Canada.*

Canc.: see *cancellation.*

cancel: to mark or perforate; make void. [61]

cancellation: the annulment or rendering void of any bank instrument upon payment; the termination of a policy or bond before its expiration, by either the bank or other party. Almost invariably, the contract states the type of notice necessary before cancellation becomes effective.

cancellation, pro rata: cancellation with a return of premium proportionate to the unexpired period for which premiums were paid. [12]

cancellation, short-rate: cancellation upon request of an insured, with a return of less than the proportionate amount. [12]

cancellation clause: a provision giving one or both parties the right to cancel the agreement in the event of a specified occurrence.

cancellation evidence: a terminated policy, or any legal notice of cancellation.

cancelled checks: checks that have been paid and charged to the depositor's account, then stamped or perforated with the date of the payment and the drawee bank's name or clearinghouse number. These checks are retained in the files of the bank until a statement of the depositor's account is sent to him or her. [31]

cancelling machine: a machine used for canceling checks, passbooks, and other records in a bank. [10]

canvass: to call on prospective customers in person or by telephone to sell banking services to determine interest or gather information.

Cap.

(1) see *capital.*

(2) see *capitalization.*

capacity

(1) *banking:* the largest amount of insurance a bank will accept on one risk.

(2) *finance:* one or the three elements of credit.

(3) *law:* competency or legal authority. cf. *non compos mentis.*

capacity costs: an alternative term for fixed costs, emphasizing that fixed costs are needed to provide operating facilities for an organization ready to produce and sell at a planned volume of activity.

capias ad respondendum: a judicial writ commencing actions at law (e.g., the order directing the sheriff to place the defendant in custody).

capital

(1) *general:* the amount invested in a venture. see *equity, fixed capital.*
(2) *banking:* describes a long-term debt plus owners' equity.
(3) *finance:* the net assets of a firm, partnership, and so on, including the original investment, plus all gains and profits.

capital account: an account maintained in the name of the owner or owners of a business and indicating his or their equity in that business—usually at the close of the last accounting period.

capital and surplus: found in a condensed statement of a bank's condition showing the bank's financial status. The two accounts, capital and surplus, are brought together because the surplus account of a bank corresponds to capital surplus, and pays no dividends.

capital appreciation: an increase or other appreciation in a capital asset's value.

capital assets: a collective term that includes all fixed assets, consisting of furniture and fixtures, land, buildings, machinery, and so on: as differentiated from property consumed; that is, property that yields income or reduces expenses. cf. *capital expenditure, capital investment.*

capital budget: a budget that itemizes expenditures to be used for building and for purchasing capital goods, and which identifies the source of the funds required to meet the expenditures.

capital charges: sums required to satisfy interest upon, and amortization of, monies invested in an enterprise. [62]

capital consumption: that portion of a firm's investment used in part or in its entirety in the process of production.

capital expenditure: an expenditure to acquire an asset with an expected useful life of more than one year. Also referred to as a capital investment because it is expected to yield revenue or reduce expenses.

capital flight: a large transfer of money from one nation to another as a hedge against poor economic or political conditions.

capital formation: the development or expansion of capital goods as a result of savings.

capital gain (or loss)

(1) *general:* the gain or loss from the sale of a capital asset above or below the cost or appraised value.
(2) *finance:* the difference (gain or loss) between the market or book value at purchase or other acquisition and that realized from the sale or disposition of a capital asset. see *long-term capital gain (loss).*

capital gains distribution: a distribution to investment company shareholders from net long-term capital gains realized by a "regulated investment company" on the sale of portfolio securities. [30]

capital gains tax: a tax that is placed on the profit from selling a capital asset, often stock.

capital goods: items ordinarily treated as long-term investment (capitalized) because of substantial value and life (e.g., industrial machinery).

capital growth: an increase in market value of securities; a long-term objective pursued by many investment companies. [23]

capital intensive: characterized by the need to use additional capital to increase productivity or profits.

capital investment: a collective term representing the amount invested in capital or fixed assets or in long-term securities, as contrasted with funds invested in current assets or short-term securities. Generally speaking, capital investments include all funds invested in assets that during the normal course of business are not expected to be returned during the coming fiscal period.

capitalism: an economic system based on freedoms of ownership, production, exchange, acquisition, work, movement, and open competition. see *laissez-faire.*

capital issues: stocks and bonds that are more or less permanent and fixed, as contrasted with short-term notes and accounts payable.

capitalist
(1) *general:* an individual investor in a business.
(2) *finance:* in Marxist terms, an individual who owns or shares in the ownership of the means of production and employs others. cf. *people's capitalism, private enterprise.*

capitalization
(1) *general:* the sum of all monies invested in a firm by the owner or owners; total liabilities.
(2) *banking:* the method of appraising property by deducting the estimated normal expenses from the amount of income the property is expected to yield. The resulting net profit does not necessarily represent the actual property value.
(3) *finance:* the total value of all securities in a firm.

capitalization of income: estimating the existing investment value of property by lowering anticipated future income to its present worth.

capitalization rate
(1) the relationship of income to capital investment or value, expressed as a percentage.
(2) the (percentage) rate at which an anticipated future income stream is discounted to present worth (i.e., market value). [6]

capitalization rate(s), basis for split: justification of the use of split rates is confined to two basic assumptions, as follows. (a) Investment in land and investment in building represent different degrees of risk and, therefore, require the application of a different rate in the capitalization of the income attributed to each: (i) land value is presumed to be stable and to earn a constant return to perpetuity; (ii) terminable lives of buildings require a higher rate to ensure return of capital investment within their estimated economic life, in addition to a return on the investment or capital value. (b) Income attributable to land and return to building are predictable, separable, and identifiable. [6]

capitalization rate(s), methods of selection of: a band of investment, sometimes designated synthetic, in which the current mortgage rate and rate for equity capital are combined in the same proportion as each (mortgage and equity) bears to the total value estimate. The accuracy of this method depends upon the correctness of the appraiser's estimate of the availability of mortgage money at the rate and long-value ratio set forth, and the degree to which the rate of return on equity capital has been verified by reference to comparable sales. [6]

capitalization rate(s), net
(1) the rate of interest expected to be earned on an investment.
(2) the rate of interest at which anticipated future net income is discounted, exclusive of provision for recapture of capital investment. [6]

capitalization rate(s), over all: net (capitalization) rate plus provision for recapture of total investment (i.e., land and improvements). This is the rate used in the property residual technique and is applied to net income before depreciation. [6]

capitalization rate(s), safe: the net rate of return on a virtually riskless and completely liquid investment, generally accepted as the savings bank interest rate or interest being paid on long-term government bonds, in a stable market; usually known as the safe rate. [6]

capitalization rate(s), source of: the market is the only source of capitalization rates which provides provable support for those rates. [6]

capitalization rate(s), split: a term used in the capitalization process denoting an application of different rates to portions of total net income presumed to be earned by fractional parts of an improved property—for example, one rate applied to claimed earnings of land and another applied to net income said to be earned by the building. [6]

capitalization ratios: the percent that each of the following or its components is of total capitalization: bonds, other long-term debt, preferred stock, common stock and retained income, capital surplus, and premium on capital stock. [3]

capitalize
(1) *general:* to classify a cost as a long-term investment item instead of a charge to current operations.
(2) *banking:* to divide income by an interest rate to obtain principal.
(3) *finance:* to convert into cash that which can be used in production; to issue shares to represent an investment.

capitalized value: the asset value (principal) of a given number of income dollars determined on the basis of an assumed rate of return. For example, the capitalized value of a $500 perpetual income at a rate of 5 percent is $10,000 (obtained by dividing $500 by 0.05). [67]

capital levy: any tax placed on capital. This tax is usually quite small, from $\frac{1}{4}$ or $\frac{1}{2}$ of 1 percent per year.

capital liability: a fixed liability (e.g., a corporate bond) that is created to acquire fixed assets or for purposes of funding.

capital loan: a loan that cannot be repaid without disposing of capital assets, in contrast to a loan, for example, to purchase merchandise, the sale of which will provide funds to repay the loan. [50]

capital loss: see *long-term capital loss.*

capital market: a place or system in which the requirements for capital of a business can be satisfied.

capital movements: the shifts in indebtedness and in gold stocks serving as balancing items when determining the international payments of a nation.

capital outlay: expenditures for the acquisition of or addition to fixed assets; included are amounts for replacements and major alterations but not for repair. cf. *operating expense.*

capital paid in: the amount paid in for Federal Reserve Bank stock owned by member banks. [40]

capital rating: a rating given by a mercantile organization when appraising the net worth of a firm.

capital readjustments: any fundamental, voluntary changes in the capital structure of a firm, involving the modification of the debt.

capital requirement: the total monetary investment needed to create and operate any business.

capital resources: resources of a fixed or permanent character, such as land and buildings, which cannot ordinarily be used to meet expenditures. [49]

capital stock: the specified amount of stock a corporation may sell as authorized by the state granting the corporate charter. If the stock has a stated value per share, such value is known as par value. Stock without a designated value is referred to as no par value stock. see *common stock.*

capital stock discount and expense: a balance sheet account. The excess of par value over the price paid in by the shareholder is capital stock discount. Expenses incurred in connection with the issuance and sale of capital stock which are not properly chargeable to "organization," and which have not been charged to "surplus" are included in capital stock discount and expense. [3]

capital structure: the distribution of a corporation's capital among its several component parts, such as stock, bonds, and surplus. [39]

capital sum: the original amount of an estate, fund, mortgage, bond, or other financial dealing, together with accrued sums not yet recognized as income.

capital surplus: the excess of assets over liabilities plus the value given to issued capital stock, less amounts in paid-in or earned surplus.

capital turnover: the rate at which an organization's assets are converted into cash.

carbon plan: a variation of the single posting plan wherein a carbonized ledger is created as a carbon copy of the original statement. [10]

card, column: lines of a punched card that are used for punching holes, with each column representing a specific symbol in data processing.

card, computer: usually, the keypunched card used in automatic data processing.

card, hopper: the portion of a card-processing machine that holds the cards to be processed and makes them available to a card-feed mechanism.

card, punch: a card that has been or will be punched with holes to represent letters, digits, or characters.

card, reproducer: a device that reproduces a punch card by punching another identical card.

Carey Street: British term for bankruptcy.

carnet: a document of international customs permitting temporary duty-free import of specific items into certain nations. see *admission temporaire.*

carrier: the bank's insurance department that writes and fulfills the conditions of the insurance policy.

carrier's lien: the carrier's right to hold the shipper's property as security until the shipping obligation is paid. cf. *general lien.*

carry

(1) *general:* to enter or post.

(2) *banking:* to supply funds to a customer.

(3) *computer:* a condition occurring during the operation of addition when the total of two digits in the same column equals or exceeds the numbering system (e.g., when 2 is exceeded in a binary system).

(4) *finance:* the act of a broker in providing money to customers who trade by margin accounts; to hold stocks; to be "long" of stock.

carry-back: in federal income taxes, the amount of a taxpayer's business loss, subject to adjustments, deductible from the net income of three preceding years. cf. *carry-over.*

carry forward

(1) *general:* to transfer the balance of an account from one balance sheet to another.

(2) *federal income taxes:* to declare an item of expense as minimal until a later time period when revenue is received.

carrying broker: any broker or commission house maintaining a client's account.

carrying charge

(1) *general:* the continuing cost of owning or holding any property or items.

(2) *banking:* the amount of charges added to the price of a service to compensate for deferred payment.

(3) *finance:* the fee charged by investment brokers for handling margin accounts.

carrying market: a market in which more distant positions are quoted at a premium over the nearby positions, and where this premium is high enough to compensate for the carrying charges. [11]

carrying-over day: any postponed day of delivery. Used on the London Stock Exchange. see *backwardation.*

carrying value: the value of a fixed asset remaining after its accumulated depreciation reserve has been deducted from its original depreciable cost. [49]

carry-over: in federal income taxes, the amount of a taxpayer's loss that was not absorbed as a carry-back; may be deducted as taxable income of succeeding years. see *carry-back.*

carry-over clause: a clause to protect a broker for a specified time, usually beyond the expiration date of the property listing.

cars: slang, used by commodity traders as a synonym for the term "contracts."

carte a memoire: a credit card developed in France which has an integrated circuit that enables a user to record more than 100 transactions on the card, updating the balance each time without the need to communicate with a central computer. see *"smart" credit cards.*

cartel: a group of separate business organizations that have agreed to institute approaches to alter competition by influencing prices, production, or marketing. Rarely as effective as a monopoly. see *monopoly, oligopoly;* cf. *consortium.*

case note: slang, a $1 bill.

Cash.: see *cashier.*

cash: an all-embracing term associated with any business transaction involving the handling of currency and coins.

cash account: a cash basis account, where all purchases are completely paid for. cf. *margin account.*

cash against documents (CAD): when the purchaser must make payment for items before the receipt of the shipping papers that will give him control of the items once they are surrendered to him.

cash assets: assets described on a financial statement represented by actual cash on hand, and the total of bank deposits.

cash audit: an examination of cash transactions during a given time period to determine whether all received cash has been documented.

cash balance: all cash on hand.

cash basis: the system of accounting under which revenues are accounted for only when received in cash, and expenditures are accounted for only when paid. [49]

cash before delivery (CBD): payment is required prior to delivery of goods.

cash board: in a commodity exchange, the area of blackboard used for the recording of sales of cash commodity contracts. see *spot commodity.*

cashbook: a book of original entry where the cash receipts journal and the cash payments journal are put together, forming one book.

cash budget: a schedule of expected cash receipts and disbursements.

cash bus: a cabinet on wheels where tellers store cash in the teller's cage or wicket during the day. This cabinet has sufficient room for the cash till and also storage under lock and key for packaged specie money that may be required for making change in large orders. The teller wheels the cash bus into the vault after balancing the cash at the end of the day. [10]

cash buying: the purchase of securities or commodities outright for immediate delivery of the item.

cash card: a card given by a retailer or store owner to a customer guaranteeing a discount for a cash payment. It is a substitute for credit cards; some merchants give cash-paying customers up to 8 percent discount.

cash commodity: a specific lot of a commodity bought through a cash transaction for immediate delivery, though delivery may be deferred.

cash credit discount: in installment cash credit, the discount is the charge for the credit service which is deducted from the total amount of the loan before the borrower receives the balance in cash. [55]

cash discount: a deduction from the selling price permitted by the seller for merchandise sold on credit, represented in terms of a percentage;

made to encourage the prompt payment of the invoice covering the goods or services purchased.

cash dispenser: a machine capable of giving out cash representing a withdrawal from a deposit account or an extension of credit. synonymous with *ATM, cashomat.*

cash dividend: declared dividends payable in cash, usually by check.

cash earnings: the profits or net income of an organization. These earnings include all depreciation and amortization accruals.

cashed check: check accepted by a bank in exchange for cash. Usually such an item can be identified by a teller's stamp or cash-out symbol. [31]

cash flow: the reported net income of a corporation, plus amounts charged off for depreciation, depletion, amortization, and extraordinary charges to reserves, which are bookkeeping deductions and not actually paid out in cash. Knowledge of these factors results in a better understanding of a firm's ability to pay dividends. cf. *net cash flow.*

cashier: a bank's officer or representative responsible for the custody of the bank's assets, and whose signature is required on official documents.

cashier's account: the ledger account of a bank that is primarily used to record cashier's checks.

cashier's check

(1) a bank's own check signed by a cashier, becoming a direct obligation of the bank. Upon issue to a customer, it becomes a loan and a debit in the cashier's account. It differs from a certified check in that it is drawn against the funds of the bank itself, not against the funds found in a specific depositor's account. cf. *certified check, register(ed) check.*

(2) synonymous with *official check* or *treasurer's check.*

cash in the chips: slang, to conclude a business transaction; to sell one's share of a company.

cash in vault: coin and currency actually held by the banks on their own premises. [40]

cash items: items listed in a firm's statement that are the equivalent of cash, such as bank deposits, government bonds, and marketable securities.

cash letter: a transit check with listing tapes, transmitting items from one bank to another for collection. Frequently, the items contained in the cash letter are grouped into several batches with a listing tape attached to each batch. The totals are recapped on the transmittal form letter. Generally, these are associated with mail deposits received from other banks. [31]

cash letter of credit: a letter addressed by a bank to its correspondent bank to make available to the party named in the letter, funds up to a specified amount within certain time limitations. The sum named in the letter is deposited with the bank before the letter is issued, hence the designation "cash letter of credit." [10]

cash loan: see *policy loan.*

cash management account (CMA): a bank-type development of Merrill Lynch in partnership with Bank One of Ohio, based in Columbus, where affluent clients are offered a Visa credit card and checking to draw against their investment balances. The account was initially offered in 206 of Merrill Lynch's 382 offices in the United States.

cash market: as contrasted with the futures market; synonymous with *spot market.*

cashomat: see *cash dispenser.*

cash on delivery (COD): describes any purchase made with the expectation that the item(s) will be paid for on delivery. cf. *franco delivery.*

cash on hand: cash drawer money, vault cash, and demand deposits in commercial banks or regional Federal Home Loan Banks. [59]

cash over: a general ledger account to which tellers' cash overages are credited. see *cash over and short.* [10]

cash over and short: the difference between the cash on hand and the balance of the cash account or cashbook. When the cash on hand is over the balance of the cash account or cashbook, the cash is over; when less than that of the balance, the cash is short.

cash position: the percentage of cash to the total net assets; the net amount after the deduction of current liabilities.

cash price: the current price of the cash commodity of a designated quality available for immediate delivery.

cash refund annuity: a life annuity providing that a lump sum payment will be made to a beneficiary in an amount equal to the excess, if any, of the amount paid by the annuitant toward the annuity over the sum of the annuity payments received by the an-

nuitant to the date of death. [52]

cash release ticket: a slip either handwritten or machine printed by which a teller charges himself for the amount of cash on a deposit. [10]

cash report: a statement, prepared on a daily basis, showing the cash position of the organization for each day.

cash reserve

(1) *banking:* refers to requirements for banks to maintain a sufficient portion of deposits as required by federal law.

(2) *finance:* funds readily available to be converted into cash in an emergency. see entries under *liquid.*

cash sale

(1) *general:* the surrender of cash at the time of sale.

(2) *finance:* a transaction on the floor of an exchange that calls for delivery of the securities the same day. In "regular way" trades, the seller is to deliver on the fifth business day.

cash short: a general ledger account to which tellers' cash shortages are charged. [10]

cash substitution ticket: see *cash release ticket.*

cash surrender value: the sum total of money paid by a bank upon cancellation of its life insurance policy. see *surrender value.*

cash ticket: a slip or ticket used as a substitute for cash included in a deposit. The teller verifies and retains the cash, recording the amount on the cash ticket. [31]

cash till: a tray built with compartment bins to help tellers sort and have ready for easy access the various denominations of currency. [10]

cash trade: any transaction in securities and commodities paid in full with cash for immediate delivery of goods. see *for cash*.

cash value: describes the amount available to the owner of a life insurance policy when the policy is surrendered to the insurer.

cash with fiscal agent: deposits with fiscal agents, such as commercial banks, for the payment of matured bonds and interest. [49]

casting: slang, any coin.

cast up: to add up a total, as "to cast up an account." synonymous with *footing*.

cathode ray tube (CRT): a visual display device that translates the data from a computer memory and visually presents the information in human language form. The CRT enables batches or blocks of information in memory to be instantly accessed, read, and displayed on a screen. In an on-line or real-time data-processing system, the device permits instant or impromptu display of any desired information.

cats and dogs
(1) *general:* items that do not have satisfactory sales turnover and accumulate inventory.
(2) *finance:* highly speculative stocks.

causa mortis: see *gift causa mortis*.

cause of action: created by intrusion on a person's legal right by a breach of contract or of a legal duty toward one's person or property.

caveat
(1) *finance:* a notice to cease payment.
(2) *law:* "let him beware" (Latin); a warning. A notice filed by an interested party with a proper legal authority directing others to cease or refrain from an act until the person filing can be heard from fully.

caveat emptor: "let the buyer beware" (Latin). When merchandise is sold without a warranty by the vendor, the purchaser takes the risk of loss as to defects. see *without recourse;* cf. *caveat subscriptor*.

caveator: one who files or sends a *caveat*.

caveat subscriptor (venditor): "let the seller beware" (Latin). Unless the seller states no responsibility, he or she is liable to the purchaser for any alterations from the written contract. cf. *caveat emptor*.

CB
(1) see *bond, callable*.
(2) see *bond, coupon*.

CBCT: see *Customer-Bank Communication Terminal*.

CBD: see *cash before delivery*.

CC
(1) see *cancellation clause*.
(2) see *cancelled checks*.
(3) see *cash commodity*.
(4) see *cashier's check*.
(5) see *cold canvassing*.

CCA: see *Credit Control Act of 1969*.

CCCS: see *Consumer Credit Counseling Services*.

CCS: see *Central Certificate Service*.

C&D: see *cats and dogs*.

CD
(1) see *cash discount*.
(2) see *certificate of deposit*.
(3) see *cum dividend*.

CE
(1) see *capital expenditure*.
(2) see *cash earnings*.
(3) see *caveat emptor*.
(4) see *commodity exchange*.

CEA

(1) see *Commodity Exchange Authority.*

(2) see *Council of Economic Advisers.*

cease and desist order

(1) *labor relations:* directions to management or the union, issued usually by the National Labor Relations Board, to halt an unfair labor practice. see *Taft-Hartley Act.*

(2) *law:* a court or governmental agency demand that a person or firm cease an activity.

CEC: see *Commodities Exchange Center.*

cede: a company reinsuring liability with another company "cedes" business to that company (i.e., it yields or grants business by agreement).

cedi: monetary unit of Ghana.

cédule: a European concept; the warehouse receipt used in transfers or assignments. see *warehouse receipt.*

CEF: see *closed-end fund.*

CEIC: see *closed-end investment company.*

ceiling price: usually during wartime, a maximum price established by government regulation on goods and services. cf. *floor.*

Celler Antimerger Act: an extension of the Clayton Antitrust Act, this 1950 addition prohibits a corporation from acquiring the stock or assets of another corporation if the effect would be a substantial lessening of competition or a tendency to monopoly.

cent: the coin of lowest worth in the United States, equal to one-hundredth of a dollar ($0.01).

Center for Financial Studies, Inc.: organized in 1977, this Connecticut nonprofit corporation directs the operation of the Center for Financial Studies on the campus of Fairfield University. The center is a joint undertaking by the university and the savings bank industry. Funds to construct the center were raised through a subscription by National Association of Mutual Savings Banks member savings banks. Upon completion of the center in late 1979, most of NAMSB's education programs were transferred there. [8]

central bank

(1) *banking:* a banker's bank. see *banker's bank.*

(2) *government:* a bank holding the main body of bank reserves of a nation and the prime reservoir of credit (e.g., Bank of England, Bank of France).

Central Certificate Service (CCS): a privately run depository through which members effect security deliveries between each other via computerized bookkeeping entries, thereby reducing the physical movement of stock certificates.

Central Industry Fund, Inc.: this nonprofit corporation was organized in 1961 to provide technical and capital assistance to new and existing savings banks. Over the years, it has assisted institutions with special problems regarding location, management succession, and overall operation. [8]

central information file (CIF): in most banks, a ledger record of the bank services used by its customers, indicating in which office or offices the business is handled. [10]

central liability: the grouping together on one record of all liabilities of a borrower, such as loans both direct and indirect, consumer credit, letters of credit, guarantees, and other accommodations. The purpose of this record is to prevent overextensions of credit to the borrower, show what is currently due from him, and provide a history of his borrowing. [10]

central processing unit (CPU): a unit of a computer that incorporates the circuits controlling the interpretation and execution of instructions.

central proof: a system for effecting economy of operation by centralizing all proof and distributing functions in a single department of a bank. see *proof department.* [31]

central rate: a rate established under a temporary regime (based on an International Monetary Fund executive board decision of December 18, 1974) by a country which temporarily does not maintain rates based on a par value in accordance with the relevant fund rules but does maintain transactions in its territories. Central rates are in certain respects treated as par values, and the concept was introduced primarily to allow fund members who, prior to August 15, 1971, had an effective par value to base their exchange rates on a stable rate subject to specified margin requirements during the period when the par value of the U.S. dollar was not effective. The temporary regime provides for the possibility of margins of $2\frac{1}{4}$ percent either side of the central rate. After the change in the par value of the U.S. dollar on May 8, 1974, a number of countries have replaced their central rates with new par values. [42]

Central Reserve Cities: established by the National Bank Act, New York City and Chicago are central reserve cities. see *reserve city bank.*

century: slang, a $100 bill.

CEO: see *chief executive officer.*

Cert.: see *certificate.*

certificate

(1) *finance:* the piece of paper that is evidence of ownership of stock in a corporation. Watermarked paper is finely engraved with delicate etchings to discourage forgery. see *savings certificates.*

(2) *government:* a form of paper money, issued against silver or gold deposited in the U.S. Treasury.

(3) *law:* any written or printed document of truth that can be used as proof of a fact.

certificate account: a savings account containing a fixed amount of funds deposited for a fixed term. The customer is charged a penalty for premature withdrawal, but is paid interest at a rate higher than that on passbook accounts if the deposit remains untouched for the full term. see also *savings certificate.* [59]

certificate check: see *certified check.*

certificated securities: the quantity of a specific commodity held in warehouses that have been approved by a commodity exchange, and which is certified as deliverable on future contracts.

certificate of analysis: to assure the importer that goods conform to ordered specifications, a document requiring an overseas seller to accompany the bill of exchange drawn against a shipment as outlined in the letter of credit. see also *certificate of inspection.*

certificate of beneficial interest: a statement of a share of a firm's business when such ownership has been deposited with a trustee. The certificate holder receives the income from and holds an interest in the firm's assets, but relinquishes management control. Used when a business is operated as a trust.

certificate of claim: a contingent promise of the Federal Housing Administration to reimburse an insured mortgagee for certain costs incurred during foreclosure of an insured mortgage provided the proceeds from the sale of the property acquired are sufficient to cover those costs. [44]

certificate of convenience and necessity: a special permit (which supplements the franchise), commonly issued by a state commission, which authorizes a utility to engage in business, construct facilities, or perform some other service. [3]

certificate of deposit (CD): a negotiable, nonnegotiable, or transferable receipt payable to the depositor for funds deposited with a bank, usually interest bearing. see also *certificate of deposit (demand), certificate of deposit (time), variable interest plus.*

certificate of deposit (demand): a negotiable or transferable receipt issued for funds deposited with a bank and payable on demand to the holder. These receipts do not bear interest and are used principally by contractors and others as a guarantee of performance of a contract or as evidence of good faith when submitting a bid. They may also be used as collateral.

certificate of deposit (time): a negotiable or transferable receipt for funds deposited with a bank, payable to the holder at some specified date (not less than 30 days after issuance) and bearing interest.

certificate of incorporation: the franchise or charter issued by a state to the original petitioners of an approved corporation. Such franchise or charter constitutes the authority granted by the state for the organization to transact business as a corporation.

certificate of indebtedness

(1) a short-term note issued by a governmental agency, describing the current debt.

(2) an unsecured promissory note, the holder having a general creditor's recourse against general assets.

certificate of inspection: a document released by a trade association or agency authorized to inspect an importer's goods to assure the purchaser that the items correspond to those identified in the letter of credit. see also *certificate of analysis.*

certificate of insurance: evidence that an insurance policy has been issued, showing the amount and type of insurance provided. It may be used as evidence of reinsurance between companies, and it is the document containing specific details of property covered by master or open policies. see *commercial set.*

certificate of no defense: when a mortgage is sold, the certificate signed by the borrower that identifies the mortgage indebtedness.

certificate of occupancy: a permit issued by a building department verifying that the work meets the local zoning ordinances and the structure ready for occupancy.

certificate of origin: a certificate declaring that goods purchased from a foreign country have indeed been produced in that country and not another.

certificate of ownership: see *proprietorship certificate.*

certificate of release: a certificate signed by the lender indicating that a mortgage has been fully paid and all debts satisfied.

certificate of title: a title company certification that the seller possesses sound, marketable, and/or insurance title to the property. If a title company issues this certificate and a defect is identified at a later time, the title company will indemnify the holder. see *title insurance.*

certificates: U.S. paper money circulated in the form of a receipt for silver or gold coins. The U.S. silver certificates are the best known. The redemption privilege was revoked by Congress on June 14, 1968. [27]

certificates of debt: certificates indicating that a loan or some other form of debts remains to be paid.

certification

(1) *banking:* an assurance by a bank that the drawer of a check has sufficient funds on deposit to cover payment on the check and that monies have been set aside to meet the incoming obligation. "Certification" is usually stamped across the face of the check. see also *cross check.*

(2) *labor relations:* determination by the National Labor Relations Board or an appropriate state agency that a particular union is the majority choice, hence the exclusive bargaining agent, of all employees in a particular bargaining unit.

certification teller: a teller whose duty is to certify or accept checks of depositors. In large banks this may be his only duty, but in smaller banks it is usually combined with others. [10]

certified check: the check of a depositor drawn on a bank; the face of the check bears the word "accepted" or "certified," with the date and signature of a bank official or authorized clerk. The check then becomes an obligation of the bank, and regulations require that the amount of the check be immediately charged against the depositor's account. cf. *cashier's check.*

certified mail: a service that provides a receipt to the sender and a record of delivery at the office of address. It is handled in the ordinary mail without insurance coverage. This service is not available to foreign countries. [24]

certified public accountant (CPA): an accountant who has been certified by the state as having met that state's requirements of age, education, experience, and technical qualifications. Not all who practice accounting are certified.

certiorari, writ of: a directive from an appellate court to a lower court declaring that the record of a case pending in the lower court is to be forwarded to the upper court for review.

cesser clause: a statement in a charter agreement that a charterer's obligation terminates when the freight is loaded. The owner of the carrier can, however, have a lien on the freight for appropriate charges.

cession number: a number assigned by an underwriting office to identify reinsurance premium transactions. [54]

cestui: a beneficiary of a trust.

cestui que trust: French adaption of a Latin phrase designating the person for whose benefit a trust has been established. synonymous with *beneficiary*.

ceteris paribus: the assumption that the values of all variables and parameters other than those being analyzed are constant.

C&F: cost and freight to named overseas port of import. Under this term, the seller quotes a price including the cost of transportation to the named point of destination. [61]

CF: see *cash flow.*

CFTC: see *Commodity Futures Trading Commission.*

CG
(1) see *capital gain (or loss).*
(2) see *capital goods.*

CGT: see *capital gains tax.*

CH: see *clearinghouse.*

chain banking: a form of multiple-office banking under which a minimum of three independently incorporated banks are controlled by one or more individuals. cf. *branch banking.*

chain of command: the organizational design for the flow of communications outlining directing toward authority, peers, and subordinates.

chain of title: the succession of conveyances from some accepted starting point from which the present holder of real property derives his title. [62]

chairman of the board: the highest ranking executive of a corporation. In some cases the firm's president is also the chairman of the board.

chamber of commerce: an organization of business executives created to advance the interests of its members.

change: money returned following a purchase, when a larger sum of money was given than was required (e.g., on a sale purchase of $0.98, a $1.00 handout returns $0.02 in change).

change in amount consumed: increase or decrease in the amount of consumption expenditures resulting from a change in personal income.

change in business inventories: represents the value of the increase or decrease in the physical stock of goods held by the business sector valued in current period prices. These inventories are in three stages of production: raw materials, semifinished goods, and finished goods ready for sale or shipment. An inventory increase is regarded as investment because it represents production not matched by current consumption; an inventory decrease is regarded as "negative investment" because it reflects consumption in excess of current production. [73]

Chapter 11: see *Bankruptcy Reform Act of 1978.*

character: a letter, digit, or other symbol that is used as part of the organization, control, or representation of data in a computer.

character and object classification of expenditures: a classification that focuses on the nature of spending apart from the functions served. It distinguishes among purchases of goods and services for current operation and capital outlay, assistance and subsidies, interest on debt, and insurance benefits and repayments.

charge

(1) *general:* a cost or expense allotted to a specific account.

(2) *banking:* to purchase for credit without making an immediate payment; usually to be paid following billing.

(3) *finance:* a demanded price.

(4) *law:* a judge's instruction to a jury.

charge account: line of credit that may be used repeatedly up to a certain specified limit. synonymous with *open-end credit, revolving credit.* [78]

charge account banking: permits consumers to arrange a line of credit with a bank or lending institution; usable to make purchases in many participating establishments. The plan may provide simply a 30-day charge account or installment payment service. [28]

charge authorization phone system: equipment permitting direct contact from a sales department to the credit office for the purpose of authorizing charges. Equipment is often selective so that calls may be directed to the individual in charge of a particular alphabetical group. [41]

charged-off paper: see *write-off.*

charge notice: see *debit memo.*

charge off: to treat as a loss; to designate as an expense an amount originally recorded as an asset. cf. *write-off.*

charge-out: a term used to designate the release of debits or credits to other departments for further handling. Before such items are released, their package totals are recorded on a charge-out sheet. Later, the totals are included in the final proof. [31]

charge-a-plate: describes a device bearing the name of the credit customer and other descriptive data.

charges and miscellaneous revenue: nontax revenue derived chiefly from fees, assessments, and other reimbursements for current services and from rents and sales of commodities or services furnished incident to the performance of particular general government functions.

charge ticket: that written memorandum which a bookkeeper uses as a guide in posting a debit item to an account. synonymous with *debit ticket.* [31]

charitable bequest: a gift of personal property to a legal charity by will. [37]

charitable devise: a gift of real property to a legal charity by will. [37]

charitable remainder: an arrangement wherein the remainder interest goes to a legal charity upon the termination or failure of a prior interest. [37]

charitable trust: a trust created for the benefit of a community ordinarily without a definite beneficiary—for example, a trust for educational purposes. synonymous with *public trust.* [32]

charter: the contract between a private corporation and the state, identifying the articles of association granted to the corporation by authority of the legislative act. Powers and privileges granted are included.

chartered accountant (CA): in the United Kingdom, Canada, and Australia, a certified accountant.

chartered banks: refers to banks that operate under a government and state charter as opposed to private banks. [27]

Chartered Life Underwriter (CLU): the professional designation awarded by the American College of Life Underwriters to those who have completed the prescribed series of examinations and have satisfied the organization's experience requirement.

Chartered Property & Casualty Underwriter (CPCU): the professional designation awarded by the American Institute for Property and Liability Underwriters to those who have completed the prescribed series of examinations and have satisfied the organization's experience requirement.

charterer: an individual or organization, usually a state agency, who grants a business the right to incorporate and transact business.

chartist: an individual who interprets stock market activity and predicts future movement, usually over a short period, from a graphic depiction of price and volume on charts. cf. *Dow theory.*

chattel: derived from "cattle." All property that is not real property. A structure on real property is a chattel real; movable properties (e.g., automobiles) are chattels personal. see *replevin;* cf. *chose(s) in action, goods and services;* synonymous with *personal property.*

chattel, personal: any item of movable property besides real estate. [62]

chattel, real: an interest in land, such as a leasehold, which is less than a freehold estate. see *tenancy at suf-ferance, tenancy at will, tenancy for years.* [32]

chattel mortgage: an instrument prepared by a debtor (the mortgagor) transferring a chattel's interest to a creditor (mortgagee) for the purposes of providing security for a debt. If the debt is not paid, the mortgagee can sell the chattel and use the monies received to satisfy the debt outstanding.

chattel mortgage agreement: a legal agreement with a purchase of merchandise on an installment basis. Provides that the buyer accepts title to goods on delivery but gives the seller a mortgage on such merchandise that may be foreclosed under certain conditions and by prescribed legal procedure. [41]

cheap money: money that is available at relatively low rates of interest.

check

(1) *general:* a process for determining accuracy.

(2) *banking:* the Federal Reserve Board defines a check as follows: "a draft or order upon a bank or banking house purporting to be drawn upon a deposit of funds, for the payment of a certain sum on money to a certain person therein named, or to his order, or to bearer, and payable instantly on demand."

(3) *computers:* the process of testing machine validity or the correctness of the results yielded by a program. cf. *debug.*

check authorization/verification: an inquiry process undertaken to reduce the risk of accepting a fraudulent check or a check written for an amount that exceeds the account balance. Check authorization systems may be provided and maintained by the party accepting the check, by a financial institution, or by a third party engaged in such a business. These systems may be designed to access bank records directly or may rely on secondary data sources. In some systems, check approval is accompanied by a guarantee of payment.

checkbook: a book containing blank checks furnished by banks to depositors to permit them to withdraw funds from their checking accounts. A customer may keep a complete record of his deposits, his withdrawals, and his balance, by means of stubs or a register book. [31]

check bouncer: slang, an individual who writes checks against nonexistent bank accounts or against accounts with insufficient funds to cover the check.

check clearing: the movement of checks from the banks where they are deposited back to those on which they are written, and funds movement in the opposite direction. This process results in credits to the accounts of the banks of deposit and corresponding debits to the accounts of the paying bank. The Federal Reserve operates a nationwide check-clearing system, though many checks are cleared by private sector arrangements. [1]

check currency: demand deposits generated by a bank loan that is subject to withdrawal by check as opposed to coin or paper money.

check desk: that section of a bookkeeping department through which all incoming and outgoing debit and credit items pass. It assembles and controls all final proof figures for the bookkeeping department. The term is also applied to a proof department for incoming and outgoing items. [10]

check files: the files in which all paid and canceled checks are stored until they are ready to be returned to the depositors with their statements. Check files may simply be drawers in a bookkeeper's desk, or in large banks a section of the bookkeeping department charged with the responsibility of filing checks and providing them with the statements before mailing. [10]

check filing: the process of placing canceled checks in storage to facilitate the periodic mailing of customers' statements. [31]

checking account: a demand account subject to withdrawal by check of funds on deposit.

checkless society: describes the predicted absence or need for checks as a medium for transferring funds. The realization of this futuristic concept will come about with the universal usage of bank credit cards, widespread adoption of common machine languages, the ability of financial and commercial concerns of all types and sizes to communicate on-line and in real-time processing, and a complete program for automatic transfer of funds within a bank or between cooperating banks. The depositor's universal bank credit card will authorize debits to his account for purchases and services which he is presently paying for with a check. Settlements between all banks, to accommodate payments of their customers, are also made automatically. [10]

checklist: an adding machine list of a depositor's checks that are to be charged to his checking account. The number of checks used to make a list varies with the individual bank. The number of checks attached to a list is usually indicated on the list to be used for account analysis. The object of a list is to cut down on the number of items posted to a depositor's account, since only the total of the list appears on the depositor's statement. [10]

checkoff: the withholding of wages by an employer for direct payments to a union of dues and assessments. The Taft-Hartley Act states the union members must give written permission for these sums to be deducted. The checkoff cannot exist for longer than one year or until the termination of the union contract, whichever date comes first. A checkoff can also be used to deduct assessments for nonunion members.

check on us: checks drawn on a bank and presented to it for deposit or payment. [50]

checkout: when a block does not prove and the difference is not located by verifying the addition of the deposit tickets and comparing the check amounts with the listings, it is necessary to resort to a checkout. This consists of matching each item shown on the deposit tickets with a similar amount appearing on the block listing tapes, which will establish that the depositor has done one of the following: included a check without listing it, listed a check but failed to include it, or listed a check incorrectly. [31]

check - protecting equipment: ma-chines that prevent a change in the check amount or in the name of the payee.

check rate: the basic rate for foreign exchange trades, used to calculate all other rates. synonymous with "demand rate."

check requisition: a written request made to the accounting department of a firm for the preparation of a check. [59]

check-routing symbol: a device to facilitate the handling and routing of transit items through banks that remit at par all over the United States. The check-routing symbol is the denominator of a fraction, the numerator being the ABA transit number. The entire fraction is located in the upper right-hand corner of a check. The check-routing symbol is composed of three or four digits. The first digit in a denominator of three figures or the first two digits in a denominator of four figures identify the Federal Reserve District (1–12) in which the drawee bank is located. The next to the last digit designates the Federal Reserve Bank head office or branch through which the item should be cleared and also any special clearing arrangement. (The head office is indicated by the number 1. Branches, if any, arranged alphabetically, are indicated by numbers 2 to 5. Numbers 6 to 9 are used to designate special collection arrangements.) The last digit shows whether the item is acceptable for immediate or deferred credit. [10]

check safeekeeping: see *free check storage account.*

check serial number: the magnetic characters imprinted in the auxiliary

On-Us field. These figures correspond to the number on each check used by the maker as identification. see *account reconciliation plan.* [31]

check trading: selling bank checks to a customer, who is expected to repay the amount of the check plus interest in installments.

check verification guarantee: systems providing retail merchants with varying degree of insurance against bad check losses by (a) verifying the authenticity of the check and/or its presenter, or (b) guaranteeing payments of the check by the bank. [33]

cheque: "check" in French or British English.

cherry pie: slang, money easily obtained or from activities other than one's regular occupation.

Chg.: see *charge.*

Chicago Board of Trade: the world's largest grain exchange where spot or futures contracts are completed in a host of agricultural products.

Chicago Mercantile Exchange: organized in 1919 as a national market place of trading in cash and futures contracts for commodity items, including butter, eggs, potatoes, pork bellies, hogs, cattle, sorghums, turkeys, and lumber.

Chicago School Theory: an economic approach stating that the basic equation controlling the macro-economic path of a state's economy is a function of the interaction between money supply and the speed of its turnover.

chicken feed: slang, small amount of money; small change.

chief clerk: usually a junior officer or a senior clerk whose duties consist of handling various transactions of an important nature, such as notary work, protests, wire transfers, and technical negotiable instruments. In branch banking, the chief clerk is a junior officer who is charged with the supervision of personnel and the general operations of the branch. [10]

chief executive officer (CEO): the person accountable to the board of directors for the activities and profits of the firm.

CHIPS: see *Clearing House Interbank Payment Systems.*

chisel: slang, borrowing money with the expectation of not paying.

chose: anything that is personal property. [37]

chose(s) in action: a right to, but not possession of, funds or property; the actual taking possession may result from some other event. The right may be enforced by a court ruling and may cover debts, mortgages, negotiable instruments, insurance policies, and warrants. see *chose.*

chose(s) in possession: tangible personal property in actual possession (e.g., an automobile), as contrasted with a *chose in action.* see chose; cf. *corporeal property, goods and services.*

Chq.: see *cheque.*

Christmas Club account: a savings account whereby a customer deposits a specified sum each week in order to accumulate a lump sum for Christmas expenditures. [31]

chumming: artificially inflating the market's volume to attract other orders in some issues which stock exchanges compete in.

churning: the repetitive buying and

selling of securities when such activity has a minimal effect on the market but generates additional commissions to a stockbroker.

CI
(1) see *capital intensive.*
(2) see *cash items.*
(3) see *compounded interest.*
CID: see *civil investigative demands.*
CIF
(1) see *central information file.*
(2) see *Corporate Income Fund.*
(3) see *cost, insurance, and freight.*
Cincinnati Stock Exchange: created 1887; most of its traded stocks are "unlisted," including securities listed and traded on other stock exchanges.
Cincotta-Conklin Bill of 1976: a New York state law permitting state savings banks and savings and loan associations to offer checking accounts like commercial banks, but at no cost.
CIO: see *Congress of Industrial Organizations.*
cipher-proof: a method of balancing whereby certain figures are automatically subtracted from a control total. If the balance results in zero, it is proved that all figures were added and listed correctly. Sometimes referred to as zero balance. [32]
circuity of action: when a bill of exchange is returned to the person who has already signed it, he may renegotiate it, but this person has no claim against individuals signing the bill between the time he initially signed it and its return to him.
circular letter of credit: a document, frequently issued by a bank, that is not addressed to any particular agency or bank. The issuing bank accepts drafts on it when they are within the terms of the letter.
circulating capital good: any capital good item when in use that is consumed by a single use (e.g., gasoline used to make a car engine function).
circulating medium: money; any form of exchange that is accepted without endorsement.
circulation
(1) *banking:* the total value of the issued bank notes of a bank that are in use, as distinguished from those being held in the bank's reserve.
(2) *finance:* the total of all currency in use at a given period. see *velocity of circulation.*
circulation statement: published monthly by the U.S. Treasury Department showing amounts of currency outstanding and in circulation, currency by denominations and coin, and the comparative sums of money in use.
circumstantial evidence: if from specific facts and circumstances, according to the experience of mankind, an ordinary, intelligent person may infer that other connected facts and circumstances must necessarily exist, the latter facts and circumstances are considered to be proved by circumstantial evidence.
City: "The City" is London's financial center. also called "The Square Mile."
city bond: see *bond, municipal.*
city collection department: a department in a bank which handles the collection of items payable within a city, and receives and collects these items by messenger. As a general rule, those items which cannot be collected through the local clearinghouse

owing to their being drawn on non-members, or drafts with documents attached which require special handling, pass through this department. [10]

city items: negotiable items, notes, and checks that are drawn upon individuals or institutions located in the same local or city in which they were deposited.

civil action: a court proceeding or suit by one person against another for protection of a private right or the prevention of a wrong. It includes actions ex contractu, ex delicto, and all equity suits.

civil bond: see *bond, civil.*

civil investigative demands (CIDs): created in legislation signed by President Ford on September 30, 1976, to give the Antitrust Division of the Justice Department added investigative authority. In civil antitrust investigations, these instruments are analogous to subpoenas issued in criminal investigations. CIDs may be issued to a company, its executives, or a third party, such as a competitor, to obtain documents or to require oral testimony.

civil law: law based on statutes, as distinguished from common law. A law that examines relationships between people, as opposed to criminal law.

civil loans: loans contracted by a federal, state, or municipal agency.

Civil Rights Act of 1964, Title VII: creating the federal Fair Employment Practices Law, covering all industries affecting interstate commerce. It bars discrimination by employers, unions, and employment agencies based on race, color, sex, religion, or national origin. Employers and unions may not discriminate in regard to apprenticeship, training, or retraining programs. Employers, unions, and employment agencies may not retaliate against any person opposing, making a charge, testifying, or taking part in probes or proceedings regarding any practice deemed to be unlawful under the act; or publishing or printing notices or advertisements indicating discrimination. Employment agencies are forbidden to discriminate by failing or refusing to refer applicants on the basis of race, color, religion, sex, or national origin. The law is administered by the Equal Employment Opportunity Commission, which has five members. see also *Civil Rights Act of 1968, Fair Employment Practices Committee.*

Civil Rights Act of 1968: guarantees to all citizens equal treatment in matters pertaining to housing and real estate. Prohibits discrimination because of race, color, religion, national origin, or sex against individuals trying to obtain financing for a home or property. see also *Civil Rights Act of 1964, Title VII.*

Ck.: see *check.*

CL
(1) see *call loan.*
(2) see *capital loss.*
(3) see *cash letter.*
(4) see *common law.*
(5) see *current liabilities.*

claim
(1) ***banking:*** a demand by an individual or a corporation to recover, under a policy of insurance, for loss that is covered by that policy.
(2) ***law:*** a demand for payment, reimbursement, or compensation for

damages or injury as identified in a contract or under law.

claim against estate: a demand made upon the estate to do or to forebear some act as a matter of duty. A common example would be the claim submitted by a creditor for a debt owed him by the decedent at the time of his death. [37]

claim audit: a survey of a policy record to determine the payment due an insured under a claim. [12]

claims reported by U.S. banks (long-term): long-term claims reported by U.S. banks represent commercial bank loans to foreigners. These loans may go to private business, individuals, or foreign governments. A large part of these comprise loans for foreign corporations, including loans to finance ship mortgages, U.S. exports, plant expansion, and to refinance debts outstanding. A loan is considered long-term if its repayment schedule is for more than one year. The flow in the opposite direction appears in long-term liabilities reported by U.S. banks. [73]

claims reported by U.S. banks (short-term): short-term claims include loans extended to foreigners with a maturity of less than one year. Loans to foreign banks for the purpose of financing general trade transactions on foreign accounts and short-term bank claims in foreign currencies that represent correspondent balances held in the bank's own account abroad are included. Nonbank claims such as outstanding collections held in the bank's custody or short-term investments in foreign money market assets are also included. [73]

claims reported by U.S. residents other than banks (long-term): those claims reported by private business firms resulting from their export transactions. These claims assume various forms. A common example is "supplier's credit." This is the long-term financing extended to a foreigner by a U.S. corporation in order that it may sell its product abroad. Long-term loans made to foreigners by insurance companies are also included. [73]

claims reported by U.S. residents other than banks (short-term): includes those claims reported by U.S. brokerage houses. These claims may be in the form of a cash account held by the broker. Also included are other short-term financial assets held abroad such as the unused proceeds of loan flotations by U.S. corporations in foreign capital markets. [73]

class
(1) *general:* to place in ranks or divisions.
(2) *banking:* a category of employees in the schedule of group insurance, denoting the amounts of coverage for which the members of the class are eligible. see also *Class A stock, classification.*

class action: a legal action in which one or more persons move against an organization on behalf of themselves as well as an aggrieved group or "class" of citizens deemed to be affected by the same condition.

Class A stock: as distinguished from Class B stock, common, a stock that usually has an advantage over other stock in terms of voting rights, dividend or asset preferences, or other special dividend provisions.

classical management: the first schools of management thought, including scientific management, functionalism, and bureaucracy.

classification: the underwriting or rating group into which a particular risk must be placed. Pertains to type of business, location, and other factors; not to be confused with "class," but see *class rate*.

classified: a securities issue of more than one class, usually presented in series from "A" on.

classified bond: see *bond, classified*.

classified loan: a loan made by a bank to a customer and subsequently criticized by examiners as being substandard.

classified property tax: the descriptions of properties by owners for the purpose of setting assessment with respect to market value and tax rates.

classified taxation: a tax structure in which real property is categorized by function, with differing tax rates applied to each class. In such situations, some classes are excluded from paying any tax.

class of options: options contracts of the same type (call or put) covering the same underlying security. [5]

class rate: a type of insurance rate applicable to risks that are so similar in character that it is unnecessary to go to the expense of differentiating among them as to varying factors of hazards.

Clayton Antitrust Act of 1914: hailed by the union movement as labor's Magna Carta. It was in part designed to remove labor from the purview of the Sherman Antitrust Act and to limit the use of injunctions against labor by the courts. The law has not been successful in the latter respect, however, because of the interpretations of the courts. cf. *Robinson-Patman Act of 1936, Sherman Antitrust Act of 1890*. see also *Celler Antimerger Act*.

clean bill of exchange: a bill of exchange having no other documents, such as a bill of lading affixed to it.

clean bill of lading: a bill of lading receipted by the carrier for goods received in appropriate condition (no damages or missing items); does not bear the notation "Shippers Load and Count." cf. *over, short, and damaged*.

clean bond: see *bond, clean*.

clean credit: any letter of credit from a bank against which the foreign seller can draw a bill without documentary support. This credit is available only to firms having the best credit reputation.

clean draft: a sight or time draft which has no other documents attached to it. This is to be distinguished from *documentary draft*. [10]

clean letter of credit: a letter of credit that does not demand such documents as bills of lading as a condition of acceptance by a bank. Such letters are issued only to prime risks.

clean up: slang, to take all available profits in a market; to make a substantial and rapid profit.

clean up fund: provided as one of the basic services of life insurance. A reserve to cover costs of last illness, burial, legal and administrative expenses, miscellaneous outstanding debts, and so on. Also called "final expenses fund."

clear

(1) *general:* to make a profit or gain.

(2) *banking:* having passed through or having been collected by a clearinghouse. see also *clearing and settlement.*

(3) *computers:* to replace information in a storage device by zero.

(4) *finance:* free from encumbrance.

clearance

(1) *general:* an act of clearing.

(2) *banking:* the adjustment of debits and credits in a clearinghouse.

(3) *finance:* a certificate of authority by a customs official permitting a ship to leave after having met customs requirements.

clearance fees: the change incurred in a commodity exchange following the clearing of a trade.

clearing

(1) *general:* freeing a machine or device from obstruction or other barriers that minimize efficiency; erasing unnecessary information or data.

(2) *investments:* the physical transfer of cash and securities between the purchasers and sellers.

clearing account: an account designed to facilitate the distribution of certain items which usually affect more than one class of accounts, such as those for the production and distribution of power, the production and handling of materials and supplies, and for shop operations. [18]

clearing and settlement: the process whereby checks or other records of financial or point-of-sale transactions are moved (physically or electronically) from the point at which they were originated to the organization (bank, thrift institution, or other agency) that keeps the accounts for, and expects to collect from and ac-

count to, the responsible payor. The settlement process completes the internal financial transactions among the (possibly) many parties involved in the clearing operation.

clearing contracts: the substitution of principals to transactions to aid in the settlement of accounts. see *futures.*

clearinghouse: an association of banks in a city, created to facilitate the clearing of checks, drafts, notes, or other items among the members. It also formulates policies and rules for the mutual welfare of all members. see *Stock Clearing Corporation.*

clearinghouse balance: the sum of the debit and credit totals or balances at the end of the banking day.

clearing house certificate: prior to the formation of the Federal Reserve System, debit balances resulting from clearinghouse exchanges were settled in gold. In times of financial stress, member banks pooled their securities with the clearinghouse, to be used for the settlement of balances in lieu of gold. Clearinghouse certificates were issued against this pool of securities by the manager of the clearinghouse association to settle the exchange balances of debtor banks whose own resources were inadequate. The New York Clearing House Association resorted to the use of clearinghouse certificates 10 times in its history, the first being at the outbreak of the Civil War in 1861. [10]

Clearing House Interbank Payment Systems (CHIPS): an automated clearing facility operated by the New York Clearing House Association which processes international funds transfers among its members.

CHIPS is a system that moves dollars between 100 New York financial institutions—mostly major U.S. banks, branches of foreign banks, and Edge Act subsidiaries of out-of-state banks. see *Edge Act.*

clearing member: a member of a clearinghouse who is also an exchange member. Since not all exchange members are members of a clearinghouse, they clear their transactions with a clearing member.

clearing member bank: a bank, though not a member of the Federal Reserve System, permitted to collect its out-of-town checks via the Federal Reserve check-collecting system. By maintaining a balance with the Federal Reserve Bank in their district a bank may be allowed to become a clearing member.

clearings: the incoming cash letters of items which must be proved, sorted, returned if necessary, and for which settlement must be made. [31]

clear title: synonymous with *good title* or *marketable title.*

Clifford trust: a ten-year trust to reduce income taxes by diverting the income from property placed in trust from the grantor to a beneficiary, usually a member of the grantor's family in a lower income tax bracket. At the end of the trust period of ten years or more, the trust property reverts to the grantor. synonymous with *"ten-year trust".*

climax: the termination of rather long-lasting rising or declining price movement, often accompanied by significant securities trading volume. synonymous with *blowing off.* see *selling climax.*

CLOB: see *composite limit order book.*

CLOC: see *clean letter of credit.*

clock stamp: a mechanical or electric time recording device for imprinting upon an inserted document the time of arrival, and frequently the date upon which the item was received or transmitted. Such devices are frequently used in safe deposit and security deposit vaults. [10]

close
(1) *general:* to transfer the balances of revenue and expense accounts at the end of an accounting period (e.g., close the books). see *accounting cycle.*
(2) *banking:* to sign legal papers indicating that the property has formally changed ownership.
(3) *finance:* to conclude a sale or agreement.
(4) *investments:* the short period before the end of the trading session when all trades are officially declared to have been confirmed "at or on the close."

closed account: an account with equal debits and credits.

closed corporation: a corporation whose shares are held by only a few people, usually in positions of management.

closed-end fund: an investment firm whose shares are traded on a securities exchange or the over-the-counter market.

closed-end investment company: a management investment company that has raised its capital by means of a public offering, over a limited period of time, of a fixed amount of common stock (and which may also have raised capital by the issuance of senior securities). The stock of a closed-end investment company is bought and sold on securities exchanges or over-the-counter markets, as are the securities of business corporations. [23]

closed mortgage: a mortgage that cannot be paid off until maturity occurs.

closed out: a situation where the margin purchaser or short seller is unable to "cover" or make up the new amount of margin resulting from the price fluctuation of his securities. He is now closed out or sold out by his broker.

closed shop

(1) *computers:* pertaining to the operation of a computer facility in which most productive problem programming is performed by a group of specialists rather than by the problem originators.

(2) *labor relations:* an agreement in which only employees who were union members in good standing before being hired could continue to work. The closed shop was outlawed by the Taft-Hartley Act.

closed trade: a transaction concluded by selling a security that has been paid for previously, or the converting of a short sale (i.e., purchasing a security that had earlier been sold short).

closely held: refers to the ownership of a company's common stock by a single individual, family, or a few holders that is not placed on the market for significant trading.

close money: term applied when changes in prices between successive stock transactions are fractional, or when the last bid and asked quotations are hardly different.

close out: to liquidate; to make a final disposition.

close (closing) the books: the date

set by a corporation's board of directors for the declaring of dividends resulting in the temporary closing of their stock transfer books.

closing a mortgage loan: the consummation of a loan transaction in which all appropriate papers are signed and delivered to the lender, the making of the mortgage becomes a completed transaction, and the proceeds of the mortgage loan are disbursed by the lender to the borrower or upon the borrower's order. [44]

closing charges: the expenses or costs incurred in the sale, transfer, or pledging of property, such as recording fees and title examination fees, which must be provided for and distributed between the parties upon the consummation of the transaction. [44]

closing costs: the expenses incurred by sellers and buyers in the transfer of real estate ownership (e.g., attorney's fee, title insurance, survey charge, recording deed and mortgage). see *Real Estate Settlement Procedures Act.*

closing entries: journal entries made at the end of an accounting period to close (bring to zero balance) all revenue, expense, and other temporary accounts.

closing price: the price of securities quoted at the end of the stock exchange day.

closing purchase: a transaction in which a writer liquidates his position by purchasing an option having the same terms as an option previously written (sold). [5]

closing range: commodities, unlike securities, are frequently traded at differing prices at the opening or close of the market. Purchasing or selling transaction at the opening can be filled at any point in such a price range for a particular commodity.

closing sale: a transaction in which an investor who had previously purchased an option demonstrates intent to liquidate his or her position as a holder by selling in a closing sale transaction an option having the same terms as the option previously purchased.

closing statement: an accounting of funds in a real estate sale.

closing (or passing) title: the formal exchange of money and documents when real estate is transferred from one owner to another. see *objection to title, paper title, presumptive title, quiet title suit, title defect.*

cloud on title: any claim or existing shortcoming that interferes with the title to real property. see *abeyance, curing title;* cf. *marketable title, perfect title.*

CLU: see *Chartered Life Underwriter.*

club account: the popularity of the Christmas Club account has led banks to open other types of club accounts on the same basis. It is a convenient method of saving small amounts regularly for a definite purpose. Popular names for the newer club accounts are ''budget savings,'' ''vacation club,'' ''travel club,'' and ''all purpose club.'' Many depositors are using these club accounts to accumulate savings for annual premiums on life insurance, taxes, and vacations. [10]

CM
(1) see *call money.*
(2) see *call of more.*
(3) see *cheap money.*

CMA: see *Cash Management Account.*

Cmdty.: see *commodity.*

Cmm.: see *commission.*

Cn.: see *consolidated.*

Cncld.: see *cancel.*

Cnl.
(1) see *cancel.*
(2) see *cancellation.*

C note: slang, a $100 bill.

Co.: see *company.*

CO
(1) see *call option.*
(2) see *coinsurance.*
(3) see *covered option.*

coassignee: a person or company to whom some property right has been assigned jointly with another person or company.

COBOL: common business-oriented language. A general-purpose (machine) language designed for commercial data utilizing a standard form. It is a language that can present any business program to any suitable computer and also act as a means of communicating these procedures among people.

COD: see *cash on delivery.*

codicil: a written instrument that is made subsequent to the will to which it applies. The codicil modifies certain desires and bequests of the testator.

COE: see *current operation expenditures.*

coefficient of cross-elasticity: the arithmetic relationship between a percentage change in the price of an item and the actual percentage change in the sales of a substitute or competitive item.

coefficient of relative effectiveness: term employed in the Soviet Union: the expected payoff or percent rate of return on capital investment. Similar to the concept of marginal efficiency of investment.

coemption: purchasing the entire supply of any commodity, usually for purposes of gaining a monopoly.

coexecutor: a trustee or person who acts jointly with another executor. see *executor.*

coffee and cake: slang, earning just enough income to pay for the necessities of life; a small salary.

cognovit: a plea used to avoid a trial, by a defendant who admits the right of the plaintiff. It is a written acknowledgment, by a defendant, of his or her liability in a civil suit to avoid the expense of contending.

cognovit note: a form of note (legal evidence of indebtedness) which is both a promissory note and chattel mortgage. The borrower, within the wording of the instrument, waives his right of action to the chattel property in case of his default in any payments agreed to in the transaction. [10]

COI
(1) see *certificate of incorporation.*
(2) see *certificate of indebtedness.*

coin: a piece of stamped metal authorized by a government for use as currency; specie.

coin-counting machine: a machine used in banks to count accurately and swiftly large volumes of specie, or coins. The machine has a hopper into which are fed all denominations of coins. The machine is regulated to sort out coins from the smallest size (dime) to the largest (half dollar). The coins are automatically counted as they are sorted, one denomination at a time, and are then packaged in coin wrappers. [10]

coin pack: a technique of roll-wrapping a cylindrical stack of disks such as coins.

coinsurance
(1) *general:* insurance held jointly with others.
(2) *banking:* a provision in a policy that requires the insured to carry additional insurance equal to a certain specified percentage of the value of the property. The inclusion of this provision, whether mandatory or optional, usually gives to the insured rates lower than would otherwise apply.

coinsurer: one who shares the loss sustained under an insurance policy or policies. Usually applied to an owner of property who fails to carry enough insurance to comply with the coinsurance provision and therefore inevitably suffers part of the loss himself.

COLA: see *cost of living adjustment.*

cold call: contacting a potential investment customer without prior notice in order to make a sale or arrange for an appointment.

cold canvassing: determining potential investment customers without assistance from others or from references (e.g., selecting every tenth name in the telephone directory within a given location and having a salesman, or other person, call on these persons).

cold in hand: slang, a person without funds.

Coll.
(1) see *collateral.*
(2) see *collection.*

collapse

(1) *general:* a sudden drop in business activity or business prices.

(2) *finance:* failure or ruin of a specific firm.

collapsible company: a firm established to manufacture, construct, produce property, or to buy inventory, stock in trade, or property held primarily for sale to customers, unrealized receivables or fees, or assets held three years.

collar pricing: rather than fix the exact stock price at the time of a merger agreement, companies agree on a range—the collar—within which the final price will fall. The actual price is based on an average of the buying company's stock price during the 10 to 20 days before the deal is actually closed. The purpose is to avoid the tendency of the buyer's stock to a dive on the merger news as traders and investors unload their shares through fears of dilution.

Collat.: see *collateral.*

collate: to combine items from two or more ordered sets into one set having a specified order.

collateral: security (e.g., one's home, automobile, jewelry) left with a creditor to assure the performance of the obligator. When the obligator has performed, the creditor must return the collateral. see *hypothecate.*

collateral bond: see *bond, collateral.*

collateral heir: a person not in the direct line of the decedent from whom he inherits real property, as, for example, a nephew of the decedent who receives a share of his uncle's estate. see *direct heir, heirs.* [37]

collateral loan: a loan obtained by the pledge of title to personal property.

see *hypothecated account.*

collateral mortgage bonds: collateral trust bonds that have been secured by a deposit of mortgage bonds.

collateral note: a promissory note secured by the pledge of specific property. [50]

collateral pledge: the agreement under which a third party pledges a savings account or other property as additional security for the lender's mortgage-secured advance of funds by check and extending credit. [59]

collateral security: property security, as distinguished from personal security.

collateral trust bond: see *bond, collateral trust.*

collectible: that which can be converted into cash. synonymous with *liquid.*

collection

(1) *general:* presentation for payment of an obligation and the payment thereof.

(2) *banking:* the getting of money for presentation of a draft or check for payment at the bank on which it was drawn, or presentation of any item for deposit at the place at which it is payable. see *float, value date.*

collection agent: a person or bank that handles checks, drafts, coupons, and related items for another person or bank with the purpose of trying to collect such instruments.

collection analyst: a person in the collection division of the credit office, responsible for determining status and subsequent collection procedure of customers' past-due accounts. [41]

collection basis of reporting: a method of reporting the receipts of takes by the Internal Revenue Service at the time of receipt of returns by collecting officers in the field (as compared with Treasury statements of receipts on the basis of reports of deposits made in Treasury accounts). The collection basis provides detail of collections by type of tax. [70]

collection charge: a bank's charge made for the collection of checks, coupons, drafts, notes, and acceptances that have been drawn on the bank, corporations, or persons out of the location of the sending bank.

collection clerk: a bank representative involved in the collection of checks, drafts, and other items drawn on out-of-town points.

collection correspondent: a person in the collection division of a credit office, responsible for handling collection matters by mail. [41]

collection cycle: the activity taking place between the extension of credit and the receipt of payment.

collection department: the department that handles checks, drafts, coupons, and other items received from a depositor with instructions to credit his or her account after final payment has been received. In large cities, the collection department is usually divided into four sections (i.e., city collection, country collection, coupon collection, and foreign collection). [10]

collection fee: the percentage paid an agent for his or her services in collecting premiums. [12]

collection item: items (drafts, notes, acceptances, etc.) received for collection and credited to a depositor's account after final payment. Collection items are usually subject to special instructions regarding delivery of documents when attached, protest, and so on, and in most banks are subject to a special fee for handling called a collection charge. synonymous with *collection.* [31]

collection ledger: a ledger that is part of the bookkeeping records of a bank transit unit showing the holding charges to other banks for checks and items while in transit or in the process of being collected. synonymous with "float ledger."

collection letter: a letter of transmittal containing special handling instructions which accompanies items to be handled for collection and credit after payment. [31]

collection manager: supervisor of the collection division of the credit office. Usually (although not always) responsible to the credit manager. Handles all collection matters. [41]

collection on delivery (COD): the request that the cost of goods and other charges be collected at the time the items are delivered.

collection percentage: the amount collected during a given period, usually one month, expressed as a percentage against the total amount owed by all customers at the beginning of a period. [41]

collection period
(1) the period of time that it takes such items as checks and notes to clear.
(2) the collection period of accounts receivable used by credit men as one measurement of their efficiency. [4]

collection reminder: reminder to customer that payment or payments are past due. Can be printed, typed, or in the form of a statement or sticker insert. [41]

collection service: a system of methods and procedures used to obtain payment of past-due consumer accounts receivable.

collection teller: a teller whose regular duty is the handling of collections. [10]

collective bargaining: negotiations between an employer or group of employers and a labor union for a contract covering employees in a bargaining unit. First established as a legal right by the National Industrial Recovery Act of 1933, and reconstituted by the Wagner Act and other subsequent legislation. The process is regulated by the National Labor Relations Board. Executive Order 10988 extended limited collective bargaining rights to federal employees.

collective investment fund: a pooled investment trust under which the funds of pension and profit-sharing plans that are approved by the Internal Revenue Service are commingled for investment. [37]

collective reserve unit (CRU): an international currency or unit of money for use along with currencies in the reserves of banks around the world.

collect shipment: a shipment for which freight charges and advances are made by the delivering carrier from the consignee.

Coll. L.: see *collection letter.*

Coll. Tr.: see *bond, collateral trust.*

collusion

(1) *general:* a secret agreement to defraud.

(2) *labor relations:* a conspiracy between an employer and the certified representative of his or her employees to defraud the employees represented while providing the semblance of a genuine bargaining relationship.

collusive bidding: bidding by suppliers who have arranged among themselves to submit to potential buyers bids that are similar or even identical.

colon: monetary unit of Costa Rica and El Salvador.

color blind: slang, an individual not opposed to cheating or stealing; a person who is unable to tell the difference between other people's money and his or her own.

Co. Ltd.: a closed corporation.

Com.: see *commerce.*

comaker: an individual who signs the note of another person as support for the credit of the primary maker. see *unsecured loan;* synonymous with "cosigner".

combination bond: see *bond, combination.*

combination orders: two orders, with the cancellation of one contingent upon the execution of the other.

combined financial statement: as distinguished from consolidated statements; used to present the financial position and the results of operations of a group of companies under common control or common management. Intercompany transactions are eliminated in the same manner as in consolidated statements. [43]

come across: slang, to pay money owed.

Comex: see *Commodity Exchange, Inc.*

comfort letter: a common condition of an underwriting agreement in connection with the offering for sale of securities registered with the SEC whereby an independent auditor issues a letter to the underwriter reporting on the limited procedures followed with respect to unaudited financial statements or other financial data. [43]

Com'l. Ppr.: see *commercial paper.*

Comm.: see *commission.*

commerce: trade between states and nations.

commercial account: in general, a checking account; a bank account established for the purpose of enabling the depositor (usually a business person) to draw checks against the balance maintained. see *checking account.*

commercial agency: an organization that offers facilities in the field of credit and collections. synonymous with *mercantile agency.*

commercial and industrial loans: loans for business purposes except those secured by real estate. [40]

commercial auction: an agent business unit that effects the sale of goods through an auctioneer, who, under specified rules, solicits bids or offers from buyers and has power to accept the highest bids of responsible bidders and, thereby, consummates the sale. [48]

commercial bank: an organization chartered either by the Comptroller of the Currency and known as a national bank or chartered by the state in which it will conduct the business of banking. A commercial bank generally specializes in demand deposits and commercial loans. see also other entries under *bank.*

commercial bills: bills of exchange resulting from a commercial business transaction as contrasted with noncommercial bills (i.e., banker's bills).

commercial borrower: one who borrows for some purpose having to do with business or commerce. [28]

commercial code: the Uniform Commercial Code, describing commercial law. It excludes laws dealing with real property.

commercial credit: credit extended by firms with which an organization does business.

commercial discounts: discounts given to encourage prompt payment of a commercial account.

commercial draft: an order for the payment of money drawn by a seller of goods on the buyer's account at a bank. Once the draft is accepted and payment made to the seller, the buyer may obtain his goods. [59]

Commercial Exchange of Philadelphia: first opened in 1854 as the Corn Exchange Association of Philadelphia, changing in 1868 to its present name. This exchange deals in grains, feeds, and flour commodities.

commercial invoice: a statement showing the record of the transaction between a buyer and seller that has been prepared by the seller.

commercial letter of credit: an instrument by which a bank lends its credit to a customer to enable him to finance the purchase of goods. Addressed to the seller, it authorizes him to draw drafts on the bank under the terms stated in the letter. [50]

commercial loan: commercial loans are principally loans made to businesses for the financing of inventory purchases and the movement of goods, as distinguished from personal loans or consumer credit loans. Commercial loans are short-term loans or acceptances (time drafts accepted). see also *loan*. *[10]*

commercial paper

(1) *general:* any notes, drafts, checks, or deposit certificates used in a business.

(2) *banking:* in 1978 the Bankers Trust Company sold several issues of clients' commercial paper—short-term IOU's issued by corporations. The securities industry has tried unsuccessfully to get the Federal Reserve Board to prohibit that sale on grounds that it violated the Glass-Steagall Act, which separates commercial from investment banking. see *Glass-Steagall Act of 1933*.

(3) *finance:* unsecured short-term (under 270 days) promissory notes issued by corporations of unquestioned credit standing and sold to corporate and individual investors.

commercial-paper house: principals and dealers who purchase commercial paper at one rate and attempt to sell it at another.

commercial property: property to be used for business purposes, as contrasted with residential, agricultural, or industrial functions.

commercial set: the four major documents covering a shipment, namely, the invoice, the bill of lading, the certificate of insurance, and the bill of exchange.

commercial stocks: U.S. Department of Agriculture stocks of grain at major grain centers.

commercial teller: an employee whose prime function is paying and receiving funds for bank customers.

commercial year: a business year; unlike the calendar year, it consists of 12 months of 30 days each, totaling 360 days.

commingled accounts: when several bank trust department accounts are managed as one account to take advantage of economies available to large investments, the accounts are referred to collectively as a commingled account. Banks may not sell shares to the public that would increase the size of these accounts and make them, in effect, open-ended investment companies or mutual funds. A recent Supreme Court decision, however, allows bank holding companies to advise, sponsor, and organize closed-end investment companies, which sell only a certain number of shares that are then traded in the open market like common stocks. Commingled accounts are testing the validity of the Glass-Steagall Act. see *Glass-Steagall Act of 1933*.

commingled fund: a common fund in which the funds of several accounts are mixed. *[37]*

commingled investment fund: a bank-operated trust fund in which accounts of individual customers are commingled and lose their identity. Each customer, in effect, owns a share of the entire fund. Such a fund differs only in detail from a mutual fund. *[74]*

commission

(1) *general:* the amount paid to an agent, which may be an individual, a broker, or a financial institution, for consummating a transaction involving sale or purchase of assets or services. cf. *override*.

(2) *banking:* agents and brokers

are usually compensated by being allowed to retain a certain percentage of the premiums they produce, known as a commission.

commission broker: an agent who executes the public's orders for the purchase or sale of securities or commodities. see *dealer*. [20]

commissioner of banking: a state's banking department manager who regulates the state chartered banks in his state. In some states, known as *superintendent of banking*.

commissioners' values: the values of securities as determined by the National Association of Insurance Commissioners to be used by insurers for valuation purposes when preparing financial statements. [12]

commission house: a broker who purchases and sells only for customers and does not trade his or her own account.

commission merchant: an agent, transacting business in his own name, who usually exercises physical control over the goods consigned to him and negotiates their sale. The commission merchant usually enjoys broader powers as to prices, methods, and terms of sale than does the broker, although he must obey instruction issued by his principal. He generally arranges delivery, extends necessary credit, collects, deducts his fees, and remits the balance to his principal.

Most definitions state that the commission merchant has possession of the goods he handles. In its strict meaning, the word "possession" connotes to some extent the idea of ownership; in its legal meaning it involves a degree of control, somewhat

of a misnomer when applied to an agent; the fact is disregarded in this definition since this usage is commonly accepted in the trade. [13]

commission trade: securities or commodities transactions where the brokerage firm receives a commission, as contrasted with tradings, usually over-the-counter, in which it serves as a principal and buys and sells for its own account and does not charge any commission.

commitment: an advance agreement to perform in the future such as by an association to provide funds for a mortgage loan. [59]

committee deed: see *deed, committee*.

committee for incompetent: an individual or a trust institution appointed by a court to care for the property or the person (or both) of an incompetent; similar to a guardian, conservator, or curator. [32]

Committee on Uniform Securities Identification Procedures: see *CUSIP*.

Commodities Exchange Center (CEC): a facility for the four major New York commodity exchanges, opened in July 1977. Each exchange retains its own autonomy, clears transactions through separate clearing units, and shares in a single computer quotation system. CEC combines the Commodity Exchange, the New York Coffee and Sugar Exchange, the New York Mercantile Exchange, and the New York Cotton Exchange. See also *New York Coffee and Sugar Exchange, New York Mercantile Exchange*.

commodity: an item of commerce of trade. cf. *spot market*.

commodity collateral loan: any loan

made with a commodity, such as cotton, coffee, or sugar, as collateral.

Commodity Credit Corporation: an instrument of the federal government, created by the Agricultural Adjustment Act in 1933 to provide financial services to carry forward public price support activities with respect to certain agricultural commodities.

commodity dollar: synonymous with *commodity theory of money.*

commodity exchange: an organization usually owned by the member-traders, which provides facilities for bringing together buyers and sellers of specified commodities, or their agents, for promoting trades, either spot or futures or both, in these commodities. see *Commodity Exchange, Inc.* [48]

Commodity Exchange Act: federal legislation of 1936 establishing the Commodity Exchange Commission to regulate trading in the contract markets and other power to prevent fraud and manipulation in commodities and set limitations in trading for the purpose of preventing excessive speculation.

Commodity Exchange Authority: a unit of the U.S. Department of Agriculture, responsible for enforcing the Commodity Exchange Act of 1936.

Commodity Exchange Commission: the U.S. secretary of commerce, secretary of agriculture, and attorney general are designated by the Commodity Exchange Act of 1936 as the Commodity Exchange Commission.

Commodity Exchange, Inc. (Comex): formed in 1933 by the merger of the New York Hide Exchange, the National Metal Exchange, the National Raw Silk Exchange, and the New York Rubber Exchange. Presently, silver, copper, and mercury are the commodities futures traded. In 1980, Comex absorbed the Amex Commodities Exchange, an offshoot of the American Stock Exchange.

Commodity Futures Trading Commission (CFTC): a federal agency established in April 1975, responsible for coordinating the commodities industry in the United States, with primary concern for detecting and prosecuting violators of the Commodity Exchange Act. see also *Tax Reform Act of 1976.*

commodity income statement: an income statement prepared for each of the major traded commodities.

commodity loan: a loan made to a grain producer by the Commodity Credit Corporation.

commodity paper: notes, drafts, or other documents with warehouse receipts or bills of lading for commodities. Should default occur, the lender can sell the commodities up to the value of the loan and the expense of collection.

commodity price: a price for a commodity is quoted on a cash (spot) basis, or on a future basis, the difference to be accounted for by the charges involved in carrying the commodity for the period of the delivery of the future.

commodity rate: the rate of interest charged by banks on notes, drafts, bills of exchange, and other related documents issued on stable commodities.

commodity standard: a suggested monetary system that proposes to substitute a commodity or commodities for the precious metal or other base of a currency.

commodity surplus: the supply of a specific commodity that exceeds the market demands for a specific time period.

commodity tax straddle: a commodity investment in which a taxpayer has real capital gain that he wants to offset with a capital loss in order to defer his current-year tax liability. see also *straddle.*

commodity theory of money: the claim that the value of money is determined by the value of the commodity of which is is composed or which it represents. synonymous with *commodity dollar.*

common business-oriented language: see *COBOL.*

common capital stock (common stock): represents the funds invested by the residual owners whose claims to income and assets are subordinated to all other claims. [3]

common disaster clause: a clause added to a life insurance policy to instruct the bank in paying the proceeds of policies when the insured and the named beneficiary die in the same disaster.

common expense: an expense arising from two or more forms of operation, the portion resulting from each form of operation not being distinguishable. For expenses common to freight and passenger service, prescribed rules are in effect with regard to their apportionment. [18]

common law: law that is based on precedent.

common law trust: see *business trust.*

common machine language (MICR): the common machine language for

mechanized check handling is a specially designed group of 10 Arabic numbers and four special symbols printed in magnetic ink in designated field locations along the bottom edge of a check. The Bank Management Commission of the American Bankers Association, in their 1959 publication number 147, stated the original intention of the MICR program as follows: "The concept of the Common Machine Language, of course, is for the amount to be encoded by the first bank receiving the item for collection. This would permit all further handling in intermediate and paying banks to be primarily mechanical, resulting in tremendous economies in the banking system." This quotation assumes that eventually all banks will at least have their transit number routing symbol encoded on their checks, regardless of whether they intend to use equipment that will read the magnetic ink characters or not. see *magnetic ink character recognition.* [31]

Common Market: see *European Economic Community.*

common property: land generally, or a tract of land, considered as the property of the public in which all persons enjoy equal rights; a legal term signifying an incorporeal hereditament consisting of a right of one person in the land of another, as common of estovers, of pasture, of piscary, property not owned by individuals or government, but by groups, tribes, or in formal villages. [62]

common size statement: refers to the device used in comparing statements, especially a statement from a small-sized concern with a statement of a concern many times larger in a similar line of business. To avoid misinterpretation and confusion frequently encountered while dealing with large amounts, the device operates as follows: the total value of each individual item (asset) is divided by the total of all like items (total assets), thus reducing each figure to a percentage of the whole. [10]

common stock: securities that represent an ownership interest in a corporation. If the company has also issued preferred stock, both common and preferred have ownership rights. The preferred normally is limited to a fixed dividend but has prior claim on dividends and in the event of liquidation, assets. Claims of both common and preferred stockholders are junior to claims of bondholders or other creditors of the company. Common stockholders assume the greater risk but generally exercise a greater degree of control and may gain the greater reward in the form of dividends and capital appreciation. Often used interchangeably with *capital stock*. see *leverage;* see also *voting right (stock)*.

common stock dividends: dividends declared on common stock during the year whether or not they were paid during the year. Unless otherwise qualified, it is the amount of such dividends charged to retained income (earned surplus) and includes those payable in cash or stock. [3]

common stock equivalent: a security which, because of its terms or the circumstances under which it was issued, is considered in computing earnings per share to be in substance equivalent to common stock, (e.g., a convertible security). [43]

common trust fund: a fund maintained by a bank or a trust company exclusively for the collective investment and reinvestment of money contributed to the fund by the bank or trust company in its capacity as trustee, executor, administrator, or guardian and in conformity with the rules and regulations of the Board of Governors of the Federal Reserve System pertaining to the collective investment of trust funds by national banks, as well as with the statutes and regulations (if any) of the several states. [37]

community bank trust department: a trust department holding less than $100 million in trust assets. A community bank holds less than $100 million in deposits. [25]

community property: property that is owned jointly by a husband and wife by fact of their marriage. The state laws vary, but in states where community property applies, a husband and wife are considered to share equally in all of each other's property that is acquired during the marriage and in any income received or increase in value occurring during the marriage.

community property law: law regarding property owned jointly by a man and wife. Insurance policies are often considered community property. [12]

Community Reinvestment Act (CRA) Statement: a description available for public inspection at each bank office indicating, on a map, the communities served by that office and the types of credit the bank is prepared to extend within the communities served. [78]

community trust: a trust ordinarily composed of gifts made by many people to a trustee for educational, charitable, or other benevolent purposes in a community. The property of the trust is trusteed, and distribution of the funds is under the control of a selected group of citizens who act as a distribution committee. There may be one trustee or, as is more often the case, several trustees (usually trust institutions of the community), each serving under identical declarations of trust in the administration of the property committee to its care and management. Some community trusts are known as foundations. [37]

commuter tax: any income tax levied by a town or city on people who work there but live elsewhere.

Comp.: see *compound.*

company: an association of people for reasons of carrying on some business activity.

company check: a check drawn by a corporation, partnership, or other business entity on its account with a bank.

company union: an employee organization, usually of a single company, that is dominated or strongly influenced by management. The National Labor Relations Act of 1935 declared employer domination to be an unfair labor practice.

comparative advantage: a country or area has such an advantage in the manufacture of a particular item when its social cost of production for that item is less than the social cost experienced by other countries or areas for the same item.

comparative statement: the income, expense, profit and loss, balance sheet, or other financial statement of the same concern for two or more consecutive years that are analyzed to determine the increase or decrease in their component items, frequently for credit purposes. [10]

comparisons: the exchange of information between a broker and his bank or between two brokers to verify that each party's records of collateral held against loan are valid and in agreement. If there is disagreement, the parties can rapidly track down any difference.

comparison shopping:
(1) *general:* evaluation of a lender's annual percentage rate (APR), which tells the borrower the relative cost of credit, against the APRs quoted by other lenders. see *annual percentage rate.* [78]
(2) *banking:* an investor who compares certificates of deposits or other rates at several banks.

compensated dollar: a monetary unit where the gold content is periodically changed to retain the purchasing power level with some commodity index.

compensating balance: the lowest percentage of a line of credit that the customer of a bank is expected to maintain at all times.

compensation
(1) *general:* payment for any services or items.
(2) *law:* the settlement of any debt by the debtor's establishment of a counterclaim against his or her creditor.

compensatory fiscal policy

(1) an approach to reverse the direction of the business cycle when it is believed that it is becoming inflationary or deflationary. cf. *archmonetarist.*

(2) synonymous with *countercyclical (policy).*

competition:

(1) *general:* any rivalry.

(2) *finance:* the situation of a large number of manufacturers serving a large number of consumers, when no manufacturer can demand or offer a quantity sufficiently large to affect the market price. see *monopoly, oligopoly;* see also *invisible hand;* cf. *cutthroat competition, imperfect competition, nonprice competition.*

competitive bid: the awarding of a new stock issue to the highest bidder. In most cases, this nonnegotiated bid is made by investment banking groups.

competitive price: a price determined in the market by the bargaining of a number of buyers and sellers, each acting separately and without sufficient power to manipulate the market.

competitive trader: a member of the exchange who trades in stocks for an account in which he has an interest. synonymous with *registered representative (trader).* [20]

compile

(1) *general:* to collect, as with data.

(2) *computers:* to prepare a machine language program by means of a compiler. see *compiler.*

compiler

(1) *general:* a machine that compiles.

(2) *computers:* a routine that yields a specific program for a particular problem. The compiler converts computer instructions into a code that can be acted on by the computer.

complaint: the initial paper filed in court by the plaintiff in a lawsuit. It is referred to as a pleading—a statement of facts on which the plaintiff rests his or her cause of action.

complete audit: an audit in which an examination is made of the system of internal control and of the details of all the books of account, including subsidiary records and supporting documents, as to legality, mathematical accuracy, complete accountability, and application of accepted accounting principles. One of the main features of a complete audit is that the auditor is not expected to make any qualifications in his report except such as are imposed by lack of information, that is physical inability to get the fact. [49]

completed transaction: a sale property that has closed. In this transaction all legal and financial aspects are identified, and title to the property has transferred from seller to buyer.

complete special audit: a complete audit of some particular phase of a governmental unit's activities, such as sinking fund transactions or a complete audit for all of a governmental unit's transactions for a shorter or longer period of time than the usual audit period. [49]

complete trust: a trust in which the trustee is not required to distribute income currently, or distribute amounts other than income, or make a charitable contribution. [37]

component operating firms: corporations that function as a unit of a holding company system. They are operating units of one parent company, which may merely hold stock in, and control the movement of, the existing operation companies or may, itself be an operating corporation.

composite check: a listing of payments to be made from an account, sent by the owner of the account to his or her depository institution with instructions to effect the payments and debit the account for the total amount. The payments are transmitted by the depository institution to the creditors for subsequent deposit by them in their respective accounts.

composite demand: the sum of demands for an item or service beginning with any number of needs, all of which can be fulfilled by that particular item or service.

composite inventory: data accumulation on bank customers, including the most pertinent information that can be obtained about them.

composite limit order book (CLOB): a central electronic repository and display that automates all orders to buy and sell securities. It could eliminate the need for any exchanges by having buying and selling done directly by brokerage offices through a central computer system.

composite supply: an indefinite number and variety of items, each of which is able to satsify a particular need.

composition: agreement between a borrower in financial difficulty and a lender, allowing the borrower to eliminate debt by paying only a portion of the total amount owed the lender. [78]

compound: to add interest to principal at time intervals for the purpose of establishing a new basis for subsequent interest computations.

compounded: indicating the frequency with which interest is computed and added to the principal to arrive at a new actual balance.

compounded interest: interest created by the periodic addition of simple interest to principal, the new base thus established being the principal for the computation of additional interest.

comprehensive income: the change in equity (net assets) due to transactions and other events and circumstances from nonowner sources during a period. Comprehensive income does not include changes resulting from investments in the enterprise by owners and distributions from the enterprise to owners. [80]

compromise
(1) *general:* any agreement between two or more persons, usually in opposition, to settle their differences on areas of controversy without resort to legal action.
(2) *labor relations:* a settlement of a union-management dispute by an adjustment of differences by both sides, rather than resorting to outside involvement by a mediator or arbitrator.

Compt.: see *comptroller.*

comptroller: an executive officer whose job embraces the audit functions of the business.

Comptroller of the Currency: a federal office created in 1863 to oversee the chartering and regulation of national banks.

comptroller's call: the Comptroller of the Currency may "call" upon all national banks to submit a complete financial report of their activities at any given date. Reports must, according to law, be submitted at his call at least three times a year. These "called reports" must also be published in all local newspapers in the town nearest to the bank. [10]

compulsory retirement: separation from employment at an age specified by union contract or company policy.

computer: a device capable of accepting information, applying a variety of actions on such data, and supplying the results of these processes. It usually consists of input and output, arithmetic, storage, communications, and control units. see *analogue computer, digital computer, first-generation computer, general-purpose computer, second-generation computer, third-generation computer.*

computer code: a machine code for a specific computer; any system of combinations of binary digits. synonymous with *machine code.*

computer science: the range of theoretical and applied disciplines connected with the development and application of computers.

concealment

(1) *general:* the willful withholding of any material fact(s) that would, if known, make the risk undesirable or would necessitate payment of a higher premium.

(2) *law:* the suppression of truth to the injury or prejudice of another. cf. *discovery practice.*

concentration ratio: in a specific industry, the breakdown of total business that is handled by a specified number of the largest organizations.

concern

(1) a business establishment, company, or firm.

(2) to be interested or anxious. [61]

concession

(1) *general:* any deviation from regular terms or previous conditions.

(2) *finance:* a reduction or rebate; an allowance from the initial price or rate.

concessionaire: the holder of a concession granted by a company, government, or other authorized body.

conciliation: in collective bargaining, the process whereby the parties seek to reconcile their differences. The discussion generated is advisory and participation is not compulsory, but under the Taft-Hartley Act a union must notify the appropriate federal agency of an impending strike. Most conciliation work is conducted by the Federal Mediation and Conciliation Service. cf. *mediation.*

concurrent authority: exists when two or more brokers are given an open listing for property.

concurrent insurance: two or more insurance policies that provide the same coverage for the same property and the same interests.

Cond.: see *condition.*

condemnation

(1) *government:* the declaration by government that a structure is unsafe for use and is a menace to the safety of people.

(2) *law:* the taking of private property for public use. Under a condemnation proceeding, the property is

taken with or without the consent of the owner, but upon the payment of just compensation. see *compensation, confiscation*; c.f. *eminent domain*. see also *excess condemnation*.

condensed balance sheet: a balance sheet where the details have been removed to give an easy, though accurate, reading of the assets, liabilities, and capital of the corporation. see *balance sheet*.

condition: a contractual clause, implied or expressed, that has the effect of investing or divesting with rights and duties the members of the contract.

conditional endorsement: an endorsement describing and imposing conditions upon a transferee. The instrument can still be negotiated within the terms of the condition, but the person who has made the conditional endorsement has the right to the proceeds of the instrument if the conditions are not fulfilled.

conditional gift: a gift of property by will which is subject to some condition specified in the will or in the trust instrument; opposed to an absolute gift. [32]

conditional sales: sales under a payment contract where title remains with the seller until final payment is made, but the property is transferred to the buyer at once. [28]

conditional sales contract: document used in installment sales credit arrangements, which withhold ownership title from the buyer until the loan has been paid in full. [78]

condition of weekly reporting member banks: the Federal Reserve System release showing the changes in the reporting banks each week. These financial data, in part, show the changes in banks which represent more than half the banking resources of the United States.

condition precedent: a contract clause stating that immediate duties and rights will vest only upon the occurrence of an event. It is not a promise; therefore, its breach is not grounds for action against damages. However, it is the basis for a defense.

condition subsequent: a contract clause for the occurrence of an event that divests rights and duties (e.g., a fire insurance policy clause excusing the insurer from paying the policy if fire occurs and combustible materials were found within 5 feet of the area.)

condominium: individual ownership of a portion of a building that has other units similarly owned. Owners hold a deed and title. Owners pay taxes independently of other owners and can sell, lease, or otherwise dispose of the portion that the individual owns. Common areas, including halls, elevators, and so on, are jointly owned by the other tenants. see *lease-purchase agreement*; cf. *cooperative building*.

confession of a judgment: an admission by a party to whom an act or liability is imputed. [76]

confidence men: professional swindlers; people who cheat and defraud.

confidential risk report: a report established through investigations, of the physical condition of an insurer or his property, made prior to the issuance of a policy.

confirmation

(1) *investments:* a written order or agreement to verify or confirm one

previously given verbally, face to face, or by telephone. Executions of orders to buy or sell securities as substantiated in writing by brokers to their customers. see *dealer.*

(2) *law:* an assurance of title by the conveyance of an estate or right from one to another, by which a voidable estate is made sure or valid, or at times increased.

confirmed letter of credit: a foreign bank wishing to issue a letter of credit to a local concern may request a local bank in the city in which the beneficiary is located to confirm this credit to the beneficiary. The purpose of this confirmation is to lend the prestige and responsibility of the local bank to the transaction because the status of the foreign bank may be unknown to the beneficiary. The confirming bank assumes responsibility for the payment of all drafts drawn under the credit and usually charges a fee for doing so. [10]

confiscation: the seizure of private property, without compensation, usually by a governmental agency. cf. *eminent domain, expropriation, nationalization.*

conformed copy: a copy of an original document with the signature, seal, and other such features being typed or otherwise noted. [37]

conforming mortgage loan: a mortgage loan that conforms to regularity limits such as loan-to-value ratio, term, and other characteristics. [59]

congeneric: meaning "of the same kind," this term has been used to designate one-bank holding companies that have diversified into areas beyond the traditional bounds of banking, but within the financial field.

This term distinguishes them from the conglomerates, which are corporations that include business enterprises of all descriptions. [74]

conglomerate: the result of the merging of organizations producing differing items and services, to secure a large economic base, acquire sounder management, and gain greater potential profit. see *merger;* cf. *consortium.*

Congress of Industrial Organizations (CIO): originally organized in 1935 as a committee (Committee for Industrial Organization) within the American Federation of Labor to spur unionization of mass production industries. Unions organized by the committee were expelled from the AFL in 1937, and the committee reorganized itself to form the Congress of Industrial Organizations in 1938.

Cons.: see *consolidate, consolidated.*

consanguinity: blood relationship; to be distinguished from *affinity.* [37]

consent decree: in a case settlement, the instrument whereby the defendant agrees to cease certain actions that caused the action to be entered.

consent trust: a trust in which the consent of the settlor or some designated person is required before specified action by the trustee. [37]

consequential damage: the impairment of value which does not arise as an immediate result of an act, but as an incidental result of it. The impairment of value to private property caused by the acts of public bodies or caused by the acts of neighboring property owners. The term "consequential damage" applies only in the event no part of land is actually taken. The damage resulting from the taking of a fraction of the whole, that is, over and above the loss reflected in the value of the land actually taken, is commonly known as severance damage. [62]

conservator: a court-appointed official responsible for the protection of the interests on an estate.

Consid.: see *consideration.*

consideration

(1) *banking:* synonymous with *premium.*

(2) *law:* a requirement of valid contracts according to which all parties must provide something of value. cf. *forbearance, nudum pactum, quid pro quo.*

consignee: the ultimate recipient of goods; a shipping term.

consignment: the act of entrusting goods to a dealer for sale but retaining ownership of them until sold. The dealer pays only when and if the goods are sold.

consignor: the originator of a shipment.

consol(s):

(1) a bond that will never reach maturity; a bond in perpetuity.

(2) the name given to British government bonds.

console: the part of a computer used for communication between the operator or maintenance engineer and the central processing unit.

consolidate: to bring together various financial obligations under one agreement, contract, or note.

consolidated: the results obtained when the accounts of a parent company and its subsidiary companies are combined to reflect the financial position and results of operations of the group as if operated as a single entity. Such a consolidation involves intercompany eliminations and minority interest adjustments. [3]

consolidated balance sheet: a balance sheet showing the financial condition of a corporation and its subsidiaries. [20]

consolidated income statement: the combined statement of profit and loss for a group of firms controlled or owned by the same interests, thus eliminating duplications and intercompany profits and losses.

consolidated limit order book (CLOB): see *composite limit order book.*

consolidated mortgage: when two or more firms, each holding a mortgage on property, combine, and then the consolidated organization takes out a mortgage, the latter mortgage is referred to as a consolidated mortgage.

consolidated sinking fund: one sinking fund that is established to serve two or more bond issues. [49]

consolidated tape: under the consolidated tape plan, the New York Stock Exchange and Amex ticket systems became the "consolidated tape" Network A and Network B, respectively, on June 16, 1975. Network A reports transactions in NYSE-listed securities that take place on the NYSE or any of the participating regional stock exchanges and other markets. Each transaction is identified according to its originating market. Similarly, transactions in Amex-listed securities, and certain other securities listed on regional stock exchanges, are reported and identified on Network B. [20]

consolidation: a combination of two or more organizations into one, to form a new entity.

consolidation loan: combines several debts into one loan, usually to reduce the annual percentage rate or the dollar amount of payments made each month, by extending them over a longer period of time. [78]

consolidation of bills: the borrowing of a lump sum of money for the payment of past-due bills; the money borrowed is then repaid in installments. [41]

consortium: a grouping of corporations to fulfill a combined objective or project that usually requires interbusiness cooperation and sharing of resources. cf. *cartel, conglomerate.*

constant dollars: the actual prices of a previous year or the average of actual prices of a previous period of years.

constant factor: the periodic amount of principal and interest that is required to retire a loan.

constant payment: a fixed or invariable payment, a continually recurring payment. [62]

constant ratio: a method of comparing mortgage amortization (principal and interest) on an annual basis to the original amount of the mortgage. Expressed as a percentage; also called the *mortgage constant.*

construction loan: funds extended on the security of real property for the purpose of constructing or improving a building. [39]

constructive side of the market: a long purchase of a stock with the anticipation that its market price will jump; a bullish position.

constructive trust: a trust imposed by a court of equity as a means of doing justice, without regard to the inten-

tion of the parties, in a situation in which a person who holds title to property is under a duty to convey it to another person; to be distinguished from an express trust and a resulting trust. [37]

consular invoice: an invoice covering a shipment of goods certified (usually in triplicate by the consul of the country for which the merchandise is destined. This invoice is used by customs officials of the country of entry to verify the value, quantity, and nature of the merchandise imported. [10]

consult account: a trust in which the trustee is required by the instrument to consult a designated party before taking action; to be distinguished from consent trust. [37]

consultant

(1) *general:* a specialist in any field of activity (e.g., psychological consultant, Wall Street consultant, engineering consultant), hired by an organization for the purpose of recommending solutions to a problem.

(2) *finance:* one with whom the fiduciary must confer in the administration of a fiduciary account. [37]

consumer: any person who uses goods and services.

consumer credit: credit extended by a bank to a borrower for the specific purpose of financing the purchase of a household appliance, alteration, or improvement, a piece of equipment, or other personal needs. This form of credit is generally extended to individuals rather than to business executives.

Consumer Credit Counseling Services (CCCS): a unit of the Federal Home

Loan Bank System. CCCS specializes in working with people who are overextended with debts and need to make arrangements with local creditors.

Consumer Credit Protection Act of 1968: see *Truth in Lending Act of 1968.*

consumer debentures: investment notes sold directly to the public by a financial institution. These notes are much like the certificates of deposit sold by banks and savings and loans. Unlike banks selling notes, these notes can be sold anywhere, at any interest rate determined to be found competitive by the institution.

consumer finance companies: companies licensed by a state for the special purpose of providing consumers with a reliable service for installment cash loans. [55]

consumer good: item bought and used by the final consumer for personal or household purposes.

consumer loan: loans to individuals or families, the proceeds to be used for consumer, as contrasted with business or investment, purposes. [28]

consumer plant and equipment: the still unused service and uses that are built into the possession of a people as individuals and families, a form of personal and family wealth. [28]

Consumer Price Index (CPI): a measurement of the cost of living determined by the Bureau of Labor Statistics. see *cost of living index.*

Consumer Protection Act: see *Truth in Lending Act of 1968.*

consumer sale disclosure statement: a form presented by a dealer giving essential details on financing charges relative to a purchase on an installment plan. This is required under the Consumer Credit Protection (Truth-in-Lending) Act.

consummation: a defined term under Regulation Z, meaning the actual time that a contractual relationship is created between borrower and lender, irrespective of the time of performance of a particular transaction. Depending upon the state law of contracts governing a particular association, consummation may occur at the time a loan is closed, at the time a lender accepts (as distinct from receives) a borrower's loan application, or at the time a firm commitment is given to make a loan. see *Regulation Z.* [59]

consumption tax: a tax on consumption. May be at the wholesale, manufacturing, or retail point.

Cont.: see *contract.*

contango
(1) *finance:* the cost factors when calculating from one given period to a future point.
(2) *investments:* a basic pricing system in futures trading. A form of premium or carrying charge; for example, instead of paying for the cost of warehousing silver bullion, paying insurance finance charges and other expenses (silver users prefer to pay more for a futures contract covering later delivery).

contemporaneous reserve accounting (CRA): a one-day lag allowing member banks of the Federal Reserve to calculate their required reserves and reserves held as vault cash for a week before making the final adjustments to their reserve balances on Wednesdays. This system is "contemporaneous" because, except for the one-day lag, assets and liabilities used in calculating reserves and required reserves are those of the same week. see *lagged reserve accounting.*

contest of a will: an attempt by legal process to prevent the probate of a will or the distribution of property according to the will. [37]

continental rate: the rate charged in Europe for foreign exchange and on bills of exchange.

contingency fund: assets set aside for use in unpredicted situations. see *contingent reserve;* cf. *sinking fund.*

contingency reserve: see *contingent reserve.*

contingent asset: an asset that may become actual or unqualified as situations presently unfulfilled are satisfied.

contingent beneficiary: the beneficiary whose interest is conditioned upon a future occurrence which may or may not take place. Unless or until the condition takes place, the interest is only contingent. [37]

contingent commission: a commission, the amount of which is dependent on the profitableness (or some other characteristic) of the business written by an agent or reinsurer. [53]

contingent executor: an executor named in a will whose capacity as executor is dependent upon the action or nonaction of the principal executor. [37]

contingent fees: renumeration based or conditioned upon future occurrence or conclusions, or results of services to be performed. [62]

contingent interest: the right to property that depends for "vesting" or re-

alization on the coming of some future uncertain occurrence.

contingent liability: the liability imposed on an individual, corporation, or partnership because of accidents caused by persons (other than employees) for whose acts the first party may be held responsible under the law. see *guaranteed debt, switch (contingent) order.*

contingent order: a request to purchase or sell a security at a specific price which in contingent upon the earlier execution of another order; for example, "Purchase 50 ABC at ____ , if you can sell 50 XYZ at ____ ."

contingent remainder: a future interest in property that is dependent upon the fulfillment of a stated condition before the termination of a prior estate; to be distinguished from vested remainder. see *remainder.* [37]

contingent reserve: the setting aside of a certain amount of profits to meet unanticipated needs of the business or some unexpected loss, the amount of which cannot be definitely ascertained at the time of budgeting.

contingent trustee: a trustee whose appointment is dependent upon the failure to act of the original or a successor trustee. [37]

continued bond: see *bond, continued.*

continuing account: a running or open book account where settlements are made regularly (e.g., 30 to 60 days).

continuing agreement: that portion of the broker's loan arrangement with a bank purporting to simplify the borrowing since the broker need not seek a loan application and sign a note each time he borrows. Following the signing of this agreement, the broker can borrow within the terms of the agreement on a continuous basis.

continuing guaranty: a form given to a bank by a person to guarantee repayment of a loan to another party. This guaranty promises payment by the guarantor in the event of default by the borrower, and is so worded that it may apply to a current loan, or to one made at a later date. The guaranty may or may not pledge collateral as security for the loan. [10]

continuity of coverage: a clause attached or contained in a fidelity bond which takes the place of another bond and agrees to pay the losses that would be recoverable under the first bond except that the discovery period has expired. This would be in a case where losses have been caused by a dishonest employee and have not been discovered, though they have occurred at various times stretching over a period of time, that time being a period under which several bonds have been insured. A chain of several bonds may be involved, each one superseding a prior obligation. Those losses will be covered if the chain of bonds is unbroken and each has included continuity of coverage clause. [56]

continuous budget: a budget that perpetually adds a month in the future as the month just ended is dropped.

continuous market: a securities or commodities market that is broad, enabling normal amounts to be sold with ease and little price variation.

contocurrent account: used in West Germany and parts of Switzerland to identify what is called in the United States a checking account.

contra: means that an account has an offsetting credit or debit entry. [59]

contraband: illegal or prohibited goods. see *smuggling*.

contract: an agreement between two or more persons, as established by law, and by which rights are acquired by one or more parties to specific acts or forbearance from acts on the part of others.

contract, breach of: failure by one party to a contract to perform his or her obligation.

contract account: general term describing a long-term credit arrangement for purchase of specific items described in the contract. Usually includes a service or carrying charge. see *chattel mortgage agreement, conditional sales contract, contract clause*. [41]

contract bond: see *bond, contract*.

contract clause: a clause in the Constitution of the United States (Article 1, Section 10) declaring that no state may pass laws diminishing the obligation of a contract. Although corporate franchises are accepted as contracts and protected by this clause, it cannot act as a bar to the regulatory and police powers of the state.

contract for deed: a written agreement between the seller and buyer of a piece of property, whereby the buyer receives title to the property only after making a determined number of monthly payments; also called an "installment contract" or *land contract*. [59]

contract grades: those grades or types of a commodity which may be delivered on the futures contract. Differentials based on federal standards have been established by the various commodity exchanges which provide premiums for superior grades or discounts for lower grades. [2]

contraction: a decline of economic activity in the business cycle. The opposite of expansion.

contract market: one of the 18 commodity exchanges, permitted under the Commodity Exchange Act to deal in futures contracts in the commodities.

contract of sale: a written document whereby an owner agrees to convey title to a property when the purchaser has completed paying for the property under the terms of the contract. [59]

contractor: a person who contracts to perform work or to supply materials under specified conditions. [44]

contract payable: sums due on contracts. [49]

contract purchasing: a form of purchasing defined in a contract for orders and deliveries, covering a time period, usually one year.

contract sale: a sale of real estate in which the seller retains title to the property until the buyer has made the required number of monthly payments. [59]

contractual liability
(1) liability assumed by contract.
(2) an additional coverage, for a specific exposure for which the basic liability policy does not provide. It may be obtained for an additional premium.

contractual plan: by common usage, an accumulation plan with a stated paying-in period and provision for regular investments at monthly or quarterly dates. Sustantially synonymous with "prepaid charge plan." [30]

contrarian: a term popularized by David Dreman to describe the small investor who makes money in the stock market at a rate that exceeds the popular averages. By purchasing unpopular stocks, the buyer looks for investment-grade stocks that are out of favor in terms of their current price-earnings ratios. Obviously, the higher the price-earnings ratio on a stock—that is, the bigger the multiple of earnings that the market is paying for it—the less likely it is to outperform both the market itself and stocks currently less in favor.

contributed capital: the payments in cash or property made to a corporation by its stockholders, in exchange for capital stock, in response to an assessment on the capital stock, or as a gift; paid-in capital; often, though not necessarily, equal to capital stock and paid-in surplus. [43]

contribution
(1) **general:** something given, such as time or money.
(2) **banking:** the bank's payment of, or obligation to pay, all or part of a loss.
(3) **law:** the sharing of a common loss or benefit, paid or to be paid by each of the parties involved.

contribution margin: the excess of total revenue over total variable cost.

contribution profit: sales revenue less the variable cost of producing the revenue.

control: a system under which all transactions or balances of a given type are included in a single total, so that the accuracy of their recording may be proved. [50]

control account: an account in the general ledger used to carry the total of several subsidiary accounts. Whenever any subsidiary account is affected, the same will be reflected in the control account total. Control accounts are also used as "total" accounts, controlling the accounts within a "book" or "ledger" in the bookkeeping department and the savings department. [10]

control card: a card which indicates the total dollar amount on deposit and the total number of accounts in a single ledger. Control cards are debited and credited according to each day's transactions and are used as a basis of proof when trial balances are taken. In addition to the control card for each ledger or section, there is a master control card for each unit, or for the bank as a whole. [39]

controlled account: where the principal authorizes the broker, with a power of attorney, to exercise his own discretion in the purchasing and selling of securities or commodities.

controlled commodities: commodities that are subject to the regulations of the Commodity Exchange Authority.

controlled company (corporation): a firm whose policies are controlled by another with ownership of 51 percent or more of its voting shares. see *Tax Reform Act of 1969;* cf. *working control.*

controlled economy: an economy that is regulated and greatly influ-

enced by government. see *statism;* cf. *laissez-faire.*

controller: see *comptroller.*

controlling account: an account, usually kept in the general ledger, which receives the aggregate of the debit and of the credit postings to a number of identical, similar, or related accounts called subsidiary accounts so that its balance equals the aggregate of the balance in these accounts. [49]

controlling interest: any ownership of a business in excess of 50 percent. However, a small percentage of shareholders may control the firm if the remainder of the stock is distributed among many owners and is not active in voting. see *working control;* cf. *minority interest.*

controlling records: a class of financial records within a bank composed of the controlling books or accounts of the bank. see *controlling account.*

controls: approaches by regulatory agencies to keep the economy in a healthy position. In most cases, governmental agencies act, by creating rules, to monitor the condition of the nation's economy.

control stock: securities belonging to those who have controlling interest in a company.

Conv.: see *convertible.*

convenience goods: products that the public wishes to purchase with a minimum of effort or time (toothpaste, cigarettes, sodas, paper, etc.).

convenient payment account: installment payment arrangement for purchase of either soft or hard goods. Usually carries a service or carrying charge. Specific payments required on specified dates. synonymous with "deferred payment account." [41]

conventional billing: a system of rendering to a customer an itemized, descriptive statement of all purchases, cash payments, merchandise returned, and allowances made during a specific period, usually one calendar month. Original sales checks and other billing media are retained by the store. [41]

conventional fixed-rate mortgage: a mortgage with a fixed term, fixed rate, and fixed monthly payments which is fully paid off within 30 years or less. It is a mortgage without government insurance or guarantee. see also *conventional loan.* [66]

conventional loan: a mortgage loan, usually granted by a bank or loan association. The loan is based on real estate as security rather than being guaranteed by an agency of the government. This loan has a fixed interest rate and fixed payments for the life of the loan. see also *conventional fixed-rate mortgage.*

conversion
(1) *general:* the process of changing from one system or one type of equipment to another.
(2) *banking:* a provision whereby a more permanent form of insurance may be elected without a medical examination if the request is made within the specified time and an additional premium is paid.
(3) *computers:* the process of changing from one method of data processing to another or from one data-processing system to another (e.g., using COBOL instead of FORTRAN).
(4) *law:* the unauthorized taking of another's goods or property.

conversion charge: the specified cost of converting from one class or series of an open-end fund to another issued by the same company or group of companies having the same sponsor. It is usually lower than the regular sales charge. [30]

conversion costs: a combination of direct labor and factor overhead in the manufacturing process.

conversion parity: the common stock price where the conversion value of a bond is equal to the existing market price of the convertible bond. see *conversion price.*

conversion price: the price for which a convertible bond, debenture, or preferred stock of a firm can be exchanged by an owner for common stock or another security of the same organization.

conversion privilege: see *exchange privilege.*

conversion ratio: the number of shares of common stock received when a convertible bond or convertible preferred stock is exchanged with the same firm. The price is frequently given at the issue date of the bond or preferred stock, and may not be the same as the market price when the conversion takes place.

conversion value: value created by changing from one state, character, form, or use to another. [62]

convertibility: ease of exchanging one currency for that of another nation or for gold. see *soft currency.*

convertible: slang, any corporate stock that can be converted to a stock of another corporation.

convertible bond: see *bond, convertible.*

convertible currencies: includes the U.S. Treasury and Federal Reserve holdings of foreign currencies that are counted as part of official U.S. reserve assets. [11]

convertible hedge: an investment strategy of selling common stock short at the same time a long position is created in convertible bonds of the same firm. This form of hedging occurs when a decline is anticipated.

convertible money: money that can be exchanged at par for the standard or legal money.

convertible preferred stock: a security that can be exchanged at the owner's option for a fixed quantity of common shares of the same corporation.

convertibles: interest-paying debentures and dividend-paying preferred shares that can be exchanged for the common stock of the issuing company on a preset basis. The conversion privilege becomes valuable only if the market value of the debenture or preferred stock is below that of the total value of the common shares into which it can be converted.

conveyance: a written statement called a deed, whereby ownership of property is passed from one person or organization to another.

conveyancing: the act of transferring title to real property.

cooling-off period: the term for the period, usually 20 days, that must elapse before the filing of a registration for a new security and public sale, as declared by the SEC.

cooperative: anything owned jointly to the same end.

cooperative bank: a term given in some states to an institution that operates as a savings and loan association. see *savings and loan association.* [39]

cooperative building: tenants residing in the building are stockholders in a corporation that owns the real estate. All are part owners of the corporation. Stockholders sign a proprietary lease with an operating organization, and in place of rent pay a proportionate fixed rate to cover operating costs, maintenance, and so on. cf. *condominium.*

cooperative central bank: a state-chartered mutual institution in Massachusetts to which all state savings associations (called cooperative banks) in Massachusetts must belong; it insures the savings accounts held by members and serves as a central credit facility. [59]

cooriginator: in bonding, where the clients of more than one surety company join for a specific contract. Such surety is known as cooriginator for its client's share. [54]

copartnership (partnership): a company of partners, as distinguished from a proprietorship or a corporation. [76]

Copeland Act of 1934: so-called antikickback law, making it illegal for an employer or his or her agent to extract a payment as a condition of continued employment. The law prohibits employers or their agents from using force, threats, or other means to secure the return of any part of a worker's wages as a condition of retaining his or her job. Violators are fined.

copper a tip: slang, a person who reacts negatively to a tipster's advice.

Cor.: see *corpus.*

cordoba: monetary unit of Nicaragua.

core inflation: the underlying rate at which prices would rise even in the absence of any excessive demand pressure or any sharp increases in prices, or strikes in key businesses.

corner the market: to purchase a security on a scale large enough to give the purchaser control over the price.

Corp.: see *corporation.*

corporate agent: trust companies act as agents for corporations, governments, and municipalities for various transactions. In each case, a fee is charged for the particular service rendered. [10]

Corporate Bankruptcy Act: see *National Bankruptcy Act. of 1898.*

corporate bond: see *bond, corporate.*

corporate depositary: a trust institution serving as the depositary of funds or other property. see also *depositary, depository.* [37]

Corporate Income Fund (CIF): a short-term series investment vehicle. It is a unit trust that is similar to a money market fund with a fixed portfolio of high-grade investment paper.

corporate profits after taxes: the earnings of U.S. corporations organized for profit after liability for federal and state taxes has been deducted. [73]

corporate profits before taxes: the net earnings of corporations organized for profit measured before payment of federal and state profit taxes. They are, however, net of indirect business taxes. They are reported without deduction for depletion charges and exclusive of capital gains and losses and intercorporate dividends. [73]

corporate profits tax liability: federal and state taxes levied on corporate earnings of a given year; a measurement of taxes for the year in which they are incurred, not necessarily for the year in which they are paid.

corporate records: the records of a corporation required by incorporation laws. A listing of all shareholders, their addresses, quantity of stock, date of purchase, and price paid for shares is obligatory.

corporate resolution: a document given to a bank by a corporation defining the authority vested in each of its officers who may sign and otherwise conduct the business of the corporation with the bank. Corporate resolutions usually are given with or without borrowing powers. These powers are granted by the board of directors of the firm. [10]

corporate shell: a firm having no fixed assets except for its name, cash, and perhaps a stock exchange listing. Some shells are illegal or carry on illegal activities.

corporate surplus: as of the date of the balance sheet, the equity in the assets not offset by the capitalization, current or deferred liabilities, or unadjusted credits. It includes appropriations for additions to property, for retirement of funded debt, reserves for sinking and other funds, and other appropriations not specifically invested. [18]

corporate trust: a trust created by a corporation, typical of which is a trust to secure a bond issue. [37]

corporate trustee: a trust institution serving as a trustee. [37]

corporation
(1) *general:* an organization having purposefulness, declared social

benefit, derived powers, legal entity, permanence, and limited liability.

(2) *law:* individuals created by law as a legal entity, vested with powers and ability to contract, own, control, convey property, and discharge business within the boundaries of the powers granted. cf. *firm.*

corporation account: a checking or savings account owned by a corporation and established in accordance with a resolution adopted by its board of directors.

corporation bond: see *bond, corporate.*

corporation de facto: despite a minor failure to comply with the regulations for incorporation, a legal entity that thereafter has exercised corporate powers.

corporation de jure: a corporation formed by fulfilling the requirements of the law permitting the formation of the corporation.

corporation sole: a one-man corporation, the authority, duties, and powers of which are attached to and go with the office and not the natural person who for the time being holds the office. [37]

corporators: the group which in certain states elects the trustees of a mutual savings bank. The number of corporators is not limited, and the group is self-perpetuating. [39]

corporeal: pertaining to a right or group of rights of a visible and tangible nature. [62]

corporeal hereditament: tangible property that can be inherited.

corporeal property: real or personal property having form or structure (e.g., house, furniture, land, fixtures). cf. *chose(s) in possession.*

corpus: a term used in trust companies and trust accounting to describe all the property in a trust, also referred to as the "body" of the trust. A corpus may consist of real estate, stocks, bonds, and other personal property, cash in the form of bank accounts, and any items that the donor may wish to have included. [10]

correction: any price reaction within the market leading to an adjustment by as much as one-third to two-thirds of the previous gain.

correction voucher: a form used by tellers to facilitate the correction of any errors made in the recording of transactions on electronic data-processing equipment. [59]

correlation: a relationship or dependence. Reflecting the principle that two things or variables are so related that change in one is accompanied by a corresponding or parallel change in the other.

correspondency system: the origination and administration of mortgage loans for investors by independent loan correspondents. [22]

correspondent: a securities firm, bank, or other financial organization that regularly performs services for another in a place or market to which the other does not have direct access. Securities firms may have correspondents in foreign countries or on exchanges of which they are not members. Correspondents are frequently linked by private wires. Member organizations of the New York Stock Exchange with offices in New York City may also act as correspondents for out-of-town member organizations that do not maintain New York City offices. [20]

correspondent bank: a bank that is the depository for another bank. The correspondent bank accepts all deposits in the form of cash letters and collects items for its bank depositor.

cosigner: see *comaker*.

cost: the value given up by an entity in order to receive goods or services. Cost is the value given up to get an item in the volume needed, shipped to the desired location. All expenses are costs, but not all costs are expenses.

cost accounting: a branch of accounting dealing with the classification, recording, allocation, summarization, and reporting of current and prospective costs. It provides the means by which management can control manufacturing costs.

cost and freight: see *C&F*.

cost approach to value: a method of estimating the value of real property by deducting depreciation from the cost of replacement and adding the value of the land to the remainder. see *appraisal*.

cost basis: the orginal price or cost of an asset usually based on the purchase price or, in the case of assets received from an estate, on the appraised value of the assets at the death of the donor or some anniversary or other fixed date. [37]

cost-benefit analysis: a branch of operations research that aids in evaluating the implications of alternative courses of action. This method is primarily concerned with the selection of equipment, products, and so on, before they become available.

cost effectiveness: see *cost-benefit analysis*.

cost factors: the various expenses that must be met by a supplier of consumer credit, and which therefore influence the charges he or she will make for credit services. [55]

costing: synonymous with *cost accounting*.

cost, insurance, and freight (CIF): a quoted price that includes the handling charges, insurance, and freight costs up to delivery, usually up to a port of entry. cf. *cost and freight* (see under *C&F*.).

cost ledger: a subsidiary record wherein each project, job, production center, process, operation, product, or service is given a separate account where all items entering into its cost are posted in the required detail. Such accounts should be so arranged and kept that the results shown in them may be reconciled with and verified by a control account or in the general books. [49]

cost of funds: interest (dividends) paid or accrued on savings, Federal Home Loan Bank advances, and other borrowed money during a period as a percent of average savings and borrowings.

cost of goods sold: the purchase price of goods sold during a specified period, including transportation costs.

cost of insurance: the cost or value of net insurance protection in a given year. [12]

cost of living

(1) *general:* the average cost to an individual of providing the basics of life. see *price control*.

(2) *finance:* the average of the retail prices of all goods and services

required for a reasonable living standard. see *Consumer Price Index.*

cost of living adjustment (COLA): an increase or decrease of wages based on the increase or decrease in the purchasing power of money. Inflation and deflation are primary causes for a cost of living adjustment. see *escalator clause.*

Cost of Living Council: established in 1971, a committee of government appointees responsible for administering a 90-day freeze on wages and prices.

cost of living index: popular term for the Consumer Price Index issued monthly by the U.S. Department of Labor, Bureau of Labor Statistics. A measurement of changes in prices of goods and services purchased by moderate-income families. Wages of workers whose union contracts contain an escalator clause fluctuate with the cost of living index.

cost of occupancy: the periodic expenditure of money necessary to occupy a property, exclusive of the expenses directly attributable to the conduct of a business. [6]

cost of reproduction: the cost of replacing a building as of any given date (usually current). [59]

cost of sales: the composite value of the product at the time it is offered for sale. This is composed of the manufacturing cost plus a proportionate percentage of selling and administrative expenses and profit. [38]

cost records: all ledgers, supporting records, schedules, reports, invoices, vouchers, and other records and documents reflecting the cost of projects, jobs, production centers,

processes, operations, products, or services, or the cost of any of the component parts thereof. [49]

cost theory of capitalization: where a firm's capitalization is determined by the out-of-pocket investments in fixed assets, the regular working capital needed to run the firm, advertising, and other related costs.

cost unit: a term used in cost accounting to designate the unit of product or service whose cost is computed. These units are selected for the purpose of comparing the actual cost with a standard cost or with actual costs of units produced under different circumstances or at different places and times. [49]

cost-volume profit analysis: a method used for measuring the functional relationships between the major aspects of profits and for identifying the profit structure of an organization.

cosurety: one of a group of surety companies executing a bond. The obligation is joint and several, but common practice provides a stated limit of liability for each surety.

cotrustee: a person, trust organization, or bank permitted to provide trust functions, acting with another as a trustee.

Cotton Futures Act: the United States Cotton Futures Act was legislated in 1915 to standardize transactions in cotton futures. In 1936, the Commodity Exchange Act was amended to cover other commodities, including cotton.

Council of Economic Advisers (CEA): in accordance with the Employment Act of 1946, a group of economists charged with advising the president on a variety of matters, including the preparation of the budget message to Congress. see also *Joint Economic Committee.*

Council on Wage and Price Stability (COWPS): a federal agency responsible for the monitoring of wage and price increases in the private sector; reviews government policies contributing to inflation and reports findings to Congress and the president. Dismantled by the President in 1981.

counter cash: that part of the actual cash of a bank kept by the tellers in their cages. [31]

counter check: a form of check provided by a bank for the convenience of the depositor. A counter check may be cashed only by the drawer personally. [50]

counterclaim: a defendant's claim that the defendant is entitled to recover from the plaintiff.

countercyclical (policy)
(1) leveling the ups and downs of the business cycle with budget deficits during depression and surpluses during prosperity.
(2) synonymous with *compensatory fiscal policy.*

counter deposits: a deposit presented at the teller's window by a customer. Other forms include deposits by mail, clearings, collections, or internal sources. [31]

countererror: in accounting, an error (over or short) that is offset by an error of equal amount, thus creating a balance which is correct without disclosing that two or more of the transactions apparently proved are actually in error. [31]

counterfeit: imitation or fraudulent money.

counter item: any item accepted or originated at the bank teller window as contrasted with those received by mail, clearings, or from internal departments. [10]

countermand: to cancel an order that has not yet been carried out.

counterpart monies: local currency equivalents of dollar assistance given to nations by the United States following World War II that are in turn used to purchase U.S. goods or services. cf. *tied loan.*

counterpurchasing: placing an order with a manufacturer in one country with the expectation that merchandise of equal value and/or quantity will be sold in the opposite direction to the other nation.

countersignature
(1) *banking:* the signature of a licensed agent or representative on a policy, which is necessary to validate the contract.
(2) *law:* a signature added to a document to authenticate it. cf. *attestation.*

country bank: a national or state bank that is not located in a Federal Reserve city. Country banks' legal reserve requirements are usually less than for large city banks.

country check: a transit check; an item drawn on an out-of-town bank; a check drawn upon a bank out of a central reserve or reserve city.

country club billing: a billing system in which the account statement is accompanied by copies of original invoices. [36]

country collections: a term describing all items that are being sent outside the city in which the sending bank is located. A banker will speak of "city collection," which are items drawn on banks and business houses upon whom drafts are to be collected within the city of the bank's location; and "country collections," which are sent out of the city to the bank's correspondents for collection and payment. [10]

country price: the price farmers receive when they sell their commodity in an area removed from the central market. It is frequently quoted as so many points or cents "on" or "off" a certain futures price.

coupon: the portion of a bond that is redeemable at a given date for interest payments. cf. *talon.*

coupon account: type of credit extension whereby books of coupons having a stated value are sold on an installment payment basis. Coupons are used in issuing stores as cash. Payment for the coupon book is stretched over a period of time. Coupon accounts are generally used for credit customers of limited responsibility, and whose buying must be closely controlled. [41]

coupon bond: see *bond, coupon.*

coupon book: a set of payment cards or computer cards that the borrower returns to the association one at a time with regular loan repayments, or with deposits for savings accounts such as a club account. [59]

coupon collection: being negotiable, coupons are collectable like any other negotiable instrument. The owner of the bond from which the coupon was clipped signs a "certificate of ownership" and attaches the coupon to this certificate. It is then either cashed by the bank, or depos-

ited by the depositor as a credit to his or her account. Coupons are collected by banks under special transit letters which require considerably more description than is required for check collections. [10]

coupon ledger: the ledger used by a bank or trust company to record the receipt of monies in order to pay coupons, disbursements for their redemption when presented for payment, and the numbers of coupons paid.

coupon-paying department: found within a bank or trust company, a department chosen as paying agent by corporations and others to pay matured coupons and bonds.

coupon payment form: a form sent to a credit bureau after an inquiry has been made by telephone. The proper coupon is attached to it. [76]

coupon payments account: to show the total coupon checks outstanding, a bank or trust company will create a general ledger account to identify coupon redemption payments.

coupon rate: the interest rate specified on interest coupons attached to a bond. synonymous with *nominal interest rate.* [49]

coupon shell: a term used in certain localities to describe the envelope in which maturing coupons are enclosed for collection. [10]

coupon teller: a bank teller responsible for controlling the redemption of matured coupons that have been presented for payment.

coupon transmittal form: a form used to request a credit report by mail. The proper coupon is attached to it. [76]

court account: accounts that require court accountings and approval in their normal conduct. Probate, guardianship, conservatorship, and testamentary trust accounts are the most common. [37]

courtage: a European term for brokerage fee.

court bond: see *bond, court.*

courtesy box: collection box equipped with mail chute for motorists. [24]

court trust: a trust coming under the immediate supervision of the court such as a trust by order of court or, in some states, a trust under will. [37]

covenant: a contract pertaining to an undertaking, a promise, or an agreement to do or forbear from doing that which has legal validity and is legally enforceable.

cover: shorts are said to cover when they buy back the contracts they had previously sold, thereby liquidating their position. [2]

coverage
(1) *general:* synonymous with *insurance* or *protection.*
(2) *finance:* the ratio of assets to cover specific liabilities.

covered option: an option in which the seller (or writer) owns the underlying security, as opposed to the uncovered (or naked) condition, under which the option is written against cash or other margin.

covered writing: the most common, and perhaps easiest to understand, strategy is writing calls against a long position in the underlying stock. By receiving a premium, the writer intends to realize additional return on the underlying common stock in his portfolio or gain some element of protection (limited to the amount of the premium less transaction costs) from a decline in the value of that underlying stock. The covered writer is long the underlying stock or a convertible security such as warrants, convertible bonds, convertible preferreds, or a listed option of the same class. He is willing to forsake possible appreciation in his underlying issues in return for payment of the premium. [15]

covering
(1) *finance:* the act of meeting one's obligation.
(2) *investments:* buying a stock previously sold short. [20]

COWPS: see *Council on Wage and Price Stability.*

CP
(1) see *closing price.*
(2) see *closing purchase.*
(3) see *collar pricing.*
(4) see *commercial paper.*
(5) see *condition precedent.*

CPA: see *certified public accountant.*

CPCU: see *Chartered Property & Casualty Underwriter.*

CPI: see *Consumer Price Index.*

CPM: see *critical path method.*

CPN: see *commercial paper note.*

CPS
(1) see *convertible preferred stock.*
(2) see *cumulative preferred (stock).*

CPU: see *central processing unit.*

Cr.
(1) see *credit.*
(2) see *creditor.*

CR: see *cash reserve.*

CRA: see *contemporaneous reserve accounting.*

crash: a sudden and disastrous drop in business activity, prices, security values, and so on, as occurred in October of 1929.

crawling peg: foreign exchange rates that permit the par value of a country's currency to change automatically by small increments, upward or downward, if in actual daily trading on the foreign exchange markets the price in terms of other monies persists on the floor or ceiling of the established range for a given period.

cream: slang, insurance policyholders having the lowest premiums, in part because they are the best risks.

creampuff sale: an expression suggesting that real property is easily sold.

creator: a trustor or settlor; a person who creates a trust by will or a voluntary trust.

Cred.
(1) see *credit.*
(2) see *creditor.*

Crediscope: a more objective system of reporting trade data from creditor's ledgers. It was introduced in 1977. [76]

credit
(1) *general:* an entry recorded on the right side of a ledger. cf. *debit.*
(2) *banking:* funds remaining in a bank account. see also *bank credit.*
(3) *finance:* sales or purchases that are accompanied by a promise to pay later.

credit acceptance: notification to a customer that his credit application has been accepted and an account is now available for his use. [41]

credit analyst: an expert who determines by examining a person's present and past activities whether the person has earned credit. [41]

credit application: a form filled out by a borrower wanting credit, or an interview, which seeks information about an applicant regarding residence, employment, income, and existing debt. [78]

credit association: a group of local retail credit granters forming a dues-paying association. In most cases the local association with 10 or more members is a unit of the National Retail Credit Association. Usually known as the Retail Credit Association. [41]

credit authorization/verification: an inquiry process undertaken to reduce the risk of credit fraud or of extending credit in excess of an imposed credit limit.

credit balance: see *balance of account.*

credit bank: synonymous with *commercial bank.*

credit bureau: an agency holding central files of data on consumers in a given trade area. These bureaus collect personal data, data on paying habits of individuals, and so on, and make impartial reports for credit granters.

credit card: a card issued by an organization entitling the bearer to credit at its establishments (e.g., Exxon's credit card used at gas stations). There are single-purpose cards issued by a specific firm, multipurpose cards (e.g., American Express, Carte Blanche), and bank cards (e.g., Master Card and Visa).

credit contract: a written statement showing how, when, and how much you will pay for goods and services.

Credit Control Act of 1969: federal legislation giving the Federal Reserve System standby authority to control the price and allocation of credit if authorized by the president, one that has never been invoked. Expected to expire June 30, 1982.

credit currency: currency that does not have full convertibility into standard money. synonymous with *fiduciary money (or standard).*

credit decline: notification to a customer that his or her credit application has not been accepted.

credit department

(1) *general:* in a nonbank the department of a company that establishes lines of credit for various customers and authorizes the extension of credit. In addition most mercantile credit departments also have responsibility for the collection of the accounts.

(2) *banking:* a department in a bank where credit information is obtained, assembled, and retained for reference purposes. Credit applications for loans are presented to this department by a loan officer. The credit department gathers all available information on the customer, and prepares it for the confidential use of the loan officer. Based upon the findings of the credit departments, which will make an analysis of the credit information, the loan officer is in a position to make a decision as to whether the loan application should be rejected. The credit department also obtains information and answers credit inquiries for its bank correspondents, who may have a business transaction pending that will involve credit knowledge on a local business. [10]

credit facilities: a business system set up to offer credit services to those who possess personal or business credit. [28]

credit file: an assembly of facts and opinions which indicates the financial resources of an individual (or an enterprise), his character, and his record of performance, especially toward financial obligations. [44]

credit grantor: a misused term indicating that credit is supplied to consumers by business. The true concept is that business supplies only the facilities through which those who possess credit can use it. [28]

credit history: a continuing record of a borrower's debt commitments and how well these have been honored. [78]

credit instrument: a written guarantee to pay, which serves the purpose of money in consummating commercial exchanges, although actual money or bank notes are not used.

credit insurance: where the insurance company reimburses a wholesaler, producer, jobber, or service organization for losses caused by the nonpayment of accounts receivable or the debtor's insolvency.

credit interchange: the sharing among suppliers of data shown by the ledger about accounts.

credit investigation: an inquiry made by a lender to verify data given in a credit application or to investigate other aspects the creditor believes to be relevant to credit worthiness. see *acid test ratio.*

creditism: a Carter administration term marking the shift to control of credit in the war against inflation.

credit letter: another title for a cash letter. see *cash letter.* [10]

credit life insurance: insurance covering the unpaid balance of a loan in the event of a borrower's death. [78]

credit limit: amount, established with or without agreement of the customer, to which credit purchases may be authorized. [41]

credit line: see *line of credit.*

credit losses: the money lost by a finance company or other credit-granting institution when a debt is not paid. This loss may be increased by the cost of collection activities before the debt is finally written off as uncollectable. [55]

credit memo

(1) a posting medium authorizing the credit to a specified account of a certain named amount that bears the complete description of the transaction, the date, and the signature of the party responsible for the authorization of the credit.

(2) a detailed memorandum forwarded from one party or firm to another, granting credit for returned merchandise, some omission, overpayment, or other cause. [10]

credit mixte: a combination of conventional government export financing and concessionary loans that are made interest free or at very low rates.

credit money: fiduciary money that is not completely backed by a precious metal.

creditor (1) one who is due money from another.

(2) synonymous with *lender.*

(3) see *guaranty.*

creditor country: a nation which on a net basis is owed more by another nation than it owes it, thereby establishing a favorable balance of trade.

creditors: those to whom one owes an obligation (usually financial).[28]

creditors' committee: a group of persons who seek to arrange some settlement on behalf of each person or firm having claims on a business in financial difficulty; the common procedure is for all claims to be assigned to this body for settlement. [76]

creditor's notice: in probate the notice published stating the decedent's death and the name of the executor or administrator to whom claims should be presented for payment. [37]

creditor's position: that portion of the market price of a property which is represented by or can be obtained through a first mortgage. [62]

credit proxy: the sum of member bank deposits plus nondeposit items. Often referred to as adjusted credit proxy.

credit rating

(1) *banking:* the amount, type, and form of credit, if any, which a bank estimates can be extended to an applicant for credit.

(2) *finance:* an estimate of the credit and responsibility assigned to mercantile and other establishments by credit investigating organizations.

credit record: a complete and permanent record of your credit performance. [41]

credit report: a confidential report made by an independent individual or organization that has investigated the financial standing, reputation, and record of an applicant for insurance.

credit reporting agencies: organizations structured to supply to business and industry the information they need to reach credit, sales, financial, and general management decisions.

credit risk: the risk assumed for the possible nonpayment of credit extended.

credit sales department: term recommended by the National Retail Credit Association to designate the place where credit and collection functions are carried on. [41]

credit scoring system: a statistical measure used to rate credit applicants on the basis of various factors relevant to credit worthiness. [78]

credit service charge: the charge made for the use of credit facilities. [28]

credit standing: one's present credit worthiness as determined by his or her past credit performance. [28]

credit terms: specification of the terms for the payment of a credit obligation.

credit ticket: a bank bookkeeping memorandum or posting medium on which the transaction leading to a credit entry in a ledger account is described in detail. [31]

credit union: a cooperative financial organization established within and listed to a specific group of people. see *Federal Credit Union, share draft.*

credit worthy (credit worthiness): receiving a favorable credit rating; an individual or business is thereby entitled to use the credit facilities of the organization(s) who requested the information. see *open credit.*

creeping inflation: a gradual but continuing increase in the general price level by as little as 2.5 percent a year. cf. *flation.*

cremation: the act of destroying by fire certain records of the bank. The legal counsel of the bank advises the bank which records and documents may be destroyed, as a result of having outrun the statute of limitations according to the laws of the state in which the bank is operating. The term also applies to the destruction by fire of certain bonds and coupons that have been redeemed by a bank acting as fiscal agent for the issuing corporation or govermental agency. The cremation of paid securities is by agreement between the bank and the issuing agency. [10]

crime of receiving: receiving, possessing, concealing, storing, bartering, selling, or disposing of any property, money, or other thing of value with the knowledge that it has been stolen. [59]

critical path method (CPM): in planning and scheduling, a complex series of operations, the sequence of events that are most critical as to timing; the longest path of activities in a system. CPM is based on the network analogue principle and was first used in 1957 by E.I. Du Pont de Nemours and Co., to improve the planning, scheduling, and coordination of its new-plant construction effort. cf. *program evaluation and review technique (PERT)*

cross check: the placing of two diagonal lines across the front of a check and the addition of a term or series of words to determine the negotiability of the check such as to one's banker if his name is inserted between the lines. Rarely used in the United States, but found in parts of Europe and Latin America.

crossed trades: forbidden by both the securities and commodities exchanges, a manipulative technique where a broker or several brokers offset an order to purchase with an offer to sell and fail to execute the orders on the exchange. The transaction, is therefore, not recorded and can suggest that one of the parties to the cross failed to obtain the price that would have been obtained on the exchange.

cross-elasticity: describes the impact on the demand for one product of price changes of a related product. For example, when the price of butter goes up, the price of margarine, a substitute, usually rises as well. see *coefficient of cross-elasticity, elastic demand.*

crossfoot: to add figures horizontally across columns. [43]

crossing: a practice by a broker who performs the act of seller and purchaser of the same stock. When a broker has such an order, he is required by the exchange to put the stock up for sale at a price that is higher than his bid price to fulfill the minimum variation permitted in the security, prior to concluding the transaction with himself.

crossrate: the determination of the rate of exchange of two foreign currencies by using the rate of exchange of each currency in a third nation's currency.

crowd

(1) *general:* the aggregate of key persons involved in any activity; those who control the day-to-day decisions of the firm.

(2) *investments:* brokers who transact business in securities on the trading floor of an exchange.

crowding out: A term used by Secre-

tary of the Treasury William Simon to describe the negative impact of large government deficits on economic growth.

CRT: see *cathode ray tube.*

CRU: see *collective reserve unit.*

Crude Oil Windfall Profit Tax Act of 1980: see *windfall profits tax.*

crunch: an economic squeeze; a crisis created by some financial pressure.

crush margin: the gross profit that a processor makes from selling oil and meal, minus the cost of buying the soybeans.

crush spread: a futures spreading position in which a trader attempts to profit from what he or she believes to be discrepancies in the price relationship between soybeans and its two derivative products.

cruzeiro: monetary unit of Brazil.

CS

(1) see *capital stock.*

(2) see *closing sale.*

(3) see *common stock.*

(4) see *condition subsequent.*

C-speck: slang, a $100 bill.

Csv.: see *cash surrender value.*

CT

(1) see *cable transfer.*

(2) see *cash trade.*

CTB: see *bond, collateral trust.*

Ctfs.: see *certificate.*

Cts.: see cent.

CU: see *credit union.*

Culpeper Switch: a computerized Federal Reserve facility located in Culpeper, Virginia, which serves as a central relay point for messages transmitted electronically between Federal Reserve districts on the Fedwire. Messages moving billions of dollars of funds and securities daily are processed by Culpeper in electronically coded form. They originate in commercial banks, are sent to Reserve Banks, and then are transmitted to Culpeper, where they are switched to other Reserve Banks and, in turn, to other commercial banks. [1]

Cum.: see *cumulative.*

cum dividend: as distinguished from the ex-dividend, the dividend included. The purchaser of a stock cum dividend has the right to receive the declared dividend.

cum right: the stockholder's right to acquire shares of a new issue of stock in a company in direct proportion to existing holdings. see also *rights.*

cumulative: an arrangement whereby a dividend or interest which, if not paid when due or received when due, is added to that which is to be paid in the future. [37]

cumulative dividend: a dividend on cumulative preferred stock payable, under the terms of issue, at intervals and before any distribution is made to holders of common stock.

cumulative preferred (stock): a stock whose holders are entitled, if one or more dividends are omitted, to be paid on the omitted dividends before dividends are paid on the company's common stock.

cumulative voting: each share of stock may cast as many votes for one director of the firm as there are directors who seek elected office.

curable depreciation: depreciated property that is still considered to be economically useful.

curator: an individual or a trust institution appointed by a court to care for the property of a minor or an incompetent person. In some states a curator is essentially the same as a temporary administrator or a temporary guardian. [37]

Curb broker: an old name for a member of the Curb Exchange. see *Curb Exchange.*

Curb Exchange: the name used before 1953 for the American Stock Exchange in New York City. See *American Stock Exchange.*

curing title: the removal of a claim from a title, to make it marketable.

Curr.: see *currency.*

currency: paper money and coin issued by a government or central bank, which circulates as a legal medium of exchange. [7]

currency band: a carefully defined area within which a nation's money fluctuates on both sides of its official parity. Set at 2.25 percent each side of the parity at the 1971 Washington Smithsonian Agreement.

currency bloc: nations that use a common currency base; for example, the British sterling bloc exists for Great Britain and many of her present and former colonies.

currency bond: see *bond, currency.*

currency convertibility: the ability to exchange for gold, as well as for other currencies.

currency parities: as agreed upon by members of the International Monetary Fund, funds of all of the world's major nations are set in relation to the U.S. dollar.

currency pouch: a zipper pouch in which a cashier places and locks the money from the cash drawer at time of closing the cash drawer. [55]

currency shipment: the responsibility

of the Federal Reserve Bank and other large city banks to supply other banks with an appropriate quantity and quality of coins, paper money, and orders for the transfer of money.

currency transferability: the ability of a currency to be easily exchanged for another currency by any and all of its owners.

current: in budgeting and accounting, designates the operations of the present fiscal period as opposed to past or future periods. [49]

current account: a running account between two companies, reflecting the movement of cash, merchandise, and so on.

current account balance: the difference between the nation's total exports of goods, services, and transfers and its total imports of them. It excludes transactions in financial assets and liabilities. [1]

current and accrued assets: generally consists of items realizable or to be consumed within one year from the date of the balance sheet. Includes cash, working funds, and certain deposits, temporary cash investments, receivables, materials and supplies including fuel, and prepayments. [3]

current and accrued liabilities generally consists of obligations incurred, accrued, or declared, including short-term borrowing, all of which are either due and payable, payable on demand or, in any event, contemplated to be paid within one year. [3]

current and collectable: money that flows or passes from hand to hand as a medium of exchange. [61]

current (floating) assets: the assets of a company that are reasonably ex-

pected to be realized in cash, or sold, or consumed during the normal operating cycle of the business.

current assets to current debt: obtained by dividing the total of current assets by total current debt. Current assets are the sum of cash, notes, and accounts receivable (less reserves for bad debts), advances on merchandise, merchandise inventories, and listed federal, state, and municipal securities not in excess of market value. Current debt is the total of all liabilities falling due within one year. [4]

current budget

(1) the budget prepared for the succeeding fiscal year, or in the case of some state governments, the budget prepared for the succeeding biennium.

(2) the budget in force during the current fiscal year or biennium. [49]

current capital: circulating capital or gross working capital.

current cost: what it would cost today to replace an asset or to require equivalent productive capacity.

current debt: the sum of all liabilities due within the year from the statement date, including current payment on mortgages, funded debts, and serial notes. Liability reserves are included, but reserves for depreciation are excluded.

current debt to inventory: dividing the current debt by inventory; yields yet another indication of the extent to which a business relies on funds from the disposal of unsold inventories to meet its debts. [4]

current debt to tangible net worth: obtained by dividing current debt by tangible net worth. Ordinarily, a business is in trouble when the relationship between current debt and tangible net worth exceeds 80 percent. [4]

current delivery: delivery during the present period such as this month for commodities. [2]

current dollars: a term used to describe the actual prices of goods and services each year.

current exit value: what a company could sell an asset for (or remove a liability) in today's market.

current income: wages, salary, profit, or other income of the immediate period of time, this month, this year. [28]

current liabilities: money owed and payable by a company, usually within one year. [20]

current operation expenditures: expenditures for salaries and wages, supplies, material, and contractual services, other than capital outlays.

current ratio: the relationship between total current assets and total current liabilities. It is calculated by dividing current assets by current liabilities.

current resources: resources to which recourse can be had to meet current obligations and expenditures. Examples are current assets, estimated revenues of a particular period not yet realized, transfers from other funds authorized but not received, and, in case of certain funds, bonds authorized and unissued. [49]

current return: the present income from any investment.

current value accounting: an accounting approach that requires the measurement of individual assets (e.g., factories, machines, and sup-

plies) in current prices rather than in terms of the actual dollar costs at which they were acquired in earlier years.

current yield: an expression as a portion of the annual income to the investment; for example, if annual income is $10 and investment is $100, the current yield is 10 percent. see *return.*

curtail schedule: a list of the amounts by which the principal of an obligation is to be reduced by partial payments and of the dates when these payments are to become due. [44]

curtesy: a husband's life interest in the property of his deceased spouse. cf. *dower.*

cushion bond: see *bond, cushion.*

cushion checking (credit): a check overdraft plan that is also an instant loan. When a check is issued in excess of the customer's account balance or a request is made to transfer from the customer's cash reserve to his or her checking account, a loan is made for up to 36 months plus a modest interest charge.

CUSIP: the American Bankers Association's Committee on Uniform Securities Identification Procedures that established alphabetical and numerical descriptions of securities traded on the exchanges and in over-the-counter markets.

custodian: a banking institution that holds in custody and safekeeping the securities and other assets of an investment company. [23]

custodian account: any financial account (i.e., bank, securities) created for a minor, as provided by state law.

custodianship: the relationship between a trust firm or bank where the bank controls the customer's property subject to the owner's instructions. To be differentiated from the safe depository function where the bank does not control the customers property but merely provided a place for safe keeping.

customer-bank communication terminal (CBCT): the name given to remote (i.e., not on bank premises) electronic devices through which customers may withdraw, deposit, or transfer funds from or to their checking or savings accounts. cf. *automated teller machine.*

customer draft: see *sight draft.*

customer ownership: the legal ownership of securities by customers of a corporation.

customer's broker(man): see *registered representative (trader).*

customer's ledger: a ledger that shows accounts receivable of each customer.

customers' liability: an account in a bank's general ledger as an offset to existing letters of credit that have not been paid but remain guaranteed. see *letter of credit.*

customers' man: synonymous with *registered representative (trader).*

customers' net debit balances: credit of New York Stock Exchange member firms made available to help finance customers' purchases of stocks, bonds, and commodities. [20]

customhouse bond: see *bond, customhouse.*

customs: taxes imposed by a government on the import or export of items. cf. *duty, tariff.*

customs duty: a tax levied and collected by custom officials in discharging the tariff regulations on imports.

customs union: an agreement by two or more trading countries to dissolve trade restrictions such as tariffs and quotas among themselves, and to develop a common external policy or trade (e.g., trade agreement).

cut: an expression used in banks to denote the taking of a total of a pack of checks sorted and going to one destination. The term is most frequently used in banks equipped with proof machines. Since these machines can list a large number of checks on a tape, it has been found more convenient to "cut a tape" by taking totals at intervals of between 100 and 200 items per total. The term also is applied to canceling checks. [10]

cut notes: paper money issues that have been officially bisected or quartered and each portion given its own value, normally indicated by overstamping. This has usually been an emergency measure due to a shortage of coins. [27]

cutoff: to effect better control over huge volumes of checks passing through the proof department in large banks, these banks have periodic "settlements" or "cutoffs" of work. Each cutoff is balanced and items are immediately released from the proof department after each settlement. This not only affords better control, but permits transit items to be mailed in several deliveries each business day. [10]

cutoff date: a specific day chosen for stopping the flow of cash, goods, or other items for closing or audit reasons. Usually this occurs if an inven tory is scheduled when sales or purchases are to take place.

cut-rate: slang, inexpensive; an item offered at less than the usual price.

cut slip: a slip of paper upon which is imprinted or written the total of a particular "cut." The cut slips are retained and used to "settle" a proof machine when the settlement is made. [10]

cutthroat competition: intensive competition that may lead to the bankruptcy of a major competitor, allowing the survivor to raise prices considerably. see *rate war.*

cutting a loss

(1) *general:* ceasing development, production, or sales of a failing item.

(2) *investments:* terminating an unprofitable market position and accepting the loss involved before it grows larger.

cutting a melon: slang, making an extra distribution of money or stock to shareholders, usually when preceded by an unusually profitable transaction (e.g., the sale of a subsidiary).

Cv.: see *convertible.*

Cvt.: see *convertible.*

Cy.: see *currency.*

CY: see *current yield.*

cycle billing: the matching of alphabetical breakdowns to specific days to assist in customer billing. Each breakdown is a cycle and occurs on the same day every month.

cycle mailing: the practice adopted by a number of banks of dividing the depositors' accounts into groups termed "mailing cycles," and the mailing of the statements at stipulated intervals during the month. Proponents of this practice claim that it decreases the cost and confusion experienced when all statements for all depositors are mailed at the same time (usually at the end of the month.) [10]

cycle posting: the practice of dividing accounts to be posted into groups termed "cycles" and posting these accounts at stipulated intervals during the month. [10]

cyclical inflation: periodic variations in a period when there is a sudden increase in the general price level. cf. *secular inflation.*

cyclical stocks: securities that go up and down in value with the trend of business, rising faster in periods of rapidly improving business conditions and sliding very noticeably when business conditions deteriorate.

cyclical theory: see *cyclical stocks.*

D
(1) see *delivery*.
(2) see *discount*.
(3) see *dollar*.

DA
(1) see *depletion allowance*.
(2) see *discretionary account*.
(3) see *dollar (cost) averaging*.
(4) see *dormant account*.

D/A: see *documents against acceptance*.

dace: slang, 2 cents.

daily interest account: a savings account that pays interest daily from the date of deposit to the date of withdrawal. [59]

daily reports: skeleton copies of insurance policies prepared for the agent and the bank, consisting of the declarations page and fill-in endorsements.

daily reserve calculation: a daily calculation to determine the "reserves" necessary to meet the "lawful reserve" requirements. see *lawful reserve*. [10]

daily statement: a daily transcript of the balances shown on the accounts in the bank's general ledger. [31]

Daily Treasury Statement: a listing of transactions that clear through the U.S. Treasurer's account. For each business day it reflects cash deposits, cash withdrawals, and the status of the Treasurer's account.

daisy chains: oil sale overcharges through transactions designed primarily to increase the price of crude oil.

dalasi: monetary unit of Gambia.

damages
(1) *banking:* loss sustained to a person or his or her property.
(2) *banking:* loss in value to remaining property when a portion of one's property is expropriated.
(3) *law:* money awarded by the court to the plaintiff to be paid by the defendant, as compensation for the plaintiff's loss.

data
(1) *general:* a representation of facts, concepts, or instructions in a formalized manner, suitable for communication.
(2) *computers:* any representation such as characters or analog quantities to which meaning is, or might be, assigned.
(3) the plural "data" is often incorrectly construed as singular. "Data" is the plural of "datum."

data bank: a comprehensive collection of information on a principal subject and related areas.

data base: a collection of information specific to an operation, business, or enterprise.

data capture: the act of collecting data into a form that can be directly processed by a computer system. Some electronic funds transfer systems are designed to capture transaction data at the precise time and place the transaction is consummated.

datamation: the flow of information by way of a computer. Formed from the words "data" and "automation."

data processing

(1) *computers:* the execution of a systematic sequence of operations performed on data.

(2) *computers:* any procedure used for receiving data and yielding a specific result.

(3) synonymous with "information processing."

data reduction: the process of transforming large masses of data into useful, condensed, or simplified intelligence.

date: the point in time, fixed by the year, month, and day, when an occurrence takes place. see also *effective date.*

date of acceptance: the date when a time draft is accepted, or honored.

date of draft: the date when a draft is drawn.

date of trade: the day when an order to buy or sell is executed.

dating: a technique of extending credit beyond the time it was originally given. Often used as an inducement to dealers to place orders far in advance of the coming season.

datum: the singular form of "data."

daylight overdraft: occurs when a bank overdraws its reserve account during the day even if the account is replenished by the end of the day; a practice frowned upon by the Federal Reserve Board.

daylight trading: making a purchase followed by a sale of a security on the same day, to avoid a holding position in the shares traded overnight or longer.

day loan: a one-day loan, granted for the purchase of stock, for the broker's convenience. Upon delivery, securities are pledged as collateral to secure a regular call loan.

day order: an order to buy or sell that, if not executed, expires at the end of the trading day on which it was entered. [20]

day points: a term used in connection with transit work and the general ledger in a bank. The term is applied to the number of days required to send transit letters to distant points geographically by the best means of transportation. Because of the adequacy of transportation today, banks average their availability for collection of transit items into one day, two days, and three days. When transit letters are sent out, the bank knows the number of days it will take to collect the items. On the day that collection should be accomplished, the totals of all transit letters scheduled for credit that day are transferred from a deferred account to the available asset account "due from banks." [10]

days of grace: the reasonable length of time allowed, without suffering a loss or penalty, for postponed payment or for the presentment for payment of certain financial documents. see *grace period.*

day-to-day loans: synonymous with *call loan.*

day-to-day money: synonymous with *call money.*

day trading: in anticipation of a rapid price change, the purchasing of a stock and selling it again, or selling it short, on the same day.

D&B: see *Dun and Bradstreet.*

Db.: see *debenture.*

DC: see *daisy chains.*

DD

(1) see *declaration date.*

(2) see *deferred delivery.*

(3) see *delayed delivery.*

(4) see *demand draft.*

(5) see *due date.*

dead asset: an asset that is not productive of income under usual operations. A standby machine tool or a high-cost facility that is not used except in emergencies is a dead asset during the time it is not in use.

deadbeat

(1) *general:* a person who tries to evade paying for things.

(2) *finance:* a person who pays his or her entire charge every billing period, thus avoiding revolving credit charges.

dead broke: slang, penniless.

dead hand: a term used to indicate the continuing hold of a settlor or a testator, who has been dead for many years, upon living individuals or organizations that are confronted with conditions which the settlor or the testator could not have foreseen. [37]

dead market

(1) *general:* a dull selling day, marked by low volume, lack of consumer interest, or other factors creating poor sales.

(2) *investments:* a market marked by minor price changes and low volume.

dead pledge: an expression for a mortgage that is paid on time.

dead president: slang, a U.S. bank-note; any piece of paper money.

deal: slang, a large transaction involving a change in ownership.

dealer: an individual or firm in the securities business acting as a principal rather than as an agent. Typically, a dealer buys for his or her own account and sells to a customer from the dealer's inventory. The dealer's profit or loss is the difference between the price he pays and the price he receives for the same security. The dealer's confirmation must disclose to the customer that he has acted as principal. The same individual or firm may function, at different times, as broker and dealer. [20]

dealer financing: a dealer of commodities, such as household appliances, may make arrangements with a bank for the bank to finance the purchase of these appliances upon their sale by the dealer. The customers who purchase these items then become borrowers of the bank under "consumer credit" or "time sales" loans. The bank usually has the dealer endorse the notes of his customers as additional security for the loans, and has the dealer maintain reserves on each note with the bank as other security. These reserves are termed "dealer holdbacks" or "dealer reserves." [10]

dealer paper: the conditional sales contract that is purchased from a merchant who assigns his rights to the finance company. [55]

dear: costly; expensive; priced unusually high.

dear money

(1) *banking:* the presence of high interest rates. see *hard money (currency).*

(2) *finance:* a situation created when loans are difficult to obtain because of the supply and demand for credit.

Deb.: see *debenture.*

debase: to reduce the quality, purity, or content, or otherwise alter the accepted intrinsic value of the coinage of a realm.

debenture

(1) *general:* the term used to describe indebtedness, usually in long-term obligations, which is unsecured.

(2) *finance:* a corporate obligation that is sold as an investment.

(3) *law:* a voucher or certificate acknowledging that a debt is owed by the signor.

debenture bond: see *bond, debenture.*

debenture stock: stock issued under a contract to pay a specified return at specified intervals. In this sense, it may be considered a special type of preferred stock. It is to be distinguished from a debenture, which represents a bond in form as compared with a share of stock. [18]

debit

(1) *general:* any amount in dollars and cents that, when posted, will increase the balance of an asset or expense account and decrease 'the balance of a liability account. All asset and expense accounts normally have debit balances, and all liability, capital, and income accounts normally have credit balances. cf. *credit.*

(2) *banking:* a weekly premium life insurance agent's list of all the premiums he or she is required to collect.

(3) *investments:* that portion of the purchase price of stock, bonds, or commodities covered by credit extended by a broker to margin customers.

debit balance: in a customer's margin account that portion of purchase price of stock, bonds, or commodities covered by credit extended by the broker to the margin customer. see *balance of account.* [20]

debit card: a cash machine automator and a check guarantee. A recent innovation permitting bank customers to withdraw cash at any hour from any affiliated automated teller machine in the country, and to make cashless purchases from funds on deposit without incurring revolving finance charges for credit.

debit memo

(1) a posting medium authorizing the debit to a specified account for a certain named amount which bears the complete description of the transaction, the date, and the signature of the party responsible for the authorization of the charge.

(2) a detailed memorandum forwarded from one party or firm to another charging for some omitted charge, disallowed or improper payment, or other causes. [10]

debit ticket: a bank bookkeeping memorandum or posting medium on which the transaction leading to a debit entry in a ledger account is described in detail. [50]

debit transfer: a voucher giving a bookkeeper authority to charge on account according to the instructions on the voucher. Opposite of "credit transfer." [41]

debt: money, services, or materials

owed to another person as the result of a previous agreement. see also *effective debt, funded debt, gross debt, total debt.*

debt capital: funds borrowed to finance the operations of a business.

debt ceiling: a level controlled by Congress: the maximum limit on the federal debt. At times Congress has raised the debt ceiling.

debt collector: anyone, other than a creditor or his attorney, who regularly collects debts for others. [78]

debtee: a creditor.

debt financing: the long-term borrowing of money by a business, usually in exchange for debt securities or a note, for the purpose of obtaining working capital or other funds necessary to operational needs or for the purpose of retiring current or other indebtedness. [35]

debt limit: a maximum amount of money that a state or local government can borrow; usually set by legislation of the state involved.

debtor: one who owes money to another.

debtor bank: a bank which, following check distribution in a clearinghouse, has fewer claims against other banks than the other banks have against it.

debtor nation: a country whose citizens, companies, and government owe more to foreign creditors than foreign debtors owe them.

debtor's position: that portion of the market price of property which is in excess of a prime first mortgage, or mortgagable interest; the equity holder's position. [62]

debt retirement: the slow reduction of a firm's debt through either a sinking fund or serial bonds. Debt reduction purports to improve the quality and the market price of a bond issue.

debt securities: fixed obligations that evidence a debt, usually repayable on a specified future date or dates and which carry a specific rate or rates of interest payable periodically. They may be non-interest bearing also. [35]

debt service: interest payments and capital reduction on government, industrial, or other long-term bonds. see *debt service fund.*

debt service fund: a fund established to finance an account for the payment of interest and principal on all general obligation debt, serial and term, other than that payable exclusively from special assessments and revenue debt issued for and services by a governmental enterprise. Formerly called a *sinking fund.* [49]

debt service fund requirements: the amounts of revenue provided for a debt service fund so that all principal and interest payments can be made on schedule. [49]

debt service requirement: the amount of money required to pay the interest on outstanding debt, serial maturities of principal for serial bonds, and required contributions to a debt service fund for term bonds. [49]

debt-to-net worth ratio: all liabilities divided by net value.

debug

(1) *computers:* to detect, locate, and remove mistakes from a routine or malfunction of a computer. see *postmortem.*

(2) *computers:* to test a program on a computer to determine whether it works properly.

(3) synonymous with "trouble-shoot."

deceased account: a bank deposit account in the name of a deceased person. Upon notification of death, the bank segregates the decedent's account and withholds release of funds until a court of law authorizes payment to the legal heirs. see *frozen account.*

decedent: a deceased person.

decedent estate account: a savings account held in the name of a deceased person. [59]

deceit: conduct in business: one person, through fraudulent representations, misleads another person who has the right to rely on such representations as the truth, or is unable to detect the fraud. see *estoppel.*

deceleration principle: an economic statement asserting that this year's increases in prices and wages should be, generally, at least a half percentage point below average increases from the previous year.

decertification: an order by the National Labor Relations Board ending the representation rights of a union, pursuant to a vote of the workers, in an NLRB election. This is done following a petition which asserts that the union no longer represents the majority of the employees. see *Taft-Hartley Act.*

decision: a court's final judgment.

deck: a collection of computer cards.

declaration

(1) *general:* the full disclosure of items, property, or income, as with a customs declaration.

(2) *banking:* a statement by an applicant for insurance, usually relative to underwriting information. Some-

times, this is copied into the policy. cf. *evidence of insurability.*

(3) *law:* the first pleading in an action.

declaration date: the date on which payment of a dividend is authorized by a corporation's board of directors.

declaration of condominium ownership: a complex legal document with appropriate addenda which provides for qualifying a multiunit property for condominium development and sale in accordance with a local state's condominium act (law). [59]

declaration of trust: a written agreement that property to which one person holds title actually belongs to another person, for whose benefit the title is maintained. see *fiduciary, trust.*

declaratory judgment: a court's determination on a question of law, stating the parties' rights without ordering any action.

declination: the rejection by a life insurance company of an application for life insurance, usually for reasons of health or occupation of the applicant. [58]

decline: a downward slump, trend. A lowering of the price for a commodity or a security. [61]

declining balance: a balance which decreases in the amount owned with each payment; the service charge is often computed on the declining balance. [41]

declining balance depreciation: a depreciation method that charges larger amounts of depreciation expense in earlier years and lesser amounts later.

decreasing costs: costs that decline as output per unit increases.

decree: the judge's conclusion in a suit in equity (e.g., an order that an agreement be put into effect immediately).

deduck: slang, an amount that is deducted from taxable income.

deduction: taking away, as from a sum or amount. Discount, rebate, method of reasoning. [61]

deductions from gross income: amounts allowed by the Internal Revenue Service, as deductions in arriving at gross income (e.g., rents, taxes, interest). see *Internal Revenue Service, itemized deductions, Tax Reform Act of 1976.*

deed: a formal, written agreement of transfer, by which title to an estate or other real property is transmitted from one person to another. see *deed, general warranty; deed, quitclaim.*

deed, administrator's: the legal instrument given by a person who is legally vested with the right of administration of an estate, especially of an estate such as that of a minor, or incompetent such as a lunatic, or of a testator having no competent executor. [62]

deed, bond for: an executory contract for the sale of land, with title remaining with the grantor until the purchase price is paid; ordinarily binding on both parties. [6]

deed, committee: a deed employed when the property of a child or a person declared incompetent is conveyed. A court-approved committee is obtained before the transfer. see *deed, guardian.*

deed, executor's: a deed by a person named by the decedent in his will to manage and settle his estate. [6]

deed, general warranty: a deed stating that a grantor is giving the grantee good title, free of debt. The most secure of deeds, it guarantees that the grantor will defend the title against any claims. It is a deed in full covenant. see *perfect title.*

deed, guardian: a deed to convey the property of an infant or incompetent. see *deed, committee.*

deed, mortgaged: a deed by way of mortgage which has the effect of a mortgage on the property conveyed and imposes a lien on the granted estate. [6]

deed, quitclaim: a document by which one's legal right to, title to, interest in, or claim to a specific property, or an estate held by oneself, or others, is forever relinquished to another; usually contains no warranty or statement against the claims that others might have in the property.

deed, special warranty: a deed in which the grantor defends property title against demands made by grantees, heirs, and other claimants. No other liability is assumed by the grantor. Trustees often use this deed when transferring title, and following a court decision, to convey tax titles.

deed, trust: a deed that establishes a trust. Generally, it conveys legal title to property to a trustee and states his authority and the conditions binding upon him in dealing with the property held in trust. Frequently, trust deeds are used to secure lenders against loss. In this respect, they are similar to mortgages. [62]

deed, trustee: a deed by a party who holds property in trust. [6]

deed absolute: see *deed given to secure a debt.*

deed description: a recitation of the legal boundaries of a parcel of land as contained in a deed of conveyance. [6]

deed given to secure a debt: a form of mortgage in which title to the property is handed over to the lender by the borrower as security for the repayment of a debt; also called a deed absolute. [59]

deed in lieu of foreclosure: a mortgagor's way of presenting title to the mortgagee to prevent foreclosure of property.

deed of assignment: the written statement, identifying an assignee, often a trust company, to be responsible for the activities of an insolvent firm.

deed of release: a deed that releases property from the lien of a mortgage.

deed of surrender: an instrument by which property is identified as an estate for life or an estate for years to a person who will receive it in reversion.

deed of trust: a deed that is placed in trust with a third party to ensure payment of the indebtedness or to assure that other conditions of the transaction are met. Upon satisfaction of the debt, the third party transmits the deed to the purchaser, freeing the third party from future responsibilities.

deed restrictions: provisions inserted in a deed limiting the use of the property conveyed by the deed. [44]

deep in money: call options give the holder the opportunity to buy 100 shares of a given stock at a predetermined price and within a limited period of time, usually months. A call is "deep in (the) money" when the exercise price of the call is well below the present market price of the underlying shares.

Def.: see *deficit.*

defaced coins: coins that have been mutilated in some manner. [10]

de facto: "in actual fact" (Latin). In reality; actually; existing, regardless of legal or moral consideration (e.g., de facto segregation; de facto discrimination in employment). cf. *de jure.*

de facto corporation: following an effort, in good faith, to form a corporation under a value statute and there is a failure in some particular, the firm is said to be de facto (in fact) when there has been an exercise of corporate power. Only the state, not a third party, can challenge the firm's existence as a de facto corporation. cf. *de jure corporation.*

defalcation: occurs when an individual in a trust or fiduciary position is unable, by his own fault, to account for funds left in his hands. Often interchangeable with embezzlement or misappropriation of funds. cf. *peculation.*

default: the failure to do that which is required by law, or to perform on an obligation previously committed. The term is commonly used when some legally constituted governing body fails to pay the principal or interest on its bond or fails to meet other financial obligations on maturity.

defaulted paper: any obligation whose principal or interest is in default. Such obligation, security, or investment should be distinguished on all financial statements where they normally appear by showing those in default separately from those not in default. [49]

defeasance: a clause that provides that performance of certain specified acts will render an instrument or contract void. [62]

defeasible: able to be annulled or made void.

defendant: an individual sued in a court of law; the individual answering the complaint of a plaintiff.

defensive investment: an investment policy that places its major effort on reducing both the risk of (eventual) loss and the need for special knowledge, skill, and continuous attention. cf. *speculation.*

defer: to delay payment to a future time. [78]

deferment charge: an additional charge on a precomputed loan which results in extending all fully unpaid installments one or more months and thus deferring the formal final interest maturity date. (This is similar to collecting interest only on a simple interest account for one month.) [55]

deferment short: a term describing the amount by which a payment is insufficient to pay the deferment charges being assessed on an account. [55]

deferrals: cash collected before revenue is recognized as being earned, or in which cash is disbursed before an expense is recognized as being incurred.

deferred annuity: an annuity contract that provides for the postponement or start of an annuity until after a specified period or until the annuitant attains a specified age.

deferred asset: an asset that is not readily convertible into cash, subject to current settlement. [19]

deferred availability cash items: checks received for collection for which credit has not yet been given. The Reserve Banks credit the banks sending in the checks according to a time schedule based on the normal time required to collect payment on the checks. [40]

deferred bond: see *bond, deferred.*

deferred charges: expenditures that are written off over a time period.

deferred compensation: the postponement of distribution of a portion of current earnings until a later date, usually at retirement. The object of deferred compensation is to reduce current income taxes by postponing receipt of taxable income until a time when the receiver will likely be in a lower income tax bracket.

deferred credit: a credit that has been delayed in posting for a reason. A deferred credit may be a deposit that came into a bank after business hours and is therefore entered on the books the next business day.

deferred debits: accounts carried on the asset side of the balance sheet in which are recorded items being amortized as charges against income over a period of years (such as debit discount and expense) and items held in suspense pending final transfer or disposition (such as extraordinary property losses, clearing accounts (net), retirement or other work in progress, etc.). [3]

deferred delivery: purchase of a cash commodity for delivery at some specified future date. synonymous with "forward delivery."

deferred dividend: a stock dividend (preferred or common) that will not be paid until some action occurs.

deferred expense: an asset that has been created through the payment of cash by an entity before the time it will obtain benefits from that payment. Basically synonymous with *prepaid expense.*

deferred income (deferred credits): any income, such as premiums received on bonds that are sold, or rent received in advance, that does not apply to the year for which it was received. Consequently, the crediting of the income is deferred until such time as it is earned. Until then it is listed on a balance sheet as a current liability.

deferred interest
(1) the delay in paying interest. see *bond, deferred.*
(2) the postponement in crediting out-of-town checks deposited by people holding interest-bearing balances for interest purposes until the required days pass to collect them.

deferred liabilities: liabilities the settlement of which is deferred. [18]

deferred maintenance: the expenditure necessary to restore a fixed asset to "like new" condition. This differs from ordinary maintenance or repairs, which, in most cases, merely restore the asset to working order. An example would be the complete rebuilding of a lathe by replacing all bearings (whether worn or not), regrinding the lead screw threads, repainting the castings, replating the fittings, and so on. [38]

deferred payments
(1) *banking:* mortgage allowances for postponement of interest payments. A type of installment plan.
(2) *finance:* delayed payments

postponed until a future time; usually against some future period.

deferred posting: a term used to describe the posting of items in the bookkeeping department on a delayed basis. All items received during one day's business are intersorted and posted on the next business day, as of the date received. [31]

deferred revenue: a liability that has been created through the receipt of cash by an entity before its performance of a service or sale of goods.

deferred serial bond: see *bond, deferred serial.*

deferred special assessments: special assessments that have been levied but are not yet due. [49]

deferred stock: stocks whose dividends are not to be paid until the expiration of a stated date, or until a specified event has taken place.

deferred tax: a tax liability accrued on income that is reported but not subject to income tax until a later time period.

deficiency
(1) *general:* the amount by which anything falls short of some requirement or expectation. The term should not be used without qualification. [49]
(2) *government:* the amount by which taxes are in excess of the taxes stated on a taxpayer's tax return, plus further earlier assessments and less earlier rebates.

deficiency contribution: that portion of the periodic payment by an employee or employer under a retirement plan which is allocated to paying or amortizing the unfunded accrued liability or actuarial reserve deficiency, or meeting the requirements for previous service. [52]

deficiency judgment: a court order authorizing collection from a debtor of any part of a debt that remains unsatisfied after foreclosure and sale of collateral. [44]

deficit

(1) *general:* the excess of liabilities over assets; the excess of obligations and expenditures affecting a given budget period which is in excess of the budget established for the period.

(2) *finance:* indicating obligations or expenditures for items that are in excess of the amount allotted for those items in a financial budget.

deficit financing: exists when government expenditures exceed revenues and the difference is made up by borrowing. The objective is to expand business activity and yield an improvement in general economic conditions. The deficit is covered by release of government bonds. cf. *deficit spending.*

deficit spending: the spending of public funds raised by borrowing rather than by taxation. A fiscal activity often associated with the government that spends more than it collects from taxes and other revenues. Some fiscal policy experts point out that an increase in the deficit stimulates the economy, whereas a decrease in the deficit has the opposite effect. cf. *deficit financing.*

defined benefit pension plan: an Internal Revenue Service ruling making possible tax-deductible pension plan contributions as high as 100% of salary for professionals and businessmen.

definitive bond: see *bond, definitive.*

deflation

(1) *general:* a decline in the general price level, resulting in an increase in the purchasing power of money.

(2) *finance:* the lessening of the amount of money in circulation.

deflationary gap: the amount by which demand falls short of full employment supply, thus lowering the real value of a nation's output.

defraud: to deprive an individual, by deceit, of some right; to cheat; to withhold improperly that which belongs to another.

defray: to pay; to carry an expense; for example, a court settlement may include an amount of money to defray the legal costs of the winning party.

defunct company: a firm that has ceased to exist; a dissolved organization.

degressive taxation: a type of progressive taxation: the rates increase as the base amount taxed increases; and each addition to the tax rate is lower than the preceding one.

de jure: "by right" (Latin); rightful, legitimate, just; according to law or equity. A term describing a state of affairs or a condition existing based on right or law, as distinguished from one that exists de facto. cf. *de facto.*

de jure corporation: a firm that has followed the law dealing with establishing incorporation. A de jure corporation exists in both law and fact. cf. *de facto corporation.*

Delaware Banking Law of 1981: a comprehensive Delaware law aimed at out-of-state banks that would grant them a wide range of credit powers, unavailable in most states. These powers include the ability to charge interest rates not subject to any legal ceiling, to raise interest rates retroactively, to charge variable interest rates, to levy unlimited fees for credit card usage and to foreclose on a home in the event of default for credit card debts. The law also includes a provision that would lower taxes. It would allow, for example, New York banks that relocate in Delaware and earn more than $30 million a year to be taxed at a rate of 2.7 percent, compared with 8.7 percent for those Delaware banks earning under $20 million and a rate of 25.8 percent for banks that remain in New York.

delayed delivery: securities that were sold with the knowledge that delivery would not occur on the regular clearance date. see *clearing*.

delayed items: items representing transactions that occurred before the current accounting year. [18]

delayed opening: the situation created when buy and sell orders accumulate prior to the opening of a stock exchange.

del credere agency: when an agency, factor, or broker attempts to guarantee to his or her principal the payment of a buyer's debt, the agent (etc.) is functioning under a del credere agency.

delectus personae: "chosen or selected person" (Latin); for example, to designate a partner.

delinquency: failure to pay a debt when due.

delinquent account receivable: a debt remaining unpaid after the due date. [43]

delinquent special assessments: special assessments remaining unpaid on and after the date on which a penalty for nonpayment is attached. [49]

delinquent tax: describing a tax that is unpaid after the date when the payment was expected.

delist: activity resulting in the removal or cancellation of rights, by the SEC, previously given to a listed security. This situation occurs usually when a security fails to meet some of the requirements for the listing privilege.

delivery
(1) *general:* the transfer of the possession of an item from one person to another.
(2) *investments:* the transmission of the certificate representing shares bought on a securities exchange; delivery is usually made to the purchaser's broker on the fourth business day after the transaction. see *good delivery, settlement day*; see also *seller's seven sale*.

delivery date: formally, the first day of the month during which delivery is to be made under a futures contract. Since sales are made at the seller's option, however, the seller can make delivery on any day of the month, following proper notification to the buyer.

delivery month: a futures contract must stipulate one of the calendar months as the month of delivery. [2]

delivery notice: the notification of delivery of the actual commodity on the contract, issued by the seller of the futures to the buyer. The rules of the various exchanges require that tender notices be issued on certain days, and in some cases, at certain hours. [2]

delivery points: those locations designated by futures exchanges at which the commodity covered by a futures contract may be delivered in fulfillment of the contract. [2]

delivery price: the price fixed by the clearinghouse at which deliveries on futures are invoiced and also the price at which the futures contract is settled when deliveries are made. [2]

Dem.

(1) see *demand.*

(2) see *demurrage.*

demand

(1) *general:* the willingness and capability to purchase goods or services.

(2) *finance:* a request to call for payment, or for the carrying out of an obligation. see *sight draft.*

(3) *law:* a claim, or the assertion of a legal right.

(4) see also *market demand.*

demand bill: any sight bill of exchange.

demand deposit: a deposit on account in a commercial bank on which checks can be drawn and funds taken out without any advance notification. Demand deposits are the greatest part of our money supply.

demand deposit (adjusted): the total of customers' deposits in reporting member banks subject to immediate withdrawal (checking accounts), excluding interbank deposits and deposits of the U.S. government, less checks in the process of collection. [40]

demand draft: a draft payable immediately upon sight or presentation to the drawee. synonymous with *sight draft.* see *draft.* [31]

demand loan: a loan that has no fixed maturity date but is payable on demand of the bank making the loan. Demand loans can be ''called'' by a bank at any time payment is desired.

demand mortgage: a mortgage that may be called for payment on demand. [44]

demand note: a note or mortgage that can be demanded at any time for payment by the holder. see also *scrip.*

demand price: the maximum price a purchaser is willing to pay for a stated quantity of a commodity or service.

demand-pull inflation: an increase in the price level created by an abundance of money pursuing too few commodities. The demand for items is greater than the capability to produce or supply them.

demand sterling: used in London and other English banks; sight bills of exchange drawn in pounds.

demonization (demonetization)

(1) *banking:* the reduction in the number of government bonds and securities by a commercial bank, resulting in an increase in the value of deposit and paper currency, including federal reserve notes.

(2) *finance:* the withdrawal of specified currency from circulation.

demonstration: the unexpected activity or sudden climb in value for any specific or group of stocks.

demonstrative gift: a gift, by will, or a specified sum of money to be paid from a designated fund or asset; as a gift of $1000 from a specified bank account. [37]

demurrage: detention of a freight car or ship beyond time permitted for loading or unloading, with additional charges for detention.

demurrer: a method of procedure in a law suit: the defendant admits the validity of all the plaintiff's complaints but denies that the facts warrant a cause of action. cf. *cognovit, nonsuit.*

denomination value: the face value of all currencies, coins, and securities.

Dep.
(1) see *deposit.*
(2) see *depositary.*

Department of Agriculture, U.S.: a federal agency established in 1889 to conduct farm educational and research programs, as well as to administer numerous federal agricultural aid programs and other projects to aid farmers and ranchers.

Department of Commerce, U.S.: a federal agency established in 1913 to promote domestic and foreign trade.

Department of Education, U.S.: this new federal agency, established in 1980, is a spinoff from the Department of Health, Education and Welfare. This agency is responsible for improving national programs in the field of education.

Department of Energy (DOE), U.S.: a federal agency established in 1977 to control oil price and allocations, to coordinate energy research and development efforts, to set rates for oil and oil-product appliances, and to fix energy conservation standards. see *Federal Energy Administration.*

Department of Health and Human Services, U.S.: following the creation of the Department of Education in 1980, this new cabinet unit replaced the Department of Health, Education and Welfare. This agency is responsible for improving national programs in health and social security.

Department of Health, Education and Welfare (HEW), U.S.: see *Department of Health and Human Services, U.S.*

Department of Housing and Urban Development (HUD), U.S.: a federal agency formed in 1965 responsible for national programs dealing with housing needs and urban renewal and development. see also *Government National Mortgage Association.*

Department of Justice, U.S.: a federal agency created in 1870 with supervisory powers over federal prosecuting agencies, representing the federal government to the courts. The department has jurisdiction over issues of antitrust and civil rights and supervises the government's activities relating to immigration.

Department of Labor, U.S.: a federal agency created in 1913 to advance workers' welfare, working conditions, and in general, employment opportunities.

Department of the Treasury, U.S.: a federal agency created in 1789 to impose and collect taxes and customs duties, to enforce revenue and fiscal laws, to disburse federal funds; to manage the public debt, and to coin and print money.

Department of Transportation (DOT), U.S.: a federal agency created in 1966 to promote a coordinated national transportation policy embracing all media except water transport. see *Federal Aviation Administration.*

department store banking: see *multiple banking.*

dependent: an individual who requires support from another, as distinguished from one who merely derives a benefit from the earnings of another. see *dependents*.

dependent covenants: two or more related agreements; the performance of one promise must take place before the performance of other promises (e.g., a buyer must pay for goods before the purchased items will be delivered).

dependents

(1) *banking:* an insured employee's spouse and unmarried children who meet certain eligibility requirements for coverage under a life plan.

(2) *taxation:* a relative or nonrelative receiving more than half of his or her support from a taxpayer; under Internal Revenue law an exemption is provided.

depletion accounting: natural resources, such as metals, oils, and gas, which conceivably can be reduced to zero over the years, present a special problem in capital management. Depletion is an accounting practice consisting of charges against earnings based on the amount of the asset taken out of the total reserves in the period for which accounting is made. A bookkeeping entry, depletion does not represent any cash outlay, nor are any funds earmarked for the purpose. [20]

depletion allowance: as permitted by the Internal Revenue Code, a deduction from taxable income derived from a wasting asset. The basis of the allowance is either a percentage of the gross income from specified property or a per-unit-of-product condition.

deposit: an amount of funds consisting of cash and/or checks, drafts, coupons, and other cash items that may be converted into cash upon collection. The deposit is given to a bank for the purpose of establishing and maintaining a credit balance.

depositary: an individual or institution identified as one to be entrusted with something of value for safekeeping (e.g., a bank or trust company).

depositary receipt: mechanism to allow for the trading of foreign stocks on U.S. stock exchanges when the overseas nation involved will not allow foreign ownership of the stock of domestic firms. The shares are therefore deposited with a bank in the country of corporation and an affiliated or correspondent bank in the United States issues depositary receipts for the securities. U.S. investors buy these receipts and can trade them on an appropriate American stock exchange in the same way as other stocks. The major purpose of the instrument is to officially identify ownership of the stock in the foreign country.

deposit banking: the activity of a commercial bank dealing with deposits, receiving checks on other banks, remitting on checks forwarded for the purpose of collection, and paying out deposits by check.

deposit book: a passbook of a customer of the bank showing the amounts of deposits made.

deposit ceiling rates of interest: maximum interest rates that can be paid on savings and time deposits at federally insured banks, savings and loan associations, and credit unions. Ceilings are established by the Federal Reserve Board, the Federal Deposit Insurance Corporation, the

Federal Home Loan Bank Board, and the National Credit Union Administration. [1]

deposit correction slip: a form used to notify a depositor of an error made by the depositor. When the error is located, the bank makes out a deposit correction slip showing what the error was and the corrected new balance of the deposit. The depositor can then correct his or her records accordingly. [10]

deposit creation multiplier: the dollars of lending generated by an independent increase of one dollar in bank deposits.

deposit currency: checks and other credit items deposited with a bank as the equivalent of cash.

deposit function: the business of receiving money on deposit for safekeeping and convenience. This function includes the receiving of demand deposits subject to check and the receiving of savings (time) deposits at interest. [31]

deposit funds: funds established to account for collection that either are held in suspense temporarily and later refunded or are paid into some other fund of the government or held by the government as banker or agent for others. cf. *escrow.*

deposit insurance: insurance to protect the depositor against bankruptcy of a bank or savings and loan institution (see, e.g., *Federal Deposit Insurance Corporation).*

deposit interest rate: limits set by the Federal Reserve System and Federal Deposit Insurance Corporation on interest rates that commercial banks can declare on time deposits. The bank is prohibited from paying any interest rates on demand deposits.

deposition: testimony not given in open court but instead taken by written or oral questionings, signed and witnessed, and ultimately used like testimony in court.

deposit liability: a bank's total liability to customers shown by all demand deposits, time deposits, certificates of deposit and so on.

deposit line: the approximate average amount that a bank's customer usually maintains in a bank account.

deposit loan: loans that are made by the banker crediting the borrower's account with a "loan deposit" for the sum of the loan. This is different from giving the borrower currency when granting a loan.

depositor: an individual, partnership, business proprietorship, corporation, organization, or association is termed a depositor when funds have been placed in bank in the name of the person or entity.

depositor's life insurance: a form of life insurance granted a depositor, without cost, by certain financial institutions, which pays the depositor's beneficiary or estate the amount on deposit—but not in excess of a certain stipulated sum—at the time of death of the depositor. Such benefits are often limited to those depositors whose accounts were opened before they attained a stipulated age. [10]

depository: a bank in which funds or securities are deposited by others, usually under the terms of a specific depository agreement. Also, a bank in which government funds are deposited or in which other banks are permitted by law to maintain required reserves. [50]

depository bond: see *bond, depository.*

Depository Institutions Deregulation and Monetary Control Act: legislation passed in the spring of 1980, the act committed the government to deregulating the banking system. It provided for elimination of interest-rate controls (known as Regulation Q) for banks and savings institutions within six years, and it authorized them to offer interest-bearing NOW accounts beginning in 1981 anywhere in the country. The act also wiped out all state usury laws on home mortgages above $25,000. It also modernized the mortgage instrument by repealing dollar limits, permitting second mortgages, and eliminating lending-territory restrictions. see *graduated-payment mortgage, pledged-account mortgage, variable-rate mortgage.*

Depository Institutions Deregulation Committee: charged with deregulating the banks and savings industry. Created by Congress in the spring of 1980, it has a panel of five voting members: the Federal Reserve Board chairman, the Treasury secretary, and the chairmen of the Federal Home Loan Bank Board, the Federal Deposit Insurance Corporation, and the National Credit Union Administration.

In June 1981, it approved a plan to phase out interest rate ceilings on deposits at banks and savings and loan associations during the following four years.

On August 1, 1981, current ceilings on 2½ year certificates were removed. Also on that date, interest rate ceilings were eliminated for ac-counts maturing in four years or more at banks or thrift institutions.

On August 1, 1982, ceilings would be eliminated for accounts maturing in three years or more. Interest on deposits maturing in two to three years would be tied to the rate on two-year Treasury securities. Thrift institutions would be allowed to pay as much as the Treasury rate, whereas commercial banks would be held to 0.25 percentage point less.

On August 1, 1983, ceilings would be eliminated on accounts maturing in two years or more, and the rates for deposits maturing in one to two years would be tied to the one-year Treasury rate, without any differential between bank and savings and loan rates.

On August 1, 1984, ceilings would be eliminated on accounts maturing in one or two years, and the rates for deposits maturing in less than a year would be tied to the comparable Treasury rate without a differential between bank and savings and loan rates.

On August 1, 1985 ceilings would be removed from accounts that mature in less than one year, except for passbook savings accounts. The committee did not decide what to do about the passbook accounts, although controls on them will end April 1, 1986, under a law passed by Congress in 1980.

depository receipt: short for American depository receipt. see *American depository receipt.*

Depository Trust Company (DTC): a central securities certificate depository through which members effect security deliveries between each other via computerized bookkeeping entries, thereby reducing the physical movement of stock certificates. [20]

deposit receipt: in banks where tellers' machines are now used, the machine issues a printed receipt for the deposit made. This receipt does away with the pen-and-ink entry made in the passbook used by checking account depositors. The bank furnishes a folder in which the depositor keeps his deposit receipts until he has received his bank statement. After verifying his statement for accuracy of entry of all deposits, he can destroy the receipts, since he has been properly credited by the bank as evidenced on his statement. [10]

deposits in federal reserve banks: deposit accounts held as follows: (a) *member banks*—deposits of member banks, which are largely legal required reserves; (b) *U.S. Treasurer*—general or checking accounts of the Treasury; (c) *foreign*—balances of foreign governments and central banks; and (d) *other*—other deposits, includes those of nonmember banks maintained for check-clearing purposes. [40]

deposit slip: an itemized memorandum of the cash and other funds which a customer (depository) presents to the receiving teller for credit to his account. [31]

deposit-taking company (DTC): a financial institution that can take deposits, make loans, discount bills, issue letters of credit, but cannot be called a bank. The concept originated in Hong Kong.

deposit warrant: a financial document prepared by a designated accounting or finance officer authorizing the treasurer of a governmental unit to accept for deposit sums of money collected by various departments and agencies of the governmental unit. [49]

depreciable plant: a utility plant. Usually a tangible plant in service which is subject to depreciation (wearing out, inadequacy, obsolescence, and other causes). [3]

depreciated cost: cost less accumulated depreciation and less other valuation accounts, having the effect of reducing the original outlay to a recoverable cost; the book value of a fixed asset.

depreciated currency: resulting from the lowering in the exchange value of currency, funds not accepted at face or par value.

depreciation

(1) *general:* normally, charges against earnings to write off the cost, less salvage value, of an asset over its estimated useful life. It is a bookkeeping entry and does not represent any cash outlay, nor are any funds earmarked for the purpose. see *book depreciation, declining balance depreciation.* [20]

(2) *banking:* a decline in the value of property.

depreciation book: accrued depreciation shown on books of account. [6]

depreciation charges: charges made by private business and not-for-profit institutions against receipts, to account for the decrease in value of capital assets as a result of wear, accidental damage, and obsolescence, plus an estimate of corresponding depreciation in owner-occupied dwellings.

depressed market: a situation created when prices of goods or services are unusually low.

depression: an economic condition: business activity is down over a long period, prices drop, purchasing power is greatly reduced, and unemployment is high.

Depression of the 1930s: the Great Depression, a severe economic crisis that afflicted the United States and also affected worldwide business, is thought to have begun with the collapse of the stock market in October 1929 and finally ended in the early 1940s, when defense spending for World War II strengthened the general economy.

Deregulation Act: see *Depository Institutions Deregulation and Monetary Control Act.*

dereliction: the intentional abandonment of property. "Derelict property" is any property forsaken or discarded in a way indicating that the owner has no further use or need of it.

derivative deposit: a deposit that is created when a person borrows money from a bank (e.g., deposit currency). A customer is lent a sum, not in money but by credit to his account, against which he or she may draw checks as required.

derived demand: the demand for an item that grows out of the wish to fulfill the demand for another item (e.g., when a demand for community tennis courts is filled, it leads to increased sales of supplies for the courts and tennis equipment).

descendant: one who is descended in a direct line from another, however remotely (child, grandchild, great-grandchild). [37]

descent: the passing of property, or title to the property, by inheritance, as contrasted with request or purchase.

description: items are sometimes described on the deposit ticket, by the teller or another clerk, as to the city or bank of payment. This provides a source reference record and assists in the calculation of uncollected funds. [31]

descriptive billing: a billing system in which an account statement is not accompanied by copies of original invoices. Instead, the statement contains sufficient detail to permit the customer to identify the nature, date, and amount of each transaction processed during the statement period. cf. *country club billing.*

desk, the: the trading desk at the New York Federal Reserve Bank, through which open market purchases and sales of government securities are made. The desk maintains direct telephone communication with major government securities dealers. A "foreign desk" at the New York Reserve Bank conducts transactions in the foreign exchange market. see also *foreign exchange desk.* [1]

de son tort: "of his own wrongdoing" (French). An expression found in such phrases as executor de son tort and guardian de son tort. [32]

destination clauses: marketing contracts to permit an oil monopoly to stipulate which countries should receive oil, preventing the oil from being diverted to the spot market. see *spot market.*

detailed audit: an audit in which an examination is made of the system of internal control and of the details of all transactions and books of account, including subsidiary records and supporting documents, as to legality, mathematical accuracy, complete accountability, and application of accepted accounting principles for governmental units. [49]

deterioration: a reduction of the quality and/or substance of a fixed asset, usually resulting from normal wear and tear from being used. The effect is to lower the value of the asset.

determination date: the latest day of the month on which savings may be deposited and still earn interest from the first day of the month; set by an association's board of directors, but usually the tenth day. [59]

detinue: a common law action to recover property.

Detroit Stock Exchange: established in Michigan in 1907, the majority of its transactions are in unlisted securities.

deutsche mark: West Germany's currency, replacing the old Reichsmark in 1948.

devaluation: an action taken by the government to reduce the value of the domestic currency in terms of gold or foreign monies.

development

(1) *general:* a gradual unfolding by virtue of which something comes to be.

(2) *finance:* a venture on a large scale.

development expense: the cost of developing products, processes, or other commercial activities to make them functional.

Development Finance Companies (DFCs): the financing of development finance companies by the World Bank commenced in 1950 with a loan of $2 million to the Development Bank of Ethiopia. By the end of fiscal 1975, bank lending to such intermediaries had reached almost $3 billion to 68 DFCs (including three regional DFCs serving the East Africa Community, Africa, and Latin America, respectively) in 44 countries and the three regions. see also *International Bank for Reconstruction and Development.* [16]

Development Loan Fund (DLF): created under the 1957 Mutual Security Act, the fund purports to administer long-range development loans. Loans, credit, and guaranties are authorized to assist private lending for economic development.

deviation

(1) *banking:* a rate or policy form differing from that published by a rating bureau.

(2) *statistics:* a measure of dispersion, calculated to be the difference between the particular number or item and the average, which is usually the arithmetic mean, or set of numbers or items.

deivse: a gift, often real property, found in a last will and testament.

devisee: any person receiving title to real property in accordance with the terms of a will. see *devisor, lucrative title.*

devisor: the donor of a gift of real property by will. see *devisee.*

devolution: the passing of real estate title by hereditary succession.

DFCs: see *Development Finance Companies.*

diary: a record kept of maturity dates for notes, bonds, and other instruments. see *tickler.*

dicta: rules or arguments given in the written statement of a judge that have no bearing on issues involved and are not critical for their determination (singular, "dictum").

dies non: Latin, a day on which no business can be transacted.

differentials: the premiums paid for the grades higher than the standard growth (basic grades) and the discounts allowed for the grades lower than the basic grades. These differentials are fixed by the contract terms. [11]

digested securities: securities owned by investors who are not expected to sell them soon. cf. *stag.*

digit: a component of an item of data; a character position in a computer that may assume one of several values; one of the symbols 0, 1, . . ., 9 (e.g., the number 557 contains three digits but is composed of two types of characters, 5 and 7).

digital computer: a computer in which discrete representation of data is mainly used; performs arithmetic and logic processes on these data. The numbers express all quantities and variables of a problem. cf. *analogue computer.*

digitizing machine: a bank machine that reproduces the signature of a customer (which is stored on a card previously signed by the customer) at the top of each check. Thus, when a customer actually countersigns a check for a cash advance, the two signatures can be corroborated.

dilution: the effect of a drop in earnings per share or book value per share, caused by the potential conversion of securities or by the potential exercise of warrants or options.

dime: a 10-cent coin, valued at 10 percent of a U.S. dollar.

diminishing returns: a condition that exists when, in successively applying equal amounts of one or two factors of production (e.g., land and capital) to the remaining factor(s), an additional application produces a smaller increase in production than the preceding application. cf. *indifference schedule.*

dinar: monetary unit of Abu Dhabi, Aden, Algeria, Bahrain, Iraq, Jordan, Kuwait, Libya, South Yemen, Tunisia, and Yugoslavia.

dip: referring to prices, a mild setback or reaction.

Dir.: see *director.*

direct cost: the cost of any good or service that contributes to the production of an item or service (e.g., labor, material); indirect costs (e.g., machinery upkeep, power, taxes) are not directly associated with the production. see *running costs*; cf. *indirect costs.*

direct debt: the debt that a unit has incurred in its own name or assumed.

direct deposit of payroll: a payroll system in which employee earnings are deposited directly to the employee's account at a depository institution.

direct earnings: earnings stated by a firm not showing any equity in the surplus earnings above dividend payments of units or affiliated companies. cf. *equity earnings.*

direct expenditures: payments to employees, suppliers, contractors, beneficiaries, and other recipients.

direct expense: synonymous with *direct cost.*

direct financing: raising capital without resorting to underwriting (e.g., by selling capital stock).

direct heir: a person in the direct line of ascent or descent of the descendent; as, father, mother, son, or daughter. see also *collateral heir, heirs.* [37]

direct inquiry: generally speaking, an inquiry about a person's credit standing made by one firm to another. As distinct from an inquiry to a credit bureau. [41]

direct investments: investments in foreign corporations where the investors have a controlling interest in the overseas firm.

direct labor: the cost of wages paid to workers.

direct liability: a debtor's obligation arising from money, goods, or services received by him or her from another.

direct loan: a loan made directly to a customer for which the customer applied in person or by mail; opposed to a "sales contract," where credit is advanced to a customer through the purchase of a conditional sales contract from a merchant. [55]

direct materials: the cost of materials which become an integral part of a specific manufactured product or which are consumed in the performance of a specific service.

direct obligation: a drawer's obligation as the instrument maker, as contrasted with the indirect obligation of an endorser of the instrument.

director: a person elected by shareholders to establish company policies. The directors appoint the president, vice-presidents, and all other operating officers. Directors decide, among many other matters, if and when dividends are to be paid. [20]

directorate: a corporation's board of directors.

direct overhead: factory, selling, or other expenses related directly to a specific product and resulting in a direct cost.

direct reduction loan: a loan repayable in consecutive equal monthly payments of interest and principal sufficient to retire the debt within a definite period. "Direct" actually means that after the monthly interest payment has been taken out of the payment, the balance of the loan payment is applied directly to the reduction of the principal of the loan. [51]

direct reduction mortgage (drm): a direct reduction mortgage is liquidated over the life of the mortgage in equal monthly payments. Each monthly payment consists of an amount to cover interest, reduction in principal, taxes, and insurance. The interest is computed on an outstanding principal balance monthly. As the principal balance is reduced, the amount of interest becomes less, thereby providing a larger portion of the monthly payment to be applied to the reduction of principal. As taxes and insurance are paid by the mortgagee (lending association), these disbursements are added to the principal balance. This procedure follows throughout the life of the mortgage. [10]

direct sendings: items that are drawn on a particular bank, and sent directly to that drawee bank by another bank, are known as direct sendings. This is to be distinguished from a transit letter, which may be sent to a "correspondent bank" and which contains items on many drawee banks within a certain area. [10]

direct tax: the burden of a tax that cannot be easily shifted or passed on to another individual by the person on whom it is levied.

direct verification: a method of bank audit whereby the auditor of a bank sends a request for the verification of the balances of deposits or loans as of a stated date to the depositors or borrowers. Verifications are returned directly to the auditor, confirming the correctness of balances or listing discrepancies. [10]

dirham: monetary unit of Morocco.

Dis.: see *discount.*

disagio: the charge made for exchanging depreciated foreign monies. cf. *agio.*

Disb.: see *disbursement.*

disburse: to pay out money; to expend. [61]

disbursement: an actual payment of funds toward the full or partial settlement of an obligation.

disbursement schedule: a list or tabular statement of the amounts to be disbursed on specific dates in accordance with agreements entered into in a mortgage loan transaction. [44]

discharge
(1) *general:* to fire. synonymous with *dismiss.*
(2) *law:* the release of one party from meeting his or her obligation under a contract because parties other to the contract have failed to meet their obligation(s).

discharge of bankruptcy: an order

that terminates bankruptcy proceedings, usually relieving the debtor of all legal responsibility for certain specified obligations. [76]

discharge of contract: the fulfillment of a contract's obligations.

discharge of lien: the recorded release of a lien when debt has been repaid. [78]

disclaimer: a document, or a clause in a document, that renounces or repudiates the liability of an otherwise responsible party in the event of (a) noncompliance by such other party to certain conditions described in the instrument, (b) named external conditions, or (c) losses incurred because of a discrepancy in the goods delivered and the weight or count made by the shipper.

disclosure: all publicly owned corporations are required by the SEC to immediately inform the public of all information, positive or negative, that may influence any investment decision. see *full disclosure, insider,* see also *discovery practice.*

discontinuous market: as differentiated from continuously listed securities, the unlisted stocks and bonds forming a separate market.

discount
(1) *finance:* the amount of money deducted from the face value of a note.
(2) *foreign exchange:* the relationship of one currency to another. For example, Canadian currency may be at a discount to United States currency.
(3) *investments:* the amount by which a preferred stock or bond sells below its par value. [20]
(4) *investments:* "to take into ac-

count," as "the price of the stock has discounted the expected dividend cut."

discount charge: a finance charge deducted in advance. [78]

discount check: as determined by the New York Fed, the difference between the purchase price and the face value of a bill purchased from a Federal Reserve Bank.

discount clerk: a bank's representative working in the discount unit. Duties traditionally include the calculations of notes, acceptances and the maintenance of records of bills discounted.

discount corporation: any banking institution involved in the buying and discounting of trade and bankers' acceptance, commercial papers, bills of exchange, and so on. synonymous with "discount house."

discounted value: the present value of future payments due or receivable, computed on the basis of a given rate of interest. [12]

discounting: occurs when an institution lends money to a business with a customer's debt obligation to the firm as security on the loan.

discounting the news: when a stock's price or the level of a major market indicator climbs or falls in expectation of a good or bad occurrence, then barely moves when the actual development takes place and is announced, the stock is said to have "discounted the news."

discount loan: a loan on which the interest and/or charges are deducted from the "face amount" of the loan at the time it is made. [55]

discount market: differing from the bank's discounts for its own clients, the open market for commercial papers and acceptances. This market deals with banks of the Federal Reserve System, other banks, discount and commercial-paper houses, dealers of notes, and so on.

discount on securities: the amount or percentage by which a security (a bond or a share of stock) is bought or sold for less than its face or par value; opposed to premium on securities. [37]

discount rate: the Federal Reserve Bank's interest rate charged to member banks for loans. In most cases, higher interest rates lead to the lowering of security prices. see *easy money, prime interest (rate), tight money.*

discounts and advances: outstanding loans of the Federal Reserve Banks, primarily to member banks. [40]

discount window: in 1980 a law was passed giving the Federal Reserve Board smoother control over the economy, requiring all banks and savings and loan associations to keep reserves behind checking-type deposits. One of the provisions of the law gives about 15,000 other banks and savings and loan associations the right to borrow from the Federal Reserve through its so-called discount window. It is felt by some analysts that this approach would hamper the Fed's ability to regulate the growth of reserves, the base for deposit and money creation.

discovery practice: the disclosure by one party of facts or statements needed by the party seeking the discovery in connection with a pending cause or action. cf. *concealment.*

discretionary account: an account in

which the customer gives the broker or someone else the authority, which may be complete or within specific limits, as to the purchase and sales of securities or commodities, including selection, timing, amount, and price to be paid or received. see *discretionary order.* [20]

discretionary fund: discretionary income enlarged by the amount of new credit extensions, which also may be deemed spendable as a result of consumer decision relatively free of prior commitment or pressure of need. [48]

discretionary income: what remains of disposable income, after essential living costs are paid. see *disposable income.* [78]

discretionary order: the customer specifies the stock or the commodity to be bought or sold, and the amount. His agent is free to act as to time and price. see *discretionary account.* [20]

discretionary policy: monetary policy, purporting to compensate for a business cycle, that leads to a decision by a person or government.

discretionary spending power: designating money available to consume after necessities have been purchased. cf. *disposable income.*

discretionary trust
(1) a trust that entitles the beneficiary to use only so much of the income or principal as the trustee in its uncontrolled discretion shall see fit to give him or to apply for his use.
(2) an investment company that is not limited in its policy to any one class, or type, of stock or security but may invest in any or all of a broad range of securities. [37]

Disct.: see *discount.*

diseconomies of scale: occur when costs increase as a business grows in size. For all firms, there is a point at which as the company becomes larger, costs also increase. see *law of increasing costs*; see also *internal economies of scale.*

dishonored: describes a negotiable instrument offered for acceptance of payment that is turned down or cannot be obtained. see *notice of dishonor.*

disinflation: the result of a strategy to reduce the general price level by increasing the purchasing power of money.

disintermediation: the taking of money out of interest-bearing time accounts (e.g., savings and commercial bank accounts) for reinvestment at higher rates for bonds and so on.

disinvestment: the reduction of capital goods.

disk: a circular metal plate with magnetic material on both sides, continuously rotated for reading in a computer network.

disk pack: a set of magnetic disks designed to be placed in a computer central processing unit for reading and writing.

dismiss
(1) *general:* to release an employee.
(2) *law:* to dispose of a case without a trial. see *nolo contendere.*

dispatch earning: a saving in shipping costs arising from rapid unloading at the point of destination.

disposable income: personal income minus income taxes and other taxes paid by an individual, the balance being available for consumption or savings. see also *discretionary spending power.*

dispositive provisions: the provisions of a will or trust agreement relating to the disposition and distribution of the property in the estate or trust; to be distinguished from administrative provisions that relate to the handling of the property while it is in the hands of the executor or trustee. [37]

dispossess: to put an individual out of his or her property by force.

dissaving: a lowering of net worth, caused by spending more than one's current income.

disseisin: the forcible explusion of an owner from his or her land; the loss of property possession by claiming ownership. see *ejectment.*

dissent: the act of disagreeing. Thus, a widow's refusal to take the share provided for her in her husband's will and assertion of her rights under the law is known as her dissent from the will. see *dower.* [32]

dissolution (corporate): termination at the expiration of a corporation's charter, by order of the attorney general of the state, by consolidation, or by action of the stockholders.

dissolution (partnership): termination by the wishes of the partners at a specified time, or by operation of law because of incapacity, death, or bankruptcy of any partner.

Dist.
(1) see *discount.*
(2) see *exchange distribution.*

distrain: to seize another's property as security for an obligation.

distress for rent: the taking of a tenant's personal property in payment of rent on real estate. see *general lien, landlord's warrant.*

distress selling: selling because of necessity; what happens when securities owned on margin are sold because lowered prices have hurt equities.

distributes: a person to whom something is distributed; frequently applied to the recipient of personal property under intestacy; to be distinguished from "heir"—a person who inherits real property. [32]

distributing syndicate: investment bankers, brokerage houses, and so on, who form a joint venture to sell an issue of securities. see *distribution.*

distribution
(1) *general:* the dividing up of something among several people or entities; the process of allocating income and expenses to the appropriate subsidiary accounts.
(2) *finance:* the division of aggregate income of a community among its members.
(3) *investments:* the selling, over a time period, of a large block of stock without unduly depressing the market price. cf. *secondary distribution.*
(4) *law:* the apportionment by a court of the personal property of a deceased person among those entitled to receive the property according to the applicable statute of distribution.

distribution cost analysis: when marketing an item in a particular location, the breaking down of all direct and indirect costs.

distribution in kind: the distribution of the assets of an estate in their original form and not the cash value of the property. Stocks and bonds are generally distributed among those entitled to receive them instead of being converted into cash for the purpose of effecting distribution. [37]

distribution of certificate account maturities: legislation of 1978; Federal Home Loan Bank System members may not accept certificate deposits that would cause the aggregate amount of certificates maturing in any consecutive three-month period to exceed 30 percent of an association's savings ($100,000 certificates excepted). [51]

distribution of risk: the spreading of investments over a number of stocks.

distribution shipment: a truckload of small goods that are transported at a truckload rate to a specified destination.

distributive share: the share of a person in the distribution of an estate. [37]

distributor: synonymous with "wholesaler."

Div.: see *dividend.*

Divd.: see *dividend.*

diversification

(1) spreading investments among different companies in different fields. Another type of diversification is offered by the securities of many individual companies whose activities cover a wide range.

(2) the purchase of varying assets in order to minimize the risk associated with a portfolio.

diversified investment company: an investment company that practices diversification. The Investment Company Act of 1940 requires such a company to have at least 75 percent of its assets represented by cash, government securities, securities of other investment companies, and other securities limited in respect of any one issuer to an amount not greater than 5 percent of the value of the total assets of such investment company and not more than 10 percent of the outstanding voting securities of such an issuer. [23]

divest: to remove a vested right.

divesture: the process of disposing of all or part of a business. see *spinoff.*

dividend: a portion of the net profits that has been officially declared by the board of directors for distribution to stockholders. A dividend is paid at a fixed amount for each share of stock held by the stockholder. cf. *Irish dividend.*

dividend appropriations: amount declared payable out of retained income (earned surplus) as dividends on actually outstanding preferred or common stock, or the amount credited to a reserve for such dividends. [3]

dividend check: a negotiable instrument in the form of a check drawn on a depository bank of the corporation issuing the dividend. It is signed by the secretary of the corporation.

dividend claim: a request made by the purchaser of stock upon the registered holder for the amount of a dividend where the transaction took place prior to the ex-dividend date, but the transfer could not be effected prior to the record date. [37]

dividend forecast chart: a chart prepared by a brokerage firm, indicating dividend yields for corporations that it considers for its customers.

dividend order: a form which, when properly filled out, instructs a corporation to forward dividend checks to a specified address. [37]

dividend-paying agent: the agent of a corporation charged with the duty of paying dividends on the stock of the corporation out of funds supplied by the corporation. [37]

dividend payout ratio: the ratio of dividends per share of common stock to earnings per share of common stock.

dividend rate: the indicated annual rate of payment to a shareholder based on a company's latest quarterly dividend and recurring extra or special year-end dividends.

dividend reinvestment plans: a service in which the bank, as agent, automatically reinvests the customer's dividends in a security. [25]

dividend requirements: the amount of annual earnings required to pay preferred dividends in full. [30]

dividends per share: the dollar amount of dividends paid to stockholders for each share owned of a corporation's common stock.

dividend warrant: any order to release a corporation's dividend to its rightful shareholder.

division of labor

(1) *general:* breaking a job down into the smallest number of operations without jeopardizing performance.

(2) *banking:* breaking a bank's job down into the smallest number of operations without jeopardizing performance.

Dix: slang, a $10 bill.

D&J: December and June (semiannual interest payments or dividends).

DJA: see *Dow Jones averages.*

DL: see *demand loan.*

DLF: see *Development Loan Fund.*

Dlr: see *dealer.*

DM: see *deutsche mark.*

DMJS: December, March, June, September (quarterly interest payments or dividends).

DNR: see *do not reduce.*

DO: see *day order.*

DOA: see *Department of Agriculture, U.S.*

dobra: monetary unit of San Tóme and Principe.

DOC: see *Department of Commerce, U.S.*

dock: slang, penalizing an employee part of his or her pay for lateness, absence, or related matters.

documentary commercial bills: bills of exchange resulting from commercial transactions that are backed by bills of lading and other related instruments.

documentary draft: a draft accompanied by a shipping document, bill of lading, insurance certificate, and so on, these documents having intrinsic value. Instructions for disposition of the document usually accompany the draft. [31]

documentray stamp: a revenue stamp issued for the payment of a tax on documents, as deeds, checks, or wills. [62]

documents

(1) *general:* anything printed or written that is relied on to record or prove something.

(2) *computers:* written evidence of transactions showing a representation of stored information (e.g., printed paper, punch cards).

documents against acceptance: referring to domestic or foreign bills of exchange, notice that supporting statements will not be given to the drawee until acceptance of the bill.

documents against payment: referring to domestic or foreign bills of exchange, notice that supporting statements will not be given to the drawee until payment of the bill.

DOE: see *Department of Energy, U.S.*

DOG: see *days of grace.*

dog: slang, a promissory note.

DOJ: see *Department of Justice, U.S.*

Dol.: see *dollar.*

DOL: see *Department of Labor, U.S.*

dollar

(1) *general:* monetary unit of the United States. Also the currency for Guam, the Marshall Islands, Puerto Rico, the Ryukyu Islands, Solomon Islands, and the Virgin Islands (U.S.).

(2) *finance:* monetary unit of other nations, including Antigua, Australia, Bahamas, Barbados, British Honduras, Brunei, Canada, Dominica, Ethiopia, Grenada, Guiana, Guyana, Hong Kong, Jamaica, Kiribati, Liberia, Montserrat, Nauru, Nevis, New Guinea, New Zealand, Singapore, Somoa (British), St. Kitts, St. Lucia, St. Vincent, Taiwan, Trinidad and Tobago, Tuvalu, and Zimbabwe.

dollar acceptance: an acceptance or any bill of exchange drawn in a foreign nation or in the United States that is payable in dollars.

dollar (cost) averaging: a system of buying securities at regular intervals with a fixed dollar amount. The investor buys by the dollars' worth rather than by the number of shares. If each investment is of the same number of dollars, payments buy more shares when the price is low and fewer when it rises.

dollar credit: a letter of credit permitting drafts to be drawn in dollars.

dollar diplomacy: the United States' attempt to influence another nation via the power of the American dollar.

dollar drain (gap): the amount by which imports from the United States into a foreign country exceed the nation's exports to the United States.

dollar exchange: banker's acceptances and bills of exchange drawn overseas that are paid in the United States or around the world in dollars, or conversely drawn in the United States and paid overseas in dollars.

dollar-month computation: a method of computing earnings on savings accounts based on the premise that every dollar held in a savings account for one full year will earn the number of cents equivalent to the earnings rate. [59].

dollar premium: a term used in Great Britain for the added premium or cost that investors are requried to pay to purchase dollars for investment outside the country.

dollar shortage: a nation's lack of sufficient money to buy from the United States, caused by a steady favorable balance of payments for the United States.

domestic acceptance: any acceptance where the drawee and drawer are situated in the United States and consequently paid in this country.

domestic bill of exchange: synonymous with *inland bill of exchange.*

domestic corporation: a corporation carrying out business in the same state where it was established or incorporated.

domestic exchange: any check, draft, or acceptance drawn in one location and paid in another within the United States. synonymous with *"inland exchange";* cf. *foreign exchange.*

domicile: a dwelling; a place of permanent residence. cf. *legal residence.*

domicile of corporation: the corporation's location for legal purposes; its legal residence.

domiciliary administration: the settlement of the portion of a decedent's estate which is located in the state of his domicile; to be distinguished from "ancillary administration," which relates to property elsewhere than in the state of the decedent's domicile. [37]

domiciliary trustee: the trustee of that portion of a decedent's or settlor's property which is located in the state of his domicile; to be distinguished from "ancillary trustee," who administers property elsewhere than in the state of the decedent's or settlor's domicile. [37]

dominion: in transferring property from one to another, the separation by the transferor from all power over the property and passing such power to the transferee.

donated stock: to raise working capital, a corporation may receive back from a shareholder any or all of the paid issues. Often done when the stock is offered as a payment for services rendered. Donated stock is nonassessable.

donated surplus: surplus arising from contributions without consideration, by stockholders and others, of cash, property, or the company's own capital stock. Donated surplus is a form of paid-in surplus. [43]

donative interest: an interest in property that is subject to gift. [37]

donee: one who receives a gift.

dong: monetary unit of Viet Nam.

donor: one who makes a gift.

donor (trust): a living person who creates a "voluntary trust." [10]

do not reduce: found in a securities limit order to buy or sell, the price given in the order is not to be lowered by the amount of cash dividend on the ex-dividend date. Does not apply to stock dividends or rights.

dormant account: an account that has had little or no activity for a period of time.

dormant partner: a partner not known to the public at large who is entitled to participate in the profits and subject to the losses.

DOT

(1) see *date of trade.*

(2) see *Department of the Treasury, U.S.*

(3) see *Department of Transportation, U.S.*

double barreled: a term applied to tax-exempt bonds which are backed by a pledge of two or more sources of payment. For example, many special-assessment or special-tax bonds are additionally backed by the full faith, credit, and taxing power of the issuer.

double counting (entry): in bookkeeping, since every transaction is entered two times, counting the same quantity twice when evolving a total; procedure used in determining the gross national product.

double eagle: a U.S. $20 gold piece.

double entry: the method of recording transactions that requires that any increase in one account reflect an increase or decrease in another account. The total debits of each entry must equal the total credits. see *journalize.*

double indemnity: a provision in a life policy, subject to specified conditions and exclusions, whereby double the face amount of the policy is payable if the death of the insured is the result of an accident.

double insurance: purchased to insure against the same risk twice. Usually, it is impossible to obtain more than the loss suffered. If a risk is insured against twice, one firm will claim contribution from the other. see *excess coverage clause, noncurrency.*

double liability: a term used to refer to the liability of the stockholders of banks before banking legislation of the 1930s brought about the elimination of this feature for all national banks and most state banks. Under the double liability provision, the stockholders of a bank, in the event of its liquidation, were held legally responsible for an amount equal to the par value of their stock in addition to the amount of their original investment. [39]

double sawbuck: a $20 bill.

double taxation: short for "double taxation of dividends." The federal government taxes corporate profits once as corporate income; the remaining profits distributed as dividends to stockholders are taxed again as income to the recipient stockholders. [20]

dough: slang, money or cash.

Douglas amendment: amendment to the Bank Holding Company Act of 1956 that prohibits bank holding companies from acquiring out-of-state banks unless laws of the host state specifically permit such entry. see *Bank Holding Company Act of 1956.*

dower: a right for life by a married woman in a portion of the land owned by her husband, which becomes vested upon his death. In some states, a wife owns one-third of her deceased husband's real estate, see *tenant in dower;* cf. *curtesy.*

Dow Jones averages: the averages of closing prices of 30 representative industrial stocks, 15 public utility stocks, 20 transportation stocks, and an average of the 65 computed at the end of a trading day on the New York Stock Exchange. cf. *NYSE Common Stock Index, Standard & Poor's 500 Stock Average.*

down and out: slang, penniless.

down payment

(1) *banking:* money deposited as evidence of good faith for purchasing property upon contract signing.

(2) *finance:* a partial payment, made at the time of purchase, to permit the buyer to take the merchandise.

downstairs merger: a merger of a parent corporation into a subsidiary.

downstream: describing movement of a business activity from a higher to a lower level (e.g., a loan from a parent company to one of its subsidiaries).

down tick: a securities transaction at a price that is lower than the last different price. synonymous with "minus tick." see *up tick.*

downturn: following a growth period, the downward movement of a business cycle or activity.

Dow theory: a theory of market analysis based on the performance of the Dow Jones industrial and transportation stock price averages. The market is said to be in a basic upward trend if one of these averages advances above a previous important high, accompanied or followed by a similar advance in the other. When both averages dip below previous important lows, this is regarded as confirmation of a basic downward trend. The theory does not attempt to predict how long either trend will continue, although it is widely misinterpreted as a method of forecasting future action. see *Dow Jones averages.* [20]

D/P: see *documents against payment.*

DPS: see *dividends per share.*

DR

(1) see *daily reports.*

(2) see *discount rate.*

drachma: monetary unit of Greece.

draft: an order in writing signed by one party (the drawer) requesting a second party (the drawee) to make payment in lawful money at a determinable future time to a third party (the payee).

drawback: any refund of taxes or duties already paid on account of imported items that have been reexported. A primary purpose of the drawback is to provide a type of government subsidy enabling the domestic manufacturer to compete more effectively with an overseas competitor.

drawee: any party expected to pay the sum listed on a check, draft, or bill of exchange.

drawee bank: the bank upon which a check is drawn. [7]

drawer: any party who draws a check, draft, or bill of exchange for the payment of funds.

drawing account: money available to owners or salespeople to be used for expenses which will be deducted from future earnings. [61]

drawn bond: see *bond, drawn.*

drayage: charges made for moving freight on carts or vehicles in a terminal location or city.

Drayton Company Ltd.: founded in 1971 to reinsure programs underwritten by U.S. insurance companies, it is geared to the special insurance needs of the savings bank industry and is wholly owned by savings banks and The Central Industry Fund, Inc. The company's primary aim is to assure that savings banks will continue to enjoy the benefit of a stable and equitable insurance market. see *Central Industry Fund, Inc.* [8]

drive-in banking: because of traffic congestion and lack of parking space, many banks now have tellers' windows facing the outside of the building, or separate outside booths, for the convenience of depositors. The bank customer drives up to a teller's window.

drop: slang, a decline in the price of a stock or commodity.

DRW: see *direct reduction mortgage.*

dry run

(1) another name used by banks for the machine pay plan of journalizing the posting media before posting to the statement. see also *machine pay.* [10]

(2) also used to mean a test period.

dry trust: see *passive trust.*

DS: see *debenture stock.*

DT: see *Dow theory.*

DTC

(1) see *Depository Trust Company.*

(2) see *deposit-taking company.*

dual banking: some banks are chartered by the state in which they operate and others by the federal government. This allows for dual banking, where each independent component cooperates with the other to offer its clientele complete banking services.

dual billing and posting: posting a customer's purchases to ledger, as independent from the preparation of a bill for the customer.

duality: effective in 1977, the ability of a single bank to be a card-issuing member of more than one credit card.

dual listing: securities listed on more than one stock exchange.

dual mutual funds: funds that divide their portfolios between capital growth investments and income investments.

dual-purpose fund: see *split investment company.*

dual savings plan: a plan whereby two separate operations are required to post a savings deposit or a withdrawal to an account.

dual system of banking: refers to the fact that banks may choose to operate under either a federal or state charter. Regulations and requirements vary, depending on whether a bank is regulated by a state or the federal government. Regulations also vary among states. [33]

Du. Dat.: see *due date.*

due (annuity): annuity payments to commence immediately. [12]

due bill: the acknowledgment of a debt that a debtor will render a service or merchandise.

due care: the standard of conduct displayed by an ordinary, reasonable, prudent individual. see also *prudent man rule.*

due date: the date on which an instrument of debt becomes payable; the maturity date.

due from banks: title of an asset account in the general ledger. Subsidiary accounts under this title include each account of funds that a bank has on deposit with other banks. Legal reserve funds and funds placed on deposit with correspondent banks are among these accounts. [31]

due from banks, collections: any contingent asset account within the bank's financial ledger showing the aggregate balances that are due from other banks.

due from Federal Reserve Bank: any asset account listed in a financial ledger of a member or clearing member bank showing the balance due from a Federal Reserve Bank. The figure shows the approximate cash reserve, as required by law, that is held with the Federal Reserve Bank.

due from Foreign Exchange Department: an asset account in the bank's financial statement showing the total funds within a foreign department for purposes of investment in foreign exchange activities.

due process of law: all actions of a court taken to ensure the rights of private individuals before the law; all legal steps to protect these rights. A court order to compel compliance with its wishes (e.g., a summons, issued to compel attendance in court).

due to banks: the title of a liability account in the general ledger. Includes subsidiary accounts of funds that one bank has on deposit with another bank. [31]

due to fiscal agent: amounts due to fiscal agents, such as commercial banks, for servicing a unit's maturing interest and principal payments on indebtedness. [49]

dull: an inactive trading period; when prices of stocks move very little.

dump

(1) *computers:* to copy the contents of all or part of a storage, usually from an internal storage into an external storage. see also *memory, postmortem;* cf. *search.*

(2) *investments:* to offer large blocks of stock for purposes of disposal, with little concern for price or the effect on the market. see *profit taking.*

dumping

(1) *finance:* selling items to other countries below cost for purposes of eliminating surplus or to hurt foreign competition.

(2) *finance:* in the United States, selling imported items at prices less than the cost of manufacture. see *boomerang;* cf. *Antidumping Act of 1974.*

dun: to press for payment of a debt; to demand repeatedly what one is owed.

Dun and Bradstreet (D&B): the oldest and largest mercantile agency in the United States, offering credit data and ratings on business concerns.

Dun's Market Identifiers: a published system identifying firms with an absolute identification number and providing regular updated economic information on each company (e.g., address code, number of workers, and corporate affiliation).

duopoly: an industry containing two businesses selling the identical items. In a duopoly, both firms exercise control.

duopsony: exists when only two buyers are seeking a similar item. cf. *monopsony, oligopsony.*

duplicate bills: any bills in a set.

duplicate deposit ticket: a copy, usually in carbon, of an original deposit ticket. [10]

duplicate documents: documents in a set.

durability

(1) *general:* the lasting quality of an item.

(2) *finance:* money that can be used over an extended period or can be replaced at minimal cost.

durable merchandise: goods that have a relatively lengthy life (television sets, radio, etc.)

duress (personal): a threat of bodily harm, criminal prosecution, or imprisonment. An individual under duress at the time of entering into or discharging a legal obligation is unable to exercise freely his or her will with respect to the transaction. see *extortion.*

duress (property): forced seizure, or withholding of goods by an individual who is not entitled to possess them, and the demands made by such a person as a condition for the release of the goods.

dutch auction: an auction sale where the price on items is continuously lowered until a bidder responds favorably and buys.

duties: see *duty.*

duty

(1) *general:* an actual tax collected.

(2) *finance:* a tax imposed on the importation, exportation, or consumption of goods.

(3) *law:* a legal requirement estab-

lished by law or voluntarily imposed by the creation of a binding promise. A legal right accompanies every legal duty.

duty card: synonymous with *tickler*.

duty drawback: a tariff concession allowing a rebate of all or part of the duty on goods imported for process-ing before being reexported.

duty free: describing items that are not affected by any customs duty. see *fee list*.

dynamiter: a securities broker who attempts to sell fraudulent or unregistered stocks and bonds over the telephone. cf. *boiler room tactic*.

EA: see *Edge Act.*

each way: trading on both the buying and selling sides of a transaction; the broker earns a commission of 3 percent each way (i.e., 3 percent for selling and another 3 percent for executing the purchase order).

eagle: a U.S. $10 gold coin, first coined in 1795. The Treasury demanded the surrender of all gold coins in 1933.

EAM: see *electrical accounting machine.*

earmarked gold: a treasury or stabilization fund; quantities of gold found in the fiduciary reserves of one nation's central bank for another nation's central bank.

earned income: income derived from goods and services rendered as well as pension and annuity income. see *Tax Reform Act of 1976;* cf. *unearned income.*

earned premium: that part of an insurance premium which pays for the protection the insurance company has already given on a policy. [56]

earned surplus: a firm's net profits available after the payment of dividends to shareholders.

earnest money: money given by a contracting party to another at the time of the signing of a contract to "bind the bargain"; this sum is forfeited by the doner if he or she fails to carry out the contract.

earning assets: loans and invest-ments that together are the assets responsible for most of the bank's earnings. [67]

earning power: an employee's potential capacity on his or her job to earn wages over a period of time—usually the normal span of years during which the worker is productive.

earnings

(1) the total remuneration received by a worker for a given period as compensation for services rendered, for work performed, as a commission, as overtime, and so on. cf. *payroll deductions, wage.*

(2) synonymous with *net income.*

earnings per share: the portion of a corporation's net income that relates to each share of a corporation's common stock that has been issued and is outstanding.

earnings price (EP) ratio: earnings per share of common stock outstanding divided by the closing stock market price (or the midpoint between the closing bid and asked price if there are no sales) on a day as close as possible after the publication of the earnings. [3]

earnings report: a statement issued by a company showing its earnings or losses over a given period. The earnings report lists the income earned, the expenses, and the net result.

ease off: a slow decline in prices. [2]

easy money: money that can be ob-

190

tained at low interest rates and with relative ease as the result of sufficient supply of a bank's excess reserves.

EC: see *ex-coupon.*

ECOA: see *Equal Credit Opportunity Act.*

econometric model: a set of related equations used to analyze economic data through mathematical and statistical techniques. Such models are devised in order to depict the essential quantitative impact of alternative assumptions or government policies, and for testing various propositions about the way the economy works. [73]

economic: describes any action having to do with the evolution of goods and services that are purported to satisfy a human condition.

economic costs: payments to the owners of the requirements for manufacturing to convince them to supply their resources in a specified activity.

economic growth rate: the percentage rate at which total annual output grows; an increase in real per capital income.

economic indicators: a classification of economic information, to be used in business cycle analysis and forecasting.

economic profit

(1) the residual profit after explicit and implicit costs have been paid.

(2) synonymous with *pure profit.*

Economic Recovery Tax Act of 1981: federal legislation, signed by President Reagan in August, 1981; includes the following provisions.

Tax rate cuts: (1981) credit of $1\frac{1}{4}$ percent against individual tax bills and 5 percent withholding rate re-

duction on October 1; (July 1982) tax rate reduction of 10 percent, followed by another in July 1983. By 1984, the top rate on $50,000 in earned income drops from 49 percent to 38 percent; (1985) cost-of-living wage and salary increases offset by widening tax brackets, raising "zero bracket" at low end, boosting personal exemptions.

Unearned income and capital gains: (June 9, 1981) the maximum tax on capital gains realized a drop from 28 percent (gain after 60 percent exclusion taxed at 70 percent) to 20 percent (gain after 60 percent exclusion taxed at 50 percent). Minimum holding period for long-term capital gain remains 12 months. (1982) top rate on dividends, interest, rents, and royalties drops from 70 to 50 percent, equal to maximum tax on salary income.

Marriage tax offset: (1982) if both spouses work, a 5 percent deduction from the salary of the lower-paid partner, up to $1,500; (1983) a 10 percent deduction, up to $3,000.

Pension deductions: (1982) tax deductions for contributions to Individual Retirement Accounts raised to $2000 and the 15 percent limitation canceled. The IRA provision is extended to employees already covered by pensions. Voluntary thrift plans as well as separate IRA accounts qualify.

Interest deductions: (1981–1982) exempt interest income up to $1000 ($2000 joint return) on special "All-Saver" savings certificates to be offered for one year only. A deduction of $750 ($1500 joint return) of public utility stock dividends is allowed if paid into a reinvestment plan; (1985) exclusion of 15 percent of savings interest, less interest paid on consumer (but not on mortgage) loans.

Estate and gift tax reductions: (1982–1986) progressive exclusion from taxation of the first $250,000 of estate up to the first $600,000 of estate; (1982) unlimited deduction for estate and gift transfers to a spouse; (1982) annual gifts excluded from taxation raised from $3000 to $10,000.

Stock option treatment: (1981) no tax at exercise on $100,000 per year in stock. Capital gains treatment on gain over option price at sale.

Depreciation and investment tax credits: (1981) accelerated depreciation rules and expanded tax credits for certain classes of real estate investment should shelter more income for investors. see also *All-Savers certificates, Individual Retirements Accounts, Keogh plan.*

economic rent: the estimated income a propety should bring in the existing rental market. The economic rent can be either above or below the amount actually received. cf. *rack rent.*

economics
(1) *general:* the branch of the social sciences concerned with the production, distribution, and consumption of goods and services.
(2) *general:* a description of events dealing with consumption, distribution, exchange, and production of goods and services. see also *labor economics.*

economic sanction: a form of economic pressure (e.g., boycott, embargo) used to compel another country or group of countries to comply with international agreement.

economic value: the value given to an item as a function of its usefulness and its scarcity.

economies of scale: the result of production functions showing an equal percentage increase in all imputs leads output to increase by a large percentage. see *natural monopoly.*

ECR: see *electronic cash register.*

ECU: the *European currency unit.*

ED: see *extra dividend.*

Edge Act: recreated a dual banking system for foreign banks by establishing a new class of Federal charters for them. It also gives the Federal Reserve Board the right to impose reserve requirements on foreign banks. The 1978 International Banking Act restated the broad purpose of the Edge Act statute, in which Congress requires the Fed to revise any of its regulations that unnecessarily disadvantage American banks in the conduct of business. The act also allowed U.S. banks to open offices across state lines to assist in foreign trade financing. see *International Banking Act of 1978.*

edge corporation: a foreign banking organization structured in compliance with the Federal Reserve Act.

EDP: see *electronic data processing.* see also ADP.

education loan: an advance of funds, insured under a program of the U.S. Department of Education, made to a student for the financing of his or her college or vocational training.

EE: see *equity earnings.*

EEOC: *Equal Employment Opportunity Commission.* see *Civil Rights Act of 1964, Title VII.*

effective date

(1) *banking:* the date on which an insurance binder or policy goes into effect and from which time protection is provided.

(2) *law:* the date on which an agreement or contract goes into effect; the starting date.

effective debt: the total debt of a firm, including the major value of annual leases or other payments that are equivalent to interest charges.

effective exchange rate: any spot exchange rate actually paid or received by the public, including any taxes or subsidies on the exchange transaction as well as any applicable banking commissions. The articles of agreement envisage that all effective exchange rates shall be situated within permitted margins around par value. [42]

effective gross revenue: total income less allowance for vacancies, contingencies, and sometimes collection losses, but before deductions for operating expenses. [62]

effective interest rate (or yield): the rate or earning on a bond investment based on the actual price paid for the bond, the coupon rate, the maturity date, and the length of time between interest dates; in contrast to "nominal interest rate." [49]

effective par: with preferred stocks, the par value that would ordinarily correspond to a given dividend rate.

EFT: Electronic Fund's Transfer.

EFTA: see *European Free Trade Association.*

EFTS: see *electronic funds transfer system.*

EI

(1) see *earned income.*

(2) see *exact interest.*

(3) see *ex-interest.*

EIB: see *Export-Import Bank.*

ejectment: the legal action brought to retain possession of property and to receive damage monies from the person who illegally retained it. see *right of possession, seisin;* cf. *landlord's warrant.*

ekuwele: monetary unit of Equatorial Guinea.

EL: see *even lots.*

elastic currency: see *elasticity.*

elastic demand: demand that changes in relatively large volume as prices increase or decrease. When a small change in price results in a greater change in the quantity people buy, the demand for the item is said to be elastic. The demand for jewelry, furs, and second homes is considered to be elastic. see *cross-elasticity.*

elasticity

(1) *general:* the impact on the demand for an item created by changes in price, production, or other factors affecting demand. see *coefficient of cross-elasticity.*

(2) *banking:* the ability of a bank to meet credit and currency demands during times of expansion and to reduce the availability of credit and currency during periods of over expansion. see *Federal Reserve Notes.*

elastic supply: supply that changes in relatively large volume with a minor change in price.

election: the choice of an alternative right or course. Thus the right of a widow to take the share of her deceased husband's estate to which she is entitled under the law, despite a contrary provision in the will, is known as the widow's election. [32]

electrical accounting machine (EAM): conventional punch-card equipment, including sorters, tabulators, and collectors.

electronic cash register (ECR): a cash register in which electronic circuitry replaces electromechanical parts.

electronic data processing (EDP): data processing largely performed by electronic devices.

Electronic Fund Transfer Act: passed by Congress in 1978, but the effective date of most of its provisions was delayed until May 10, 1980, to allow time for the federal bank regulatory agencies to develop a comprehensive set of implementing regulations. Essentially a consumer protection measure, the art requires financial institutions to disclose to new customers the terms and conditions of EFT services, including the consumer's liability for unauthorized transfers; and to describe the type and availability of EFT services offered, and the service charges. The law covers the consumer's right to receive documentation of transfers and to have errors corrected promptly; preauthorized transfer procedures; and the institution's liability if it fails to make or stop transfers. see *Regulation E.* [14]

electronic funds transfer system(s) (EFTS): a loose description of computerized systems that process financial transactions or process information about financial transactions, or effect an exchange of value between two parties. see *Bank Wire System, Fedwire, Hinky Dinky,*

paperless item processing system, pre-authorized payment, prestige card, service counter terminal.

electronic handshake: see *Intermarket Trading System.*

eleemosynary: describes the classification of quasi-public corporations and organizations engaged in charitable work. cf. *not-for-profit corporation.*

eligible commercial paper: a negotiable instrument, having met certain requirements, that is eligible for rediscounting at a special rate by member banks of the Federal Reserve System.

eligible investment: any income-producing investment that is considered to be a sound repository for the funds of savings banks and similar institutions.

eligible paper: instruments, securities, bills, and so on, accepted by a financial institution (i.e., a Federal Reserve Bank) for the purpose of rediscounting.

embargo

(1) *finance:* a condition resulting in the failure to accept freight at a specified location because of some crisis at the point of destination; the prohibition of handling certain goods.

(2) *government:* an official order prohibiting the entry or departure of commercial ships at its ports, especially as a wartime measure. see *blockade, sanction.*

embezzlement: the fraudulent appropriation "to one's own use" of the money or property entrusted to an individual's care. see also *defalcation.*

Emergency Banking Relief Act of 1933: federal legislation returning to the president World War I power relating to transactions in credit, currency, silver and gold, and foreign currencies, and the fixing of a $10,000 fine and 10 years of imprisonment for violators. Also authorized the president to fix regulations on Federal Reserve member banks.

emergency dispute: a strike or the threat of a strike that would affect the national welfare and/or safety. Under the Taft-Hartley Act, the president is authorized to determine whether a dispute imperils the nation's well-being, and if it does, to take appropriate action, which is usually to create a fact-finding board.

Emergency Home Finance Act: federal legislation of 1970; created the Federal Home Loan Mortgage Corporation, under the Federal Home Loan Bank System, to provide a secondary market for conventional loans as well as Federal Housing Administration and Veterans Administration mortgages; extended from 20 to 30 years the period allowed for associations to accumulate Federal Savings and Loan Insurance Corporation-required reserves. [51]

eminent domain: the inherent right of certain legally constituted governing bodies to take title to and possession of real property, for the public good, with just compensation to the owner. cf. *confiscation.*

emolument: compensation for personal services in the form of wages, commissions, awards, or other personal benefits.

emphyteutic lease: a perpetual lease whereby the owner of an uncultivated parcel has granted it to another in perpetuity or for a lengthy period on condition the leasee will improve the land.

empirical credit system: a credit scoring system, based on creditors; experience with borrowers, allotting certain points to attributes describing the applicant. [78]

employ: to hire or engage the services of an individual or his or her equipment.

employable: describes people in the population who are able to work and fall within certain age limits. cf. *hard-core unemployed.*

employee: a general term referring to all those who work for a wage or salary and perform services for an employer.

employee benefit trust: a trust that holds the assets of a pension, profit-sharing, stock bonus, or thrift plan, operated for the benefit of a corporation's employees or a labor union's members. [25]

Employee Retirement Income Security Act of 1974 (ERISA): on Labor Day, 1974, President Ford signed into law the Employee Retirement Income Security Act. The purpose of ERISA is to protect the interests of workers who participate in private pension and welfare plans and their beneficiaries. ERISA reaches 1.5 million plans and approximately 40 million workers and affects assets now held in private pension and welare plans totaling more than $200 billion.

Title I, administered by the Department of Labor, deals with protection of employee benefit rights. Title II is composed of amendments to the Internal Revenue Code. Title III deals with the division of responsibilities among the Department of Labor, the

Internal Revenue Service, and the Pension Benefit Guaranty Corporation. Title IV deals with plan termination insurance and establishes the Pension Benefit Guaranty Corporation.

ERISA is designed to guarantee that workers are not required to satisfy unreasonable age and service requirements before becoming eligible for pension plan participation, that persons who work for a specified minimum period under a pension plan are assured of at least some pension at retirement age; that the money will be there to pay pension benefits when they are due; that plans and plan funds are administered and managed prudently; that employees know their rights and their obligations under the plans; that spouses of pensioners are given adequate protection; that the benefits of workers in certain defined benefit pension plans are protected in the event of a plan termination; and that the federal taxing power is protected by ensuring the equitable operation and soundness of pension plans.

The law also allows an employee not covered by a pension plan other than Social Security to put aside, on a tax-defered basis, a certain amount of money for retirement. see *Individual Retirement Account;* see also *Keogh plan.*

employee stock ownership plans (ESOPs): programs created to give the worker a feeling of participation in the management and direction of a company. Thus workers are encouraged to purchase stock of the company. see *compensation, retirement, self-employed.*

employees trust: a trust established by an employer (usually a corporation) for the benefit of employees. [37]

employer rights: see *management prerogatives.*

Employment Act of 1946: a law designed to seek the federal government's promotion of full employment. Provision is also made for continuing study of economic trends and the submission of the President's Economic Report by the Council of Economic Advisers. The act also direct the president to present an annual economic report to Congress with legislative recommendations. see *reconversion.*

EMS: see *European Monetary System.*

EMU: see *European Monetary Union.*

encipher: synonymous with *encode.* see *encode.*

enclosure sale: a sale in which property placed as security for a debt is sold to pay the debt.

encode

(1) to place magnetic ink characters of the E 13B type font specified by the ABA on the face of a document during the processing of items through an encoding machine.

(2) to apply a code, frequently one consisting of binary numbers, to represent individual characters or groups of characters in a message. synonymous with *encipher.*

(3) to substitute letters, numbers, or characters for other numbers, letters, or characters, usually with the intent of hiding the meaning of the message from everyone except those who know the enciphering scheme. synonymous with *encipher.* [21, 31]

encroachment

(1) *general:* the gradual expansion of a low-value district into a higher economic residential section.

(2) *law:* the infringement of another's property without the owner's consent.

encumbered: property to which one has title, but against which a claim has been made or granted to another.

encumbrance (incumbrance)

(1) *general:* that which holds back or weighs down.

(2) *banking:* a claim or interest in land or other property that although its value depreciates, does not prevent transfer or sale.

(3) *finance:* the amount expected to be paid for items ordered before they are received.

End.: see *endorsement.*

end money: a special fund created in the event that the costs of a project exceed original estimates.

endogeneous: those variables or facts explained within the framework of an economic model. [57]

endorse: the act of placing one's name on an instrument, usually on the back, either by signing or by rubber stamping, so as legally to pass title of the instrument to another party. May also refer to the endorsing of a note by a second party guaranteeing payment in the event of default by the maker. Also spelled "indorse." [31]

endorsed bond: see *bond, endorsed.*

endorsee: the person to whom a negotiable item payable or endorsed to order is negotiated by endorsement and delivery. Also spelled "indorsee."

endorsement

(1) *general:* a show of support, a verification.

(2) *finance:* a signature written on the back of an instrument constitutes an endorsement. An endorsement is required on a negotiable instrument in order to transfer and pass title to another party, who becomes a "holder in due course." The endorser, in signing the endorsement, guarantees that he or she is the lawful owner of the instrument, knows of no infirmity in the instrument, accepted it in good faith for the value received, and is a holder in due course and has the legal capacity to transfer title to another party in the normal course of business.

(3) *insurance:* when circumstances require that a policy be changed (e.g., change of name, addition of property, or change in coverage), such changes are made by attaching to the policy an endorsement—a form bearing the language necessary to record the change. cf. *scratch endorsement.*

(4) also spelled "indorsement."

endorser: one who endorses; the person who transfers his or her title to an instrument to another by endorsement. Also spelled "indorser."

endowment

(1) *general:* a gift to an institution, usually for a specific purpose. In most cases, the gift permits the giver to declare a deduction on his taxes.

(2) *insurance:* a life term contract providing for the payment of the face amount of the policy at a specified age, at the end of a specified period, or upon the death of the insured.

endowment, pure: an insurance plan,

that provides for payment of the face amount to the insured only upon survival to the end of a fixed period. Does not allow for payment of benefits to a beneficiary on prior death of the insured. [12]

endowment insurance: life insurance on which premiums are paid for at a given period, during which the insured is covered. If the person survives beyond the end of the premium period, he or she collects the face value.

endowment term: period of time from date of issue to maturity of an endowment contract. [12]

Energy Research and Development Administration (ERDA): federal agency, in the Department of Energy, responsible for government activities in energy research and development, including demonstration of commercial feasibility and practical application of fossil, nuclear, solar, and geothermal energy, and programs of energy conservation.

Energy Tax Act of 1978: federal legislation dealing with excise taxes imposed on gas guzzlers; changes in motor fuels excise taxes; the repeal of excise taxes on buses; benefits of van pooling among employers and employees; additional investment credits to encourage business energy conservation; a push for geothermal exploitation and development; elimination of the excise tax on rerefined lubricating oil; and tax credits for energy saving in the home. Housing credits apply to qualified energy-saving devices installed in a personal residence after April 19, 1977. An individual received 1978 credits for 1977 expenditures if the work was done after April 19, 1978. See *Revenue Act of 1978.*

enfeoff: to give a gift of ownership to property.

English disease: synonymous with *stagflation.* see *stagflation.*

engross: to purchase a sufficient quantity of a commodity to secure a monopoly for purposes of reselling at a higher price.

enjoin
(1) *general:* to command or direct.
(2) *labor relations:* a court action to prevent a union from engaging in an illegal stoppage or strike action. An employer or corporation may also be enjoined during a labor dispute. see *injunction.*
(3) *law:* to stop, to forbid.

entail: to limit or curtail the succession to property by ordinary rules of inheritance. cf. *primogeniture.*

enterprise: any business venture requiring risk.

enterprise debt: debt that is to be retired primarily from the earnings of publicly owned and operated enterprises. see also *bond, revenue.* [49]

entirety (estate by): the property of husband and wife passed on to the survivor on the death of one. The estate is called "entirety" because the law looks on the husband and wife as one.

entity: see *corporation.*

Entree: a debit card produced by Visa (formerly BankAmericard).

entrepot trade: reexporting imports from a warehouse. When the items are not sold from bonded warehouses, and duty has been paid, the reexporter may be entitled to a refund of the duty.

entrepreneur: one who assumes the financial risk of the initiation, operation, and management of a given business or undertaking. see *threshold companies.*

entry

(1) *general:* a recording of data in an account or account book.

(2) *computers:* an input received from a terminal device attached to a computer.

Environmental Protection Agency (EPA): federal agency founded in 1970. It develops and enforces standards for clean air and water, establishes standards to control pollution from pesticides, toxic substances, and noise, and approves state pollution abatement plans. see *Noise Control Act of 1972, Toxic Substances Control Act of 1976.*

EOM dating: a policy of commencing credit terms as of the month's end. For example, 7/20 EOM means that a 7 percent cash discount is taken if the invoice is paid by the 20th of the month following the invoice date. Invoices dated after the 25th of the month are considered to be dated in the following month.

EP

(1) see *earning power.*

(2) see *effective par.*

EPR: see *earnings-price ratio.*

EPS: see *earnings per share.*

EPT: see *excess profits tax.*

Equ.: see *equity.*

equal coverage: a corporation indenture protective clause providing that in the case of an additional issue of bonds, the subject bonds shall be entitled to the same security as that of the earlier issue.

Equal Credit Opportunity Act (ECOA): federal legislation prohibiting creditors from discriminating against credit applicants on the basis of sex or marital status. After March 1977, discrimination in credit on the basis of race, color, religion, national origin, age, and receipt of public assistance was prohibited. Compliance with the law comes under the jurisdiction of the Federal Trade Commission.

equal dignity: a reference to mortgages or other legal obligations so that all have equal ranking to prevent one from taking precedence over another. see *parity clause;* cf. *first lien, overlying mortgage, second lien, subordinated interest, tacking, underlying mortgage.*

Equal Employment Opportunity Commission (EEOC): see *Civil Rights Act of 1964, Title VII.*

Equal Pay Act of 1963: a federal law requiring that men and women performing equal work be paid equal wages, and applying to employers and workers covered by the Fair Labor Standards Act. The act prohibits lowering pay for men to equalize rates.

equal pay for equal work: the concept, frequently written into contract language, that like work shall command like pay, regardless of sex, race, or other individual characteristics of the employees.

equation price: a price attained by the adjusting action of competition in any market at any time, or in a unit of time, such that the demand and supply become equal at that price.

equilibrium price

(1) *general:* the price that maximizes a firm's profitability.

(2) *finance:* the price of goods determined in the market by the intersection of a supply and demand curve.

equilibrium quantity

(1) *general:* the quantity that maximizes a firm's profitability.

(2) *finance:* the quantity of goods determined in the market by the intersection of a supply and demand curve.

equipment leasing: the renting of expensive equipment to save a substantial and immediate cash outlay. In most cases the leasing agreement includes a maintenance arrangement with the lessor on the leased items.

equipment obligations: equipment bonds, equipment notes, or car-trust notes secured only by lien on specific equipment. [18]

equipment trust

(1) a corporate trust established for the purpose of financing the purchase of equipment.

(2) a device or trust used to help firms obtain equipment by either the Philadelphia-Lease Plan or the New York Conditional Sales Plan. see *equipment trust certificate.* [37]

equipment trust certificate: a type of security, generally issued by a railroad, to pay for new equipment (e.g., locomotives). Title to the equipment is held by a trustee until the notes are paid off. An equipment trust certificate is usually secured by a first claim on the equipment. [20]

equitable conversion: permitting real property to be converted into personal property. Real property owned by a partnership is, for the purpose of the partnership, personal property, because to determine a partner's interest, the real property must be reduced to cash.

equitable mortgage: a written statement making certain property security for a debt.

equitable ownership: the estate or interest of a person who has a beneficial right in property, the legal ownership of which is in another person. For example, a beneficiary of a trust has an equitable estate or interest in the trust property. [37]

equitable right of redemption: a defaulted borrower's right to redeem his property, by full payment of the mortgage debt, up to the date of the mortgage foreclosure sale. [59]

equitable title: the right that exists in equity to secure total ownership to property when its title is in someone else's name.

equities: a term used synonymously with common stocks or capital stocks to designate securities that are owned capital rather than owed capital. The stockholders' equity in a company may be stated inclusive or exclusive of preferred stock. [67]

equity

(1) *general:* the value placed on the distribution of income.

(2) *banking:* the difference between liens against property and the current market value.

(3) *investments:* the ownership interest of common and preferred stockholders in a company. [20]

(4) *investments:* the excess of value of securities over the debit balance in a margin account. see *margin call.*

(5) *law:* the law of trusts, divorce, injunctions, and other rules of performance are enforced in courts of

equity to determine fairness, right, and justice.

equity capital: stockholders' or owners' investments made in an organization.

equity earnings: a portion of surplus earnings of a subsidiary company, over dividend payments, that are unreported by the parent company. synonymous with "indirect earnings," "undisclosed earnings," "unreported earnings."

equity financing: the selling of capital stock by a corporation.

equity funding: any combination of mutual fund shares and insurance. In such a plan, the buyer purchases his mutual fund shares and then the shares are pledged as collateral for the loan that is used to defray the cost of the premium on an insurance policy. see *investment company.*

equity of redemption: see *equitable right of redemption.*

equity securities: any stock issue, common or preferred.

equity stake mortgage: low interest rates on a mortgage, one-third less on the average, in return for one-third of the profits when the property is sold.

equity transaction: a transaction resulting in an increase or decrease of net worth or involving the transfer between accounts making up the net worth.

equity turnover: the ratio that measures the relationship between sales and the common stockholders' equity. It is used to compute the rate of return on common equity.

ER

(1) see *earnings report.*

(2) see *ex-rights.*

ERDA: see *Energy Research and Development Administration.*

ERISA: see *Employee Retirement Income Security Act of 1974.*

erratic fluctuations: short-term changes that are difficult to measure and predict because they tend to be unexpected.

errors and omissions: referring to insurance coverage for liability arising out of errors or omissions in the performance of professional services other than in the medical profession; applicable to such services as engineering, banking, accounting, insurance, and real estate.

ES

(1) see *earned surplus.*

(2) see *exempt securities.*

escalator clause

(1) *general:* provides for an adjustment of wages in accordance with such factors as cost of living, productivity, or material costs. Escalator clauses are designed to keep real wages reasonably stable during the term of a contract.

(2) *banking:* provides for increased payments in the event of unforeseen occurrences (e.g., increased fuel or maintenance costs).

(3) *finance:* permitting adjustments of price or profit in a purchase contract, under specified conditions.

escape law

(1) *general:* in a maintenance-of-membership agreement, a provision setting a period during which union members may withdraw from membership without effect on their employment.

(2) *law:* a contractual provision outlining the circumstances under

which either party may be relieved of any obligation previously incurred or agreed to.

escheat: the reversion of property to the government when a person dies without leaving a will and has no heirs, or when the property is abandoned.

escheat law: pertaining to the reversion of land to the state by the failure of persons having legal title to hold the same.

escrow: a written agreement or instrument setting up for allocation funds or securities deposited by the giver or grantor to a third party (the escrow agent), for the eventual benefit of the second party (the grantee). The escrow agent holds the deposit until certain conditions have been met. The grantor can get the deposit back only if the grantee fails to comply with the terms of the contract, nor can the grantee receive the deposit until the conditions have been met. see also *billed escrow;* cf. *deposit funds.*

escrow agreement: an arrangement whereby two parties agree to place a sum of money in the hands of a third party for conditional delivery under specified circumstances.

escrow bond: see *bond, escrow.*

escrow closing: a type of loan closing in which an escrow agent accepts the loan funds and mortgage from the lender, the down payment from the buyer, and the deed from the seller. [59]

escrow funds: as applied to mortgage loans, represents reserves established for the repayment of taxes and insurance when due. Reserves are collected monthly by the mortgagee as part of the regular payment. [31]

escrow officer: an officer of a financial institution designated as the escrow agent or the custodian of the funds, securities, deeds, and so on, deposited until their release by agreement upon the completion of the agreed-upon act. [10]

escudo: monetary unit of Azores, Cape Verde Islands, Guinea-Bissau, Madeira, Mozambique, Portugal, Portuguese East Africa, and Timor.

ESD: see *ex-stock dividend.*

ESOPs: see *employee stock ownership plans.*

Est.: see *estate.*

estate

(1) *general:* any right, title, or other interest in real or personal property.

(2) *law:* all assets owned by an individual at the time of his or her death. The estate includes all funds, personal effects, interests in business enterprises, titles to property (real estate and chattels), and evidence of ownership, such as stocks, bonds, and mortgages owned, and notes receivable.

estate account: an account in the name of the estate of a decedent, administered by the executor or administrator of the estate. [39]

estate at will: of indefinite duration; the estate allows the lessee possession as long as both lessor and lessee mutually agree to it.

estate duty: a British term for the tax on property of a deceased individual. synonymous with *inheritance tax* in the United States.

estate in common: see *tenancy in common.*

estate in reversion: the remaining

portion of an estate that the grantor retains after certain interests in it have been transferred to another.

estate in severalty: an estate held by one person only. No other party has any part of it.

estate in tail: see *entail.*

estate plan: a definite plan for the administration and disposition of one's property during one's lifetime and at one's death; usually set forth in a will and one or more trust agreements. [37]

estate tax: a state or federal excise tax placed on an estate, to be paid before property is transferred to heirs. This is different from an inheritance tax, which is levied against the receivers of the estate. see *Tax Reform Act of 1976.* cf. *succession tax.*

estate tax bond: see *bond, estate tax.*

estimated cost: the expected cost of a product to be manufactured. It includes standard costs projected to future operations.

estimated revenues: the account title used in governmental accounting to set up the budgeted revenues for a period. The estimated revenues are compared against the actual revenues at the end of the period.

estimated tax: for corporations, the projected tax liability, minus tax credits permitted by law, above $100,000.

estoppel: a legal stoppage; when an individual who knows the truth but does not reveal it makes another believe something to be truthful, and that person acts to his detriment based on belief of the facts given to him, the giver of the untruthful information must reveal the full details of the situation. see *deceit.*

estoppel certificate: an instrument in-

dicating the unpaid principal balance of a mortgage plus the amount and rate of interest thereon.

ET: see *estate tax.*

ETA: see *Energy Tax Act of 1978.*

et al.: (abbreviation of *et alii,* Latin) "and others" (who are specified elsewhere in the document.)

Eurobond: a bond released by a U.S. or other non-European company for sale in Europe. In this market, corporations and governments issue medium-term securities, typically 10 to 15 years in length. see *Eurocredit sector.*

Eurocard: a European credit card developed by the West German banking system that is accepted in most western European countries.

Eurocheque: a credit card for purchasing goods in several western European countries.

Eurocredit sector: a sector of the Euromarket, where banks function as long-term lenders by constantly rolling over short- and medium-term loans at rates that fluctuate with the cost of funds. see *Eurobond.*

Eurocurrency: monies of various nations deposited in European banks that are used in the European financial market. synonymous with "Euromoney."

Eurodollar collaterized certificates of deposits (CDs): certificates of deposit of at least $100,000 to foreign investors issued by federally chartered and Federal Savings and Loan Insurance Corporation-insured institutions.

Eurodollars: European claims for U.S. dollars. These claims arise when, through the purchase of a bill of exchange or other financial transaction, a foreign bank debits the account of a U.S. bank and credits a dollar deposit account (Eurodollars).

Euromarket (Euromart):
(1) see *Eurobond.*
(2) see *Eurocredit sector.*
(3) see *European Economic Community.*

Euromoney: see *Eurocurrency.*

European Coal and Steel Community (ECSC): known as the Schuman Plan, it was proposed in 1950 by Jean Monnet, a leader in European confederation; its major functions are the pooling of resources and the placement of duty restrictions on coal, iron, and steel in trade among the nations of France, West Germany, Italy, Belgium, The Netherlands, and Luxembourg. see *European Economic Community.*

European Common Market: see *European Economic Community.*

European Economic Community (EEC): an agreement made in 1957 among France, Italy, West Germany, Belgium, The Netherlands, and Luxembourg (the original "Inner Six" nations) for the purposes of establishing common import duties and the abolishing of tariff barriers between borders. Denmark, Ireland, and England joined the EEC in 1973, and in 1975 many countries of Africa and the Caribbean became members. Greece became a member in 1981. synonymous with "Common Market," "Euromarket (Euromart)." see *European Free Trade Association.*

European Free Trade Association (EFTA): in 1959 Austria, Denmark, Norway, Portugal, Sweden, Switzerland, and the United Kingdom (the original "Outer Seven") established common regulations for tariffs and trade. Subsequently, Iceland became a member and Finland an associate member. see *European Economic Community.*

European Investment Bank: created by the Rome Treaty as a finance institution of the European Economic Community, this bank assists in financing projects within the Common Market.

European Monetary System (EMS): intended to move Europe toward closer economic integration and to avoid the disruptions in trade that can result from fluctuating currency values. France, West Germany, Belgium, Luxembourg, The Netherlands, Ireland, and Denmark all plan to prevent their currencies from rising or falling in value against each other any more than 2.5 percent. Italy will keep its lira from fluctuating against the other currencies by more than 6 percent. see *European Monetary Union.*

European Monetary Union (EMU): created on January 1, 1979, the union is Europe's response to U.S. monetary profligacy. Under EMU, currencies of member nations would rise together, rather than fluctuating separately. Founding members were Germany and France, but the expectation is that all nine Common Market members will join, with invitations going out to non-Common Market countries as well. see *European Monetary System.*

evening up: a profit to offset a loss.

even lots: lots or number of stock shares sold in units of 100 or multiples thereof. see also *board lot.*

even up: a securities term describing an evenly divided balance of security buyers and sellers. Prior to the opening of the exchange, it refers to the opening prices of the day which show minimal changes from the closing prices of the previous days trading.

eviction: the depriving by due process of law land or property in keeping with the judgment of a court. see *disseisin, ejectment.*

Evid.: see *evidence.*

evidence: the testimony of witnesses and information presented to a court.

evidence of insurability: any statement or proof of a person's physical condition and/or other factual information affecting his acceptability for insurance. cf. *declaration.*

EW: see *ex-warrants.*

Ex.: see *exchange.*

exact interest: interest compounded on a 365-days-per-year basis. see *compounded interest, ordinary interest, simple interest.*

ex-all: indicates that the seller has sold a security but reserved for himself the right to all pending advantages. These would include rights, warrants, and dividends in money or kind which may be granted to the security.

examine for bank endorsement: an act performed generally in a bank's proof department or bookkeeping department whereby clerks examine the backs of all checks to see that the bank which forwarded the items has properly endorsed them. The bank endorsement is very important because banks use it to trace the path of an item through the banks through which it has passed. The whole system of returning items for infirmity through the channels from which they came relies to a great extent upon clear, legible bank endorsements. [10]

examine for endorsements: an act performed to determine whether an item has been properly endorsed so as to complete its negotiability. Tellers, or clerks who receive the items from tellers, check endorsements so that the depositor of any item can be readily determined. It is the responsibility of bookkeepers to see that items are properly endorsed before they are paid by the bank. Many cases involving the negotiability of an instrument have arisen because of improper, incomplete, or faulty endorsements on the instrument. [10]

examine for missorts: bookkeepers are required to examine checks before posting them to determine that they are drawn on accounts in their particular ledger, or that they are actually drawn on the drawee bank. There are two types of missorts: checks sorted to the wrong ledger, or checks drawn on another bank where a depositor may maintain another account but is using a similar style of check. [10]

exception: in title-insuring practice, an item that may not be covered by title insurance because it limits in some way the owner's right to his property; exceptions may include easements, liens, and deed restrictions. [59]

excess condemnation: in condemnation proceedings, taking more land or property than is truly required for the government project in question.

excess coverage clause: a statement

that in the event of a loss, a specific insurance will be considered in excess of any other insurance held against the identical risk. see *double insurance.*

excess demand curve: reflects the quantity demanded less the quantity offered at each price.

excess equity: a situation where the cash value of an account is in excess of the amount required for margin in the buying of securities.

excess insurance: a policy or bond covering the insured against certain hazards, applying only to loss of damage in excess of a stated amount. The risk of initial loss or damage (excluded from the excess policy or bond) may be carried by the insured himself or may be insured by another policy or bond, providing what is known as primary insurance.

excess loan: an illegal bank loan made to one customer that is in excess of the maximum stated by law. Directors of banks approving such loans have been held by court decisions to be personally liable for the bank's losses.

excess of loss reinsurance: reinsurance that indemnifies the ceding company for the excess of a stipulated sum or primary retention in the event of loss.

excess profits tax: a tax added to the normal tax placed on a business. It is usually levied on profits above what the law declares as normal during periods of wartime.

excess reserves: designates the amount of funds held in reserve in excess of the legal minimum requirements, whether the funds are on deposit in a Federal Reserve Bank, in a bank approved as a depository, or in the cash reserve carried in its own vaults.

Exch.: see *exchange.*

exchange
(1) *general:* an organization or place for carrying out business or settling accounts.
(2) *finance:* the volume of monies available for use.
(3) *investments:* any exchange for trading in securities or commodities. see *clearinghouse, foreign exchange, stock exchanges.*

exchange acquisition: a method of filling an order to purchase a block of stock on the floor of an exchange. Under certain circumstances, a member broker can facilitate the purchase of a block by soliciting sell orders. All orders to sell the security are lumped together and crossed with the buy order in the regular auction market. The buyer's price may be on a net basis or on a commission basis. [20]

exchange charge: the term "exchange charge" has a variety of meanings. Sometimes it refers to a remittance charge, which is a charge that some banks deduct in paying checks drawn upon themselves when they are presented through the mails from out-of-town points for the service of remitting the proceeds to these distant points. The term may also refer to a charge for drafts on other cities or to a charge which banks make for collecting out-of-town items. Generally called collection charges. [50]

exchange current: the current rate of exchange.

exchange distribution: a method of

selling large blocks of stock on the floor of an exchange. Under certain circumstances a member-broker can facilitate the sale of a block of stock by soliciting and inducing other member-brokers to solicit orders to buy. Individual buy orders are lumped together with the sell order in the regular auction market. A special commission is usually paid by the seller; ordinarily the buyer pays no commission. [20]

exchange of securities: resulting from a merger or consolidation, a technique where the securities of one corporation are exchanged for those of a second firm on a mutually agreeable basis.

exchange of spot (or cash commodity) for futures: the simultaneous exchange of a specified quantity of a cash commodity for the equivalent quantity in futures, usually due to both parties' carrying opposite hedges in the same delivery month. Also known as "exchange for physical" or "exchange against actuals." In grain the exchange is made outside the "pit." [2]

exchange privilege: enables a mutual fund shareholder to transfer his investment from one fund to another within the same fund group if his needs or objectives change, generally with a small transaction charge. [23]

exchange rate: refers to the price of one currency in relation to that of another.

exchanges: all checks, drafts, notes and other instruments that are presented to a clearinghouse for collection. synonymous with "clearinghouse exchanges."

Excise, Estate and Gift Tax Adjustment Act of 1970: federal legislation; extended excise tax rates on automobiles and telephone service until January 1972. Sped up collections on estate and gift taxes.

excise taxes: taxes levied by the federal and state governments on the manufacture, sale, or consumption of commodities, or taxes levied on the right, privilege, or permission to engage in a certain business, trade, occupation, or sport.

Excise Tax Reduction Act of 1954: federal legislation; dismantled Korean War excise tax structure. All excise tax rates in excess of 10 percent were reduced to 10 percent, except for the 20 percent cabaret tax. see *Excise Tax Reduction Act of 1965.*

Excise Tax Reduction Act of 1965: federal legislation; repealed excise taxes on several items and provided for systematic reductions in the rates on transportation equipment and communication services. see *Excise Tax Reduction Act of 1954.*

exclusion

(1) *general:* any restriction or limitation.

(2) *banking:* a provision of an insurance policy or bond referring to hazards, circumstances, or property not covered by the policy.

exclusive allowance: the portion of an annuity payment that can be excluded from taxable income each year. This amount is determined by dividing the annuitant's investment in the contract by his life expectancy. In a tax-deferred-annuity (TDA) program, the amount of annual contribution that may be excluded from taxable income by a participant is specified by law.

exclusive listing: an arrangement whereby a broker becomes the sole agent of the owner of a property, assuming the sole right to sell or rent the property within a specified time period.

ex-coupon: without the coupon. A stock is sold ex-coupon when the coupon for the existing interest payment has been removed.

Exctr.: see *executor.*

exculpatory clause: a clause that relieves the landlord of liability for personal injury to tenants as well as for property damages. The clause does not necessarily protect the landlord against liability to a third party.

Ex. D.: see *ex-dividend.*

Ex. Div.: see *ex-dividend.*

ex-dividend (ex div; XD): identifying the period during which the quoted price of a security excludes the payment of any declared dividend to the buyer, and the dividend reverts to the seller.

ex-dividend date: the day on and after which the right to receive a current dividend is not transferred automatically from seller to buyer. [37]

execute

(1) *computers:* to carry out an instruction or perform a routine.

(2) *law:* to complete or make valid, as by signing, sealing and delivering.

executed: signed, sealed, and delivered, as of contracts or other written agreements.

execution: the actual filling of a customer's order.

executive compensation: the total monies paid to an executive, including the regular salary, plus additional payments (e.g., bonuses or director's fees). It does not include warrants or options to purchase stock. see *compensation.*

executor: a party (person, bank, etc.) identified in a will to administer the estate upon the death of the maker of the will (the testator) and to dispose of it according to the wishes of the testator.

executor de bonis non: the individual or corporation named in the will to take over and complete the settlement of an estate in those cases in which the original executor, for one reason or another, has failed or been unable to do so. Unless the testator himself names such a successor executor, the court appoints an administrator de bonis non. [37]

executor de son tort: one who, without legal authority, assumes control of a decedent's property as if he were executor and thereby makes himself responsible for what comes into his possession. [37]

executor of an estate: the person appointed by a testator to execute his will or to see its provisions carried into effect after his decease. [76]

executor's deed: see *deed, executor's.*

executory: until all parts of a contract are performed, the contract is said to be executory as to the part not performed.

executrix: a woman identified in a will to administer the estate upon the death of the maker of the will (the testator) and to dispose of it according to the wishes of the testator.

exemplary damages: monies or fines imposed by a court (a) in punishment of the defendant, (b) to make an example of the wrongdoers, and (c) to deter others from doing the same thing.

exemplified copy: a copy of a record or document witnessed or sealed certified to as required by law for a particular transaction. [37]

exempt employees

(1) *general:* employees who are not subject to the rulings of seniority.

(2) *labor relations:* employees not subject to wage and overtime provisions of the Fair Labor Standards Act. Such employees may or may not be covered by a union contract. see *Fair Labor Standards Act of 1938.*

exemption

(1) *income taxes:* a token deduction from gross income allowed for the taxpayer and others in his family where at least half of their support can be shown. Additional deductions are given for people over 65 years of age and for blindness. see *Tax Reform Act of 1976.*

(2) *law:* a person free from a duty required by some law (e.g., one relieved from jury duty because of prejudice of the subject).

exempt securities: stocks that do not require the regular margin when bought on credit.

exercise notice: a notice issued by a clearinghouse that was formed to ensure stock deliveries, obligating a customer to send the securities covered by an option against payment of the exercise price. see *exercise price.*

exercise price: the fixed price for which a stock can be purchased in a call contract or sold in a put contract. see *puts and calls.* synonymous with "striking price."

ex gratia payment: a payment made by an insurance company, but one for which it is not liable under the terms of the insurance policy.

exhaust price: the price at which a broker is forced to sell a security that was margined and subsequently dropped in price.

exhibit

(1) *general:* a display or public show.

(2) *law:* anything presented in a court to assist in proving a set of allegations.

Eximbank (Ex-Im Bank): see *Export-Import Bank of the United States.*

Ex. Int.: see *ex-interest.*

ex-interest: having no interest. synonymous with *flat.*

existing mortgage: a mortgage that is encumbering a property. After the property has been sold, the mortgage may or may not remain.

exogenous: those variables or facts not explained within an economic model but imposed upon the model by outside forces. [57]

exonumia: a numismatic term applicable to all nongovernment monetary issues. [27]

Exor.: see *executor.*

Exp.

(1) see *expense.*

(2) see *exports.*

expansion

(1) *general:* extending or broadening the operation or area of a business.

(2) *finance:* a business cycle fluctuation characterized by an increase in industrial activity.

ex parte: upon, from, or in the interest of one side only. Ordinarily implies a hearing or examination in the presence of, or on papers filed by, one party and in the absence of, and often without notice to, the other. [18]

expected exit value: the nondiscounted amount of cash a company expects to realize from holding a particular asset. cf. *present value of expected cash flow.*

expected return: the profit that is anticipated from a business venture.

expected yield: the ratio of expected return over the investment total, usually expressed as a percentage on an annual basis.

expendable fund: a fund whose assets may be applied by administrative action for general or specific purposes.

expenditure: an actual payment, or the creation of an obligation to make a future payment, for some benefit, item, or service received. If the expenditure is for the purpose of acquiring or improving a relatively permanent asset, it is termed a "capital expenditure." If the amount involved is charged to some operating account, it is a "revenue expenditure."

expense: the cost of resources used to create revenue. Expense is the amount shown on the income statement as a deduction from revenue. Expense should not be confused with cost. All expenses are costs, but not all costs are expenses.

expense account
(1) *general:* an account carried in the general ledger in which all operating expenses are recorded. Expenses are deducted from gross profits, or the total of all income accounts, to compute the net profit of the business for the period.

(2) *finance:* money advanced to an employee, usually an executive, for travel, daily costs, and other items that are accepted by the organization as justified; monies paid by an employee that are reimbursed by the employer after the expenditures have been accepted.

expense constant: a flat amount included in some premiums, which covers the minimum expense of an insurance transaction.

expense fund: a fund, required by law, held by a mutual savings bank or directors of a nonstock bank to ensure the financial stability of the bank at the time of its dealings with the public.

expense loading: a term used in rate making to denote the amount which is added to the pure premium in order to provide for the expenses of the insurance company. see *pure premium.* [56]

expense ratio: the percentage of the premium used to pay all operating costs.

experience
(1) *general:* events during one's lifetime; usually pertaining to acquired knowledge or skill.

(2) *banking:* the premium and loss record of an insured or of a class of coverage.

experience rating
(1) *general:* the basis for an adjustment, according to the employer's unemployment or accident record, of the rate the employer pays for unemployment insurance or workmen's compensation insurance.

(2) *banking:* a type of individual risk rating that, based on insured experience on the risk, measures the

extent to which a particular risk deviates from the average of its class and reflects this deviation in the rate for the risk. see *basic rating,* cf. *judgment rates.*

expiration

(1) *general:* termination, cessation.

(2) *banking:* the date on which a policy will cease to be in effect, unless previously canceled.

(3) *investments:* the last day on which the option may be exercised. [5]

expire: to arrive at the termination period of an agreement, contract, or other instrument.

expired account: an account on which the originally agreed period for payment has elapsed, but an unpaid balance remains due. [55]

ex-pit transaction: the buying of cash commodities at a specified basis outside the authorized exchange.

explicit interest: the amount of money or goods paid on a loan.

export: to ship an item away from a country for sale to another country.

export credit: a commercial letter of credit issued for the purpose of financing a shipment of goods to a foreign country. [50]

Export-Import Bank of the United States (Eximbank) (Ex-Im Bank): this independent federal banking corporation, established in 1934, facilitates and aids in financing exports and imports and the exchange of commodities between the United States and foreign nations; it offers direct credit to borrowers outside the United States as well as export guarantees, export credit insurance, and discount loans.

exports: items produced in one country and sold to another.

Export Trade Act: see *Webb-Pomerene Act of 1918.*

ex-post facto law: "after the fact" (Latin). A law applying retroactively: forbidden by Article 1 of the U.S. Constitution. That is, a law that would serve to convict an individual for an activity that had not been declared illegal when the person is accused of having performed it.

Express Company money orders: money orders, similar to postal and bank money orders.

express trust: a trust stated orally or in writing, with the terms of the trust definitely prescribed; to be distinguished from a *resulting trust* and a *constructive trust.* [37]

expropriation: the act of taking private property for public purpose, or the modification of the right to private property by a sovereignty or any entity vested with the proper legal authority; for example, property under eminent domain is expropriated. cf. *confiscation.*

Ex. R.: see *ex-rights.*

ex-rights: without the rights. Corporations raising additional money may do so by offering their stockholders the right to subscribe to new or additional stock, usually at a discount from the prevailing market price. The buyer of a stock selling ex-rights is not entitled to the rights. see *ex-dividend, rights.* [20]

ex-stock dividend: without any stock dividend; for example, when the stock dividend is held as the property of the seller. cf. *ex-dividend.*

ex-store: selling term for commodities in warehouse. [11]

Extd.: see *extended.*

extend(ed)

(1) *general:* to multiply the unit price by the quantity of units to ascertain the total cost on an invoice.

(2) *banking:* to allow a period of time for the payment of a debt beyond the date originally set.

(3) *law:* describes a contractual obligation that has been prolonged beyond the originally stated date of maturity or termination.

extended bond: see *bond, extended.*

extended term insurance: permanent plans of life insurance providing term coverage for the face amount of policy, in lieu of cash settlement, when premiums are discontinued for a fixed period.

extension

(1) *banking:* moving the maturity date to a later time, resulting in prolongation of the terms of a loan. see *lockup.*

(2) *finance:* the granting of borrowing rights, or the permission to buy without immediate payment.

(3) *law:* a postponement by agreement of the parties of the time set for any legal procedure.

extension of mortgage: an agreement which prolongs the terms of a mortgage.

external audit: an examination intended to serve as a basis for an expression of opinion regarding the fairness, consistency, and conformity with accepted accounting principles of statements prepared by a corporation or other entity for publication. [43]

external bond: see *bond, external.*

externalities: external benefits or costs of activities for which no compensation is offered. synonymous with "spillovers."

extinguish: to wipe out, settle, or conclude, as with a debt or obligation.

extortion: the taking of something of value from someone by force; fear of exposure and threat of force are also instruments of extortion, which is sometimes aimed at inducing the victim to pay the extortioner more than is due him or her in a legitimate connection. cf. *duress (personal).*

extra: short form of "extra dividend." A dividend in the form of stock or cash in addition to a company's regular or usual dividend. Not to be confused with *ex-dividend.*

extractive industry: a business that takes products directly from nature, especially from land or water (e.g., lumber, coal, or oil).

extra dating: adding days beyond the regular date for invoice payment. Extensions are usually for 3- or 60-day periods.

extra dividend: a second dividend paid in cash or in stock, and tendered in addition to the regular dividend.

extra expense insurance: designed for the business firm (e.g., a bank) that must continue to operate following a loss, usually at great additional expense. It is not to be confused with business interruption insurance because it does not protect against interruption of business.

extraordinary gain or loss: income or loss to an entity caused by an unusual and infrequent event, unrelated to the ordinary activities of the entity.

extraordinary items: income statement captions (extraordinary income and extraordinary deductions) which segregate material gains and losses, less applicable income taxes, arising out of current-year transactions that are of a character significantly different from the typical or customary activities of the company. Included would be such items as the sale or abandonment of a plant or a significant segment of the company's investments or business, major changes in accounting procedures, and condemnations. [3]

extraordinary property losses: an amortizable (deferred debit) account, which includes the depreciated value of property abandoned or damaged by circumstances that could not have been reasonably anticipated and which is not covered by insurance. [3]

extrapolation: the estimate of an unknown value beyond the range of a series of identifiable values (e.g., projecting the world's population in A.D. 2500).

ex-warrants: without warrants. When a security is sold ex-warrants, the warrants are retained (exercised) by the seller. see *ex-rights*.

F: used on a ticker tape after a foreign stock symbol to show that the stock has been sold by a foreign owner.

F&A: February and August (semiannual interest payments or dividends).

FA

(1) see *face amount.*

(2) see *facilitating agency.*

(3) see *fixed assets.*

(4) see *floating assets.*

(5) see *frozen asset.*

FAA: see *Federal Aviation Administration.*

face amount: the principal sum involved in a contract. The actual amount payable by the company may be decreased by loans or increased by additional benefits payable under specified conditions or stated in a rider.

face of policy: the first or front page of the insurance policy. It usually includes the name of the insurance company and the insuring clauses. [56]

face value

(1) the principal value of an instrument. It is one the face value that interest is computed on interest-bearing obligations such as notes and bonds. The legal entity issuing a note, bond, or other obligation contracts to repay the face value of the obligation at maturity.

(2) synonymous with *par value.*

facilitating agency: any organization aiding an individual or firm in taking title to goods (i.e., a stock exchange).

facsimile signature: a mechanically imprinted signature placed on an instrument, check, bond, security, and the like. Although such signed checks are accepted as equal to hand-signed ones, banks usually have certain stipulations that must be met prior to honoring them.

factor

(1) *general:* an individual who carries on business transactions for another. see also *factors.*

(2) *finance:* an agent for the sale of goods or services, authorized to sell and receive payment for the times or services.

factorage: the commission collected by a factor.

factoring

(1) *banking:* a method commonly employed by an installment loan department of a bank for computing the amount of interest to be refunded or credited because a 12-month loan is being liquidated before maturity. It is also a method for accruing earned discount.

(2) *finance:* selling accounts before their due date, usually at a discount.

factors

(1) *general:* ingredients needed for the production of any good or service. The primary factors are land, labor, capital, and enterprise.

(2) *finance:* limited agents who

buy accounts receivables from small firms at a discount. Funds are advanced upon the delivery of duplicate invoices as evidence of sale and delivery of the goods. Factors frequently perform all accounting functions in connection with the accounts receivable, in which case purchasers are notified to remit directly to the factor. see also *factor*.

factor, 78th: a method commonly employed by the installment loan and other departments of a bank for computing the amount of interest to be refunded or recredited when a 12-month loan is liquidated prior to maturity. Also, a method used for accruing earned discount. [10]

factor's lien: a factor's right to retain the merchandise consigned to him or her for reimbursal for all advances previously made to the consignor. cf. *particular lien*.

factory overhead: manufacturing costs, excluding direct material and direct labor.

factory overhead incurred: manufacturing costs accumulated during a given accounting period.

facultative: describes a specific transaction, one risk at a time, with the ceding and acceptance being optional on the part of the ceding company and the reinsurer. That is, the reinsuring company may exercise its "faculty" to accept or reject the risk offered.

fail(s)

(1) *general:* a business venture that does not prove financially viable.

(2) *investments:* a broker's inability to deliver stocks he or she owes another broker within the required five business days. One broker's fail-

ure to deliver results in another broker's failure to receive.

failure: the inability to fulfill normal business obligations; becoming insolvent or bankrupt.

FAIR Certificate: *f*ree from tax *a*ffordable, *i*nsured *r*ewarding; the 1981 Savings and Loan Association strategy with Congress to allow a savings certificate that would be free from federal income tax, offered in affordable denominations, insured by a federal agency, and pay a significant net turn. see *All-Savers certificates*.

Fair Credit Billing Act: an amendment to the federal Truth in Lending Law that protects charge account customers against billing errors by permitting credit card customers to use the same legal defenses against banks or other "third party" credit card companies that they previously could use against merchants.

Fair Credit Reporting Act of 1971: federal legislation giving the user of credit, the buyer of insurance, or the job applicant the right to learn the contents of his or her file at any credit bureau. see also *Freedom of Information Act of 1966*.

Fair Debt Collection Practices Act: an amendment to the Consumer Practices Act, signed by President Carter, its basic objective is to eliminate abusive and bitterly unfair debt collection practices, such as threats of financial ruin, loss of job or reputation, and late evening telephone calls. The law became effective in March 1978.

Fair Employment Practices Committee: a committee set up by Executive Order 8802 in 1941 to "investigate complaints of discrimination." Fair employment practices were made part of federal law by the Civil Rights Act of 1964. see *Civil Rights Act of 1964, Title VII.*

Fair Labor Standards Act of 1938: a federal statute setting minimum hourly wages, providing for payment of time and one-half for work beyond 40 hours a week, and regulating employment of those under 18 years of age. Known as the Wage and Hour Law, it is administered by the U.S. Department of Labor. The act has been amended to include standards for computing working time and increases of the minimum wage, rules for computing overtime pay, and requirements for equal pay for equal work without regard to sex. There are more than 40 exemptions applying to professionals, executives, and salespersons. Similar statutes have been passed by state legislatures.

fair market value: a value arrived at by bargaining between informed buyers and sellers.

fair price: the price that results in a fair return on funds invested or which has an appropriate markup on goods or services sold to claim a reasonable profit.

fair rate of return: the profit that a public utility can earn to pay interest and dividends and expand facilities, as determined by federal and state law. see *rate regulation.*

fair trade acts: laws passed by various states in which retailers are obliged to maintain specified prices on select goods. In recent years fair trade pricing has been withdrawn by a great number of retailers and manufacturers.

fair value: under the Investment Company Act, value determined in good faith by the board of directors for those securities and assets for which there is no market quotation readily available. [30]

fairy godfather: slang, a potential business supporter.

fall out of bed: a crash in stock prices; a sharp drop in the market.

false pretense: refers to any untrue statements or representations made with the intention of obtaining property or money. [56]

family allowance plan: a scheme providing every family, rich or poor, with a certain amount of money based exclusively on the number and age of its children. Family units above specified levels would return all or a portion of the money with their income taxes; those below specified income levels would retain the funds.

family income rider: a special policy provision added to a basic term life insurance policy, stating that a specified monthly income is to be paid to the beneficiary for the remainder of the income period if the insured dies before the expiration of the term.

Fannie Mae: see *Federal National Mortgage Association.*

Farm Bankruptcy Act of 1933: federal legislation that allowed farmers added time to pay off their debts. The provisions of the act expired in 1949.

Farm Credit Administration: the U.S. agency responsible for the cooperative farm credit system, providing long- and short-term aid to farmers.

Farmers Home Administration: an agency of the federal government that makes, participates in, and insures loans for rural housing and other purposes. [59]

farm out: to subcontract.

farm price: the price received by farmers for their products as reported each month by the U.S. Department of Agriculture.

Farm Relief Act of 1933: see *Agricultural Adjustment Act of 1933.*

farm stock: the grain stock held by farmers.

farm subsidies: monies given or loaned, under stringent regulation, by the U.S. Department of Agriculture to producers of certain farm products when the market price drops below the percentage of agricultural parity or if a portion of acreages is used for pasturage or for purposes of conservation. see *price support*; cf. *Brannan plan.*

farm surplus: farm products purchased by the U.S. government for purposes of keeping agricultural prices stable. These surpluses remain in warehouses until disposed of (e.g., as overseas sales or as food distributed to needy people).

FAS: see *free alongside ship.*

Fas-Cash: a copyrighted system designed to expedite the handling of cash by the teller. Currency is precounted and strapped by the teller before banking hours. The currency is strapped in packages of from $2 through $9, and from $10 through $100. This permits the teller to select rapidly nearly any combination of precounted packages of currency, and he or she is required only to get the correct change from an automatic cashier. For example, a customer wants to cash a check for $38.75. The teller selects a $30 and an $8 package of currency and selects $0.75 from the automatic cashier. This is a very fast method of handling customers at the teller's window. [10]

fat snake: slang, a monetary union to create a European fixed system. see *European Monetary System, European Monetary Union.*

favorable trade balance: when a nation's total value of exports is in excess of its total value of imports.

FB: see *bond, fidelity.*

FBA: see *Farm Bankruptcy Act of 1933.*

FC
(1) see *fixed capital.*
(2) see *fixed charges.*
(3) see *floating capital.*
(4) see *futures contract.*

FCA: see *Farm Credit Administration.*

FCBA: see *Fair Credit Billing Act.*

FCC: see *Federal Communications Commission.*

FCI: see *Federal Crime Insurance.*

FCPA: see *Foreign Corrupt Practices Act of 1977.*

FCRA: see *Fair Credit Reporting Act of 1971.*

Fcs.: see *franc.*

FCU: see *Federal Credit Union.*

Fd.
(1) see *fund.*
(2) see *funding.*

FDCPA: see *Fair Debt Collection Practices Act.*

Fdg.: see *funding.*

FDIC: see *Federal Deposit Insurance Corporation.*

FE
(1) see *foreign exchange.*
(2) see *futures exchange.*

FEA: see *Federal Energy Administration.*

feature
(1) *general:* the components of an

item or service that yield a benefit.

(2) *investments:* the more active stocks in the general list.

Fed: slang, the Federal Reserve System.

Federal Advisory Council: a committee of the Federal Reserve System that advises the Board of Governors on major developments and activities.

Federal Aviation Administration (FAA): in the U.S. Department of Transportation, the agency chartered "to provide for the regulation and promotion of civil aviation in such manner as to best foster its development and safety, and to provide for the safe and efficient use of the airspace by both civil and military aircraft." The FAA was established in 1959.

federal bonds: see *bond, federal.*

federal budget expenditures: in the unified budget concept, expenditures of all federal agencies and trust funds. Expenditures are distinguished from net lending, and total budget outlays are the sum of expenditures and net lending. Expenditures of public enterprise funds and trust revolving funds are shown net of the receipts of such funds.

federal budget receipts: in the unified budget concept, receipts, net of refunds, of all federal agencies and trust funds. Interfund and intragovernmental transactions are excluded. Proceeds of borrowing or receipts of public enterprise and revolving funds are not included.

Federal Communications Commission (FCC): established in 1934 to regulate interstate and foreign commerce in communications by both wire and radio activity. Jurisdiction now includes radio, television, wire, cable, microwave, and satellite. The FCC consults with other government agencies on matters involving radio communications and with state regulatory commissions on telegraph and telephone matters; it also reviews applications for construction permits and relevant licenses.

Federal Contract Compliance Office (OFCC): a unit of the U.S. Department of Labor, created in 1962; responsible for drawing up uniform sets of rules to guide the government agencies that enforce affirmative action programs. Prohibits discrimination by race or sex by employers holding federal contracts.

Federal Corrupt Practices Act: see *Hatch Act.*

Federal Credit Union: a cooperative association organized under the Federal Credit Union Act for the purpose of accepting savings from people, making loans to them at low interest rates, and rendering other financial services to members.

Federal Crime Insurance: insurance against burglary, larceny, and robbery losses offered by the federal government in which the Federal Insurance Administration has determined that such insurance is not readily available from commercial companies. This Department of Housing and Urban Development program began in 1971.

federal debt limit: a limit imposed by law on the aggregate face amount of outstanding obligations issued, or guaranteed as to principal and interest, by the United States; guaranteed obligations held by the secretary of the Treasury are exempted.

federal deficit: a public or federal debt; the difference that exists between revenue and government expenditures.

Federal Deposit Insurance Corporation (FDIC): a government corporation that insures the deposits of all banks that are entitled to the benefits of insurance under the Federal Reserve Act. The FDIC was created through the Banking Act of 1933 and was affected by amendments of 1935. All national banks and all state banks that are members of the Federal Reserve System are required by law to be members of the FDIC. Mutual savings bank are also encouraged to join.

Federal Energy Administration (FEA): a federal agency launched in 1973 to develop and implement federal energy policy, including the allocation of resources. Absorbed in 1977 into the U.S. Department of Energy.

Federal Equal Credit Opportunity Act of 1977: legislation prohibiting discrimination when responding to credit requests on the basis of race, color, religion, national origin, sex, marital status, or age; because all or part of a person's income derives from any public assistance program; or because a person in good faith has exercised any right under the Truth in Lending Law. Gives married persons the right to have credit information included in the name of both the wife and the husband if both use or are responsible for the account. The right was created, in part, to ensure that credit histories will be available to women who are later divorced or widowed.

federal expenditures: federal purchases of goods and services, transfer payments, grants-in-aid to state and local governments, net interest paid, and subsidies, less current surplus of government enterprises.

Federal Farm Loan Act: established in 1916, this legislation was passed to provide long-term credit for farmers, to provide capital for agricultural development, to create standard forms of investment based upon farm loans, to furnish a market for U.S. bonds, to create government depositaries and financial agents for the United States, and for other purposes.

federal funds: funds available at a Federal Reserve Bank, including excess reserves of member banks and checks drawn in payment for purchases by the Federal Reserve Bank of government securities.

federal funds rate: the interest rate charged on loans by banks that have excess reserve funds (above the level required by the Federal Reserve) to those banks with deficient reserves. The Fed funds rate is closely watched as an early warning indication of major changes in the national economy. see *legal reserve*. [33]

federal government securities: all obligations of the U.S. government. see *Treasury bill, Treasury note.*

Federal Home Bank: one of 11 regional banks established in 1932 to encourage local thrift and home financing during the Depression. The banks are owned jointly by various savings and loan associations. The Federal Home Loan Bank Board serves as a management body.

Federal Home Loan Bank System: a system established in 1932 to serve as a mortgage credit reserve system for home mortgage lending institutions. Members may obtain advances on home mortgage collateral and may borrow from home loan banks under certain conditions. [44]

Federal Home Loan Mortgage Corporation: established in 1970, responsible for aiding the secondary residential mortgages sponsored by the Veterans Administration and Federal Housing Administration in addition to nongovernment protected residential mortgages.

Federal Housing Administration (FHA): the government agency that carries out the provisions of the National Housing Act, approved in June 1934. The FHA promotes the ownership of homes and also the renovation and remodeling of residences through government guaranteed loans to home owners.

Federal Housing Administration mortgage: a mortgage made in conformity with requirements of the National Housing Act and insured by the Federal Housing Administration. [22]

Federal Housing FHA Insured Loans: insured mortgages from private lending institutions to stimulate homeownership and rental opportunities to American families. Applicants who wish to participate in a single-family mortgage insurance program must apply to a HUD-approved mortgage lender, who then applies to HUD. Interest rates are set by the FHA on these loans. [66]

Federal Insurance Contributions Act (FICA): federal legislation that defines Social Security taxes and benefits. FICA deductions are made on paychecks to support this program. see *payroll tax.*

federal insurance reserve: a general loss reserve required to be established by a federal association under the rules and regulations of the Federal Savings and Loan Insurance Corporation. [59]

Federal Intermediate Credit Banks: regional banks created by Congress to provide intermediate credit for ranchers and farmers by rediscounting the agricultural paper of financial institutions.

federal internal revenue collections: total federal taxes collected through the Internal Revenue Service. These monies make up 99 percent of all federal taxes (customs and a few miscellaneous taxes are excluded). see *federal tax collections.*

Federal Labor Relations Authority: created on January 1, 1979, one of the major agencies to replace the Civil Service Commission, it is responsible for overseeing labor-management relations.

Federal Land Bank (FLB): supervised by the Farm Credit Association, one of 12 banks that offers long-term credit to farmers. Strictly speaking, the Land Banks are a competitor to thrifts. However, regulations limit their participation in housing loans to 15 percent of their total investments. Also, their money is limited to farmers and ranchers.

Federal Loan Bank: one of 12 district banks, originally established in 1916, to make available long-term mortgage loans, at equitable terms, to farmers to enable them to own their own farms. The Federal Loan Bank System is the largest holder of farm mortgages in the world.

Federal Maritime Commission: an

agency created in 1936 to regulate foreign and domestic ocean commerce, mainly by overseeing agreements reached by a variety of rate-making conferences of ship carries.

Federal Mediation and Conciliation Service (FMCS): an independent agency created in 1947 as the successor to the U.S. Conciliation Service. Its functions include providing mediators for labor-management disputes in which interstate commerce is involved.

Federal National Mortgage Association (FNMA): an independent agency, originally chartered in 1938 and reconstituted in 1954. Its major function is to purchase mortgages from banks, trust companies, mortgage companies, savings and loan associations, and insurance companies to help these institutions with their distribution of funds for home mortgages. Nicknamed "Fannie Mae."

Federal Open Market Committee (FOMC): the Federal Reserve System's most important policy-making group, with responsibility for creating policy for the system's purchase and sale of government and other securities in the open market.

Federal Power Commission (FPC): an agency established in 1930 to regulate interstate operations of private utilities in matters of their issuance of securities, rates, and location of sites. In 1977 the FPC was made part of the Department of Energy.

Federal Reserve Act: legislation signed by President Wilson on December 23, 1913, establishing the Federal Reserve System to manage the nation's money sypply.

Federal Reserve agent: chairman of the board of a Federal Reserve District Bank (a Class "C" director) who is responsible for maintaining the collateral for all Federal Reserve notes held within his bank.

Federal Reserve Bank: one of 12 banks created by and operating under the Federal Reserve System. Each Federal Reserve Bank has nine directors. The banks and districts are listed under *banker's bank.*

Federal Reserve Bank account: as mandated by Federal Reserve regulations, the account kept by all member banks and clearing member banks with a Federal Reserve Bank in its district. It shows the cash balance due from a Reserve Bank to guarantee that the member bank has sufficient legal reserves on hand.

Federal Reserve Bank collections account: shows the sum of monies for out-of-town checks distributed for collection by a Federal Reserve check collection system that are not presently available in reserve but being collected.

Federal Reserve Board: the seven-member governing body of the Federal Reserve System; the governors are appointed by the President, subject to Senate confirmation, for 14-year terms. Created in 1913 to regulate all national banks and state-chartered banks that are members of the Federal Reserve System, the board possesses jurisdiction over bank holding companies and also sets national money and credit policy.

Federal Reserve branch banks: see *banker's bank.*

Federal Reserve Bulletin: a monthly journal issued by the Board of Governors of the Federal Reserve System dealing with issues in banking and finance.

Federal Reserve Chart Book: a monthly and semiannual publication of the Board of Governors of the Federal Reserve System, presenting charts of interest to the financial community.

Federal Reserve check collection system: the system, established in 1916, by which the Fed accepts out-of-town checks from the banks at which they were deposited or cashed, routes the checks to drawees, and credits the sending bank. It handles over 60 million checks each business day.

Federal Reserve cities: see *banker's bank.*

Federal Reserve credit: the sum of the Federal Reserve credit as measured by the supply that its banks have given to member bank reserves. It is composed primarily of earning assets of the Federal Reserve Banks.

Federal Reserve notes: when certain areas require large volumes of currency, or in seasons of the year when the public demand for currency is very heavy, Federal Reserve Banks have the power under the Federal Reserve Act to issue notes. When the need for currency relaxes, Federal Reserve Banks retire these notes. Federal Reserve notes are issued to member banks through their respective Federal Reserve Banks in denominations of $1, $5, $10, $20, $50, $100, $500, $1000, $5000, and $10,000. Federal Reserve notes answer the need for an elastic currency with full legal tender status.

Federal Reserve notes of other banks:
the total amount of Federal Reserve notes held by Reserve Banks other than the Reserve Bank that issued them. [40]

Federal Reserve Open Market Committee: a committee of the Federal Reserve System that has complete charge of open market operations, through which the Fed influences the growth of the nation's money supply. It includes the members of the Board of Governors of the Federal Reserve System and five representatives of the 12 Federal Reserve Banks. [33]

Federal Reserve routing symbol: see *American Bankers Association.*

Federal Reserve System: the title given to the central banking system of the United States as established by the Federal Reserve Act of 1913. The system regulates money supply, determines the legal reserve of member banks; oversees the mint, effects transfers of funds, promotes and facilitates the clearance and collection of checks, examines member banks, and discharges other functions. The Federal Reserve System consists of 12 Federal Reserve Banks, their 24 branches, and the national and state banks that are members of the system. All national banks are stockholding members of the Federal Reserve Bank of their district. Membership for state banks or trust companies is optional. see *Federal Reserve Board.* see also *banker's bank.* [31]

Federal Reserve Wire Network: see *Fedwire.*

Federals: a name given to items drawn on banks in a large city in which a Federal Reserve Bank is located, although the banks do not belong to the city's clearinghouse association.

Federal Savings and Loan Association: one of the associations established by the Home Owners' Loan Act of 1933, and amended in the Home Owners' Loan Act of 1934, which brought existing and newly formed mutual savings banks and building and loan associations under a federal charter. see *Federal Savings and Loan Insurance Corporation.*

Federal Savings and Loan Insurance Corporation: an organization created in 1934 for the purpose of insuring the shares and accounts of all federal savings and loan associations and of such state-chartered savings and loan associations as apply for insurance and meet the requirements of the corporation. [39]

Federal Savings Association: a savings association chartered and regulated by the Federal Home Loan Bank Board. [59]

federal tax collections: all internal revenue collections, plus customs collections and railroad unemployment insurance taxes collected by the Railroad Retirement Board, before refunds.

Federal Tort Claims Act of 1946: permits the United States to be sued for property or personal damages under circumstances such that if the federal government were an individual, it would be liable. Before passage of this act, the government could be sued only with its permission.

Federal Trade Commission (FTC): established in 1914; the enabling legislation also declared unfair methods of competition illegal. Amended by the Wheeler-Lea Act of 1930; en-

forces antitrust laws; seeks voluntary compliance or civil remedies. see *Equal Credit Opportunity Act.*

Federal Wage-Hour Act: see *Fair Labor Standards Act of 1938.*

Fedwire: a communications network linking Federal Reserve Banks, branches, and member banks; used both to transfer funds and to transmit information. cf. *Bank Wire System.*

fee

(1) *banking:* an inheritable estate in land. cf. *fee simple estate, freehold.*

(2) *finance:* a remuneration for services.

fee checking account: a type of checking account on which a fixed fee is charged for each check written or item deposited. This distinguishes it from the regular checking account plan, which sometimes requires a minimum balance and the service charge is computed on a measured activity analysis of the account. The fixed fee may be charged before any checks are written, in which case the book of blank checks is sold to the depositor. The fixed fee may be charged at the time the checks or deposits are posted to the account, in which case the bookkeeper posts the service charge immediately after posting the check or deposit to the account. [10]

fees and royalties from direct investments: reported by companies with direct investments abroad. They represent income received by U.S. parent companies from their foreign affiliates for patent royalties, licensing fees, rentals, management services, other home office charges, and research and development. [73]

fee simple estate: an absolute fee; an estate of inheritance without limitation. This form of estate is not qualified by any other interest and upon the owner's death passes unconditionally to the heirs.

FEIA: see *Foreign Earned Income Act of 1978.*

felony: any major crime (e.g., murder, arson, rape) punishable by a greater penalty than for a misdemeanor or minor offense. In many states of the United States, felony is defined by statute as crimes punishable by imprisonment or death. see also *misdemeanor, tort.*

feoffment

(1) *general:* the granting of a fee.

(2) *banking:* the granting of land by the act of taking possession. see *enfeoff.*

FEPC: see *Civil Rights Act of 1964, Title VII.*

FF.&C.: see *full faith and credit.*

FFLA: see *Federal Farm Loan Act.*

FHA: see *Federal Housing Administration.*

FHB: see *Federal Home Bank.*

FHLBS: see *Federal Home Loan Bank System.*

FHLMC: see *Federal Home Loan Mortgage Corporation.*

FI: see *foreign investment.*

fiat money: money circulated by government decree and having no precious metal backing. see *gold exchange standard;* cf. *full-bodied money, real money.*

FICA: see *Federal Insurance Contributions Act.*

FICB: see *Federal Intermediate Credit Banks.*

Fid.: see *fiduciary.*

fidelity bond: see *bond, fidelity.*

fidelity insurance: coverage against loss from embezzlement or theft by employees.

fiduciary: an individual, corporation, or association, such as a bank, to whom certain property is given to hold in trust, according to an applicable trust agreement. The property is to be utilized or invested for the benefit of the property owner to the best ability of the fiduciary. Administrators and executors of estates, and trustees of organizations, are common examples of fiduciaries. Investments of trust funds, are usually restricted by law.

fiduciary accounting

(1) *general:* maintaining property accounts in the hands of a trustee, executor, or administrator.

(2) *banking:* estate accounting.

fiduciary bond: see *bond, fiduciary.*

fiduciary money (or standard): currency not secured completely by any precious metal. synonymous with *credit money.*

fiduciary return: an income tax return prepared by a fiduciary on behalf of a trust or estate, as distinguished from an "individual return." [37]

fiduciary service: a service performed by an individual or corporation acting in a trust capacity. A banking institution authorized to do a trust business may perform fiduciary services, for example, by acting as executor or administrator of estates, guardian of minors, and trustee under wills. [50]

field warehousing: an approach for receiving collateral pledged in business loans. The warehouseman usually leases part of the borrower's facility and appoints a custodian to care for the items.

fieri facias: "that you cause it to be made" (Latin). A court order directing the sheriff to impose a tax on goods or personal property of the defendant, to satisfy the judgment of a plaintiff.

FIFO (first in, first out)

(1) *general:* the term relates to inventory valuations, and the balance sheet figures for inventory should be qualified accordingly. This simply means that the cost shown for the first shipment of a particular item is used for valuations. This could inflate or deflate profits.

(2) *finance:* a method of computing dividends or interest and the effect withdrawals have on earnings for the period. The FIFO method is considered to be using the oldest money on deposit for withdrawals during the interest period. It was originally designed to discourage withdrawals by exacting the maximum penalty.

(3) see *LIFO.*

file

(1) *general:* any collection of informational items similar to one another in purpose.

(2) *law:* to place a legal document on public record.

fill

(1) *general:* to complete an order for goods or services.

(2) *investments:* to satisfy the demand for a security at a specific time by selling an amount equivalent to the quantity of shares bid for at the highest quoted price. see *hit the bid.*

fill (or kill) order: an order that must be filled immediately (or cancelled).

fin.: see *finance.*

final sales: the total of net sales to consumers, governments, and foreigners. Final sales exclude sales made to producers except sales of durable plant and machinery.

finance

(1) *general:* to raise money by sale of stock, bonds, or notes.

(2) *finance:* describes the theory and practice of monetary credit, banking, and comprehensive promotion methods. This theory covers investment, speculation, credits, and securities.

(3) *government:* to raise money by taxation or bond issue, and to administer revenue and expenditures in a governmental organization. More recently, this activity has become known as public finance.

finance, public: a special branch of finance dealing with the provision of means of payment to meet public or government expenditures.

finance bill: any draft drawn by one bank on a foreign bank against securities retained by the overseas institution.

finance charge: the cost of a loan in dollars and cents as required by the Truth in Lending Act. see *Truth in Lending Act of 1968.* [78]

finance company: any institution other than a bank that makes loans to businesses or individuals. see *sales finance company.*

finance unit: a nondelivery postal branch or station for financial services and acceptance of mail. [39]

Financial Accounting Standards Board (FASB): an independent accounting organization formed in 1973, responsible for creating "generally accepted accounting principles." FASB is a self-regulatory organization whose impact is on accounting firms and practitioners.

Financial Center Development Act of 1981: legislation of the State of Delaware, the act has provisions designed to alter the state's banking and tax codes in order to convince out-of-state banks to establish subsidiaries in Delaware. The tax provision, replacing a flat 8.7 percent franchise tax on banks, calls for a regressive income tax on banks starting at 8.7 percent and declining to 2.7 percent for all income over $30 million. The bill also includes an elimination of interest rate ceilings on all consumer transactions; permission for banks to charge customers additional expenses, such as cash withdrawal fees and transaction fees, on top of interest costs; permission for a lender to foreclose on a borrower's home in the event of default, and an allowance for a retroactive raise in interest rates on credit card transactions.

financial counseling: expert advice given to a family with respect to money and credit management. [55]

financial expense: the interest expense on long-term debts.

financial flexibility: the ability of an enterprise to take effective actions to alter the amount and timing of future cash flows so that it can respond to unexpected needs and opportunities. [80]

financial institution: an institution that uses its funds chiefly to purchase financial assets (deposits, loans, bonds) as opposed to tangible property. Financial institutions can be classified according to the nature of the principal claims they issue: nondeposit intermediaries include, among others, life and property/casualty insurance companies and pension funds, whose claims are the policies they sell, or the promise to provide income after retirement; depositary intermediaries obtain funds mainly by accepting deposits from the public.

Financial Institutions Regulatory and Interest Rate Control Act: federal legislation of 1978; modified authority to invest in state housing corporation obligations; increased Federal Savings and Loan Insurance Corporation insurance limits for IRA and Keogh accounts from $40,000 to $100,000; permitted FSLIC to issue cease-and-desist orders against associations, directors, officers, employees, and agents; authorized cease-and-desist orders against associations, holding companies, their subsidiaries, and service corporations; expanded criteria for removal of a director interlocks among depository institutions; created interagency Federal Bank Examination Council to encourage uniformity in financial institutions supervision; authorized Federal Home Loan Mortgage Corporation pruchase of secured home improvement loan packages; amended Consumer Credit Protection Act establishing rights and responsibilities for electronic funds transfer; established procedural safeguards for dissemination of financial institution records to federal agencies; extended Regulation Q authority for rate control and rate differential until December 15, 1980. [51]

financial intermediaries: organizations operating in money markets that permit buyers and sellers, borrowers, and lenders, to meet easily. see *financier.*

financial markets: the money and capital markets of the economy. The money markets buy and sell short-term credit instruments. The capital markets buy and sell long-term credit and equity instruments.

financial position: the status of a company, combining the assets and liabilities as listed on a balance sheet.

financial ratios: the relationship that exist between various items appearing in balance sheets and income accounts and occasionally other items. These ratios are used to measure and evaluate the economic condition and operating effectiveness of a firm.

financial reports: reports of union financial affairs required to be filed with the U.S. secretary of labor by the Taft-Hartley Act. [5].

financial solvency: a normal business condition: current assets are above current liabilities. cf. *insolvency.*

financial statement: any statement made by an individual, a proprietorship, a partnership, a corporation, an organization, or an association, regarding the financial status of the "legal entity."

Financial Times (of London): considered by professionals as one of the best English-language newspapers for business and financial news.

financier: an individual who earns a living by supplying money for other people's businesses and in turn receives a cash profit or retains a percentage of the business. see *financial intermediaries.*

finder's fee

(1) *general:* payment given to an individual for bringing together a buyer and seller.

(2) *banking:* payment to someone for acquiring a potential buyer with a property. A fee is usually paid when the seller and the buyer conclude an arrangement.

fine: a penalty charged a violator by a government, court, or other authority for breaking a law or rule.

fine tuning: the manipulation of discretionary monetary and fiscal policy to offset changes in the level of economic activity.

fireworks: slang, the rapid climb in price for a security or group of securities.

firm

(1) *general:* the acceptance of an obligation to perform, deliver, or accept, as "a firm bid," "a firm offer."

(2) *finance:* any business, corporation, proprietorship, or partnership.

(3) *law:* an unincorporated business or a partnership. Unlike a corporation, a firm is not recognized as a separate person apart from those managing it (i.e., it is not an entity).

firming of interest rate: a period during which interest rates are rising and the supply of money tends to become less plentiful. [67]

firming of the market: a period when security prices tend to stabilize around a certain level after a downward movement. [67]

firm order: a definite order than cannot be canceled. It may be written or verbal.

first board: the delivery dates for futures as determined by the administration of an exchange.

first deed of trust: a deed of trust that is recorded first and is the first lien.

first-generation computer: a computer utilizing vacuum tube components. This equipment was predominantly made from 1953 to 1960.

first in, first out: see *FIFO*.

first lien: a first mortgage. cf. *equal dignity*.

first mortgage: the mortgage on property that takes precedence over all other mortgages. A first lien. see also *prior lien, underlying mortgage*.

first notice day: first day on which transferable notices can be issued for delivery in a specified delivery month. [11]

first preferred stock: dividend stocks that are preferred over common stock of the corporation. It ranks ahead of the second preferred issue.

firsts: the top grade of any item.

first teller: the paying teller in a bank.

fiscal: relating to financial matters.

fiscal agency services: services performed by the Federal Reserve Banks for the U.S. government. These include maintaining accounts for the Treasury Department, paying checks drawn on the Treasury, and selling and redeeming Savings Bonds and other government securities. [1]

fiscal agent: a bank or trust company acting under a corporate trust agreement with a corporation. The bank or trust company may be appointed in the capacity of general treasurer of the corporation, or may be appointed to perform special functions as fiscal agent. The principal duties of a fiscal agent include the disbursement of funds for payment of dividends, redemption of bonds and coupons at maturity, and the payment of rents. [10]

fiscal charges: expenses or charges that are normal for a given type of business and must be incurred in order to engage in a given type of business.

fiscal dividend: the increase in federal revenues resulting from an increase in gross national product at any given level of tax rates.

fiscal drag: the tendency of a high-employment economy to be restrained from its full growth potential because it is incurring budgetary surpluses.

fiscalists: believers who insist that fiscal policy is the primary means for altering the level of economic activity by the government.

fiscal period: A 12-month accounting period for which business activities are reported.

fiscal policy: a planned course of action on budgetary issues.

fiscal year (FY)
(1) *general:* a corporation's accounting year. It can be any 12 consecutive months (e.g., February 1 of one year through January 31 of the next). Most companies operate on a calendar year basis.
(2) *government:* the fiscal year of the U.S. government begins October 1. Before 1976 the government's FY began on July 1.

five-case note: slang, a $5 bill.

five percent redemption fund: the amount of funds retained by all Federal Reserve Banks held on deposit with the U.S. Treasury.

five-spot: slang, a $5 bill.

fix: setting the cost of an item or service. cf. *price fixing*.

fixation: the setting of a price in the future, as used in commodity call purchase and call sale trades.

fixed annuity: an annuity contract providing payments that remain constant throughout the annuity period. These payments do not vary with investment experience.

fixed assets: permanent assets required for the normal conduct of a business, which normally are not converted into cash during the period after they were declared fixed (e.g., furniture, land, buildings). see *illiquid.*

fixed-balance bonus account: a savings account that pays earnings above the passbook rate if the balance in the account exceeds a specified minimum for a specified term. [59]

fixed budget: a corporation's budget, set for a specific time period in advance that is not subject to change during the budgetary period.

fixed capital: capital invested, usually by stock-and bondholders; as distinguished from current assets, which are partly supplied by banks.

fixed charges: business expenses that are not related to the level of operations.

fixed cost or expense: a cost or expense, for a fixed period and a range of activity, that does not change in total but becomes progressively smaller per unit as the volume increases. synonymous with "*period costs*"; see also *capacity costs;* cf. *direct cost.*

fixed exchange rate: a concept within the European Monetary System, where all members except Britain maintain fixed exchange rates be- tween their currencies, promoting monetary stability in Europe and throughout the world. see also *European Monetary System.*

fixed income: income that does not fluctuate with the general price level. People on fixed income have the most difficulty when prices are rising (e.g., retired pensioners in a period of inflation).

fixed-income market: any debt-bearing instrument, among them U.S. Government bonds, tax-exempt bonds, corporate bonds, financial futures, and money market funds.

fixed investment: measures additions to and replacements of private capital brought about through purchase of durable equipment and structures for business and residential purposes. Fixed investment expenditures are reflected in GNP in two ways. First, capital investment increases GNP by the value of the asset in the period in which the investment is made. Second, the effects of previous years' fixed investments show in the products produced with the help of the capital. These products are of all types: consumer goods, additional capital goods, exports, and government purchases. [73]

fixed liabilities: all liabilities that will not mature within the ensuing fiscal period (e.g. mortgages due 20 years hence, bonds outstanding).

fixed price: the lowest sale price of a new issue, below which a purchase cannot be made. This price is usually set by the underwriter of the security.

fixed rate: see *fixed exchange rate.*

fixed register asset: a record (book, card, or sheet) that contains the details of the cost price and the depreciation of the fixed assets. [73]

fixed test asset: the ratio of fixed assets to fixed liabilities.

fixed-to-tangible-net-worth asset: fixed assets represent depreciated book values of buildings, leasehold improvements, machinery, furniture, fixtures, tools, and other physical equipment, plus land, if any, and valued at cost or appraised market value. The ratio is obtained by dividing fixed assets by tangible net worth. Ordinarily, the relationship between fixed assets and tangible net worth should not exceed 100 percent for a manufacturer, and 75 percent for a wholesaler or retailer. Beyond these limits, so disproportionate an amount of capital is frozen into machinery or "brick and mortar" that the necessary margin of operating funds for carrying receivables, inventories, and day-to-day cash outlays, as well as maturing obligations, becomes too narrow. This not only exposes the business to the hazards of unexpected developments, such as a sudden change in the business climate, but creates possible drains on income in the form of heavy carrying and maintenance charges should a serious portion of fixed assets lie idle for any length of time. [61]

fixing the price

(1) *finance:* establishing a price on something arbitrarily rather than through the free enterprise system.

(2) *investments:* computing the price at which a commodity will be billed for rapid delivery. see *spot market.*

fixture

(1) *general:* any equipment or furnishing (e.g., lamps, shelves) added to rented space for purposes of aiding in business acitivity.

(2) *law:* any chattle or personal property that is attached to real property in a permanent fashion.

flagging an account: temporarily suspending activity on an account until brought up to date or for other relevant reason. see *rubricated account.*

flag of convenience: the national flag flown by a ship that is registered in a country other than that of its owners (e.g., to escape taxes and high domestic wages).

flat

(1) *finance:* with no interest.

(2) *investments:* describes the price at which a bond is traded, including consideration for all unpaid accruals of interest. Bonds that are in default of interest or principal are traded flat. Income bonds, which pay interest only to the extent earned, are usually traded flat. cf. *loaned flat.*

flat broke: slang, penniless.

flat cancellation: the cancellation of a policy as of what would have been its effective date, before the company has assumed liability. This requires the return in full of any paid premiums. cf. *pro rate cancellation.*

flat income bond: see *bond, flat income.*

flation: neither inflation or deflation; a period of economic stability. cf. *creeping inflation.*

FLB

(1) see *Federal Land Bank.*

(2) see *Federal Loan Bank.*

fleece: slang, to take money or property from an unknowing person (the "sheep") by unfair activity. synonymous with *swindle.*

Fletcher-Rayburn Act: see *SEC*.

flexible account: see *charge account*.

flexible budget: a budget, usually referring to overhead costs, that is established for a range rather than for a single level of activity. Direct materials and labor are sometimes included in the flexible budget.

flexible exchange rates: where exchange rates of varying world currencies freely change in reaction to supply and demand conditions, free from governmental maneuvers to hold a fixed rate where one currency is exchanged for another.

flexible loan insurance plan: a new type of mortgage, this device calls for using a portion of the borrower's down payment to set up a savings account. The account is then pledged over to the lender and gradually drawn upon to supplement the low monthly payments made by the borrower during the initial years of the loan. Popularly referred to as "flip." An example of a *pledged-account mortgage*.

flexible mortgage: there are two types. see *renegotiable-rate mortgage* and *variable-rate mortgage*.

flexible-payment mortgage: an interest-only type of loan for the first five years. Two major restrictions apply: each monthly payment must cover at least the interest due, and after five years, payments must be fully amortizing. A rarely used mortgage because it offers the home buyer only a slight reduction in monthly payments during the early years. see also *graduated-payment mortgage, pledged-account mortgage, reverse-annuity mortgage, rollover mortgage, variable-rate mortgage*.

flier: a speculative purchase of investment, usually made by an individual who does not usually speculate or actively trade in the market.

flight of capital: the movement of capital, which has usually been converted into a liquid asset, from one place to another to avoid loss or to increase gain.

flip: acronym for *flexible loan insurance plan*.

float

(1) *banking:* describes the amount of funds in the process of collection represented by checks in the possession of one bank but drawn on other banks, either local or out of town; the value of checks that have been covered by the Federal Reserve but for which the Federal Reserve has not yet collected from the bank on which the check was written. see *uncollected funds*.

(2) *investments:* the portion of a new security that has not yet been bought by the public. cf. *undigested securities*.

floatation (flotation)

(1) *finance:* the process of financing a business activity.

(2) *investments:* launching an issue of securities. see *float*.

floating assets: synonymous with *current assets*.

floating capital: funds that are not a permanent investment, (i.e., invested in items manufactured). synonymous with *working capital*.

floating charge: a business loan that is secured on assets rather than on a particular item. The lender has priority of repayment from the fund of assets that exist when a receiving order is made against the firm.

floating currency: one whose value in terms of foreign currency is not kept stable (on the basis of the par value or a fixed relationship to some other currency) but instead is allowed, without a multiplicity of exchange rates, to be determined (entirely or to some degree) by market forces. Even where a currency is floating, the authorities may influence its movements by official intervention; if such intervention is absent or minor, the expression "clean float" is sometimes used. [42]

floating debt: any short-term obligation; usually, the portion of the public debt held in Treasury bills or other short-term obligations.

floating-rate notes: tradable-like bonds, but with interest rates adjusted every six months to reflect a six-month interbank offered rate.

floating rates: the automatic determination of appropriate exchange rates by market forces, not a nation's reserve holdings. Nations that do not follow these rates are pressured into line; otherwise, they would see the value of their currency driven to unacceptably low levels or driven up to the point where no other nation would be able to purchase their goods.

floating securities

(1) securities purchased for speculation and resale, retained in the name of a broker.

(2) stock of a corporation ready for sale on the open market.

(3) new issues of securities that have not been completely purchased.

floating supply: in municipal bond terminology, the overall amount of securities believed to be available for immediate purchase, in the hands of dealers and speculators who wish to sell as distinct from investors who may be willing to sell only for a special reason. [67]

float one: slang, to cash a check or take a loan.

floor

(1) *government:* as distinguished from ceiling, the minimum level determined by regulation, law or contract for wages, prices, and so on.

(2) *investments:* the huge trading area where stocks and bonds are bought and sold on an exchange. see also *pit*.

floor broker: a member of a stock exchange who executes orders on the floor of the exchange to buy or sell listed securities.

floor limit: the largest amount for which a merchant may accept noncash payment (check or credit card) without obtaining an authorization. A zero floor limit calls for authorization for every transaction, and this is becoming more feasible as the time and cost of obtaining authorization decline.

floor trader: any member of the stock exchange who trades on the floor for his own account. An exchange member who executes his own trades by being personally present in the pit or place provided for futures trading. [20]

flotation: see *floatation*.

flowchart

(1) *general:* a graphical representation of the definition, analysis, or solution of a problem, in which symbols are used to represent opera-

tions, data, flow, equipment, and other variables.

(2) **operations research:** a system analysis tool that displays a picture of a procedure. May be general or detailed. see *methods study.*

flower bond: see *bond, flower.*

flow-through method: an accounting method under which decreases or increases in state or federal income taxes resulting from the use of liberalized depreciation and the investment tax credit for income tax purposes are carried down to net income in the year in which they are realized. [3]

FLRA: see *Federal Labor Relations Authority.*

FLSA: see *Fair Labor Standards Act of 1938.*

fluctuation: the ups and downs of prices (see, e.g., *erratic fluctuations*). see *hedging, yo-yo stocks.*

fluid capital: see *floating capital, working capital.*

fluid savings: savings that have neither been spent nor invested.

flurries: unexpected, short-lived price fluctuations in the trading of securities, usually brought on by news.

fly-by-night activity: figuratively, an unsound operation; literally, one that is expected to move under cover of darkness to avoid payment to creditors.

FMAN: February, May, August, November (quarterly interest payments or dividends).

FMC: see *Federal Maritime Commission.*

FMCS: see *Federal Mediation and Conciliation Service.*

FMV: see *fair market value.*

FNMA: see *Federal National Mortgage Association.*

FOB: freight (free) on board: a term identifying the point from which a store is to pay transportation on incoming shipments. When the shipping point is FOB, the store must pay all charges from the vendor's shipping point. When the shipping point is FOB store, the vendor must pay all charges up to the store's receiving dock. cf. *free alongside ship.*

FOIA: see *Freedom of Information Act.*

fold: slang, to go into bankruptcy.

folding money: slang, paper banknotes.

FOMC: see *Federal Open Market Committee.*

for a turn: a commitment in a stock made with the expectation of gaining a quick, though small profit.

forbearance: surrendering the right to enforce a valid claim in return for a promise. This consideration binds a promise.

forbearance agreement: a verbal or written agreement providing that the association will delay exercising its rights (in the case of a mortgage loan, foreclosure) as long as the borrower performs certain agreed-upon actions. [59]

for cash

(1) **general:** items or services sold for 100 percent of funds.

(2) **investments:** a transaction demanding that sold stocks be delivered to the purchaser on the same day.

force account: a method employed in the construction and/or maintenance of fixed assets whereby a governmental unit's own personnel are used instead of an outside contractor. [49]

forced billing: a means used to secure payments for freight delivery when no bill can be found.

forced loan: any draft drawn against uncollected funds that is honored by a bank with the expectation that the uncollected monies will clear, becoming a forced loan should the uncollected funds not clear for reasons of insufficient balance, forgery of the draft, and the like.

forced sale: the sale or loss of property when one does not wish to dispose of it, as in bankruptcy. synonymous with *judicial sale.* see *involuntary alienation.*

forced saving: occurs when consumers are prevented from spending a portion of their income on consumption.

forecasting: projecting events of the future utilizing current data.

foreclose (foreclosure): a legal process whereby a mortgagor of a property is deprived of his or her interest therein, usually by means of a court-administered sale of the property. see *deed in lieu of foreclosure, referee's foreclosure deed;* cf. *mother hubbard clause;* see also *equity of redemption, shortcut foreclosure.*

foreign bank: any bank other than the subject bank. Items of other banks included with the bank's are considered to be on a "foreign bank." The term may also refer to a banking concern outside the continental limits of the United States. [31]

foreign bill of exchange
(1) the system by which the balances arising out of transactions between countries are settled.
(2) the currency used in making the settlement. [50]
(3) a draft, directing that payment be made in a foreign currency.

foreign company: a company in any other state than the one in which it is incorporated or chartered.

foreign correspondent: a bank in another nation serving as agent for a U.S. bank maintaining sufficient balances.

Foreign Corrupt Practices Act of 1977: federal legislation designed to avoid improper corporate payments abroad. Under the act, corporate violators can be fined up to $1 million and others are liable for fines up to $10,000—not payable by the company—and five years in prison.

foreign crowd: the name given for New York Stock Exchange traders of foreign bonds.

foreign currency: the currency of any foreign country which is the authorized medium of circulation and the basis for record keeping in that country. Foreign currency is traded in by banks either by the actual handling of currency or checks, or by establishing balances in foreign currency with banks in those countries. [10]

foreign currency account: an account maintained in a foreign bank in the currency of the country in which the bank is located. Foreign currency accounts are also maintained by banks in the United States for depositors. When such accounts are kept, they usually represent that portion of the carrying bank's foreign currency account that is in excess of its contractual requirements. [10]

foreign direct investments: the flow of foreign capital into U.S. business enterprise in which foreign residents have significant control. [73]

Foreign Earned Income Act of 1978: extends pre-1976 tax rules for U.S. citizens working abroad to tax years commencing with 1978. Thereafter, a whole new set of deductions reflect excess living costs abroad.

foreign exchange (F/X): instruments used for international payments (i.e., currency, checks, drafts, and bills of exchange).

foreign exchange desk: the foreign exchange trading desk at the New York Federal Reserve Bank. The desk undertakes operations in the exchange markets for the account of the Federal Open Market Committee, as agent for the U.S. Treasury and as agent for foreign central banks. see also *desk, the.* [1]

foreign exchange markets: those in which the monies of different countries are exchanged. Foreign exchange holdings—sometimes referred to as foreign exchange—are holdings of current or liquid claims denominated in the currency of another country. [73]

foreign exchange rate: the price of one currency in terms of another.

foreign exchange transactions: the purchase or sale of one currency with another. Foreign exchanges rates refer to the number of units of one currency needed to purchase one unit of another, or the value of one currency in terms of another. [1]

foreign income: income earned by Americans from work performed in another country. Under the Tax Reform Act of 1976, the amount of annual income that can be excluded from taxable income by Americans working abroad was reduced from $20,000 (in some cases from $25,000) to $15,000. Foreign employees of U.S. charitable organizations are able to exclude $20,000 each year.

foreign inquiry: an inquiry made to a credit bureau for information on a person or firm from an other-than-normal service area of the bureau. [41]

foreign investment: the purchase of assets from abroad.

foreign items
(1) transit items payable at an "out-of-town" bank.
(2) bills of exchange, checks, and drafts that are payable at a bank outside the jurisdiction of the U.S. government. [10]

foreign trade multiplier: the concept that fluctuations in exports and/or imports may lead to significant variations in national income.

forex: short, for *foreign exchange.*

forfeit: a thing lost to its owner by way of penalty for some default or offense.

forfeiture: the automatic loss of cash, property, or rights, as punishment for failure to comply with legal provisions and as compensation for the resulting losses or damages.

Forg.: see *forgery.*

forged check: one on which the drawer's signature has been forged. [50]

forgery: false writing or alteration of an instrument to injure another person or with fraudulent intent to deceive (e.g., signing, without permission, another person's name on a check to obtain money from the bank).

forgery bond: see *bond, forgery.*

forint: monetary unit of Hungary.

form: the insurance policy itself and any endorsements or riders that may be included. [56]

formula clause: the provision of a will or trust agreement stating a formula whereby the executor or trustee can determine the federal estate-tax value of property; usually employed in connection with the marital deduction under the Revenue Act of 1954. [37]

formula investing: an investment technique. One formula calls for the shifting of funds from common shares to preferred shares or bonds as the market, on average, rises above a certain predetermined point—and the return of funds to common share investments as the market average declines. see *dollar (cost) averaging.* [20]

FORTRAN: acronym for the formula translation system. A language primarily used to express computer programs by arithmetic formulas.

forward buying: the buying of an actual or spot commodity where delivery is for the future rather than as a current delivery.

forward commitment: an investor's agreement to make or purchase a mortgage loan on a specified future date. [22]

forward delivery: see *deferred delivery.*

forward exchange: a foreign bill of exchange purchased or sold at a stated price that is payable at a given date.

forward exchange transaction: a purchase or sale of foreign currency for future delivery. Standard periods for forward contracts are one, three, and six months. [42]

forwarding: carrying information from one page to another in an account or journal.

forward market: the claim to sell or purchase securities, foreign currencies, and so on, at a fixed price at a given future date. This market is one that deals in futures.

forward prices: a proposal for minimizing price uncertainty and encouraging greater stability in farming by utilizing the price system as an adjustment mechanism.

foul bill of lading: a bill of lading identifying shortage or damage that existed at the time of shipment.

founder's stock: stock given to the developers or founders of a new corporation for services rendered by them.

fourth market: the buying and selling of unlisted securities directly between investors.

FP: see *fixed price.*

FPC: see *Federal Power Commission.*

FPS: see *first preferred stock.*

Fr.: see *franc.*

FRA: see *Federal Reserve Act.*

fraction: a term generally applied to holdings of less than one share, resulting from rights and stock dividends. Because they are not entitled to dividends, they are usually disposed of by sale or rounded out, by the purchase of additional fractions, to full shares. [37]

fractional currency: any currency that is smaller than a standard money unit (e.g., any coin worth less than $1).

fractional lot: less than a round lot. see *fraction.*

fractional reserve: under the U.S. commercial banking system, a bank is required by law to maintain only a portion of any deposit as reserves. The difference is then permitted to be lent to borrowers.

franc: monetary unit of Belgium, Benin, Burundi, Cameroons, Central African Empire, Chad, Comoros, Congo (Brazzaville), Dahomey, Djibouti, France, French Somaliland, Gabon, Guadeloupe, Ivory Coast, Liechtenstein, Luxembourg, Madagascar, Malagasy, Mali, Martinique, Monaco, New Caledonia, New Hebrides Islands, Niger, Oceania, Reunion Island, Rwanda, Senegal, Switzerland, Tahiti, Togo, and Upper Volta.

franchise
(1) *general:* a privilege given to a dealer for the distribution of a manufacturer's product.
(2) *government:* a privilege given by a government to utilize public property or to create a monopoly.
(3) *law:* a certificate of incorporation.

franchise clause: provides that payment shall not be made unless the loss or damage equals or exceeds a specified amount, known as the "franchise."

franchise tax: the tax levied on a corporation to conduct business under its corporate name.

franco delivery: the full delivery of items to a consignee, with all charges paid, as with a prepaid delivery.

franken: monetary unit of Liechtenstein.

fraud: intentional misrepresentation of the truth in order to deceive another person. Aspects of fraud include the false representation of fact, intentionally made (see *scienter*), with the intent that the deceived person act thereon; knowledge that

the statement would deceive; and knowledge that the person deceived acted leading to his injury. see also *bad faith, deceit, lapping, voidable contract.*

fraudulent conveyance: conveyance of property entered into by a debtor with the objective of defrauding creditors.

Frazier-Lemke-Long Act: see *Farm Bankruptcy Act of 1933.*

FRB: see *Federal Reserve Bank.*

Freddie Macs: the participation certificates guaranteed by the Federal Home Loan Mortgage Corp. The minimum investment is $100,000 and there is virtually no odd-lot market.

free alongside ship (FAS): when an exporter delivers merchandise "free alongside ship," he pays all charges involved up to the moment of delivery. cf. *FOB, free overside.*

free and open market: a market in which supply and demand are freely expressed in terms of price. Contrasts with a controlled market, in which supply, demand, and price may all be regulated. [20]

free astray: freight that is miscarried or delivered at the wrong location, then is billed and forwarded to the correct location without additional charge.

free balance: the minimum balance that a commercial bank allows a checking account customer to maintain without being charged a service fee. The free balance varies by commercial bank.

free bond: see *bond, free.*

free check storage account: an example of what the banking industry calls check safekeeping, or truncation. It is a process that cuts off the normal cycle of check flow—from check to payee to bank and back to the check-writer—before it is completed.

free crowd: see *active crowd.*

Freedom of Information Act (FOIA) of 1966: federal legislation, amended in 1974 and 1976, establishing the principle that the public has the right, with certain exceptions, to information collected and kept by federal government agencies. Its aim is to make government records and decision making more accessible to public scrutiny by preventing agencies from arbitrarily withholding information. see also *Fair Credit Reporting Act of 1971.*

freedom shares: U.S. savings notes sold from 1967 through the mid-1970s.

free enterprise: the condition under which a firm or individual is able to function competitively without excessive government restrictions.

free goods: items that are so abundant that it is not profitable to attempt to charge for them (e.g., sunlight).

freehold: the holding of a piece of land, an office, and so on, for life, or with the right to pass it on through inheritance.

free list: a statement prepared by a customs department of items that are not liable to the payment of duties.

free market: describes the unrestricted movement of items in and out from the market, unhampered by the existence of tariffs or other trade barriers.

free (freight) on board: see *FOB.*

free overside: in export price quotations: the seller pays all costs and accepts full responsibility for the goods until they have been safely unloaded at the place of importation in a foreign country; thereafter, the buyer will pay all costs such as customs duty.

free port: a port where no duties are paid on either imports or exports.

free reserves: a Federal Reserve Bank term describing the margin by which excess reserves exceed the bank's borrowings.

free riding

(1) *investments:* prohibited by law, the buying and rapid sale of securities, where no personal funds are given for the original purchase.

(2) *investments:* the withholdings by brokerage firms of new stocks that are expected to climb higher than the initial public offering. Prohibited by the SEC.

free supply: a term in the commodities industry where total stocks less what is owned or controlled by the government.

free surplus: that portion of retained earnings available for common stock dividends, that is, after deducting any amounts appropriated or legally restricted by reason of such items as preferred stock dividends in arrears, the repurchase of treasury stock, or loan agreements calling for a minimum cash balance or a minimum liability ratio. Dividends payable in common stock are a general exception to most restrictions on dividends arising from loan agreements. [43]

free trade: trade among countries in the absence of policy restrictions that may interfere with its flow.

free trade zone: where imports are distributed with little or no customs duties and regulations.

free working capital: synonymous

with *working capital* and *net current monetary assets.*

freeze

(1) *general:* to fix prices at present levels. as with a price freeze. A freeze rarely takes place except during national crises or wartime.

(2) *government:* governmental seizure or impounding of property, goods, and so on. This action demands an executive order or the passage of a law, usually during emergencies.

(3) see also entires under *frozen.*

freight: all merchandise, goods, products, or commodities shipped by rail, air, road, or water, other than baggage, express mail, or regular mail.

freight absorption: when a seller does not charge a customer with freight out, the seller is said to have absorbed the freight.

freight allowed: an agreement whereby a business pays the transportation charges on incoming goods but is permitted to charge back all or part of that cost to the vendor.

freight inward: freight paid on shipments received.

freight outward: freight paid by a seller on outgoing customer shipments.

Friedmanite: one who upholds the monetary theories of Milton Friedman, who advocates direct control of money supply by governments in lieu of tax manipulations, government projects, and so on. cf. *neo-Keynesian.*

friendly counter: a newer trend in bank lobby design. The friendly counter is an open counter where depositors and customers of a bank may transact business with the teller. The counter has no grille work other than a gate that the teller may open for the depositor to pass large packages over the counter. The friendly counter has a ledge constructed over the counter. Forms, working supplies, etc., are under this ledge, and are beyond the reach of persons who might try to perpetrate illegal acts in the bank. [10]

fringe benefits: nonwage benefits (paid vacations pensions, health and welfare provisions, life insurance, etc.) whose cost is borne in whole or in part by the employer.

frozen

(1) *general:* not easily available.

(2) *finance:* when the conversion of something of value into money is impossible, the thing is said to be frozen. cf. *liquid.*

frozen account

(1) an account on which payments have been suspended until a court order or legal process again makes the account available for withdrawal. The account of a deceased person is frozen pending the distribution by a court order grant to the new lawful owners of the account. see *deceased account, sequestered account;* cf. *blocked accounts.*

(2) where a dispute has arisen regarding the true ownership of an account, it is frozen to preserve the existing assets until legal action can determine the lawful owners of the asset.

frozen asset: any asset that cannot be used by its owner because of pending or on-going legal action. The owner cannot use the asset; nor can he or she dispose of it until the process of the law has been completed and a decision passed down from the courts.

FRS: see *Federal Reserve System.*

FS

(1)   see *financial statement.*

(2)   see *futures spread.*

FSLA: see *Federal Savings and Loan Association.*

FSLIC: see *Federal Savings and Loan Insurance Corporation.*

FTC: see *Federal Trade Commission.*

FTCA: see *Federal Tort Claims Act of 1946.*

fudge factor: to offset errors made by economists, an adjustment of model findings to fit known facts. This factor is introduced whenever its forecasts appear to be suspiciously out of line with the real world.

full-bodied money: gold; currency that is worth its face value as a commodity. cf. *fiat money.*

full-cost pricing: the practice that includes all appropriate manufacturing costs in determining inventory.

full coverage: any form of insurance coverage that provides for payments of losses in full, subject to the limit of the policy, without application of a deductible. cf. *ordinary life.*

full disclosure: as described by the Securities Exchange Act of 1934; every company that has securities listed on an exchange must register with the SEC and file annual and other reports disclosing financial and other data for the information of the investing public. Management must also disclose basic financial information used in stockholder's meetings.

full faith and credit: a pledge of the general taxing power for the payment of obligations.

full faith and credit debt: a municipality's debt that is a direct obligation of the municipality.

full liability: liability not shared with others.

full lot: usually, 100 shares of stock traded on the New York Stock Exchange. synonymous with *round lot* or *board lot.* cf. *odd-lot orders.*

full-service bank: a commercial bank that is capable of meeting the total financial needs of the banking public. Because the charters of some financial institutions limit their activities, this term draws attention to the advantages enjoyed by customers of a commercial bank. cf. *Hinky Dinky, multiple banking, one-stop banking.*

full stock: an equity stock with a par value or $100.

fully funded: a method of financing a pension or annuity plan whereby its entire cost is fully provided on an accrual basis. [52]

fully paid stocks: legal issues where the corporation has received at least the equivalent of its par value in goods, services, or currency.

fully registered: a term generally applied to bonds that are registered as to principal and income. In this form, a bond is not negotiable and interest is remitted by the disbursing agent to the registered owners. [37]

fully vested: describes an employee covered by a pension plan who has rights to all the benefits bought with the employer's contributions to the plan, even when the worker is not employed by that employer at retirement.

functional costing: classifying costs by allocating them to the various functions performed (warehousing, delivery, billing, etc.).

functional discount: a deduction taken to effect differing prices to different customers (e.g., retailers get 40 percent off the list price, wholesalers 40 to 50 percent off).

functional income distributions: wages, rents, interests, and profits paid to manufacturers in return for supplying their labor, land, capital, and management talents.

functional obsolescence: created by structural defects that reduce a property's value and/or market ability.

fund

(1) *general:* an asset of any organization set aside for a particular purpose. Not to be confused with general fund. see *sinking fund.*

(2) *finance:* cash, securities, or other assets placed in the hands of a trustee or administrator to be expanded as defined by a formal agreement.

fund accounts: all accounts necessary to set forth the financial operations and financial condition of a fund. [49]

fundamental research: an analysis of industries and companies based on such factors as sales, assets, earnings, products or services, markets, and management. As applied to the economy, fundamental research includes consideration of gross national product, interest rates, unemployment, inventories, and savings, see also *technical research.* [20]

fundamentals: a Wall Street school of thought that purports to predict stock market behavior by examining the vital statistics of a stock, the frim's management, earnings, and so on.

fund balance: the excess of the assets of a fund over its liabilities and reserves except in the case of funds subject to budgetary accounting where, prior to the end of a fiscal period, it represents the excess of the fund's assets and estimated revenues for the period over its liabilities, reserves, and appropriations for the period. [49]

fund balance receipts: receipts that increase the fund balance of a fund but which are not property included in current revenues. Examples are taxes and accounts receivable previously written off as uncollectible. [49]

fund balance sheet: a balance sheet for a single fund. see *fund.* [49]

funded debt

(1) *general:* exists when the method of paying off the debt and its interest is determined for specific periods.

(2) *finance:* usually, interest-bearing bonds of debentures of a company; may include long-term bank loans but does not include short loans or preferred or common stock. [20]

funded debts to net working capital: funded debts are all long-term obligations, as represented by mortgages, bonds, debentures, term loans, serial notes, and other types of liabilities maturing more than one year from the statement date. This ratio is obtained by dividing funded debt by net working capital. Analysts tend to compare funded debts with net working capital in determining whether or not long-term debts are in proper proportion. Ordinarily, this relationship should not exceed 100 percent. [4]

funded debt unmatured: unmatured debt (other than equipment obligations), maturing more than one year from date of issue. [18]

funded deficit: a deficit eliminated through the sale of bonds issued for that purpose. see also *bond funding.* [49]

funded insurance trust: an insurance trust in which, in addition to life insurance policies, cash and securities have been placed in trust to provide sufficient income for the payment of premiums and other charges on or assessments against the insurance policies. [32]

fund group: a group of funds which are similar in purpose and character. For example, several special revenue funds constitute a fund group. [49]

funding: the gathering together of outstanding debts of a business, leading to a reissuing of new bonds or obligations for the purpose of paying off debts.

funding bond: see *bond, funding.*

funds: a sum of money or stock convertible to money, assets. [61]

funds, corporate: a general funds mix of industrial and utility issues of varying maturities. Typically, about half the securities mature in more than 20 years. High-yield funds have less than 20-year maturity periods.

funds, government: the U.S. government has a large selection of load and no-load funds of high quality.

funds, municipal: most big fund sponsors have muncipal bond funds, some general funds with securities of good grade, and some "high-yield" filled with speculative issues.

fund surplus: see *fund balance.*

fungible: describes goods or securities, any unit is the equal of any other like unit (e.g., wheat, corn).

funny money: convertible preferred stocks, convertible bonds, options, and warrants that appear to have characteristics of common stock equity but which did not reduce reported earnings per share before 1969.

future depreciation
(1) that loss from present value which will occur in the future.
(2) sometimes used to indicate the future annual charge necessary to recapture the present building value over its economic life or the annual amount necessary to amortize total investment. [6]

future estate
(1) *general:* an estate developed for the purpose of possession, to be taken at an identified later date or upon occurrence of a future event.
(2) *law:* referred to as a nonpossessory estate.

future income: earnings or other income which seems to be reasonably certain for some time to come. [41]

futures
(2) *finance:* foreign currencies bought or sold based on a rate that is quoted as of some future date.
(2) *investments:* contracts for the sale and delivery of commodites at some future time, made with the expectation that no commodity will be received immediately. see *gray market, hedging, Tax Reform Act of 1976.*

futures call: the sale of commodities where delivery is made upon the request of the seller on any trading date for a specified month.

futures commission broker: a firm or party engaged in soliciting or accepting and handling orders for the purchase or sale of any commodity for future delivery on or subject to the rules of any contract market and who, in or in connection with such solicitations or acceptance of orders, accepts any money, securities, or property (or extends credit in lieu thereof) to margin any trades or contracts that result therefrom. They must be licensed under the Commodity Exchange Act when handling business in commodities covered thereby. [2]

futures commission merchant: see *futures commission broker.*

futures contract: the right to buy or sell a commodity at a specified price on a specified future date. The price is established when the contract is made in open auction on a futures exchange.

futures exchange: an organization created for the trading of commodity futures.

futures market: any commodity exchange trading in futures.

futures spread: the simultaneous purchase and sale of contracts in either the same or different commodities. In the case where one commodity is involved, the contracts must be in different delivery months. The aim of a futures spread is to take advantage of the difference, or spread, in the prices of two future contracts that have some direct economic relation to each other. A trader buys one contract, and sells the other short—sells it without owning it—in the hope that one part will move more than the other. see *spread, straddle.*

future sum: the money that a borrower agrees to repay for an obligation. It is the interest or discount, plus service or other charges, added to the total amount borrowed.

future worth: the equivalent value at a future date on time value of money.

FV: see *face value.*

F/X: see *foreign exchange.*

FY: see *fiscal year.*

G: gold.

GA

   (1) see *general account.*

   (2) see *general average.*

   (3) see *gross asset.*

GAAP: generally accepted accounting principles. see *Financial Accounting Standards Board.*

gain: any benefit, profit, or advantage, as opposed to a loss.

gain on disposal: the sale of a noncurrent asset for more than book value.

galloping inflation: the rapid and unlimited rise of prices; swiftly increasing inflation that, if not controlled and minimized, could lead to a major crisis in the economy. synonymous with "hyperinflation," "runaway inflation."

GAD: see *General Accounting Office.*

garbage: unwanted and meaningless information in computer memory or on tape. see *GIGO.*

garnishee: a debtor of a defendant who possesses money or property that a third party (a plaintiff) wishes to acquire to satisfy a debt due him or her by the defendant; an individual upon whom a garnishment is served.

garnishment: a writ from a court directing an employer to withhold all or part of the money due an employee in wages and to pay such funds to the court or to the plaintiff in the action (the person to whom the employee is indebted) until a given debt is liquidated. cf. *offset.*

gateway: a place at which freight is interchanged or interlined between carriers or where a carrier joins two operating authorities for the provision of through service.

gather in the stops: to sell a security in sufficient supply to lower the price to a level where numerous stop orders are known to be entered. synonymous with *uncover the stops.* see *snowballing.*

GATT: see *General Agreement on Tariffs and Trade.*

GAW: see *guaranteed annual wage.*

GB: see *bond, guaranteed.*

GD

   (1) see *good delivery.*

   (2) see *gross debt.*

GE: see *gross earnings.*

geets: slang, money, purchasing power.

gelt: slang, money.

general account: an account appearing in the bank's general ledger; all accounts other than those of depositors and depositories.

General Accounting Office: an independent nonpolitical agency established in 1921 that audits and reviews federal financial transactions and examines the expenditures of appropriations by federal units. The GAO is directly responsible to Congress.

General Agreement on Tariffs and Trade (GATT): a 1947 arrangement among 23 nations to make numerous mutual tariff concessions. Additional countries have joined GATT. see *Kennedy round.*

general asset currency: see *asset currency.*

general audit: an audit that embraces all financial transactions and records and which is made regularly at the close of an accounting period. [49]

general average: a contribution by all the parties in a sea adventure to make good a loss sustained by one of their number because of sacrifices voluntarily made of part of the ship or cargo to save the remaining part and the lives of those on board from an impending peril.

general banking law: the banking law of an individual state under which the banks organized in that state are authorized to do business. [50]

general control expenditures: expenditures (for personnel administration and other general administration) of the legislative and judicial branches of the government, the office of the chief executive, auxiliary agencies, and staff services.

general deposit: funds of banking deposits that are combined in the bank, as differentiated from special deposits that are kept separately and for which the bank serves as a bailee.

general depository: any Federal Reserve member bank authorized to handle deposits of the Treasury.

general equilibrium analysis: an economic inquiry in which the interaction of all markets is considered.

general expenditures: total expenditures less utility, sales of alcoholic beverages, and insurance trust expenditures when used in reference to

state or local governments separately. When combined for state-local totals, these items become direct general expenditures to avoid duplicating intergovernmental payments. cf. *general revenue.*

general fixed assets: those fixed assets of a governmental unit which are not accounted for in an enterprise, trust, or intragovernmental service fund. [49]

general fund: money that can be utilized (i.e., money that has not already been authorized for a particular project).

general gift: a gift, by will, of personal property which is not a particular thing as distinguished from all others of the same kind. [32]

general journal: an accounting record into which journal entries are made.

general ledger: the most important bank record. Every transaction that takes place in the bank during the business day is reflected through various departmental subsidiary records to the general ledger. see also *suspense account.*

general legacy: a gift of personal property by will which is not a particular thing as distinguished from all others of the same kind; to be distinguished from *specific legacy.* [37]

general lien: a lien against an individual but not against his real property. It gives the right to seize personal property until a debt has been paid. The asset involved does not have to be that which created the debt. see *distress for rent, vendor's lien;* cf. *particular lien.*

general loan and collateral agreement: synonymous with *broker's loan.*

general long-term debt: a long-term debt legally payable from general revenues and backed by the full faith and credit of a governmental unit. see *long-term debt.* [49]

general management trust: a trust that is not limited to any particular stock in which to invest.

general mortage: a mortgage covering all properties of a debtor and not restricted to one parcel.

general partner: a partner who, along with others, is liable for the partnership debts.

general power of appointment: the power of the donee (the one who is given the power) to pass on an interest in property to whomsoever he pleases, including himself or his estate. see *power of appointment.* [37]

general property tax: a tax on the assessed value of property, computed as a percentage of the total value.

general-purpose computer: a computer designed to handle a wide variety of problems (e.g., sorting, or a file processing activity).

general reserves: funds set aside for the sole purpose of covering possible losses. Includes the Federal Insurance Reserve, reserve for contingencies, and any reserve "locked up" for losses. [59]

general revenue: total revenue less utility, sales of alcoholic beverages, and insurance trust revenue when used in reference to state or local governments separately. When combined for state-local totals, it refers only to taxes and charges and miscellaneous revenue, to avoid duplicating intergovernmental revenue. cf. *general expenditures.*

general revenue sharing: funds distributed to states and local general-purpose governments by the federal government under the State and Local Fiscal Assistance Act of 1972. [70]

general sales tax: a tax on most items, collected at the time of purchase. In many states purchases of food and medicine are excluded from this law. see also *sales tax.*

general warranty deed: see *deed, general warranty.*

Gen. Led.: see *general ledger.*

Gen. Mtge.: see *general mortgage.*

gentlemen's agreement: an unsigned, unsecured contract based on the faith of the involved parties that each will perform.

GES: see *gold exchange standard.*

gestor: one who acts for another, in law. [61]

GICs: see *guaranteed income contracts.*

gift: the value of a donated asset acquired without cost to the recipient or regard to its donor. The use of the gift may or may not be restricted. [49]

gift causa mortis: a gift made in the anticipation of death to avoid inheritance taxes. cf. *gift inter vivos.*

gift certificate: a certificate having an identified cash value, to be used in purchasing goods or services from the issuing store or business.

gift inter vivos: a gift of property given during the donor's life to another living person. cf. *gift causa mortis.*

gift tax: a graduated, progressive tax imposed by some state governments and the federal government. This tax is paid by the donor, or individual making the gift, not the donee, the recipient of the gift.

GIGO: garbage in, garbage out; the acronym for the concept that results produced from unreliable or useless data are equally unreliable or useless.

gilt-edged bond: see *bond, gilt-edged.*

Ginnie Mae: see *Government National Mortgage Association (GNMA).*

Ginnie Mae trusts: closed-end unit investment trusts made up of Ginnie Mae certificates. The cost is $1000 per unit with a sales charge of around 4 percent. The monthly payments cover earned interest and amortization—the same as having direct participation in Ginnie Mae certificates, which are available only in the larger denominations. see *Government National Mortgage Association.*

giro: developed in the banking system of Germany, the payment system in which a bank depositor instructs his or her bank to transfer funds from his account directly to creditor accounts and to advise the creditors of the transfer.

give-up: occurs when a member of a stock exchange on the floor acts for à second member by executing an order for him with a third member. see *two-dollar brokers.*

GL: see *go long.*

glamour stock

(1) *general:* any popular security.

(2) *investments:* a successful security that attracts a substantial following and whose price rises on a continuous basis.

Glass-Steagall Act of 1933: a legislative saefguard designed to prevent commercial banks from engaging in investment banking activities; also authorized deposit insurance. In re-

cent years, attempts have been made to change this act. After a long period of contentment with the restrictions, the banking industry, especially the American Bankers Association, has begun to test the limitations on several fronts, including commercial paper, commingled accounts, money market funds, municipal revenue bonds. see *bond, municipal revenue; commercial paper; commingled accounts; money market funds.*

glut: to oversupply (e.g., a glut of oil on the market).

GNMA: see *Government National Mortgage Association.*

gnomes of Zurich: those financial and banking people of Zurich, Switzerland, involved in foreign exchange speculation. The term was coined by Great Britain's Labour ministers during the 1964 sterling crisis.

GNP: see *gross national product.*

GO: see *government obligations.*

go-down: in the Far East, a commercial storage warehouse.

go-go fund: an investment purporting to acquire sizable earnings in a short time period, resulting in risky, speculative market activity.

going ahead: when a broker decides to make a trade for his own account, fair practice requires that he fill all his customer's orders first. A dishonest broker will "go ahead" (i.e., transact his own business first).

going public: describes a situation when a firm's shares become available on a major exchange, as distinguished from being held by a few shareholders.

going short: selling a stock or commodity short.

gold brick: slang, worthless, and often fraudulent, securities that initially appear sound and worthy.

gold bullion standard: a monetary standard according to which (a) the national unit of currency is defined in terms of a stated gold weight, (b) gold is retained by the government in bars rather than coin, (c) there is no circulation of gold within the economy, and (d) gold is made available for purposes of industry and for international transactions of banks and treasuries.

gold certificate account: gold certificates on hand and due from the Treasury. The certificates, on hand and due from the Treasury, are backed 100 percent by gold owned by the U.S. government. They count as legal reserve, the minimum the Reserve Banks are required to maintain being 25 percent of their combined Federal Reserve note and deposit liabilities. (40)

gold clause: contract term defining a money debt in terms of a U.S. dollar of a specified weight and quality of gold.

gold clearance fund: today, known as the *Interdistrict Settlement Fund.*

gold exchange standard: an international monetary agreement according to which money consists of fiat national currencies that can be converted into gold at established price ratios.

gold fixing: in London, Paris, and Zurich, at 10:30 A.M. and again at 3:30 P.M., gold specialists or bank officials specializing in gold bullion activity determine the price for the metal.

gold hoarding: with the hope of guaranteeing the value of their money, people who convert their funds into gold bullion and hold on to it over an extended time period.

gold points: the range within which the foreign exchange rates of gold standard countries will differ. Gold points are equal to the par rate of exchange plus and minus the cost of transporting gold. The cost of insurance is included.

gold production: as listed by the *Federal Reserve Bulletin,* appearing monthly, the estimated gold production in countries of the free world.

gold reserves: gold, retained by a nation's monetary agency, forming the backing of currency that the nation has issued.

gold standard: applied to a monetary agreement according to which all national currencies are backed 100 percent by gold and the gold is utilized for payments of foreign activity. cf. *limping standard.*

gold stock: value of gold owned by the government. [40]

gold tranche position in International Monetary Fund: represents the amount that the United States can draw in foreign currencies virtually automatically from the International Monetary Fund if such borrowings are needed to finance a balance-of-payments deficit. The gold tranche itself is determined by the U.S. quota paid in gold minus the holdings of dollars by the fund in excess of the dollar portion of the U.S. quota. Transactions of the fund in a member country's currency are transactions in monétary reserves. When the fund sells dollars to other countries to enable them to finance their international payments, the net position of the United States in the fund is improved. An improvement in the net position in the gold tranche is similar to an increase in the reserve assets of the United States. On the other hand, when the United States buys other currencies from the fund, or when other countries use dollars to meet obligations to the fund, the net position of the United States in the fund is reduced. [73]

go long: purchasing stock for investment or as speculation. see *short sale.*

good deal: slang, a desirable business opportunity.

good delivery: certain basic qualifications must be met before a security sold on an exchange may be delivered; the security must be in proper form to comply with the contract of sale and to transfer title to the purchaser. [20]

good faith: trust. [28]

good faith bargaining: applied to the requirement that both parties to a labor dispute meet and confer at reasonable times, with minds open to persuasion with a view to reaching agreement on new contractual terms. A requirement to reach agreement on any proposal is not implied.

good-fors: a term usually applied to emergency low-denomination notes, which state on the face that they are "good for" a specified amount. [27]

good money: if two kinds of money of equal nominal value are in circulation, the general public may prefer one over the other because of metal content and will tend to hoard the "good money" and spend the "bad money," driving the good money out of circulation. see *Gresham's Law.*

goods and services
(1) *general:* the result of industrial work, equaling the gross national product for one year.
(2) *law:* any movable personal property, excluding livestock and excluding intangible property such as leases. cf. *chattel, chose.*

goods on approval: obtained when a potential buyer requests and receives from a seller the right to examine items for a stated time period before deciding whether to purchase the goods.

good-this-month order (GTM): a customer's request to a broker for the purchase or sale of stocks or commodities, the order being good this month only. see *day order, open order.*

good-this-week order (GTW): a customer's request to a broker for the purchase or sale of stocks or commodities, the order being good this week only. see *day order, open order.*

good through: a request to purchase or sell stock at a stated price limit for a stated time period, unless it is executed, canceled, or altered as to price. May appear as GTW (good through week), GTM (good through month), and so on.

good ticket: slang, financially successful.

good-'til-canceled order (GTC): an order to buy or sell that remains in effect until it is either executed or canceled. cf. *orders good until a specified time, resting order.* [20]

good title: see *just title.*

good-to-the-last-drop method: an approach in banking where every clearing member is liable to be assessed to make good on any individual member's default.

goodwill: the intangible possession that enables a business to continue to earn a profit in excess of the normal or basic rate of profit earned by other businesses of similar type.

go public: to raise money for a corporation by offering stock for public sale. see *new issue, registration.*

Gosplan: the state planning commission of the Soviet Union responsible for general economic planning.

gouge: slang, to acquire an excessive profit, by either overcharging or defrauding.

gourde: monetary unit of Haiti.

governmental accounting: the composite activity of analyzing, recording, summarizing, reporting, and interpreting the financial transactions of governmental units and agencies. [49]

government bond: see *bond, government.*

government deposits: funds of the U.S. government and its agencies which are required to be placed in depositories designated by the secretary of the Treasury.

government expenditures: gross expenditure amounts without deduction of any related receipts.

government monopoly: a monopoly owned and controlled by either a local, state, or federal government (e.g., U.S. Postal System, water supply systems).

Government National Mortgage Association (GNMA): an agency of the Department of Housing and Urban Development. Its primary function is in the area of government-approved special housing programs, by offer-

ing permanent financing for low-rent housing. Nickname, Ginnie Mae. see *Ginnie Mae trusts.*

government obligations: instruments of the U.S. government public debt that are fully backed by the government, as contrasted with U.S. government securities—that is, Treasury bills, notes, bonds, and savings bonds.

government revenue: all money received other than from issue of debt, liquidation of investments, and agency and private trust transactions. Includes tax collections, charges and miscellaneous revenue, intergovernmental revenue, utility, sales of alcoholic beverages, and insurance trust revenue for all funds and agencies of a government. Revenue is net of refunds and other correcting acts.

"governments": as used in the United States, all types of securities issued by the federal government (U.S. Treasury obligations), including, in its broad concept, securities issued by agencies of the federal government. [67]

government saving: tax receipts less government expenditures.

government securities: securities issued by U.S. government agencies for example, Federal Land Bank bonds and Federal Home Loan Bank notes. These securities are not guaranteed by the federal government.

GP
(1) see *going public.*
(2) see *gold points.*
(3) see *grace period.*
(4) see *gross profit.*

GPAM: see *graduated-payment adjustable mortgage.*

GPMs: see *graduated-payment mort-gage.*

GR

(1) see *gross receipts.*

(2) see *gross revenue.*

grace period

(1) *general:* most contracts pro-vide that the policy will remain in force if premiums are paid at any time within a period (the "grace period") varying from 28 to 31 days following the premium-due date.

(2) *banking:* the period when a mortgage payment becomes past due, before it goes into default.

grade creep: slang; in personnel com-pensation systems, the tendency to upgrade the rating and pay for a spe-cific job. Under this concept, a high-ly inflationary trend is encouraged.

graded tax: a form of local taxation; an attempt to place an increasingly heavy burden on land values and at the same time a lessening burden for land improvements. The primary ob-jective is to dissuade owners from keeping their land unimproved—spe-cifically, by building on the property.

grades (grading): the classification into well-defined grades of major commodities. The standardization in quality difference of staple commodi-ties for purposes of identification during trading periods.

graduated-payment adjustable mort-gage (GPAM): a GPM with an ad-justable rate; the borrower and lender share interest rate risk. see *graduated-payment mortgages, price-level-adjusted mortgage.*

graduated payment adjustable mort-gage loan: a new type of mortgage instrument that combines features of the graduated payment mortgage

and the adjustable mortgage loan was authorized by the Federal Home Loan Bank Board in July 1981. Lend-ers are now able to offer mortgage loans where the interest rate may change to reflect changes in the mar-ket place and where the monthly pay-ments for the first 10 years may be set at a lower amount than required to fully amortize the loan.

graduated-payment mortgage (GPM): first insured by the Federal Housing Administration in 1977, where pay-ments are much lower at first than for traditional level-payment mortgages. Prices then rise gradually and level off after a few years. The idea is to put home ownership within reach of young people who might otherwise be forced by spiraling housing prices and high interest rates to remain rent-ers. see also *flexible-payment mort-gage, pledged-account mortgage, price-level-adjusted mortgage, re-verse-annuity mortgage, rollover mortgage, variable-rate mortgage.*

graduated securities: stocks that have moved from one exchange to another (e.g., from the American Stock Exchange to the New York Stock Exchange).

graduated tax: a progressive tax; the rate of tax per unit of the tax base in-creases as the number of units in-creases.

graft: a financial or other gain achieved through the abuse of a per-son's position or influence.

grain exchanges: commodity ex-changes that trade in spot and fu-tures of grain.

grand: slang, $1000.

grandfather clause: any condition that ties existing rights or privileges to previous or remote conditions or acts. More popularly used when a new regulation goes into effect, to exempt people already engaged in the activity being regulated.

grandfathered activities: nonbank activities, some of which would normally be impermissible for bank holding companies, but which were acquired or engaged in before a particular date. Such activities may be continued under the "grandfather" clause of the Bank Holding Company Act—some until 1981 and some indefinitely. [1]

grant: a clause in a deed reflecting the transfer of title to real property.

grantee: an individual to whom a grant is made; the person named in a deed to receive title to property.

granter: a person who offers credit.

grantor: an individual who makes a grant; a person who executes a deed giving up title to property.

grants-in-aid: payments made by one government unit to another for specified purposes. They represent federal support for a state or locally administered program, or state support for a local program. cf. *revenue sharing.*

gratuitous coinage: a government policy of producing coins from metal without cost to the owner of the metal.

gratuity: a gift or donation.

graveyard market: a securities market where those who are in cannot get out and those who are out cannot get in.

gravy: money that is in excess of what is anticipated; money easily earned.

gravy train: slang, a chance to receive excessive funds for little or no work.

gray knight: an opportunistic second bidder in a company takeover, not sought out by the target, who attempts to take advantage of the problems between the target and the initial bidder. cf. *white knight.*

gray market: sources of supply from which scarce items are bought for quick delivery at a premium well above the usual market price. Individuals engaged in this legal activity speculate on future demands. cf. *black market.*

green: slang, paper money.

greenlining: a response of community citizens who withdraw their accounts from lending institutions that they believe practice redlining. see *redlining.*

green power: the power of money.

Gresham's law

(1) describes the fact that bad money tends to drive out good money. Refers to the way in which people protect themselves from loss by spending money of questionable value and holding onto money of known better value. cf. *quantity theory.*

(2) see *good money.*

grift: slang, money made dishonestly, especially by swindling.

gross

(1) *general:* 12 dozen.

(2) *finance:* the total amount before any deductions have been made.

gross asset: all property in possession of a company. Gross assets are the total of the ledger and nonledger assets. [42]

gross bonded debt: the total amount of direct debt of a governmental unit represented by outstanding bonds before deduction of sinking fund assets. see *direct debt*. [49]

gross charge: the ratio between the interest charge on a discount interest loan and the discounted amount disbursed to the borrower. [59]

gross debt: all long-term credit obligations incurred and outstanding, whether backed by a government's full faith and credit or non-guaranteed, and all interest-bearing short-term credit obligations.

gross deposits: all deposits, without any exclusions or deductions. This would include all forms of demand and time deposits (i.e. those due banks and government deposits).

gross earnings: the total income of a business, usually segregated as to type in financial income statements.

gross estate: all of a person's property before debts, taxes, and other expenses or liabilities have been deducted; to be distinguished from *net estate,* which is what is left after these items have been taken into account. [37]

gross income: revenues before any expenses have been deducted.

gross income multiplier: a figure by which effective gross income is multiplied to obtain an amount that indicates the capital value of property. [44]

gross lease: a lease of property under which the lessor agrees to meet all charges which would normally be incurred by the owner of that property. [62]

gross line: the amount of insurance a company has on a risk, including the amount it has reinsured. "Net lines" plus reinsurance equals the "gross line."

gross margin
(1) the amount, determined by subtracting the cost of goods sold from net sales, which covers operating and financial expenses and provides net income. synonymous with *gross profit.*
(2) the dollar difference between the net sales and the net cost of goods sold during a stated time frame. Gross margin percentage is calculated by dividing net sales into this figure.

gross national debt: the total indebtedness of the federal government, including debts owed by one agency to another.

gross national disproduct: the total of all social costs or reductions in benefits to the community that result from producing the gross national product (e.g., the pollution of rivers is part of the gross national disproduct).

gross national expenditure: the full amount spent by the four sectors of the economy (household, government, business, and foreign) on the nation's output of goods and services. It is equal to the gross national product.

gross national income: synonymous with *gross national product.*

gross national product (GNP): the total retail market value of all items and services produced in a country during a specified period, usually one year. Distribution is presented in terms of consumer and government purchases, gross private national and foreign investments, and exports.

gross operating income: an accounting term that includes income received from the ordinary operation of the business before deducting expenses of operation. [59]

gross private domestic investment: purchases of newly produced capital goods plus the value of the change in the volume of inventories held by business. Purchases include all new private dwellings, whether leased to tenants or owner occupied.

gross profit: operating revenue less the cost of goods sold. see *gross margin.* [77]

gross rate: see *flat rate.*

gross receipts: total receipts prior to deducting expenses.

gross revenue: total revenues received from selling goods or performing services. A revenue before any deductions have been made for returns, allowances, or discounts. Often called *gross sales.*

gross sales: total sales, over a specified period, before customer returns and allowances have been deducted.

gross savings: the sum of capital consumption (depreciation), and personal and corporate savings.

gross spread: a banking term used to determine underwriting fees. see *underwriter.*

gross variance: the total difference between actual and standard attainment under a standard cost system. Gross variance is generally broken down into volume and efficiency components. [38]

gross yield: the return obtained from an investment before the deduction of costs and losses involved in procuring and managing the investment. see *net yield.* [44]

ground floor: slang, a low price security with expectations of considerable increase in value.

group banking: a form of banking enterprise whereby a group of existing banks form a holding company. The holding company supervises and coordinates the operations of all banks in the group. A majority of the capital stock of each bank in the group is owned by the holding company.

group enrollment card: a document signed by an individual eligible for group insurance as notice of his or her wish to participate in the group plan. In a contributory case, this card also provides an employer with authorization to deduct contributions from an employee's pay.

group insurance: any insurance plan under which a number of employees and their dependents are covered by a single policy, issued to the employer or often to an association with which the employees are affiliated, with individual certificates given to each insured person. see *noncontributory.*

group life insurance: life insurance, usually without medical examination, on a group of people under a master policy. It is typically issued to an employer for the benefit of employees. The individual members of the group hold certificates as evidence of their insurance. [58]

Group of Ten: composed of the prosperous countries of the world who fix and regulate their policies in international monetary activities. Members are Belgium, Britain, Canada, France, Italy, Japan, The Netherlands, Sweden, the United States, and West Germany. Switzerland is an unofficial member.

growth fund: a mutual fund whose holdings are made up primarily of growth stocks. The more speculative of these are often referred to as go-go stocks.

growth in earnings per share: annual percentage growth in primary earnings per share for the restated five-year period ending December 31, based on the least-squares method.

growth stock: stock of a corporation whose existing and projected earnings are sufficiently positive to indicate an appreciable and constant increase in the stock's market value over an extended time period, the rate of increase being larger than those of most corporate stocks.

GS
(1) see *glamour stock.*
(2) see *government securities.*
(3) see *gross sales.*
(4) see *gross spread.*
(5) see *growth stock.*

GSA: see *Glass-Steagal Act of 1933.*
GSL: see *guaranteed student loans.*
GT: see *gift tax.*
GTC: see *good-'til-canceled order.*
Gtd.: guaranteed.
GTM: see *good-this-month order.*
GTW: see *good-this-week order.*
Guar.: see *guarantee.*
guarani: monetary unit of Paraguay.
guarantee
(1) a written statement assuring that something is of stated quantity, quality, content, or benefit, or that it will perform as advertised for a stated period. In some cases, all or part of the purchaser's money will be refunded if the item fails to meet the terms of a guarantee.
(2) see *guaranty.*

guaranteed account: an account, the prompt and full payment of which is guaranteed by a responsible agency or person. Usually, guaranteed accounts are those for minors whose legal credit responsibility is deemed insufficient for granting unsupported credit or individuals whose payment record or other factors make necessary the guarantee of a more responsible person. [41]

guaranteed annual wage (GAW): a plan whereby an employer agrees to provide his employees a special minimum of employment or income for a year. Unions argue that GAW plans add to income and employment stability. Management argues that GAW does not take into account the fluctations in demand for goods, and is thus a poor business practice. cf. *Halsey premium plan.*

guaranteed bond: see *bond, guaranteed.*

guaranteed debt: obligations of certain semipublic and public corporations that are guaranteed by the federal government as contingent liabilities.

guaranteed deposits: see *Federal Deposit Insurance Corporation.*

guaranteed income contracts (GICs): agreements that promise a rate of return no matter how well or poorly an insurance company's investment portfolio performs.

guaranteed interest
(1) rate of interest return specified in the policy as the rate at which reserves will be accumulated.
(2) rate of interest paid on funds deposited with the company, either for advance premium deposits or in accordance with the settlements options. [12]

guaranteed letter of credit: travelers' letters of credit or commercial letters of credit; the party requesting the credit issuance does not pay the bank in cash for the equivalent amount of the credit upon its issuance. The bank substitutes its own credit for people or firms, to encourage more domestic and foreign trade.

guaranteed stock: usually, preferred stock on which dividends are guaranteed by another company; under much the same circumstances as a bond is guaranteed. [20]

guaranteed student loans (GSL): loans primarily made by banks, savings and loan associations, and credit unions, and some colleges. The federal government pays the full 9 percent interest on loans for college students while they are enrolled.

guarantee of signature: a certificate affixed to the assignment of a stock certificate or registered bond or to other documents by a bank or stock exchange house, vouching for the genuineness of the signature of the registered holder. [37]

guarantees: federal credit aid in which the federal government pledges its financial liability for loans made by private or state or local government institutions.

guarantees against price decline: guarantees given by a manufacturer to distributors that if his price to them declines within a given period after purchase, he will reimburse them for the amount of the decline on remaining stock. [9]

guarantor: one who makes a guaranty; an individual who by contract is prepared to answer for the debt, default, and miscarriage of another. see *guaranty.*

guaranty: a contract, agreement, or undertaking involving three parties. The first party (the guarantor) agrees to see that the performance of a second party (the guarantee) is fulfilled according to the terms of the contract, agreement, or undertaking. The third party is the creditor, or the party, to benefit by the performance.

guaranty fund: a fund which a mutual savings bank in certain states must create through subscriptions or out of earnings to meet possible losses resulting from decline in value of investments or from other unforeseen contingencies. In other states, such a fund is known as the surplus fund. [39]

guaranty stock: basic stock that is not withdrawable and which protects the interest of all other investors against losses. [59]

guardian: an individual chosen by a court to oversee the property rights and person of minors, persons adjudged to be insane, and other incompetents.

guardian account: an account in the name of a guardian who acts on behalf of and administers the funds for the benefit of the ward. [39]

guardian ad litem: a particular guardian chosen for the single purpose of carrying on litigation and preserving a ward's interests but who has no control or power over the ward's property.

guardian deed: see *deed, guardian.*

GUC: see *good-'til-canceled order.*

guerrilla financing: loans devised on their own outside conventional channels. A strategy to protect an individual seller who lends money privately to the individual buyers who might get saddled with a risky, illiquid asset when cash comes in gradually as the buyer pays off the note.

guerrillas: municipal bond syndicates that attempt to outbid independent bidders on new bond issues. synonymous with "barracudas."

guilder: monetary unit of The Netherlands, Netherlands Antilles, and Surinam.

gulf riyal: monetary unit of Dubai and Qatar.

gunslingers: Wall Street slang for speculators.

gyp 'ems: slang, for graduated-payment mortgages. see *graduated-payment mortgages.*

HA: see *house account.*

habeas corpus: a writ ordering an official having custody of a person alleged to be unlawfully detained to return the individual before a court to determine whether the imprisonment was legal.

habendum clause: a deed of mortgage clause that defines the extent of the property being transferred. It reads: "To have and to hold the premises herein granted unto the party of the second party (i.e., the grantee), his heirs and the assigns forever."

hacking the pie: slang, what occurs at the end-of-the-year meeting of partners when they divide up a firm's profits.

haggle: see *higgling.*

haircut: slang, describes the amount of capital a brokerage firm must hold to meet New York Stock Exchange capital requirements.

half-buck: slang, a half-dollar (50 cents).

half-stock: common or preferred stock having a par value of $50.

hallmark: an impression made on gold and silverware introduced in the beginning of the fourteenth century in England to identify the quality of the metal used.

Halsey premium plan: incentive wage plan which provided for a guaranteed wage in addition to an extra bonus for performance in excess of the norm.

hammering the market: the persistent selling of securities by speculators operating on the short side who believe that prices are inflated and that liquidation is imminent. When the market is primarily affected by the bears, these individuals are said to be "hammering the market."

handbill: paper currency.

hang-out loan: a loan lasting longer than its lease.

hard cash: metallic currency, as distinguished from paper money.

harden: following a drop in the price for securities, a surge in buying leading to a price increase.

hard loan: a foreign loan that must be paid in hard money.

hard money (currency)
(1) *finance:* currency of a nation having stability in the country and abroad.
(2) *finance:* coins, in contrast with paper currency, or soft money.
(3) *finance:* describes a situation in which interest rates are high and loans are difficult to arrange. synonymous with *dear money.*

hard sell: slang, attempting to sell goods or services in an aggressive, often unpleasant fashion.

hard spot: a security or group of securities holding strong in a generally weak market.

hard stuff: slang, money.

hardware
(1) *general:* mechanical equip-

ment used for conducting an activity. (2) *computers:* the electric, electronic, and mechanical equipment used for processing data, consisting of racks, tubes, transistors, wires, and so on. cf. *software.*

Harter Act: legislation protecting a ship's owner against claims for damage resulting from the behavior of the vessel's crew, provided the ship left port in a seaworthy condition, properly manned and equipped.

Hart-Scott-Rodino Act: federal legislation of 1976, requiring companies to notify the Federal Trade Commission and the Justice Department of their plans to buy more than $15 million or 15 percent of a company.

Hatch Act: the Federal Corrupt Practices Act; Section 313 of this law was amended by Section 304 of the Taft-Hartley Act to make it unlawful for (a) banks and corporations authorized by Congress to make a contribution or expenditure in connection with election to any political office or activity; and (b) any corporation or labor organization to make a contribution or expenditure in connection with any election or political activity.

Hawley-Smoot Act: legislation of 1930 that raised tariffs, spurring foreign retaliation and a decline in world trade.

hazard insurance: a form of insurance coverage for real estate that includes protection against loss from fire, certain natural causes, vandalism, and malicious mischief. see also *homeowner's insurance.* [59]

HC: see *holding company.*

head tax: a tax imposed on immigrant aliens on their entry to the United States.

head teller: a teller in a bank who sometimes has the title of assistant cashier. The head teller is usually custodian of the reserve cash in the bank's vault. It is his or her responsibility to see that an "economical" quantity of cash is on hand at all times to meet the normal demands of the banks customers. It is his responsibility to assemble the cash figures for all tellers at the end of the business day, and prepare the cash report for the general ledger. He is also responsible for the work of all tellers in the bank, and he must recount cash for a teller who comes up with a difference at the end of the day. He must fully report any overage or shortages that may appear, and assist where possible to locate the difference. [10]

heavy market: a declining securities and commodities market created when the supply of bids for buying shares exceeds the demand for them, resulting in a price drop.

hedge: to offset. Also, a security that has offsetting qualities. Thus one attempts to "hedge" against inflation by the purchase of securities whose values should respond to inflationary developments. Securities having these qualities are "inflation hedges." see *arbitrage, puts and calls, short sale.* [30]

hedge fund: a partnership of people who pool their resources for purposes of investment. cf. *investment company.*

hedger: an individual who is unwilling to risk a serious loss in his or her cash position and takes a counterbalancing position in order to avoid or lessen loss.

hedging: a type of economic insurance used by dealers in commodities and securities, manufacturers, and other producers to prevent loss due to price fluctuations. Hedging consists of counterbalancing a present sale or purchase by a purchase or sale of a similar commodity or of a different commodity, usually for delivery at some future date. The desired result is that the profit or loss on a current sale or purchase be offset by the loss or profit on the future purchase or sale.

hedging clause: a protective statement of warning for securities customers that customarily reads: "The information furnished herein has been obtained from sources believed to be reliable, but its accuracy is not guaranteed."

heirs: people who receive(d) the title to property upon the death of an ancestor or other testator.

hereditament: property that can be inherited.

hesiflation: a concept suggested by former Secretary of the Treasury Henry H. Fowler for a reduced growth pattern in the economy combined with strong inflationary pressures. cf. *stagflation.*

HHFA: see *Housing and Home Finance Agency.*

HI: see *hot issue.*

hiccup: slang, a short-lived drop in the stock market.

hidden amenities: desirable aspects of property that are provided but not always given attention on first inspection.

hidden assets: assets of a firm that are not easily identifiable by examining the balance sheet.

hidden clause: in a contract, any obscure provision that stipulates requirements that may be against the buyer's interests.

hidden tax: a tax included in the price of goods and services that is not easily identifiable by the payer of the tax.

higgling
(1) when the buyer offers a low price and the seller asks a high price, and through bargaining, a third price is arrived at to satisfy both parties.
(2) sometimes referred to as haggling.

high credit: highest amount of credit extended to a particular customer at one time. [41]

highest credit: the greatest amount owed by the consumer within the last year or on the last installment contract. [76]

high finance
(1) *general:* utilizing another's funds in a speculative fashion, which may result in a loss to the funds' owner.
(2) *finance:* borrowing to the maximum of one's credit.
(3) *finance:* extremely complicated transactions.

high flyers: high-priced speculative securities that move up or down several points in a trading day.

high grade: describes an item of superior quality (e.g., high-grade stock).

high-premium convertible debenture: a bond with a long-term equity kicker packaged to offer some protection against inflation. Designed primarily for the bond buyer, it carries a higher return than conventional convertible debentures.

high-volume accounts: an account

whose activity is so unusually large as to warrant special handling. [31]

highway trust fund: a trust fund through which is financed the expanded program of federal highway aid. Appropriations based on certain highway user tax collections are made to the fund, and from it, federal payments to states for highways are made.

H. in D.C.: see *holder in due course.*

Hinky Dinky: the name of a Nebraska supermarket chain whose employees operate in-store terminals provided by First Federal Savings and Loan of Lincoln, Nebraska, to permit First Federal customers to make deposits and withdrawals in the store. This service is significant because (a) it enables off-premises access to accounts maintained at a depository institution, and (b) the accounts bear interest. see *service counter terminals.*

hire purchase: a term used in Great Britain for purchases made on time payments or on the installment plan.

historical cost: the principle requiring that all information on financial statements be presented in terms of the item's original cost to the entity. The dollar is assumed to be stable from one time period to another.

historical rate: assets such as inventories, property, plant, and equipment are translated into dollars at the rate in effect when the assets were acquired.

hit the bid: selling at the highest bid price quoted for a stock.

hoarding: to collect for the sake of accumulating; a planned effort by persons to accumulate items beyond normal need (e.g., purchasing doz-

ens of cartons of cigarettes in anticipation of a price hike).

HOI: see *house of issue.*

hokeys: see *Home Owners' Loan Corporation Bonds.*

hold: a term used to indicate that a certain amount of a customer's balance is held intact by the bookkeeper until an item has been collected, or until a specific check or debit comes through for posting. [31]

holder: the bearer possessing an instrument.

holder in due course: a person who has taken an instrument under the following conditions; (a) that it is complete and regular upon its face; (b) that he or she become a holder of it before it was overdue, and without notice that it had been previously dishonored, if such was the fact; (c) that the holder took it in good faith and for value; and (d) that at the time it was negotiated to him, the holder had no notice of any infirmity in the instrument or defect in the title of the person negotiating it. see *endorsement.*

holder of record: dividends are declared payable to stockholders owning shares on a specific date. Such stockholders are said to be "holders of record."

holding company: a corporation that owns the securities of another, in most cases with voting control. synonymous with *parent company* and *proprietary company.* see *group banking, holding company (multiple-bank), holding company (one-bank).*

holding company (multiple-bank): a bank holding company, however defined, that owns or controls two or more banks. [74]

holding company (one-bank): at present, there is no legal definition of a one-bank holding company. A very broad definition would be any company that owns or controls a single bank. Several alternative legal definition have been proposed in bills now pending before Congress. [74]

holding company affiliate: a legal term fully defined in the Banking Act of 1933. Generally, it pertains to any organization that owns or controls any one bank either through stock ownership or through any means that allows it to elect a majority of the bank's directors. [74]

holding the market: to minimize the decline in the price of a security, a sufficient quantity of the stock is purchased to support the interest in a particular share.

holdovers: a term used, usually in large banks, to describe a portion of work that has to be processed by a twilight shift or a night force. The 40-hour workweek makes it frequently necessary for the bank to employ three shifts. Since the business day starts officially at midnight, work that has not been processed by the twilight force is "held over" to the night force, which starts processing the remaining work. The work, for control purposes, is credited to the twilight force, and recharged as "holdovers" to the night force. [10]

hollow note: a $100 bill.

home banking: a new concept in banking, pioneered in 1980 by Banc One Corporation in Columbus, Ohio. By connecting a device to TV sets and telephones, customers will be able to call up information about bills and bank accounts on their TV screens and pay bills with a push of a button. Since this approach does not allow deposits and cash withdrawals, it isn't considered a branch bank.

home debit: a self-check; any draft or check drawn upon a bank and subsequently brought to the same institution for deposit or payment.

home financing: the providing of funds, secured by a mortgage, for the purchase or construction of a residential structure containing one, two, three, or four dwelling units. [59]

home improvement loan: an advance of funds, usually not secured by a mortgage and usually short-term, made to a property owner for the upgrading of his property, such as maintenance and repair, additions and alterations, or replacement of equipment or structural elements. [59]

Home Loan Bank Act (System): see *Federal Home Loan Bank System.*

homeowner's insurance: a broad form of insurance coverage for real estate that combines hazard insurance with personal liability protection and other items. [59]

Home Owners'Loan Act of 1933: federal legislation establishing the Home Owners' Loan Corporation with $200 million from the Reconstruction Finance Corporation; the corporation was authorized to release up to $2 billion in bonds to exchange for mortgages. see *Federal Savings and Loan Association.*

Home Owners' Loan Corporation Bonds: authorized by the Home Owners Loan Act of 1934, $2 billion of bonds could be sold or exchanged for mortgages by the Home Owners Loan Corporation. Nicknamed "hokeys." The Corporation is now defunct and all bonds have been re-called.

homestead association: the name used by some savings associations in the state of Louisiana. [59]

homestead estate: a type of estate ownership in land, permissible in a number of states, that protects the possession and enjoyment of the owner against the claims of creditors and from execution and sale for his general debts, provided that he has a family. [59]

homogenization: the blurring of the traditional distinctions among a nation's financial institutions, where banks, thrift institutions, and credit unions have moved onto each other's turf but increasingly are facing stiff competition from nonregulated, nonfinancial institutions.

Hon'd.: honored.

honeycombed with stops: a securities market containing entries of many stop orders.

honor: to pay or to accept a draft complying with the terms of credit.

honor bond: see *bond, honor.*

HOR: see *holder of record.*

horizontal merger: a combination formed when two or more businesses producing the same goods or service merge.

horizontal price fixing: an agreement on prices among competitors at similar levels of distribution.

hot issue: a stock in great demand, often when sold for the first time. A typical symptom is a rapid price rise with the original purchaser making a quick profit.

hot money: money that is received through means that are either illegal or of questionable legality.

house account

(1) *general:* any account belonging to a client that has not been nor ever may be assigned to a firm's representative.

(2) *investments:* an account created by a brokerage company for its own use.

house bill: any bill of exchange drawn by a central office against a branch or affiliate.

house cleaning: slang, the reorganization of a firm, by rearranging positions and often releasing employees.

household saving: household disposable income less the existing household consumption.

house of issue: an investment banking firm engaged in underwriting and distribution of security issues.

house organ: a publication (newspaper, magazine) issued periodically by a company to its employees to keep them informed about the company, its personnel, and pertinent activities.

Housing Act of 1949: established national housing goals of "a decent home and suitable living environment for every American family"; provided grants to municipalities for public housing and slum clearance; set up a program of financial assistance for rural areas. [51]

Housing Act of 1961: authorized new programs for federal involvement in housing, including subsidized rental housing for low- and moderate-income families, and Federal Housing Administration insurance of liberal term loans for repair and modernization in declining urban areas; expanded funds for Federal National Mortgage Association special assistance functions. [51]

Housing and Community Development Act of 1977: raised ceilings on single-family loan amounts for association lending, federal agency purchases, Federal Housing Administration insurance and security for Federal Home Loan Bank advances; raised ceilings on conventional and FHA home improvement loans. [51]

Housing and Home Finance Agency: a single agency created in 1977, responsible for major housing programs and activities of the federal government.

HR 10: see *Keogh Plan (HR 10)*.

HSA: see *Hawley-Smoot Act*.

HUD: see *Department of Housing and Urban Development, U.S.*

human resource accounting: the reporting and emphasis of the relevance of skilled and loyal employees in a firm's earning picture.

hung up: a situation of an investor whose money is tied up in securities that have dropped in value below the original purchase price, the selling of which will lead to a major loss.

hush money: slang, money given to assure the silence of the receiver; a bribe.

hybrid basis accounting: a system of accounting that combines cash basis and accrual basis accounting. [59]

hybrid computer: a computer for data processing using both analog and digital representations of data.

hyperinflation: see *galloping inflation*.

hypothecate: to promise and place property to secure a loan. The identified property is said to be hypothecated.

hypothecated account: an account that is pledged or assigned as collateral for a loan. Savings accounts and trust accounts are usually selected for purposes of hypothecation.

hypothecated asset: things pledged without transferring possession or title.

hypothecation

(1) *banking:* an agreement or contract that permits a bank or a creditor to utilize the collateral pledge to secure a loan, in case the loan is unpaid at maturity. see *respondentia*.

(2) *investments:* the pledging of securities as collateral, for example, to secure the debit balance in a margin account. [20]

I

I: see *interest.*

IA

(1) see *inactive account.*

(2) see *intangible asset.*

IAA: see *Investment Advisers Act.*

IADB: *Inter-American Development Bank.*

IBA

(1) see *Independent Bankers Association of America.*

(2) see *International Banking Act of 1978.*

(3) see *Investment Bankers Association.*

IBFs: see *international banking facilities.*

IBRD: see *International Bank for Reconstruction and Development.*

ICA

(1) see *Interstate Commerce Act of 1887.*

(2) see *Investment Company Act of 1940.*

ICC: see *Interstate Commerce Commission.*

ICE: see *International Commercial Exchange.*

ICS: see *issued capital stock.*

ID

(1) see *immediate delivery.*

(2) see *income debenture.*

(3) see *interim dividend.*

(4) see *interlocking directorate.*

idemsonans: describes a legal document in which absolute accuracy in the spelling of names is not demand-ed. (e.g., "Eliot" or "Elliott" would be acceptable as designation of a person named Elliott).

identification: the procedure by which a bank teller or other employee assures himself as far as possible (through documents, contact with another bank, and other means) that the person with whom he is dealing is the person he or she claims to be. [39]

idle money

(1) *banking:* inactive bank deposits. see *unclaimed balances.*

(2) *finance:* uninvested available funds.

idle time

(1) *general:* time when an employee is unable to work because of machine malfunction or other factors not within the control of the worker. Usually the worker receives compensation during idle time.

(2) *computers:* the part of available time during which the computer is not in use.

IDP (integrated data processing)

(1) *computers:* a collection of data-processing techniques built around a common language, in which duplication of clerical operations is minimized. Also referred to as automatic data processing.

(2) *systems:* data processing carried out, organized, and directed according to a systems approach.

IEEPA: see *International Emergency Economic Powers Act of 1977.*

IF: see *insufficient funds.*

IFC: see *International Finance Corporation.*

IFE: see *Institute of Financial Education.*

if issued: see *when issued.*

ignorantia juris neminem excusat: "ignorance of the law is not excuse" (Latin). The principle according to which you can be cited for parking illegally even if you say you didn't see the "No Parking" sign.

II: see *institutional investor.*

IID: see *investment in default.*

illegal: describes behavior contrary to the basic principles of law. An illegal act is forbidden by law, whereas an unlawful act, though not forbidden by law, is not given the protection of the law.

illegal operation: the process resulting when a computer either cannot perform the instruction part or will perform it with incorrect and irrelevant results. This shortcoming is often caused by built-in computer limitations.

illiquid
(1) *finance:* not easily convertible into cash; the opposite of liquid. Illiquid assets can be converted into cash, but usually at a major loss in value. Fixed assets are illiquid assets.
(2) *law:* not established by any documentary evidence.

illusory: appearing false. If that which seems to be a promise is found not to be a promise, it is said to be illusory.

IMF: see *International Monetary Fund.*

immediate and deferred credit: items sent to a Federal Reserve Bank are generally divided into separate cash letters which contain items for immediate credit and items for deferred credit. [31]

immediate annuity: an annuity commencing one month, one quarter, half a year, or one year after the effective date of payment.

immediate beneficiary: a beneficiary of a trust who is entitled to receive immediate benefits from the trust property, whether or not limited to income; opposed to ultimate beneficiary. synonymous with "primary beneficiary." [37]

immediate delivery: an arrangement whereby an investor selects mortgages, generally from a mortgage banker's off-the-shelf inventory, for delivery, acceptance, and payment within a limited period, usually 30 days. [22]

immigrant remittances: funds of immigrants that are sent out of the country.

immovable: describes real property that cannot be moved (e.g., land, trees, structures).

immunity: that which confers the ability to escape from the legal duties or penalties imposed on others (see, e.g., indemnity).

immunization fund: a technique to protect pension-fund bond investments from sharply rising interest rates. To eliminate the risk of losing principal, the fund invests in government securities. The bank's actuaries fix the proportions of longer-term, medium-term and short-term securities by formulas that take into account differences in yields and the timeliness of cash flows from the securities.

Imp.

(1) see *import.*

(2) see *improvement.*

impaired capital: when the capital of a firm is indeed less than the capital stated.

impaired credit: the reduction of credit given to a corporation resulting from the bank's decision that its credit worthiness has weakened. see *credit, line of credit.*

impairment

(1) *general:* the total, where liabilities exceed assets by reason of losses.

(2) *finance:* the amount by which stated capital is reduced by dividends and other distributions, and by losses.

imperfect competition: circumstances under which prices are usually altered by one or more persons. This occurs because of unusual conditions in the market or advantages secured by some buyers or sellers.

implicit costs: costs originating within the business that are the responsibility of the owner (e.g., time, money).

implicit price deflator for gross national product: a measure of the average change in market prices of goods and services represented in the national income and product accounts, compared to average levels in a base period.

implied easement: infringement on property that has been left unchallenged over a period of time. The infringement is apparent from continued and lengthy use.

implied trust: a trust created by operation of law or by judicial construction, to be distinguished from an express trust, which is created by express language, oral or in writing. [37]

import: to receive goods and services from abroad; an imported item.

import credit: a commercial letter of credit issued for the purpose of financing the importation of goods. [50]

import duty: any tax on items imported.

import letter of credit: see *import credit.*

import quota: a protective ruling establishing limits on the quantity of a particular product that can be imported.

imports of goods and services: represent the sum of all payments for merchandise imports, military expenditures, transportation and travel costs, other private and U.S. government services, and income and service payments to foreign parent companies by their affiliates operating in the United States. By far the largest component of this category is merchandise imports, which includes all goods bought or otherwise transferred from a foreign country to the United States. [73]

imposition: a demand or tax (e.g., bridge tolls, tariffs) on items or property made by a taxing authority.

impost: a tax, usually an import duty.

impound: to seize or hold; to place in protective custody by order of a court (e.g., impounded property, impounded records).

imprest (petty cash) fund: a fund of a designated amount out of which payments for expenses of small amounts are made; a system commonly employed in business.

imprinting: to place on the face of a document the magnetic ink characters specified by the American Bankers Association. synonymous with "encoding." [31]

improvement: a change made in an asset to improve its condition with the expectation that it will also increase its value.

improvement lien: see *special assessment.*

improvement mortgage bond: see *bond, improvement mortgage.*

imputed: describes a value estimated when no cash payment is made, in order to establish that value.

imputed cost: a cost that is not specified but instead is implied to exist by the policies of the organization (e.g., interest that would have been earned on cash spent to purchase inventories).

In.: see *income.*

inactive account: an account that has little or no movement. The balance may be stationary, neither deposits nor withdrawals having been posted to the account for a period of time. cf. *idle money.* synonymous with *dormant account.*

inactive asset: that part of total assets that are not in continuous productive use in any business. An emergency generator not in use for an extended time period would be an inactive asset.

inactive bad debt account: an account charged off and judged to be uncollectible. [55]

inactive corporation: one which neither operates property nor administers its financial affairs. If it maintains an oganization, it does so only for the purpose of complying with legal requirements and maintaining title to property or franchises. [18]

inactive post: a trading post on the floor of the New York Stock Exchange where inactive securities are traded in units of 10 shares instead of the usual 100-share lots. Better known in the business as Post 30. see *round lot.* [20]

inactive stock (bond): an issue traded on an exchange or in the over-the-counter market in which there is a relatively low volume of transactions. Volume may be a few hundred shares a week or even less. see *cabinet crowd.*

inactive trust: a trust in which the trustee has no duty except to hold title to the property. [37]

inadvertent error: a mechanical, electronic, or clerical error that is not intentional. [78]

inalienable: not able to be sold or transferred. synonymous with "non assignable."

in-and-out: the purchase and sale of the same security within a short period—day, a week, even a month. An in-and-out trader is generally more interested in day-to-day price fluctuations than dividends or long-term growth. [20]

INAS: see *Interbank National Authorization System.*

Inc.
(1) see *income.*
(2) see *incorporate.*

incentive: a motivational force that stimulates people to greater activity or increased efficiency.

incentive pay: a wage system based on the productivity of a worker above a specified level. It may take the form of a piece rate, rate for performance above a fixed standard, or rate arrived at by some other method agreed upon.

incestuous share dealing: the buying and selling of one another's company securities for purposes of creating a tax or other financial advantage.

inchoate: newly begun or incomplete.

inchoate interest: a future interest in real estate.

incidence of taxation: see *tax incidence.*

in-clearing items: items received by a bank as a result of a clearinghouse exchange are commonly called incoming clearings, or shortened to "in-clearings." [31]

income: money or its equivalent, earned or accrued, arising from the sale of goods or services. see *gross income, net income, profit, revenue.*

income account: an account in the general ledger of a bank. Expenses are listed under the assets, and the total expenses are usually deducted from the income accounts total to show the net profit to date as a portion of the undivided profits accounts.

income and expense statement
(1) a summary of the incomes and costs of operation over a specified time period.
(2) synonymous with *profit and loss statement.*

income and profit: income and profit involve net or partially net concepts and refer to amounts resulting from the deduction from revenues, or from operating revenues, of cost of goods sold, other expenses, and losses, or some of them. The terms are often used interchangeably and are generally preceded by an appropriate qualifying adjective or term such as "gross," "operating," "net . . . before income taxes," and "net." [77]

income approach to value: a procedure for property appraisal in which the value on the net amount of income produced by the property is used. This value is determined by subtracting the total income of the property from expenses to determine net profit.

income available for fixed charges: total income less miscellaneous deductions, which consist of expenses of miscellaneous operations, taxes on miscellaneous operating property, miscellaneous rents and tax accruals, loss on separately operated properties, maintenance of investment organizations, income transferred to other companies, and miscellaneous income charges. [8]

income averaging: see *averaging.*

income beneficiary: a person who, by the terms of a will or a trust instrument, is entitled to receive income from property for a specified number of years or for life. [37]

income bond: see *bond, income.*

income capital certificates: Federal Home Loan Bank Board Certificates that are agreements to pay back a corporation's loan, plus interest, when and if associations in financial difficulty get into a better position. Payments are installments, and are always less than the association's net income. Income capital certificates were initiated in September 1981.

income coverage
(1) *direct:* the extent to which net income from portfolio investments

(after deduction of any prior interest or preferred dividend requirements) covers the requirements of a specific senior obligation, whether bank loans, debentures or preferred stock; in computing the coverage for bank loans or debentures, interest actually paid is added back to net income. The coverage figure may be expressed in dollars, as a percentage, or as a ratio.

(2) *overall:* the amount by which net income from portfolio investments plus interest actually paid covers total interest charges, if any, senior preferred dividends, if any, and the dividend requirement of the subject issue. [30]

income debenture: a corporate bond paying interest only when earned. By means of a subordinate venture, the interest it bears is senior to stock dividends.

income deductions: includes interest on long-term debt, amortization of debt discount, expanse and premium-net, taxes assumed on interest, interest on debt to associated companies, other interest charges, interest charged to construction (credit), miscellaneous amortization and income deductions (any nonrecurring income deductions of a material amount should be noted). [3]

income distribution: the way in which personal income is dispensed throughout the various socioeconomic levels in a nation.

income dividends: payments to mutual fund shareholders of dividends, interest, and short-term capital gains earned on the fund's portfolio securities after deduction of operating expenses. [23]

income effect: the change in the quantity of an item demanded because a person's purchasing power has been altered.

income fund: an investment company whose primary objective is generous current income. May be a balanced fund, common stock fund, bond fund, or a preferred stock fund. [30]

income property: property, usually commercial, industrial, or residential, owned or purchased for a financial return expected.

income return: monies earned from an investment over the period of one year. see *yield.*

income statement

(1) *general:* the profit and loss statement of a given concern for a particular period of time.

(2) *banking:* a copy of the income cash ledger for a particular trust account.

income tax: a tax on annual earnings and profits of a person, corporation, or other organization. Traditionally, there are federal, state, and city taxes, although not all states and not all cities tax income.

income velocity of money: the average number of times each year that a dollar is spent on purchasing the economy's annual flow of final goods and/or services—its gross national product.

incoming clearings: checks and drafts received from other banks in the same city. [31]

incoming exchanges: those checks presented by member banks to a clearinghouse for clearing purposes. see *clearinghouse.*

incoming mail: checks and drafts received through the mail for deposit from other banks and depositors. [31]

incompetent: one who is incapable of managing his affairs because of mental deficiency or undeveloped mentality. Children and idiots are incompetents in the eyes of the law. [62]

incontestable: a clause stating that after a certain period, the insurance policy may not be disputed except for nonpayment of the premiums.

inconvertible money: irredeemable funds; circulating money that cannot be converted into the standard. United States money has been inconvertible since 1933 because it is not redeemable in gold. see *fiat money.* synonymous with "irredeemable money."

incorporate: to form into a corporation; become a corporation. [62]

incorporated trustee: any trust company or bank under its charter and by law that can serve as a fiduciary.

incorporation: the procedure in obtaining a state charter to form a corporation.

incorporation by reference: a reference in one document to the contents of another document in such a manner as to give legal effect to the material to which reference is made. [32]

incorporeal: of no material substance; existing with no physical properties (e.g., rights, privileges).

incorporeal property: intangible, personal property (i.e., without body); includes property rights, mortgages, and leases. see *choses in action.*

increasing-cost industry: an industry that experiences increases in re-

source prices or in manufacturing costs as it expands when new firms enter it.

incremental: describes the additional investment required for a project or additional cash flows resulting from a project.

incumbrance: see *encumbrance.*

incurably depreciated: describes damaged property that is beyond rehabilitation or property that is uneconomical to repair.

incurred losses: loss transactions occurring within a fixed period, usually a year. For example, calendar-year incurred losses are customarily computed in accordance with the following formula: losses paid during the period, plus outstanding losses at the end of the period, less outstanding losses at the beginning of the period.

indebtedness: a debt is owed; any form of liability.

indefeasible: incapable of being annulled or rendered void; as, an indefeasible title to property. [37]

indemnify: to compensate for actual loss sustained. Many insurance policies and all bonds promise to "indemnify" the insureds. Under such a contract, there can be no recovery until the insured has actually suffered a loss, at which time he or she is entitled to be compensated for the damage that has occurred (i.e., to be restored to the same financial position enjoyed before the loss).

indemnity

(1) *general:* payment for damage; a guarantee against losses.

(2) *finance:* a bond protecting the insured against losses from others failing to fulfill their obligations. see *bond, indemnity.*

(3) *investments:* an option to buy or sell a specific quantity of a stock at a state price within a given time period.

(4) *law:* an act of legislation, granting exemption from prosecution to certain people.

indemnity bond: see *bond, indemnity.*

indent: the request from a purchaser to an importer to import specific items at a stated price. The importer has a given time period in which to accept or refuse the offer.

indent.: see *indenture.*

indenture

(1) *finance:* a written agreement under which debentures are issued, setting forth maturity date, interest rate, and other terms. [20]

(2) *law:* an agreement binding one person to work with or without pay for another for a stated period (e.g., apprenticeship). An obsolete agreement.

(3) see *trust indenture.*

indenture bond: see *bond, indenture.*

independent audit: an audit performed by an independent auditor. see also *audit report, independent auditor.*

independent auditor: an auditor who is independent of the governmental unit or agency whose accounts are being audited.

independent bank: a bank that operates in one locality. The directors and officers are generally local to the community.

Independent Bankers Association of America: created in 1930, an association to promote the interest of independent banking in the United States as a vibrant, contributing force within the economy.

independent broker: members on the floor of the New York Stock Exchange who execute orders for other brokers having more business at that time than they can handle themselves, or for firms who do not have their exchange member on the floor. Formerly known as the two-dollar brokers—from the time when these independent brokers received $2 per 100 shares for executing such orders. Their fees are paid by the commission brokers. see *commission broker.* [20]

independent executor: an executor of a will, who, after filing has inventory, does not make further accounting to the probate court; recognized by statute in only a few states. [37]

indeterminate appropriation: an appropriation that is not limited either to any definite period of time or to any definite amount, or to both time and amount. [49]

index

(1) *general:* an ordered reference list of the contents of a file or document, together with keys or reference notations for identification of location of those contents.

(2) *government:* a statistical yardstick expressed in terms of percentages of a base year or years. For example, the Federal Reserve Board's index of industrial production is based on 1967 as 100. In April 1973 the index stood at 121.7 which meant that industrial production during that month was about 22 percent higher than in the base period.

indexation: formally adjusting wages and other kinds of incomes such as rents, pensions, or interest payments to changes in inflation.

index fund: a mutal fund whose investment objective is to match the composite investment performance of a large group of publicly traded common stocks, generally those represented by the Standard & Poor's 500-Composite-Stock Index. [23]

indexing: an increasingly popular form of investing: investments are weighted in line with one of the major stock indices (e.g., Standard & Poor's 500-Composite-Stock Index.).

Index of National Enervation and Related Trends (INERT): a U.S. Department of Commerce measure of the rate of increase of the figure for the gross national product.

indicated yield: a term used to describe the current return or yield to maturity of stocks and bonds.

indifference schedule: a table illustrating all combinations of two commodities that are equally satisfactory or yield the same total utility to a recipient at a specified time.

indirect business tax and nontax liability: all tax liabilities incurred by business, except for corporate income and social insurance taxes, plus general government nontax revenues from business. Nontax liabilities consist mainly of certain charges for government products and services, fines and penalties, donations, and special assessments by state and local governments.

indirect control: control of an individual, a corporation, or other legal person, as exercised through an intermediary. [18]

indirect costs: costs not usually identifiable with or incurred as the result of the manufacture of goods or services, but applicable to a productive

activity generally. Included are costs from manufacturing operations (wages, maintenance, overhead, etc.). see *running costs.*

indirect expense: expenses such as rent, taxes, and insurance which cannot be specifically charged to the department or cost center that benefit from them. They are generally accumulated for a period and the total then distributed on some equitable basis. [38]

indirect labor costs: wages of non-production employees, such as maintenance crews, inspectors, timekeepers, tool crib attendants, and sweepers.

indirect liability: a party who endorses the note of a maker for a bank or guarantees a note as guarantor for a maker is said to have indirect liability on the note.

indirect origination: the purchase of a ready-made loan from a source other than a regular lender (such as a subdivision contractor, or a mobile home or home improvement dealer), usually as part of an on-going business relationship between the association and the seller. see also *loan origination.* [59]

individual account: an account in the name of one individual, as contrasted with an account or a corporation, a partnership, or an account in two or more names. [50]

individual banker: a private banker; an unincorporated bank, found in only a few states.

individual policy pension trust: a type of pension plan, frequently used for small groups, administered by trustees who are authorized to purchase individual level premium policies or annuity contracts for each member of the plan. The policies usually provide both life insurance and retirement benefits. [58]

Individual Retirement Accounts (IRA): originally, individual pension accounts available to anyone not covered at work by a qualified pension plan. Effective January 1, 1982, all wage earners, including those already in company pension plans are able to make tax-deductible contributions to IRAs. An individual can now put away an extra $2000 a year, or a total of $2250 if there is a non-working spouse, and let the earnings accumulate tax-free until age 59½. see *Employer Retirement Income Security Act of 1974*; see also *Economic Recovery Tax Act of 1981, Keogh plan.*

Indm.: see *indemnity.*

indorsee: see *endorsee.*

indorsement: see *endorsement.*

indorser: see *endorser.*

induced investment: new capital formation caused by an upturn in consumer buying.

industrial bank: a financial instutition originally organized to extend loans to employees. The bank derives its funds through a form of worker savings. Most industrial banks have now been merged into commercial banks. cf. *labor banks.*

industrial collateral: a category of stock exchange collateral where brokers who borrow in the call money market present to the lending institution either industrial or regular collateral. This collateral is represented by the firm's traded stocks.

industrial credit: debt incurred by industrial or business firms to meet payrolls, buy raw materials, build new plants. [55]

industrial insurance
(1) life insurance on an individual in an amount under $1000, with premiums payable weekly to an agent who calls at the insured's home to collect. see *debit.*
(2) also called weekly premium insurance.

industrialist: an individual who owns, controls, or plays a critical role in the operation of an industrial organization.

industrial life insurance: see *industrial insurance.*

industrial loan commitments: amount of loans to industrial borrowers which have been approved but for which the funds have not yet been advanced to them. [40]

industrial loans: loans outstanding to industrial borrowers under an amendment to the Federal Reserve Act which authorized the Federal Reserve Banks to make loans to certain business firms unable to get credit from other financial institutions on reasonable terms. This authority was terminated in August 1959. [40]

industrial production: a measure issued by the Federal Reserve mid-month for the previous month, of the physical output of factories and mines.

industrial psychology: the branch of applied psychology concerned with the behavior and motivation of individual workers. Activities include testing, selection, training, and other aspects of individual and/or group interactions on the job.

industrial relations: any activity, event, or interaction between employer and employee. It commences with the job interview and lasts throughout the working lifetime of an employee. The most popular usage of the term limits it to union-management relations.

industrials: corporate securities of firms involved in the production and/or sale of services or commodities.

industry

(1) *general:* trade, business, production, or manufacture.

(2) *government:* as determined by the Standard Industrial Classification (SIC) system of the U.S. Bureau of the Census, any commercial activity identified by this listing.

inelastic demand (inelasticity): exists when a price increase leads to a higher total sales, revenue, or a price decrease leads to a lower sales revenue. A perfectly inelastic demand occurs when the demand for an item does not change with changes in price.

inelastic supply: a condition in which the quantity of an item produced does not alter, or changes minimally, with a price change.

inequities: rates or conditions substantially out of line with those paid or existing for comparable work in a plant, locality, or industry.

INERT: see *Index of National Enervation and Related Trends.*

infant industry argument: a dispute in support of import restrictions, claiming that specific new domestic firms have not reached their ultimate level of technical superiority and consequently required temporary protection from products from abroad.

infirmity: in the creation or transfer of title, any known act or visible omis-

sion in detail, that would invalidate the instrument.

inflation: an increase in the price level creating a decrease in the purchasing power of the monetary unit. cf. *deflation, flation, hesiflation, hyperinflation, overheating, prime interest (rate), simultaneous inflation and unemployment, speculation, stagflation.*

inflation, runaway: see *galloping inflation.*

inflation accounting: the bookkeeping practice that shows the impact of inflation on corporate assets and profits.

inflationary gap: the amount by which government and private spending exceeds the amount needed to maintain a stable price level and full employment.

inflationary spiral: in a time of rising prices, employees demand higher wages, which in turn increases costs, leading sellers and producers then to demand still higher prices. see *stabilization policy, wage stabilization*; cf. *Pigou effect concept.*

inflationitis: slang for "the dollar-ain't-worth-a-hill-o'-beans blues."

inflump: see *simultaneous inflation and unemployment.*

informatics: see *information science.*

information

(1) *general:* the meaning that a human assigns to data by means of the conventions used in their representation.

(2) *computers:* the collection of data, numbers, characters, and so on, which is processed or produced by a computer.

information processing: same as *data processing.*

information retrieval

(1) *general:* the methods and procedures for recovering specific information from stored data.

(2) *general:* a technique for cataloguing data all related to one field so that such data can be called for at any time with speed.

(3) *computers:* a branch of computer science relating to the methods for storing and searching quantities of information.

information science: the study of how data are processed and transmitted through digit processing equipment. synonymous with *"informatics."*

infrastructure: the basic structure of a nation's economy, including transportation, communications, and other public services, on which the economic activity relies.

infringement

(1) *general:* encroaching on someone else's property (i.e., trespassing). cf. *intrusion.*

(2) *law:* the production of an item that yields the same results by the same action as a patented item. A patent infringement.

(3) *law:* the reproduction of a registered trademark and its use on merchandise to mislead the public into believing that the items bearing the reproduced trademark are the product of the true owner of the trademark. A trademark infringement.

in gear: the parallel rise of two or more indicaters of an economic condition or activity; for example, when the Dow Jones Industrial Average and the Transporatation Averages both rise, they are "in gear."

ingress: the ability to enter property or land.

inherit: to acquire the property of a person who dies intestate. see also *devolution.*

inheritance: the act of inheriting; any possession coming as a gift; any characteristic passed on by heredity. see *Tax Reform Act of 1976.*

inheritance taxes: taxes levied by the states on property received by inheritance or by succession; a tax on inherited property. cf. *estate tax, succession tax.*

inheritance tax return: the return that the executor or administrator is required to make to the state on the basis of which the inheritance tax due the state is calculated and paid; to be distinguished from the federal estate tax return. [37]

inheritance tax waiver: a release, signed by the appropriate state taxing official, relinquishing any claim of the state to the assets of an estate, or a portion thereof, under consideration. [59]

initial margin: the amount a buyer is requested to deposit with a broker before commencing trading. cf. *maintenance margin.* see also *margin, margin call.*

Inj.: see *injunction.*

injunction: a court order advising the party that if it does commit the enjoined-against act, there will be a penalty. A temporary restraining order is issued for a limited time. A permanent injunction is issued after a full hearing. In 1932 the Norris-La-Guardia (Anti-Injunction) Act forbade the federal courts to issue injunctions unless certain conditions were fulfilled first. see also *blanket injunction.*

injunction pendente lite: a court remedy before the hearing of the merits of a suit, for the express purpose of preventing the doing of any act whereby the conditions in the conflict might be substantially altered. see also *lis pendens.*

inland bill of exchange: a bill drawn and payable in the same state. [39]

innocent purchaser: an individual who in good faith does not expect any hidden property defects to appear when he has gained title to real property.

in personam: a legal judgment binding the defendant to a personal liability. cf. *in rem.*

input/output (I/O): a general term for equipment used to communicate with a computer.

in rem: a legal judgment that binds, affects, or determines the status of property. cf. *in personam.*

Ins.: see *insurance.*

in shape for sale: a term describing the condition in which a security will make a good delivery. [37]

insider: an individual who, because of his or her employment position, has special information dealing with the financial status of a firm before that information is released to the public or to stockholders. see *smart money.*

in sight: a commodities term describing the quantity of goods that are to be delivered to a particular location.

insolvency: the inability to pay one's debts as they mature. Even though the total assets of a business might exceed its total liabilities by a wide margin, the business is said to be insolvent if the assets are such that they cannot be readily converted into cash to meet the current obligations of the business as they mature.

insolvent: an individual who has ceased to pay his or her debts or is unable to pay such debts as demanded by creditors. see *bankrupt, bankruptcy.*

inspection report: information gathered by a mercantile source and compiled in report form to be used to supplement underwriting material in the selection of risks. The primary purpose of the report is to verify information given on the application. [12]

Inst.
(1)   see *installment (instalment).*
(2)   see *instant.*
(3)   see *instrument.*

installment (instalment): a partial payment on the purchase price for any item, sold with the agreement that the remaining monies will be paid on a specified due date.

installment account: see *charge account.*

installment bond: see *bond, serial.*

installment buying: acquiring goods or services with no down payment or a small down payment; to be followed by payments at regular intervals.

installment cash credit: money loans directly to an individual and repaid through periodic payments over a specified length of time. [55]

installment credit: a form of consumer credit involving regular payments; permitting the seller to reacquire the item bought if the buyer fails to meet the payment schedule.

installment financing: that form of financing which involves the repayment or amortization of an obligation by payments of fixed amounts at regular intervals. [55]

installment loan: synonymous with *personal loan.*

installment refund annuity: a live annuity providing that, upon the premature death of the annuitant, benefit payments will be continued to a specified beneficiary until the total of payments to the retirant and to the beneficiary equals the consideration paid for the annuity. [52]

Installment Sale Revision Act of 1980: this legislation liberalized the rules for postponing tax on property that is sold on the deferred-payment basis.

installment-sales (homes): homeowners wanting to sell their homes who act as lenders can reap a tax benefit by allowing purchasers to pay in installments. The Internal Revenue Service allows sellers to spread their gain over a number of years instead of reporting it all in the year of sale, and thus to defer most of the capital gains tax on the profit.

installment sales credit: a one-shot loan used to buy "big ticket" items, such as cars or appliances. A down payment is usually required and a contract is signed for the balance due, plus interest and service charges. The debt is repaid in equal installments over a specified period of time. Generally involves three parties: the buyer, the seller, and the lender. [78]

instant (inst.): a business term designating the present month (e.g., on the 10th inst.) cf. *proximo.*

Institute of Financial Education: a national educational organization, affiliated with the United States League of Savings Association, dedicated to increasing the professional skills of savings association personnel through classroom courses, home study, executive training programs, seminars, workshops, clinics, and other methods. Formerly called the American Savings and Loan Institute. [59]

institution: an organization (e.g., bank, insurance company, investment company pension fund) holding substantial investment assets, often for others.

institutional investor: a company having substantial funds invested in securities (e.g., a bank, labor union, college).

Instl.: see *installment (instalment).*

instrument: any written document that gives formal expression to a legal agreement or act.

instrumentalities: agencies of the federal government whose obligations are not the direct obligation of the federal government.

insufficient funds: a term used when a depositor's balance is inadequate for the bank to pay a check that has been presented. A service charge is often placed on the customer when the balance is not sufficient to pay the check.

insular bond:see *bond, insular.*

insurable interest (life version): the monetary interest of the beneficiary of a life insurance contract in the continued life of the person insured. Insurable interest exists only to the extent that the beneficiary will suffer financial loss as the result of the death of an insured.

insurable interest (property and liability version): any interest in or relation to property of such nature that the occurrence of an event insured against would cause financial loss to the insured.

insurance

(1) *general:* a method whereby those concerned about some form of hazard contribute to a common fund, usually an insurance company, out of which losses sustained by the contributors are paid. see also *self-insurance.*

(2) *law:* a contractual relationship that exists when one party (the insurer), for a consideration (the premium), agrees to reimburse another party (the insured) for loss to a specified subject (the risk) caused by designated contingencies (hazards or perils), or to pay on behalf of the insured all reasonable sums for which he may be liable to a third party (the claimant).

insurance company: an organization chartered under state or provincial laws to act as an insurer. In the United States, insurance companies are usually classified as fire and marine, life, casualty, and surety companies and may write only the kinds of insurance for which they are specifically authorized by their charters.

insurance coverage: the total amount of insurance that is carried.

insurance policy: broadly, the entire written contract of insurance. More specifically, it is the basic written or printed document, as well as the coverage forms and endorsement added to it.

insurance premium: see *premium.*

insurance trust: an instrument composed wholly or partially of life insurance policy contracts.

insurance trust expenditures: cash payments to beneficiaries of contributory social insurance programs (employee retirement funds, unemployment compensation, sickness insurance, etc.). Excludes cost of administration, intergovernmental expenditures for social insurance, and noncontributory payments to former employees.

insurance trust revenue: revenue from contributions required of employers and employees for financial social insurance programs operated by state and local governments, plus earnings on assets held for such systems.

insured: the person(s) protected under an insurance contract.

insured account: a savings account, up to but not exceeding the prescribed maximum amount, that is held in an association whose accounts are insured by the Federal Savings and Loan Insurance Corporation or a bank belonging to the Federal Deposit Insurance Corporation.

insured association: an association whose savings accounts are insured by the Federal Savings and Loan Insurance Corporation. [59]

insured bank: a bank that is a member of the Federal Deposit Insurance Corporation.

insured life: the person on whose life the policy is issued. [58]

insured member: an individual, a partnership, an association, a corporation, a trustee under a trust or a custodian of public funds, holding an account at an insured association. [59]

insurer: the party to the insurance contract who promises to indemnify losses or provide service.

intangible asset: an asset that has no substance or physical body; it is incorporeal. The most widely known types of intangible asset are goodwill and patented rights. These assets are purchased, sometimes for very substantial outlays of capital. Their value to the purchaser lies in the use he or she can make of them, although they cannot be seen. see *chose(s) in action.*

intangible tax: a state tax levied on all deposits in a bank (stocks, bonds, notes, etc.), excluding certain exempted items. The tax is against the individual accounts.

integrated company: a firm that has united its multiple units or items for the purpose of widening its market territory to achieve efficiency, and improve costs.

integrated data processing: see *IDP.*

inter alia: among other things.

Inter-American Development Bank: established in 1959 to encourage economic development of 21 member nations in Latin America. Twenty representatives from Latin American countries and the United States initiated this effort. see also *Alliance for Progress.*

Interbank: the New York-based originator of Master Card. Interbank is a nonprofit institution originally formed by a group of banks to combat Bank of America's credit card system.

interbank borrowing: usually done when banks find themselves temporarily low on liquidity and approach banks that have an excess of liquidity in order to borrow funds.

interbank demand deposits: deposits held for other commercial or savings banks; the breakdown shows the amounts for domestic (United States) and foreign banks. [40]

Interbank National Authorization System (INAS): the national authorization network used to approve Master Card credit transactions. [36]

interbranch: a term associated with any action or function that takes place between or among the various branches of a bank. As an example, an interbranch memorandum would be sent to all branches within a banking organization to inform them of some action, function, or decision to be instituted. All branches would receive the same message, so that all would be coordinated and put the action into effect at the same time in the same manner. [10]

interchangeable bond: see *bond, interchangeable.*

intercommodity spread: a position between two related commodities; for example, a long wheat and a short corn position is an intercommodity spread. see *interdelivery spread, intermarket spread.*

intercorporate stockholding: an unlawful condition where a corporation holds stock in other corporations and this interferes with competition (e.g., restraint of trade).

interdelivery (or intramarket) spread: the most common type of spread consisting of buying one month and selling another month in the same commodity. An example of such a spread would be long December corn/short September corn. see also *intercommodity spread, intermarket spread.*

Interdistrict Settlement Fund: a U.S. Treasury gold certificate fund held for the account of and subject to the control of the Federal Reserve System to minimize the time and expense of settlement of the inter-Federal Reserve Bank transactions.

interest: the price paid for the borrowed use of a commodity, usually money. see *money rates;* cf. *pure interest.*

interest and penalties receivable on taxes: the uncollected portion of interest and penalties receivable on taxes. [49]

interest coverage: applies to the frequency with which interest charges are earned; found by dividing the sum of the fixed charges into the earnings available for such charges, either before or after deducting income taxes.

interest earned but not collected: represents interest on loans which has not been collected in advance, but is due and payable at specified times. Interest on demand loans usually comes into this class, collection being made each month, each quarter, or longer period of time, based upon bills being sent to the borrower for interest due. This is an asset (resources) account in the general ledger. synonymous with "interest receivable." [10]

interest equalization tax: a form of foreign-exchange control established by the U.S. government in the early 1960s whereby any U.S. resident has to pay a special tax on any purchase of overseas securities.

interest on long-term debt: interest on outstanding bonds (mortgage and debenture), receivers' certificates, and miscellaneous long-term debt, notes, and so on, issued or assumed by the utility and which are due one year or more from date of issuance. [3]

interest only account: an account which in the last two calendar months has made one or more payments of which nothing was applied to principal (ledger card balance). Loans made during the last two calendar months are excluded. [55]

interest only mortgage: where mortgage payments are smaller for a set period, with the principal paid off when the property is sold.

interest-rate peg: monetary policy followed from 1942 to 1951 where the Federal Reserve System adjusted the amount of money in order to maintain a constant interest rate on Treasury securities. see *Monetary Accord of 1951.*

interest receivable on investments: the amount of interest receivable on investments, exclusive of interest purchased. Interest purchased should be shown in a separate account. [49]

interest receivable on special assessments: the amount of interest receivable on unpaid installments of special assessments. [49]

interest short: a term describing the amount by which a payment is insufficient to pay the accrued interest on an account. [55]

interest table: a broad term given to any mechanical indexing device, or chart, permitting independent calculation of simple or compound interest, the discount or present value, and the like, on varied amounts for certain or varied times. [10]

interest waived: refers to the amount of interest due on an account which is relinquished due to certain circumstances and arrangements made for repayment of an account. [55]

interest warrant: a firm's request for payment of interest due on its notes, debts, and so on. see *warrant.*

interest yield: the uniform rate of interest on investments computed on the basis of the price at which the investment was purchased, giving effect to the periodic amortization of any premiums paid or to the periodic accrual of discounts received. [52]

interfund accounts: accounts in which transactions between funds are reflected. see *interfund transfers.* [49]

interfund loans: loans made by one fund to another. [49]

interfund transfers: amounts transferred from one fund to another. [49]

intergovernmental expenditures: payment to other governments as fiscal aid or as reimbursements for the performance of services for the paying government. synonymous with *revenue sharing.* cf. *direct expenditures.*

intergovernmental revenue: revenue received from other governments as fiscal aid, shared taxes, and reimbursements for services performed. synonymous with *shared revenue.*

interim bond: see *bond, interim.*

interim borrowing: the sale of short-term paper in anticipation of bond issuance. see also *bond anticipation notes.* [49]

interim certificate: see *bond, interim certificate.*

interim dividend: any dividend given to shareholders ahead of the full (regular) dividend.

interim loan: a short-term construction loan made to finance improvements on real property. [22]

interim receiver: a court-appointed individual asked to protect a debtor's property until an official receiver is appointed.

interim statement: a financial statement prepared before the end of the current fiscal year and covering only financial transactions during the current year to date. see *statement.* [49]

interim warrants: see *interim borrowing.*

interlocking directorate: the condition in which one or more members of the board of directors of one business also are members of the board of directors of other corporations.

interlocutory decree: issued before a final court decree; an intermediate decree that does not resolve the matter but settles some portion of it.

intermarket spread: involves purchasing a commodity deliverable on one exchange and selling the same commodity deliverable on another exchange (e.g., long Chicago December wheat/short Kansas City December wheat). see *intercommodity spread, interdelivery spread.*

Intermarket Trading System: a computerized system connecting the six exchanges in the nation (American Stock Exchange, Boston Stock Exchange, Midwest Stock Exchange, New York Stock Exchange, Philadelphia Stock Exchange, and Pacific Stock Exchange) which transmits commitments to buy or sell to each simultaneously. Price information is displayed on a video screen at each exchange where traders then accept or reject the prospective transaction on the basis of the price. sometimes referred to as "electronic handshake."

intermediate bond: see *bond, intermediate.*

intermediate-term credit: credit that is generally extended over a period of 3 to 10 years.

intermediation: the investment process in which savers and investors place funds in financial institutions in the form of savings accounts and the financial institutions in turn use the funds to make loans and other investments. [59]

internal audit: a business audit carried out by the firm itself on a continuous basis. cf. *look back.*

internal bond: see *bond, internal.*

internal check: coordinated methods and measures adopted by an organization to check the accuracy and validity of data and to safeguard assets.

internal controls: methods and measures employed to promote efficiency, encourage acceptance of managerial procedures and policies, check the validity of management data, and protect assets.

internal debt: the debt of a nation.

internal economies of scale: factors that bring about increases or decreases to an organization's long-run average costs or scale of operations resulting from size adjustments with the company as a product unit. They occur primarily because of physical economies or diseconomies. see *diseconomies of scale.*

internal items: debit or credit memoranda prepared by or for an officer of the bank to adjust the balance in the general ledger and for a customer's account. Examples include corrections, loan proceeds, special customer charges, and certification entries. [31]

internal memory: the internal parts of a data-processing machine capable of retaining data.

internal revenue bond: see *bond, internal revenue.*

Internal Revenue Code of 1954: federal legislation; provided for a complete revision of the Internal Revenue Code of 1939. Includes provisions for dividend credit and exclusion, retirement income credit, and accelerated depreciation. Changes in tax laws since 1954 have been enacted as amendments to this code.

Internal Revenue Service (IRS): the federal agency empowered by Congress to administer the rules and regulations of the Department of the Treasury, which includes the collection of federal income and other taxes. It is divided into 9 regions with 64 districts and is also responsible for the investigation and prevention of tax frauds.

International Bank for Reconstruction and Development (IBRD—The World Bank): proposed at Bretton Woods in July 1944, commencing operation in June 1946. After phasing out activities of reconstruction, primary efforts are made to provide loans for economic development. see *International Monetary Fund.* see also *Development Finance Companies.*

International Banking Act of 1978: federal legislation designed to remove many of the competitive advantages that foreign banks had over their domestic counterparts. The Federal Reserve Bank is now authorized to impose reserve requirements on foreign banks, for example, and for the first time there are restrictions on their ability to take deposits nationwide. Its basic purpose is to apply the McFadden Act of 1927, which forbids branching by American banks across state lines, to foreign banks. Until passage of this new act, foreigners have been free to open branches in any state which allowed them in. see *Edge Act.*

international banking facilities (IBFs): specially designated offices in the United States, identified by the Federal Reserve Board, permitting banks to take deposits from and make loans to nonresidents, including overseas subsidiaries of U.S. companies.

International Commercial Exchange: established in 1970, following the passage of the Commodity Exchange Act, to create a currency futures trading market. An international commercial exchange clearing association was also formed. This institution replaced the New York Produce Exchange.

International Emergency Economic Powers Act of 1977: this federal law grants the president authority "to deal with any unusual and extraordinary threat, which has its source in whole or substantial part outside the United States, to the national security, foreign policy, or economy of the United States, if the president declares a national emergency with respect to such a threat." President Carter, utilizing this law in November 1979 froze all official Iranian assets in the United States.

International Finance Corporation: established in 1956, this investing organization purports to aid in the expansion of private business in less developed industrial nations.

international liquidity: the total for all internationally acceptable currencies in the monetary system of the world.

International Monetary Fund (IMF): to restore orderly exchange practices following World War II, the IMF was formed and became operational on March 1, 1947. Member nations can borrow foreign currencies from the fund under specified conditions. Membership in the fund is a prerequisite to membership in the International Bank for Reconstruction and Development. see *Bretton Woods Agreement of 1944, special drawing rights.*

international payments mechanism: the organization of markets whereby the monies of different nations are exchanged. see *swap.*

interpleader: when an individual who has an obligation to pay for services or goods does not know which of two or more claimants should receive his or her obligation, he or she brings a suit requiring the claimants to litigate between themselves.

interpositioning: when brokerage houses create an arrangement to create business when acting in behalf of two principal companies in a stock transaction. Abuses of interpositioning are illegal under SEC regulations.

in terrorem clause: a provision of a will or trust agreement intended or, at any rate, calculated to frighten a possible beneficiary into doing or refraining from doing something at the peril of forfeiting his possible benefits—such as a provision that would disinherit any named or potential beneficiary who contested the will. [37]

interrupt

(1) *computers:* to stop a process in such a way that it can be resumed without destroying work already done.

(2) *operations research:* to stop a current control sequence.

(3) *systems:* a break in the normal flow of a system or routine, permitting the flow to be restarted from that point at a later time.

interstate branching bill: a concept that allows banks from other states to open branches with broad services in a different state, and vice-versa. In principle, interstate branch banking creates a free trade zone, but presently remains prohibited by the McFadden Act of 1927.

interstate carrier: a common carrier whose business extends beyond the boundaries of one state.

interstate commerce: commerce, including the transporting of goods and services across the boundaries of more than one state.

Interstate Commerce Act of 1887: federal legislation regulating the practices, rates, and rules of transportation carriers engaged in handling interstate shipments or the movement for a fee of people across state lines.

Interstate Commerce Commission (ICC): a federal agency established to enforce the Interstate Commerce Act and other related acts affecting common carriers engaged in interstate commerce.

Interstate Land Sales Full Disclosure Act of 1968: federal legislation requiring all large land-sales promoters to furnish prospective buyers with a detailed and accurate report on the land and to spell out buyers' rights in the transaction.

intervention currency: the foreign currency a country uses to ensure by means of official exchange transactions that the permitted exchange rate margins are observed. Intervention usually takes the form of purchases and sales of foreign currency by the central bank or exchange equalization fund in domestic dealings with commercial banks. [42]

interview: a conversation designed to yield information for purposes of research or assistance in guidance, counseling, or treatment. see *interview, structured; interview, unstructured.*

interview, exit: a conference with an employee before termination of his or her relationship with the organization to determine reasons for leaving, future plans, and general attitudes toward the job and company.

interview, structured: an interview in which the asking of definite questions closely controls the subjects discussed.

interview, unstructured: an interview in which the interviewer does not determine the format or subject to be discussed, thus leaving the interviewee in major control of the conversation.

interview bias: influence resulting from the presence of personal prejudice of the individual conducting the interview.

inter vivos: "between living persons" (Latin). In the term "trust inter vivos" or "inter vivos trust," the same as living trust. see also *gift inter vivos.* [32]

intestacy: the condition resulting

from a person's dying without leaving a valid will. [32]

intestate: not having a valid will; when a person dies intestate, his or her estate is persented for settlement to administrators. see *escheat.*

intestate succession: the descent and distribution of property of a person who dies without a valid will. [37]

in the black: slang, describing a business that is functioning with a profit.

in the money: a situation in which the striking price is below the market price of the underlying stock for a call, or the striking price is above the market price of the underlying stock for a put. [5]

in the red: slang, describes a business that is functioning at a loss.

Intl.: *international.*

in toto: in the entire amount.

intrabranch: a term used to express an action or function that is ordered to take place within an individual branch or office, and does not affect the action of other branches or offices of an organization. An example would be a personnel problem such as tardiness or absenteeism that applies only to one office or branch of an organization. An intrabranch memorandum would be sent to all departments within the one office or branch involved. [10]

intracity: an action or function taking place within one city. As an example, intracity clearings between banks within one city. This is to be distinguished from intercity clearings or collections, which means the exchange of items through transit between different cities. [10]

intracommodity spread: a position in the same commodity but different months on the same exchange.

intragovernmental service fund: a fund established to finance and account for services and commodities furnished by a designated department or agency to other departments and agencies within a single governmental unit. Amounts expended by the fund are restored thereto either from operating earnings or by transfers from other funds, so that the original fund capital is kept intact. Formerly called a "working capital fund." [49]

intramarket spread: see *interdelivery spread.*

intrastate commerce: commerce conducted solely within a state's geographic borders.

intrastate securities: over-the-counter shares issued and distributed within only one state.

intrinsic value

(1) *general:* the market value of the material in a thing (e.g., the value of the metal in a gold tooth filling).

(2) *investments:* the excess of the market value of the underlying stock over the striking price of the option for a call, or the excess of the striking price of the option over the market value of the underlying stock for a put. [5]

intrusion: forcefully taking possession of another's real property.

Inv.: see *invoice.*

inventory: the name given to an asset of a business. Inventories are of two general types: direct and indirect. (a) Direct inventory in an industrial concern consists of raw materials, work-in-process, and finished goods. Direct inventories represent various stages of fabrication; in commercial and retail businesses, they are inventories purchased for resale. (b) Indirect inventories, in general, are all supplies used to carry on the business and not purchased for resale. Indirect inventories are usually considered as deferred assets.

inventory financing: the attempt to find the necessary capital for a firm by borrowing funds with inventory used as collateral.

inventory of stores for resale: the value of goods held by a governmental enterprise for resale rather than use in its own operations. [49]

inventory of supplies: the cost value of supplies on hand. [49]

inventory to net working capital: merchandise inventory is divided by net working capital. This is an additional measure of inventory balance. Ordinarily, the relationship should not exceed 80 percent. [4]

inventory turnover: the number of times, on the average, that inventory is replaced during a period. It is calculated by dividing cost of goods sold by average inventory.

inventory valuation adjustment: corporate profits and income of unincorporated enterprises include inventory profit or loss in customary business accounting. Current output in the national income accounts, however, includes only the value of the change in volume in inventories.

inverse demand pattern: exists when price and volume vary at the same time and more is sold at a high price than at a lower one.

inverted market: a commodity futures market where distant-month contracts are selling lower than near-month contracts.

invested capital: the amount of capital contributed to a company by its owners.

investment: the use of money for the purpose of making more money, to gain income or increase capital, or both.

Investment Advisers Act: federal legislation of 1940 to regulate investment advisers, in order to protect the public from misrepresentation and dishonest investment tactics, by identifying specific unlawful activities. All investment advisers are required to register with the SEC, the administrator of the Investment Advisers Act.

investment banker: the middleman between the corporation issuing new securities and the public. The usual practice is for one or more investment bankers to buy outright from a corporation a new issue of stock or bonds. The group forms a syndicate to sell the securities to individuals and institutions. The investment banker is the underwriter of the issue.

Investment Bankers Association: a national fraternity of investment bankers engaged in investment banking activities. The IBA was founded in 1912.

investment banking: the financing of the capital requirements of an enterprise rather than the current "working capital" requirements of a business.

investment banking house: one that engages in the merchandising of corporate and government securities by purchasing them in large blocks and selling them to investors. It helps to finance the capital, or long-term, credit requirements of business organizations, whereas the commercial bank finances their short-term credit requirements. [50]

investment certificate: a certificate issued by an association which shows the amount of money an individual has invested with it. Such certificates do not carry any stockholders' liability and have no voting rights. Not to be confused with investment accounts. [51]

investment club: a voluntary grouping of people who pool their monies to build up an investment portfolio, which it is hoped, will give members a better return per individual than each would have expected separately.

investment company: a company or trust that uses its capital to invest in other companies. There are two principal types: the closed-end type and the open-end, or mutual fund. (a) Shares in closed-end investment companies are readily transferable in the open market and are bought and sold like other shares. Capitalization of these companies remains the same unless action is taken to change, which is seldom. (b) Open-end funds sell their own new shares to investors, stand ready to buy back their old shares, and are not listed. Open-end funds are so called because their capitalization is not fixed; more shares are issued as people want them. see *reinvestment privilege*; cf. *hedge fund, monthly investment plan, no-load funds, regulated investment company, split investment company.*

Investment Company Act of 1940: federal legislation requiring the registration and regulation of investment companies with the SEC.

investment counsel: one whose principal business consists of acting as investment adviser; a substantial part of the person's business consists of rendering investment services. [20]

investment credit: credit given to a firm for the purchase of property, equipment, or other identified fixed assets.

investment income: any income resulting from monies invested in securities or other property.

investment in default: investment in which there exists a default in the payment of principal or interest. [49]

investment in fixed assets: the book value of fixed assets. [49]

investment objective: the goal (e.g., long-term capital growth, liberal current income, etc.) which an investor (whether an individual, an investment company, or other institution) pursues. [23]

investment policy: the means employed in pursuit of an investment objective. [23]

investment portfolio: the list of securities owned by a bank, an individual, or a business enterprise.

investment powers: the power of a fiduciary regarding the investments in the account. [37]

investment property: real estate acquired for profit.

investment savings account: a savings account, usually represented by a certificate for each unit of savings placed in the account, on which earnings ordinarily are mailed to the account holder when payable rather than credited to the account. [59]

investment trust: any firm, company or trust that takes its capital and invests it in other companies. see *closed-end investment company, mutual fund.*

investor: an individual whose principal concerns in the purchase of a security are regular dividend income, safety of the original investment, and if possible, capital appreciation. see *long position*; cf. *speculator.*

investors funds: actually retail (repos) or repurchase agreements that are not funds at all. synonymous with *money funds.* see terms above.

Investors Service Bureau: a facility of the New York Stock Exchange which answers written inquiries from individual investors on all aspects of securities investing. Major areas of inquiries involve finding local brokerage firms that take small orders or accounts, explaining investing methods and listed securities, clarifying exchange operations, and providing instructions for tracing dubious securities. [20]

invisible hand: a term first used by Adam Smith to describe the ability of the perfectly competitive market to bring about the greatest benefit for all, even when all merchants selfishly maximize their own profits.

invisible trade balance: as contrasted with the import and export of goods, the trade balance created by the import and export of services, (i.e., consulting and advisory services).

invoice: an instrument prepared by a seller of goods or services and rendered to the buyer. The instrument usually lists all items making up the bill for the convenience of the buyer, and to prevent disagreements, the amount is stated on the instrument.

involuntary alienation: forced sale of real estate.

involuntary bankruptcy: see *bankruptcy.*

involuntary investor: an investor who has purchased securities at a high price and therefore cannot sell his shares without a substantial loss; he becomes an investor. see *locked in, trader.*

involuntary lien: a lien on property demanded without the consent of the owner. Construction of sewers and sidewalks near an owner's property and property tax increases are examples. synonymous with *lien in invitum.*

I/O: see *input/output.*

IOU: an informal written agreement acknowledging a cash debt (i.e., I owe you).

IP: see *issue price.*

IRA: see *individual retirement accounts.*

Irish dividend: a trade term for an assessment imposed on a security instead of a dividend.

iron law of wages
(1) the concept that wages tend to equal what the employee needs to maintain a subsistence level of living.
(2) synonymous with *subsistence theory of wages.*

iron man: slang, a silver dollar.

irredeemable bonds: see *bond, irredeemable.*

irredeemable money: see *inconvertible money.*

irregular savings account: a savings account containing a contractual variation as to time, notice, systematic buildup, additional earnings, earnings penalty, or similar provision. [59]

irreparable harm: injury or damage that is so constant and universal that no fair of reasonable redress can be achieved in court. Therefore, the plaintiff seeks resolution by injunction.

irrevocable trust: a trust that cannot be set aside by its originator.

IRS: see *Internal Revenue Service.*

IS: see *income statement.*

ISB: see *Investors Service Bureau.*

ISF: see *Interdistrict Settlement Fund.*

issue: any of a company's securities, or the act of distributing such securities. [20]

issued capital stock: a portion of a firm's stock retained by stockholders or repurchased by the firm to be held as treasury stock. Such stock represents the difference between authorized and unissued capital stock.

issue price: the price for a new security sold to the public, determined by an underwriter or syndicate. see *syndicate, underwriter.*

issuer: with reference to investment company securities, the company itself. [30]

IT: see *income tax.*

itemized appropriation: a restriction of an appropriation to be made only for and in the amounts listed. A step-by-step listing of all pertinent funds set aside to pay a specific cost.

itemized deductions: a listing of allowed expenses which are subtracted in arriving at taxable income. see *Tax Reform Act of 1976.*

items: as used in bank collections, a flexible term broad enough to include instruments payable in money generally. The term is often used in combinations such as cash items, noncash items, collection items, city items, and out-of-town items. [50]

ITS: see *Intermarket Trading System.*

IVA: see *inventory valuation adjustment.*

J: see *judgment.*

JA: see *joint account.*

jack: slang, money.

jacket: a wrapper or enclosure for an official document. [49]

JAJO: January, April, July, October (quarterly interest payments or dividends).

jawbone: slang, establishing financial credit by presenting clear, objective information.

jawboning: slang, pressured urging by an influential individual to submit to specific rules and regulations. cf. *moral suasion.*

J&D: June and December (semiannual interest payments or dividends).

JD: see *job description.*

jeeps: 9.5 percent GPMs. see *graduated-payment mortgages.*

jell: slang, to complete a business transaction or sale of goods.

JIT: see *Job Instruction Training.*

Jnt. Stk.: see *joint stock company.*

JO: see *joint ownership.*

job account: an account pertaining either to an operation that occurs regularly or to a specific piece of work, showing all charges for material and labor used and other expenses incurred, together with any allowances or other credits. [49]

job analysis: a systematic study of the specific tasks required for a particular job, set of conditions, rate of pay, and so on. Usually, a statement of the personal qualities needed to perform a given job.

job classification: evaluation of job content and required skills, for the purpose of setting up wage brackets for each classification.

job content: for a given classification, the duties, functions, and responsibilities.

job definition: the statement of task requirements; there is a job definition for each job in the company.

job depth: refers to the amount of control an employee can exert to alter or influence his or her job and the surrounding environment.

job description: a statement, usually in writing, of the responsibilities, approaches, conditions, and other relevant factors built into a job.

job dilution: the approach of dividing the tasks of a job into levels of skill. The parts needing higher skill are to be performed by skilled employees and the remaining tasks are carried out by relatively unskilled employees who have a lower level of training.

job enlargement: a procedure for increasing the scope and responsibilities of a job to increase satisfaction to the employee. cf. *loose jobs (rate).*

job evaluation: a systematic rating of job content on factors such as skill, responsibility, and experience. The evaluation is primarily used to minimize wage inequities.

Job Instruction Training (JIT, J.I.T.): a program of training workers within industry based on a specific outline of procedures, including rules for getting ready to instruct and rules on how to train.

job lot: a form of contract having a smaller unit of trading than is featured in the regular contract.

job placement: the assignment of a person to a job.

job range: the number of operations a job occupant performs to complete his or her work.

job rotation: a personnel practice that involves moving an employee from one work station to another to increase overall performance by promoting a greater understanding of the multiple tasks in the organization.

job satisfaction: given in terms of the positive or negative aspects of an employee's attitude toward his or her job or some part of it.

job security: usually described in a union contract, a means of protecting a worker's job. Often invoked when new methods or machines are introduced.

job specification (specs): a carefully written description of a specific job with duties and opportunities described. It identifies the requirements of the job and the desired qualifications needed for a worker to perform effectively. see also *job standardization.*

job standardization: the use of clearly defined techniques for work procedures and the requirements to be met to reduce individual variations to be found in a specific work task. cf. *job classification.*

John Doe: a name given in legal proceedings to a party whose true name is unknown. [61]

joint account: an account owned by two or more people, subject to deposit or withdrawal by all signatures of all joint owners. In banks, any account owned by two or more parties is referred to as a joint account regardless of whether all parties or any one of the parties may sign checks.

joint adventure: two persons entering into a single business for their mutual benefit, as with partners.

joint and last survivor (annuity): payments made jointly to two or more annuitants, and continuing until death of the last survivor. [12]

joint and several account: when two or more persons desire to deposit in a jointly owned account, and the account is drawn against either by check or withdrawal order, the signature of any one of the owners will be honored.

joint and severally: a term frequently encountered in loan transactions when several persons sign a note for a loan. When the term "jointly and severally" is used, each person is legally obligated to become liable for the payment of the note; the group involved must also become liable.

joint bond: see *bond, joint and several.*

Joint Commission on the Coinage: created by the Coinage Act of 1965, to determine whether the nation requires new coinage and if so, what form it should take.

joint contract: two or more people who make a promise to another are joint obligors to the contract and to the other party identified.

joint control bond: see *bond, joint control.*

joint cost: a cost that is common to all the segments in question that can be assigned to the segments only by means of arbitrary allocation.

Joint Economic Committee: created under the Employment Act of 1946, the Congressional counterpart to the president's Council of Economic Advisers, to gather appropriate data on economic matters, to make recommendations, and so on.

joint endorsement: an endorsement made by two or more payees or endorsees.

joint life insurance: insurance on two or more persons, the benefits of which are payable on the first death to occur.

joint mortgage: any mortgage that has been signed by two or more mortgagors, being the joint obligation of all signers.

joint ownership: the interest in property of two or more people.

joint production costs: the costs of two or more produced goods that are made by a single process and are not identifiable as individual products up to a certain stage of production, known as the split-off point.

joint-stock banks: in England, the name for all commercial banks. This term does not apply to the Bank of England, private banks, and so on.

joint stock company: an association that is neither a partnership nor a corporation but has some of the characteristics of each.

joint tenancy: two or more people holding equal ownership of property. Upon the death of one of the parties, the decedent's interest automatically passes on to the surviving owner(s). see *undivided right.*

joint venture: a commercial undertaking by two or more people, differing from a partnership by relating to the disposition of a single lot of goods or the termination of a specific project.

joint will: a single will of two or more individuals.

JOJA: July, October, January, April (quarterly interest payments or dividends).

Jour.: see *journal.*

journal: a record of original entry. This record may be written in pen and ink at the time a transaction is made, or may be created either in original printing or carbonized as the posting of the entry is made by machine. cf. *ledger.*

journalize: the process of recording a transaction in an entity's records using the double-entry system. Debits, credits, and any necessary explanations are recorded in the journal.

journal voucher: a voucher provided for the recording of certain transactions or information in place of or supplementary to the journals or registers. The journal voucher usually contains an entry or entries explanations, references to documentary evidence supporting the entry or entries, and the signature or initials of one or more properly authorized officials. [49]

Jr.: see *junior.*

JSC: see *joint stock company.*

JSDM: June, September, December, March (quarterly interest payments or dividends).

judgment: a debt or other obligation, as determined by the decision or decree of a court.

judgment account: an account on which legal action has been taken and judgment obtained. [55]

judgmental system: a nonstatistical measure of evaluating credit worthiness. [78]

judgment bond: see *bond, judgment.*

judgment creditor: an individual who has proved a debt in court or has won an action for the recovery of a debt.

judgment debt: any debt contested in a suit at law and proved to be valid.

judgment debtor: an individual who has been ordered by the court to make a payment to another.

judgment in personam: a judgment against a person, directing a specific defendant to do or not to do something.

judgment in rem: a judgment against a thing, as contrasted with a judgment against an individual (e.g., bank account, personal property). see *judgment lien.*

judgment lien: a charge rendered in a state or federal court on a piece of land or personal property against one who owes a debt. When applied to personal property, it is generally termed an attachment. [51]

judgment note: a note authorizing a creditor to enter a judgment against a debtor in case of nonpayment, without the need for court action.

judgment rates: rates established by the judgment of the underwriter utilizing his or her professional skills and experience, without the application of a formal set of rules or schedule.

judgments payable: amounts due to be paid by a governmental unit as the result of court decisions, including condemnation awards in payment for private property taken for public use. [49]

judicial accounting: an account of proceedings prepared for submission to a court having jurisdiction. [37]

judicial review

(1) *labor relations:* an action brought before a court to determine the legality of decisions issued by a labor relations board. The review is concerned only with whether the decision is in violation of a statute; the merits of the case are not at issue.

(2) *law:* a legal examination of a situation ordered, sanctioned, prescribed, or enforced by a judge or court (e.g., a judicial proceeding).

judicial sale: a sale of real or personal property ordered by a legal body or court. synonymous with *forced sale.*

judicial settlement: the settlement of an account in accordance with the order, judgment, or decree of a proper court, the effect of which in many states is determined by statute. [32]

juice man: slang, a loaner of money at exorbitant interest rates. synonymous with *loan shark.*

jumbo CDs: certificates of deposit in minimum denominations of $100,000.

jumbo certificates: bank certificates earning in excess of 10 percent interest.

junior: an exchange by holders of securities maturing within one to five years for issues with original maturities of five or more years. [71]

junior advance refunding: an operation where the securities eligible for exchange mature in from one to five years. [65]

junior bond: see *bond, junior.*

junior issue: an issue whose claim for dividends or interest, or for principal value, comes following that of another issue, called a senior issue.

junior mortgage: a second or third mortgage that is subordinated to a prior mortgage. cf. *equal dignity.*

junior refunding: an exchange by holders of securities maturing within one to five years for issues with original maturities of five or more years. [71]

junior securities: common stocks and other issues whose claims to assets and earnings are contingent upon the satisfaction of the claims of prior obligations. [30]

jurisdiction

(1) *government:* authority given by the Constitution to the courts to try cases and determine causes. Different courts get differing cases, based on the nature of the offense, the amount of the claim involved, and other factors.

(2) *labor relations:* the area of work or group of employees for which a union claims the right to bargain collectively.

jury of executive opinion: a forecasting approach utilizing the opinions of senior executives.

justified price: a fair market price that a buyer will give for property.

just title: a title that will be supported against all claims. Considered to be a proper title. synonymous with "clear title," " good title."

JV: see *joint venture.*

Kaffirs: a term used by European investors who deal in South African mining shares.

kale seed: slang, money.

kameralism: a concept of mercantilism concerned with the production of wealth by the state and how the wealth is used; sometimes spelled "cameralism."

KD: see *knocked-down price.*

keelage: the charges paid by a ship entering or remaining in certain ports.

Kennedy round: during President Kennedy's Administration, a 1964 series of world tariff negotiations to reduce tariffs. The sixth round of tariff reductions under the auspices of the General Agreement or Tariffs and Trade.

Keogh plan (HR 10): a form of tax-qualified retirement plan established by a nonincorporated business or self-employed individual. Investment contributions and appreciation are generally tax deferred until actually received in the form of benefits. Formerly defined under the Self-Employment Individuals Tax Retirement Act of 1962. Until January 1, 1982, in each taxable year, the contributed amount could not exceed $7500 or 15 percent of annual earned income, whichever was less. Under the Tax Reform Act of 1976, for individuals with less than $15,000 of adjusted gross income, the minimum contribution would remain at the lesser of $750 or 100 percent of self-employed income. Effective January 1, 1982, a self-employed person or an individual who has outside self-employment income can put as much as $15,000 every year in a Koegh plan, double the old limit. But the 15 percent of earnings restrictions stays in effect for Keoghs. see *Economic Recovery Tax Act of 1981, Individual Retirement Accounts.*

Kerr-Smith Tobacco Control Act of 1934: federal legislation, amended in 1935, provided for processing taxes in the tobacco industry to finance a quota system for growers, including penalties for marketing beyond individual quotas.

key industry: an industry that because of a unique characteristic, holds major importance in the country's economy (e.g., steel, automobile).

Keynesian economics: developed by the British economist John Maynard Keynes, a system showing that national income and employment are dependent upon real investments and consumer spending. see *liquidity preference, New Economics, paradox or thrift, savings and investment theory;* cf. *Friedmanite, quantity theory.*

KI: see *key industry.*

kickback

(1) *government:* an illegal rebate given secretly by a seller for granting an order or contract, as with a payoff.

(2) *labor relations:* the racketeering practice of forcing employees, as a condition of employment, to return a part of the wages established by law or by union contract to the employer. Outlawed in federally financed employment. see *Antikickback Law.*

kick in: slang, to contribute money, to pay one's share.

killing: slang, describes an unusually profitable trade.

kin: persons of the same blood or members of the same family. [37]

kind: monetary unit of Papua.

kind: when used in "distribution in kind" the distribution of the property itself; not its cash value.

kip: monetary unit of Laos.

kite (kiting)

(1) *banking:* writing a check in an amount sufficient to overdraw the account, but making up this deficiency by depositing another check, likewise in excess of deposits, and issued on some other bank. This unorthodox procedure is considered to be evidence of fraudulent intent (e.g., mailing in the rent when your account has insufficient funds, but counting on receiving and depositing some money before the landlord has a chance to present the check for collection;. see *forgery.*

(2) *finance:* a term sometimes used for an accommodation bill.

kiting stocks: the manipulation of stock prices to unprecedented high levels.

knocked-down price: a lowered or reduced price; a seller's asking price that has been lowered for purposes of making the sale.

Kondratyev wave: a major contribution of the Russian economist Nikolai Dmitriyevich Kondratyev, whose theseis was that business activity in the major western nations assumes a rhythmic wave pattern over very long periods. Using price indexes and other economic gauges for such countries as the United States, Britian, and France, he contended that sort of "super" business cycle exists, extending over roughly over half a century.

koruna: monetary unit of Czechoslovakia.

KP: see *Keogh Plan.*

krona: monetary unit of Iceland and Sweden.

krone: monetary unit of Denmark and Norway.

KS: see *kiting stocks.*

kwacha: monetary unit of Malawi and Zambia.

kyat: monetary unit of Burma.

kwanza: monetary unit of Angola.

L: a new definition of money supply of the Federal Reserve Board: a broad measure of liquid assets, equaling M3 plus other liquid assets not included elsewhere, such as term Eurodollars held by U.S. residents other than banks; bankers' acceptances; commercial paper; Treasury bills and other liquid Treasury securities; and U.S. Savings Bonds. see also *M3*.

LA

(1) see *legal asset.*

(2) see *liquid assets.*

labor banks: banks whose stock is owned by labor unions and their membership. cf. *industrial bank.*

Labor Department, U.S.: see *Department of Labor, U.S.*

labor economics: a specialty in the field of economics concerned primarily with the relationship between the worker and his or her job. Areas covered include supply of labor, hours and wages, conditions of work, and other forces relating to the general economic welfare of the worker.

labor force: defined by the U.S. Bureau of the Census, people over 14 years of age who are gainfully employed, looking for work, or absent from work (e.g., because of illness or vacation).

labor grade: job or job groups in a rate structure, set usually through job classifications and evaluations, or by agreement with a union.

labor intensive: describing the use of additional manpower to increase output or earnings. see also *labor pool.*

Labor-Management Relations Act of 1947: see *Taft-Hartley Act.*

labor mobility: the ease with which workers change positions and jobs. Horizontal mobility pertains to the way workers move from job to job at a similar skill level. Vertical mobility pertains to the way workers change jobs by moving up and sometimes down the occupational ladder.

labor pool: the established source of trained people from which prospective workers are recruited. see also *labor intensive.*

labor relations: a general term to identify all matters arising out of the employer-employee relationship. see also *industrial relations.*

labor-saving equipment: any machine or mechanized equipment that reduces the need for labor by a reduction of workers or by curtailing the number of hours of potential employees. In the 1960s automation was considered to be a technological breakthrough that would result in displacement of workers. cf. *automation.*

labor theory of value: expounded by Karl Marx to describe the exploitation of workers in a capitalist system. He claimed that the exchange value of any good was measured by the amount of labor required for its manufacture. Since labor was not only the measure but also the source of all value, every product could be identified as relating directly to the human effort or the quantity of labor involved in production.

labor turnover: see *turnover.*

lag: the delay between two computer events.

lagged reserve accounting (LRA): a Federal Reserve ruling of September 1968, changing the timing of reserve accounting by extending the one-day lag to a two-week lag. Under this system, required reserves for each settlement week (seven days ending each Wednesday) are based on deposit liabilities held two weeks earlier. Average vault cash held two weeks earlier is counted as a part of reserves in the current week, and vault cash in the current week is counted as reserves two weeks in the future.

lagged values of variables: values of variables pertaining to previous time periods. For example, consumption expenditures today might be related to both today's income and yesterday's income. Yesterday's income is a lagged variable. [57]

laissez-faire

(1) *general:* a term used to describe a leadership style of minimal involvement.

(2) *finance:* a policy of the classic capitalistic model, suggesting that government should not interfere with the economy. cf. *controlled economy, statism.*

lamb: an inexperienced speculator.

lame duck

(1) *general:* an individual going out of office shortly; thus thought to be ineffectual or helpless.

(2) *investments:* a speculator whose venture has failed.

(3) *investments:* a member of a stock exchange who is unable to meet his or her debts.

land banks: see *Federal Land Bank.*

land certificate: a legal document indicating proof of ownership of land or property. Contains a description of property and the owner's name and address.

land contract: installment contract drawn between buyer and seller for the sale of property. Occasionally used as a substitute for a mortgage, except that ownership of the property does not pass until payment of the last installment. [78]

land development loan: an advance of funds, secured by a mortgage, for the purpose of making, installing, or constructing those improvements necessary to produce construction-ready building sites from raw land. [59]

land freeze: government limit on the sale or transfer of land.

landlord: the owner of leased property; the lessor.

landlord's warrant: to obtain overdue rental payments, the landlord secures a court-approved warrant that permits him or her to take possession of the lessee's personal property in the leased premises until the debt is paid. Should the debt remain, the landlord can sell the personal property at public auction. see *distress for rent*; cf. *ejectment, reentry.*

land patent: a governmental document providing proof of title to land. cf. *land warrant.*

land poor: usually refers to a person who owns land but because of taxes or other obligations is short of funds.

land revenue: any form of payment derived from ownership of land. It may take various forms (farm produce, forest rights, mineral deposits, ect.).

land tax

(1) a tax levied on the ownership of real property. An assessed valuation determines the rate of the tax. see also *cadastre.*

(2) synonymous with *ad valorem taxes* or *"property tax."*

land trust: title to land held by a trustee in the interest of the beneficiaries of a trust.

land value tax: a governmental levy on the value of land only (i.e., not including structures or agricultural produce on it).

land warrant: a government document given as proof of ownership to anyone buying public land.

language

(1) *general:* a set of representations, conventions, and rules used to convey information.

(2) *computers:* a defined character set used to form words, symbols, and so on, and the rules for combining these into useful communications.

language translator: a general computer term for any assembler, compiler, or other routine that accepts statements in one language and produces equivalent statements in another language.

Lanham Act of 1947: federal legislation governing trademarks and other symbols for identifying goods sold in interstate commerce. As amended, it allows a manufacturer to protect his brand or trademark in the United States by having it recorded on a government register in the U.S. Patent Office, provides for the legal right to register any distinctive mark, and so on. see *trademark.*

lapping: theft from a customer that is covered by theft from another customer by placing false entries in account books. see *fraud.*

lapse

(1) *banking:* the failure of the insured to pay the cost of the premium when due, or within the days of grace allowed.

(2) *banking:* the discontinuance of a right by the passage of time, as when the grace period of a mortgage ends or the date of a lease has passed.

(3) *law:* the termination of a right through disuse or failure to meet standard obligations over a fixed time period.

lapsing schedule: a form on which are recorded the costs of fixed assets or the total yearly additions to a group of fixed assets, together with the details of the distribution of their costs over accounting periods succeeding their purchase.

larceny: the unlawful taking of the personal property of another without the individual's consent and with intent to deprive him or her of the ownership and use of it. This offense is defined by statute in nearly all states and provinces, but there are some differences in the definitions.

last in, first out: see *LIFO.*

last trading day: the last day during which trading in a futures contract is permitted during the delivery month. All contracts which have not been offset by the end of trading on that day must therefore be settled by delivery or agreement.

last will: the will last executed by an individual; all former wills are revoked by the last one.

late charge: a special fee demanded in connection with any payment on a mortgage loan or other obligation that is not made when due. [44]

late payment: a payment made after the due date on which an additional charge may be imposed. [78]

latifundism: the holding of land in sizable estates.

lawful money: all forms of money that are endowed by federal law with legal tender status for the payment of all debts, both public and private.

lawful reserve: banking laws establish the lawful reserves that must be maintained by banks for the protection of depositors' accounts. These reserves were established by the Federal Reserve Act of 1933 and 1935 for national banks, and by the banking laws of the various states for state-chartered banks. The Federal Reserve Board is vested by law with power to change the lawful reserve for national banks in order to control the supply of credit throughout the United States. This board may increase the reserve requirements in order to curtail the extension of credit, or it may decrease the reserve requirements in order to permit the expansion of credit. The various state laws follow a similar pattern, being more strict in some respects and less strict in others. The lawful reserves are required to be available at all times in the form of cash, and under certain conditions, government securities, either in the vaults of the bank, or in lawful bank depositories authorized by government or state officials. [10]

law of increasing costs: that the average total unit cost in a production process increases as the volume of a firm increases. see *diseconomies of scale, marginal cost.*

laws of descent: laws governing the descent of real property from ancestor to heir; to be distinguished from laws, rules, or statutes of distribution governing the disposition of personal property. [32]

lawsuit: a claim in a court of law. [61]

lay days: agreed-upon days that a chartered vessel is permitted without penalty to remain in port for loading and unloading.

LB: see *bond, legal.*

L/C

(1) see *letter of credit.*

(2) see *line of credit.*

LC

(1) see *leverage contract.*

(2) see *loan capital.*

(3) see *loan crowd.*

L. Cr.: see *letter of credit.*

L&D: see *loans and discounts.*

LDC: see *less developed country.*

leader: a person who at a given time and place, by his or her actions, modifies, directs, or controls the attitudes or behavior of others, often referred to as followers.

leaders

(1) *general:* any item that shows strong selling power in a market situation.

(2) *investments:* individual securities or groups of shares that set the

pace of a climbing or declining market.

leadership: in a group or organization, the exercise of command and direction in a skillful and responsible fashion.

leadership training: provided by means of workshops, conferences, seminars, and other programs designed to upgrade skills and to offer information of use to those in leadership positions.

leading indicators: 12 indicators, issued by the Bureau of Economic Analysis, chosen for their record in predicting turns in the business cycle, released late in the month for the previous month.

leakage: any factor or pressure that prevents new capital formation from exerting its full effect on the national income.

lease: a form of contract transferring the use or occupancy of land, space, structures, or equipment, in consideration of a payment, usually in the form of rent. Leases can be for a short period or as long as life. In a lease, the lessor gives the use of the property to a lessee.

lease (regular or commercial): agreement to occupy and use space for a definite term at a fixed monthly rental. [24]

leaseback: a seller who remains in possession as a tenant after completing the sale and delivering the deed. cf. *sell and leaseback agreement.*

leased fee interest: an interest of the owner in a leased property.

lease ground: a lease that provides for occupancy and use of a parcel of unimproved land often, though obviously not always, for the construction

of a building. In the event the lessee is to assume all property charges, more descriptive terminology would be "net ground lease." [6]

leasehold: an estate or interest a tenant holds for a number of years in the property he or she is leasing.

leasehold obligation: an obligation in a leasehold, to pay a specified rental for a specified number of years.

leasehold value: the market value of a lease may increase or decrease over what was originally paid.

lease-purchase agreement: an agreement providing that a portion of a tenant's rent can be applied to the price of purchase.

Led.: see *ledger.*

ledger: a record of final entry in bookkeeping. An account is established for every type of transaction, and a ledger account is posted with every transaction affecting this particular account. cf. *journal.*

ledger asset: those assets for which accounts are maintained in the general ledger. [42]

ledger control card: a monthly record to date of the total debits, credits, and balances of the customer accounts it represents. In demand deposit accounting, this card is the final record of its group to be updated. [31]

ledger proof card: a record prepared daily containing total debits and credits affecting a given group of accounts. In demand deposit accounting, this card follows the customer account cards. Its reconciliation with the daily updating totals is the control for its group. [31]

legacy (bequest): a gift of personal property made in a will. There are four common types of legacy: (a) *specific legacy*—a gift of a particular piece of property, as an automobile, or an investment that has been specifically described; (b) *demonstrative legacy*—one payable in cash out of a particular designated fund; (c) *general legacy*—a gift of money in a certain sum; and, (d) *residual legacy*—includes all the remaining personal property after the payment of all obligations, charges against the estate, and all other legacies.

legal asset: any property, including securities, that can be used for payment of a debt.

leagl bond: see *bond, legal.*

legal common trust fund: a common trust fund invested wholly in property that is legal for the investment of trust funds in the state in which the common trust is being administered. The term is employed most often in or with respect to common trust funds in states that have a statutory or court-approved list of authorized investment for trustees where the terms of the trust do not provide otherwise. [37]

legal entity: any individual, proprietorship, partnership, corporation, association, or other organization that has, in the eyes of the law, the capacity to make a contract or an agreement and the abilities to assume an obligation and to discharge an indebtedness. A legal entity is a responsible being in the eyes of the law and can be sued for damages if the performance of a contract or agreement is not met.

legal interest: the maximum rate of interest permitted by state law; this rate is used in contracts in which no rate has been stated. cf. *usury.*

legal investments

(1) investments that savings banks, insurance companies, trustees, and other fiduciaries (individual or corporate) are permitted to make by the laws of the state in which they are domiciled, or under the jurisdiction of which they operate or serve. Those investments which meet the conditions imposed by law constitute the legal investment list.

(2) investments that governmental units are permitted to make by law. see *legal list.* [49]

legal list: a list of investments selected by various states in which certain institutions and fiduciaries, such as insurance companies and banks, may invest. Legal lists are often restricted to high-quality securities meeting certain specifications. see *prudent man rule.* [20]

legal monopoly: a privately owned organization that is granted an exclusive right by the government to function in a specified market under strict control and pricing by the government (e.g., public utilities).

legal obligations: a debt or promise to perform, that can be enforced by legal means if necessary. [28]

legal opinion

(1) the opinion of an official authorized to render it, such as an attorney general or city attorney, as to legality.

(2) in the case of municipal bonds, the opinion, usually of a specialized bond attorney, as to the legality of a bond issue. A preliminary legal opinion is made in advance of the original sale of the bonds, a final opinion, after the bonds have been issued and sold. [49]

legal ownership: an estate of interest

in property which is enforceable in a court of law; to be distinguished from equitable ownership. [37]

legal rate of interest: the maximum rate of interest that is permitted by the laws of the state having jurisdiction over the legality of a transaction. Interest in excess of this legal rate is termed usury. see *usury*. [10]

legal reserve: part of a bank's cash assets that must be retained as protection for depositors; ruling from the Federal Deposit Insurance Act.

legal residence: where a person lives. The law does not require anyone to spend a majority of his or her time in a certain place for it to be categorized as a legal residence. However, federal law recognizes only one legal residence for an individual. cf. *domicile.*

legal security: a stock or bond that can be bought by a fiduciary and retained for beneficiaries.

legal tender: any money that is recognized as being lawful for use by a debtor to pay a creditor, who must accept same in the discharge of a debt unless the contract between the parties specifically states that another type of money is to be used.

legal title: the claim of right to property that is recognized by law.

legatee: an individual to whom a legacy is given by will.

legend: the text on a bank note. [27]

lek: monetary unit of Albania.

lempira: monetary unit of Honduras.

lend: to give up something of personal value, for a definite or indefinite period of time, without relinquishing ownership. see *loan.*

lender: an individual or financial institution making a trade of placing an interest on money, as with a money lender, with the expectation that the money (or other item) will be returned with the interest. see *note.*

lender-dealer agreement: in mobile home lending, a document that spells out the exact conditions under which lender and dealer will do business, and the rights and responsibilities of each. [59]

lender of last resort: the name given to a central bank that will lend to individual banks whenever they experience large withdrawals.

lender's loss payable clause: a provision in an insurance policy that establishes a lender's interest in real property for insurance purposes; once such endorsement has been added to the policy, any claim drafts are written to the mortgagor and mortgagee as joint payees. [59]

lending institution: a finance company, bank, loan or other organization that lends money and makes money by advancing funds to others. see also *personal finance company.*

lending securities: securities that can be borrowed by a broker representing a short seller.

leniency clause: in a promissory note, a clause spelling out the association's willingness to adjust loan payments temporarily if a borrower is experiencing several financial difficulties through no fault of his or her own. [59]

leone: monetary unit of Sierra Leone.

less developed country (LDC): a country showing (a) a poverty level of income, (b) a high rate of population increase, (c) a substantial portion of its workers employed in agriculture, (d) a low proportion of adult literacy,

(e) high unemployment, and (f) a significant reliance on a few items for export. see also *underdeveloped country.*

lessee: a tenant.

lessor: a landlord.

letter of administration: evidence of appointment issued by a court to an individual or a trust instruction to settle the estate of a decedent who failed to name an executor. [37]

letter of attorney: a document showing a power of attorney.

letter of conservatorship: a certificate of authority issued by the court to an individual or corporate fiduciary to serve as conservator of the property of a person; corresponds with letters of guardianship. [37]

letter of credit: an instrument or document issued on behalf of a buyer by a bank on another bank or banks, or on itself. It gives a buyer the prestige and the financial backing of the issuing bank. The acceptance by the bank of drafts drawn under the letter of credit satisfies the seller and the seller's bank in the handling of the transaction. The buyer and the accepting bank also have an agreement as to payment for the drafts as they are presented. see *authority to purchase, guaranteed letter of credit, revolving letter of credit;* cf. *traveler's letter of credit.*

letter of demand: see *payoff statement.*

letter of indication: a bank's letter of identification given to a traveler who has bought a letter of credit.

letter of intention: a pledge to purchase a sufficient amount of open-end investment company shares within a limited time (usually 12 or 13 months) to qualify for the reduced selling charge that would apply to a comparable lump-sum purchase. [30]

letters testamentary: a certificate of authority to settle a particular estate issued by the appointing court to the executer named in the will; to be distinguished from letters of administration. [37]

letter stock: an unregistered stock, usually issued by a new, small firm to avoid the expense of a formal underwriting. These securities are sold at a discount to mutual funds and investors specializing in speculative purchases.

lettuce: slang, money, especially paper money.

leu: monetary unit of Romania.

lev: monetary unit of Bulgaria.

level-payment plan: an amortization plan that provides for equal monthly payments covering both principal and interest during the term of the mortgage. Part of each payment is applied to interest as earned, and the rest of the payment is credited to principal. [44]

level-premium life insurance: life insurance for which the premium remains the same from year to year. The premium is more than the actual cost of protection during the earlier years of the policy and less than the actual cost in the later years. The building of a reserve is a natural result of level premiums. The overpayments in the early years, together with the interest that is to be earned, serve to balance out the underpayments of the later years. [58]

leverage: the effect on the per share earnings of the common stock of a company when large sums must be paid for bond interest or preferred stock dividends, or both, before the common stock is entitled to share in earnings. Leverage may be advantageous for the common stock when earnings are good but may work against the common stock when earnings decline. [20]

leverage charge plan: an accumulation plan under which the selling charges are spread over the entire life of the program; that is, a sales charge obtains on each separate purchase, the amount varying with the size of the purchase. [30]

leverage contract: the right to buy or sell a commodity at a specified price on a specified future date without rigid variation margin requirements of recognized commodity exchanges. The customer puts up 25 percent of the value of the contract and pays a premium of 2 percent over the prevailing market price, commissions, and interest on the unpaid balance of the contract.

leverage factor: the ratio of working assets to price of the leverage security. [30]

leverage stock: junior security of a multiple-capital-structure company, generally a common stock, but the term may also be applied to a warrant, or to a preferred stock if the latter is preceded by funded debt or bank loans. [30]

levy
(1) *general:* a tax assessment.
(2) *finance:* a demand made on the members of a company for a contribution of added working capital or to make good on a loss.
(3) *government:* to assess, de-

clare, and receive a sum of money against a person or property for public objectives.

levy (writ of)
(1) *general:* placing a lien on land or other property of a defendant.
(2) *law:* the instrument authorizing the sheriff to take a defendant's property to satisfy a plaintiff's judgment.

Li.: see *liabilities.*

liabilities
(1) *banking:* the funds a bank owes. The largest liability for a bank is deposits. see *accrued liabilities, capital liability, contingent liability, current liabilities, deferred liabilities, fixed liabilities, long-term liabilities reported by U.S. banks.*
(2) *finance:* all the claims against a corporation. see *indirect business tax and nontax liability.*

liability hedge: a strategy for a bank to make its liabilities less sensitive to rate changes. When a bank takes in interest-sensitive deposits (e.g., six-month money market certificates, it can fix, or very nearly fix, the cost of reissuing or rolling over the certificates simply by short-selling securities for future delivery.

lien affidavit: an affidavit either stating that there are no liens against a particular property or documenting and describing any existing liens. see *recordation; cf. no lien affidavit.*

lienee: a person possessing a right of lien on the property of another person.

lien in invitum: a lien placed on property without the owner's approval. synonymous with *involuntary lien.*

lienor: the holder of a lien. see *voluntary conveyance or deed.*

lien placement fee: cost of recording with the secretary of state the security interest of a bank on the title of any new or used car. [78]

lien theory: a theory of real estate law which holds that a mortgage conveys to the mortgagee a claim to, or lien on, the mortgaged property. [59]

life annuity: a contract that provides an income for life. [58]

life beneficiary: a person who receives benefits from an estate, generally in the form of income, during his or her lifetime; sometimes called a life tenant if the estate consists of real property. [37]

life contingency: probability of living or dying. Tables relating to life contingency may be found in rate manuals. [12]

life cycle hypothesis: a theory of the saving decision stating that consumers save to be able to maintain a stable level of consumption in the future. see also entries under *marginal propensity.*

life estate: an estate in real or personal property that terminates when the owner dies. The future of the property (i.e., after the owner's death) is usually provided for when the estate for life is prepared.

life insurance: insurance providing for payment of a stipulated sum to a designated beneficiary upon the death of the insured. Various plans of life insurance are available to fit the differing needs of many classes of insureds—for example, endowment plans, which pay back the face amount of the policy to the insured if he or she survives the specified period of the policy, or annuity contracts, under which savings are accumulated and paid back in periodic payments of guaranteed lifetime income to the annuitant if he or she survives the specified period.

life insurance in force: the sum of the face amounts, plus dividend additions, of life insurance policies outstanding at a given time. Additional amounts payable under accidental death or other special provisions are not included. [58]

life insurance trust: a trust created by an individual for the benefit of his or her heirs, the major portion of which is in the form of life insurance.

life of delivery: the time period from the beginning of commodity trading in the delivery to the date of the last transaction.

life tenant: a beneficiary having possession of certain property for the duration of his or her life. An estate or interest in property held during the life of a specified person, called *life estate.*

LIFO (last in first out)

(1) *general:* dealing with the valuation of inventories: the price shown on the last incoming shipment of a particular item is the one that will be used for current valuations and cost.

(2) *banking:* a method of determining the effect of withdrawals on savings account dividends or interest computations. With LIFO, withdrawals are made from money that was deposited last. The withdrawal penalty under this plan is loss of interest on the last money deposited. cf. *FIFO.*

lift check: a check that is not drawn on a bank but through the bank against the maker. Many corporations issue payroll checks in the form of lift checks. The bank through which the items are drawn accumulates a group of these items and delivers them to the maker upon receipt of a regular check in payment of the total. [31]

light gold: gold coins that have been reduced in weight, either by error of the mint or as the result of usage.

light piece: slang, a silver coin, usually a 25-cent piece.

lilangeni: monetary unit of Swaziland.

limitations of actions (statutes of): the law for each state identifying the definite time limit to the period within which a law suit can be brought under law. The terms within the statutes vary by state; however, the time within which a commercial case action should be brought is usually six years.

limited (Ltd.): see *limited company.*

limited audit: an audit in which the effectiveness of the system of internal control and the mathematical accuracy, legality, propriety, and completeness of all transactions are determined by examining only selected items. The assumption is that the transactions selected for examination are representative of the entire group from which selected, and, therefore, if no errors are found in them, the unchecked items in the group are also correct. see also *complete audit.* [49]

limited check: a check limited as to the amount. Such checks have inscribed on their face a legend that the item is void if for more than a certain amount. Limited checks are frequently used in payroll payments by check, with the maximum amount

shown on the face. This is done to frustrate attempts to raise the amount of the check. The date by which a check must be presented for payment also constitutes a limitation. [10]

limited coinage system: the U.S. Mint's program under which the right of the individual to bring bullion for purposes of being coined is limited.

limited company: a British business corporation; "Ltd." indicates registration under the Companies Act and formally establishes the limited liability of stockholders.

limited depositary: a Federal Reserve System member bank which under stated restrictions can receive governmental deposits.

limited facility branch office: a branch office that operates subject to certain limitations, such as the services it may offer or the number of its personnel. [59]

limited liability: the legal exemption of stockholders from financial liability for the debts of the firm beyond the amount they have individually invested. see *partnership;* cf. *nonassessable stock.*

limited life: a characteristic of a single proprietorship or partnership; in both cases the business ceases to exist on the death of either of the owners.

limited open-end mortgage: an indenture under which additional bonds may be issued, but which establishes certain limits, or measures, of maximum amounts that may be issued. [37]

limited order: an order in which the customer has set restrictions with respect to price. see *composite limit order book, market order, no-limit* *order, percentage order, stop limit order.*

limited partner: a member of a partnership who is not personally liable for incurred debts of the partership. By law, at least one partner must be fully liable.

limited payment life: a policy providing permanent protection, but premiums are payable only for a specified, limited number of years.

limited power of appointment: a power of the donee (the one who has the power) to pass on an interest in property that is limited in some way—as to or for whom or to the time within which he must exercise the power; also known as special power; the opposite of general power of appointment; all powers that are not general are special or limited powers. [37]

limited price order: an order to buy or sell a stated amount of a security at a specified price, or at a better price according to the directions within the order. cf. *limited order.*

limited tax bond: see *bond, limited tax.*

limit move: the greatest change in the price of a futures contract allowed during any trading period, as determined by the contract market's regulations.

limit order: see *limited order.*

limit up, limit down: commodity exchange restrictions on the maximum upward or downward movement permitted in the price for a commodity during any trading session day.

limping standard: a modification of the gold monetary standard leading to the acceptance of certain silver coins as standard money to the extent that they are made unlimited le-gal tender and not required to be redeemed in gold.

Lincoln Incentive Management Plan: a combination profit-sharing and incentive plan, developed by J.F. Lincoln in 1934, leading to better worker performance and sizable extra payments for the employee.

lineal descendant: a person in the direct line of descent, as child or grandchild; opposed to collateral heir. [37]

line and staff authority: a part of the organization identified by those having the right to decide and to order others to perform activities (line), and those having the right to plan, recommend, advise, or assist, but not empowered to order others to perform activities (staff).

linear programing: a mathematical technique used in operations research to optimize a business operation subject to given resources and restraints; bears no relation to computer programming. [45]

line authority: authority that is exerted downward (i.e., over subordinates) in an organization.

line manager: a high-level officer having direct responsibility for carrying out a superior's requests and authorized to pass along his or her own orders to subordinates. see also *line organization, middle management.*

line of credit: an agreement between a bank and a customer: the bank agrees, over a future period, to lend the customer funds up to an agreed maximum amount. The bank has the option to withdraw from the agreement if the financial status of the borrower changes, or if the borrower fails to use the line of credit for its intended use as set forth in the agreement. The customer may borrow as much of the "line" as is required and pay interest on the borrowed portion only. A line of credit is widely used by large organizations to finance future commitments and for purchases of inventory. May be "advised"—that is, the customer is officially notified of the existence of the line—or "guidance"—that is for the bank's internal use only.

line of discount: the maximum credit that a bank will extend to a retailer on the basis of his or her accounts payable, which the merchant discounts with the bank.

line organization: the oldest and least complex company structure, where top officials have total and direct authority and subordinates report to only one supervisor.

linkage
(1) *computers:* coding that connects two separately coded routines.
(2) *finance:* the pressures an industry can exert on the rest of the economy.

liquid: capable of being readily converted to cash. Usually the assets of an entity are considered to be most liquid when they are in cash or marketable securities. synonymous with *collectible.*

liquid.: see *liquidation.*

liquid asset fund: see *money market fund.*

liquid assets: those assets that are easily converted into cash (e.g., government bonds). see also *flight of capital.*

liquidate
(1) *general:* to convert (assets) into cash.

(2) *banking:* to discharge or pay off an indebtedness.
(3) *finance:* to settle the accounts of, by apportioning assets and debts.

liquidated damages: the payment by all parties of an agreed-upon sum of money as damages for breaching their contract. The courts can declare the amount to be a penalty and unenforceable if the amount is excessive.

liquidating dividend: the declared dividend in the closing of a firm, to distribute the assets of the organization to qualified stockholders.

liquidating market: a securities market where aggressive selling occurs at relatively low prices.

liquidating value: the anticipated value of a particular asset that will be realized in case of liquidation of a business. [10]

liquidation: the winding up of the affairs of a business by converting all assets into cash paying off all outside creditors in the order of their preference, and distributing the remainder, if any, to the owners in proportion, and in the order of preference, if any, of ownership.

liquidator: a person who liquidates; a person legally in charge of liquidating a business.

liquidity
(1) *finance:* the solvency of a business, which has special reference to the speed with which assets can be converted into cash without loss.
(2) *investments:* the ability of the market in a particular security to absorb a reasonable amount of buying or selling at reasonable price changes. [20]

liquidity preference: part of Keynesian theory; the preference of people to hold their assets in cash rather than in a less liquid form, as with an investment. see *Keynesian economics;* cf. *marginal propensity to invest.*

liquid ratio: the ratio of readily available current assets to current liabilities.

liquid saving: individuals' saving consisting of, or easily and quickly convertible into, cash. These consist of currency, bank deposits, shares in savings and loan associations, and securities. Included are holdings of persons, unincorporated businesses, trusts, and not-for-profit institutions. [70]

liquid securities: stocks, bonds, and so on, easily marketable and converted to cash. [28]

liquid trap: the liquidity preference theory of John Maynard Keynes. The concept that at some low interest rate, the speculative desire for cash becomes infinitely elastic. cf. *quantity theory.*

lir.: see *lira.*

lira: monetary unit of Italy, San Marino, Turkey, and Vatican City.

lis pendens: a pending suit. see also *injunction pendente lite, pendente lite.*

listed securities (stocks): any bonds or stocks that have been admitted for trading on a stock exchange and whose issues have complied in every way with the listing requirements of the exchange.

lister: a broker who sells property from a listing.

listing: a seller's preference to offer a property with one or more real estate brokers; the broker who successfully sells the property receives a commission.

listing agreement: a mutual agreement between a firm seeking to have its securities identified on that exchange and the sponsoring stock exchange. see *listed securities (stocks), listing requirements.*

listing requirements: securities listed on the New York Stock Exchange require that (a) the corporation have net tangible assets of $16 million; (b) the corporation issue a minimum of 1,000,000 publicly held shares, including at least 2000 round-lot shareholders; (c) the publicly held shares have a market value of at least $16 million; (d) the corporation have had $2.5 million of net income or more prior to federal taxes in the latest year and $2 million or more in each of the preceding two years; and (e) the corporation fulfill certain other requirements as to debt, capital, national interest, and so on.

LIT: see *life insurance trust.*

litigant: a person engaged in a law suit.

litigation: the act of carrying on a lawsuit.

Little Board: the American Stock Exchange. cf. *Big Board.*

Little Steel: a description used in World War II to identify all steel companies, excluding the U.S. Steel Corporation (Big Steel).

lives in being: lives in existence at a given time. see *rule against perpetuities.* [37]

living trust: a voluntary trust created from the assets of a living person.

LL: see *limited liability.*

Lloyds: an association of English insurance underwriters, the oldest of its kind in the world. The Corporation of Lloyds also provides a daily newspaper *(Lloyds List and Shipping Gazette),* a clasification of ships *(Lloyds Register of Shipping),* and other publications.

L.M.E.: see *London Metal Exchange.*

LO

(1) see *limited order.*

(2) see *lowest offer.*

load: the portion of the offering price of shares of open-end investment companies that cover sales commissions and all other costs of distribution. The load is usually incurred only on purchase; there is seldom any charge when the shares are sold. cf. *no-load funds.*

load funds: mutual funds sold by sales representatives. For the shares they sell, there is a sales charge or load. cf. *no-load funds.*

loading

(1) *general:* the amount added to net premiums to cover a company's operating expenses and contingencies; includes the cost of securing new business, collection expenses, and general management expenses. Precisely: the excess of the gross premiums over net premiums.

(2) *finance:* money added to an installment agreement to cover selling and administrative overhead, interest, risk, and so on.

(3) *investments:* monies added to the prorated market price of underlying securities, representing fees and overhead.

loading charge: a premium, usually from 6 to 8 percent, charged by open-end investment funds on selling new securities, to cover selling costs.

load up: to buy a security or commod-

ity to one's financial limit, for purposes of speculation.

loan: a business transaction between two legal entities whereby one party (the lender) agrees to "rent" funds to the second party (the borrower). The funds may be "rented" with or without a fee. This fee is called interest or discount. Loans may be demand or time loans, depending on the agreement as to maturity. Loans may also be short-term or long-term. cf. entries under *lend.*

loanable funds theory of interest: a concept that the interest rate is determined by the demand for, and supply of, loanable funds only, as distinguished from all money.

loan application: a form used by banks to record the formal request for a loan by a borrower. The form is specially designed by each bank to incorporate the necessary information that the bank desires having on record. The loan application may be a simple form or a more complex one, containing information relative to the assets, liabilities, income, insurance, and contingent obligations of the borrower, as well as the purpose for which the loan is intended. [10]

loan capital: part of a corporation's capital formed by long- and short-term creditors (i.e., banks, noteholders).

loan-closing payments: expenses incurred when a mortgage loan is set (mortgage costs, legal fees for preparing the papers, appraisal and recording fees, etc.).

loan committee: the group of persons responsible for approving applications for loans and thereby committing the institution to making those loans, subject to the applicants' acceptance of the loan terms. [59]

loan consent agreement: the agreement that a securities broker must receive authorizing him to lend securities carried for a customer's account. A loan consent agreement is required by the SEC.

loan crowd: stock exchange members who will borrow or lend securities to investors who have sold short. These individuals usually meet at a designated place of the exchange. see *short sale.*

loan department: the department of the bank where all the paperwork as well as the actual loan transactions are handled. All notes and other negotiable instruments and all collateral securities are filed in this department, which is bailee or custodian of these instruments and securities. The "loans made register," the record of original entry for all loans, is created here. The note notice and maturity tickler are filed here for ready reference. The liability ledger containing the complete loan record of each borrower is made and kept in this department. This department is the principal source of revenue for the operations of the bank. [10]

loaned flat: sometimes securities are sold short, requiring the seller to borrow them if this becomes necessary to make delivery. When he or she is able to borrow without making an interest payment for the shares, the seller is dealing in a stock that is "loaned flat." see *loan stock.*

loan fee: any charge made to the borrower in connection with an association loan, and particularly a charge made in connection with a new mortgage loan; in the latter case, also called a loan origination fee or premium of initial servicing fee. [59]

loan fund: a fund whose principal and/or interest is loaned to individuals in accordance with the legal requirements and agreements setting up the fund. Such a fund is accounted for as a trust fund. see also *trust fund.* [49]

loan information sheet: in secondary market transactions, a listing of loans being offered for sale, showing principal balance, term, loan-to-value ratio and other items. [59]

loan-in-process account: an accounting category representing funds remaining to be disbursed on mortgage loans that have been closed. [59]

loan interest: the amount of money paid for the use of capital or borrowed funds.

loan loss provision: a charge for anticipated loan losses, which appear on an income statement as an operating expense.

loan modification provision: a clause in a mortgage permitting the borrower to defer one or more payments in the event of financial difficulties.

loan officer: an officer of the bank who is designated with the responsibility of interviewing customers who may become borrowers. Certain officers have the power to grant loans. Large loans are approved by a loan committee consisting of appointed officers and directors of the bank. [31]

loan origination: all the steps taken by an association up to the time a loan is placed on its books, including solicitation of applications, application processing, and loan closing. see also *indirect origination.* [59]

loan participation agreement: in secondary market transactions, a contract under which the seller-servicer agrees to supply, and the buyer to purchase, interests in blocks of loans at a future date; the agreement sets forth the conditions for individual transactions, and the rights and responsibilities of both parties. [59]

loan passbook: a book in which loan payments, escrow account disbursements, and other loan account transactions are entered for the customer's records. [59]

loan policy: a title insurance policy prepared by a title insurance company to a holder of a mortgage.

loan price: the price at which growers can secure government loans under a price support system.

loan proceeds: the net amount of funds that banks disburse from the borrower's loan account.

loan processing: all the steps taken by banks from the time a loan application is received to the time it is approved, including application taking, credit investigation, evaluation of the loan terms, and other steps.

loan rate: the rate charged for borrowing money at a specific date for a stated period. cf. *legal interest.*

loan register: a loose-leaf or bound journal in which the details of loans are entered, usually in the order in which they are granted. [10]

loan relief: when the principal walks away via a cash or an exchange deal from an encumbrance that he or she had on a particular piece of property. [62]

loan repayments: repayments of out-standing loan principal to the association, whether in the form of regular installments or prepayments; excludes payments of interest, loan fees, and similar items of income. [59]

loans adjusted: the face value of customers' notes held (including bankers' acceptances and commercial paper purchased in the market) less interbank loans and reserves for losses on loans. [40]

loans and discounts: used by banks to designate all funds outstanding on loans. [31]

loans and investments adjusted: the total of loans adjusted, U.S. government securities, and other bank eligible securities. [40]

loans and notes payable: obligations outstanding in the form of loans and notes payable or other similar evidences (except interest coupons) of indebtedness payable on demand or within a time not exceeding one year from date of issue. [18]

loans and notes receivable: obligations in the form of demand or time loans and notes receivable, or other similar evidences (except interest coupons) of money receivable within a time not exceeding one year from date of issue. [18]

loans and other long-term assets: a part of total transaction in U.S. government assets, this account includes the flow of capital abroad resulting from all loans and credits with an original maturity of more than one year made by the federal government to foreign countries. Most of these credits finance U.S. exports of goods and services. [73]

loan servicing: all the steps taken to

maintain a loan, from the time it is made until the last payment is received and the loan instruments are canceled. [59]

loan settlement statement: a document, prepared for and presented to the borrower at a loan closing, showing all disbursements to be made from the loan proceeds. [59]

loan shark: an unauthorized moneylender who charges excessive interest for instant cash, accepting poor credit risks, and so on. A racketeer who threatens punishment if the repayment is not on schedule. see also *usury.*

loans in process: loans on which the bank has made a definite commitment but has not disbursed the entire loan proceeds.

loans receivable: amounts that have been loaned to persons or organizations, including notes taken as security for such loans. The account is usually found only in the trust and agency funds balance sheet. [49]

loan stock: securities that have been loaned to a broker or short seller to fulfill the terms of a short-selling contract by delivering shares.

loans to nonbank financial institutions: loans outstanding to nonbank financial institutions, subdivided as follows: sales finance, personal finance, factors, business credit companies; and others, including mortgage companies, mutual savings banks, savings and loan associations, insurance companies, and federal agencies. [40]

loan teller: an employee in the loan department who handles loan transactions. This teller is the custodian of cash in the loan teller's cash till (except in larger banks), and handles all direct transactions involving loans for the loan officer, upon the officer's recommendations and approval. The teller usually computes the interest based upon the rate set by the loan officer, accepts collateral over the counter, and performs all duties of a regular teller, but dealing specifically with the functions of the loan department. [10]

loan term: the time period granted for repayment of a loan. [59]

loan to facilitate: a mortgage loan in which the association provides the borrower with funds to purchase real estate that the association has acquired in salvage of mortgage loans. [59]

loan value

(1) *general:* the amount of money that can be borrowed on a life insurance policy.

(2) *banking:* the amount a lending organization will lend on property.

loan-value ratio: the ratio of a property's appraised value in proportion to the amount of the mortgage loan.

loan voucher: a document required by some state laws, itemizing, identifying, and detailing the distribution of funds covered by the face amount of the note, including such items as discount or loan charges, fees, insurance premiums, rebates, and checks issued. [55]

lobby: the main banking room of a bank where depositors and customers of the bank may transact business with the bank. The ordinary business is transacted through the teller, whereas loans, credit extensions, trust operations, and the more complex matters of finance are handled in privacy in offices away from the bank lobby. [10]

LOC: see *letter of credit.*

local clearings: see *local items.*

local items: refers to checks drawn on other banks in the same city as the bank currently holding them. synonymous with "local clearings." [31]

lock-away: a British term for a long-term security.

lock box: a specialized service by which a bank acts as an agent in directly receiving and collecting a customer's incoming payments.

locked in: an investor is said to be locked in when he or she does not sell a security because its profit would immediately become subject to the capital gains tax. see *Tax Reform Act of 1976.*

lockup

(1) *banking:* a note or obligation that has been renewed, the time of repayment having been extended beyond the original due date.

(2) *investments:* securities that have been withdrawn from circulation and placed in a safe deposit box as a long-term investment.

lombard loan: a central bank loan supported by collateral such as stock and bonds. Term used primarily in England and parts of Europe.

Lombard Street: the financial area in London.

London interbank offered rate (LIBOR): a measure of what major international banks charge each other for large-volume loans of Eurodollars, or dollars on deposit outside the United States.

London Metal Exchange: members, approximately 110, deal in copper, lead, zinc, and tin.

London Stock Exchange: a major European stock exchange, formed in 1773.

long: signifies ownership of stocks. "I am long 100 U.S. Steel" means that the speaker owns 100 shares. Specifically, holding a sizable amount of a security or commodity in anticipation of a scarcity and price rise. see *carry.*

long account: synonymous with *long interest.*

long-form mortgage clause: provides for the assumption of responsibility, for the satisfaction of the mortgage by the mortgagor when he or she takes title; the mortgagor does not simply acquire the property.

long green: slang, paper money.

long hedge: the buying of futures made as a hedge against the sale of a cash commodity.

long interest: the collective retention of a particular stock, or group of stock. symonymous with "long account."

long market: an overbought market.

long of exchange: when a trader in foreign currency holds foreign bills in an amount exceeding the bills of his or her own that have been sold and remain outstanding, the trader is long of exchange.

long on the basis: one who has bought cash or spot goods and has hedged them with the sale of futures. He has therefore bought at a certain basis on or off futures and expects to sell at a better basis with the future for a profit. [2]

long position: describes a holder of securities who expects an increase in the price of his or her shares or holds these securities for income.

long pull: the buying of a security with

the expectation of a holding position over a period of time hoping for a rise in the value of the stock.

long-range planning: a systematic procedure for directing and controlling future activities of a firm for periods longer than a year. It predicts the future and establishes a strategy of action and expected results.

long sale: in the commodities market, hedging sales or sales created due to spot commitments. see *short sale.*

long side: a long interest.

long squeeze: a market situation in which longs are forced to liquidate their positions because of falling prices.

long stock: securities that have been bought in anticipation of increasing prices.

long-term budget: a budget prepared for a period longer than a fiscal year, or in the case of some state governments, a budget prepared for a period longer than a biennium. If the long-term budget is restricted to capital expenditures, it is called a capital program or a capital improvement program. [49]

long-term capital gain: realized when capital assets that have been held for longer than 12 months are sold at a profit. see *Tax Reform Act of 1976.*

long-term capital loss: realized when capital assets that have been held for longer than 12 months are sold at a loss. see *Revenue Act of 1978, Tax Reform Act of 1976.*

long-term corporate bond: see *bond, long-term corporate.*

long-term debt: liabilities that become due more than one year after the signing of the agreement. Usually, these are formal legal agreements

demanding periodic payments of interest until the maturity date, at which time the prncipal amount is repaid.

long-term financing: the issuance and sale of debt securities with a maturity of more than one year and preferred and common stock for the purpose of raising new capital, refunding outstanding securities, or for the divestment of investments in securities not permitted to be held under the Public Utility Holding Company Act of 1935. [3]

long-term liabilities reported by U.S. banks: include long-term deposits—in excess of one year—by foreigners in U.S. banks, mainly by foreign officials or international agencies. Some of these liabilities consist of deposits used to finance U.S. imports, plant expansion, and other financial transactions which would involve U.S. banking services, such as a foreign government's line of credit to a U.S. bank. The flow in the opposite direction appears in claims reported by U.S. banks: long-term. [3]

long-term mortgage: a home mortgage running 40 or more years.

look back: the auditing of past records to locate errors that have come to the attention of a bank's auditing department. cf. *internal audit.*

loophole certificate (CD): under present regulations, federally insured banks are permitted to pay the market interest rate—that pegged to the weekly auction of Treasury bills—only on deposits of $10,000 or more. With the loophole certificate of deposit, the saver is loaned, generally at an annual rate of 1 percent, the difference between his or her deposit sum and the $10,000. For example, if the depositor has only $5000, the bank issues a passbook loan for the other $5000. The loan is automatic and requires no collateral. It is only a paper transaction and the consumer never touches the money. It is credited to his account at the beginning and extracted six months later.

loose jobs (rate):   exist when the earnings for a worker are not in line with pay for similar positions requiring similar skills. see *incentive pay, piece rate (wage)*.

loot: slang, money, especially large sums of it.

Lorenz curve: a graphic device for plotting the degree of inequality in the distribution of income.

Los Angeles Stock Exchange: see *Pacific Coast Stock Exchange*.

loss
(1)   *general:*   any item that can be listed as an expense.
(2)   *finance:*   the excess of the cost or depreciated cost of an asset over its price of sale.

loss on disposal: the result of a sale of noncurrent asset for less than the book value or unrecovered cost.

loss payable clause: provides for payment to a party (e.g., mortgagee or lienholder) in addition to the insured, for any losses to the insured property according to the extent of that party's interest in the property at the time of the loss.

loss ratio: a percentage arrived at by dividing the amount of the losses by the amount of the insured premium. Various loss ratios are computed (e.g., earned premium to incurred losses, written premium to paid losses).

loss reserve: a part of assets retained by a bank in available form to meet expected claims (i.e., insurance coverage on a mortgage).

lost opportunity: a professional money managers description for investments that are not earning the current available rate of interest.

lost policy release: a statement signed by the insured releasing the bank from all liability resulting from a lost or mislaid contract of insurance.

lot
(1)   *general:*   any group of goods or services making up a single transaction.
(2)   *banking:*   a parcel of land having measurable boundaries.
(3)   *investments:*   a quantity of shares, usually 100. cf. *block, odd-lot orders*.

low: the lowest price paid for a purchase of securities at a specific time period.

lowest offer: the lowest price that a person will accept in the sale of a stock at a specific time.

low grade: of inferior quality, applied to merchandise, stocks, and so on.

low interest: an account on which the rate has been reduced to 12 percent per annum simple interest or less. [55]

LP
(1)   see *limited partner*.
(2)   see *linear programming*.
(3)   see *long position*.

LR
(1)   see *listing requirements*.
(2)   see *loan rate*.

LRA: see *lagged reserve accounting*.

LS
(1)   see *letter stock*.
(2)   see *listed securities (stocks)*.

LSE: see *London Stock Exchange.*

Lshld.: see *leasehold.*

LT

   (1) see *legal tender.*

   (2) see *legal title.*

LTCG: see *long-term capital gain.*

LTCL: see *long-term capital loss.*

Ltd.: see *limited company.*

LTD: limited to any security or purpose.

lucrative title: a title that is obtained by a person who pays less than the true market value of the property; title to property obtained as a gift. see *devise, gift causa mortis, gift inter vivos.*

lump sum: full payment made in one sum, and at one time. [12]

lump sum purchase: a group of assets obtained for an indicated figure, without breakdown by individual assets or classes of asset.

luxury tax: a tax imposed on items not considered essential for daily living. In most cases, goods so taxed are expensive.

M1: see *M-1A*.

M-1A: recent money supply definition of the Federal Reserve Board (1980), replacing the old M1 definition; currency plus demand deposits at commercial banks. This is essentially the same as the old M1 with one exception: it excludes demand deposits held by foreign banks and official institutions. see also *L, M-1B, M2, M3, M4, M5*.

M-1B: recent money supply definition of the Federal Reserve Board (1980); equals M-1A plus other checkable deposits at all depositary institutions, including NOW accounts, automatic transfer service, credit union share drafts, and demand deposits at mutual savings banks. see also *L, M-1A, M2, M3, M4, M5*.

M2: recent money supply definition of the Federal Reserve Board (1980); equals M-1B plus savings and small-denomination time deposits at all depositary institutions, overnight repurchase agreements (RPs) at commercial banks, overnight Eurodollars held by U.S. residents other than banks at Caribbean branches of member banks, and money-market mutual fund shares. see also *L, M-1A, M-1B, M3, M4, M5*.

M3: recent money supply definition of the Federal Reserve Board (1980); equals M2 plus large-denomination time deposits at all depositary institutions and term repurchase agree-

ments at commercial banks and savings and loan associations. see also *L, M-1A, M-1B, M2, M4, M5*.

M4: (defunct) includes M2 plus large negotiable CDs at banks. [33]

M5: (defunct) includes M3 plus large negotiable CDs at banks, savings banks, credit unions, and savings and loans. [33]

MA

(1) see *margin account*.

(2) see *market averages*.

machine: any piece of equipment used to regulate force or motion; a combination of mechanical devices and powers to carry out a task. cf. *hardware*.

machine, scanning: a machine that facilitates the input of data by reading printed data and converting them into machine language.

machine accounting: a record-keeping system that uses electromechanical, but not electronic, machines for the posting of account records and ledgers. [59]

machine address: the direct, absolute, unindexed address expressed as such or resulting after indexing has been carried out.

machine code: an operation code that a machine is designed to recognize. synonymous with *computer code*.

machine instruction: an instruction that a machine can recognize and execute.

machine language: information or data expressed in a code that can be read by a computer or by peripheral equipment without further interpretation.

machine-oriented language: a programming language that is more like a machine language than a human language.

machine pay: a plan of checking account posting whereby all media, both checks and deposits, are posted to a journal only on the first "run" of the media. The old balances of all affected accounts are picked up, the media posted, and new balances extended as in any posting run. The affected accounts may or may not be offset, depending upon the using bank's preference. The machine pay journalizing mechanically shows up items to be returned for insufficient funds, or paid as overdrafts. The run also establishes totals for checks, deposits, and new balances of affected accounts. The subsequent run on the depositor's statements must then prove to the machine pay run for checks, deposits, and new balances, verifying that the items were posted correctly, checks as checks, deposits as deposits, and the right accounts selected. [10]

machine readable: describing material that can be sensed or read by a specific device.

macroeconomics
(1) the study of statistics (e.g., total consumption, total employment) of the economy as a whole rather than as single economic units.
(2) synonymous with *aggregate economics.*

magnetic disk: a storage device in which information is recorded on the magnetizable surface of a rotating disk. A magnetic disk storage system is an array of such devices, with associated reading and writing heads which are mounted on movable arms. [45]

magnetic ink character recognition (MICR): the recognition by a computer of characters printed with magnetic ink. cf. *optical character recognition.*

magnetic tape
(1) *computers:* a tape with a magnetic surface on which data can be stored by selective polarization of portions of the surface.
(2) *computers:* describes a storage system in which information is recorded on the magnetizable surface of a strip of synthetic or steel tape.

mail deposit: a deposit received by the bank through the mail rather than over the counter. The bank credits the customer's account and mails a receipt back to the customer. [31]

mailgram: a low-cost, written message transmitted electronically by Western Union and delivered by the U.S. Postal Service. [24]

mail teller: this name is used to designate the teller or division that handles deposits received by mail. [31]

main frame
(1) the major part of the computer, the arithmetic or logic unit.
(2) Synonymous with *central processing unit.*

main storage: the general-purpose storage of a computer.

maint.: see *maintenance.*

maintenance
(1) *general:* the upkeep of any form of property (land, machinery, tools, etc.).

(2) **banking:** all expenditures made to preserve an asset's value.

(3) **computers:** the updating of object program master files, selection of programs, and control of production procedures.

(4) **computers:** any activity intended to eliminate faults or to keep hardware or programs in satisfactory working condition, including tests, measurements, replacements, adjustments, and repairs. see *debug.*

(5) **investments:** the sum of cash or securities deposited in a brokerage account to fulfill the broker's margin requirements.

(6) **law:** support or sustenance that a person is legally bound to give to another.

(7) **law:** interfering unlawfully in a suit between others by assisting either party (e.g., giving one party money).

maintenance bond: see *bond, maintenance.*

maintenancé margin: the amount of money required by a clearinghouse to retain a futures position. It is less than the initial margin and allows the flexibility needed to permit minor price fluctuations.

maintenance of investment organization: the charges to income for the directly assignable organization and administration expenses that are incident to the carrier's investments in leased or nonoperating physical property, and in stocks, bonds, or other securities. [18]

maintenance reserve: an amount reserved to cover costs of maintenance. [62]

majority stockholders: those who own more than 50 percent of the vot-

ing stock corporation, thus having controlling interest. see *working control.*

make a market: to stand ready to buy or sell, adjusting bid and offer prices to balance purchases and sales. [67]

make good: to discharge an obligation or debt.

maker

(1) **general:** a manufacturer, processor, or producer of merchandise or products.

(2) **law:** an individual, firm, or other legal entity who signs a note, check, or other negotiable form as a responsible party.

make the cash: to decide whether the funds on hand, following receipts and payments, balance with the record of sales payments of obligations.

making a market

(1) **general:** the promotion or stimulation of interest in any good or service.

(2) **investments:** the coming to terms between two brokers, one attempting to buy and the other to sell a particular security.

making a price: the price a seller gives indicating a willingness to accept at the request of the purchaser, or vice versa.

making-up price: the price of a delivered security.

mala fides: see *bad faith.*

malfeasance: a wrong doing; a criminal act (e.g., a public official taking graft). cf. *misfeasance.*

malicious: describes an improper act done purposefully without excuse. "Maline" suggests a state of mind that is noncaring of the law and other's rights.

Maloney Act: see *National Association of Securities Dealers.*

management: the individual or group of individuals responsible for studying, analyzing, formulating decisions, and initiating appropriate actions for the benefit of an organization.

management accounting: a resource of management that supplies financial information at all levels to be used in the planning and administering of the business.

management audit: a system for examining, analyzing, and appraising a management's overall performance. Ten categories of the audit are economic function, corporate structure, health of earnings, service to stockholders, research and development, directorate analysis, fiscal policies, production efficiency, sales vigor, and evaluation of executive performance.

management by crisis: a leadership style that purports to clear away shortcomings and failures by waiting until things get so bad that people will accept drastic measures. It is usually destructive and fails to attain stated organizational goals.

management by exception: the practice, by an executive, of focusing attention primarily on significant deviations from expected results.

management by objectives: see *MBO.*

management company: a firm that manages and sells the shares of open-end investment companies and claims a fee or commission.

management development: leadership training for middle- or top-level personnel to upgrade their skills.

management fee: the charge made to an investment company for supervision of its portfolio. Frequently includes various other services and is usually a fixed percentage of average assets at market. [30]

management game: a dynamic training approach utilizing a model of the business world. In most cases, this problem-solving technique attempts to examine broad business issues in a classroom setting free of real-world consequences.

management information system (MIS): a specific data-processing system that is designed to furnish management and supervisory personnel with current information in real time. In the communication process, data are recorded and processed for operational purposes. The problems are isolated for referral to upper management for higher-level decision making, and information is fed back to top management to reflect the progress in achieving major objectives.

management science: the formulation of mathematical and statistical models applied to decision making and the practical application of these models through the use of digital computers.

managing agency accounts: an agency account concerning which the agent has managerial duties and responsibilities appropriate to the kind of property and in conformity with the terms of the agency; to be distinguished from a safekeeping or custody account. [37]

managing underwriter: the syndicate organizer, also referred to as the syndicate manager or the principal underwriter. [26]

mandate: a court order to an authorized agency or officer to enforce a decree, judgment, or sentence to the court's satisfaction.

mandatory: obligatory; as a power of a trustee which the trustee must exercise, mandatory power, the equivalent of a direction. [37]

MANF: May, August, November, February (quarterly interest payments or dividends).

manipulation

(1) *general:* artful approach, often in an unfair or fraudulent fashion.

(2) *investments:* an illegal operation. Buying or selling a security for the purpose of creating a false or misleading appearance of active trading or for the purpose of raising or depressing the price to induce purchase or sale by others. see *rigged market, stock jobbing;* see also *SEC.* [20]

manual: a listing of information, instructions, prices, and so on, that is a handy reference book; a handbook.

manual accounting: a record-keeping system of hand-posting account transactions to the proper subsidiary ledgers, journals, and general records. [59]

manual of operation: the written instructions, usually prepared by, or with the approval of, the accounting, auditing, comptroller's, or methods department, covering the procedure to follow and the responsibilities of the party or parties in the handling of the transactions within and affecting the operations of a given business or financial institution. [10]

MAPS

(1) acronym for multivariate analysis, participation, and structure. A management-development tech-

nique allowing members to define their task groups and choose the people most appropriate for working in them.

(2) see *Monetary and Payments System Planning Committee.*

Marg.: see *margin.*

margin

(1) *general:* the difference between the cost of sold items and the total net sales income. see *contribution margin, profit.*

(2) *finance:* the difference between the market value of collateral pledged to secure a loan and the face value of the loan itself. see also *remargining.*

(3) *investments:* the amount paid by the customer when he or she used a broker's credit to buy a security. Under Federal Reserve regulations, the initial margin required in past decades has ranged from 50 to 100 percent of the purchase price. see *Regulation T.*

margin account: any brokerage account where listed stocks can be bought with the aid of credit given by the buyer's broker.

marginal analysis: the analysis of economic information by examining the results of the value added when one variable is increased by a single unit of another variable. see *direct cost.*

marginal borrower: a borrower who will reject an opportunity to borrow if the interest charge is increased.

marginal buyer: a buyer who will refuse to buy at any given price if the price is increased.

marginal cost: the increase in the total cost of production that results from manufacturing one more unit output. see *law of increasing costs.*

marginal land: land that will merely repay the cost of products grown on it and will not yield increased revenue.

marginal lender: a lender or investor who will refuse to lend or invest if the rate of interest is lowered.

marginal producer: a producer who is just able to meet his costs of production with little actual profit.

marginal propensity to consume (MPC): reflected by the percentage of increases in income that is spent for consumption purposes.

marginal propensity to invest (MPI)
(1) reflected by the percentage of increases in sales that is spent on investment items. cf. *liquidity preference, oversaving, quantity theory.*
(2) synonymous with *accelerator.*

marginal propensity to save (MPS): reflected by the percentage of increases in income that individuals save. cf. *life cycle hypothesis, multiplier principle, oversaving, quantity theory.*

marginal revenue: the added revenue a business receives from the sale of one additional unit. In the short run, under conditions of competition, this is the same as the market price.

marginal seller: a seller who refuses to sell if the price is lowered.

marginal trading: the purchase of a security or commodity by one who borrows funds for part of the purchase price rather than paying for the entire transaction with his or her own money.

margin buying: using credit given by a broker to purchase securities.

margin call
(1) *banking:* if a borrower has securities pledged as collateral for a loan, and a declining market for the securities forces the value of the securities downward, the bank is responsible for seeing that the margin requirements are maintained. The bank will request more margin from the borrower, who will either have to pledge more collateral or partially pay the loan, to meet the established margin requirements.
(2) *investments:* a demand upon a customer to put up money or securities with a broker. The call is made when a purchase is made or when a customer's equity in a margin account declines below a minimum standard set by the exchange or firm. [20]

margined securities: stocks purchased on credit or held as collateral in a margin account. The securities cannot be withdrawn until the debit balance owing in the account has been fully paid.

margin of profit: operating income divided by sales. Income taxes are usually excluded, and depreciation is usually included in the operating expenses.

margin of safety
(1) *general:* the balance of income left after payment of fixed charges.
(2) *finance:* the difference between the total price of a bond issue and the true value of the property for which it is issued.

margin requirement: the portion of a total purchase price of securities that must be put up in cash.

marine protection and indemnity insurance: insurance against legal liability of the insured for loss, damage, or expense arising out of or incident to the ownership, operation, chartering, maintenance, use, repair, or construction of any vessel, craft, or instrumentality in use in ocean or inland waterways, including liability of the insured for personal injury or death, and for loss of or damage to the property of another person.

marital deduction: assured by provisions in federal tax laws to prevent double taxation of an estate at the time of the death of a spouse. It permits the deceased to leave up to one-half of his or her estate to the spouse, with this amount deductible from the taxable estate. see *Tax Reform Act of 1976.*

Mark.: see *market.*

markdown

(1) *general:* a reduction of an originally established selling price.

(2) *investments:* a revaluation of stocks based on a decline in their market quotations.

market: people possessing the ability and desire to purchase, or prospects for a product or service; an estimated or realized demand for an item or service.

marketability: the rapidity and ease with which a given asset can be converted into cash. cf. *liquid.*

marketable: that which can be sold, e.g., property that can be sold to a purchaser within a reasonable period.

marketable title: title to property that is free of defects and will be accepted by a lawyer without objection. cf. *cloud on title, perfect title.* synonymous with "clear title," *good title.*

market analysis: an aspect of market research involving the measurement of the extent of a market and the de-

termination of its characteristics. see *chartist, Dow theory.*

market audit: a method for studying the marketing activities and structure of a bank or financial institution. It is designed primarily to identify areas in which improvements are necessary to boost profits. cf. *management audit.*

market averages: a major securities barometer showing the trend and conditions of the market; that is, the American Stock Exchange Index, the Dow Jones averages, the New York Stock Exchange Index, and Standard & Poor's 500-Corporate-Stock Index.

market data approach to value: in appraising, the estimation of the market value of a property by comparing it with similar properties sold recently. [59]

market demand: the total amount of a bank service that is wanted at a specified price at a specific time.

market equilibrium: the balance that occurs when buyers and sellers decide to stop trading at the prevailing prices.

market factors: statistical series such as population, number of families, and income, which are used for setting sales potential for any selection of the market. [9]

market financing: that part of the general business function of providing and managing funds and credit which is directly related to the transactions involved in the flow of goods and services from producer to consumer or industrial user. [13]

market-if-touched order (MIT): an order to buy or sell at the market immediately if an execution takes place at a certain price stated in the order.

marketing: activities that accelerate the movement of goods or services from the manufacturer to the consumer; that is, everything connected with advertising, distribution, merchandising, product planning, promotion, publicity, research and development, sales, transportation, and warehousing of goods or services.

marketing research

(1) the process of gathering, recording, and analyzing information pertaining to the marketing of the services of banks and financial institutions.

(2) see *market research.*

market liquidity: the condition of a securities market reflecting the supply and demand forces, assisting an investor to purchase or sell stocks at prices relatively close to the previous sale.

market off: an expression indicating that prices on the various stock exchanges were down for the day.

market order: an order to buy or sell stocks or bonds at the price prevailing when the order reaches the market. cf. *limited order, no-limit order, percentage order, stop order.*

market out clause: found in underwriting statements of securities; the underwriter reserves the privilege of terminating an agreement to sell securities at a stated price if unfavorable market conditions occur, rendering sale at this price unprofitable.

market oversight surveillance system: see *MOSS.*

marketplace: a general term identifying business and trade activities.

market potential: the expected sales of a commodity, a group of commodities, or a service for an entire industry in a market during a stated period. [13]

market price

(1) *finance:* the price established in the market where buyers and sellers meet to buy and sell similar products; a price determined by factors of supply and demand rather than by decisions made by management.

(2) *investments:* the last reported price at which the stock or bond sold.

market rate: the interest rate charged a firm in order to borrow funds.

market research

(1) that part of marketing research dealing with the pattern of a market, measuring the extent and nature of the market, and identifying its characteristics. Market research precedes marketing research.

(2) see *marketing research.*

market sentiment: the public or mass psychology that affects the buying or selling trend of securities. They may be positive, negative, or mixed.

market share: a bank's percentage of the industry's total sales.

market value

(1) *finance:* the price that property will command on the open market. The price for which an owner is prepared to sell property and the amount a purchaser is willing to pay. see *reasonable value.*

(2) *investments:* the price of a security or commodity on the daily quotation, indicating the amount required for buying or selling.

markka: monetary unit of Finland.

mark signature: when a person is unable to write his own name, a mark or other indication (e.g., an "X") is affixed to a legal instrument.

mark the market: checking the last sale prevailing for stocks retained in a margin account to determine if the account fulfills minimum margin requirements of the Federal Reserve Board, the Stock Exchange, and/or the brokerage house involved.

markup

(1) *general:* an increase, in dollars or percentage, between cost and selling price.

(2) *finance:* increasing the value of assets (i.e., securities) to show an improvement in their market value.

Maryland Savings-Share Insurance Corporation: a state-chartered mutual corporation in Maryland that insures the savings deposits held by member savings associations and serves as a central credit facility. [59]

Massachusetts rule: a term frequently applied to a rule for the investment of trust funds enunciated by the Supreme Judicial Court of Massachusetts in 1830; now commonly referred to as the prudent man rule. see *prudent man rule.* [32]

Massachusetts trust: see *business trust.*

master budget: comprised of all the departmental budgets in a bank or financial institution.

master card: a card that contains fixed or indicative information for a group of punched cards. It is usually the first card of the group.

master in chancery: an official appointed by a court to assist by taking testimony, calculating interest, projecting damage costs, determining liens, and so on, as requested by the court. cf. *referee.*

master lease: an original lease.

master policy

(1) *general:* a policy issued to cover the interest of a lender or lessor of property in the possession of others.

(2) *banking:* a policy issued to an insured to cover property at more than one location. If locations are in more than one state, it is customary to issue underlying policies to meet the states' legal requirements.

master tariff: a tariff controlling the use of other tariffs.

Mat.

(1) see *matured.*

(2) see *maturity.*

matched and lost: when two bids of the same stock are made on the trading floors simultaneously, and each bid is equal to or larger than the amount of stock offered, both bids are considered to be of an equal basis. The two bidders then flip a coin to decide who buys the stock. Also applies to "offers to sell." [20]

matched sale-purchase agreements: when the Federal Reserve makes a matched sale-purchase agreement, it sells a security outright for immediate delivery to a dealer or foreign central bank, with an agreement to buy the security back on a specific date (usually within seven days) at the same price. The reverse of repurchase agreements, matched sale-purchase agreements allow the Federal Reserve to absorb reserves on a temporary basis. [1]

materialmen's lien: see *mechanic's lien.*

matured: fully paid up, fully carried out as to terms, completed as to time or as to contract. [28]

matured bonds payable: see *bonds payable, matured.*

mature economy: describing the conditions of a nation's economy with a declining rate of population growth and a decrease in the proportion of national income utilized for new capital investment accompanied by a relative increase of national income used in purchasing consumer goods. cf. *underdeveloped country.*

maturity

(1) *finance:* the date on which a note, time draft, bill of exchange, bond, or other negotiable instrument becomes due and payable. A note, time draft, or bill of exchange drawn for a future date has a maturity date that is set starting with the date of the loan or acceptance and runs the specified number of days from date of loan or acceptance of maturity. Presentation and request for payment of the instrument are made on the maturity date.

(2) *law:* the completion of a contract, as with an insurance policy.

maturity date: the date on which a financial obligation becomes due for payment and/or an obligation or contract expires.

maturity distribution of loans and securities: shows the amounts of loans, holdings of acceptances, and government securities that mature or are payable within the various periods specified. [40]

maturity index: see *maturity tickler.*

maturity tickler: a form made and used in the loan department of a bank. The maturity tickler is usually a copy of the "note notice" and contains all information as to the amount, due date, maker, address, collateral, and so on. It is filed according to the due date of the note. This permits ready access to the number and total value of all notes maturing on any day. The maturity ticklers are generally used by bank officials and the loan committee in daily meetings when the maturing notes are under review and discussion for official reference and action. synonymous with "maturity index." [10]

maturity value: the money that is to be paid when a financial obligation or other contract becomes due.

MB

(1) see *bond, municipal.*

(2) see *merchant bank.*

MBA: see *Mortgage Bankers Association of America.*

MBO (management by objectives): a type of management in which superiors and those who report to them jointly establish objectives over a specified time frame, meeting periodically to evaluate their progress in meeting these goals.

MC: see *margin call.*

McFadden Act of 1927: federal statute that banned interstate banking. Recently, new legislation has been proposed to encourage competition in banking by permitting interstate banking as a way to stimulate competition for consumer loans.

McLean-Platt Act: superseded by the Edge Act. See *Edge Act.*

MD: see *maturity date.*

measure of value: a function of money that gives the standard for identifying the results of production using the monetary unit as the common denominator.

mechanic's lien: the legal, enforceable claim of a person who has performed work on or provided materials for a given property. Such claims are permitted by law in certain states as a claim against the title to the property. A mechanics' lien may also grant the claimant a degree of preference in case of liquidation of an estate or business. cf. *particular lien.*

medium of exchange: any commodity (commonly money) which is widely accepted in payment for goods and services and in settlement of debts, and is accepted without reference to the standing of the person who offers it in payment. [39]

meeting bond interest and principal: an expression indicating that payments are being made when due. [67]

megabuck: slang, $1 million dollars.

melon:

(1) slang, unusually large profits that have not been dispersed to eligible persons. see *cutting a melon.*

(2) slang, the profits gained from any business venture.

member bank: a commercial bank that is a member of the Federal Reserve System. All national banks are automatically members of the system, while state banks may be admitted. By law, member banks must hold reserves (consisting of their own vault cash and deposits with their Federal Reserve Bank) equal to a percentage of their customer's deposits. [7]

member-bank reserves: currency maintained by banks who are members of the Federal Reserve System, in addition to their deposits at Federal Reserve Banks.

member corporation: a securities brokerage firm, organized as a corporation, having at least one person who is a member of a stock exchange as a director and a holder of voting stock in the corporation.

member firm: a securities brokerage firm organized as a partnership and having at least one general partner who is a member of a stock exchange.

member's rate: the amount of commission charged a member of an exchange who is not a member of the clearing association. This amount is less than the regular charge paid by the average customer.

memorandum account: the record of an account maintained by a bank which is not included in its assets or liabilities. An example is the record of a bad debt written off, on which subsequent recoveries are anticipated. [10]

memory: computer storage; a device into which a unit of information can be copied, held, and retrieved at another time. see *random access.*

mercantile agency: an organization that supplies to its subscribers credit data on individuals and firms. In addition, some mercantile agencies gather statistical information and serve as collection depositories of past-due accounts. see *Dun and Bradstreet.*

mercantile rate of return: the ratio, expressed in percentages, between the figure showing on the contemporary income statement and the figure appearing on the contemporary balance sheet.

mercantilism: the economic policy under which nations measure their power by the amount of precious metal they have acquired. see *kameralism.*

merchant: an individual who takes title to goods by buying them, for the purpose of resale.

merchantable title: that condition of title which is acceptable in the market. [44]

merchant bank: a term used in Great Britain for an organization that underwrites securities for corporations, advises such clients on mergers, and is involved in the ownership of commercial ventures (i.e., Rothschild's, Hambro's).

merge

(1) *general:* to combine two or more into one.

(2) *computers:* to combine items from two or more similarly ordered sets into one set that is arranged in a specified order.

merger: the combining of two or more entities through the direct acquisition by one of the net assets of the other. A merger differs from a consolidation in that no new entity is created by a merger, whereas in consolidation a new organization comes into being and acquires the new assets of all the combining units. see *conglomerate;* cf. *takeover.*

merit increase (pay): an individual wage increase in recognition of superior performance or service, commonly specified as negotiable in a contract between union and management. cf. *incentive pay.*

metered mail: any class of mail with postage printed by a U.S. Postal Service-approved meter. The same privileges and conditions apply as to all material to which stamps have been affixed. [24]

metes and bounds: real property boundary lines.

methods study: the analysis of the flow of work; in particular, the utilization of materials to permit more efficient use of manpower.

methods-time measurement (MTM): the listing of basic human movements, and the assignment of time values to each. MTM is used in establishing time standards for varying tasks.

MF: see *mutual fund.*

MFN: see *most favored nation (clause).*

Mgmt.: see *management.*

MI: see *minority interest.*

Michigan roll: slang, a wad of paper money, usually, smaller denomination notes wrapped by larger value ones.

MICR: see *magnetic ink character recognition.*

microeconomics: the examination of the economic behavior of individual units in the economy, such as households or corporations.

middle management: management personnel who report directly to top management; a level of management responsible for carrying out the directives of top management.

Midwest Stock Exchange: formed in 1949 with the merger of the Cleveland, Minneapolis–St. Paul, and St. Louis Stock Exchanges with the Chicago Stock Exchange (1882). In trading volume, this exchange is the second largest among the "regional" securities exchanges.

milking: slang, management's attempt to squeeze the last remaining profits from the firm without, for example, leaving sufficient reserves for improvements preparing for a downturn period.

milling: the corrugated edge found on a coin.

minimum charge (rate): the lowest rate a public utility company charges for a commodity or service, even though on a per unit, per hour basis the amount of the charge would be less (e.g., there is a minimum monthly charge for your telephone, regardless of the frequency of telephone calls made).

minimum lending rate (MLR): a bank lending rate for its customers below which the financial institution will refrain from loaning money. MLRs have been popularized by the Bank of England.

minimum premium: the smallest premium an insurance company may charge under the manual rules for writing a particular policy or bond for a designated period. It is calculated to allow the defraying of the necessary expenses of the insurance transaction and to leave an adequate amount to contribute to the payment of losses.

minimum subscription: the figure given in a firm's prospectus identifying the minimum that must be raised for the organization to become operational.

minimum wage: the lowest allowable rate, by union contract, or by federal or state law, for a given job. The term is most widely used, however, in reference to the federal Wage and Hour Law (Fair Labor Standards Act), which sets a minimum hourly rate for all workers to which it applies, and to supplementary state and municipal statutes. see *union rate.*

minor coins: U.S. penny and 5-cent coins.

minority interest: the part of the net worth of a subsidiary relating to shares not owned by the controlling company or other members of the combined group.

minority investment: retaining less than 50 percent of a corporation's voting stock.

minority stockholder: a shareholder with less that 50 percent of a corporation's stock, individually or collectively.

mint: where metallic money is coined or manufactured.

mint ratio: the ratio of the weight of one metal to another, and their equivalent in terms of the national unit of currency, such as the dollar (e.g., x grains of silver = x grains of gold = $1.00).

MINTS: see *Mutual Institutions National Transfer System, Inc.*

minus asset: a term applied to the amount that must be subtracted from the original value of an asset in order that the present value of the asset may be known. [73]

minute book: an official record of a corporation's scheduled meetings (stockholders' gathering, board of director's meeting, etc.).

MIP: see *monthly investment plan.*

MIS: see *management information system.*

miscellaneous chattel mortgage: a chattel mortgage taken on items other than household goods or a licensed automobile or truck. [55]

Miscellaneous Revenue Act of 1980: federal legislation that lets companies write off, over a period of 60 months, new business startup costs that heretofore had to be capitalized.

miscellaneous stock: a security that

does not properly belong to any particular industrial grouping.

misdemeanor: a criminal offense, less than a felony, not punishable by imprisonment or death.

misfeasance: illegal or improper exercise of a legal responsibility; failure to properly perform a lawful act, or the performing of an action without proper notice of those involved. cf. *nonfeasance.*

misrepresentation: the giving of a positive statement or the claim to an alleged fact that is not true, thus leading to a false conclusion.

missent item: an item that has been sent in error to another bank.

missort: generally, a check drawn by a depositor which is wrongly sorted to a "book" or bank other than that in which the account is kept. [31]

miss the market: allowing a particular advantage to buy or sell a good or service to slip by.

MIT: see market-if-touched order.

mixed collateral: different forms of securities that are pledged against the payment of borrowed funds.

mixed property: property having characteristics of both personal and real property (e.g., house fixtures).

mixing rates: used in the foreign exchange rate system, the use of varying rates of exchange for specific categories of overseas traded goods.

MJSD: March, June, September, December (quarterly interest payments or dividends).

Mkr.: see *maker.*

Mkt.: see *market.*

MLR: see *minimum lending rate.*

MM: see entries under *money market.*

MMC: see *money market certificate.*

MMF: see *money market fund.*

M&N: May and November (semi annual interest payments or dividends).

MO: see *money order.*

mobile home: a movable, portable dwelling without permanent foundation, designed for year-round living. [59]

Mobile Home Certificates: lesser known variations of the Ginnie Mae. They are fully guaranteed pass-through securities consisting of mobile home mortgages carrying shorter maturities.

mobile home loan: a nonmortgage loan to an individual for the purchase of a mobile home, secured by the lender's claim on the mobile home. [59]

modeling: the identification of the fixed and variable components in a system, assigning them numerical or economic values and relating them to one another in a logical fashion so that solutions to operational problems can be obtained.

model savings association act: a model for a code of state law providing for the organization, operation, and supervision of state thrift and home-financing institutions. [59]

modification agreement: any agreement between the association and borrower that alters permanently one or more of the terms—interest rate, number of years allowed for retirement, monthly payment amount and the like—of an existing mortgage loan. [59]

modified accrual basis: the basis of accounting under which expenditures other than accrued interest on general long-term debt are recorded at the time liabilities are incurred and revenues are recorded when received in cash, except for material and/or available revenues which should be acrued to reflect properly the taxes levied and the revenues earned. [49]

modified cash refund annuity: a form of annuity in which, if death of the annuitant occurs before he has received annuity payments equal to the amount of his own contributions at date of retirement, his designated beneficiary, or his estate, will receive the remainder in a single sum. [52]

momentum: the rate of acceleration in price or volume expansion, best noted by developing gaps in velocity figures, or gaps in an on-balance volume series. Upside momentum is greatest just short of price maturity, and downside momentum tends to reach a peak at or near an important bottom.

monetarist: a believer in the concept that balanced economy depends on the supply of money. cf. *archmonetarist.*

monetary: a country's currency and/ or coinage.

Monetary Accord of 1951: an agreement between the Federal Reserve System and the Treasury which permitted monetary policy to react to objectives, other than the interest-rate peg. The accord terminated the interest-rate peg. see *interest-rate peg.*

Monetary and Payments System (MAPS) Planning Committee: a committee established by the American Bankers Association in 1969 to conduct extensive research and planning efforts related to the nation's payments system. The four task forces of the committee pro-duced detailed recommendations which were consolidated into a summary report by the committee, stressing the importance of preauthorized payments and bank charge cards as building blocks in a future electronic payments system. [36]

monetary asset: money or a claim to receive a sum of money, the amount of which is fixed or determinable without reference to future prices of specific goods or services. see *monetary liability.* [80]

monetary base: a monetary aggregate composed of funds retained by banks, by the public, and including member-bank deposits at the various Federal Reserve Banks. Measures "high powered money"—bank reserves and currency, serving as a guide to potential money creation. Issued each Thursday for the week that ended the day before.

Monetary Control Act: requires that all banks and all institutions that accept deposits from the public make periodic reports to the Federal Reserve System. Starting in September 1981, the Fed charged banks for a range of services that it had provided free in the past, including check clearing, wire transfer of funds, and the use of automated clearinghouse facilities. see *Depository Institutions Deregulation and Monetary Control Act.*

monetary liability: the promise to pay a claim against a specified quantity of money, the amount of which is unaffected by inflation or deflation. see *monetary asset.*

monetary multiplier: a number showing the anticipated change in income-per-unit change in the money supply.

monetary policy: a policy of the Federal Reserve System that attempts to affect the terms on which credit can be obtained in private markets; its purpose is to regulate the nation's sales level, level of employment, and prices. see *discretionary policy, Operation Twist (Nudge); cf. fiscal policy.*

monetary reserve: the amount of bullion held by the government or banks as security for fiduciary or credit money in circulation. see *reserve.*

monetary working capital: items that are related to operations and not, for example, liquid assets that are surplus to operating requirements. [80]

money: any denomination of coin or paper currency of legal tender that passes freely as a medium of exchange; anything that is accepted in exchange for other things (e.g., precious metals). Major characteristics of money include easy recognition, uniformity in quality, easy divisibility, and a relatively high value within a small area. cf. *currency.*

money broker: a person or institution serving as a go-between for borrowers and lenders of money.

money funds: a type of mutual fund. Though they have been marketed practically as bank accounts, the individual owns shares in a fund. The value is usually $1 per share, to make the accounting simple. The purchaser doesn't actually have a cash balance. The shares owned purchased prior to March 14, 1980 were free from new Federal Restrictions. see *mutual fund.*

money illusion: perceived when an increase in all prices and incomes by the same proportion produces an increase in consumption, although real incomes remain the same.

money in circulation: the total amount of currency and coin outside the Treasury and the Federal Reserve Banks.

money income: the amount of money received for work performed.

money management: financial planning with the aim of gratifying long-range as well as immediate needs and of maintaining a sound relationship among income, savings, and spending. [55]

money market (brokers): all financial organizations that handle the purchase, sale, and transfer of short-term credit instruments and notes.

money market certificate (MMC): six-month Federal Home Loan Bank Board certificate at federally insured savings and loan associations.

money market fund (MMF)

(1) *banking:* many investment banking firms sponsor money-market mutual funds, which invest in such short-term credit instruments as Treasury bills. Customers earn high interest rates on the accounts and can write checks against their investment. Commercial banks contend that these accounts are offering traditional commercial banking services without the restrictions that apply to commercial banks, such as reserve requirements on deposits. see *Glass-Steagall Act of 1933, reserve requirements.*

(2) *finance:* an investment vehicle whose primary objective is to make higher-interest securities available to the average investor who wants im-

mediate income and high investment safety. This is accomplished through the purchase of high-yield money market instruments, such as U.S. government securities, bank certificates of deposit, and commercial paper. synonymous with *liquid assets.*

money market securities: high-quality and generally accepted senior securities whose market prices expressed on a yield basis relate more closely to the prevailing interest rate for money than to the risks in a company's operations or in general business conditions. [67]

money order: postal money orders and bank money orders are instruments commonly purchased for a fee by people who do not maintain checking accounts and wish to send money to others. The names of the purchaser and the payee are shown on the face of the money order. An advantage of the money order over checks is that presentation to their original place of purchase for payment, is not required. A disadvantage is that a bank or other financial institution may charge for the service of supplying a money order.

money price: the number of money units that must be sacrificed to purchase a particular commodity.

money rates: interest rates that lenders charge their borrowers.

money stock: see *M-1A, M2, M3.*

money supply: a general term for the total sum of currency circulating in a country. see *price;* see also money supply (Federal Reserve).

money supply (Federal Reserve): measures several variants in the amount of money in the economy, issued each Thursday for the week that ended eight days earlier. It has been criticized as very erratic, subject to frequent revision.

money talks: slang, money is power and can therefore buy anything.

monger: any trader or seller; often used in a derogatory fashion.

monometallism: a monetary system: the monetary component is defined in terms of only one metal that is accepted in unlimited quantities for producing coins. see *real money;* cf. *bimetallism.*

monopoly
(1) ***general:*** ownership of the source of a commodity or the domination of its distribution. see *competition, engross.*
(2) ***finance:*** exclusive dominance of the supply and price of a commodity that is acquired by a franchise or government patent. cf. *bilateral monopoly, legal monopoly, natural monopoly, partial monopoly, perfect (pure) monopoly, strategic resource monopoly.*

monopsony: a market situation in which there is only one buyer for an item. cf. *duopsony, oligopsony.*

monthly investment plan (MIP): a pay-as-you-go method of buying odd lots of exchange listed shares on a regular payment plan for as little as $40 a month or every three months, and up to $1,000 per payment. Under MIP the investor buys a stock designated by a securities broker by the dollar's worth. If the price advances, he or she gets fewer shares; if it declines, more shares. The investor may discontinue purchases at any time without penalty. cf. *investment company.*

monthly payment bonus account: a

savings account that pays bonus earnings if the customer makes a specified number of fixed monthly deposits. [59]

Moody's Bond Ratings and Stock Quality Groups

(a) bonds

Aaa: best quality, generally referred to as "gilt edge."

Aa: high quality by all standards; generally known as high-grade bonds.

A: possessing many favorable investment attributes and considered as high-medium-grade obligations.

Baa: considered as lower-medium-grade obligations—that is, neither highly protected nor poorly secured. Such bonds lack outstanding investment characteristics as well.

(b) preferred and common stocks

high quality: high quality by all standards.

good quality: possesses many favorable high-grade investment attributes.

medium quality: medium-grade equity securities. [3]

Moody's Bond Yield (Annual Averages of Monthly Yield): represents the average yield on 40 operating utility companies' bonds (10 each of Class Aaa, Aa, A, and Baa) as determined and rated by Moody's Investors Service. This "yield" is the arithmetical average of 12 months and is calculated on the basis of market price, coupon rate, and on being "held to maturity." [3]

moola (moolah): slang, money.

moonlight: slang, working at a second job, usually to supplement the income from a permanent position.

moot: in law, not covered, debatable, or made clear by earlier cases or decisions of the court (e.g., there is no uniform or clear-cut opinion on a moot point).

MOP: see *margin of profit.*

moral hazard: the possibility of loss being caused by or aggravated by dishonesty or carelessness of the insured, his or her agents, or employees, it arises from the character and circumstances of the insured, as distinguished from the inherent nature of the property covered, or its location.

moral obligation: a debt or responsibility whose payment or fulfillment is not based on legal rights or action. [28]

moral suasion: Federal Reserve System pressure exerted on U.S. banking, unaccompanied by an effort to compel compliance with the suggested action. see also *jawboning.*

morning loan: bank loans to stockbrokers on an unsecured basis enabling the broker to handle stock deliveries until reimbursed by the customer.

Morris plan bank: those banks that handle small loans and consumer credit involving insurance of the debtor's life.

mortality: the expectancy of an asset or class of aspects to expire or depreciate by use or the passage of time.

mortgage

(1) *general:* a written conveyance of title to property, but not possession, to obtain the payment of a debt or the performance of some obligation, under the condition that the conveyance is to be void upon final payment.

(2) *finance:* property pledged as security for payment of a debt. see *chattel mortgage;* cf. *conventional loan.*

mortgage administration: the part of a mortgage banker's service involving all clerical and supervisory functions necessary to ensure prompt repayment of mortgage loans, and to protect and enforce all rights of investors thereunder. [22]

mortgage-backed certificates: several banks, notably the Bank of America, have issued certificates covering pools of conventional mortgages insured by private mortgage insurance companies. These certificates are issued in big denominations, so the market is limited mainly to institutions.

mortgage banker: a banker who specializes in mortgage financing; an operator of a mortgage financing company. Mortgage financing companies are mortgagees themselves, as well as being mortgage agents for other large mortgages.

Mortgage Bankers Association of America (MBA): the professional and business organization of persons operating under the correspondency system whose major purpose is continuing improvement in the quality of service to investors. [22]

mortgage bond: see *bond, mortgage.*

mortgage certificate: an interest in a mortgage evidenced by the instrument, generally a fractional portion of the mortgage, which certifies as to the agreement between the mortgagees who hold the certificates and the mortgagor as to such terms as principal, amount, date of payment, and place of payment. Such certifi-cates are not obligations to pay money, as in a bond or note, but are merely a certification by the holder of the mortgage, generally a corporate depository, that he or she holds such mortgage for the beneficial and undivided interest of all the certificate holders. The certificate itself generally sets forth a full agreement between the holder and the depository, although in some cases a more lengthy document, known as a depository agreement, is executed. [62]

mortgage clause: a provision attached to a fire or other direct damage insurance policy covering mortgaged property, stating that (a) the loss shall be payable to the mortgagee according to the amount of his or her interest, (b) the mortgagee's right of recovery shall not be defeated by any act or neglect of the insured, and (c) the mortgagee has other rights and privileges.

mortgage company: mortgage financing companies are mortgages themselves, as well as being mortgage agents for other large mortgagees. Serving as mortgage agents, these mortgage bankers collect payments, maintain complete mortgage records, and make remittances to the mortgagees for a set fee or service charge. [10]

mortgage credit: money that is owed for the acquisition of land or buildings (frequently of a home) and which is paid back over an extended period of time; hence, long-term debt. [55]

mortgaged deed: see *deed, mortgaged.*

mortgage debenture: a mortgage bond. see *bond, mortgage.*

mortgage debt: an indebtedness created by a mortgage and secured by the property mortgaged. A mortgage debt is made evident by a note or bond.

mortgage department: a department in banks, building and loan, savings and loan associations, and trust companies, where mortgage counselors, mortgage loan officers, and mortgage recording personnel handle all phases of mortgage work for mortgagors. This department may also act as "escrow agents" for mortgagors, in that they collect in the monthly payment from the mortgagor a portion of the real estate taxes, assessments on real estate, and hazard insurance. They hold these in escrow funds until payable, and then disburse the funds for the benefit of the mortgagor, and also the mortgagee, to prevent the development of liens against the property. In some states, they administer escrow funds in connection with closing mortgages, whereas in other states mortgage closings are required to be handled by attorneys-at-law. [10]

mortgagee: the creditor or lender, to whom a mortgage is made. The mortgagor retains possession and use of the property during the term of the mortgage (e.g., the bank holds the mortgage on your house).

mortgagee clause: a clause in an insurance contract making the proceeds payable to a named mortgagee, as his or her interest may appear, and stating the terms of the contract between the insurer and the mortgagee. This is preferable usage but the same as mortgage clause. [53]

mortgage guarantee policy: a policy issued on a guaranteed mortgage. [62]

mortgage insurance policy: issued by a title insurance firm to a mortgage holder, resulting in a title policy.

mortgage investment trust: a specialized form of real estate investment trust that invests in long-term mortgages, usually Federal Housing Administration-insured or Veterans Administration-guaranteed, and makes short-term construction and development loans. [59]

mortgage lien: in a mortgage given as security for a debt, serving as a lien on the property after the mortgage is recorded.

mortgage life insurance: insurance on the life of the borrower that pays off a specified debt if he dies. synonymous with credit life insurance. [59]

mortgage loan: a loan made by a lender, called the mortgagee, to a borrower, called the mortgagor, for the financing of a parcel of real estate. The loan is evidenced by a mortgage. The mortgage sets forth the conditions of the loan, the manner of repayment or liquidation of the loan, and reserves the right of foreclosure or repossession to the mortgagee. In case the mortgagor defaults in the payment of interest and principal, or if he permits a lien to be placed against the real estate mortgaged due to failure to pay the taxes and assessments levied against the property, the right of foreclosure can be exercised. [10]

mortgage loan commitment: written statement by lender to grant a specific loan amount, at a given rate, for a certain term, secured by a specific property, if the real property transaction is closed before the expiration date. [78]

mortgage loan ledger record: a document that contains a complete record of all transactions—payments of principal and interest, special disbursements, fees, charges, and the like—on a particular mortgage loan. [59]

mortgage loan report: an updated report that requires the same kind of information as the full report plus a statement certifying that all Federal Housing Administration or Veterans Administration specifications, including public record items have been met. [76]

mortgage note: a note that offers a mortgage as proof of an indebtedness and describes the manner in which the mortgage is to be paid. This note is the actual amount of debt that the mortgage obtains, and it renders the mortgagor personally responsible for repayment.

mortgage origination: the part of a mortgage. banker's service involving performance of all details concerned with the making of a real estate loan. [22]

mortgage pattern: the arrangement or design of payments and other terms established by a mortgage contract. [44]

mortgage portfolio: the aggregate of mortgage loans or obligations held by a bank as assets. [44]

mortgage premium: an additional bank fee charged for the giving of a mortgage when the legal interest rate is less than the prevailing mortgage market rate and there is a shortage of mortgage money.

mortgager(or): a debtor or borrower who gives or makes a mortgage to a lender, on property owned by the mortgagor.

mortgage risk: the hazard of loss of principal or of anticipated interest inherent in an advance of funds on the security of a mortgage. [44]

mortgage securities: see *Freddie Macs, Gennie Mae trusts, Government National Mortgage Association, mortgage-backed certificates.*

mortgaging future income: pledging income not yet earned. [28]

Mos.: months

MOS: see *margin of safety.*

MOSS: market oversight surveillance system; proposed by the chairman of the Securities and Exchange Commission, a $12 million computerized surveillance network capable of monitoring every facet of securities trading in the country.

most favored nation (clause): in international business treaties, a provision against tariff discrimination between two or more nations. It provides that each participant will automatically extend to other signatories all tariff reductions that are offered to nonmember nations. see *retaliatory duty.* cf. *open door policy.*

mother hubbard clause: a mortgage provision permitting the lender, upon default of the conditions of the mortgage, to foreclose on the overdue mortgage. Courts around the country have questioned the legality of this clause.

movement: an increase or decrease in the price of a specific stock.

moving average: a technique for correcting small fluctuations of the stock market indicator to yield a general market trend.

MP: see *market price.*

MPC: see *marginal propensity to consume.*

MPI: see *marginal propensity to invest.*

MPS: see *marginal propensity to save.*

MS

(1) see *majority stockholders.*

(2) March, September (semiannual interest payments or dividends).

(3) see *margin of safety.*

(4) see *minority stockholder.*

(5) see *money supply.*

M&S: March and September (semiannual interest payments or dividends).

MSB: see *mutual savings bank.*

MSE: see *Midwest Stock Exchange.*

Mtg.: see *mortgage.*

Mthly.: monthly.

MTM: see *methods-time measurement.*

multicompany: diverse organizations or a variety of firms under a single management.

multi-industry: the management of firms involved in different activities.

multilingual notes: paper money issued with a legend in two or more languages, as in India, Belgium, or Cyprus. [27]

multinational corporation: a corporation that participates in international business activities. A firm that produces, markets, and finances its operations throughout various nations of the world. cf. *production sharing.*

multiple banking: the offering of all types of banking services to a bank's customers, as distinguished from specialization in a few services as offered by savings and loan associations, and other banking institutions. Often referred to as department store banking. cf. *full-service bank.*

multiple currency practice: arises when two or more effective exchange rates exist simultaneously, at least one of which, as the result of official action, is more than 1 percent higher or lower than the par value. Such practices are usually to be found where a dual exchange market exists or where the monetary authorities set different exchange rates for imports, exports, current invisibles, and capital. They often result from taxes or subsidies on specified exchange transactions. [42]

multiple exchange: three or more principals involved with various pieces of property. [62]

multiple expansion of bank deposits: occurs when a loan made by one bank is used to finance business transactions and becomes a deposit in another bank. A portion of this loan can be used by the second bank as a required reserve, and the remainder can be loaned out for business use, so that it is eventually deposited in a third bank.

multiple management: a description of worker participation in a firm's management by assisting in the development and execution of policy.

multiple ownership: ownership by two or more parties. synonymous with "co-ownership." [59]

multiplier principle: the reciprocal of the marginal propensity to save. The multiplier is a figure that identifies the changes in investment and spending to alterations in aggregate incomes. see *Keynesian economics.*

multiprocessing

(1) *computers:* using several computers to logically divide jobs or

processes, and to execute programs simultaneously.

(2) *systems:* loosely, parallel processing.

(3) *systems:* two or more processors in a system configuration.

multiprogramming: pertaining to the concurrent execution of two or more programs by a computer.

multivariate analysis, participation, and structure: see *MAPS.*

Munic.: municipal.

municipal bond: see *bond, municipal.*

municipal improvement certificates: certificates issued in lieu of bonds for the financing of special improvements. [49]

municipal revenue bond: see *bond, municipal revenue.*

municipals: a popular word for the securities of a governmental unit.

munifunds: synonymous with *mutual funds.* see *investment company.*

muniment of title

(1) *general:* anything that protects or enforces; written proof that enables an owner to defend his or her title to property.

(2) *law:* deeds and contracts that show conclusive proof of ownership (e.g., warranty deed).

munis: Wall Street slang for municipal bonds. see *bond, municipal.*

mutual assent: agreement by all parties to a contract to the same thing. Each must know what the other wishes.

mutual association: a savings association that issues no capital stock, but is owned and controlled solely by its savers and borrowers, who are called members. Members do not share in profits, because a mutual institution operates in such a way that it makes

no "profit," but they exercise other ownership rights. [59]

mutual company: a corporation without capital stock (e.g., mutual savings bank): the profits, after deductions, are distributed among the owner-customers in proportion to the business activity carried with with the corporation.

mutual fund: an investment company which ordinarily stands ready to buy back (redeem) its shares at their current net asset value; the value of the shares depends on the market value of the fund's portfolio securities at the time. Also, mutual funds generally continuously offer new shares to investors. see also *investment company, money funds.* [23]

Mutual Institutions National Transfer System, Inc. (MINTS): an organization affiliated with the National Association of Mutual Savings Banks (NAMSB). The MINTS Money Transfer Card is intended to become part of a future nationwide Mutual Savings Bank EFT system. [36]

mutuality: equality of status and opportunity among members of a savings association. [59]

mutual savings bank: a banking organization without capital stock, operating under law for the mutual benefit of the depositors. The depositor is encouraged to practice thrift, and the savings of these small depositors are invested in very high grade securities and some first-class mortgages. Dividends from these investments are mutually distributed after deduction of expenses of the association and reserves for a guaranty fund for depositors. The principal idea of a mutual savings bank is to perform a social service for small depositors who cannot invest their savings at high yield. see also *mutual company.*

Mutual Savings Foundation of America, The: based in Washington, D.C., this nonprofit organization was established in 1961 as a vehicle to enable savings bankers to promote and improve education in the field of economics. The foundation assists educational institutions with grants-in-aid, gifts and loans to support research, and also grants scholarships, fellowships, and loans to students in the field of economics. It also provides aid to developing nations to assist them in accumulating domestic savings. Contributions to the foundation qualify as charitable contributions for federal income tax purposes. [8]

mutual wills: a common arrangement executed pursuant to an agreement in which the husband and wife leave everything to each other.

MV: see *market value.*

N

N: see *note.*

NA

(1) see *net assets.*

(2) see *no account.*

(3) no approval required (full discretion).

(4) see *nostro account.*

naird: monetary unit of Nigeria.

naked calls: the selling of options on stock that is not owned by a customer.

"naked" reserve: an adjusted reserve of each of the Federal Reserve Banks showing the true reserve position of the bank. see *reserve requirements.*

name day: see *settlement day.*

named insured: any person or firm or corporation or any of its members, specially designated by name as insured(s) in a policy, as distinguished from others who, although unnamed, are protected under some circumstances.

NAMSB: see *National Association of Mutual Savings Banks.*

narrow market: a condition that exists when the demand for a security is so limited that small alterations in supply or demand will create major fluctuations in the market price.

NASD: see *National Association of Securities Dealers.*

NASDAQ: see *National Association of Securities Dealers Automated Quotations.*

National Association of Mutual Savings Banks (NAMSB): exists to serve its member banks. It provides services to individual member banks which they would find impractical to provide for themselves, and it serves the savings bank industry as a whole, through national-level programs and activities to further industry goals and objectives and to meet needs common to all savings banks. [8]

National Association of Securities Dealers (NASD): the Maloney Act, passed in 1938, which amended the Securities Exchange Act of 1934, provides for self-regulation of the over-the-counter securities market by associations registered with the SEC. The NASD is the only association so registered. Most companies offering variable annuities are NASD members.

National Association of Securities Dealers Automated Quotations (NASDAQ): an automated information network that provides brokers and dealers with price quotations on securities traded over the counter.

national bank: a commercial bank organized with the consent and approval of the Comptroller of the Currency and operated under the supervision of the federal government. National banks are required to be members of the Federal Reserve System and must purchase stock in the Federal Reserve Bank in their district.

National Bank Act of 1863: the act of Congress providing for the incorporation of banks under federal supervision. Such national banks are now under the supervision of the Federal Reserve System.

national bank association: synonymous with *national bank.*

national bank call: the report, submitted four times each year, to the Comptroller of the Currency on the well-being of the bank's commercial department.

national bank note: a type of currency issued in the United States. National bank notes are backed by two types of U.S. government bonds—2 percent consols of 1930, and the 2 percent Panama Canal bonds of 1916–1936 and 1918–1938. These bonds were called for redemption by the Bank Act of 1935, and no further issuance of national bank notes was authorized. They are being retired from circulation. National bank notes are in denominations of $5, $10, $20, $50, and $100, and each has a brown seal and the issuing bank's charter number on its face. [10]

National Bankruptcy Act of 1898: federal law stating the conditions under which an individual or business may declare bankruptcy, and the procedures for declaration. see *reorganization.*

National Commission on EFT: a commission authorized by a 1974 Act of Congress to conduct a two-year investigation into electronic funds transfer system policy and planning issues, concluding with reports and recommendations for congressional action. [36]

National Consumer Cooperative Bank: federal legislation signed by President Carter in 1978 creating a national bank to provide credit for consumer cooperatives.

National Credit Union Administration (NCUA): the federal government agency that supervises, charters, and insures federal credit unions. NCUA also insures state-chartered credit unions that apply and qualify for insurance. As of October 1979, the NCUA also operates a credit facility for member credit unions. [1]

national currency: all Federal Reserve Bank notes and national bank notes that are now retired.

national debt: the debt owed by the federal government.

National Housing Act of 1934: created the Federal Housing Administration to insure home mortgage, low-income housing project, and home improvement loans made by private lenders; established the Federal Savings and Loan Insurance Corporation to insure savings accounts at member savings associations up to $5000. [51]

national income: the total of the incomes received by all the people of a country over a stated period. It is equal to the gross national product minus depreciation minus sales taxes and other small items.

national income and product accounts: accounts prepared and published by the U.S. Department of Commerce showing various aspects of the total output of the economy and of the total income received in the economy.

nationalization: takeover by the government, with or without compensation, of a public or private activity. cf. *confiscation, eminent domain.*

national liquidity: a nation's monetary situation as determined by its rates of interest on all loans and deposits.

National Stock Exchange: the third stock exchange of New York City, established in 1960.

national wealth: the combined monetary value of all the material economic products owned by all the people.

nationwide loan: a conventional loan made or purchased upon improved real estate located outside the insured institution's normal lending territory but within any state of the United States. [59]

Natl.: national.

natural business year: a 12-month period usually selected to end when inventory or business activity is at a low point.

natural capital: land that is used as a factor of production.

natural financing
(1) a real estate transaction requiring no outside financing, as is demanded in cash sales.
(2) the selling of properties that do not call for a third party.

Natural Gas Policy Act: federal legislation passed in October 1978 which created whole new categories for natural gas and raised ceiling prices on some of them.

natural monopoly
(1) *general:* a monopoly due to natural conditions (e.g., a crop that demands special climate is subject to monopolization by a grower in the area having that climate.
(2) *finance:* among industries that experience economies of scale, the cost per unit is lowest when there is only one company in the industry.

natural resources: all materials fur-

nished by nature (minerals, timber, water, etc.).

NAV: see *net asset value.*

navicert: an official document released by a belligerent country authorizing specified items to be transported overseas by a neutral nation through a blockade to a named neutral port of entry.

NBA
(1) see *National Bank Act of 1863.*
(2) see *National Bankruptcy Act of 1898.*

NC
(1) see *net capital.*
(2) see *net cost.*

NCB: see *bond, noncallable.*

NCCB: see *National Consumer Cooperative Bank.*

NCF: see *net cash flow.*

NCS: see *noncallable securities.*

NCUA: see *National Credit Union Administration.*

ND: see *net debt.*

NE: see *net earnings.*

nearby delivery: the closest active month of delivery, as stated in a commodity futures agreement.

near money: highly liquid assets (e.g., government securities) other than official currency.

negative amortizer: when a home buyer gets a bank mortgage below the going rate and the difference is added to the principal. Payments are low to start but much higher later.

negative file: an authorized system file containing a simple list of accounts for which credit, check cashing, and other privileges, should be denied. cf. *positive file.*

negative income tax: proposed by some to provide financial aid to individuals with incomes below a certain minimum. Rulings of the Internal Revenue Service would be followed, but the procedure would be to distribute rather than collect revenue.

negative investment: see *disinvestment.*

negative pledge clause: a covenant in an indenture to the effect that the corporation will not pledge any of its assets unless the notes or debentures outstanding under the particular indenture are at least equally secured by such pledge. synonymous with "covenant of equal coverage." [37]

negative verification: many banks have a legend printed on the statement form going to the depositor to the effect that "if no difference is reported within 10 days, the account will be considered correct." If the bank does not hear from the depositor, it assumes that the depositor finds no discrepancies between its statement and his or her records.

Negb.: see *negotiable.*

Neg. Inst.: see *negotiable instrument.*

Negl.: see *negligence.*

negligence: failure to do that which an ordinary, reasonable, prudent person would do, or the doing of some act that an ordinary, prudent person would not do. Reference is made of the situation, circumstances, and awareness of the parties involved.

negotiable

(1) *general:* anything that can be sold or transferred to another for money or as payment of a debt.

(2) *investments:* refers to a security, title to which is transferable by delivery. [20]

negotiable certificate of deposit: a bank technique to expand loan vol-

ume despite government efforts to tighten credit. The certificates normally are issued in denominations of $1 million. The advantage of large CDs for the banks are great, as the certificates provide a quick and easy way to raise needed funds.

negotiable instrument: the Uniform Negotiable Instruments Act states: "An instrument, to be negotiable, must conform to the following requirements: (a) it must be in writing and signed by the maker or drawer; (b) it must contain an unconditional promise or order to pay a certain sum in money; (c) it must be payable on demand, or at a fixed or determinable future time; (d) it must be payable to order or to bearer; and (e) where the instrument is addressed to a drawee, he must be named or otherwise indicated therein with reasonable certainty."

negotiable order of withdrawal: see *NOW account.*

negotiable paper: negotiable instruments that are used in the borrowing of money on a short-term period for business objectives.

negotiable warehouse receipt: a certificate issued by an approved warehouse that guarantees the existence and the grade of a commodity held in store.

negotiated price: the result obtained by a purchaser who desires something different from what is available or is powerful enough to force the seller to accept prices lower than those usually charged.

negotiation

(1) *finance:* the act by which a negotiable instrument is placed into circulation, by being physically passed

from the original holder to another person.

(2) *labor relations:* the deliberation or discussion by representatives of labor and management to set conditions of work (e.g., wages, hours, benefits, working conditions, machinery for handling grievances); the bargaining that goes on between these parties.

neoclassical economics: an economic approach developed between 1870 and 1918, utilizing mathematics in the analysis of data and models. Neoclassicists were primarily concerned with refining the concepts of price and allocation theory, marginalism, and the theory of capital.

neo-Keynesian: a follower of concepts dealing with tax adjustment and government spending as primary forces of economic expansion. see *Keynesian economics.*

nest egg: slang, money saved, often deposited in a savings bank in preparation for retirement.

net: that which remains after certain designated deductions have been made from the gross amount.

net assets: the property of a business, corporation, organization, or estate, remaining after all obligations have been met.

net asset value: it is common practice for investment companies to compute assets daily, or even twice daily, by totaling the market value of all securities owned. All liabilities are deducted; the balance is divided by the number of shares outstanding. The resulting figure is the net asset value per share.

net avails: the funds given to a borrower in the discounting of a note. It is equal to the face value of the note minus the discount.

net balance: the amount due at a particular time, after all refunds have been calculated. Often called the payoff balance or net payoff. [55]

net bonded debt: gross bonded debt less applicable cash or other assets. [49]

net capital: a firm's net worth (assets minus liabilities) minus certain deductions, for assets that may not be easily converted into cash at their full value. In the securities industry, net capital is used to determine whether a brokerage house can be considered solvent and capable of operating.

net cash flow: the net cash consumed or produced in a period by an activity or product during a unit of time, including all revenue and expenses except noncash items such as depreciation.

net change: the change in the price of a security between the closing price on one day and the closing price on the following day on which the stock is traded. The net change is ordinarily the last figure on the stock price list. The mark $+1\frac{1}{4}$ means "up $1.250 a share from the last sale on the previous day the stock had been traded."

net charge-offs as percent of average net loans: loan charge-offs less recoveries as percent of net average loans outstanding. Net loans are gross loans outstanding minus unearned income and the valuation portion of loan loss reserves on an average daily basis for the year. A minus sign indicates that recoveries exceeded charge-offs.

net cost

(1) *general:* the true cost of an item. The net cost is determined by subtracting all income or financial gain from the gross cost.

(2) *banking:* the total premiums paid on a policy less any dividends, and the surrender value as of the time the net cost is determined.

net current monetary assets: equals monetary assets less monetary liabilities. The main difference between net current monetary assets and working capital is that the former definition of funds excludes inventory. see *working capital.* [80]

net debt: the sum of fixed and existing liabilities less the sinking fund and other assets that are earmarked for payment of the liabilities.

net earnings: the excess of gross operating income over gross operating expenses is referred to as "operating earnings before taxes." Income taxes applicable to operating earnings are deducted, to arrive at "net earnings" or "net operating earnings."

net estate: the part of an estate remaining after all expenses to manage it have been taken out.

net export of goods and services: the excess of exports of goods and services (domestic output sold abroad, and the production abroad credit to U.S.-owned resources) over imports (U.S. purchases of foreign output, domestic production credit to foreign-owned resources, and net private cash remittances to creditors abroad).

net federal funds borrowed as percent of average net loans outstanding: net federal funds borrowed are the bank-calculated average federal funds purchased and securities sold under agreements to repurchase, less the bank-calculated average federal funds sold and securities purchased under agreements to resell. A minus sign indicates that the bank was a net seller of federal funds. see *net charge-offs as percent of average net loans.*

net for common stock: net income less dividends on preferred stock applicable to the period on an accrual basis. [3]

net foreign investment: the net change in the nation's foreign assets and liabilities, including the monetary gold stocks, arising out of current trade, income on foreign investment, and cash gifts and contributions. It measures the excess of (a) exports over imports, (b) income on U.S. public and private investment abroad over payments on foreign investment in the U.S., and (c) cash gifts and contributions of the U.S. (public and private) to foreigners over cash gifts and contributions received from abroad. [70]

net free (or net borrowed) reserves: excess reserves less member-bank borrowings from Federal Reserve Banks. The resulting difference is called net free when positive and net borrowed when negative. [72]

net income: the remains from earnings and profits after all costs, expenses, and allowances for depreciation and probable loss have been deducted.

net income after dividends: net income less dividends on preferred stock applicable to the period and dividends declared on common stock during the period. [3]

net income multiplier: a figure which, times the net income of a property, produces an estimate of value of that property. It is obtained by dividing the selling price by the monthly net rent (net income). [52]

net indebtedness: see *net debt.*

net interest: measures the excess of interest payments made by the domestic business sector over its interest receipts from other sectors, plus net interest received from abroad. Interest paid by one business firm to another business firm is a transaction within the business sector and has no effect on the overall interest payments or receipts of the sector. The same is true of interest payments within other sectors as from one individual to another, or one government agency to another. [73]

net investment income per share: the net amount of dividends and interest earned during an accounting period on an investment company's portfolio securities (after deduction of operating expenses) divided by the number of shares outstanding. [23]

net lease: a lease stating that the landlord will incur all maintenance costs, taxes, insurance, and other expenses usually paid by the owner.

net line: the amount of liability retained on a property by a company for its own account. [54]

net listing: the broker receives as commission all monies received above minimum sales price agreed to by owners and broker. [62]

net long-term debt: total long-term debt, less cash and investment assets of sinking funds and other reserve funds specially held for redemption of long-term debt.

net loss: the excess of expenses and losses during a specified period over revenues and gains in the same time frame.

net national product: gross national product minus capital consumption (depreciation). The market value of the net output of goods and services produced by the nation's economy.

net-net income: the repetition of the word "net" emphasizes the actual profit, resulting in usable cash, after all expenses have been paid.

net operating income: net current operating income after minority interest and taxes but before securities gains and losses and preferred dividends for the year ending on December 31.

net position: the difference between the open contracts long and the open contracts short held in any one commodity by an individual or group. [11]

net price: the price after deductions, allowances, and discounts have been made.

net profit: the excess of all revenues over all costs and expenses incurred to obtain the income in a given enterprise during a given period of time. If the total expenses exceed the income, such amount is known as the net loss. synonymous with *net revenue.*

net profit on net sales: obtained by dividing the net earnings of the business, after taxes, by net sales (the dollar volume less returns, allowances, and cash discounts). This is an important yardstick in measuring profitability. [4]

net profits on net working capital: net working capital represents the equity of the owners in the current assets, as obtained by subtracting total current debt from total current assets. This equity, or margin, represents the cushion available to the business for carrying inventories and receivables, and for financing day-to-day operations. To illustrate how net working capital is computed: if a concern has current assets of $1,000,000 and current debt of $400,000, its net working capital is $600,000. [4]

net profits on tangible net worth: tangible net worth is the equity of stockholders in the business, as obtained by subtracting total liabilities from total assets, and then deducting intangibles. The ratio is obtained by dividing net profits after taxes by tangible net worth. The tendency is to look increasingly to this ratio as a final criterion of profitability. Generally, a relationship of at least 10 percent is regarded as a desirable objective for providing dividends plus funds for future growth. [4]

net realized capital gain per share: the amount of net capital gains realized on the sale of portfolio securities during an accounting period after deducting losses realized, divided by the number of shares outstanding. [23]

net revenue: see *net income.*

net revenue available for debt service: gross operating revenues of an enterprise less operating and maintenance expenses but exclusive of depreciation and bond interest. "Net revenue" as thus defined is used to compute "coverage" on revenue bond issues. [49]

net sales: gross sales, minus returns and allowances, over a stated period.

net sales to inventory: obtained by dividing annual net sales by merchandise inventory as carried on the balance sheet. This quotient does not yield an actual physical turnover. It provides a yardstick for comparing stock-to-sales ratios of one concern with another or with those for the industry. [4]

net sales to net working capital: net sales are divided by net working capital. This provides a guide as to the extent the company is turning its working capital and the margin of operating funds. [4]

net sales to tangible net worth: obtained by dividing net sales by tangible net worth. The result gives a measure of the relative turnover of capital. If capital is turned over too rapidly, liabilities build up excessively, as amounts owed to creditors become a substitute for permanent capital. And if capital is turned too slowly, funds become stagnant, and profitability suffers. [4]

net savings inflow: the change in an association's savings account balances over a given period, determined by subtracting withdrawals during the period; also called net savings gain or net savings receipts. When interest credited to accounts during the period is excluded, the resulting figure is customarily referred to as net new savings. [59]

net surplus: the earnings or profits remaining to a corporation after all operating expenses, taxes, interests, insurance, and dividends have been paid out. The surplus is determined before deducting dividends while the net surplus is determined following the deduction of dividends.

net working capital: the excess of existing assets over present liabilities.

net worth

(1) *general:* the owner's equity in a given business, represented by the excess of the total assets over the total amounts owing to outside creditors at a given moment of time.

(2) *finance:* refers to the "net worth" of an individual, as determined by deducting the amount of all his or her personal liabilities for the total value of personal assets.

net yield: the return from an investment following subtractions for costs and losses incurred in operating the investment.

neutral spread: an investment strategy, since on the downside it is impossible to lose more than commission costs. It involves buying a call option on a stock for a specific time period and selling two call options on the same stock for the same period, but at a higher exercise price. The idea is to pick a stock whose options at the high exercise price are trading at about half the price, or premium, of the option bought. The out-of-pocket costs are just the commissions on doing the deal. synonymous with *ratio bull spread, twofer.*

new business venture group: a separate company unit with a mandate to develop one or more new businesses or items that fall outside the natural charter of the firm's existing activities.

new cedi: monetary unit of Ghana.

new cruzeiro: monetary unit of Brazil.

New Economics: economic thought, initially developed by John Maynard Keynes in the 1930s, which states that an economy may be in equilibrium at any level of employment. Appropriate government fiscal and monetary policies are required to maintain full employment and keep economic growth with minimal inflation. see *Keynesian economics.*

New England NOW Accounts: a 1979 federal law that expanded NOW account authority to federally chartered associations in Connecticut, Maine, Rhode Island, and Vermont. see also *NOW account.* [51]

new high: usually, the highest price that a security has attained since its exchange listing.

new issue: a stock or bond sold by a corporation for the first time. Proceeds may be issued to retire outstanding securities of the company to finance new plant or equipment, or to secure additional working capital.

new issue market: the market for new issues of securities (as opposed to the secondary market on securities already issued). [52]

new rupiah: monetary unit of Indonesia.

New York Coffee and Sugar Exchange: founded in 1882, when it was originally known as the New York Coffee Exchange, it is the principal U.S. exchange for the trading of coffee and sugar futures contracts. see *Commodities Exchange Center.*

New York Curb Exchange: former name for the American Stock Exchange.

New York Futures Exchange: created in 1980, resulting from the absorption of the Amex Commodities Exchange (ACE). The new exchange began with trading futures in Treasury bonds, and contracts in five foreign currencies: British pounds, Canadian dollars, Japanese yen, Swiss francs and West German marks.

New York Insurance Exchange: opened in March 1980, allows insurance brokers to place large business orders with a variety of underwriters on one exchange floor.

New York Mercantile Exchange: founded in 1872 as a market for cheese, butter, and eggs, its principal commodities include potatoes, silver coins, and platinum. see *Commodities Exchange Center.*

New York NOW accounts: legislation passed in 1978 permitting FSLIC-insured institutions in New York State to offer NOW accounts. see *NOW account.* [51]

New York Stock Exchange (NYSE): the largest, most prestigious security exchange in the world, reorganized under its existing name in 1863. In 1817, the New York Stock and Exchange Board moved indoors to a second-floor room at 40 Wall Street in New York City. On January 2, 1863, the title was changed to the New York Stock Exchange, and on the next day, the first subsidiary, the New York Stock Exchange Building Company, was created. see also *NYSE Common Stock Index.*

next friend: one who, although not regularly appointed a guardian, acts for the benefit of a minor or incompetent person or, in some instances, a married woman or for any person who, for some legal reason, cannot appear for himself. [37]

next of kin: the person or persons in the nearest degree of blood relationship to the decedent. As the term is usually employed, those entitled by law to the personal property of a person who has died without leaving a valid will (such persons do not include the surviving husband and wife except where specifically so provided by statute); to be distinguished from the heirs, who take the real property. [37]

nexus: a relationship used in tax laws to express a connection between a tax and the activities of the individual or group being taxed. see *tax incidence.*

NF: see *no funds.*

NGPA: see *Natural Gas Policy Act.*

ngultrum: monetary unit of Bhutan.

NH: see *new high.*

NI
  (1)   see *national income.*
  (2)   see *negotiable instrument.*
  (3)   see *net income.*
  (4)   see *net interest.*

NICs: newly industrializing countries (e.g., Mexico, South Korea, Brazil, and Taiwan).

night depository: a small vault located on the inside of a bank, but accessible to the streetside of the bank. To use this vault, depositors are given a passkey to the outer door of the night depository vault. When this door is opened, the package of money properly identified by the depositor is dropped down a chute into the night depository vault. This convenience is used by merchants who do not wish the day's receipts to remain in their place of business, and so have this means of protecting their deposits after the regular business hours of the bank. The vault is opened by a bank attendant, and the deposits properly counted and credited to the depositor's account. [10]

NINOW's: non-interest-bearing NOW accounts.

NL
  (1) see *net loss*.
  (2) see *no-load funds*.
NLF: see *no-load funds*.
NLO: see *no-limit order*.
N&M: November and May (semiannual interest payments or dividends).
NM: see *narrow market*.
NMF: see *nonmember firm*.
NNI: see *net-net income*.
No.: number.
N/O: registered in name of.
No. AC: see *no account*.
no account: a situation when the
  drawer of a check fails to possess an
  account in the drawee bank and the
  drawee returns the check to the presenting bank for credit with a statement reading "no account."
no funds: a situation when the drawer
  of a check fails to possess needed
  funds in the drawee bank and the
  drawee returns the check to the presenting bank for credit with a statement reading "no funds."
no lien affidavit: a written document
  by a property owner that the work has
  been finished on an identified property and that no liens or mortgages
  encumber it. cf. *lien affidavit*.
no-limit order: a request to buy or sell
  a security without any stipulation
  about price. cf. *limited order, market
  order*.
no-load funds: mutual funds that are
  not sold by a salesperson. They do
  not involve extensive marketing
  schemes and contain no sales
  charge or load.
nolo contendere: "I will not contest
  [it]" (Latin). In a criminal case, a form
  of guilty plea on the basis of which a
  sentence may be passed. By pleading, the defendant admits to the facts

of the case without admitting his formal guilt of a crime. The plea is most
often used when a guilty plea would
affect other interests (e.g., a contract,
insurance).
nominal asset: an asset whose value
  is inconsiderable, to be questioned,
  or difficult to evaluate such as claims
  or judgments in reorganization. Accounting tradition suggests that
  nominal assets be written down and
  carried as some token value, usually
  one dollar. Copyrights, goodwill and
  other such assets can be considered
  nominal assets.
nominal income: the dollar value of
  income. Shifts in nominal income
  arise from changes in either real income or in price levels.
nominal interest rate: the contractual
  interest rate shown on the face and in
  the body of a bond and representing
  the amount of interest to be paid, in
  contrast with the effective interest
  rate. see *coupon rate*. [49]
nominally issued: capital stock, funded debt, and other securities when
  they are signed and sealed or certified and placed with the proper officer for sale and delivery, or pledged
  or placed in some special fund of the
  issuing corporation. [18]
nominally outstanding: securities reacquired by or for the issuing corporation under each circumstance as
  requires them to be considered as
  held alive, and not canceled or retired. see *actually outstanding*. [18]
nominal partner: an individual who
  lends his or her name to a business
  organization but is not a true partner
  because he may not have given sufficient financial backing or he does not
  take a full share of the profit.

nominal price

(1) *finance:* an amount of money so small in relation to the item purchased that it hardly justifies the use of the word "price."

(2) *investments:* an estimated price for a security or commodity that is not traded often enough to warrant the setting of a definite market price.

nominal value: term used in the United Kingdom for face value, or par value. In the United States, this term is equivalent to par value. see *par value.* [43]

nominal yield: the rate of return stated on a security calculated on its par or face value.

nomination: the naming or proposal of a person for an office, position, or duty; to be distinguished from appointment. Thus the testator nominates but the court appoints the executor under a will. [32]

nominee: an official of a bank or trust company, or an appointed agent into whose name securities or other funds are transferred by agreement. This is done to facilitate the purchase or sale of securities, when it may be inconvenient to obtain the signature of the principal to make such transfers. It also facilitates the collection and distribution of income from securities when these securities are held in the name of a nominee. Nominee arrangements also apply to custodianships. [10]

no more credit: instruction to authorizers that no further credit be allowed a particular customer. [41]

nonaccrual asset: an asset, such as a loan, that has been questioned on bank examination is known to be a "slow" or "doubtful" (of payment)

loan. A reserve is set up or applied on this type of loan, and it is excluded from the earning or accrual assets.

nonassessable stock: most securities; stock whose owners cannot be assessed in the event of failure or insolvency. cf. *limited liability.*

nonassignable: see *inalienable.*

nonborrowed reserves: total reserves less member-bank borrowings from reserve banks. [72]

noncallable bond: see *bond, noncallable.*

noncallable securities: stocks that cannot be redeemed prior to maturity, even if the issuing company can afford to do so. They are not subject to call.

noncompetitive tender: the submission to a bank when wishing to purchase Treasury bills directly from a Federal Reserve Bank, indicating the willingness to pay the average price of all the competitive offers from large institutions that buy millions of Treasury bills each week. The minimum purchase is $10,000, with multiples of $5,000 above that.

non compos mentis: describing an individual not possessing sufficient understanding to comprehend the nature, extent, and meaning of his or her obligations or contracts.

noncontributory: describing a group insurance plan under which the policyholder (employee) pays the entire cost.

Non. Cum.: see *noncumulative.*

noncumulative: a preferred stock on which unpaid dividends do not accrue. Omitted dividends are, as a rule, gone forever. [20]

noncumulative quantity discount: a price reduction that is given based on the size of the individual order placed.

noncurrency: the situation that exists when two or more policies provide differing coverages on the same risk. see *double insurance.*

noncurrent: that which is due more than one year after the date of issuance.

noncurrent liabilities: claims against the assets of an entity that will become due a year or more later.

nonexpendable disbursements: disbursements that are not chargeable as expenditures; for example, a disbursement made for the purpose of paying off an account payable previously recorded on the books. [49]

nonexpendable fund: the principal, and sometimes also the earnings, of which may not be expended. [49]

nonexpenditure disbursements: disbursements that are not chargeable as expenditures; for example, a disbursement made for the purpose of paying off an account payable previously recorded on the books. [49]

nonfeasance: failure to perform a legal duty. cf. *malfeasance.*

nonforfeiture options: privileges allowed under terms of a life insurance contract after cash values have been created. Four privileges exist: (a) surrender for full cash value; (b) loans up to the full amount of the cash value; (c) paid-up policy for the amount of insurance that cash value, as a single premium, will buy at net rates; and (d) term insurance for full face amount of the original policy for as long as the cash value will last to pay necessary premiums.

nonguaranteed debt: debt payable solely from pledged specific sources which does not constitute an obligation on any other resources of the government if the pledged sources are insufficient. [70]

noninstallment credit: credit granted, with payment to be made in a lump sum, at a future date.

noninsured fund: pension or other fund invested through channels other than deposit with an insurance company. [22]

non-interest-bearing note: a note whose maker does not have to pay any interest.

noninvestment property: property that will not yield income.

nonledger asset: assets not carried in the general ledger, such as accrued dividends, uncollected and deferred premiums, and excess of market value of securities over book value. [42]

nonlegal investment: an investment that is outside the classes designated by statute or by some governmental agency as proper for the investment of trust funds. [37]

nonlegals: securities that do not conform to the requirements of the statutes, in certain states, concerning investments for savings banks and for trust funds; opposed to legals. see *legal list.* [67]

nonmarketable liabilities of U.S. goverment (including medium-term securities): other medium-term securities include foreign holdings of nonmarketable, medium-term U.S. government securities, payable before maturity only under special conditions. Examples of these are nonconvertible ''Roosa Bonds'' issued by the Treasury, and Certificates of Participation representing

Export-Import Bank loans sold mainly to foreign governments and central banks. [73]

nonmember bank: U.S. banks that are not members of the Federal Reserve System. These institutions are either state or private banks.

nonmember firm: any brokerage firm that is not a member of the New York Stock Exchange. Usually such houses sell securities in the third market, often at lower fees than those charged by New York Stock Exchange members. see *member firm.*

nonmerchantable title: an unmarketable title that is legally unsound because it shows property defects. see *cloud on title.*

nonmortgage loan: an advance of funds not secured by a real estate mortgage. [59]

nonnegotiable title: a title that cannot be transferred by delivery or by endorsement.

nonoperating expense: the outlays and losses of a savings association that are nonrecurring in nature and that do not result from the ordinary savings and lending operations of the institution, such as the expense of maintaining real estate owned or a loss taken on the sale of a nonmortgage investment. [59]

nonoperating income: the receipts and profits of a savings association that are nonrecurring in nature and that do not result from the ordinary savings and lending operations of the institution, such as a profit on the sale of a nonmortgage investment. synonymous with "nonrecurring income." [59]

non-par item: a check that cannot be collected at the par or face value when presented by another bank. All checks drawn on member banks of the Federal Reserve System, and nonmember banks that have met the requirements of the Federal Reserve System, are collectible at par. Some nonmember banks in certain regions of the United States levy an exchange charge against the check presented for collection and payment. These banks are called non-par banks, and deduct the exchange charge when remitting the payment to the bank requesting collection and payment. see *par list.* [10]

nonpayment: the failure to pay as agreed. [28]

nonperformance: the failure of a contracting party to provide goods or services according to an agreement.

nonprice competition: applied to markets in which a seller maneuvers for influence on the basis of special aspects of the items to be sold, promotion, or marketing strategy. Most larger organizations avoid price competition by emphasizing nonprice marketing forces.

nonprofit corporation: see *not-for-profit.*

nonrecourse loan: the type of loan that the government makes to farmers under its price-support program. In the event the farmer defaults on the loan, the government has no recourse against the farmer if the security the farmer has put up (his crop) fails to bring the amount of the loan when sold.

nonrecurring charge: any cost, expense, or involuntary loss that will not, it is felt, be likely to occur again.

nonresidential mortgage loan: a mortgage loan secured by nonresidential property such as an office building, store, factory, or church. [59]

nonrevenue receipts: collections, other than revenue, such as receipts from loans where the liability is recorded in the fund in which the proceeds are placed and receipts on account of recoverable expenditures. see also *revenue receipts.* [49]

nonstandard payment: any amount of payment other than the exact contract payment. see *standard payment.* [55]

nonsuit: a court judgment against the plaintiff when he or she is unable to prove the case or for failure to continue with the trial once it has commenced.

nontaxable income: incomes that are not liable to income tax.

nonvoting stock: securities of any class within a firm other than voting stock. They cannot be listed by the New York Stock Exchange. see *listing requirements.*

no-par-value stock: stock of a corporation without designated par value.

no-passbook savings: the same as a regular passbook savings account, except that no passbook is used. Deposits and withdrawal slips are receipted by the teller, with a copy returned to the depositor for personal records. A periodic statement is rendered in place of a passbook. Withdrawals must be made by the depositor personally.

no protest: instructions given by one bank to another collecting bank not to object to items in case of nonpayment. The sending bank stamps on the face of the item the letters ''NP.'' If the item cannot be collected, the collecting bank returns the item without objecting.

no record: the report given to a credit grantor by a credit bureau when no record exists in the bureau files regarding a particular customer. [41]

normal good: an item whose consumption changes directly with money income, where prices remain constant (e.g., consumer goods). synonymous with ''superior good.''

normal price: the price to which the market price tends to return following fluctuations up or down.

normal profit: the lowest price that an entrepreneur will accept as compensation for his or her activity. It is part of an organization's total economic costs, since it is a payment that must be received by the owner to keep him from withdrawing capital and effort that might have to be used in another way.

normal sale: a transaction that pleases both the seller and buyer of property and in which no unforessen or abnormal situations surface.

normal value: the price or a property commanded on the open market.

nostro account: ''our'' account; an account maintained by a bank with a bank in a foreign country. Nostro accounts are kept in foreign currencies of the country in which the monies are held, with the equivalent dollar value listed in another column. cf. *vostro account.*

nostro overdraft: part of the bank's statement indicating that it has sold more foreign bills of exchange than it has bought, resulting in the domestic bank's owing currencies to foreign banks in the amount of the nostro (our) overdraft.

notarial acknowledgment: the acknowledgment of the due execution of a legal instrument before a notary public. The statement of the notary public as to the face and date of the acknowledgment, with the notary public's signature and seal of office and date of expiration of commission to serve as notary public. [37]

notarial certificate: the certificate of the notary public as to the due acknowledgment of the instrument. [37]

notarial protest certificate: see *notice of dishonor (protest jacket).*

notarized draft: a withdrawal order signed and acknowledged before a notary public, who affirms that the person who signed the draft personally appeared before him or her, was known to be the person indicated, and executed the draft for the purpose indicated. [39]

notary public: a person commissioned by a state for a stipulated period (with the privilege of renewal) to administer certain oaths and to attest and certify documents, thus authorizing him or her to take affidavits and depositions. A notary is also authorized to "protest" negotiable instruments for nonpayment or nonacceptance. see *notice of dishonor (protest jacket).*

note: an instrument, such as a promissory note, which is the recognized legal evidence of a debt. A note is signed by the maker, called the borrower, promising to pay a certain sum of money on a specified date at a certain place of business, to a certain business, individual, or bank, called the lender.

note loan: the classification of an unsecured loan. [55]

note notice: a form made and used by the loan department of a bank. The note notice contains all information as to the amount: due date, maker's name and address, securities pledged, if any, and so on. It is mailed to the borrower several days before the maturity of the note, as a reminder of the due date of the note. If the bank is posting the "liability ledger" by machine, the "loans made register," customer's liability ledger card, note notice, and maturity tickler are all created in one posting operation. [10]

note of hand: any promissory note.

note payable: a liability, evidenced by a formal written promise to pay a specified sum at a fixed future date. Notes may be either short (one year or less) or long term.

note receivable: a promissory note collected by a business from a customer.

note teller: synonymous with *loan teller.*

not-for-profit: describes an activity of an organization established with the sole goal of providing service for society rather than for the purpose of making a profit. see *eleemosynary.*

notice account: a passbook savings account on which the customer agrees to give the association specified notice before making a withdrawal. As long as he gives the agreed notice, his funds earn at a higher interest rate than that paid on passbook accounts; insufficient notice for a withdrawal may incur a penalty. [59]

notice day: the day on which notices of intention to deliver may be issued.

notice of dishonor (protest jacket):

when a "holder in due course" presents an instrument for payment or acceptance by a drawee, and the maker or drawee fails to honor the instrument, the holder in due course gives it to a notary public. The notary public also presents the instrument to the maker or drawee as a legal formality. If the maker or drawee again dishonors the instrument by refusing to pay for or to accept it, the notary public prepares a "notice of dishonor," or in the terminology of some states, a "mandate of protest" or a "notarial protest certificate." cf. *acceptance for honor.*

notice of intention to deliver: a certificate supplied by a short seller indicating his intention to fulfill his contract obligation by delivering the actual commodity.

notice of withdrawal: a notice that may be required by a mutual savings bank or other recipient of savings deposits before a withdrawal of funds is permitted. The length of time required before the notice becomes effective varies in the several states. [39]

notice price: the fixed price at which futures deliveries are invoiced.

notice to creditors: the notice in writing by posting in public places or by notice in newspapers to creditors of an estate to present their claims for what the executor or administrator owes them; it usually is also a notice to debtors to come in and pay what they owe the estate. [37]

no-ticket savings plan: a variation of the "unit-savings plan" whereby the normal savings account transaction, either deposit or withdrawal, is accomplished without the use of either a deposit ticket or a withdrawal slip. A deposit is recorded just as in the unit-savings plan, but the depositor is not required to make out a deposit ticket under this machine-printed entry plan. In place of a withdrawal slip, the depositor merely writes his signature on the same line as the machine-printed entry of withdrawal. As in the unit savings plan, the passbook, ledger card, and lock-protected audit tape are posted in original printing in one operation directly in front of the depositor, who is the "auditor" of the transaction. [10]

not subject to call: those bonds or notes that cannot be paid off and retired prior to their maturity date. cf. *callable.*

novation

(1) *general:* the replacement of a new debt or obligation for an older one. see *open-end mortgage;* cf. *renewal, standstill agreement.*

(2) *finance:* the replacement of a new creditor or debtor for a former creditor (or debtor).

NOW (negotiable order of withdrawal) account: a savings account from which the account holder can withdraw funds by writing a negotiable order of withdrawal (NOW) payable to a third party. [59] Until January 1, 1980 NOW accounts were available only in New England, New York, and New Jersey. Effective with new federal regulations, all savings and loans as well as banks, for the first time nationally, are allowed to offer interest-bearing checking accounts (NOW accounts).

NP

(1) see *net position.*

(2) see *net profit.*

(3) see *no protest.*

(4) see *notary public.*

(5) see *note payable.*

NPVS: see *no-par-value stock.*

NR: see *note receivable.*

NS: see *net surplus.*

NSE: see *National Stock Exchange.*

NSF: not sufficient funds.

NT Dollar: monetary unit of China (Taiwan).

nudge: see *Operation Twist (Nudge).*

nudum pactum: "an empty promise" (Latin); a statement for which no consideration has been given.

nuisance tax

(1) *government:* any tax the revenue from which does not justify the inconvenience to a person subject to the tax.

(2) *government:* a tax that yields a low return following deduction of the costs of handling and administration.

nullification of agreement: setting aside the terms of an agreement. cf. *repudiation.*

numerical control: programming equipment by means of coded numbers, stored on magnetic tapes or cards, according to the needs of different items.

numerical transit system: see *American Bankers Association number.*

numeric character: any allowable digit in a machine's number system.

nuncupative will: a will given orally before witnesses, which is reduced to writing at a later time.

nursery finance: institutional loans to profitable organizations that plan to go public shortly. see *adventure, risk capital, venture capital.*

NVS: see *nonvoting stock.*

NW: see *net worth.*

NWC: see *net working capital.*

NY: see *net yield.*

NYCE: see *New York Curb Exchange.*

NYFE: see *New York Futures Exchange.*

NYSE: see *New York Stock Exchange.*

NYSE Common Stock Index: a composite index covering price movements of all common stocks listed on the "Big Board." It is based on the close of the market December 31, 1965, as 50.00 and is weighted according to the number of shares listed for each issue. The index is computed continuously and printed on the ticker tape each half-hour. Point changes in the index are converted to dollars and cents, to provide a meaningful measure of changes in the average price of listed stocks. The composite index is supplemented by separate indices for four industry groups: industrials, transportation, utilities, and finances. cf. *Dow Jones averages.* [20]

O&A: October and April (semiannual interest payments or dividends).

OA
   (1) see *open account.*
   (2) see *operational analysis.*

OASI: see *old-age and survivors' insurance.*

OB
   (1) see *bond, obligation.*
   (2) see *operating budget.*

object: as used in expenditure classification, this term applies to the article purchased or the service obtained (as distinguished from the results obtained from expenditures). Examples are personal services, contractual services, materials, and supplies. [49]

object classification: a grouping of expenditures on the basis of goods or services purchased; for example, personal services, materials, supplies, and equipment. [49]

objection to title: a weakness in a title for property, requiring adjustment. see *cloud on title.*

objective value: the price that an economic good can command in terms of other goods in the market. [44]

objects of expenditure: see *object.*

Oblg.: see *obligation.*

Oblig.: see *obligation.*

obligation: the legal responsibility and duty of the debtor (the obligor) to pay a debt when due, and the legal right of the creditor (the obligee) to enforce payment in the event of default.

obligation bond: see *bond, obligation.*

obligator: synonymous with *obligor.*

obligatory maturity: the compulsory maturity of any bond or note, as distinguished from optional maturity dates or early redemption dates.

obligee: a creditor or promisee.

obligor: a debtor or promisor; principal.

OBR: see *Overseas Business Reports.*

obsolete securities: abandoned or defunct corporation securities. Any bond that has matured or been withdrawn.

obverse: the front or face of a note, as opposed to the reverse or back. It usually bears the value of the note, its date, and the principal vignette. [27]

OC
   (1) Office of Commissioner.
   (2) see *operating company.*
   (3) see *organizational chart.*

OCC: see *Options Clearing Corporation.*

occupational analysis: a descriptive approach for determining the jobs that have common activities, to permit grouping them under a common occupation.

occupational information: information resulting from analysis of questionnaires and other materials (e.g.,

Dictionary of Occupational Titles) that describe the functions and characteristics of specific occupations.

Occupational Safety and Health Act of 1970: federal legislation providing for health and safety standards for individuals in the performance of their labors; created the Occupational Safety and Health Administration (OSHA) of the Department of Labor to set the rules and enforce the laws. OSHA also administers training and education programs on occupational safety and health standards for employers and workers, supervises regional inspections, and issues citations to employers not meeting federal standards.

occupation currency: military currency introduced to a country by occupying forces. [27]

OCO: see *one-cancels-the-other order.*

OCR: see *optical character recognition.*

Od.
(1) see *overdraft.*
(2) see *overdraw.*
(3) see *overdue.*

OD
(1) see *on demand.*
(2) see *organizational development.*

odd lot: an amount of stock less than the established 100-share unit or 10-share unit of trading: from 1 to 99 shares for the greatest majority of issues, 1 to 9 for so-called inactive stocks. see *inactive stock (bond), round lot.* [20]

odd-lot dealer: a member firm of an exchange that buys and sells odd lots of stock—1 to 9 shares in the case of stocks traded in 10-share units and 1

to 99 shares for 100-share units. The odd-lot dealer's customers are commission brokers acting on behalf of their customers.

odd-lot orders: any purchase or sale of stock not in 100-share units. cf. *full lot.*

OE: see *operating expense.*

OECD: see *Organization for Economic Cooperation and Development.*

OEEC: see *Organization for Economic Cooperation and Development.*

OEF: see *open-end funds.*

OEIC: see *open-end investment company.*

OEIT: see *open-end investment trust.*

OF: see *offshore funds.*

OFCC: see *Federal Contract Compliance Office.*

Ofd.: see *offer(ed).*

off: describes a given day on which the prices of stocks and commodities drop. see also *on.*

off-board: describes over-the-counter transactions in unlisted securities, or a transaction involving listed shares that was not executed on a national securities exchange.

off-budget programs: a miscellany of government programs or agencies whose outlays are by law accounted for outside the budget.

offer(ed)
(1) *general:* to present for acceptance or refusal.
(2) *investments:* the price at which a person is ready to sell. Opposed to bid, the price at which one is ready to buy. [20]

offered ahead: a situation created when an individual who has placed an order to sell at a given price finds that other or lower offers have been given earlier on the same security; these obviously take precedence over his offer.

offered down: securities that are offered for sale at levels lower than the last sale or quoted price of the same stock.

offering: a term used to indicate an issue of securities or bonds offered for sale to the public. see *secondary offering, special offering.*

offering price: the price per share at which investment shares are offered to the public. The offering price usually consists of the net asset value per share plus a sales charge. synonymous with *asked (asking) price.*

offer wanted: a request made by a buyer for a security for which no apparent market exists. Such a potential buyer is seeking a potential seller. see *bid wanted.*

off-exchange: commodity firms registered with the Commodity Futures Trading Commission that are not members of any of the 10 regulated futures exchanges that keep an eye on the daily operations of their members. In fact, these "off-exchange" houses, in practice, are barely regulated.

Office of Federal Contract Compliance Programs: see *Federal Contract Compliance Office.*

Office of Management and Budget (OMB): a federal agency that prepares the president's budget; with the Council of Economic Advisers and Treasury Department, develops the government's fiscal program; oversees the administration of the federal budget.

office paper: see *finance bill.*

officer's check: synonymous with *cashier's check.*

official check: a check drawn by an official of a commercial bank on the bank itself, used by a bank to pay its bills and other obligations; sometimes provided to the bank's customers for transactions in which a personal check might not be acceptable. synonymous with *cashier's check* or *treasurer's check.* [7]

off-line computer system: a computer system that processes previously collected data in batches rather than at the time the data are produced. [59]

offset

(1) *general:* either of two equivalent entries on both sides of an account.

(2) *banking:* the right accruing to a bank to take possession of any balances that a guarantor or debtor may have in the bank to cover a loan in default. cf. *garnishment.*

(3) *banking:* a depositor who has both a deposit credit balance and a loan balance is denied the right of offset if the bank becomes insolvent and closes.

offsets to long-term debt: cash and investment assets of sinking funds, bond reserve, and other reserve funds held specifically for the redemption of long-term debt, and assets of credit funds that are pledged to redeem debt incurred to finance loan activities of such funds.

offshore funds: as they affect U.S. citizens, mutual funds that have their headquarters outside this country or off its shores. Usually, such funds are not available to Americans but are sold to investors in other parts of the world.

off the board: referring to a transaction made over the counter or involving a block of listed securities that were not executed on an organized exchange. synonymous with *off-board*; see *secondary distribution, third market.*

off time: describing a computer that is not scheduled for use, maintenance, alteration, or repair.

of record: as shown by the record; usually employed in such entries as "attorney of record," showing that the one named is the recognized representative of the party at interest. [37]

Ohio Deposit Guarantee Fund: a state-chartered mutual institution in Ohio that insures the savings accounts held by member savings associations and serves as a central credit facility. [59]

OI

(1) see *operating income.*

(2) see *ordinary interest.*

OJAJ: October, January, April, July (quarterly interest payments or dividends).

OJT: see *on-the-job training.*

OK: correct.

ok packages: a list or package of checks that has been processed in a branch office, proved for accuracy, checked for date and endorsement, and considered OK by the branch office. The total on the package is used at the main office for the final consolidation of totals without the main office having to rerun the items in the package. [10]

OL

(1) see *odd lot.*

(2) see *operating losses.*

old-age and survivors' insurance (OASI): the source of retirement income and other payments made to survivors of those eligible under Social Security legislation.

old and new balance proof: a method of proof used in a bank, especially in savings departments, to prove the correct pickup of old balances, and to establish the net amount of increase or decrease to ledger controls. An adding machine tape, or a columnar journal sheet is used as a permanent record of this proof. All affected ledger cards are sorted by account number, and then run on an adding machine. Generally, the new balances are run in the first column. In the next column, the old balances are run so that the old balances appear opposite the new balances and the old balances must equal the difference in the totals of the deposits and the withdrawals. If these two differences agree, it is proof that the old balance was picked up correctly on every account affected in the day's business. [10]

Old Lady of Threadneedle Street: a popular name for the Bank of England.

oligopoly: an industry in which a small number of producers sell identical products. cf. *monopoly.*

oligopoly price: a price that develops when there is a market of numerous buyers and few sellers, thus resulting in the sellers having the greatest power.

oligopsony: control by a number of buyers, who attempt to influence the demand for a specific commodity.

oligopsony price: a price that develops when there is a market of few buyers and numerous sellers, thus resulting in the buyers having the greatest power.

OM

(1) see *on margin.*

(2) see *open market.*

OMB: see *Office of Management and Budget.*

omnibus account: an account carried by one futures commission merchant with another in which the transactions of two or more persons are combined rather than designated separately and the identity of individual accounts is not disclosed. [2]

Omnibus Reconciliation Act of 1980: federal legislation; imposed restrictions on use of mortgage subsidy bonds plus other miscellaneous tax changes.

on: the number of points that a cash commodity is higher than a specified futures month. see also *off.*

on account

(1) *general:* describes a payment made toward the settlement of an account.

(2) *finance:* a purchase or sale made on *open account.*

on a scale: in buying or selling securities: the customer purchases or sells equal amounts of a stock at prices that are spaced by a constant interval, as the market price rises or drops.

on balance

(1) *general:* the net effect or result.

(2) *investments:* the difference between offsetting sales and purchases; for example, if an investor sells 1000 shares of securities, then purchases 2200 shares of the same security, he has purchased 1200 shares on balance.

on-balance volume: an indicator that attempts to pinpoint where futures contracts are being accumulated or bought, and when they are being distributed or sold by controlling market forces, the hedgers, and large traders.

on demand: describing a bill of exchange that is payable on presentation. see *demand note.*

one-bank holding company: a corporation that owns control of one commercial bank.

one-cancels-the-other order (OCO): a contingency order in which one part is automatically canceled as soon as the other part is filled.

one-day certificates: authorized by Congress in 1971, the Federal Reserve Banks buy and sell guaranteed obligations of the government directly from or to the United States. By law, these certificates cannot exceed $5 billion.

one-day loans: see *day loan.*

one hundred percent reserve: a banking system that can be substituted for the fractional reserve system. Commercial banks can be required to hold reserves for the full amount of their deposits and would not be able to make loans with any funds except those available from paid-in capital and surplus.

one-stop banking: provided by a bank whose clients can do all banking business at that bank. cf. *full-service bank.*

on-line computer system: a computer system that is available at all times for receiving data and making calculations. [59]

on margin: describes securities purchased when the buyer has borrowed part of the purchase price from the broker.

on opening: a term used to specify execution of an order during the opening call. [11]

on-the-job training (OJT): using the actual work site as a proper setting to instruct workers while at the same time engaging in productive work.

on-us check: any depositor's check drawn on and payable at the bank wherein the account is carried is termed an "on us" check when presented for payment to the drawee bank. [10]

OO: see *open order.*

ooftish (offtish): slang, money, usually to be used for speculation.

OP
    (1)   see *offering price.*
    (2)   see *opening price.*
    (3)   see *opening purchase.*
    (4)   see *operating profit.*

Op. D.: delayed opening.

OPEC: see *Organization of Petroleum Exporting Countries.*

open account: credit extended that is not supported by a note, mortgage, or other formal written evidence of indebtedness (e.g., merchandise for which a buyer is billed later).

open charge account: see *charge account.*

open contracts: contracts that have been bought or sold without the transaction having been completed by subsequent sale or repurchase or actual delivery or receipt of the commodity. [11]

open credit: credit that is allowed without immediate proof of a customer's credit worthiness.

open door policy: a condition where citizens and products of foreign countries receive the same treatment as domestic citizens and products. cf. *most favored nation (clause).*

open economy: an economy free of trade restrictions.

open-end bond: see *bond, open-end.*

open-end clause: an optional mortgage clause, used in states that recognize its validity, which provides that the pledge of real estate will cover additional advances of funds that the borrower may request and the lender agrees to grant at unknown times in the future. Under the terms of this clause, all subsequent advances represent a claim on the property dating from the time of recording of the original mortgage. [59]

open-end credit: a line of credit that may be used repeatedly up to a certain limit. synonymous with *charge account* or *revolving credit.* [1]

open-end funds: mutual funds where new shares of the fund are sold whenever there is a request, with the expectation that the seller will eventually request to buy back the shares, at no additional charge. see *investment company.*

open-end investment company: an investment firm that sells and reclaims its capital stock continuously, selling it at book value, adding a sales charge, and redeeming it at a slight discount or at book value.

open-end investment trust: an investment trust in which the trustee, by the terms of the trust, is authorized to invest in shares of stock other than those in the trust at the time of the inception of the trust or of the participation in the trust. [37]

open-end lease: a lease that may involve an additional payment based on the value of property when returned. [78]

open-end mortgage: a mortgage that permits the borrower to reborrow money paid on the principal up to the original amount.

opening price

(1) *general:* the first price given in an auction or sales marketplace.

(2) *investments:* the initial price at which a transaction in a security takes place on every day; the first quoted price of a new stock issue.

opening purchase: a transaction in which an investor becomes the holder of a security or an option.

opening range: commodities, unlike securities, are often traded at several prices at the opening or close of the market. Buying or selling orders at the opening might be filled at any point in such a price range for the commodity. [2]

opening sale: a transaction in which an investor becomes the writer of an option. [5]

open interest: the number of outstanding contracts in the exchange market, or in a particular class or series.

open market: a general term describing a condition of trading that is not limited to any area or persons.

open-market credit: short-term financing enabling commercial paper houses to purchase notes and resell them in the open market.

open-market operations: operations carried out by the Federal Reserve System, in which it buys or sells government bonds in the same market other institutional investors use.

open-market rates: the money rates set for classes of paper in the open market, as distinguished from banks rates offered to customers, and rates for advances and rediscounts set by Federal Reserve Banks for all member banks.

open mortgage: a mortgage that can be paid off, without penalty, at any period prior to its maturity.

open order: an order to buy or sell securities that has not yet been executed. Orders may be placed at market price or at a fixed price. synonymous with *good-'til-canceled order.*

open outcry: see *outcry market.*

open prospectus: a brochure that aims to obtain financial backing and does not clearly identify the use to be made of the investment.

open to buy: the currently unused portion of a total dollar credit line agreed upon. [28]

open trade: any transaction that has not yet been closed.

operating budget: a budget that applies to all outlays other than capital outlays. see *budget.* [49]

operating company: a company whose officers direct the business of transportation and whose books contain operating as well as financial accounts. [18]

operating earnings before taxes: see *net earnings.*

operating expense

(1) *general:* actual expense incurred in the maintenance of property (e.g., management, repairs, taxes, insurance); not included as operating expenses are mortgage payments, depreciation, and interest paid out.

(2) **finance:** any expense incurred in the normal operation of a business. This is to be distinguished from expenditures, which are disbursements that are capitalized and depreciate over a period of years. see *margin of profit.*

operating income
(1) **general:** income to a business produced by its earning assets and by fees for services rendered.
(2) **finance:** rental monies obtained from the operation of a business or from property.

operating income as percent of net interest income: net operating income before securities gains and losses, divided by total interest income, minus total interest expense, minus provision for loan losses.

operating losses: losses incurred in the normal (i.e., nonnegligent) operation of a business.

operating officer: the officer who heads up an operating department in a large bank. He is in complete charge of the operations of his or her department. A distinction is to be made between an operating officer and the other officials, such as the vice-presidents, who are specialists in their fields. The cashier of the bank can be considered the senior operating officer in charge of the overall operations of the bank in its routine work. The vice-presidents are specialists in the fields of loans, credits, investments, and trusts. In smaller banks, it is not uncommon for vice-presidents to be in charge of certain operations as well as being specialists in their field. Any decision regarding the operation of a department is usually left to the oper-

ating officer in charge of the department. His or her recommendations regarding personnel requirements, equipment purchases, type and quantity of supplies used, and so on, carry great weight with higher officials. [10]

operating profit: profit arising from the regular operation of an enterprise engaged in performing physical services (e.g., public utilities), excluding income from other sources and excluding expenses other than those of direct operation. [62]

operating profit (for purposes of marketing): gross margin (gross profit), less operating expenses (including salaries of managers, whether proprietors or employees), fixed plant and equipment cost, and sometimes interest on invested capital. [13]

operating profit ratio: the ratio of a firm's operating profit to its net sales. see *turnover ratio.*

operating reserves: a group of balance sheet accounts reflecting the net accumulated balances provided for property insurance, injuries and damages, pensions and benefits, and amortization. [3]

operating return: operating income before income taxes and depreciation and amortization expense. [3]

operating statement: a statement providing net sales, costs, expenses, and the net operating profit or loss for a fixed period.

operating surplus: the remaining profit after deducting all operating costs of the business over a given time period. Items such as interest on capital and indebtedness are not deducted prior to determining the operating surplus.

operating system: software that controls the execution of computer programs and that may provide scheduling, debugging, input/output control, accounting, compilation, storage assignment, data management, and related services. [34]

operation

(1) *general:* any process or action that is part of a series in work.

(2) *computer:* the act specified by a single computer instruction.

(3) *computer:* a defined action of obtaining a result from one or more operands in accordance with a rule that completely specifies the result for any permissible combination of operands.

operational analysis (OA): a form of industrial engineering that separates work into activities and designs the work flow to construct the most efficiently scheduled sequences of output. synonymous with *operations research.* cf. *MAPS.*

operational control: the influence by management over the inputs and activities in the daily performances in a firm.

operations analysis: a system of analyzing specific savings association operations in order to establish norms, appraise efficiency, improve operations, and reduce costs accrued. [59]

operations research (OR): the application of scientific methods, techniques, and tools to problems involving the operation of a system, to provide those in control of the system with optimum solutions to the problems. see *cost-benefit analysis;* cf. *organizational analysis and planning.*

Operation Twist (Nudge): in 1961 the Federal Reserve and the U.S. Treasury attempted to raise short-term interest rates relative to long-term rates to harmonize domestic and foreign objectives. Bank time-deposit interest rates were increased, and funds were redirected from short- to long-term goals.

operator: slang, any person who makes a career in speculation on the prices of securities or commodities.

OPIC: see *Overseas Private Investment Corporation.*

opinion of title: legal opinion stating that title to property is clear and marketable; serves the same purpose as a certificate of title. [62]

OPM

(1) operations per minute.

(2) other people's money.

opportunity cost: a maximum alternative profit that could have been obtained if the productive good, service, or capacity had been applied to some other use.

opportunity cost of capital: the expected rate of return from effectively employing funds in the company.

Opt.: see *option.*

optical character recognition (OCR): the machine identification of printed characters through the use of light-sensitive devices. cf. *magnetic ink character recognition.*

optical reader: a device that interprets handwritten or machine-printed symbols into a computing system.

optical scanner: a device that scans optically and usually generates an analog or digital signal.

optimum capacity: the quantity of output that permits the minimum cost per unit to be incurred.

option

(1) *general:* a privilege to buy or sell, receive, or deliver property, given in accordance with the terms stated, with a consideration for price. This privilege may or may not be exercised at the option holder's discretion. Failure to exercise the option leads to forfeiture.

(2) *banking:* the right of an insured or a beneficiary to select the form of payment of the proceeds of an insurance contract.

(3) *investments:* an agreement, often for a consideration, to buy or sell a security or commodity within a stipulated time in accordance with the agreement. see *puts and calls*; cf. *covered option, straddle.*

option account: a charge account in which the consumer may choose either to pay at the end of 30 days or to spread payments over a longer period of time. If he chooses to spread his payments beyond 30 days, he pays a service charge. [40]

optional bond: see *bond, callable.*

optional (revolving) credit: a regular open or 30-day charge account to which the customer has requested to have the "option" added. That is, he may pay the whole balance within 15 or 20 days of receipt of his bill (when there will be no credit service charge) or may pay any portion of it that is convenient. Then on any amount not paid by the time the next bill is made out (which would be after the 15- to 20-day period following the first bill), a charge of 1 percent, of $1\frac{1}{2}$ percent, or the like is added. As in other revolving credit plans, this charge would not be applied to purchases or additions in the then-current month but just to the sum left unpaid from the last billing. [28]

optional dividend: the stockholder has the choice of receiving either a stock dividend or a cash dividend.

optional payment bond: see *bond, optional payment.*

optional valuation date: the date on which the size of an individual's estate is computed for purposes of tax payment. It can be set at the date of death or as of six months following death, provided the assets are not disposed of in the interim.

option day: the specified date when an option expires unless exercised.

optionee: the holder of an option; a prospective buyer.

optioner: any property owner.

option income fund: the investment objective of these funds is to seek a high current return by investing primarily in dividend-paying common stocks on which call options are traded on national securities exchanges. Current return generally consists of dividends, premiums from expired call options, net short-term gains from sales of portfolio securities on exercises of options or otherwise, and any profits from closing purchase transactions. [23]

Options Clearing Corporation: the issuer of all options contracts on the American Stock Exchange. [5]

option spreading: the simultaneous purchase and sale of options within the same class. The options may be either at the same striking prices with different expiration months, or at different striking prices with the same or different expiration months. The spread is the dollar difference between the buy and sell premiums.

OR
(1) see *operating reserves.*
(2) see *operations research.*
oral will: see *nuncupative will.*
order
(1) *general:* a request to deliver, sell, receive, or purchase goods or services.
(2) *finance:* identifying the one to whom payment should be made: "Made to the order of."
(3) *investments:* a request to buy or sell. see *buy, day order, discretionary order, limited order, open order, stop order.*
order of distribution: an order by a probate or other court having jurisdiction of an estate directing distribution of estate property to persons or others entitled thereto. [37]
orders
(1) *general:* requests made for the delivery of goods or services.
(2) *investments:* instructions to a broker to buy or sell shares.
orders good until a specified time: a market or limited price order that is to be represented in the "trading crowd" until a specified time, after which such order or the portion not executed is treated as canceled. cf. *good-'til-canceled order.* [20]
ordinary asset: an asset that is bought and sold as a regular component of a continuing business activity. What may be an ordinary asset to one firm may be a capital asset to another. A real estate broker selling property would be selling an ordinary asset, whereas a retailer would be selling a capital asset if he sold land.
ordinary income: in income tax filing, reportable income that does not qualify as capital gains.

ordinary interest: interest that is calculated based on 360 days to the year.
ordinary life
(1) a type of insurance policy continuing in force throughout the policyholder's lifetime and payable on his death or when he attains a specified age.
(2) also referred to as whole life or straight life.
ordinary stock: refers to common or equity stock.
organic structure: an organization design characterized by a decentralized hierarchy, flexible work procedures, and democratic leadership, with informal and open communications. cf. *organization, formal.*
organization: any structured system of roles and functional relationships designed to carry out a firm's policies, or more precisely, the programs such policies inspire.
organization, formal: a highly structured organization with little flexibility in the delegation of authority and assignment of tasks and responsibilities.
organization, informal: a flexibly structured organization, free of rigid rules for governing its activity and authority. synonymous with *organic structure.*
organizational analysis and planning: the study of the objectives, the surroundings, and the human, physical, and financial assets of a business to determine the most effective design for using the creative ideas and power generated by the firm's ultimate authority toward the accomplishment of its stated goals.
organizational chart: a graphic pres-

entation of the relationships and interrelationships within an organization, identifying lines of authority and responsibility.

organizational climate: a set of properties of the work environment perceived by employees and assumed to be a major factor in influencing their behavior.

organizational development (OD): a planned process of reeducation and training designed by administrative personnel to facilitate adaption to demands placed on the environment of the company. see *multiple management.*

organization certificate: in the formation of a bank, one of the statements that must be filed, usually with the Comptroller of the Currency.

organization expense: direct costs when forming a new corporation (incorporation fees, taxes, legal fees, etc.).

Organization for Economic Cooperation and Development (OECD): created in 1948, an organization of 17 European nations (including the German Federal Republic) and known until 1960 as the Organization for European Economic Cooperation. Initially, OEEC developed and implemented economic recovery programs following World War II. It was enlarged to 24 members, including the United States, Canada, and Japan, with the changing of its name to OECD. Headquartered in Paris, it promotes the economic growth of member nations, the expansion of world investment and trade, and the economic development of emerging countries.

Organization for European Economic

Cooperation (OEEC): see *Organization for Economic Cooperation and Development.*

Organization of Petroleum Exporting Countries (OPEC): the group's 13 members are concentrated in the Middle East but also include countries in Africa, South America, and the Far East. By virtue of their large exports, Saudi Arabia and Iran have been the most powerful influences. see also *petrodollars.*

organized market: a group of traders, operating under recognized rules, for the purpose of buying and selling a single commodity or a small number of related commodities—for example, the Chicago Board of Trade. [13]

original asset: stocks, bonds, or other property received in a trust at the time of its creation, or an estate at the time of appointment of the executor or administrator. [37]

original balance: the beginning debt or obligation before any payment has been made on it to reduce it. [28]

original cost: the actual cost of construction or acquisition, or, in other words, the actual original cost of property to the carrier at the time of its dedication to public use. [18]

original investment: an investment received by the trustee as part of the decedent's estate or from the settlor of a living trust. [32]

original margin: margin required at the onset of a transaction. [11]

origination fee: a charge made for initiating and processing a mortgage loan.

originator: the banking house or individual investment banker who is the first to promote a proposed new issue for a corporation.

orphan's court: in many states the court that has jurisdiction over matters pertaining to the settlement of estates and sometimes over guardianships and trusts. [37]

O&S: see *over and short account.*

OS: see *option spreading.*

OS&D: see *over, short, and damaged.*

OSHA: see *Occupational Safety and Health Act of 1970.*

OTB: see *off the board.*

OTC: see *over the counter.*

other income: a general heading on the income statement under which are grouped revenues from miscellaneous operations, income from the lease of road and equipment, miscellaneous rent income, income from nonoperating property, profit from separately operated properties, dividend income, interest income, income from sinking and other reserve funds, release of premiums on funded debt, contributions from other companies, miscellaneous income, and delayed income credits. [18]

other liabilities and accrued dividends: miscellaneous liabilities plus dividends accrued but unpaid on Federal Reserve Bank stock owned by the member banks. [40]

other loans: mostly loans to individuals, except farmers, for consumption purposes. [40]

other long-term debt: long-term debt other than mortgage bonds and debentures. This includes serial notes and notes payable to banks with original maturity of more than one year. [3]

other securities: all securities other than U.S. government obligations—that is, state, municipal, and corpo-rate bonds. (Member banks are generally not permitted to invest in stocks other than Federal Reserve bank stock). [40]

ouguiya: monetary unit of Mauritania.

outbid: to offer a higher price for an item than that offered by other bidders.

out card: a card substituted for a ledger card when the latter is removed from the file. The out card should contain the balance, the date the ledger card was removed, by whose authority, and the person in whose possession the ledger card is held. There are occasions when ledger cards must be removed from the ledger trays for reference—for example, when a borrower who is already borrowing funds from the bank requests a large loan. The ledger card is the record that must be used to review the borrower's use of credit, how the loans in the past were liquidated, and when the customer last completely liquidated his borrowings. This information supplements other available credit information held by the bank and is used by the loan committee in arriving at decisions. [10]

outcry market: commodity tradings by private contract that must be shouted out, as on the floor of an exchange, in order that the agreement be recorded. synonymous with *open outcry.*

outgo: slang, any expense or other cost in running a business.

outlays

(1) *general:* any expenditures.

(2) *government:* disbursements or spending either for the government as a whole or for a particular de-

partment or function, such as health care.

out of line: a stock whose price is determined to be either too low or too high. This is often determined by noting the corporation's price-earnings ratio.

out-of-pocket expense: a cost incurred by an individual, often when on a business trip; the item or service is paid for in cash or by check or charge account, and the employee expects reimbursement from the company.

out of the money: a situation in which the striking price is above the market price of the underlying stock for a call, or the striking price is below the market price of the underlying stock for a put. [5]

out-of-town item: see *foreign items, transit letter.*

output

(1) *general:* the quantity yielded in any operation.

(2) *computers:* information transferred from the internal storage of a computer to output devices or external storage.

(3) *finance:* the average dollar gross domestic product produced in a stated period.

outside borrowing: borrowing funds from sources other than a Federal Home Loan Bank or a state-chartered central reserve institution.

outside broker: not a member of a regular stock exchange; a dealer in unlisted stocks.

outside collector: a person employed by a store or firm to make personal calls on debtors for the purpose of securing payment or a promise of payment. [41]

outside market: an over-the-counter market, or a market where unlisted securities are handled.

outsiders: the general investing public.

outside securities: any security not listed or quoted on a major local exchange. For example, a security for the City of Los Angeles not traded on the Pacific Stock Exchange is an "outside security."

outstanding

(1) *general:* any unpaid or uncollected debt.

(2) *investments:* stock in the hands of stockholders, as distinguished from stock that has not yet been issued or, if issued, has not been released by the corporation. cf. *absorbed.*

Outstg.: see *outstanding.*

out the window: a term for a new issue of securities or bonds that moves out rapidly or is sold quickly to investors.

overage

(1) *general:* items additional to those shown on a bill of lading.

(2) *government:* created by a spending program that exceeds a specified budget target during a specified time period.

(3) see *shortfall.*

overall market price coverage: the ratio of net assets to the sum of all prior obligations at liquidating value plus the issue in question taken at market price. [30]

over and short account: an account carried in the general ledger. Overages and shortages from all sources, and their nature, are posted to this account, which is also termed a "suspense" or "differences" account in banks. At the end of the fiscal period, this account is closed out to profit and loss and becomes either an increase or a decrease to the undivided profits account in the general ledger. In larger banks, a subsidiary ledger is carried on this account so that the overages and shortages of all departments are carried as separate accounts. In this way, the frequency of any differences can be localized to a department and this department brought under control. [10]

overapplied overhead: the excess of amount of overhead cost applied to a product over the amount of overhead cost incurred.

overbought: reflecting an opinion about price levels. May refer to a security that has had a sharp rise, or to the market as a whole after a period of vigorous buying, which some are arguing, has left prices "too high."

overbought market: see *oversold market.*

overcapitalize

(1) *general:* to provide an excessive amount of capital to a business. see *capitalize, watered stock.*

(2) *banking:* to set too high a value on property.

(3) *finance:* to place too high a value on the nominal capital of a company.

overcertification: a rarely used certification by the bank of a customer's check where the collected balance in the person's account is less than the amount recorded on the check.

overcheck: a check drawn against an uncollected or insufficient balances; an overdraft.

overdraft: when a depositor draws a check for more than the balance on

deposit with a bank and the bank honors that check, he or she is said to be "overdrawn." The bank can either return the check to the bank from which it came or to the person who presented it for payment, marked "insufficient funds." The bank can also elect to render the customer a service and pay the check.

overdraft checking account: a line of credit that allows a person to write checks for more than the actual balance, with a finance charge on the overdraft. [1]

overdraw: to write a bank check for an amount exceeding the deposit in the bank on which the check is drawn. see *cushion checking (credit), kite (kiting), overdraft.*

overdue: a payment that has not been made at the time it was due.

overextension

(1) *general:* the expansion by a business concern of buildings, equipment, and so on, in excess of the company's present or prospective future needs.

(2) *finance:* credit received or extended beyond the debtor's ability to pay.

(3) *investments:* the condition of a dealer in securities who becomes obligated for an amount beyond his or her borrowing power or ability to pay.

overhead: a general term for costs or materials and services not directly adding to or readily identifiable with the product or service of the entity. see *conversion costs*; cf. *direct overhead, factory overhead.*

overhead expenses: a term applied to certain costs that do not vary much, regardless of business conditions, sales, and so on, such as rent, heat, the salaries of office clerks and company officers—as contrasted to the wages of those who are paid for what they make or sell. [28]

overheating: excessive price or money activity that some economists believe will lead to inflation.

overinvestment theory: a business cycle concept which holds that economic variations are a function of too much investment in the economy as business managers try to measure increasing demands during an upswing, and of major cutbacks in investment during a downswing when they realize that they expanded too much in the previous prosperity.

overissue: the release of stock in excess of the authorized or ordered amount. see *registrar, undigested securities.*

overlapping debt: the proportionate share of the debts of local government units located wholly or in part within the limits of the reporting government which must be borne by property within each governmental unit. [49]

overlying bond: see *bond, overlying.*

overlying mortgage: a junior mortgage subject to the claim of a senior mortgage, which has a claim prior to the junior mortgage. cf. *equal dignity.*

over on bill: additional freight described on the bill of lading.

overplus: synonymous with *surplus.*

overprints: official marks on a current paper money issue for the reason indicated: for purposes of revaluation, cancellation, and so on. [27]

override: a commission paid to managers that is added to their salary.

oversaving: when planned saving exceeds planned investment, oversaving is said to occur, and the quantity of cash removed from income movement exceeds the amount returned to it, resulting in the decline of income. cf. *marginal propensity to invest, saving.*

Overseas Business Reports (OBR): a publication of the U.S. Department of Commerce providing basic background data for businesspeople who are evaluating various export markets or are considering entering new areas. [61]

Overseas Private Investment Corporation (OPIC): a federal agency that insures U.S. companies against seizure of their overseas property by foreign governments, damage to property from acts of war, or conditions under which they are unable to take their profits out of the foreign country. see *nationalization, seizure.*

over, short, and damaged (OS&D): the discrepancy between the amount and/or condition of cargo on hand and that shown on the bill. cf. *clean bill of lading.*

oversold

(1) *general:* the situation of a manufacturer who has become obligated to deliver more than he or she is able to supply within the stated period.

(2) *investments:* an opinion—the reverse of overbought. A single security or a market that is believed to have declined to an unreasonable level. [20]

oversold market: when the speculative long interest has been drastically reduced and the speculative short interest increases, actually or relatively, a market is said to be oversold. At such times, sharp rallies often materialize. On the other hand, when the speculative short interest decreases sharply, a market is said to be overbought. At such times, the market is often in a position to decline sharply. [2]

overstay the market: holding a position in stocks for too long a period of time—for example, a sustained advance when the market appears overbought and about to have a price correction.

oversubscribed: a situation in which, for a given issue of shares, more orders have been received than can be filled. cf. *undigested securities.*

overt act: an act done openly in pursuance of an avowed interest or design; in contradistinction to a threat without any act to carry it out. [37]

over the counter (OTC)
(1) securities not listed or traded on any of the regular exchanges. Such securities are traded through dealers in unlisted stocks. Sales or purchases are arranged by these dealers or through a chain of them until the desired securities and prices are obtained. However, members of regular stock exchanges also handle trades in unlisted securities, but not through the exchange. see *National Association of Securities Dealers Automated Quotations*; cf. *off-board*; see also *third market.*
(2) synonymous with *unlisted.*

over-the-counter market: a securities market conducted by dealers throughout the country through negotiation rather than through the use of an auction system as represented by a stock exchange. [26]

overtrading: the activity of a firm that even with high profitability cannot pay its own way for lack of working capital and finds itself in a liquidity crisis.

overturn: synonymous with *turnover.*

over without bill: freight without its bill of lading.

owe: to be obliged to pay something to someone for something received; an indebtedness.

owl: slang, any business activity that operates during the evening hours.

owner: a person possessing title to property.

owner financing: a creative home-financing approach where the potential buyer bypasses the bank and borrows money directly from the person selling the house. Owners often find that this type of financing is the only way they can sell their houses because so many potential buyers cannot qualify for bank loans. The buyer, for example, might borrow half the needed money from the owner at 8 percent interest and the rest from a bank at 14 percent.

ownership certificate: a form required by the government and furnished by the Collector of Internal Revenue which discloses the real owner of stocks registered in the name of a nominee. Such a form must also accompany coupons presented for collection on bonds belonging to nonresident aliens, or partially tax-free corporate bonds issued prior to January 1, 1934. [37]

owner's paper: all forms of mortgage debt, including second mortgages, held by the seller of a house, rather than a bank.

P
(1) see *partnership.*
(2) see *payee.*
(3) see *peso.*
(4) see *private trust.*
(5) see *purchaser.*

PA
(1) see *paying agent.*
(2) see *per annum.*
(3) see *power of attorney.*

pa'anga: monetary unit of the Tonga Islands.

Pacific Coast Stock Exchange: formed in January 1957, by a consolidation of the San Francisco Stock Exchange (1882) and the Los Angeles Stock Exchange (1899), it is the most active U.S. securities exchange outside New York City.

package mortgage: a home-financing mortgage covering appliances and other household items (e.g., air conditioners, refrigerators, dryers).

paid check: a check that has been canceled and paid.

paid-in capital: capital contributed by stockholders and assigned to accounts other than capital stock.

paid-in surplus: excesses of a business arising from sources other than profits; the surplus from the sale of capital stock at a premium.

paid-up capital: the total of par value stock and the given value of no-par securities for which full consideration is received by a corporation.

paid-up insurance: a policy on which no further premium payments need to be made; the company will be held liable for any benefits claimed under terms of the contract.

paid-up stock: capital stock on which the initial buyer has paid in services, goods, or funds an amount at least equal to the par value.

painting the tape
(1) *investments:* creating an interest in a particular stock by trading constantly in it, thus causing it to appear on the ticker tape at frequent intervals.
(2) *investments:* unusual public interest in a specific security.

panic: a sudden, spreading fear of the collapse of business or the nation's economy, resulting in widespread withdrawal of bank deposits, stock sales, and similar transactions. A depression may but does not always follow a panic.

paper: a loan contract; commercial paper, short-term evidence of a debt.

paper basis: indicating that a nation does not employ a metallic basis for its currency. see *paper money.*

paper gain or loss: an expression for unrealized capital gains or losses on securities in a portfolio, based on comparison of current market quotations and the original costs. [67]

paper hanger: slang, an individual who attempts to pass or forge worthless checks on a nonexistent bank account.

paperless item processing system (PIPS): an electronic funds transit system that is capable of performing transit functions by establishing accounting transactions by which bank funds are shifted from one ledger or subledger to another.

paper money: currency on which a value is printed, although unlike coins, the bills have no value in themselves; usually represents bullion held in government vaults. cf. *fiat money.*

paper profit: an unrealized profit on a security still held. Paper profits become realized profits only when the security is sold. see *short sale.* [20]

paper standard: a monetary system, based on paper money, that is not convertible into gold or any other item of intrinsic value.

paper title: a written document that appears to convey proof of ownership but may not in fact show proper title. cf. *cloud on title.*

paper truncation: the act terminating the flow of paper in a transaction-processing system. For example, in an Electronic Funds Transfer system, once pertinent data from checks or credit card sales drafts are captured electronically, the paper records would be stored and would not be required in subsequent system operations. Paper truncation mandates a descriptive statement in lieu of the return to the customer of individual records of each transaction. [36]

paper wars: attempting to drown the other side in motions, interrogatories, depositions, pleadings, cross-claims and countersuits, using every conceivable procedure to attempt to avoid or delay trial on the merits. Often used in complex antitrust cases.

par
(1) when the exchangeable value of an instrument is equal to that expressed on its face without consideration of any premium or discount.
(2) see also *face value.*

paradox of thrift: a concept of John Maynard Keynes that any effort by society to raise its savings rate can lead to a reduction in the amount it can really save.

parallel standard: a monetary standard; two or more metals are coined and authorized unconditionally as legal tender. cf. *bimetallism.*

paramount title: the foremost title, a title that is superior to all others. Often the original title used to prepare later ones.

par clearance: any check that clears at par as contrasted with a check that is non par. see *par.*

par collection: the process of check collections as stated in the "par collection requirements" of the Federal Reserve Act. see *par.*

parent company: a controlling organization that owns or manages business properties. synonymous with *proprietary company.*

Pareto optimality
(1) distribution of resources that will make at least one person better off and no one else worse off.
(2) synonymous with "economic efficiency."

Pareto's law: the theory of Vilfredo Pareto, Italian sociologist and economist, that income tends to become distributed in the same proportion among consumers throughout the world, regardless of differing forms of taxation.

par exchange rate: the free market price of one country's money in terms of the currency of another.

pari delicto: fault or blame that is equally shared.

Paris Bourse: the national stock exchange of France, established in 1724.

par item: any item that can be collected at its par or face value upon presentation.

parity

(1) *finance:* the equivalence established between the wage schedules of some categories of employees.

(2) *government:* a farm policy established to keep the purchasing power of a unit of farm output equal to the purchasing power of the units of production bought by a farmer in the same ratio that existed during a chosen period. see *farm subsidies*; cf. *Brannan plan.*

(3) *investments:* the state or quality of being equal or equivalent; equivalence of a commodity price expressed in one currency to its price expressed in another.

(4) *investments:* equality of purchase power established by law between different kinds of money at a given ratio.

parity clause: a mortgage clause by virtue of which all notes obtained by the mortgage have "equal dignity"; that is, none has priority.

par list: a Federal Reserve System list of banks that will remit in full for items that are payable to the system.

par of exchange: the market price of money in one national currency that is exchanged at the official rate for a specific amount in another national currency, or another commodity of value (gold, silver, etc.).

parol evidence: oral testimony or evidence, as contrasted with written or documentary evidence. [37]

Part.: see *participation.*

partial audit: see *limited audit.*

partial equilibrium analysis: an inquiry that looks at only one market of an economy under the assumption that solutions in other markets will not be altered by a change in the market examined.

partial monopoly: exists when there are so few sellers of an item or service that each may alter the price and market. cf. *perfect (pure) monopoly.*

partial payment: a payment that is not equal to the full amount owed and is not intended to constitute the full payment.

partial release: the giving up of a claim to a portion of the property held as security for the payment of a debt. [51]

participant: a bank, brokerage house, or investment firm that has agreed to sell a stock issue to the public as part of a syndicate.

participating bond: see *bond, participating.*

participating life insurance: insurance on which the policyholder is entitled to receive policy dividends reflecting the difference between the premium charged and actual experience. The premium is calculated to provide some margin over the anticipated cost of the insurance protection. [58]

participating preferred: describing a preferred stock that is entitled to its stated dividend and, also, to additional dividends on a specified basis (i.e., with respect to the plan participated in) on payment of dividends on the common stock.

participation: an ownership interest in a mortgage. [51]

participation agreement: an understanding, the terms of which are usually specified in writing between institutional investors, to buy or sell partial ownership interests in mortgages. [51]

participation loan: a loan having two or more banks as creditors. Laws prohibit banks from lending more than a fixed percentage of their capital and surplus to any one borrower. Thus banks invite other banks to participate in making large loans.

particular lien: a right to keep something valuable that belongs to another person as compensation for labor, supplies, or money spent in his or her behalf. Also referred to as a special lien. cf. *factor's lien, general lien, mechanic's lien;* see also *voluntary conveyance or deed.*

partisan issues: paper money for limited circulation issued by partisans fighting the forces occupying their country. [27]

partnership: a contractual relationship between two or more people in a joint enterprise, who agree to share, not necessarily equally, in the profits and losses of the organization. cf. *joint venture.*

partnership certificate: a certificate filed with a bank showing the interest of each partner in a business enterprise operating as a partnership. This certificate also shows the limited partners (partners who specify a maximum amount for which they may be held responsible in settlement of obligations incurred by the partnership), and also "silent partners" (partners who have invested funds in the partnership, but who, for certain reasons, do not wish to be publicly known as partners). [10]

party at interest: individual or group of individuals having a vested interest in a commercial enterprise.

par value: face value; the par value of stocks on the date of issuance is the principal.

par value (of currency): the value of a currency in terms of gold as formally proposed to the International Monetary Fund, normally subject to fund concurrence. The fund's Articles of Agreement envisage that each member country shall have an effective par value, i.e., a unitary, fixed exchange rate for spot transactions that is established and maintained in accordance with the provisions of the Articles. [42]

pass(ing) a dividend: a corporation's decision to omit the declaration of an expected dividend.

passbook: a book record prepared by a bank for a depositor, listing date and amount of deposits, with an initial or identifying symbol indicating the teller who received the deposit. In the case of savings accounts, the passbook lists deposits, withdrawals, interest paid by the bank, dates of all transactions, each new balance, and the initial or identifying symbol of the teller handling each transaction. The passbook shows the depositor's name or names and account number. cf. *no-passbook savings.*

passbook account: a savings account that normally requires no minimum balance, no minimum term, no specified deposits, and no notice or penalty for withdrawals. [59]

passbook loan: see *savings account loan.*

passed dividend: a regular or scheduled dividend that has been omitted.

passing title: the handling over of title to a new owner. Also referred to as *closing (or passing) title.*

passive bond: see *bond, passive.*

passive trade balance: an unfavorable balance of trade.

passive trust: one whose trustee has no tasks to perform and merely retains title to the trust property.

pass no more: see *no more credit.*

pass-through certificates: synonymous with "Ginnie Maes," guaranteed by the Government National Mortgage Association. see *Government National Mortgage Association.*

past due: an account on which payment has not been made according to agreement and owes a given amount which is in arrears. [41]

past-due item: any note, acceptance, or other time instrument of indebtedness that has not been paid on the due date.

pataca: monetary unit of Macao.

pawn: the pledge to pay a debt.

pay
(1) to pay a check in cash, as when a check is paid by the paying teller.
(2) to charge a check against a customer's account, as in the case of a check coming through the clearings. [50]

payable in exchange: the requirement that a negotiable instrument be paid in the funds of the place from which it was originally issued.

pay-as-you-go accounts: a variation of "special checking accounts" or "special fee accounts." Under the pay-as-you-go plan, the special-checking-account depositor purchases a checkbook, usually at the rate of 5 or 10 cents per check. The fee or service charge is therefore prepaid to the bank, and the depositor can control the cost of his checking account by the number of checks he writes. In this plan, no service charge is posted as checks are posted against the account. [10]

payback period: the period of time that passes before the incoming cash equals the outgoing cash on a specific project, order, or other effort.

pay-by-phone: a service enabling customers to instruct their financial institution via telephone to initiate one or more payments from their accounts. [33]

payee: the person or organization to whom a check or draft or note is made payble. The payee's name follows the expression "pay to the order of." [7]

payer: the party primarily responsible for the payment of the amount owed as evidenced by a given negotiable instrument.

paying agent: an agent to receive funds from an obligor to pay maturing bonds and coupons, or from a corporation for the payment of dividends. [37]

paying bank: a bank upon which a check is drawn and pays a check or other draft to the holder and/or collecting bank.

paying teller: a representative of the bank who is responsible for the proper paying or cashing of checks presented at the window. see *unit teller system.* [50]

pay-in warrant: see *deposit warrant.*

pay loans: computing and counting out the currency (and/or issuing the checks) to be paid out to a customer in closing his loan. [55]

payment: total sum of money borrowed, plus all finance charges, divided by the number of months in the term of the loan. [78]

payment date: the date on which a customer has agreed to make his payment each month. synonymous with *due date.* [55]

payment for honor: paying a bill by another other than the one on whom it is drawn, when the latter has defaulted, to save the reputation or credit of the original drawee.

payments deficit: the excess of the value of a nation's imports over its exports.

payments mechanism: systems designed for the movement of funds, payments, and money between financial institutions throughout the nation. The Federal Reserve plays a major role in the nation's payments mechanism through distribution of currency and coin, check processing, wire transfers, and automated clearinghouses. Various private associations also perform many payments mechanism operations. [1]

payments surplus: the excess of the value of a nation's exports over its imports.

payments system: a system (composed of people, machines, and procedures) used to transfer value from one party to another. [36]

payment voucher: usually the upper part of a customer's monthly statement presented or mailed together with remittance. Becomes the posting medium for the accounts receivable bookkeeper. [41]

payoff

(1) *banking:* the complete repayment of loan principal, interest, and any other sums due; payoff occurs either over the full term of the loan or through prepayments. [59]

(2) *finance:* money given for an unethical or illegal service.

(3) *systems:* the result of a decision problem transformed to represent its true utility to the decision maker.

payoff statement: a formal statement prepared when a loan payoff is contemplated, showing the current status of the loan account, all sums due, and the daily rate of interest. synonymous with *letter of demand.* [59]

payola: slang, any gift or other valuable item offered to people who have the potential for using their influence in the promotion or sale of a product or service.

payor: a person who makes, or is to make, a payment. [59]

payroll

(1) *general:* the wages or salary earned by a firm's employees for a certain period of time. Various deductions for withholding tax, health benefits insurance, and so on, are identified on the employee's record affixed to his or her payroll check.

(2) *general:* a list of employees receiving pay during a wage period.

payroll deduction plan (mutual fund): an arrangement whereby an employee may accumulate shares in a mutual fund by authorizing his employer to deduct and transfer to a fund a specified amount from his salary at stated times. [23]

payroll deductions: sums withheld from an employee's gross pay for federal and state income taxes, social security, or other governmental levies; may include, on authorization of employees, deductions for union dues and assessments, premiums for group insurance, contribution for pension plan, and so on.

payroll savings plan: a plan whereby an employee authorizes his employer to deduct from his wages or salary each pay period a specified amount and to forward that amount to his savings association for deposit to his savings account. [59]

payroll tax: used to finance an employer's contribution to the Social Security program, a tax levied on a company's payroll. see *Federal Insurance Contributions Act.*

Payt.: see *payment.*

PB: see *Paris Bourse.*

PBWSE: see *Philadelphia-Baltimore-Washington Stock Exchange.*

P&C: see *puts and calls.*

PC: see *petty cash.*

PCS: see *preferred capital stock.*

Pd.: paid.

PD

(1) see *past due.*

(2) see *per diem.*

PE: see *price-earnings ratio.*

peak: an exceptionally busy period in a business.

peculation: the embezzlement of funds or goods, especially public funds or goods, by an individual in whose care they have been entrusted. see *defalcation.*

pecuniary exchange: any trade using money.

pecuniary legacy: a gift of money by will. [37]

peg (pegging): to fix or stabilize the price of something (e.g., stock, currency, commodity) by manipulating or regulating the market. For example, the government may peg the price of gold by purchasing all that is available at a stated price. see also *adjustable peg, crawling peg.*

penal bond: see *bond, penal.*

penalty: see *liquidated damages.*

penalty clause

(1) a clause in a promissory note specifying a penalty for late payments.

(2) a clause in a savings certificate specifying a penalty for premature withdrawal from such an account. [59]

pendente lite: Latin, pending during the progress of a suit at law. see also *lis pendens.*

pending claim: a claim submitted to a company by a policyholder which is in the process of consideration of preparation for payment. [12]

Pennsylvania Rule: a rule that requires credit of extraordinary dividends received in trust on the basis of the source of such dividends; to income if declared from earnings of the corporation during the life of the trust, and to principal if from earnings accumulated before commencement of the trust. [37]

penny ante: slang, involving an insignificant amount of cash.

penny stocks: low-priced issues, often highly speculative, selling at less than $1 a share. Frequently a term of disparagement, although a few penny stocks have developed into investment-caliber issues. [20]

Pension Benefit Guaranty Corporation: see *Employee Retirement Income Security Act of 1974.*

pension fund: a fund out of which pensions are to be paid either to those entitled thereto under specific agreement or to those who may be selected by persons in control of the fund. [49]

pension plan: a method used by a firm or union to pay annuities or pensions to retired and/or disabled employees. Sections 401 and 404 of the Internal Revenue Code identify conditions enabling an organization to establish a pension plan. see *Employee Retirement Income Security Act of 1974, trust agreement (trust instrument).*

pension reserve: an actuarial computation of the financial obligation for future payments to be made on account of a pension or retirement allowance or benefit. [52]

pension trust: a trust established by an employer (commonly a corporation) to provide benefits for incapacitated, retired, or superannuated employees, with or without any contributions made by the employees. [37]

people's capitalism: the full range of income levels in the population of a community is represented in the ownership of the business.

Pepper-McFadden Act: see *McFadden Act of 1927.*

PER
(1) see *par exchange rate.*
(2) see *price-earnings ratio.*

per annum: by the year.

Per. Cap.: per capita.

per capita output: the gross national product of a nation divided by its population; often used to identify a country's standard of living.

per capita tax: by the individual; a tax based on the result of dividing stated sums of money by a specified group of people to show the amount to be paid by each person.

percentage lease: a lease providing for payment of rent based on a percentage of the gross sales or the sales over a fixed amount. [37]

percentage order: either a market or a limited price order to buy (or sell) a stated amount of a specified stock after a fixed number of shares of such stock have traded.

per cent per month: the method of computing loan interest in which the charge is specified as a monthly percentage of the outstanding balance, as "1 percent per month on the unpaid balance." The effective yield to the lender is 12 times the monthly rate. [59]

per centum: by the hundred.

per contra item: a balance in one account that is offset by a balance from another account.

per curiam: a full court's decision (e.g., to remand), when no opinion is given.

per diem: for each day.

perfect competition: a description for an industry or market unit consisting of a large number of purchasers and sellers all involved in the buying and selling of a homogeneous good, with awareness of prices and volume, no discrimination in buying and selling, and a mobility of resources.

perfect (pure) monopoly: one person or organization has total control over the manufacture and marketing of an item. see *monopoly, oligopoly.*

perfect title
(1) *general:* property displaying total right of ownership.
(2) *law:* a title that is not open to dispute or challenge because it is complete in every detail, and has no legal defects. see also *marketable title, muniment of title, quiet title suit, warranty deed*; cf. *cloud on title.*

performance appraisal: a methodical review of an employee's performance on the job to evaluate the effectiveness or adequacy of the person's work.

performance bond: see *bond, performance.*

performance budgeting: grouping of budget accounts into categories related to a specific product or service that is produced and the evolution of product-cost measurements of these activities.

performance fee: fees charged by some mutual fund managers when their purchasing and selling for the fund portfolio helps it to outperform certain market averages over a stated time period. synonymous with "incentive fee."

performance fund: a mutual fund that places more of its monies into speculative risky investments, such as some common stocks, rather than more conservative investments, such as bonds.

performance report: a comparison of actual results against those anticipated in a stated budget.

peril point: the greatest reduction in U.S. import duty that could be made for a stated item without creating a major hardship to domestic manufacturers or to makers of a closely related item.

period cost: see *fixed cost or expense.*

periodic payment plan: see *contractual plan.*

period of digestion: a time immediately following the release of a new or large security offering, during which sales are made primarily to regular investment customers.

period of redemption: the length of time during which a mortgagor may reclaim the title and possession of his property by paying the debt it secured. [51]

peripheral equipment: any of the units of computer equipment, distinct from the central processing unit, that provide outside communication. Not all systems have peripheral equipment. see *auxiliary operation.*

perjury: knowingly false testimony delivered under an oath that has been properly administered in a judicial proceeding.

perks: compensations given by corporations to executives (e.g., home repairs, company owned cars) that are not considered as taxable income. short for "perquisites."

permanent accounts: see *real accounts.*

permanent asset: any fixed or capital asset.

permanent capital: common and preferred stock as well as retained earnings that do not have to be paid back.

permanent financing: a long-term mortgage, amortized over 15, 20, or more years at a fixed rate of interest.

permanent income: the average income anticipated to be received over a number of years.

permanent life insurance: a phrase used to cover any form of life insurance except term; generally insurance that accrues cash value, such as whole life or endowment. [58]

permanent stock association: see *stock association.*

permissible nonbank activities: financial activities closely related to banking that may be engaged in by bank holding companies, either directly or through nonbank subsidiaries. Examples are owning finance companies and engaging in mortgage banking. The Federal Reserve Board determines which activities are closely related to banking. Before making such activities permissible, the board must also determine that their performance by bank holding companies is in the public interest. [1]

permit bond: see *bond, permit.*

permit mail: mail with printed indicia in lieu of a stamp, showing that postage was paid by the sender. [24]

perpetual bond: see *bond, perpetual.*

perpetuity

(1) *general:* endless; the quality of going on forever (e.g., an estate willed in perpetuity).

(2) *finance:* anything that is removed from the ordinary channel of commerce by limiting its capacity to be sold for a period longer than that of a life or lives in being and 21 years thereafter, plus the period of development, is said to be removed in perpetuity. see *consol(s), emphyteutic lease.*

perquisites: see *perks.*

personal asset: an asset that is owned for personal use. [73]

personal check: a check drawn by someone as an individual (i.e., not acting as an employer or in a fiduci-

ary capacity).

personal consumption expenditures: the sum of money and imputed expenditures made by consumers (individuals, not-for-profit institutions such as hospitals, etc.) for goods and services. It excludes purchases of dwellings (included in gross private domestic investment) but includes rental value of owner-occupied houses.

personal distribution of income: the distribution of natural income among individuals or households.

personal finance company: a business that lends small sums of money to people, usually for personal needs, at relatively high interest rates. Most states require these organizations to be licensed.

personal income: national income less various kinds of income not actually received by individuals, nonprofit institutions, and so on (e.g., undistributed corporate profits, corporate taxes, employer contributions for social insurance), plus certain receipts that do not arise from production (i.e., transfer payments and government interest).

personal installment loan: funds, borrowed by an individual for personal needs, which are repaid in regular monthly installments over a specified period.

personal loan: a type of loan generally obtained by individual borrowers in small amounts, usually less than $1000. A personal loan is often secured for the purpose of consolidating debts, or paying taxes, insurance premiums, or hospital bills.

personal outlays: made up of personal consumption expenditures, interest paid by consumers, and personal transfer payments to foreigners. They represent the disbursements made by individuals of that portion of personal income available after payment of personal taxes. The residual is personal saving. [73]

personal property: the rights, powers, and privileges an individual has in movable things such as chattels, and choses in action.

personal representative: a general term applicable to both executor and administrator. [37]

personal saving: the difference between disposable personal income and personal consumption expenditures; includes the changes in cash and deposits, security holdings, indebtedness, reserves of life insurance companies and mutual savings institutions, the net investment of unincorporated enterprises, and the acquisition of real property net of depreciation.

personalty: personal property.

personnel psychology: a subdivision of applied psychology that treats an individual's psychological qualities in relation to his or her job. It deals with employment procedures, selection, placement, training, promotion, supervision, morale, and other personal aspects of job attitude and behavior.

PERT: see *program evaluation and review technique.*

PERT/COST: a modified PERT system that in addition to time, deadlines, and schedules, includes all cost considerations.

peseta: monetary unit of Andorra, Balearic Island, Canary Islands, and Spain.

peso: monetary unit of Argentina, Bo-

livia, Chile, Colombia, Cuba, Dominican Republic, Mexico, Republic of the Philippines, and Uruguay.

petition in bankruptcy: the form used for declaring voluntary bankruptcy. see *bankruptcy.*

petrobonds: instruments that are backed by a specific number of barrels of oil. Since 1977, the Mexican government has been raising money by selling these bonds that trade in direct relations to the rapidly rising official price of Mexico's crude oil. see also *petrodollars.*

petrodollars: huge sums of money from oil-producing nations other than the United States or Great Britain. These funds are initially converted into Eurocurrency and deposited with international banks to be used for future investment and for paying debts. These banks traditionally set limits on the sum they will accept from any one country. see *Organization of Petroleum Exporting Countries.*

petty cash: cash kept on hand for the payment of minor items. [59]

Pfd.: preferred.

phantom stock: used in executive compensation programs, the executive is granted a number of shares of the company; each shares entitles the executive to the amount, if any, by which the market price of the stock at some future time exceeds the current market price.

Philadelphia - Baltimore - Washington Stock Exchange: in 1919, the Philadelphia Stock Exchange became the Philadelphia-Baltimore Stock Exchange. In July 1953, the Washington Stock Exchange merged with the PBSE and in 1969, the Pittsburgh

Stock Exchange consolidated with the Philadelphia-Baltimore-Washington Stock Exchange.

Philadelphia bank roll: slang, a $10 or $20 bill wrapped around a roll of $1 bills.

Phillips curve: a correlation between the unemployment level and the rate of wage changes. The curve shows that it is possible to lower unemployment only at the expense of a climbing price level, thereby making it necessary to trade off between lowering unemployment and maintaining the price level stable.

phony dividends: rather than paying dividends from stock earnings, dividends that are paid immediately from a portion of the money that comes in from the public's purchasing of that stock. This is an illegal activity.

physical value: a term erroneously used to designate an estimate of reproduction or replacement cost, or the estimated value of physical assets as distinct from nonphysical assets. [62]

PI: see *prime interest (rate)*.

piece-of-the-action financing: a lending arrangement in which the mortgagee receives, besides regular loan interest, a negotiated percentage of the gross income of an income property, of increases in rentals over a stated period of the life of an income property, or the gross or net profit of a commercial or industrial enterprise. [59]

piece rate (wage): the amount of money received for each unit of output; when wages are so determined, an incentive wage system is in operation.

Pigou effect concept: a theoretical countercyclical force which, under an extreme condition, might provide some stimulus to an economy in a depression. synonymous with *wealth effect*.

pilgrims' receipts: currency on which an overprint indicated that the notes were for use by pilgrims in another country. Pakistan, for example, overprinted some notes "for use in Saudi Arabia by pilgrims only." [27]

pinch
(1) *general:* a bind or tight situation.
(2) *finance:* a sudden, unanticipated rise in prices; when money rates go up suddenly, it is called a "money pinch."

pink sheets: price quotations of many over-the-counter stocks that are published on pink sheets. synonymous with "the sheets."

PIPS: see *paperless item processing system*.

pit: a circular area in the middle of the floor of a stock exchange; steps lead down into the pit, giving greater visibility to the trading action occurring there. Also called the ring. see *floor, open order, outcry market*.

PITI: common abbreviation for principal, interest, taxes, and insurance, used when describing the monthly carrying charges on a mortgage.

pivotal stock: a stock that is accepted as the leader of its group and often influences the activity of other stocks.

P&L: see *profit and loss statement (operating statement)*.

PL: see *place*.

place: to locate a market for a security; to sell it to an investor.

placement: negotiating for the sale of

a new securities issue, or the arranging of a long-term loan.

plain bond: see *bond, plain.*

plaintiff: a complaining party or the person who begins a legal action against another person or organization, seeking a court remedy.

PLAM: see *price-level-adjusted mortgage.*

planholder: a pension plan shareholder.

planning – programming – budgeting (PPB): mainly in government accounting, a system of administration for federal agencies. Concepts included are (a) long- and short-range planning of objectives and end products, (b) realistic cost estimates, (c) a search for greater efficiency, (d) budgetary projections of outputs in terms of goods and services, and (e) reports on current and prospective outlays, designed to service management controls and to supply information on budgetary administration for all levels of government.

plate numbers: figures in extremely small print on the side of some notes, to identify the printing plate from which they were made. [27]

Plcy.: see *policy.*

pledged-account mortgage: a variation on graduated-payment mortgages, where a portion of the borrower's down payment is used to fund a pledged savings account, which is drawn on to supplement the monthly payment during the first years of the loan. The net effect to the borrower is lower payments at first. Payments gradually rise to slightly above those on conventional mortgages. see also *flexible-payment mortgage, graduated-payment mortgage, reverse-annuity mortgage, rollover mortgage, variable-rate mortgage.*

pledged assets: securities owned by a bank, generally U.S. government bonds and obligations, specified by law, which must be pledged as collateral security for funds deposited by the U.S. government, or state or municipal governments.

pledged loan: a mortgage loan that has been pledged as security for a borrowing; particularly, one that has been pledged as security for a Federal Home Loan Bank advance. [59]

pledged securities: securities issued or assumed by the accounting company that have been pledged as collateral security for any of its long-term debt or short-term loans. [18]

pledging: the offering by a borrower of his or her assets as security for the repayment of a debt. cf. *distrain, hypothecation.*

plow back: to put earnings from sales back into the business operation.

plum: slang, extra profits or additional stock dividends.

plunger: an individual speculator who takes great risks, resulting in substantial profits or losses.

plunk down: slang, to make a payment in cash.

plus tick: see *up tick.*

PM
   (1) see *primary market.*
   (2) see *purchase money.*

PMM: see *purchase-money mortgage.*

PN: see *promissory note.*

PO
   (1) see *public offering.*
   (2) see *purchase order.*

POA: see *power of attorney.*

POC: see *preservation of capital.*

point of sale (POS): systems that permit bank customers to effect transfers of funds from their bank accounts and other financial transactions at retail points of sale. [33]

Point-of-Sale Terminal (POST): a communication and data capture terminal located where goods or services are paid for. POST terminals may serve merchant accounting needs and may assist in processing financial transactions. In the latter case, the terminal may operate as part of an authorization/verification system or initiate direct exchanges of value among merchants, customers, and financial institutions. [36]

point
(1) in shares of stock, a point means $1.
(2) a loan discount, which is a one-time charge, used to adjust the yield on the loan to what market conditions demand. Each point equals one percent of the principal amount. [78]
(3) the minimum unit in which changes in futures price may be expressed ($^1/_{000}$ cent, equivalent to $3.00). [11]

Pol.: see *policy.*

policy
(1) *general:* any plan of action.
(2) *banking:* a written contract of insurance.

policy dividend: a refund of part of the premium on a participating life insurance policy reflecting the difference between the premium charged and actual experience. [58]

policyholder
(1) a person or company protected by an insurance contract.
(2) synonymous with "the insured."

policy loan: funds borrowed from a life insurance organization, usually at low interest rates, using as security the cash value of the holder's policy.

policy reserves: see *reserve.*

policy value: the amount of money available to the insured upon the maturity of the policy.

pool
(1) *general:* any combination of resources of funds, and so on, for some common purpose or benefit.
(2) *finance:* an agreement between two or more companies to curtail output, divide sales areas, or in any other way avoid competition.
(3) *finance:* firms joined to share business over a fixed time.
(4) *investments:* a combination of persons (brokers, traders) organized for the purpose of exploiting stocks. The SEC prohibits pool operations. see *SEC.*

pooling of interests: a method of accounting for business combinations under which the net assets are accounted for in the combined corporation's financial statements at their book value as recorded in the combining corporations, and comparative figures are restated on a combined basis. [43]

pooling operation: a business similar to an investment trust or syndicate, which solicits, accepts, or receives from others funds for the purpose of trading in any commodity for futures delivery. see *pool.*

portability: a characteristic of valuables that allows them to be carried easily (e.g., diamonds or stamps are more portable than bullion).

portfolio: holdings of securities by an individual or institution. A portfolio may contain bonds, preferred stocks, and common stocks of enterprises of various types.

POS: see *point of sale.*

POSDCORB: the seven functions of administration: planning, organizing, staffing, directing, coordinating, reporting, and budgeting.

position

(1) *general:* a job; an employment situation.

(2) *investments:* a stake in the market. see *technical position.*

position sheet: an accounting statement, indicating the bank or foreign exchange firm's commitment in overseas currencies.

position traders: traders who take the long-term approach to the commodity markets, meaning anywhere from six months to a year or more.

positive file: an authorization system file that contains information about every account holder and is capable of providing a variety of data to be evaluated in responding to a request for authorization of credit, check cashing, or other privileges. see *ratio of accounts payable to purchases*; cf. *negative file.*

positive verification: see *direct verification.*

post

(1) *general:* to record onto detailed subsidiary records (ledgers) amounts that were recorded in chronological records of original entry. see also *suspense account.*

(2) *investments:* the horseshoe-shaped fixture on the New York Stock Exchange trading floor where 100-share unit stocks and active 10-share unit stocks are bought and sold.

(3) see *point-of-sale terminal.*

postage currency: U.S. fractional currency issued in 1862 and 1863, deriving its name from the facsimile of a postage stamp on the reverse. Not to be confused with stamp money. [27]

postal money order: a checklike instrument sold by U.S. post offices for payment of a specified sum of money to the individual or firm designated by the purchaser. [59]

postaudit: an audit made after the transactions to be audited have taken place and have been recorded or have been approved for recording by designated officials, if such approval is required. see *preaudit.* [49]

postdated check: a check bearing a date that has not yet arrived. Such a check cannot be paid by a bank before the date shown and must be returned to the maker or to the person attempting to use it. If presented on or after the date shown, the same check will be honored if the account contains sufficient funds.

posting: the act of transferring to an account in a ledger the data, either detailed or summarized, contained in a book or document of original entry. [49]

postlist: a term used generally in the bookkeeping department of banks. Many banks use a posting plan whereby the old balances are listed *after* a posting run to prove the correct pickup of old balances, and to catch any "high posting" (posting over or above the last previous balance). When this type of proof is used, the bookkeeper is said to create a postlist of the previous old balances. The total of the postlist is the total of all old balances of accounts affected by the posting run. [10]

postmortem: pertaining to the analysis of an operation after its completion. [34]

potentially dilutive: see *dilution.*

potential output (potential gross national product): the value of the final output of goods and services produced in a year if all resources (land, labor, and capital) are fully utilized. [57]

potential value: a loose term signifying a value that would or will exist if and when future probabilities become actualities. [62]

pound (pound sterling): monetary unit of Great Britain. Also the currency of Bermuda, Cyprus, Eygpt, Fiji Islands, Gibraltar, Grand Cayman Island, Ireland (Republic), Lebanon, Malta, Sudan, and Syria.

pourover: a term referring to the transfer of property from an estate or trust to another estate or trust upon the happening of an event as provided in the instrument. [37]

power: the authority or right to do or to refrain from doing a particular act, as a trustee's power of sale or power to withhold income. [37]

power in trust: a power that the donee (the trustee) is under a duty to exercise in favor of the beneficiary of the trust. [37]

power of alienation: the power to assign, transfer, or otherwise dispose of property. [37]

power of appointment: the equivalent of total ownership of part or all of a trust, since the individual having this power can identify the ultimate recipients of the trust's assets.

power of attorney: a written statement identifying a person as the agent for another with powers stated in the document. Full power may be granted, or the authority may be limited to certain functions, such as making deposits and withdrawals from a checking account. The statement must be executed before a notary and the signature of the agent is then placed on file with the bank. [29]

power of retention: the power expressed or implied in will or trust agreement permitting the trustee to retain certain or all of the investments comprising the trust property at inception, even though they may not be of a type suitable for new investments made by the trustee. [37]

power of sale: a clause included in a mortgage giving the holder or trustee the right to seize and sell the pledged property upon default in payments or upon the occurrence of any other violation of the conditions in the mortgage. see *shortcut foreclosure.*

POW money: paper money issued during World War II, valid for circulation in specified prisoner-of-war camps. [27]

pp
(1) see *paper profit.*
(2) see *partial payment.*
(3) see *purchase price.*

PPB: see *planning-programming-budgeting.*

PPBS: programming, planning, and budgeting systems; see *planning-programming budgeting.*

PPS: see *prior preferred (stock).*

Pr.
(1) preferred.
(2) see *principal.*

PR: see *pro rata.*

PRD: see *payroll deductions.*

preaudit: the examination of a creditor's invoices, payrolls, claims, and expected reimbursements before actual payment, or the verification of sales transactions before delivery.

preauthorized payment: a service that enables a debtor to request funds to be transferred from the customer's deposit account to the account of a creditor.

Prec.: precedent.

precatory words: expressions in a will praying or requesting (but not directing) that a thing be done or not done. [37]

procedence of order: the priority that one security has over another for buying or selling. When bids arrive, a priority exists to determine whose buy or sell order is accepted first.

preclusive purchasing

(1) *finance:* buying materials with the expectation of denying their use to a competitor.

(2) *government:* the activity of a belligerent country, aimed at preventing neutrals from selling the items purchased to an enemy. cf. *blockade.*

precomp: precomputation or precomputed loan. [55]

preconstruction affidavit: an affidavit, required by the lender on a construction loan, in which the borrower and contractor affirm that up to a specific date no work has been started on the lot and no materials delivered, prepared for use, or used.

preemptive right: the privilege of a stockholder to buy a portion of a new issue of stock equal to his or her existing percentage holding.

Pref.: preference.

preference as to assets: in the event of dissolution of a firm, before disbursement of a declared dividend, stockholders holding preferred shares are entitled to claim payments before payments are made to common stockholders.

preference bond: see *bond, preference.*

preference shares (preferred stock): shares that receive a dividend at a stated rate prior to the paying out of any dividend on the firm's common shares.

preferred capital stock: capital stock to which preferences or special rights are attached (i.e., preferred as to dividends and/or proceeds in liquidation) as compared to another class of stock issued by the same company.

preferred creditor: a creditor whose claim takes legal preference over the claim of another (such as government taxes over the amount owed to an individual). [10]

preferred debt

(1) *banking:* a first mortgage.

(2) *finance:* a debt that takes precedence over others.

preferred shares: a portion of the capital stock of a corporation which ranks after all bonds or other debt but has certain preferences over common stock. see *preferred stock.* [26]

preferred stock: corporate stock whose owners have some preference as to assets, earnings, and so on, not granted to the owners of common stock of the same corporation. see also *adjustment preferred securities, Class A stock, cumulative preferred (stock), effective par, guaranteed stock, privileged issue, voting right (stock).*

preferred stock, cumulative: a stock having a provision that if one or more dividends are omitted, the omitted dividends must be paid before dividends may be paid on the company's common stock. [20]

preferred stock, noncumulative: provides that dividends, if passed, do not have to be paid later. [68]

preferred stock, participating: under certain conditions, shares in earnings beyond the stated dividend. [68]

preferred stock, prior: ranks ahead of any other preferred and common in claim on dividends and assets. [68]

preliminary expenses: expenses incurred in the establishment of an organization (e.g., costs for developing and circulating a prospectus).

prelist: a term used generally in bookkeeping in a bank as a part of the bank's posting plan. After offsetting the ledger sheets to be affected by a posting run, the bookkeeper makes a prelist run of the balances, thus creating a total of all balances that will be affected by the run to be made. This is the opposite of postlist, but has the same effect in the proof of pickup of old balances. [10]

Prem.: see *premium.*

premium

(1) *banking:* the sum paid for a policy, not to be confused with premiums. An earned premium is the portion of the written premium covering the part of the policy term that is included in the time period. The pure premium is found by dividing losses by a hazard or contingency, and to which no operating expenses of the firm has been added (e.g., commissions, taxes).

(2) *finance:* the amount by which one form of funds exceeds another in buying power.

(3) *investments:* the amount by which a preferred stock or bond may sell above its par value. In the case of a new issue of bonds or stocks, a premium is the amount the market price rises over the original selling price.

(4) *investments:* a charge sometimes made when a stock is borrowed to make delivery on a short sale.

(5) *investments:* the redemption price of a bond or preferred stock, if this price is higher than face value.

(6) *investments:* the price of a put or call determined through the auction process. [5]

premium audit: an examination by a representative of the insurer of the insured's records, insofar as they relate to the policies or coverages under consideration. see *audit.*

premium bond: see *bond, premium.*

premium finance: a facility that allowed an insured to finance his or her payment over a specified period within the term of the policy.

premium loan: a policy loan made for the purpose of paying premiums. [58]

premium on capital stock: the excess of the cash or cash value of the consideration received from the sale of capital stock (excluding accrued dividends) over the par or stated value of such stock. [3]

premium on funded debt: the excess of the actual cash value of the consideration received for funded debt securities (of whatever kind) issued or assumed over the par value of such securities and the accrued interest thereon. [18]

premium on securities: the amount by which a security (a bond or a share of stock) is bought or sold for more than its face or par value; opposed to discount on securities. [37]

premium pay: a wage rate higher than straight time, payable for overtime work, work on holidays, or scheduled days off, or for work on evening shifts.

premium raids: the unannounced, lightning-quick buying sprees that several companies have mounted to build up large stakes in other companies by offering a bonus over the prevailing stock market share price.

premiums on bonds: the amount or percentage by which bonds are bought, sold, or redeemed for more than their face value. [37]

prenuptial agreement: a contract made before marriage; each future spouse forfeits any interest in the other's estate.

prepaid: indicating that shipping charges have already been paid or are to be paid at the point of delivery. see *franco delivery.*

prepaid expense: payment for items not yet received; a charge deferred for a period of time until the benefit for which payment has been made occurs (e.g., rent paid for future months). cf. *accrued liabilities.*

prepay: to pay before or in advance of receipt of goods or services.

prepayment: the payment of a debt before it actually becomes due.

prepayment clause
(1) *general:* the privilege of repaying part or all of a loan in advance of date or dates stated in a contract.
(2) *banking:* a clause in a mortgage allowing the mortgagor to pay off part or all of the unpaid debt before it becomes due. This affords a saving for the mortgagor.

prepayment of taxes: the deposit of money with a governmental unit on condition that the amount deposited is to be applied against the tax liability of a designated taxpayer after the taxes have been levied and such liability has been established. [49]

prepayment penalty: a penalty placed on a mortgagor for paying the mortgage before its due date. This applies when there is no prepayment clause to offset the penalty.

prerefunding: an exchange by holders of securities maturing in less than one year for securities of longer original maturity, usually due within 10 years. [71]

prerogatives: the rights, powers, privileges (e.g., diplomatic immunity) of an individual that others do not possess.

Pres.: see *president.*

presentation: a legal term used in connection with negotiable instruments. The act of presentation technically means the actual delivery of a negotiable instrument by a holder in due course to the drawee for acceptance, or to the maker for payment. Upon presentation, the holder in due course requests acceptance of a draft, or requests payment of the instrument from the maker of a note, check, or whatever. see *negotiable.* [10]

present beneficiary: synonymous with *immediate beneficiary.* [32]

presentment: synonymous with *presentation.*

present value: the discounted value of a certain sum due and payable at a certain specified future date.

present value of expected cash flow: the net cash that a company expects to realize or pay out from holding an asset or liability, discounted by an appropriate rate of interest.

preservation of capital: a form of investment, with the objective of preserving capital by way of avoiding high-risk situations. cf. *go-go fund.*

president: the highest ranking executive responsible for the policy decisions of an organization; the president reports to a board of directors.

prestige card: a plastic identification card issued by savings and loan associations to their customers to be used in electronic funds transfer systems.

presumptive title: possession of property that leads others to presume ownership, where in fact ownership may not exist. cf. *cloud on title.*

pretax earnings: income which is subject to federal income tax.

pretermitted child: a child to whom the parent's will leaves no share of his or her estate without affirmative provision in the will showing an intention to omit. It frequently is an afterborn child, a posthumous child, a child erroneously believed to be dead or unintentionally omitted. [37]

pretermitted heir: an heir not included in the descent or devolution of the parent's estate. [37]

price: the amount of money the seller receives for goods or services at the factory or place of business. Price is not what the seller asks for the product, but what is actually received.

price clearing: the settlement price at which a clearinghouse clears all the buy and sell orders for the day, or at which an exchange settles unliquidated contracts.

price control
(1) *finance:* the result of the demand by a manufacturer that the buyer for resale not be able to determine a resale price for the goods.
(2) *government:* regulation of the prices of goods and services with the intent to reduce increases in the cost of living, to fight inflation, or during emergencies. see *rollback.*

price-earnings (P/E) ratio: the price of a share of stock divided by earnings per share for a 12-month period. For example, a stock selling for $50 a share and earning $5 a share is said to be selling at a price-earnings ratio of 10:1. [20]

price elasticity: reflected in a reduction in sales when the price of an item is raised.

price fixing: an agreement by competing organizations to avoid competitive pricing by charging identical prices or by changing prices at the same time. Price fixing is in violation of the Sherman Antitrust Act. cf. *price stabilization.*

price index: a measure used to illustrate the changes in the average level of prices. see *purchasing power of the dollar, wholesale price index.*

price leadership: a situation in which prices can be determined by one major manufacturer in an industry, thus influencing others to accept the prices as determined. see *administered price.*

price level: a relative position in the scale of prices as determined by a comparison of prices (of labor, materials, capital, etc.) with prices as of other times. [62]

price-level-adjusted mortgage (PLAM): a unique mortgage plan in which the outstanding loan balance is indexed. The interest rate is a rate net of any inflation premium. The payments on a PLAM are based on this real rate, and at the end of each year, the then outstanding balance is adjusted by an inflation factor. The principal benefit of a PLAM is the much lower initial payment than either a GPM, GPAM, or a shared appreciation mortgage. see *graduated-payment adjustable mortgage, graduated-payment mortgage, shared-appreciation mortgage.*

price limit: the price that is entered on the trading floor of an exchange for placing an order to buy or sell. see *limited order, market order.*

price loco: the price at the place where a purchase occurs.

price-special flow theory: a theory stating that imports of precious metals increase the supply of funds and therefore advance the price level of items using these metals.

price spreading: the simultaneous purchase and sale of options in the same class with the same expiration date but with different striking prices. see *spread.*

price stabilization: keeping prices at a stated level. Primarily a government strategy, especially during wartime or periods of rapid inflation, but illegal when practiced by private companies. see *Sherman Antitrust Act of 1980;* cf. *price fixing.*

price support: subsidy or financial aid offered to specific growers, producers, or distributors, in accordance with governmental regulations to keep market prices from dropping below a certain minimum level. see *farm subsidies;* cf. *Brannan plan.*

prima facie: at first view; that which appears to be true until contrary evidence is given.

primary beneficiary: one who the insured designates as first in order of time, or development, in the payment of policy benefits see *beneficiary.* [12]

primary boycott: see *boycott.*

primary deposits: cash deposits in a bank.

primary distribution: the original sale of a company's securities. synonymous with "primary offering." [20]

primary market
(1) *general:* the initial market for any item or service.
(2) *investments:* the initial market for a new stock issue.
(3) *investments:* a firm, trading market held in a security by a trader who performs the activities of a specialist by being ready to execute orders in that stock.

primary money: standard money.

primary offering: see *primary distribution.*

primary reserves: a bank's legal reserves of cash and demand deposits with the Federal Reserve Bank and other banks.

primary trend: the direction in stock values that last for many months and usually for years.

prime bill of exchange: a draft or trade acceptance which states on the face of the instrument that it was created through a business transaction inolving the movement of goods. Bankers' acceptances are considered prime bills of exchange, although smaller banks must generally have the endorsement without recourse of a large bank enjoying high financial recognition in order to give the instrument "prime status." Prime bills of exchange are acceptable for rediscount with the Federal Reserve Bank, and therefore can be construed as a "secondary reserve" for banks. [10]

prime cost: the sum of direct labor expenditures plus direct materials cost that are identified with a product. see also *loading.*

prime interest (rate): the rate of interest charged by a commercial bank for large loans made to its most creditworthy business and industrial customers; it is the lowest interest rate charged by the bank. The prime rate level is determined by how much banks have to pay for the supply of money from which they make loans. In an inflated economy, banks pay increasingly higher rates for funds, and the prime rate rises. When inflation subsides, the prime rate usually drops. The Federal Reserve Bank's charge for negotiable business instruments, which is publicly established, influences the rate for all other business interest payments.

prime investment
(1) *general:* quality, first-class investment.
(2) *investments:* a high-grade investment, considered so safe and sound that dividends or interest payments are assumed.

prime maker: the party (or parties) signing a negotiable instrument and becoming the original party responsible for its ultimate payment. see *liabilities.*

prime rate: see *prime interest (rate).*

primogeniture: under common law, the right of the eldest child to inherit all real property of the parent; the estate usually passes to the son, but daughters are increasingly inheriting under this right. cf. *entail.*

Prin.: see *principal.*

principal
(1) *general:* one of the major parties to a transaction; either the seller or purchaser.
(2) *banking:* the original amount of a deposit, loan, or other amount of money on which interest is earned or paid. see also *billed principal.*
(3) *finance:* the face value of an instrument, which becomes the obligation of the maker or drawee to pay to a holder in due course. Interest is charged on the principal amount.
(4) *investments:* the person for whom a broker executes an order, or a dealer buying or selling for his or her own account.

principal beneficiary
(1) the beneficiary who is ultimately to receive the principal of the estate.
(2) the beneficiary who is the settlor's primary concern. [37]

principal only: an account on which payment is being credited to principal; that is, interest is no longer being charged on remaining balance. [55]

principal sum: the amount specified under a life insurance policy, such as the death benefit.

prior deductions method: an improper method of determining bond interest or preferred dividend coverage: the requirements of senior obligations are first deducted from earnings and the balance is applied to the requirements of the junior issue.

prior lien: a mortgage that ranks ahead of another.

prior-lien bond: see *bond, prior-lien.*

prior preferred (stock): see *preferred stock, prior.*

prior redemption privilege: a privilege frequently extended by a debtor to the holders of called bonds permitting them to redeem their holdings prior to the call date or maturity. There are chiefly three types of offers prior redemption: (1) with interest in full to the call date; (2) with interest in full to the call date less a bank discount (usually $\frac{1}{4}$ percent per annum) based on the period from the date of collection to the date of call; and (3) with interest to the date of collection only. [37]

prior stock: any preferred stock.

prior years' tax levies: taxes levied for fiscal periods preceding the current one. [49]

private bank: a bank chartered by the state in which it operates, subject to state laws and regulations, and subject to examinations by the state banking authorities. The principal distinction between private banks and other state banks is that the private bank may arise from a partnership, in which there is no capital stock.

private enterprise: the organization of production in which the business is owned and operated by people taking risks and motivated by the wish to make a profit. see *capitalist;* cf. *people's capitalism.*

private financing (private placement): the raising of capital for a business venture via private rather than public placement, resulting in the sale of securities to a relatively few number of investors. Such investments do not have to be registered with the SEC since no public offering is involved.

private lender: an individual who lends money from institutional funds (insurance companies, banks, etc.).

private mortgage insurance: insurance offered by a private company that protects an association against loss up to policy limits (customarily 20 to 25 percent of the loan amount) on a defaulted mortgage loan. Its use is usually limited to loans with a high loan-to-value ratio; the borrower pays the premiums. [59]

private notes: paper money issued by merchants, shopkeepers or anyone other than the legally authorized government agency. [27]

private property: all land not owned by the government.

private rate of return

(1) *general:* the financial rate of return anticipated by business-people prior to investing their monies.

(2) *finance:* the expected net profit after taxes and all costs, including depreciation, expressed as a percentage annual return on the total cost of an effort or the net worth of the stockholder owners. see *ROI.*

private remittances: represent transfers or transmissions of cash and goods by individuals and by charitable and nonprofit institutions to individuals or groups residing abroad. Personal remittances include all noncommercial transfers of funds to be sent abroad by means of customary bank drafts and money orders. [73]

private sector: the segment of the total economy composed of businesses and households, but excluding government. cf. *public sector.*

private trust

(1) a trust created for the benefit of a designated beneficiary or designated beneficiaries; as, a trust for the benefit of the settlor's or the testator's wife and children; opposed to a charitable (or public) trust.

(2) a trust created under a declaration of trust or under a trust agreement; as, a living trust or an insurance trust; opposed to a trust coming under the immediate supervision of a court. see *court trust*. [32]

private trust fund: a trust fund that will ordinarily revert to private individuals or will be used for private purposes. For example, a fund that consists of guarantee deposits. [49]

private wire firm: brokerage companies that are sufficiently large to allow them to rent telegraph wires for their own branch office communications.

privileged bond: see *bond, privileged*.

privilege issue: a preferred stock or bond having a conversion or participating right, or having a stock purchase warrant on it.

privileges: options such as puts, calls, and straddles.

Pr. In.: see *prior lien*.

Pro.: see *protest*.

probate

(1) *general:* the right or jurisdiction of hearing and determining questions or issues in matters concerning a will.

(2) *law:* the action or process of proving before a court of law that a document offered for official recognition as the last will and testament of a deceased person is genuine.

probate court: the court that has jurisdiction with respect to wills and intestacies and sometimes guardianships and adoptions; also called *court of probate, ordinary court, orphan's court, perfect's court,* and surrogate's court. [37]

probate in solemn form: the probate of a will in a formal proceeding after notice to the interested parties; opposed to probate in common form, which is an informal proceeding without such notice. [37]

probate of will: presentation of proof before the proper officer or court that the instrument offered is the last will of the decedent. [37]

Proc.: procedure.

proceeds

(1) *finance:* the actual amount of funds given to a borrower, following deductions for interest charges, fees, and so on.

(2) *finance:* the funds received by a seller after deductions for the payment of commissions, as with proceeds from a sale.

procuration: the authority given to another to sign instruments and to act on behalf of the person giving the procuration.

producer prices: the successor to the wholesale price index, this measure contains data on prices by stage of processing, sector, industry, and commodity. Bureau of Labor Statistics measure issued the first week of the month for the previous month.

product: goods and services made available to consumers. The total of benefits offered.

production costs: factory costs plus administrative expenses.

productivity: a measurement of the efficiency of production: a ratio of output to input (e.g., 10 units per man-hour).

professional: in the securities business, a student of the market or a person who makes a living buying and selling securities. A professional may direct the investments of a pension fund or other institution, or be a member of a brokerage firm who advises or acts for his firm's clients. [20]

profit

(1) *general:* the excess of the selling price over all costs and expenses incurred in making a sale.

(2) *banking:* the monies remaining after a business has paid all its bills. see also *contribution profit.*

(3) *finance:* the reward to the entrepreneur for the risks assumed by him or her in the establishment, operation, and management of a given enterprise or undertaking.

profit, gross (margin, gross): net sales less cost of goods sold (before consideration of selling and administrative expenses). Gross profit is expressed in dollar figures; gross margin is expressed as a percentage of net sales. [9]

profit, net (or income, net): revenue remaining after deduction of all costs, but before taxes; usually designates the final figure on a profit and loss statement. [9]

profitability: a firm's ability to earn a profit and the potential for future earnings.

profit and loss account: an account transferred from accounts receivable to a separate ledger. An amount deducted from the accounts receivable balance. An account deemed to be uncollectable, or a certain number of months past due, becomes eligible for transfer to the "profit and loss account" ledger. [41]

profit and loss reserve: an amount set aside by a firm to provide for anticipated "P & L accounts" during the fiscal period. Usually calculated as given percentage of the total "accounts receivable." [41]

profit and loss statement (operating statement; P & L): the summary listing of a firm's total revenues and expenses within a specified time period. synonymous with *income and expense statement.*

profit center: a segment of a business that is responsible for both revenues and expenses.

profit margin: the ratio of sales less all operating expenses divided by the number of sales.

profit sharing: an arrangement under which employees share in company profits, based on company successes, according to a plan. This compensation is paid in addition to wages. There are cash plans (giving a share of profits in cash) and deferred plans (setting up a trust for payment upon retirement, death, or disability). see *employee stock ownership plans, Lincoln Incentive Management Plan.*

profit-sharing trust: a trust established by an employer (usually a corporation) as a means of having the employees share in the profits of the enterprise. [37]

profit squeeze: profit shrinkage resulting from stable prices and increasing costs.

profits tax: a tax on business profits, excluding income taxes.

profit taking: the sale of stock that has appreciated in value since purchase, in order to realize the profit that has been made possible. This activity is often cited to explain a downturn in the market following a period of rising prices. cf. *unloading.*

pro forma invoice: a preliminary invoice indicating the value of the items listed and informing the recipient that all have been sent. It is not a demand for money.

program

(1) a set of step-by-step instructions that prepares a computer to perform an operation; also, the operation itself, performed upon the date for which it is designed.

(2) to prepare instructions for a specific operation or to enter these instructions into the computer. [59]

program budgeting: a long-range approach to budgetary decision making that relates future expenditures to broadly defined objectives of the organization.

program evaluation and review technique (PERT): an approach to facilitate planning and to give management tools for the control of specific programs. Original PERT programs were developed by the U.S. Navy. cf. *critical path method, PERT/COST.*

programmer: a person who designs, writes, and tests computer programs. see *analyst, program.*

programming: the art of reducing the plan for a solution to a problem to instructions that can be fed to a computer. see *programmer.*

progressive tax: an income tax that rises as income increases. The rate of increase varies. see *ability to pay, degressive taxation, graduated tax;* cf. *regressive taxes.*

progress payment plan: a method of construction loan payouts in which the contractor presents to the association all bills and lien waivers from time to time as construction progresses. [59]

Project Link: a huge econometric model of the global economy that generates consistent forecasts for individual economies while considering the feedback effects among countries. The popularizer of this concept is the 1980 Nobel Prize winner in economics, Dr. Lawrence R. Klein, of the University of Pennsylvania.

promissory note: any written promise to pay; a negotiable instrument that is evidence of a debt contracted by a borrower from a creditor, known as a lender of funds. If the instrument does not have all the qualities of a negotiable instrument, it cannot legally be transferred see *accommodation paper, note.*

proof

(1) an operation for testing the accuracy of a previous operation—for example, relisting the checks and adding their amounts to determine the accuracy of the total shown on a deposit slip.

(2) applied to the proof sheet, the record on which the test is made.

(3) also used to describe the method by which a type of transaction is proved, as in transit proof. Proof is generally affected when a total agrees with another total of the same items arrived at in a different manner; it is then said to be in balance. [32]

proof department: a department of a bank charged with the duties of sorting, distributing, and proving all transactions arising from the commercial operations of the bank. The proof function involves the creation of adequate records of all transactions, showing the proper distribution of all items going to other departments for further processing, and proof of the correctness of all transactions passing through the bank. The records created by the proof department are of vital importance, since examination of these records may be made months after a transaction occurs, in order to substantiate the accuracy of deposits made by customers and to establish legally that deposits were made by certain individual depositors. [10]

proofs: the final design of an issue prepared by a printing company as a sample for the issuing authority, but not of course intended for circulation. Proofs are always printed on a different type of paper from that used for the final issue, whereas specimen notes are always on the same paper. [27]

Prop.: see *property.*

property
(1) *general:* the exclusive right or interest of a person in his or her belongings.
(2) *law:* that which is legally owned by a person or persons and may be used and disposed of as the owner(s) see fit.

property, intangible: property that cannot be touched (e.g., choses in action) or has no physical structure. see *intangible asset.*

property, personal: chattels, choses in possession; everything that is owned except real estate.

property, real: land, including that which is naturally growing on it, and any improvements made to the land, including structures.

property, tangible: property that is touchable or has a physical structure; choses in possession.

property assessment: the valuation of real property for tax purposes. [59]

property dividends: dividends paid by one corporation in the form of stocks of another corporation, which the former may have acquired by purchase or received from the sale of property.

property search report: a type of credit bureau report that deals specifically with details of real property owned by a subject of inquiry. Frequently involves a search of country courthouse records for details of purchase, title, mortgage, or other encumbrance on property. [41]

property tax: see *land tax.*

proportional tax: a tax whose percentage rate stays constant as the tax base increases, resulting in the amount of paid tax being proportional to the tax base (e.g., property tax).

proprietary accounts: those accounts which show actual financial condition and operations such as actual assets, liabilities, reserves, surplus, revenues, and expenditures, as distinguished from budgetary accounts. [49]

proprietary company: a nonfunctioning parent company of a nonfunctioning controlling company, formed for the purpose of investing in the securities of other companies, and for controlling these companies through such holdings. synonymous with *holding company* and *parent company.*

proprietor: a person who has an exclusive right or interest in property or in a business.

proprietorship: a business owned by one person. The individual owner has all the rights to profits from the business as well as all the liabilities and losses. synonymous with "individual proprietorship."

proprietorship certificate: a certificate filed with a bank showing the ownership of a privately owned business enterprise.

pro rata: "according to the rate" (Latin); in proportion to a total amount. For example, if a contract is terminated prior to the end of the period for which payment has been given, a pro rata return of the payment is made, in proportion to the unused period of time remaining.

pro rata rate: a premium rate charged for a short term at the same proportion of the rate for a longer term as the short term bears to the longer term. see *short-rate cancellation.* [53]

prorate: to redistribute a portion of a cost to a department or product in accordance with an agreed-upon formula.

pro rate cancellation: the termination of an insurance contract or bond, with the premium charge being adjusted in proportion to the exact time the protection has been in force. cf. *flat cancellation, short-rate cancellation.*

prospect: a potential customer. see *qualified prospect.*

prospectus

(1) *general:* a plan of a proposed enterprise.

(2) *banking:* a description of property for sale or lease.

(3) *investments:* a written offer to sell a security; it provides information about the quality of the stock that is regulated by the SEC. cf. open *prospectus, red herring.*

prosperity: the uppermost phase of a business cycle. cf. *depression.*

protected check: a check that is prepared in such a manner as to prevent alterations. For example: *machine protection*—perforating the paper with pressure and indelible ink. *Paper protection*—any erasure of matter written in ink, by rubber eraser, knife, or chemical eradicator will remove the sensitive color and show instantly that an alteration has been attempted. *Machine printing protection*—the machine automatically prints stars or asterisks between the dollar sign and first digit of the amount. An indelible ink ribbon is used, or a ribbon treated with a acid that eats into the paper. [10]

protection

(1) *banking:* synonymous with *coverage.*

(2) *government:* the imposition of high (i.e., protective) tariffs on imports that are presumed to compete with domestic items, with the objective of giving the domestic manufacturer an advantage. see *infant industry argument.*

protectionists: people who favor high tariffs and other import restrictions to enable domestic items to compete more favorably with foreign items.

protective committee: a committee formed to represent security holders in negotiations on defaulted securities. [39]

protective tariff: a tax on imported goods designed to give domestic manufacturers an economic shield against price competition from abroad. cf. *revenue tariffs*.

protest: a written statement by a notary public, or other authorized person, under seal for the purpose of giving formal notice to parties secondarily liable that an instrument has been dishonored, either by refusal to accept or by refusal to make payment. [50]

protest jacket: synonymous with *notice of dishonor (protest jacket)*.

prove: in banking, the act of creating a record, to show by a list or run of the items, the accuracy of a list or deposit created by another person. The list shows that each item is listed correctly as to amount, and that the amounts listed add up to an exact total. The two lists, one made by the bank as a record, and the other created by another person, such as a depositor, must agree in total to be "in proof." [10]

provision: a charge for an estimated expense or liability or for the diminution in the cost or value of an asset. [43]

provision for loan loss: a charge for anticipated loan losses, which appears on the bank's income statement as an operating expense.

proximate clause: defining the cause that directly produces a loss.

proximo: in the following month. cf. *instant (inst.)*.

proxy: a power of attorney given by a stockholder to an individual or individuals to exercise the stockholder's rights to vote at corporate meetings.

proxy statement: printed information required by the SEC to be given to potential holders of securities traded on a national exchange, supplying minimum descriptions of the stock, timing of the proposed sale, and so on.

prudent investment-cost standard: a means of defining the value of an organization by subtracting the costs of unwise, inappropriate, or wasteful investments from the original costs of the assets.

prudent man rule: an investment standard. In some states, the law requires that a fiduciary, such as a trustee, may invest the fund's money only in a list of securities designated by the state—the so-called legal list. In other states, the trustee may invest in a security if it is one that would be bought by a prudent person of discretion and intelligence, who is seeking a reasonable income and preservation of capital.

P&S: see *purchase and sale statement*.

PS
(1) see *penny stocks*.
(2) see *pink sheets*.
(3) see *preferred stock*.
(4) see *price spreading*.
(5) see *profit sharing*.

PSE: see *Pacific Coast Stock Exchange*.

PST: see *profit-sharing trust*.

PT
(1) see *paper title*.
(2) see *passing title*.
(3) see *perfect title*.
(4) see *profit taking*.

Ptas.: see *peseta*.

PTE: see *pretax earnings*.

P. Tr.: see *private trust*.

public administrator: in many states, a county officer whose main duty is to settle the estates of persons who die intestate, when there is no member of the family, creditor, or other person having a prior right of administration who is able to administer the estate. [32]

public bond: see *bond, public.*

public debt transaction: see *back-door financing.*

public deposits: any bank deposit made by a federal, state, or municipal government.

public finance: see *finance.*

Public Law 94-455: see *Tax Reform Act of 1976.*

public offering: new or subsequent issues of stocks sold to the general public. cf. *private financing (private placement).*

public ownership: ownership by the public of the common or other equity stock of a New York Stock Exchange firm.

public relations department: a department within a bank or other business institution created and maintained to promote and encourage better harmony and relationships between that particular institution and the general public by offering a wide variety of services—educational and other—to the public without cost to the recipient. Such departments operate under a variety of names such as "courtesy," "customer's service," "public aid," and "public service." [10]

public revenue: income received by a governmental agency (taxes, tariffs, customs, etc.).

public sector: a segment of the total economy including all levels of government and excluding businesses and households. cf. *private sector.*

public trust: the same as a charitable

trust; opposed to a private trust. [37]

public trust fund: a trust fund whose principal, earnings, or both, must be used for a public purpose—for example, a pension or retirement fund. [49]

pula: monetary unit of Botswana.

pull: raising the offering price, or lowering the bid price of a stock, or if neither, then to cancel completely.

pull down: slang, the sum of money earned from working (e.g., one's weekly salary).

punch card check: a check that has perforations either in the body of the check or around a portion of its border. These perforations are used to re-sort and correlate the checks after they have been canceled and returned with the bank statement. This type of check must be canceled in some special manner agreed upon by the banker and the depositor. Punch card checks are used to correlate the checks by number or some other coding; thus facilitating the reconcilement of the depositor's bank statement. [10]

punched card: a card punched with a pattern of holes to represent data.

punched tape: a tape on which a pattern of holes or cuts is used to represent data.

punt: slang, shares that will rarely turn out to be profitable.

pup: slang, a low-priced, inactive security.

Pur.: purchase.

purchase and sale statement: a statement sent by a commission merchant to a customer when his or her futures position has been reduced or closed out. It shows the amount involved, the price at which the position was acquired and reduced or closed out, respectively, the gross profits or loss, the commission charged, and the net profit or loss on the transaction. Frequently referred to as a P&S. [11]

purchased funds: large-denomination certificates of deposits held by banks.

purchased paper: as distinguished from paper that has been discounted, any commercial paper that has been bought outright.

purchase money: monies paid to obtain ownership of property.

purchase-money bond: see *bond, purchase-money.*

purchase-money mortgage: for those who put their homes on the market and find that, to sell their property, they must act as the lender themselves. The mortgage is actually a short-term instrument, that runs no more than five years and often only a year or two. In most cases, a purchase-money mortgage is a second mortgage, supplementing the buyer's partial bank financing.

purchase order: a document that authorizes the delivery of specified merchandise or the rendering of certain services and the making of a charge for them. [49]

purchase outright: to pay the full amount in cash for purchased stocks.

purchase price
(1) *general:* the amount for which any item is bought.
(2) *banking:* the combination of monies and mortgages given to obtain a property.

purchaser: a buyer; a person who obtains title to or an interest in property by the act of purchase.

purchasing power: the value of money measured by the items it can buy. cf. *money, real value of money, wages.*

purchasing power of the dollar: a measurement of the quantity of goods and services that a dollar will buy in a specified market compared with the amount it could buy in some base period. It is obtained by taking the reciprocal of an appropriate price index. see *money, wage.*

pure interest
(1) the price paid for the use of capital, not to include monies for risk and all other costs incurred because of the loan.
(2) synonymous with *net interest* or *true interest.*

pure market economy: a competitive economic system of numerous buyers and sellers, where prices are determined by the free interaction of supply and demand. see *free enterprise.*

pure monopoly: see *perfect (pure) monopoly.*

pure premium: premium arrived at by dividing losses by exposure, and to which no loading has been added for commission, taxes, and expenses.

pure profit: see *economic profit.*

put out a line: the selling short of a considerable amount of the stock of one or more firms over a period of time with the hope of falling prices. cf. *take on a line;* see *short sale.*

puts
(1) an option contract that entitles the holder to sell a number of shares of the underlying stock at a stated price on or before a fixed expiration date. [5]
(2) see *puts and calls.*

puts and calls: options that give the right to buy or sell a fixed amount of certain stock at a specified price within a specified time. A put gives the holder the right to sell the stock; a call conveys the right to buy the stock. Puts are purchased by those who think a stock may go down. A put obligates the seller of the contract, commonly known as the option writer, to take delivery of the stock and to pay the specified price to the owner of the option within the time limits of the contract. The price specified in a put or call is usually close to the market price of the stock at the time the contract is made. Calls are purchased by those who think a stock may rise. A call gives the holder the right to buy the stock from the writer at the specified price within a fixed period of time. Put and call contracts are written for 30, 60, or 90 days, or longer. Six months and 10 days is the most common term. If the purchaser of a put or call does not wish to exercise the option, the price paid for the option becomes a loss. see *spread*.

PV

(1) see *par value*.

(2) see *present value*.

PY: prior year.

Pymt.: see *payment*.

pyramiding: employing profits of open or unliquidated positions to add to the holder's original position; buying additional stocks or commodities by offering unrealized paper profits as additional margin. Used with commodities; rarely with stocks.

pyramid ratio: a tool used in the analysis of management and income ratio between profits and capital.

pyramid selling (schemes): business opportunity frauds, usually promoted through advertisement for job opportunities guaranteed to yield enormous or quick profits—requiring little education or demanding a minimal personal investment. There are government regulations against certain pyramid schemes. The pyramider induces people to buy his products, which they are to resell at a higher price. For example, if 10 people buy 50 units each and sell only 15 each, the pyramider is still ahead because he has sold 500 units. see *fraud*.

Q

(1) in receivership or bankruptcy proceedings.

(2) quarterly.

QA: see *quick assets.*

QC: see *quasi-contract.*

QP: see *quoted price.*

QPC: see *quasi-public company.*

Q-ratio: developed in the early 1960s by Yale University economist James Tobin, a way of explaining how the level of stock market prices affects capital spending—and thus the overall economy—even though the vast majority of firms never consider raising fresh equity capital. The *Q*-ratio relates the market value of a company's physical assets to the cost of replacing those assets. A ratio greater than 1 means that the stock market values a dollar of a company's assets at more than a dollar. Conversely, if *Q* is less than 1, the assets are being valued at less than dollar for dollar.

QS: see *quality stock.*

QT: see *quotation ticker.*

Qtly.: quarterly.

Qtr.: quarter.

qualified acceptance: any counteroffer.

qualified endorsement: an endorsement by which the endorser seeks to avoid the usual liabilities inherent in his act. ''Without recourse'' is the most common example. If the instru-

ment is not honored, the endorser does not want to become responsible for it. cf. *recourse.*

qualified plan (or trust): an employer's trust or plan that qualifies under the Internal Revenue Code of 1954 for the exclusive benefit of his or her employees or their beneficiaries in such manner and form as to entitle the employer who makes the payments to the plan or trust to the deductions and income tax benefits as set forth in that Code. [37]

qualified prospect: a potential customer who is able to buy a product or service and has the authority to make a decision to purchase. This conclusion is often arrived at following a check on the individual's credit.

qualified retirement plan: a private retirement plan that meets the rules and regulations of the Internal Revenue Service. Contributions to a qualified retirement plan are in almost all cases tax deductible, and earnings on such contributions are always tax sheltered until retirement. [23]

qualifying period: see *waiting period.*

quality of estate: the form in which an estate is to be owned, including type of possession and time. No indication of property value or physical characteristics is given.

quality stock: a stock of high grade, of superior merit. synonymous with ''blue chip stock.'' see *blue chip.*

411

quantity discount: a reduction given for volume buying.

quantity theory: a theory stating that a special relationship exists between the quantity of money and money income. People spend excess money holdings irrespective of the interest rate and the manner in which the new money holdings were received. cf. *Gresham's law, liquid trap, marginal propensity to invest, marginal propensity to save.*

quantum meruit: "as much as he deserved" (Latin); a principle of business law providing that when a service is given without a written estimate of price, there is an implied promise by the purchaser of the service to pay for the work as much as it is worth.

Quar.: quarter.

quarter stock: stock with a par value of $25 for each share.

quasi: as if; that which resembles.

quasi-arbitrage: see *arbitrage.*

quasi-contract: an obligation similar in character to that of a contract, but which arises not from an agreement between the parties but from some relationship between them or from a voluntary act by one or more of them—for example, the management of the affairs of another without authority or the management of a common property without authority. [37]

quasi-corporation: any political subdivision of an organization or group (e.g., an unincorporated town).

quasi-public company: a corporation operated privately in which the public has a special interest (e.g., eleemosynary institutions).

quasi-reorganization: a restructuring that does not lead to the formation of a new company, undertaken for purposes of absorbing a deficit, avoiding bankruptcy, and affording an opportunity to begin again.

quetzal: monetary unit of Guatemala.

queue: a line or group of items or people in a bank waiting for service.

quick assets
(1) *general:* assets that in the ordinary course of business, will be converted into cash within a reasonably short time.
(2) *finance:* assets that can be readily converted into cash without appreciable loss. see *liquidity.*

quick (quickie) buck: slang, money made rapidly; a windfall.

quick ratio: the ratio between existing liabilities and quick assets; shows a firm's ability to pay off its liabilities rapidly with available funds.

quick turn: any quick buy and sale transaction over a brief time period, often within hours. see *day trading.*

quid pro quo: "something for something" (Latin): a mutual consideration; securing an advantage or receiving a concession in return for a similar favor.

quiet title suit: a legal action to remove a defect or any questionable claim against the title to property. cf. *cloud on title.*

quitclaim deed: see *deed, quitclaim.*

quit rent: the last rental payment made by a tenant before leaving the property.

quotation: the highest bid to buy and the lowest offer to sell a security in a given market at a given time. For example, if you ask a broker for a "quote" on a stock, the reply may be something like "45¼ to 45½." This means that $45.25 is the highest price any buyer wanted to pay at the time the quote was given on the floor of a stock exchange, and $45.50 was the lowest price any seller would take at the same time. The word is often shortened to "quote." see *bid and asked*.

quotation ticker: the ticker of an exchange carrying prices of actual transactions.

quote: see *quotation*.

quoted price: the stated price of a security or commodity.

R

(1) see *range.*
(2) see *rate of interest.*
(3) see *right.*

RA

(1) see *restricted account.*
(2) see *Revenue Act of 1962, Revenue Act of 1964, Revenue Act of 1971, Revenue Act of 1976, Revenue Act of 1978.*

rack: a term used to describe the "rack department," which sorts, distributes, and proves items in the commercial operations of the bank.

racket: slang, a dishonest business activity. synonymous with *swindle.*

rack rent: an unusually high rent in an amount equal to or nearly equal to the total value of the items produced on the rented property. cf. *economic rent.*

rag money: American term for paper money. [27]

raid: a deliberate attempt by professionals, traders, and others to depress the market price of a stock.

raise

(1) *general:* any increase in value or amount (e.g., wages or prices).
(2) *investments:* a fraudulent increase in the face value of a negotiable instrument.

raised bills: the denomination of paper money that has been illegally raised.

raised check: a check on which the amount has been illegally increased.

raised notes: those on which there is an overprint indicating that the denomination has been increased as a result of government revalidation. [27]

rally: a brisk rise following a decline in the general price level of the market, or in an individual stock. [20]

RAM

(1) random-access memory; cf. *ROM.*
(2) see *reserve adjustment magnitude.*

rand: monetary unit of Lesotho, Republic of South Africa, and South-West Africa.

random access: a quality of a computer's memory device allowing data to be written in or read from the memory through direct locating rather than locating through reference to other data in the memory. synonymous with *"direct access."*

random walk: name given to the theory that price movements have no memory and occur at random.

range: the difference between the high and low price of the future during a given period. [11]

rank

(1) *general:* a title or position in an organization.
(2) *computers:* to arrange in an ascending or descending series according to importance.
(3) *investments:* see *restricted shares.*

ratable distribution: the proportionate distribution of an estate according to a percentage. For example, if all the legacies cannot be paid in full and each of them is reduced by the same percentage, there is ratable distribution. [37]

rate

(1) *general:* to categorize and rank in terms of special qualities or properties.

(2) *banking:* the cost of a unit of insurance. cf. *premium.*

(3) *finance:* a charge, fee, or price.

rate base: the value established by a regulatory authority, upon which a utility is permitted to earn a specified rate of return. [3]

rate discrimination: charging different prices for almost identical services. When this action tends to lessen competition, it may be illegal under antitrust laws.

rate of exchange: the amount of funds of one nation that can be bought, at a specific date, for a sum of currency of another country. Rates fluctuate often because of economic, political, and other forces.

rate of inflation: the average percentage rate of increase of the price of money, weighted and stated in annual terms.

rate of interest: the charge for borrowing money.

rate of return

(1) the yield obtainable on a security based on its purchase price or its current market price. This may be the amortized yield to maturity on a bond or the current income return.

(2) the income earned by a public utility company on its property or capital investment, expressed as a percentage. [67]

(rate of) return on investment (capital): see *ROI.*

rate regulation: the determination by a commission or public service agency of the maximum, and at times the minimum, charge that public utility corporations may demand for their services. see *fair rate of return, utility.*

rate-sensitive assets: bank loans. see *liability hedge.*

rate-sensitive liabilities: bank deposits and borrowings. see *liability hedge.*

rate setting: the establishment of rates by agreement between labor and management or by an employer alone.

rate variance: in accounting procedures, the difference between actual wages paid and the standard wage rate, multiplied by the total actual hours of direct labor used.

rate war: a negative form of competition; sellers drop their prices below their costs for purposes of putting the competition out of business.

rating (bonds): a system of rating that provides the investor with a simple system of gradation by which the relative investment qualities of bonds are indicated. [3]

ratio

(1) *general:* a number relationship between two things (i.e., ratio of births to deaths).

(2) *finance:* any relationship that can be used in measuring the rating or financial position of a firm (e.g., the relationship of a company's earnings to the firm's market price for its stock).

(3) *finance:* one of the various analyses made by a money-lending

or credit agency, of the financial statements of a given individual, company, or other business enterprise seeking credit, to determine the desirability of granting the requested credit.

(4) *finance:* the relative values of silver and gold in a monetary system based on both. see *bimetallism.*

ratio analysis: analysis of the relationships of items in financial statements. see listings under *ratio.*

ratio bull spread: see *neutral spread.*

ratio of accounts payable to purchases: this ratio, determined for the present period and compared with a similar ratio for previous periods, indicates the trend toward or from prompt payment of current obligations.

ratio of capital to fixed assets: this ratio is usually determined for a number of years to ascertain whether there is a trend toward converting the investment of the owners into fixed assets, thereby indicating a possible reliance on creditors for furnishing the required working capital.

ratio of collateral to debt: a measure for determining how effectively stock margin is achieved. It is shown as a fraction with full collateral value as the numerator and the total securities margin as the denominator.

ratio of finished goods inventory to the cost of goods sold: this ratio is determined by dividing the cost of goods sold by the average finished goods inventory. The resulting figure is the number of times the investment in the finished goods inventory has turned over during the period under consideration. The present ratio is compared with a similar ratio for several previous periods, since it tends to portray the stability and trend of sales, or the possible overstated or expanded inventory.

ratio of fixed assets to fixed liabilities: this ratio tends to indicate the margin of safety to the present mortgage and bond holders, if any. Failure of the ratio to meet the minimum requirement frequently suggests that additional funds should be raised from the owners rather than by mortgaging fixed assets.

ratio of notes payable to accounts payable: three quantitative factors are frequently considered when determining whether the resulting ratio (notes payable/accounts payable) is desirable: (a) notes issued in payment of merchandise, (b) notes issued to banks and brokers, and (c) notes issued to others. If a relatively large amount of the outstanding notes was issued to merchandise creditors, this might indicate that the firm is unable to take advantage of the cash discounts offered in the trade, and, also, that other lending agencies might consider the firm's credit unfavorably.

ratio of notes receivable to accounts receivable: if a financial statement discloses a large ratio of notes receivable to accounts receivable, as compared with other firms in a similar line of business, the firm with the high ratio may have a lax credit policy, or it may be extending credit to customers whose ability to pay promptly is dubious.

ratio of owned capital to borrowed capital: this ratio is considered to be important in determining the advisability of extending additional long-term credit to an applicant. If this ratio is not considered favorable, it frequently suggests that the funds desired should be raised from the owners of the business (i.e., the applicants themselves) rather than through the additional pledging of any assets.

ratio of raw materials inventory to cost of manufacture: this ratio is determined by dividing the cost of goods manufactured by the average raw materials inventory. The resulting figure is the number of times the investment in the raw materials inventory has turned over during the period under consideration. When the present ratio is compared with a similar ratio for previous periods, it tends to portray the trend and steadiness of production, or to indicate an overstated or overexpanded inventory.

Ravenswood plan: the combination of a checking account with a bank repurchase agreement. A high-yielding checking account first developed by the Bank of Ravenswood on Chicago's North Side.

RB
(1) see *bond, redeemable.*
(2) see *bond, revenue.*

RC
(1) see *recurring charges.*
(2) see *register(ed) check.*
(3) see *reserve currency.*
(4) see *risk capital.*

Rcd.: received.

RCPC: see *Regional Check Processing Center.*

Rcpt.: see *receipt.*

Rct.: see *receipt.*

R&D: see *research and development.*

RE
(1) see *rate of exchange.*
(2) see *real estate.*

reacquired securities: securities, once outstanding, that have been acquired by the issuing corporation and are legally available for reissue or resale (in some states these securities cannot be reissued without approval of regulatory authorities). [3]

reaction: a drop in securities prices following a sustained period of increasing prices.

reader
(1) *computers:* a device that converts information in one form of storage to information in another form of storage.
(2) *computers:* a part of the scheduler that transfers an input stream into the system.

read(ing) the tape: a technique for judging the performance of various stocks by following their price changes as given on the ticker tape.

real accounts: those accounts—asset, liability, reserve and capital—whose balances are not canceled out at the end of an accounting period but are carried over to the next period. These accounts appear on the postclosing trial balance and the statement of condition. Sometimes called permanent accounts. [59]

real earnings: earnings adjusted to exclude the effects of price change.

real estate: tangible land and all physical property. Includes all physical substances below, upon, or attached to land; thus houses, trees, and fences are classified as real estate. All else is personal property.

real estate bond: see *bond, real estate.*

real estate investment trust: an unincorporated trust or association set up to invest in real property and which has centralized management, issues beneficial interest to 100 persons or less, and meets other strict requirements of the income tax laws; 90 percent of income must come from real property rentals, dividends, interests, or gains from sale of securities or real estate. [62]

real estate loans: loans secured by real estate, regardless of the purpose. see *mortgage.* [40]

real estate owned: a term that applies to all real estate directly owned by a bank, usually not including real estate taken to satisfy a debt. [44]

Real Estate Settlement Procedures Act: federal legislation of 1974, this act provided comprehensive guidelines for loan closing costs and settlement practices; effective in June 1975. see *Real Estate Settlement Procedures Act amendments.* [51]

Real Estate Settlement Procedures Act amendments: federal legislation of 1976 which eased the requirement of the Real Estate Settlement Procedures Act by permitting lenders to disclose good faith estimates of closing costs instead of actual charges, and by tying disclosure timing to receipt of the application instead of the date of closing; also eliminated disclosure of the property's previous selling price. see *Real Estate Settlement Procedures Act.* [51]

real estate sold on contract: real estate that has been sold for which the buyer does not have sufficient down payment to warrant the seller giving title; the contract generally provides that when the contract balance is reduced to a certain amount, the buyer may refinance the contract to get title to the property. [59]

real estate tax: a pecuniary charge laid upon real property for public purposes. [62]

real income: the sum total of the purchasing power of a nation or individual.

real interest rate: the rate at which a person earns future purchasing power on monetary assets. It equals the money rate minus the rate of inflation.

real investment: an expenditure that establishes a new capital asset, thus creating a new capital formation.

realization (realize)
(1) *finance:* the act or process of converting into cash an asset, or the total assets, of an individual or business.
(2) *investments:* receiving a profit from selling a security following an increase in its price.

realized profit (or loss): a profit or loss resulting from the sale or other disposal of a security, as distinguished from a paper profit or loss. [67]

realizing: when a profit is realized either by a liquidating sale or the repurchase of a short sale. [11]

real money: money containing one or more metals having intrinsic value, as distinguished from representative money such as currency issued by a realm, and checks, drafts, and so on, issued by legal entities. see *bimetallism, monometallism;* cf. *fiat money.*

real-money balances: the amount of goods and services that can be bought from a given stock of money retained by individuals. Shifts in real-money balances are computed by adjusting changes in the amount of money held for changes in the level of prices.

real price: the price of goods and services measured by the quantity of labor needed to earn sufficient money to purchase the goods or services.

real property: the property that is devised by will to a party known as the devisee; or all fixed, permanent, immovable property, such as land and tenements.

real spendable earnings: a U.S. Bureau of Labor Statistics measure of the economy; successor to the wholesale price index. It contains a wealth of data on prices by stage of processing, sector, industry, and commodity. This index is issued the first week of the month for the previous month.

real stock: as contrasted with stock that is sold short, any long stock.

real time
(1) *computers:* the actual time during which a physical process transpires.
(2) *systems:* "in real time" refers to the performance of a computation during the same time that the related physical process transpires, allowing the results of the computation to be used in guiding the physical process.

realty: synonym for *real estate.*

real value of money: the price of money measured in terms of goods. cf. *purchasing power.*

real wages: the cost of items and services that can be purchased with money wages. It is useful for compar-

ing changes in the standard of living by eliminating the effect of changes in the general price level.

reappraisal: the term applied when property is appraised a second time.

reasonable value: a value placed on property that parallels the existing market value.

reassessment: the result of a change in the assessed value of property or reappraisal of property.

rebate
(1) *finance:* unearned interest that may be returned to a borrower if his or her loan is paid off before the maturity date.
(2) *finance:* any deduction made from a payment or charge. As contrasted with a discount, the rebate is not deducted in advance but is returned to the consumer following payment of the full amount (e.g., a General Electric appliance costs $24 with a rebate of $5 after the consumer has mailed in a coupon from the appliance package). cf. *discount.*

rebating: the illegal and unethical practice of selling a policy at less than the legal rate, or allowing the insured a refund of the premium, or giving him or her the goods of any value, thus avoiding payment of the full legal premium.

Rec.: see *receipt.*

recap: an abbreviated term for "recapitulation" (or assembling) of totals taken from "batch proof" sheets or from proof machines which must be assembled in proper order so as to build up control totals for the various departments charged with the items. Recap sheets may be used in all departments of the bank, and all recap sheets assembled into a final recap sheet for the settlement of the entire bank. see also *settlement clerk.* [10]

recapitalization: altering the capital structure of a firm by increasing or decreasing its capital stock.

recapitulation: see *recap.*

recapture clause: a clause in an agreement providing for retaking or recovering possession. As used in percentage leases, to take a portion of earnings or profits above a fixed amount of rent. [62]

recast: see *recomputation.*

recasting a mortgage: reconstructing an existing mortgage by increasing its amount, interest rate, or time period.

Recd.: received.

recede: any drop in prices.

receipt: any written acknowledgment of value received.

receipts outstanding for funded debt: receipts for payments on account of subscriptions to funded debt. [18]

receipts outstanding for installments paid: receipts for payments on account of subscriptions to capital stock. [18]

receivables: accounts receivable owned by a business. These may be pledged as collateral for a loan secured from a bank or other financial institution.

receiver: a court-appointed, neutral party named to handle property under litigation or the affairs of a bankrupt person. The receiver is required to maintain the property and its assets for the benefit of those having equity in it until a court decision as to its disposition is made. see also *bailee, interim receiver, remaindermen, sequestered account.*

receivers' and trustees' securities: evidences of indebtedness (other than equipment securities or obligations) issued by a receiver or trustee acting under orders of a court. [18]

receivership: the state of being under the care or administration of a receiver.

receiving teller: a bank employee assigned to the duties of accepting deposits from depositors. This teller is responsible for counting all cash received, and for verification of the count to the customer's deposit. The teller should also see that all checks deposited are properly endorsed by the depositor. The receiving teller enters the amount of the deposit in the depositor's passbook, or issues a receipt from a teller's machine for the depositor's record. [10]

recession: a phase of the business cycle that shows a downswing or contraction of the economy.

recession (growth): period of sluggish growth in output—up to 2.5 or 3 percent without six months of actual decline.

reciprocal business: a business favor where a request to purchase or sell stocks by one person is expected from another in return for a similar order.

reciprocal statutes: similar statutes in two or more states providing mutual provisions or reciprocal treatment within the states affected concerning the subjects treated in such statutes; for example, similar provisions with regard to corporations or inheritance taxes, a trust institution, bank, or business in another state. [37]

reciprocal trade agreement: an international agreement between two or more countries to establish mutual trade concessions that are expected to be of equal value.

reclamation

(1) *general:* a business term to describe the act of obtaining useful materials from waste products.

(2) *banking:* a sum of money due or owing by a bank resulting from an error in the listing of the amount of a check on a clearinghouse balance.

reclassification of stock: a change or modification of the capital structure of an organization.

recompense: a payment or award made to anyone to make amends for a loss or damage. see *compensation.*

recomputation: to refigure and reapply, on a simple interest basis, all payments made on a precomputed loan. see *acceleration.* [55]

reconciliation: a process for determining the differences between two items of an account so as to bring them into agreement (e.g., a bank statement and an up-to-date checkbook). see *adjustment.*

reconditioning property: improving a property's value by repairing it or making changes to enhance it.

reconveyance: the transfer of title of property back to a former owner.

recordation: the public acknowledgment in written form that a lien exists against a specific property that is identified in a mortgage. see *lien affidavit.*

record date: the date on which a person must be registered as a shareholder on the stock book of a company in order to receive a declared dividend, or among other things, to vote on company affairs. cf. *ex-dividend.*

recording fee: cost of recording nec-essary documents with the appropriate state or county administrative office. [78]

records of original entry: the general journal, the cash receipts record, and the cash disbursement record. All transactions must first be analyzed and recorded in one of these records before posting to the general ledger accounts. [59]

recourse: a term used to define the rights of a holder in due course of a negotiable instrument to force prior endorsers on the instrument to meet their legal obligations by making good the payment of the instrument if dishonored by the maker or acceptor. The holder in due course must have met the legal requirements of presentation and delivery of the instrument to the maker of a note or acceptor of a draft, and must have found that this legal entity has refused to pay for, or defaulted in payment of the instrument. see also *notice of dishonor (protest jacket).* [10]

recoverable expenditure: an expenditure made for or on behalf of another governmental unit, fund, or department, or for a private individual, firm, or corporation which will subsequently be recovered in cash or its equivalent. [49]

recovery

(1) *finance:* the period of the business cycle that follows a depression.

(2) *investments:* following a period of declining prices, the rise in stock prices. synonymous with *expansion.*

Recovery Act: see *Economic Recovery Tax Act of 1981.*

Rect.: see *receipt.*

recurring charges: those financial obligations of a recurring nature that a potential borrower must pay or has obligated himself to pay, including taxes, debt repayments, legal obligations such as alimony, and other items. [59]

red, in the: slang, losing money from operating a business.

redeemable bond: *bond, redeemable.*

redeemable rent: payments of rent that can be recovered (i.e., with a rental agreement containing the option to buy the property). When such an option is exercised, the purchaser receives all or a portion of the rents, or the monies may be applied to the sales price.

redeemable stock: a preferred stock that can be called in, at the option of the issuing company. see *redemption price.*

Redem.: see *redemption.*

redemise: to renew a lease.

redemption

(1) *finance:* the liquidation of an indebtedness, on or before maturity, such as the retirement of a bond issue prior to its maturity date.

(2) *banking:* purchasing back; a debtor redeems his mortgaged property when he has paid his debt in full.

redemption bond: see *bond, redemption.*

redemption fund: a fund created for the purpose of retiring an obligation.

redemption price

(1) the price (usually at its par value) at which a bond may be redeemed before maturity, when retired at the option of the issuing company.

(2) the amount a company must pay to call in certain types of preferred stock.

redemption right: a defaulted mortgagor's right to redeem his property after default and court judgment, both before and after its sale. see also *equitable right of redemption.* [59]

redemptions: cash-ins made of investment company shares.

redemption value bond: see *bond, redemption value.*

red herring: a financial prospectus. On the first page, printed in red, is a cautionary statement. It is informational and not to be intended as an offer to sell the securities described. see *open prospectus.*

Redi Check Plan: the customer arranges a top credit limit with the bank. He is issued a book of special checks (usually of a type prepared for automated bookkeeping). It is his privilege to write checks as he wishes, up to the total of his line of credit, which may be for $300, $500, $1000, and at times as high as $5000. Each month he receives a statement which records all of his checks that have "cleared" the bank. A service charge may be added but usually is not if he makes a deposit to cover the statement within 10, 15, or 20 days; except perhaps 25 cents for each check that has been drawn, to cover the bookkeeping. [28]

Redisc.: see *rediscount.*

rediscount

(1) *banking:* a negotiable instrument that has been discounted by a bank and subsequently discounted a second time by a Federal Reserve bank or another bank for the benefit of the bank that originally discounted the instrument. see *bank credit.*

(2) *finance:* to discount for the second time.

rediscount rate: the rate set by the Federal Reserve Bank for discounting a second time monies offered by their district member banks; the interest rate charged for discounting a negotiable instrument that has already been discounted.

redlining: the alleged practice of certain lending institutions of making it almost impossible to obtain mortgages, improvement loans, and insurance by homeowners, apartment house landlords, and businesses in neighborhoods outlined in red on a map, usually areas that are deteriorating or considered by the lending institution as poor investments. cf. *greenlining.*

reduced rate average: see *coinsurance.*

reentry: a landlord's right to reacquire leased property if terms in the lease, such as the making of rent payments, are not satisfied. A reentry clause must be inserted by the landlord in the original lease. cf. *landlord's warrant.*

reexport: to export already imported items without duty charges, in basically similar form, to a third country.

Ref.

(1) see *referee.*

(2) see *refunding.*

refer authorizer: a person in a credit office with the authority to approve or disapprove credit transactions which need special attention. The person is usually a section supervisor. [41]

referee: when a case is pending in court, the presiding officer requests an individual (the referee) to receive testimony from the parties and pre-

sent the information to the court. When appropriate, the referee can accept foreclosed property and make a deed. see *bankruptcy, foreclose (foreclosure);* cf. *master in chancery.*

referee's foreclosure deed: a deed made by a court official that forecloses the mortgage on a property and passes the title on to the referee.

referee's partition deed: a deed made by a referee, conveying title to property when co-owners choose to divide their interest.

refinance

(1) *banking:* to extend existing financing or to acquire new monies. Usually done when a mortgage is withdrawn so that a larger one can be placed on the property. see *refunding mortgage.*

(2) *finance:* to revise a payment timetable and, frequently, to modify interest charges on the obligation.

refinanced loan: a loan that has had an addition to the principal balance. Such increases are usually for property improvements such as an added room. Normally the term and/or payment amount is also affected.

refinancing: synonymous with *refunding.*

reflation: upon recovering from a depression or a recession, the period during which prices are returned to the level they had attained during a period of prosperity by lowering the purchasing power of money.

refund

(1) an amount paid back of credit allowed because of an overcollection or on account of the return of an object sold.

(2) to pay back or allow credit for an amount because of an overcollection

or because of the return of an object sold.

(3) to provide for the payment of a loan through cash or credit secured by a new loan.

(4) to replace one bond issue with another, usually in order to extend the maturity, to reduce the interest rate, or to consolidate several issues. "Advance refunding" is an offer to exchange new securities for outstanding securities prior to their maturity dates. [49]

refundable interest: the unearned portion of interest previously charged that will be returned to the debtor (maker of a note) if the indebtedness is liquidated prior to maturity.

refund check

(1) *general:* a check or other instrument of currency that is repayment of money for any reason. see *rebate.*

(2) *finance:* a statement for a customer's purchase that is returned.

(3) *taxes:* a check from a governmental tax agency.

refunding

(1) *investments:* replacing an old bond issue with a new issue, either before or at maturity of the older one. It is often done to change the interest rate on the debt.

(2) *finance:* the act of returning a portion of money to the giver from an amount already paid out. see *debt.*

refunding bond: see *bond, refunding.*

refunding certificates: U.S. $10 certificates of deposit, which had an interest of 4 percent for an indefinite period of time. They were issued in 1879 and intended to induce people not to redeem them but to keep them in circulation. [27]

refunding mortgage: refinancing a mortgage with monies derived from a new loan.

Reg.

(1) see *register.*

(2) see *registrar.*

regional bank: one of the 12 Federal Reserve District or Regional Banks around the United States.

Regional Check Processing Center (RCPC): a Federal Reserve facility in which check-processing operations are performed. These centers serve a group of banks located within a specified area of a Federal Reserve District. They expedite collection and settlement of checks within the area on an overnight basis. [7]

regional differential: among broad geographical subdivisions, the difference in prevailing wages for equal work.

register

(1) *general:* the making of a permanent record of events.

(2) *computers:* a device capable of storing a specified amount of data (e.g., one word).

(3) *finance:* a written document prepared by a customs official allowing a ship to engage in foreign trade.

(4) *systems:* a unit or machine for temporarily storing information while or until it is used.

register(ed) check: the title given to a check prepared by a teller, using funds recorded and placed aside in a special register, for the convenience of members of the general public who may wish to make a payment by check, but who do not maintain a checking account. The check has two stubs: one is for the purchaser and the other is used by the bank for record keeping. It is actually a money order, prepared in the form of a check, and the bank usually charges a small fee for each registered check sold.

registered as to principal: a term applied to a coupon bond, the name of the owner of which is registered on the bond and on the books of the company. Such bonds are not negotiable and cannot be sold without an assignment. [37]

registered bond: see *bond, registered.*

registered check: see *register(ed) check.*

registered investment company: an investment company which has filed a registration statement with the SEC, fulfilling the requirements of the Investment Company Act of 1940. [30]

registered mail: mail recorded in a U.S. Post Office at the mailing and at each successive point of transmission, to guarantee special care in delivery. Registered mail can be insured to guarantee indemnity in case of loss, fire, or damage. cf. *certified mail.*

registered representative (trader): present name for "customer's man," a full-time employee of a stock exchange member organization who has met the requirements of the exchange with respect to background and knowledge of the securities business. Also known as an account executive or customer's broker.

registered warrant: a warrant registered by the paying officer for future payment on account of present lack of funds and which is to be paid in the order of its registration. In some cases, such warrants are registered when issued; in others, when first presented to the paying officer by the holders. see also *warrant.* [49]

register of wills: in some states (Delaware, for example), the name of the officer before whom wills are offered for probate and who grants letters testamentary and letters of administration. [32]

registrar: an agency, usually a trust company or a bank, charged with the responsibility of preventing the issuance of more stock that has been authorized by a company. The registrar's primary function is to authenticate the issuing of securities. see *overissue.*

registration: before a public offering may be made of new securities by a company, or of outstanding securities by controlling stockholders, the securities must be registered under the Securities Act of 1933. A registration statement is filed with the SEC by the issuer, disclosing pertinent information relating to company's operations, securities, management, and purpose of the public offering. On security offerings involving less than $300,000, the information required is less detailed.

regressive supply: when the price of an item drops, a greater quantity of the item is offered.

regressive taxes: rates in a tax system that decrease as the base amount taxed increases (a rate of 5 percent applied to a base of $500, 4 percent applied to a base of $2000, etc.). A sales tax is a regressive tax. cf. *progressive tax.*

regs: slang, regulations.

regular dating: referring to terms of a sale under which the period for discount and the date on which payment is required are determined from the date of the invoice. cf. *ROG dating.*

regular dividend: the established rate of dividend set by a firm on its stock which is usually paid every three or six months.

regularity of dividends: the pattern of constant payment of dividends by a corporation. Confidence by the public is often related to a firm's regularity of dividends.

regular lending area: the geographical boundaries within which a security property must be located in order for a savings association to invest in a mortgage loan secured by the property, without the loan and the association being subject to special limitations set by regulatory and supervisory agencies. synonymous with "normal lending territory." [59]

regular lot: the unit of trading on a specific stock or commodity exchange; the full or board lot.

regular mortgage: the legal document used in most states to pledge real estate as security for the repayment of a debt. [59]

regular savings account: a savings account to which additions or withdrawals may be made in any amount at any time; earnings typically are credited directly to the account at the appropriate earnings distributions times rather than mailed to the account holder. [59]

regular serial bond: see *bond, regular serial.*

regular warehouse: a government-authorized warehouse for commodity deliveries under futures contracts.

regular-way delivery: unless otherwise specified, securities (other than government) sold on the New York Stock Exchange are to be delivered to the buying broker by the selling broker and payment made to the selling broker by the buying broker on the fourth business day after the transaction. Regular-way delivery for government bonds is the following business day. see *delivery, transfer.* [20]

regular-way sale: any securities transaction that is not a short sale.

regulated commodities: those commodities over which the Commodity Exchange Authority has supervision are known as "regulated." This does not means that the prices are controlled. The CEA simply concerns itself with the orderly operation of the futures market and, at times, investigates abnormal price movements. Under the Commodity Exchange Act, approved June 15, 1936, definite regulations are established providing for the safeguarding of customers' money deposited as margin. Commodities currently supervised by the CEA are wheat, cotton, corn, rice, oats, barley, rye, flaxseed, grain sorghums, bran, shorts, middlings, butter, eggs, potatoes, onions, wool tops, wool futures, lard, tallow, soybean oil, cottonseed meal, cottonseed, peanuts, soybeans, and soybean meal. [2]

regulated investment company: an investment company that can avoid income tax on its ordinary income and capital gains by distributing profits as dividends and by conforming to other statutory rules.

Regulation D: the regulation of the

Federal Reserve Board which defines and prescribes legal reserve requirements of member banks. [36]

Regulation E: for financial institutions, implementing the Electronic Fund Transfer Act, which covers the limits of consumer liability and rules on the issuance of cards; adopted in March 1979. In January 1980, the Federal Reserve Board adopted additional amendments to its Regulation E proposals to become effective in May 1980. The more recent actions deal with documentation of transfers, preauthorized credits, and procedures for processing errors. see *Electronic Fund Transfer Act.* [14]

Regulation F: a regulation issued by the Board of Governors of the Federal Reserve System under authority of Section 11(k) of the Federal Reserve Act, as amended, relating to the conduct of fiduciary business by national banks. The full title of the regulation is Regulation F—Trust Powers of National Banks. [37]

Regulation J: the regulation of the Federal Reserve Board containing the terms and conditions governing collection of checks and other items by Federal Reserve Banks. [36]

Regulation Nine (9): a regulation issued by the Comptroller of the Currency under authority of Section 1(j) of the act of September 28, 1962 (76 Stat. 668, 12 U.S.C. 92a) relating to the conduct of fiduciary business by national banks. The full title of the regulation is Regulation 9—Fiduciary Powers of National Banks and Collective Investment Funds. [37]

Regulation Q: as established by the Federal Reserve Board, a formula it uses to determine the maximum in-terest that can be paid by commercial banks to their customers on time deposits.

Regulation T: the Federal Reserve Board criterion governing the amount of credit that may be advanced by brokers and dealers to customers for the purchase of securities. see *margin.*

Regulation U: the Federal Reserve Board criterion governing the amount of credit that may be advanced by a bank to its customers for the purchase of listed stocks when the requested loan is to be secured by listed stocks.

Regulation Z: this so-called truth-in-lending regulation was adopted, effective July 1, 1969, by the Board of Governors of the Federal Reserve System to implement Title I (Truth in Lending Act) and Title V (General Provisions) of the Consumer Protection Act. Dealing with the information customers of consumer credit should be given, it specifies, among other things, that they must be told the exact dollar amount of the finance charge and the annual percentage rate computed on the unpaid balance of the loan. [33]

rehypothecate: to pledge a second time.

reimbursement: cash or other assets received as a repayment of the cost of work or services performed or of other expenditures, made for or on behalf of another governmental unit, or department, or for an individual, firm, or corporation. [49]

reindustrialization: a term often used for resuscitating industries and modernizing factories, in part by marshaling capital for new businesses.

Amitai Etzioni is credited with having coined the term, which was later popularized by President Carter.

reinstatement: the payment of a claim reduces the principal amount of the policy by the amount of the claim. Provision is usually made for reestablishing the policy to its original amount. Depending on policy conditions, it may be done automatically, either with or without premium consideration, or it may be done at the request of the insured.

reinsurance: the assumption by one insurance company of all or part of a risk undertaken by another.

reinvestment privilege: the automatic investment of dividends from holdings in a mutual fund in additional shares of the fund, at times without a sales charge.

reissues: issues replaced into circulation after a specific lapse of time and usually with an overprint. [27]

REIT: see *real estate investment trust.*

reject: to refuse or decline a risk. [12]

related funds: funds of a similar character which are brought together for administrative and reporting purposes; for example, sinking fund. [49]

relationship banking: a strategy to attract investors, where a customer deals with just one officer who can handle all services—and who becomes a salesperson in the process.

relative income concept: the hypothesis that spending is a function of a family's relative place in the income distribution of similar family units (i.e., people who earn the same tend to spend the same amount of money).

release

(1) *general:* the written statement of a claim's settlement.

(2) *banking:* the discharge of property from a mortgage lien; a written statement that an obligation has been satisfied.

(3) *law:* the cancellation or resolution of a claim against another person. [59]

release clause: a clause in a mortgage permitting payment of a part of the debt in order that a proportionate part of the property can be freed.

release of mortgage: dropping a claim against property established by a mortgage.

release of premiums on funded debt: a credit to income each fiscal period of a proportion of the premium realized at the sale of funded securities, based on the ratio of such fiscal period to the remaining life of the securities. [18]

reloader: slang, an individual who is clever in selling further securities to a person who has just purchased a small amount of the same stock.

Rem.: see *remittance.*

remainder: upon completion of a life estate, the property reverts to the owner or goes to an heir. If the owner does not take the property back, a remainder estate is created by the same instrument. This estate begins upon the termination of the temporary estate (i.e., the life estate) that preceded it.

remainder beneficiary: the beneficiary of a trust who is entitled to the principal outright after the prior life beneficiary or other prior beneficiary has died or his or her interest has been terminated. [32]

remainder estate: an estate in property created simultaneously with other estates by a single grant and consisting of the rights and interest contingent upon and remaining after the termination of the other estates. [58]

remainder interest: a future interest which will become an interest in possession after the termination of a prior interest created at the same time and by the same instrument as the future interest. For example, H leaves his estate in trust with income to be paid to W, and on her death the trust is to terminate and the property is to be delivered to C. C has a remainder interest. [37]

remaindermen: those persons who receive the proceeds from the final distribution of a trust or estate. [25]

remainder notes: unissued and unsigned notes of a bank which either closed down or changed its design, leaving a supply of unwanted notes. With few exceptions, these should be in absolutely perfect condition. [27]

remand: the action of an appellate court in sending a cause back to the lower court that sought the appeal, accompanied by the instructions of the higher court.

remargining: placing added margin against a loan. Remargining is one option when brokers require additional cash or collateral when their securities have lost some of their value.

remise: to give or grant back; to discharge or release. synonymous with "quit claim."

Remitt.: see *remittance.*

remittance: funds forwarded from one person to another as payment for bought items or services.

remittance letter: a transit letter containing a list of checks sent for collection and payment by a sending bank to a receiving bank. The sending bank does not maintain an account with the receiving bank, and hence requests the latter to remit payment for the items sent. The receiving bank pays for the checks by remitting a bank draft to the sending bank. This is to be distinguished from a cash letter of credit, in which case the receiving bank credits the account of the sending bank in its "due to banks" ledger. [10]

remitting: paying, as in remitting a payment; also canceling, as in remitting a debt. [28]

remonetization: the reinstatement of a coin as standard money after it has been demonetized.

remote electronic banking: electronic funds transfer systems through which bank customers conduct banking business at a location other than a bank office, for example, point-of-sale or CBCT. [33]

remoteness of vesting: see *rule against perpetuities.* [37]

remote service unit: the terminology used by savings and loan associations that corresponds to the customer-bank communication terminal (CBCT) that may be employed by banks. see *customer-bank communication terminal.* [36]

remuneration: wages and other financial benefits received from employment.

renege: to go back on a promise; to pull out of an agreement. see also *repudiation.*

renegotiable-rate mortgage (RRM): authorized by the Federal Home Loan Bank Board, requires home buyers to renegotiate the terms of the loan every three to five years—a distinct advantage if interest rates drop but a poor hedge against inflation if they go up. cr. *variable-rate mortgage*; sometimes called the *rollover mortgage*.

renewal: extending the maturity of an existing loan obligation, or other document of relationship. cf. *novation.*

renewal certificate: an insurance policy is sometimes renewed by issuing a certificate rather than writing out a new policy. The certificate refers to the policy but does not enumerate all its items.

renounce

(1) an act by which an individual or trust institution named under a will as executor or trustee declines to accept such appointment.

(2) the act of a surviving husband or wife under the decedent's state law declining to take the provision made for him or her under the other's will and taking his or her share of the estate had the other died without a will.

(3) any action by which the beneficiary of any interest in real or personal property therewith refuses to accept such interest. [37]

rent: income received from leasing real estate.

rentier: a person living on income received from fixed investments.

renunciation: giving up a right or claim, without any reservation, or without naming the person who is to assume the title.

REOP: reopening after a halt in trading.

reorganization: the altering of a firm's capital structure, often resulting from a merger, that affects the rights and responsibilities of the owners. The objectives of a reorganization are to eliminate the cause of failure, settle with creditors, and allow the firm to remain in business. see *National Bankruptcy Act of 1898*; cf. *quasi-reorganization.*

reorganization bond: see *bond, reorganization.*

repatriated earnings: a U.S. Department of Commerce definition in services (not manufacturing, agriculture, or raw materials) where most of the dollar total in the service group is attributable to investment income earned on American-owned assets and enterprises abroad.

repatriation: the liquidation of overseas investments and the return of the proceeds to the country of the investor.

repayments: see *loan repayments.*

replacement-cost standard: the cost of replacing equipment with new equipment for tasks identical to those performed by worn or obsolete equipment; it provides a way of determining a firm's value.

replacement notes: those which do not run in serial sequence and which have been issued to replace a damaged or misprinted note. They usually bear an indicative symbol of some sort, such as the asterisk used in the United States as part of the serial number. [27]

repledge: synonymous with *rehypothecate.*

replevin: a statute remedy for the recovery of the possession of a chattel. The right of possession can be tried only in such action. cf. *seisin (seizin).*

report (or certificate): the report (or certificate) of an independent accountant (or auditor) is a document in which he indicates the nature and scope of the examination (or audit) that he has made and expresses the opinion that he has formed in respect of the financial statements. [77]

reporter: person employed by a credit bureau. Makes reports on credit inquiries. [41]

repossession: the reclaiming or taking back of items that were bought on an installment sales contract on which the buyer has fallen behind in payments.

representations and warrants: the promise or pledge by a seller made prior to or in connection with a sale to induce the buyer to purchase. Also the guarantees the seller gives the guarantees the seller gives to the purchaser of its installment notes, relating to such matters as signatures, validity of obligation, and legal sufficiency of the notes. [55]

representative

(1) a general term designating either an executor or an administrator.

(2) the person who acts or speaks for another under his or her authority. [37]

representative money

(1) *finance:* paper money secured by monetary metal (i.e., gold or silver certificates) deposited in the treasury of a country.

(2) *investments:* funds that are backed in full by a commodity.

reproduction value: the sum of money which would be required to reproduce a building less an allowance for depreciation of that building. [44]

repudiation: the intentional and willful refusal to pay a debt in whole or in part. The term usually refers to the willful act of a government or a subdivision thereof. cf. *nullification of agreement.*

repurchase agreement: see *retail repo.*

repurchases: in closed-end companies, refers to voluntary open market purchases by investment companies of their own securities, usually for retirement. In open-end funds, the term represents stock taken back at approximate liquidating value. [30]

required reserves: liquid assets that state-chartered banks must hold in accordance with regulations of state banking agencies and Federal Reserve officials.

required return: the lowest return of profit needed to justify an investment.

Res.: see *reserve.*

res: in the phrase trust res, the same as trust property. The corpus of the trust. [37]

res adjudicata: Latin; the principle according to which a controversy that has once been decided is deemed to be settled forever; that is, the courts will not hear claims to which the issue adjudicated applies.

rescind: see *right of rescission.*

rescission: making void or annulling (e.g., the rescission of a law or judgment). see *right of rescission.*

research and development

(1) *general:* applying the findings of science and technology to create a firm's products or services.

(2) *investments:* the dollar amount spent on company-sponsored research and development for the year as reported to the SEC. The total excludes any expenditures for research and development performed

under contract for others, such as U.S. government agencies.

reservation price: the highest offered price at which a seller will continue to hold back from selling. The seller will, however, sell at any offer above the reservation price.

reserve

(1) *finance:* a portion of the profits allocated to various reserve accounts to protect any depreciation in asset values. The reserves are taken from profits before any declaration of dividends by the board of directors.

(2) *banking:* assets in the form of cash maintained in a bank's own vault. see *reserve requirements.*

(3) *banking:* refers to funds earmarked for specific purposes. For example, reserves for unearned premiums and reserves for losses in process of adjustment. cf. *legal reserve.*

reserve adjustment magnitude (RAM): measures the impact of changes in reserve requirements by simply subtracting the current period's required reserves from those that would have been required if some base period's reserve requirements were, instead, in effect. The purpose of a RAM is to capture in the adjusted monetary base those total reserve changes that arise from changes in reserve requirements by the Federal Reserve. [79]

reserve bank: any one of the 12 Federal Reserve Banks. see *banker's bank, Federal Reserve Bank.*

reserve city bank: a member bank of the Federal Reserve System located in cities identified by the Federal Reserve Act as amended as reserve cities. These banks are divided for reserve requirements by the act into reserve city banks and country banks.

reserve currency: foreign funds retained by a nation's central bank as a vehicle for settling international financial obligations. The U.S. dollar and the pound sterling are the dominant reserve currencies today.

reserve depository: an authorized bank serving as depository for part of the legal reserves against deposits other banks must hold, under law.

reserve for bad debts: a reserve account to which bad debt losses are charged. Under federal tax laws, savings associations are allowed to build up such reserves by making tax-deductible allocations of earnings according to a specified formula. [59]

reserve for encumbrances: a reserve representing the segregation of a portion of a fund balance to provide for unliquidated encumbrances. see also *reserve.* [49]

reserve for retirement of sinking fund bonds: a reserve that indicates the amount of cash and other resources that should have been accumulated at a certain date in order eventually to redeem bonds outstanding. [49]

reserve for revenue bond contingency: a reserve in an enterprise fund which represents the segregation of a portion of retained earnings equal to current assets that are restricted for meeting various contingencies as may be specified and defined in the revenue bond indenture. [49]

reserve for revenue-bond-debt-service: a reserve in an enterprise fund which represents the segregation of a portion of retained earnings equal to current assets that are restricted to current servicing of revenue bonds in accordance with the terms of a bond indenture. [49]

reserve for uncollected taxes: a reserve representing the segregation of a portion of a fund balance equal to the amount of taxes receivable by a fund. [49]

reserve ratio (requirement): see *reserve requirements.*

reserve requirements: percentage of customer deposits that banks must set aside in the form of reserves. The reserve requirement ratio determines the expansion of deposits that can be supported by each additional dollar of reserves. The Board of Governors can raise or lower reserve requirements for member banks within limits specified by law. Reserve requirements act as lending controls (lowering reserve requirements allows more bank lending; raising requirements, less lending). [1]

reserves: see *reserve.*

reserve split: reduction in the number of shares of a class of capital stock, with no reduction in the total dollar amount of the class, but with an increase in the par or stated value of the shares. This is achieved by substituting one new share for so many outstanding shares. [43]

reserves with Federal Reserve Banks: deposits of reporting member banks with the Federal Reserve Banks. Members banks are required by law to hold an amount equal to a percentage of their deposits as reserve (a deposit) in the Reserve Banks. [40]

residual legacy: personal property of an estate remaining after all claims to the estate have been properly disposed of.

residual securities: stocks that derive most of their value from conversion rights. see *conversion price, conversion ratio.*

residuary bequest: the part of a will that gives instruction for the disposal of any portion of an estate remaining after payments of debts and other obligations.

residuary clause: the provision in the will or trust agreement that disposes of all of the decedent's property remaining after the payment of all taxes, debts, expenses, and charges and the satisfaction of all other gifts in the will or trust agreement. [37]

residuary devise: a gift by will of the real property remaining after all specific devices have been made. [37]

residuary devisee: a recipient by will of any real property after all other claimants to the estate have received payment.

residuary estate: what remains in an estate after all claims to the estate have been properly disposed of.

residuary legatee: a person to whom is given the remainder of a testator's personal property after all other legacies have been satisfied. [37]

residuary trust: a trust composed of the property of the testator that remains in the estate after the payment of all taxes, debts, expenses, charges, and the satisfaction of all other gifts under the will. [37]

residue: (rest, residue, and remainder); that portion of a decedent estate remaining after the payment of all debts, expenses, and charges and the satisfaction of all legacies and devises. [37]

resolution: a formal document expressing the intention of a board of directors of a corporation. [37]

resources: the bank's title for assets owned. The resources of a bank are offset by the liabilities and capital accounts as listed on the daily statement of condition. The major resources of a bank are cash on hand and due from banks; investments held; loans and discounts; and buildings, furniture, fixtures, and equipment. [10]

RESPA: see *Real Estate Settlement Procedures Act.*

respondentia: under conditions of hypothecation, the security offered against a loan (e.g., the goods on a truck).

resting order: an order that can remain open or good until canceled when (a) an order to purchase securities is limited to a price lower than the market, or (b) an order to sell is limited to a price above the market.

restitution: the enforced payment of money, or its equivalent, to its rightful owner as established by law. cf. *replevin.*

restoration premium: the premiun charged to restore a policy or bond to its original value after payment of a loss.

restraining order: a court order in aid of a suit to maintain the status quo until all parties can be heard from. see also *injunction.*

restraint of trade: the effect of any contract, combination, or agreement (e.g., a monopoly) that impedes free competition. see *Robinson-Patman Act of 1936. Sherman Antitrust Act of 1890.*

restraint on alienation of property: a limitation on the right of a person to transfer title to property or property rights. [37]

restricted account: any margin account where the debit balance exceeds the maximum loan value of stocks retained in that account.

restricted assets: money or other resources, the use of which is restricted by legal or contractual requirements. The most common examples of restricted assets in governmental accounting are those arising out of revenue bond indentures in enterprise funds. synonymous with "restricted funds," but this terminology is not preferred. [49]

restricted securities: see *restricted shares.*

restricted shares: common stock shares released under an agreement whereby they do not rank for dividends until some event has taken place—usually the attainment of certain levels of earnings. Any unregistered stock acquired in private transactions as employment bonuses and the like.

restricted stock option: a privilege granted to an employee of a corporation to purchase during a specified period, at the market price at the date of the option, a specified number of shares of its capital stock. synonymous with "qualified stock options." [43]

restricted surplus: that portion of retained earnings which is not regarded as available for dividends. This may be because of legal requirements or loan agreements. [43]

restrictive covenants: written agreements limiting the use of property.

restrictive endorsement: an endorsement that limits the negotiability of an instrument, or contains a definite condition as to payment; it purports to preclude the endorsee from making any further transfer of the instrument. [59]

resulting trust: a trust that arises in law from the acts of the parties, regardless of whether they actually intend to create a trust—as when a person disposes of property under circumstances that raise an inference that he or she does not intend that the person taking or holding the property shall have the beneficial interest in it; to be distinguished from an *express trust* and a *constructive trust*. [32]

retail repo: repurchase agreement; arrangements in which a lender lends the bank cash for a flexible period—usually a week to 89 days, and the bank promises to return the principal to the lender, plus interest. They are more liquid than bank savings certificates because there are usually no penalties for early withdrawal. The interest rate is competitive with money market mutual funds and much higher than the rate on passbook savings. The minimum denomination is typically $1000. However, a retail repo is an investment, not a deposit, and the money is not insured.

retail sales (index): a U.S. Bureau of the Census measure of sales of all types of retail establishments. It is issued around the 10th of the month for the previous month.

retained earnings, appropriated: the net accumulated balance reflecting reservations of retained earnings bring held for a special purpose, and not available for dividends. [3]

retained earnings, restricted: retained earnings restricted, usually against payment of dividends, by cor-

porate indentures and other covenants and/or by orders of regulatory authorities. [3]

retained earnings, unappropriated: formerly earned surplus; accumulated net income less distribution to stockholders and transfers to other capital accounts. It is the connecting link between the income account and the balance sheet and represents the excess of the book value of the depreciated assets (and other debits) over the sum of long-term debt, current and accured liabilities, deferred credits, operating reserves, contributions in aid of construction, accumulated deferred income taxes (when used by the company), and proprietary capital other than retained earnings. [3]

retainer: payment to cover future services and advice, submitted in advance to the individual expected to render service.

retaliatory duty: a differential duty designed to penalize foreign nations for alleged discriminatory commerce activity or to force them into making trade concessions. see *tariff war;* cf. *most favored nation (clause).*

retirement: the paying off of a debt prior to or at maturity.

retirement fund: monies set aside by an organization; the fund builds up value over the year to provide income for employees eligible to retire and receive income from it.

retirement income: a stipulated amount of income starting at a selected retirement age. This is derived by exercising one of the settlement options available against the policy or annuity cash value. see also *Individual Retirement Accounts.*

retirement plan trusts: trusts established to enable the employees on retirement to receive a pension from funds created out of payments made by the employees, their employers, or both. [37]

retiring a bill: paying a bill of exchange on its due date or beforehand, at a discount.

retreat: any drop in the price level of securities or commodities.

retrieval: see *information retrieval.*

retroactive restoration: a provision in a policy or bond whereby, after payment of a loss, the original amount of coverage is automatically restored to take care of prior undiscovered losses as well as future losses.

return: a statement of financial and related information required by government tax agencies (e.g., tax return). see *yield.*

returned check: a check the bank refused to accept and returned unpaid. [55]

return item: a negotiable instrument, principally a check, that has been sent to one bank for collection and payment and is returned unpaid to the sending bank.

return on investment: see *ROI.*

return on net worth: the ratio of an organization's net profit following taxes to its net worth, providing a measure of the rate of return on a shareholder's investment.

return on total assets: the ratio of an organization's net profit following taxes to its total assets, providing a measure of the rate of return on, or productivity of, total assets.

return premium: the amount due the insured if a policy is reduced in amount, canceled, or—if subject to

audit—the audit yields a finding of less exposure(s) than the original estimate(s).

revalidated notes: paper money bearing an official overprint, stamp, or other mark to indicate its renewed status as legal tender, despite the invalidity of the original note. [27]

revaluation (revalorization): the restoration (by lowering the request for, or raising the supply of foreign currencies by restricting imports and promoting exports) of the value of a depreciated national currency that has previously been devalued.

revenue: the grand total of all resources received from the sale of a firm's product or service during a stated period. Not to be confused with general revenue. cf. *gross revenue*; see also *government revenue.*

Revenue Act of 1962: federal legislation; provided investment tax credit of 7 percent on new and used property other than buildings. see also *Revenue Act of 1964, Revenue Act of 1971, Revenue Act of 1978, Revenue Adjustment Act of 1975.*

Revenue Act of 1964: federal legislation; provided for two-stage cut in personal income tax liabilities and corporate-profits tax liabilities in 1964 and 1965. see also *Revenue Act of 1962, Revenue Act of 1971, Revenue Act of 1978, Revenue Adjustment Act of 1975.*

Revenue Act of 1971: federal legislation; accelerated by one year scheduled increases in personal exemptions and standard deduction. Repealed automobile excise tax retroactive to August 15, 1971; on small trucks and buses to September 22, 1971. Reinstated 7 percent investment tax credit and incorporated depreciation range guidelines.

Revenue Act of 1976: much of this act was revised by the Revenue Act of 1978. see *Revenue Act of 1978.*

Revenue Act of 1978: federal legislation affecting the following areas.

(a) *Individual and corporate tax cuts:* lowers tax rates and widens brackets so that raises will not bring people so quickly into higher tax levels; the personal exemption deduction goes to $1000 beginning with 1979; the top corporate rate will be 46 percent in 1979 and after, with new graduated rates for lower income corporations.

(b) *Capital gains:* sellers of capital assets held more than a year can exclude 60 percent of the gain for sales on or after November 1, 1978. Capital gains have no adverse impact on the maximum tax on earned income on or after that date; nor are they subject to the add-on 15 percent preference tax in 1979 and later.

(c) *New alternative tax on capital gains:* the excluded portion of capital gains and adjusted itemized deductions are no longer subject to the regular add-on preference tax to be replaced by a new alternative minimum tax. If a person has heavy capital gains or itemized deductions, he or she must now figure two taxes—regular taxes and an alternative tax, which is at graduated rates (25 percent maximum) above an exclusion base of $20,000; the individual pays whichever is higher.

(d) *Homeowners:* personal residence sales will no longer produce gains subject to the old add-on minimum tax or to the new alternative

minimum tax described above. There is also the right to exclude all gain up to $100,000 if the individual is 55 years of age or over. Both changes apply to home sales after July 26, 1978.

(e) *Tax shelter rules:* these are broader, causing more entities to be subject to the "at risk" rules that keep people from deducting more than their equity investment. Entertainment facilities such as hunting lodges and yachts are no longer to be accepted as business deductions. Partnerships face more stringent reporting requirements, with stiff new penalties if partnership returns are not sent in on time.

(f) *Carry-over basis rules postponed:* a stepped-up basis for inherited property is back. The carry-over basis rules enacted in 1976 did not apply until 1980. Refund possibilities abound for those who have reported gains using carry-over basis for assets inherited from someone who died in 1977 or 1978.

(g) *Other provisions:* there are changes on deductions and credits—for example, there is a new targeted jobs credit, and the investment credit is set permanently at 10 percent. The new law also contains important changes for employee benefits. See *Tax Reform Act of 1976*; see also *Energy Tax Act of 1978.*

Revenue Adjustment Act of 1975: federal legislation; provided extensive redrafting of tax laws. Restricted use of tax shelter investments and made changes in taxing of gifts and estates. Increased taxes on very wealthy. Continued tax cuts passed in 1975.

Revenue and Expenditure Control Act of 1968: federal legislation; levied 10 percent surtax on personal income taxes effective April 1, 1968, and on corporate taxes effective January 1, 1968. Postponed reduction in excise tax rates on automobiles and telephone service.

revenue bond: see *bond; revenue.*

revenue bonds payable: a liability account which represents the face value of revenue bonds issued and outstanding. [49]

revenue from own sources: total revenue consisting of taxes and charges and miscellaneous revenues, and revenue from utility, liquor stores (where applicable), and insurance trust.

revenue receipts: a term used synonymously with "revenue" by some governmental units which account for their revenues on a "cash basis." see also *nonrevenue receipts.* [49]

Revenue Reconciliation Act of 1980: grants a credit of up to $1000 for the windfall profits tax imposed on oil royalty holders.

revenues collected in advance: a liability account which represents revenues collected before they become due. [49]

revenue sharing: the return by a larger unit of government, with greater taxing powers, of a part of its revenue to a smaller component of government. see *highway trust fund, intergovernmental expenditures, shared revenue;* cf. *grants-in-aid.*

revenue stamps: documentary stamps; adhesive stamps issued by the federal or state government, which must be purchased and affixed, in amounts provided by law, to documents or instruments representing original issues, sales, and transfers of stocks and bonds, deeds of conveyances, and certain types of foreign insurance policies. [37]

revenue tariffs: duties placed on imports with the goal of increasing revenues rather than protecting domestic industries.

reverse: the back of a note. see *obverse.* [27]

reverse-annuity mortgage: designed for retirees and other fixed-income homeowners who owe little or nothing on their houses. Typically, it permits them to use some or all of the equity already in the home as supplemental income, while retaining ownership. In effect, they are borrowing against the value of the house on a monthly basis. The longer they borrow, of course, the less equity they retain in the house. The loan becomes due either on a specific date or when a specified event occurs such as the sale of the property or death of the borrower. see also *flexible-payment mortgage, graduated-payment mortgage, pledge-account mortgage, rollover mortgage, variable-rate mortgage.*

reverse stock split: the reduction of the number of outstanding shares. see *stock split down.*

reversing entries: an accounting procedure by which equal and opposite entries are made to an account to adjust the financial records of an association. This normally occurs after closing procedures. [59]

reversion: the interest in an estate remaining in the grantor after a particular interest, less than the whole estate, has been granted by the owner to another person; to be distinguished from remainder. The reversion remains in the grantor; the remainder goes to some grantee. [37]

reversionary interest: a claim or interest that an individual can keep to property or income that has been assigned to someone else. cf. *estate in reversion, remainder.*

reverter: the interest which the grantor retains in property in which he has conveyed an interest less than the whole to another party. If the grantor makes the conveyance subject to a condition which may or may not be broken sometime in the future, he retains a possibility of reverter. [37]

revocable beneficiary: a beneficiary whose rights in the policy are subject to the insured's right of change. see *beneficiary.*

revocable letter of credit: any letter of credit that may be canceled.

revocable living trust: the income from such a trust is paid to the grantor during his or her lifetime, and to the family following the grantor's death. It can be canceled by the person granting or initiating the trust.

revocable trust with consent or approval: a trust which may be terminated by the settlor or by another person but only with the consent or approval of one or more other persons. For example, A creates for his son B a trust which may be revoked by B with C's consent (in this case C may be B's mother). To be distinguished from an irrevocable trust. [37]

revocation: the act of annulling or making inoperative a will or a trust instrument. [37]

revolving account: a line of credit that may be used repeatedly up to a certain specified limit. [78]

revolving credit
(1) see *open-end credit.*
(2) see *optional (revolving) credit.*

revolving fund: money that is renewed as it is used, either by additional appropriations or by income from the programs it finances; thus the fund retains a balance at all times.

revolving letter of credit: a letter of credit issued for a specific amount that is automatically renewed for the same amount over a given period. Usually the unused renewable portion of the credit is cumulative, as long as drafts are drawn before the expiration of the credit.

revolving loan: a loan that is automatically renewed (upon maturity) without additional negotiation.

reward account: a type of checking account that gives no-charge checking to anybody with a minimum (e.g., $2000) savings account.

RF: see *revolving fund.*

RFC: Reconstruction Finance Corporation (defunct).

Rfg.: see *refunding.*

RH: see *red herring.*

rial: monetary unit of Iran, Oman, and Yemen.

rich: an expression applied to security prices when the current market quotation appears to be high (or the income return low) in comparison with either the past price record of the individual security or the current prices of comparable securities. [67]

riel: monetary unit of Cambodia and Kampuchea.

rigged market: the situation that exists when purchases and sales are manipulated to distort a normal supply and demand price.

right

(1) the privilege attaching to a share of stock to subscribe to other securities in a fixed ratio.

(2) that which is reserved by a settlor, as the right of amendment or revocation; opposed to the power granted to the trustee. [37]

right of action: the right to enforce a claim in court.

right of curtesy: see *curtesy.*

right of dower: see *dower.*

right of election: the right of a surviving husband or wife, under the decedent's estate law, to take his or her intestate share in preference to the provision made in the deceased person's will. [37]

right of foreclosure: the right of the association to take over property and close out the mortgagor's interest in it if the mortgagor violates the provisions of the mortgage or note. [59]

right of redemption: the right to free a property from foreclosure by paying off all debts.

right of rescission: the privilege, guaranteed by the Truth in Lending Act to cancel a contract under certain circumstances within three business days, without penalty and with full refund of all deposits submitted. see *voidable contract.*

right of survivorship: the right establishing a surviving joint owner as holder of the title to the property jointly owned. see *tenancy by the entirety*; cf. *tenancy in common.*

right of withdrawal: the privilege of an insured or beneficiary permitting withdrawal of funds placed on deposit. [12]

rights: when a company wants to raise more funds by issuing additional securities, it may give its stockholders the opportunity, ahead of others, to buy the new securities in proportion to the number of shares each owns. The piece of paper evidencing this privilege is called a right. Because the additional stock is usually offered to stockholders below the current market price, rights ordinarily have a market value of their own and are actively traded. In most cases they must be exercised within a relatively short period. Failure to exercise or sell rights may result in actual loss to the holder. see also *cum right.* [20]

ring: synonymous with *pit.*

ringgit: monetary unit of Malaysia.

ringing out (or up): a practice of commodity brokers and commission merchants of settling existing futures contracts by exchanging sale and purchase contracts among themselves before the instruments mature and become deliverable. For example, A has agreed to purchase in the future from C and at the same time to sell the same item to C. In the meantime, B has agreed to sell the item to C. The ring is complete and the transaction can be approved. The ringing-out process permits incomplete ring participants to clear up their responsibilities and commitments.

rising bottoms: a bullish formation that reveals the ability of a futures contract to turn up above each preceding important low point. To be complete, however, there should also be an accompanying series of rising tops. Rising bottoms precede rising tops and are thus the first technical requirment that must be met if a situation is to be termed bullish.

risk: the possibility of loss; specifically chance of nonpayment of a debt. [59]

risk analysis: an examination of the elements or sources of risk in a mortgage loan and of their efforts both separately and in combination. [44]

risk capital

(1) *general:* capitalization that is not secured by a lien or mortgage.

(2) *finance:* long-term loans or capital invested in high-risk business activities.

(3) *investments:* common stock from a new enterprise.

risk category: a class or group into which related elements affecting mortgage risk are placed for purposes of convenience in analysis. [44]

rivets: slang, money.

riyal: monetary unit of Saudi Arabia.

RL: see *round lot.*

Rmdr.: see *remainder.*

Robinson-Patman Act of 1936: federal legislation amending the Clayton Antitrust Act of 1914. Price discrimination practices are more clearly identified. Quantity discounts in excess of the cost savings realized by selling in such quantities are declared illegal, as are false brokerage deals. Promotional allowances must be made to all buyers on a proportionately equal basis, and price discrimination is acceptable if made to meet a proper low price of a competitor so long as the price does not restrict competition.

rock: slang, any quantity of money.

rock bottom: slang, the lowest level

that will be entertained in a business transaction (e.g., the rock-bottom price is the lowest price at which a seller will agree to sell his or her goods).

ROE: see *rate of exchange.*

ROG dating: receipt-of-goods dating. Under this condition of sales, the date for payment and discount period are determined from the date when the buyer obtains shipment, rather than from the invoice date.

ROI: return on investment; the amount earned in direct proportion to the capital invested. see *private rate of return.*

rollback

(1) *computers:* a program returned to a prior point that has been verified.

(2) *government:* an effort to create, as the legal price, a price lower than the existing market price—that is, to return to a price that existed earlier.

roll over: renewing a loan contract to extend the term. It is often used to put off payments of balloons. see *balloon, buy down.*

rollover mortgage: a short-term mortgage where the unpaid balance is refinanced, or "rolled over," every few years; at that time, the interest rate is adjusted up or down, depending on prevailing market conditions. Before the Depression of 1929, such loans were common, but since then the fixed-rate mortgage has generally been standard. During the early 1980s, the rollover mortgage again became popular. see also *flexible-payment mortgage, graduated-payment mortgage, pledged-account mortgage, reverse-annuity mortgage,* *variable-rate mortgage.* synonymous with *renegotiable-rate mortgage.*

rook: slang, to misrepresent, overcharge, or cheat another.

ROR: see *right of rescission.*

Rouble: see *ruble.*

round lot: this is a unit of trading. On the New York Stock Exchange, the unit is generally 100 shares. In some inactive stocks, the trading unit could be 10 shares. An amount of stock less than the established unit of trading is called an odd lot. [29]

round trip trade: any complete transaction, made up of a buy followed by a sale of the same stock, or vice versa. synonymous with "round turn."

round turn: see *round trip trade.*

royalty: compensation for the use of a person's property based on an agreed percentage of the income arising from its use (e.g., to an author on sales of his book, to a manufacturer for use of his machinery in the factory of another person, to a composer or performer, etc.). It is a payment reserved by the grantor of a patent, lease, or similar right, while a residual payment is often made on properties that have not been patented or are not patentable. see also *syndicate.*

RPQ: request for price quotation.

RR

(1) see *rediscount rate.*

(2) see *registered representative (trader).*

(3) see *required reserves.*

RRM: see *renegotiable-rate mortgage.*

RS: see *redeemable stock.*

RSU: see *remote service unit.*

Rt.: see *right.*

RTA: see *reciprocal trade agreement.*

rubber check: slang, a check that bounces, that is returned for lack of sufficient bank funds.

ruble: monetary unit of Union of Soviet Socialist Republics.

rubricated account: any earmarked account.

rule against accumulations: the limitation imposed by common law or by statute upon the accumulation of income in the hands of a trustee. [37]

rule against perpetuities: a rule of common law that makes void any estate or interest in property so limited that it will not take effect or vest within a period measured by a life or lives in being at the time of the creation of the estate plus 21 years and the period of gestation. In many states the rule has been modified by statute. Sometimes it is known as the rule against remoteness of vesting. [37]

rule in Shelly's case: a rule of law that nullifies a remainder interest in the heirs of the grantee. For example, A conveys Blackacre to B for life, the remainder to heirs of B. Under this rule, B's heirs received nothing and B took a fee-simple absolute interest in Blackacre. This rule has been abolished by statute or judicial decision in many states. [37]

rules of the class: the terms and conditions, established by the association's board of directors and included in the savings account contract, applicable to each savings account classification, such as time and amount of deposit, rate of interest, penalty provisions, and the account designation. [59]

run

(1) *general:* an action of a large number of people (e.g., a run on a bank occurs when a great many customers make massive withdrawals of funds).

(2) *computers:* one routine automatically connected to another form on an operating unit, during which manual interruptions are not normally required.

(3) *computers:* a single, continuous performance of a computer program or routine.

runway: the condition in which part of a system undergoes a sudden or undesirable and often destructive increase in activity.

runaway inflation: synonymous with *galloping inflation.*

runner: an employee of the bank who delivers items to other banks in the same community, and who in turn may receive and bring back to his bank the items that the other banks may wish delivered there. The runner's duties may involve all types of messenger service for his bank. [10]

running costs: direct or indirect costs incurred when keeping an operation and/or machinery functioning. These costs include wages, rent, and taxes.

running days: consecutive days including Sundays, as distinguished from working days, which excludes Sundays.

running in the shorts: purchasing different securities where there is a substantial short position for the purpose of advancing the price so that those short will purchase their securities back, or cover their short selling contracts, and hence lead to an additional climb in price. see *short covering, short sale.*

runoff: the closing prices printed by the stock exchange ticker following the closing of the daily market. During a heavy trading session, the runoff may be hours late.

run on a bank: see *run.*

rupee: monetary unit of India, Maldives, Mauritius, Nepal, Pakistan, Seychelles, and Sri Lanka.

rupiah: monetary unit of Indonesia.

SA: see *savings account.*

saddle blankets: nickname for the large-size U.S. paper money before 1929. [27]

saddled: a situation describing an individual holding an undesirable security purchased at a price above the prevailing market price.

safe deposit box: a metal container that remains under lock and key in a section of a bank vault when the person who rents it is not handling or inspecting the jewelry, stock certificates, or other valuables it contains. The boxes are kept in small compartments, each with two separate locks. A box is rented with its compartment to a customer, not necessarily a depositor, for an annual fee.

safe deposit company: any financial warehouse, retaining securities, wills, and other documents.

safe deposit vault: a section of the bank's vault set aside for the use of customers who may rent space in the vault for the safekeeping of valuable securities, papers, and small objects of value. see also *safe deposit box.* [10]

safekeeping: a service rendered by banks, especially banks in large metropolitan areas, where securities and valuables of all types and descriptions are protected in the vaults of the bank for the customer for a service fee. (These valuables may include se-curities, precious gems, valuable paintings, collection pieces of great value, silver and gold services, etc.) Many of these items are too large to be placed in safe deposit boxes. In the case of securities, some customers "buy" security counselor services of large banks, requesting the banks to handle their securities to the best advantage. The banks will buy and sell, collect dividends and interest, and credit the depositor's account with this income. Many clients of this type are foreign citizens, and wealthy Americans who spend a good portion of their time abroad, traveling or living in foreign countries. Since they cannot have constant access to safe deposit boxes, they appoint banks to act as their fiscal agents to protect and control their holdings for them in their absence. [10]

safekeeping account: an agency account concerning which the duties of the agent are to receipt for, safekeep, and deliver the property in the account on demand of the principal or on his or her order; to be distinguished from a custody account and a managing agency account. [32]

safekeeping (deposit for): the receipt by a bank of custody of specific property to be returned, as contrasted with an ordinary deposit to be repaid in money and with a safe deposit box, rented to a customer, to which the renter rather than the bank has access. [50]

safety factor: the ratio of the interest on a funded debt to the net income following the payment of the interest.

safety of principal: the major characteristic of a sound investment.

sag: a minimal drop or price weakness of shares, usually resulting from a weak demand for the securities.

sale

(1) *banking:* the transfer of title for a sum of money and conditions, for the change of ownership of property.

(2) *finance:* the transfer of title to an item or items or the agreement to perform a service in return for cash or the expectation of cash payment.

sale and servicing agreement: in secondary-market transactions, a contract under which the seller-servicer agrees to supply, and the buyer to purchase, loans from time to time; the contract sets forth the conditions for the transactions, and the rights and responsibilities of both parties. [59]

sales

(1) *general:* the sum of the income received when goods and services are sold.

(2) *finance:* revenue received from the sale of goods.

sales agreement: a written document by which a seller agrees to convey property to a buyer for a stipulated price under specified conditions. [44]

sales charge: the amount charged in connection with the issuance of shares of a mutual fund and their distribution to the public. It is added to the net asset value per share in determining the offering price. [23]

sales finance company: a financial organization that purchases installment contracts from dealers and finances dealers' inventories.

sales literature: literature used by an issuer, underwriter, or dealer to inform prospective purchasers concerning an investment company the shares of which are offered for sale. Such literature is governed by the SEC's Statement of Policy and various regulations issued by the state. [23]

sales tax: a tax placed by a state or municipality on items at the time of their purchase. It may be a tax on the sale of an item every time it changes hands, or only upon its transfer of ownership at one specific time. The sales of manufacturers are taxed when the items are considered to be completed goods; the sales of wholesalers are taxed when their goods are sold to retailers; and retail sales are taxed when the goods are purchased by consumers. see *tax.*

Sallie Mae: see *Student Loan Marketing Association.*

salt-down stock: buying securities and keeping them over a long time period, disregarding paper profits that evolve.

sampling

(1) *general:* choosing a representative portion of a population to characterize a larger population.

(2) *computers:* a random method of checking and controlling the use of data by obtaining the values of a function for regularly or irregularly spaced, discrete values.

(3) *computers:* a method of communication control in which messages are selected by a com-

puter that chooses only those for which processing is needed.

sanction

(1) *finance:* a coercive measure, usually undertaken by several nations, to force another country to cease violation of a treaty or international agreement. see *embargo.*

(2) *law:* a penalty for the breach of a rule of law.

sandwich lease: a leasehold in which the interest of the sublessor is inserted between the fee owner and the user of the property. The owner A of a fee simple leases to B, who in turn leases to C. The interest of A may be called the leased fee; that of B the sandwich lease, and that of C the leasehold. [62]

San Francisco Stock Exchange: see *Pacific Coast Stock Exchange.*

SARs: see *stock-appreciation rights.*

satellite office: a convenience facility of fewer than four teller stations where any business of a federal association can be transacted; such an office must be located in retail stores, or, in the case of a fully automated satellite, in office buildings, shopping centers, or transportation centers. [59]

satellite processor: a processor that is under the control of another processing piece of equipment and performs subsidiary operations. The function of this unit is to process programs which are subsidiary to the main work of the system.

satisfaction of judgment: the legal procedure followed when a debtor pays the amount of judgment, together with interest and costs. "Satisfaction of judgment" is then entered on records of the court of record. [41]

satisfaction of mortgage: a document issued by mortgagee when a mortgage is paid off. [62]

saturation point: the time when the supply of stocks for purchase starts to exceed the public demand. see *distribution, undigested securities.*

Saturday night special: a direct tender offer, made without any forewarning, that expires in one week. Such offerings were made possible by the Williams Act of 1968, which permits tender offers to run as short as seven days and does not require the bidder to tip his hand in advance with any notification.

Sav.: see *saving.*

saving: the amount of existing income that is not spent on consumption.

savings account: money that is deposited in a bank, usually in small amounts periodically over a long period, and not subject to withdrawal by check. Savings accounts usually bear interest and some banks levy a service charge for excess withdrawal activity on an account.

savings account contract: the contractual relationship encompassing all the terms and conditions to which the customer and the association are subject when the customer opens a savings account. [59]

savings account ledger card: the association's complete record of account transactions on a particular savings account. [59]

savings account loan: a loan secured by the pledging of savings funds on deposit with the association. [59]

savings and investment theory: developed by John Maynard Keynes and D. H. Robertson: business cycles occur because people save either more or less than the amounts invested in new capital. cf. *veil of money theory.*

savings and loan association: a mutual, cooperative quasi-public financial institution, owned by its members (depositors), and chartered by a state or by the federal government. The association receives the savings of its members and uses these funds to finance long-term amortized mortgage loans to its members and to the general public. Such an association may also be organized as a corporation owned by stockholders. see *Cincotta-Conklin Bill of 1976.*

savings bank: a banking association whose purpose is to promote thrift and savings habits in a community. It may be either a stock organization (a bank with a capital stock structure) or a "mutual savings bank." Until passage of the Cincotta-Conklin Bill in New York State or other similar bills, a savings bank had no power to perform commercial functions, but specialized in interest-bearing savings accounts, investing these savings in long-term bonds, mortgage loans, and other investment opportunities for the benefit of all depositors. see *NOW accounts.*

Savings Bank Life Insurance (SBLI): insurance written in several states through savings banks. Characterized by having no agents selling the insurance. It is bought over the counter and is available in statutory limited amounts in the form of whole life, limited-payment life, endowment, term, and annuities on a participating basis.

Savings Bond: see *Bond, Savings (U.S.).*

savings certificate: evidence of the ownership of a savings account typically representing a fixed amount of funds deposited for a fixed term. [59]

savings deposits: a deposit of funds to the credit of one or more individuals or to a nonprofit institution which may be subject to 30 days written notice prior to withdrawal. In practice, commercial banks have not required this notice. [69]

savings liability: the aggregate amount of savings accounts of an association's members, including earnings credited to such accounts, less redemptions or withdrawals. [59]

savings rate: a ratio showing the portion of income saved to income earned.

sawbuck: slang, a $10 bill.

SBA: see *Small Business Administration.*

SBLI: see *Savings Bank Life Insurance.*

SC
(1) see *silver certificates.*
(2) see *stock certificate.*

scale order: an order to buy (or sell) a security specifying the total amount to be bought (or sold) and the amount to be bought (or sold) at specified price variations. [20]

scaling: trading in securities by placing orders for purchase or sale at intervals of price instead of giving the order in full at the market or at a stated price.

scalper: a speculator who constantly sells his or her shares at fractional profit or at one or two points profit per share.

Scanlon plan: designed by Joseph Scanlon of MIT; a management incentive scheme created to achieve increased productivity with improved efficiency and the chance for accrued savings to be distributed among the employees.

scanner: see *optical scanner.*

scavenger sale: property taken over by the state as the result of nonpayment of taxes (e.g., failure of a state resident to pay state income taxes). After full notice, the state may hold a public sale of the property to recover monies entitled to it, and the excess of the sale beyond the taxes and penalties due the state are returned to the resident.

SCC: see *Stock Clearing Corporation.*

schedule: a systematic plan for future operations over a given period.

schedule bond: see *bond, schedule.*

scheduled items: an FSLIC regulatory category in which every insured association is required to include the total amount of its slow loans, real estate owned as a result of foreclosure, and real estate sold on contract or financed at a high loan-to-value ratio. [59]

scheduled payment: a payment promised at a particular time, or one of several payments scheduled as to due date. [28]

schedule of distribution: a form of accounting which sets forth in detail the estate property contained in each share to be distributed. [37]

schilling: monetary unit of Austria.

school savings: a plan designed to promote the lesson of thrift in children in schools. A bank representative will call at the school one day a week, and assist teachers in accepting deposits in any small amount for the account of the pupil. [10]

scienter: awareness by a defrauding party of the falsity of a representation.

scientific management: a term popularized in the work of Frederick W. Taylor, this theory proposes approaches for increased efficiency, cost reductions, and maximum utilization of human and material resources.

scientific tariff: a duty to cover foreign and domestic manufacturing costs.

scoop

(1) *general:* to beat out a rival.

(2) *finance:* a considerable profit following a transaction that is likely to involve advance notice over, or exclusion of competitors.

scratch: slang, available money.

scrip: any temporary document that entitles the holder or bearer to receive stock or a fractional share of stock in a corporation, cash, or some other article of value upon demand, or at some specified future date. Some industries issue scrip to their employees as a supplement to salary for use in company-owned stores.

scrip dividend: a type of dividend issued by a corporation to its stockholders, entitling the holder or bearer to receive cash, stock, or a fractional share of stock, or one or more units of the product manufactured, upon presentation or at a specified future date.

scrivener's error: a typographical error introduced when reducing an oral agreement to writing or when an agreement is typed or printed in final form.

SCT: see *service counter terminals.*

SD

(1) see *secondary distribution.*

(2) see *sight draft*.

(3) see *stock dividend*.

SD. CO.: see *safe deposit company*.

SDMJ: September, December, March, June (quarterly interest payments or dividends).

SDR: see *special drawing rights*.

SE: see *stock exchanges*.

sealing: concealed bids that are simultaneously revealed; the most attractive one is accepted on the spot, without further bidding.

search

(1) *general:* the process of recruiting executive talent for a specific organization.

(2) *banking:* in the consideration of property transfer, the examination of records for evidence of encumbrances (unpaid taxes, mortgages, etc.) against the property. synonymous with *title search*.

(3) *computers:* to locate a desired word or record in a set of words or records. cf. *dump*.

seasoned issues: securities from well-established corporations that have been favorably known to the investment population over time, including good and bad periods.

seasoned loan: a loan that has been on the association's books long enough to demonstrate that the borrower's credit is sound. [59]

seasoned mortgage: periodic payments of a mortgage that are made over a long span based on the borrower's payment structure.

seasoned security: a security possessing a fine performance record in the paying of dividends or interest; one that has been listed for a considerable period of time and sells at a relatively stable price.

seat: a traditional figure of speech designating a membership on an exchange. Price and admission requirements vary. [20]

SEC: the Securities and Exchange Commission, established by Congress to protect investors. The SEC administers the Securities Act of 1933, the Securities Exchange Act of 1934, the Trust Indenture Act, the Investment Company Act, and the Public Utility Holding Company Act. The principal provisions of these acts are: (a) the Securities and Exchange Commission, created in 1934, administers the federal laws applying to securities; (b) corporations issuing securities and investment bankers selling them must make "full disclosure" of the character of the securities (i.e., they must state all relevant facts in registration statements to the SEC and in prospectuses submitted to the public). see also *waiting period;* (c) any omission of fact or insertion of false information makes all persons (bankers, lawyers, accountants, etc.) whose names appear on the prospectus and the registration statement liable to the purchasers of the securities for any losses suffered; (d) the organization of people (brokers, traders, etc.) to manipulate the price of securities is forbidden. see *pool;* (e) dealings by corporation officers in securities of their own corporations are restricted; (f) the Board of Governors of the Federal Reserve System is given power to fix margin requirements on loans secured by bonds and stocks. see also *National Association of Securities Dealers, unlisted trading privileges*.

secondaries: slang, for smaller companies to which investors are attracted. They usually involve considerable risk but offer the opportunity for possible large gains.

secondary beneficiary: a beneficiary whose interest in a trust is postponed or is subordinate to that of the primary beneficiary. [37]

secondary boycott: see *boycott.*

secondary distribution: the redistribution of a block of stock sometime after it has been sold by the issuing company. The sale is handled off the exchange by a securities firm or group of firms, and the shares are usually offered at a fixed price that is related to the current market price.

secondary financing: see *junior mortgage.*

secondary market: the market, referred to as the aftermarket, that exists for a new stock issue following distribution to the public. see *primary market.*

secondary mortgage market: an informally constituted market that includes all activity in buying, selling and trading mortgages among originators and purchasers of whole loans and interests in blocks of loans. [59]

secondary offering: the selling by a large stockholder of a large block of shares. Such a sale is frequently made on an exchange, to minimize the impact on the general market. synonymous with *secondary distribution.*

secondary rental: a lease determined in part by the landlord's costs. As the landlord's costs (taxes, fuel, etc.) increase, proportionate rent increases are demanded.

secondary reserves: assets other than primary reserves retained by banks and capable of being rapidly converted into cash. Government bonds are a prime example of these assets.

second-generation computer: a computer utilizing solid-state components.

second lien: a lien that ranks following the first lien and is to be fulfilled next.

second mortgage: a mortgage on real property that already possesses a first mortgage.

second-mortgage bond: see *bond, second-mortgage.*

second partner: an active partner in an organization whose capacity as a partner is not known to the public. cf. *silent partner.*

second preferred stocks: a series of preferred security issues that rank behind first preferred stock but in front of any third preferred issue or common stock in dividends or assets.

secretary: an officer of a trust company whose signature is necessary on all official documents. In large trust companies where a secretary's duties are too numerous, the board of directors may appoint assistant secretaries to perform specific duties in connection with his official functions. [10]

Section 403(b) plan: Section 403(b) of the Internal Revenue Code permits employees of certain charitable organizations and public school systems to establish tax-sheltered retirement programs which may be funded with annuities and mutual fund shares. [23]

secular inflation: the most serious economic problem of the late 1960s and the 1970s. In contrast to cyclical inflation, which moves in and out of the economic system roughly every two years, secular inflation is primarily a long-term social phenomenon. see *cyclical inflation*.

secular stagnation: a low level of economic movement measured over an extended time period.

secured: guaranteed as to payment by the pledge of something valuable. [28]

secured bond: see *bond, secured*.

secured creditor: a creditor whose obligation is made safe or backed by a pledge or collateral. see *collateral*.

secured debt: any debt for which some form of acceptable collateral has been pledged see *hypothecation*.

secured deposits: bank deposits of state or local government funds which, under the laws of certain jurisdictions, are secured by the pledge of acceptable securities or by a surety contract (known as a depository bond) for the direct protection of these funds. [67]

secured loan: a loan that is made safe, or backed, by marketable securities or other marketable values.

secured note: a note containing a provision that, upon default, certain pledged property may be claimed by the lender as payment of a debt. [78]

securities: any documents that identify legal ownership of a physical commodity or legal claims to another's wealth.

Securities Act of 1933: federal legislation dealing with full disclosure of material facts and antifraud. see also *SEC*.

Securities and Exchange Commission: see *SEC*.

securities company: an organization that relies for its income on other firms' securities, which it retains for investment. It may also issue stocks and bonds of its own. synonymous with *investment company*; see *holding company*.

securities depository: a physical location or organization where securities certificates are deposited and transferred by bookkeeping entry. [25]

Securities Exchange Act: see *SEC*.

Securities Investor Protection Corporation: see *SIPC*.

securities trading: anyone who sells or buys securities through recognized channels is said to engage in securities trading. The term also applies to the operations of brokers in the various exchanges.

security
(1) *general:* property pledged as collateral.
(2) *investments:* stocks and bonds placed by a debtor with a creditor, with authority to sell for the creditor's account if the debt is not paid.
(3) *law:* any evidence of debt or right to a property.
(4) *law:* an individual who agrees to make good the failure of another to pay.

security capital: low-risk capital (e.g., government bonds, mortgages).

security element: the property that will secure a loan. [59]

security exchange: see *stock exchanges*.

security interest: an interest that a lender has in the borrower's property to assure repayment. [78]

security loan: any loan secured by the pledge of securities collateral.

security price level: the existing price level for a specified stock, any group of stocks, or the general securities market at a given period.

security ratings: ratings placed on securities according to the degree of investment risk incurred by the purchaser. [3]

security record: this term is applied to any accounting record relative to the custody of securities, whether it be for safekeeping, collateral, or trust ownership. [10]

segmentation: a bank marketing strategy involving figuring out who the richest and biggest customers are, showering them with favors, freebies, and other inducements to open or increase their accounts and, if necessary, as it often is, raising rates and fees among the less affluent to pay for it all.

segregated account: a term used to describe funds segregated to meet obligations which the bank has assumed for a customer. Usually it applies to cash set aside to meet drafts drawn under a letter of credit issued by the bank. It may also apply to funds set aside to honor checks certified by the bank. It is a liability account. [10]

segregation: separating from an operating or holding firm one or more of its subsidiaries or operating divisions, effected by distributing stock of the subsidiary to the parent company's shareholders.

seignorage: a government's profit from issuing coins at a face value higher than the metal's intrinsic worth. It is the difference between the bullion price and the face value of the coins made from it. see *brassage.*

seisin (seizin): taking legal possession of real estate. The rightful owner seizes the property. cf. *disseisin, replevin.*

seizure: the act of taking possession of property, see *condemnation.*

selection check: a check, usually automatic, to verify that the correct register or other device has been selected in the performance of an instruction. [21]

self-check: a check deposited in a bank for credit, or one presented for payment in the banking institution on which it was drawn.

self-employed: the gainfully occupied part of the work force whose members work for themselves, as opposed to salaried or commissioned workers who are the employees of others.

self-insurance: a system whereby a firm or individual, by setting aside an amount of monies, provides for the occurrence of any losses that could ordinarily be covered under an insurance program. The monies that would normally be used for premium payments are added to this special fund for payment of losses incurred.

self-liquidating: describing an asset that can be converted into cash or subject to the total recovery of invested money, over a period of time.

self-liquidating loan: a short-term commercial loan, usually supported by a lien on a given product or on the sale of the product or commodities.

self-reducing clause: a life insurance statement that has the effect of lowering an obligation or mortgage: the amount of insurance automatically drops during the term of the policy, matching the lowering amount of the debt involved.

self-supporting (self-liquidating) debt: debt obligations whose principal and interest are payable primarily or solely from the earnings of the municipal utility or enterprise for the construction or improvement of which they were originally issued. [49]

sell and leaseback agreement: an arrangement whereby a business owning and occupying improved real estate sells it to an investor, (e.g., an insurance company) and takes back a long-term lease on the property and usually an option to buy it, at the termination of the lease. cf. *repurchase agreement.*

seller's call: the buying of a commodity of a given quality identified in a contract that freezes the future price.

sellers' market: a descriptive term: demand is greater than supply in this type of market, resulting in seller's setting the prices and terms of sale. It is a market characterized by rising or high prices.

seller's option: a special transaction on an exchange: the seller holding the option can deliver the stocks or bonds at any time within a specified period, ranging from not less than 6 business days to not more than 60 days.

seller's seven sale: an agreed-upon delay of several or more days for the delivery of a security. see *settlement day.*

seller's surplus: the difference between the price a seller acutally receives and the lowest price that he or she would accept.

selling below the market: an expression indicating that a security is currently quoted for less than similar securities of comparable quality and acceptance. [67]

selling charge: see *load.*

selling climax: the unsystematic dumping of stocks; a burst of panic selling indicating the termination of a declining period, as in a bear market. The rebounding rally after this climax is often short-lived, but strong. see *blowing off.*

selling group: syndicated dealers of an underwriting company that operates in the public sale of an issue of securities.

selling hedge: synonymous with *"short hedge."* see *short hedges.*

selling off: descending prices of an issue, group of stocks, or the general market. When there are fewer offers to purchase stock at the time that more stocks are being offered for sale, prices usually drop and the market is said to be selling off.

selling price: the cash price that a customer must pay for purchased items.

selling short: a technique employed with the expectation of a drop in the market with the expectation of a drop in the market price of the security. A temporarily borrowed stock is sold to effect delivery. If the price drops, the trader can purchase the security for less than he or she sold it, pay the borrowing cost, and clear a profit. see *bear position, loaned flat.*

sell out

(1) *general:* to betray a person, organization, or cause, usually for profit or special treatment.

(2) *investments:* to close out a

customer's account by selling held securities or commodities.

send money: funds set aside to commence an activity.

senior bond: see *bond, senior.*

senior refunding: an exchange by holders of securities maturing within 5 to 12 years for issues with original maturities of 15 years or longer. [17]

senior securities: preferred securities and bonds that receive consideration before common stock when a firm is at the point of being dissolved or actually fails. synonymous with "senior obligations." see also *junior securities.*

sensitive market: characterized by fluctuations determined by the announcement of favorable or unfavorable news.

SEP: see *Simplified Employee Pension.*

separate property: property that is owned individually and is not jointly held.

sequential computer: a computer in which events occur in time sequence, with little or no simultaneity or overlap of events. see also *serial computer.*

sequestered account: an account that has been impounded under due process of law. Since disbursement of such an account is subject to court order, the account is usually set up in a separate control. see *frozen account, receiver.*

sequestration: legal appropriation of property by a third party until there is a settlement of a stated dispute.

Ser.: see *serial.*

serial
(1) *general:* one after the other.
(2) *computers:* the sequential or

consecutive occurrence of two or more related activities in a single device or channel.

serial annuity bond: see *bond, serial annuity.*

serial bond: see *bond, serial.*

serial bonds payable: a liability account that records the face value of general obligation serial bonds issued and outstanding. [49]

serial computer: a computer having a single unit that performs arithmetic and logic functions.

serial issue: a bond issue with a staggered maturity, usually due in equal annual amounts over a period of successive years. [67]

serial letters and numbers: the system of numbering notes assists the checking of quantities put into circulation as well as guarding against counterfeits and forgeries. Misprints whereby different serial numbers appear on the same note are often collected as curiosity items, as are particular combinations of serial numbers. [27]

series: options of the same class having the same exercise price and expiration time. [5]

service charge: a payment by a financial institution against an individual or organization for services rendered or are about to be rendered.

service corporation: a corporation, owned by one or more savings associations, that performs services and engages in certain activities for its owners, such as originating, holding, selling, and servicing mortgages; performing appraisal, brokerage, clerical, escrow, research, and other services; and acquiring, developing, or renovating, and holding real estate for investment purposes. [59]

service counter terminals (SCT): a device for handling information, located in retail stores and similar places, through which individuals can obtain access to funds and possible credit at their disposal, for purposes of making deposits and withdrawals, and for making third party payments. see *electronic funds transfer system(s), Hinky Dinky.*

service credit: a credit arrangement allowing bills to be paid at month-end for services provided during the month. Utility companies and medical professionals extend this type of credit. [78]

service life: the anticipated time of usefulness of an asset.

Servicemen's Readjustment Act of 1944: (The GI Bill of Rights) established a program of loan guarantees under Veterans Administration auspices to encourage private lending on generous terms to veterans of the armed forces. [51]

service value: the difference between the ledger value of a unit of property and its salvage value. [18]

servicing
(1) *finance:* in mortgage financing, the performance by the mortgagee or his agent of the many services which must be taken care of while the mortgage is held by the institution, such as title search, billing, collection of interest and principal payments, reinspections and reappraisals of the real property, readjustment of the terms of the mortgage contract when necessary, and tax followup work.

servicing contract: in secondary-market transactions, a document that details servicing requirements and legally binds the servicing institution to perform them. Such a contract refers to the seller of mortgage participations, binding it to continue accepting loan payments. see also *loan servicing.* [59]

setback: a reversal or partial loss in an activity.

settlement
(1) The winding up and distribution of an estate by an executor or an administrator; to be distinguished from the administration of an estate by a trustee or a guardian.
(2) A property arrangement, as between a husband and wife or a parent and child, frequently involving a trust. [37]

settlement check: a memorandum issued by the manager of a clearinghouse association to settle the results of a clearinghouse exchange between the member banks. This memorandum is sent to the local Federal Reserve Bank, which adjusts the accounts of the clearinghouse banks to settle the debits and credits, or "wins and losses" in the exchange each day. The term may also be used with reference to checks and drafts received in payment of items sent for collection under remittance letters. [10]

settlement clerk: a senior clerk in the proof department of a bank who is responsible for assembling totals obtained in the proof department. These totals, showing all credits and charges to all departments, are assembled and written on a "settlement sheet," or recap sheet of the proof department. It is from this source that the proof department shows a settlement of the day's work. The settlement sheet then becomes a subsidiary record for the general ledger, and the general ledger bookkeeper may use all final totals shown on this record. [10]

settlement day: the deadline by which a purchaser of stock must pay for what has been bought and the seller must deliver the certificates for the securities that have been sold. The settlement day is usually the fifth business day following the execution of an order. cf. *shave.*

settlement options: provisions in a life policy or annuity contract for alternative methods of settlement in place of lump-sum payments.

settlement price: the daily price at which the clearinghouse clears all the day's trades. It may also refer to the price established by the exchange to settle contracts unliquidated because of acts of God, such as floods or other causes. [2]

settlements bank: see *Bank for International Settlements.*

settlor: one who finalizes a property settlement (e.g., creator of a trust).

severalty: property owned by one person only. see *singular property title, sole owner.*

S/F: see *statute of frauds.*

SF: see *sinking fund.*

SH.: see *stockholder.*

shading: giving a small reduction in a price or terms of a sale.

shake out

(1) *finance:* a trend or shift in a industry that forces weaker members toward bankruptcy.

(2) *investments:* any shift in activity that forces speculators to sell their shares.

share: a unit of stock naming the holder and indicating ownership in a corporation.

share account: see *savings account.*

Sharebuilder Investment Plan (SIP): developed by Merrill Lynch and Chase Manhattan Bank, a plan whereby a depositor's account is debited automatically on a prescribed date and the money transferred to a special sharebuilder account at Chase. The broker buys stock for the depositor the next morning. Chase and Merrill Lynch split the commissions on sales of the plan. There is a three-way split if a correspondent institution makes the sale. Customers benefit from rates discounted from the standard Merrill Lynch schedule, and they can buy stock with weekly or monthly installments too small to cover investments made through normal channels.

share capital: the total direct ownership in a corporation. When all stock to be issued by a firm is ordered and paid for, the funds collected constitute the share capital of the corporation.

shared-appreciation mortgage: a home-financing technique whereby the borrower receives a mortgage rate that is one-third lower than the prevailing level. But the borrower must agree to give the lender one-third of the profits from the eventual sale of the house. A shared-appreciation mortgage has payments that are based on a long amortization schedule, but the loan becomes due and payable no later than at the end of 10 years. It has an interest rate below that on a conventional mortgage. It has a contingent interest feature, whereby at either the sale or transfer of the property or the refinancing or maturity of the loan, the borrower must pay the lender a share of the appreciation of the property securing the loan.

share draft: an order by a credit union member to pay a third party against funds on deposit with the credit union and cleared through a commercial bank.

shared revenue: payments to the states and localities of a portion of the proceeds from the sale of certain federal property, products, and services, and payments to the territories of certain federal tax collections derived within their boundaries or from transactions affecting them. synonymous with *intergovernmental revenue,* cf. *revenue sharing.*

shareholder: the possessor of shares or stocks in an organization (company, corporation, etc.).

share loan: a simple interest loan secured by funds on deposits at a credit union or a savings and loan institution. One purpose of a share loan is to preserve dividends due on deposits by not withdrawing the funds until the date on which the dividend payment is due.

share register: the records of a corporation indicating ownership of shares of that firm by the public. A share register is required by law for every corporation.

shares outstanding: the shares issued by a corporation, excluding treasury stock.

shark repellent: a state statute that demands strict notification and disclosure of tender offers for compa-

nies incorporated or transacting business within its boundaries.

shave
(1) *finance:* a charge that is higher than the accepted rate, made for the handling of a note or other instrument of low quality or when the seller will take a smaller amount for any other reason.
(2) *investments:* the additional charge (premium) made for the right to extend the delivery time on a security.

shekel: the official currency of Israel, resurrected from Biblical times, that replaced the pound in 1980. On October 1, 1980, one shekel equaled 10 pounds.

shelf distribution: a method of selling securities. Stocks, owned by stockholders, are placed on the shelf for sale at a later time. To be contrasted with the usual public offering of stocks to when all are sold at one time at a fixed price through underwriters.

shell firm: an organization that is incorporated but does not function or produce any goods or services.

shelter trust: synonymous "spendthrift trust." see *spendthrift provision.*

sheriff's deed: an instrument drawn under order or court to convey title to property sold to satisfy a judgment at law. [62]

Sherman Antitrust Act of 1890: federal legislation aimed at the prevention of business monopoly. Some courts, however, applied the sanctions of the law against strikes, and unions where fined triple damages for acts that were considered to be in restraint of trade. New legislation (see *Clayton Antitrust Act of 1914*) was required to protect the unions against further such misinterpretations since in the absence of legislative action, antiunion rulings would continue to be sustained under the principle of res adjudicata. see *res adjudicata.*

shift differential: additional pay for working more than one shift.

shifting loan: the act of securing funds from other lending banks for assistance at the time banks ask their borrowers to pay their loans.

shifting tax: a tax whose burden is transferred from the original taxpayer (individual or organization) to another.

shift premium: extra compensation given to a shift worker for the inconvenience of altering his daily working hours. see *shift differential.*

shilling: monetary unit of Kenya, Somalia, Tanzania, and Uganda.

shinplaster

(1) *general:* any money made worthless either by inflation or by inadequate security.

(2) *banking:* a pre-Civil War term used to deprecate the value of paper money.

(3) *finance:* paper money, usually of less than one dollar face value, once used by some private financial institutions.

shock loss: a loss larger than expected.

shoestring: slang, a tiny amount of money.

shoestring trading: existing on minimal, barely adequate margin.

short: an individual who sells a futures contract in anticipation of purchasing it back at a lower cost. see *short hedges, short interest, short sale.*

short against the box: see *short sale.*

short and intermediate term credit: debt repaid over a relatively short span of time. [55]

short bill: a bill of exchange payable upon request, at sight, or within a brief period, usually less than 10 days.

short certificate: a certificate by the proper officer of a court as to the appointment and authority of a fiduciary, as distinguished from a full certified copy of letters testamentary, administration, or trusteeship. [37]

short covering: buying a stock to return stock previously borrowed to make delivery on a short sale. [20]

shortcut foreclosure: a method of foreclosure in which a power of sale clause in the mortgage allows the lender to sell a property if it goes into default. The borrower must be informed, but the issuing of a public statement need not be carried out. Upon property foreclosure, the junior mortgage holders' positions are wiped out, unless the sale yields more than the outstanding first mortgage.

shortfall: spending, usually in a governmental agency, that falls sharply below projections, thus contributing to an economic sluggishness. cf. *overage.*

short-form credit report: a type of credit bureau report, usually combining certain features of an oral report and a written report in abbreviated form. [14]

short-form mortgage clause: a mortgage clause permitting the buyer to take over the mortgage, subject to and not assuming liability for its payment.

short hedges: sales of futures created as hedges against holdings of the spot commodity or product. see *hedge.*

short interest: the sum of the short sales outstanding in a security or commodity or on an exchange.

short of exchange: the position of a foreign exchange trader who has sold more foreign bills than the quantity of bills he or she has in possession to cover sales.

short of the basis: said of a person or firm who has sold cash or spot goods and has hedged them with purchases of futures. He has therefore sold at a certain "basis" and expects to buy back at a better basis for a profit. [2]

short of the market: holding a short position in stock with the expectation that lower prices will occur. see *short sale.*

short position

(1) stocks sold short and not covered as of a particular date. On an exchange, a tabulation is usually issued once a month listing all issues on the exchange in which there was a short position of 5000 or more shares and issues in which the short position had changed by 2000 or more shares in the preceding month.

(2) the total amount of stock an individual has sold short and has covered, as of a particular date.

short purchase: buying a stock to cover an earlier short sale of the same stock.

short-rate cancellation: describes the charge required for insurance or bonds taken for less than one year. Also in some cases, it denotes the earned premium for insurance or bonds canceled by the insured before the end of the policy period or term of bond. cf. *pro rate cancellation.*

short run

(1) *general:* a one-time job.

(2) *finance:* the time during which a firm can alter the price or output of its goods but not change the size of its plant or close down operations.

short sale: a transaction made by a person who believes a stock will decline and places a sell order, though he or she does not own any of these shares. Stock exchange and federal regulations govern and limit the conditions under which a short sale may be made. Sometimes a person will sell short a stock already owned to protect a paper profit. This is known as "selling against the box."

short selling: selling a stock and purchasing it at a lower price to receive a profit.

short side: pessimists who sell short as contrasted with being on the long side. see *short sale.*

short squeeze: a sharp runup of prices that forces shorts to make offsetting purchases in order to avoid larger losses. A short squeeze occurs when people who have sold borrowed shares, in anticipation of replacing them at lower prices, are forced to cover those borrowed shares by buying shares, even at higher price. When a confluence of short covering occurs, price tend to jump because of the increased demand.

short stock: securities that have been sold short and not yet covered. see *short covering, short sale.*

short-term debt: an obligation that is usually due within the year.

short-term funds: money borrowed from 30 days up to one year.

short-term savings account: ordinarily, an account that is to be withdrawn within less than 24 months from the date the account is opened. [59]

short-term securities: securities payable on demand or which mature not more than one year from date of issue. [18]

short-term trust: an irrevocable trust running for a period of 10 years longer, in which the income is payable to a person other than the settlor, and established under the provisions of the Revenue Act of 1954. The income from a trust of this kind is taxable to the income beneficiary and not to the settlor. The agreement may provide that on the date fixed for the termination of the trust, or on the prior death of the income beneficiary, the assets of the trust shall be returned to the settlor. [37]

Shr.: see *share.*

shrinking stocks: stocks of corporations that are bought by the firms of their own shares, thus drastically reducing the number of shares outstanding. These corporations feel that they can earn a higher return on the money spent for their stock than on investing in new business schemes.

shut-off rates: high mortgage rates that are designed to turn away prospective buyers.

SI: see *simple interest.*

SIC

(1) see *split investment company.*

(2) see *Standard Industrial Classification System.*

sideliner: any person who withdraws temporarily from an active role in the market after closing out his long and/or short position.

Sig.: signature.

Sig. Cd.: see *signature card.*

sight bill of exchange: any bill of exchange that becomes due and payable when presented by the holder to the party on whom it is drawn. see also *short bill.*

sight draft: a draft payable upon delivery and presentation to the drawee, or "upon sight."

sight rate: the exchange rate tied to a demand draft or check. synonymous with *check rate.*

signature card: a card signed by each depositor and customer of the bank. The signature card is technically a contract between the bank and its customer, in that it recites the obligations of both in their relationship with each other. The principal use of the signature card is that of identification of the depositor. Signature cards are made out in at least two sets, one for the signature file department, where all signatures are kept for ready reference, and the other for the file at the teller's window where the depositor will most frequently transact his business. [10]

signature file department: this department is the custodian for all signature cards. The employees of this department issue daily reports on all accounts opened and all accounts closed. As a part of the public relations and "new business" work, the signature file department may write "thank you" letters to new depositors. [10]

signed instrument: any legal agreement, or note which is written and signed. [28]

silent partner: an individual who gives funds for a business partnership but takes no part in the management of the firm.

silver certificates: U.S. paper money since 1873 issued as receipts for the stated amount of silver in the U.S. Treasury. The redemption privilege was revoked by Congress in 1968. [27]

Silver Thursday: March 27, 1980, when the commodity industry and the entire financial community was imperiled after a major brokerage house, Bache Halsey Stuart Shields, was momentarily unable to get a commodity customer, the billionaire Hunt brothers, to cover a margin call for $100 million.

silver wing: slang, a half-dollar (50 cents).

simple interest: interest calculated on a principal sum and not on any interest that has been earned by that sum. cf. *compounded interest.*

simple trust: a term used only in tax laws to describe a trust that is required to distribute all of its income currently and that does not provide for any charitable distribution; opposed to complex trust. [37]

Simplified Employee Pension (SEP): made possible by the Revenue Act of 1978; a retirement plan that increases the limit on yearly contributions to $7500 an employee. This plan combined element of both Keogh plans and Individual Retirement Accounts. The SEP option permits an employee to establish an IRA whether or not the worker is covered by a company pension plan. An SEP also increases the amount that can be contributed annually to an IRA from the usual $1500 to $7500. Earnings from investments are tax-free until after age $59\frac{1}{2}$. Upon the death of the person, any undistributed funds can escape the estate tax by going to the heirs in installments over at least 36 months.

simulation: the process of imposing various hypothetical conditions on a model in order to observe their effects on certain variables. [57]

simultaneous inflation and unemployment (inflump): a situation calling for a value judgment of whether inflation or unemployment is the more serious problem and whether the economy is moving toward worse inflation or worse unemployment.

sinecure: a position of limited or nonexistent responsibility demanding little or no labor or service.

single capital structure company: company having only one class of security outstanding. [30]

single debit reporting: normal method used by mortgage bankers for reporting the current status of its mortgages when making a regular remittance to an investor. [22]

single entry: a bookkeeping approach in which each transaction is entered only once on the account books. The single-entry system is primarily used by small businesses. cf. *double entry.*

single-family dwelling: a housing unit designed for ownership and occupancy by one individual or family. [59]

single-lump-sum credit: a closed-end credit arrangement whereby the total outstanding balance is due on a specified date. [78]

single-name paper: a note for which only one legal entity—the maker—is obligated to make payment at maturity. A legal distinction exists in single-name paper, in that if the obligation is incurred for one purpose, or one common interest, the paper may have more than one maker or endorser, and still be termed single-name paper. Such a case would be two or more partners making a note for a loan to the common partnership or a subsidiary company making a note endorsed by the parent company. Single-name paper is also frequently termed *straight paper*. [10]

single option: as contrasted from a spread or straddle, any put or call. see *option*.

single-payment loan: a loan whose entire principal is due on one maturity date.

single-posting system: a plan of posting used in the bookkeeping department of a bank. Single posting generally means the posting of a depositor's statement only. The ledger record may be either a carbonized ledger created with the posting of the statement, or a photographed record of the statement (under the unit-photographic plan) made on microfilm. This posting plan is to be distinguished from the dual plan where the statement is posted in one run and the ledger is posted in another. [10]

single proprietorship: ownership of a business by one person.

singular property title: property title granted to only one person. see *severalty*.

sinkers: synonymous with "sinking fund bonds." see *bond, sinking fund.*

sinking fund: a fund used to accumulate the cash needed to pay off a bond or other security. By accumulating cash in a sinking fund, the firm is in a better position to pay its securities when due, and the risk is therefore reduced to the security holder.

sinking fund bond: see *bond, sinking fund.*

sinking fund depreciation: a system for calculating depreciation: the yearly amount is presumed to be deposited in a sinking fund that will also increase as a result of earnings from the fund investment.

sinking fund requirements: the amount by which a sinking fund must be increased periodically through contributions and earnings so that the accumulation thereof will be sufficient to redeem sinking fund bonds as they mature. [49]

sinking fund reserve: see *reserve for retirement of sinking fund bonds.*

SIP: see *Sharebuilder Investment Plan.*

SIPC: Securities Investor Protection Corporation; provides funds for use, if necessary, to protect customers' cash and securities which may be on deposit with an SIPC member firm in the event the firm fails and is liquidated under the provision of the SIPC Act. SIPC is not a government agency. It is a nonprofit membership corporation created, however, by an act of Congress. [20]

situs: Latin, a place or situation where a thing is located. An owner's home is the situs of his personal property.

six and seven nations of (economic) Europe: see *European Economic Community, European Free Trade Association.*

six bits: the equivalent of 75 cents.

sixty-day notice: notice required to be given to the Internal Revenue Service in those cases where the decedent's gross taxable estate exceeds or may exceed the exemption under the federal estate tax law. [37]

Sk.: see *safekeeping.*

skate: slang, avoidance of a creditor; the attempt to avoid payment.

Skg.: see *safekeeping.*

skimming prices: a high introductory price followed by a series of price reductions, designed to get all the trade the market will bear at one price level before lowering the price, as well as to appeal to the more price-conscious consumer.

skip: person owing money who has moved leaving no forwarding address. [41]

skip-payment privilege: a privilege provided in certain mortgage contracts that allows the borrower to skip monthly payments at any time the loan is paid ahead of schedule as long as the loan is prepaid. [59]

skunk: slang, to fail to pay a debt.

S & L Assn.: see *savings and loan association.*

slack
(1) the time in which a minor operation can be completed in advance of the next major operation that depends on it.
(2) a dull or inactive business period, a "slack season."

slander: an oral utterance that tends to harm the reputation of another.

Sld.: sold.

sleeper: a slow-moving security that has a sound potential for growth.

slice: slang, having a portion or interest in a business venture or activity.

slide: a posting error by which an amount is wrongly recorded by a bookkeeper who unintentionally places the decimal one or more digits to the right or left of the true decimal position.

slid off: a drop in the price of stocks.

slow asset: an asset that can be converted into cash, near its book value, usually after a lengthy passage of time.

slow loan: a Federal Savings and Loan Insurance Corporation regulatory category in which every insured savings association is required to list its delinquent loans. The regulations spell out what constitutes a slow loan in terms of the loan's age and length of delinquency. Loans less than one year old are slow when 60 days delinquent, those between one and seven years old are slow when 90 days delinquent, and so on. [59]

sluggish market: a slow-moving, inactive securities trading where volume is unusually low. Few stocks are traded with only minimal price fluctuations.

slump: a short-lived decline in the activity of a business or economy.

slush fund: slang, monies given for political purposes with the expectation that it will influence the receiver to favor the giver.

S & M: September and March (semiannual interest payments or dividends).

SM
(1) see *secondary market.*
(2) see *second mortgage.*

small bread: slang, a small amount of money.

Small Business Administration (SBA): a federal agency established in 1953 solely to advise and assist the nation's small businesses. The SBA provides loans, loan guarantees, and offers loans to victims of floods, riots, and other catastrophes and to those who have suffered economic harm as a result of federal programs. The SBA also conducts research on conditions affecting small businesses.

small loan: a term sometimes used to designate a personal cash loan. [41]

small loan law: a regulatory code covering cash installment loans, administered by the state, and protecting both the borrower and the lender. [55]

small potatoes: slang, a small amount of money.

small-saver   certificates: certificates issued in denominations of less than $100,000 with maturities of 2.5 years or more.

small-size   notes: American paper money since 1928, characterized by new designs and a smaller size. [27]

"smart" credit cards: originally developed in France, a credit card that deducts charges from a customer's bank balance. For banks and stores, the advantage of "smart" credit cards is increased automation and expected lower costs. see *carte à mémoire.*

smart money: experienced and professional security traders who expolit inside information to make profits at the expense of other investors.

smash: a severe drop in the market, approaching a panic.

smuggling: conveying goods or persons, without permission, across the borders of a country or other political entities (e.g., cigarette smuggling across state lines).

snake system: an international agreement between Belgium, The Netherlands,   Luxembourg,   Denmark, Sweden, Norway, and West Germany, linking the currencies of these countries together in an exchange rate system. The signatories have agreed to limit fluctuations in exchange rates among their currencies to 2.25 percent above or below set median rates. The snake was designed to be the first stage in forming a uniform Common Market currency. Members maintain fairly even exchange rates among themselves by buying or selling their currencies when the rates threaten to drop or rise beyond the 2.25 percent limits specified.   see   *European   Economic Community, European Free Trade Association, swap.*

snowballing: resulting   transaction following stop orders that become market orders, during periods of either advance or decline.

SO

(1)   see *seller's option.*

(2)   see *standing order.*

(3)   see *stock option.*

Social Security: the combination of social insurance plans sponsored by the Federal government, and including old age and survivors' insurance and unemployment insurance. Wage and payroll deductions are made to finance these programs. Federal employees are exempt from having to contribute to the costs of such coverage.

Social Security Act of 1935:   resulted in a national social insurance program providing old age and survivor benefits, public assistance to the aged, the blind, and needy children, unemployment insurance, and disability benefits.

Social Security Payment Program: a cooperative effort between the Social Security Administration and the U.S. Treasury Department devoted to planning and implementing a system for direct deposits of Social Security benefit payments to individuals, initially by distributing checks directly to recipients' banks, to be followed by gradual conversion from checks to tape. [36]

Society for Worldwide Interbank Financial Telecommunications (SWIFT): an organization developing a system for the electronic transfer of funds among participating banks in Europe and North America. [36]

Society of Savings and Loan Controllers: formed in 1950 under the sponsorship of the American Savings and Loan Institute as a professional organization, the society is devoted to improving the professional status of accounting and auditing officers through the development of better accounting methods and new aids to management. The society presently exists as a separate organization closely allied to institute activities and interests. This organization consists of more than 1500 of the principal accounting and chief auditing officers in savings associations. The society's technical publications are available on a subscription basis to nonmembers. [51]

SOE: see *short of exchange.*

soft: a security or general market that moves toward a lower price level.

soft currency: the funds of a country that are controlled by exchange procedures, thereby having limited convertibility into gold and other currencies.

soft landing: when an economy slows down from a period of unsustainable growth to a slower but more manageable growth rate, and does so without a recession.

soft loan: a loan whose terms of repayment are generous, at times holding a low rate of interest.

soft money: paper currency, as contrasted with coinage (hard money).

soft spot: while the general securities market is holding or even moving ahead, the sudden decline in specific stocks or groupings of securities.

software

(1) *computers:* a set of programs or procedures concerned with the operation of a data-processing system.

(2) *computers:* a set of coded instructions prepared to simplify programming and computer operations.

(3) *computers:* a term applied to computer operations that include compilers, assemblers, executive routines, and input and output libraries.

soil bank: a farm program established by the government to pay farmers for removing land from cultivation.

sol: monetary unit of Peru.

sola: any overseas bill of exchange or check made up on one document instead of a check or bill drawn together.

sold loan: a mortgage loan that has been sold to another institution but is still serviced by the seller. [59]

sold-out market: a market in which liquidations of weakly held contracts has largely been completed and offerings have become scarce. [2]

sole owner: the only person holding the title to a specific property or business. see *severalty.*

sole proprietorship: a proprietorship in which all equity lies with one individual.

solicit: to offer additional credit to a customer. [55]

solid-state computer: a computer that uses solid-state, or semiconductor, components; a second-generation computer.

solvency: exists when liabilities, other than those of ownership, amount to less than the total assets; the ability to pay debts.

solvent: the condition of an individual who is able to pay his or her debts.

solvent debtor section: a part of the Bankruptcy Tax Act of 1980 whereby a company that buys back its own bonds at a discount price must pay income tax on the spread between the face value of the bonds, or the original sales price, and the discount repurchase price.

Sonnie Mae: synonymous with the "New York State Mortgage Authority."

SOP: see *statement of policy.*

SOR: see *stockholder of record.*

So. shilling: monetary unit of Somalia.

source document: a record used by the association ofr the initial recording of a transaction. [59]

SP

(1) see *selling price.*

(2) see *short position.*

(3) see *spot price.*

(4) see *stop payment.*

special administrator: an administrator appointed by the court to take over and safeguard an estate pend-ing the appointment of an executor or administrator; sometimes known as *temporary administrator.* [37]

special assessment: a compulsory levy made by a local government against certain properties to defray part or all of the cost of a specific improvement or service which is presumed to be of general benefit to the public and of special benefit to such properties. [49]

special assessment bond: see *bond, special assessment.*

special assessment liens: claims which governmental units have upon properties until special assessments levied against them have been paid. [49]

special assessment roll: the official list showing the amount of special assessments levied against such property presumed to be benefited by an improvement or service. [49]

special bank credit plans: lines of credit extended to borrowers by banks. Based upon a prearranged limit, the borrower may use all or part of the credit by writing a check. Interest charges are based on the amount of credit used during the month and the total amount outstanding. [78]

special bid: a method of filling an order to buy a large block of stock on the exchange floor. The bidder for the block of stock pays a special commission to the broker who represents him or her in making the purchase. The seller does not pay a commission. The special bid is made on the floor of the exchange at a fixed price, which may not be below the last sale of the security or the current bid in the regular market, whichever is higher. Member firms may sell this stock for customers directly to the buyer's broker during trading hours. [20]

special deposit: a fund established for the payment of interest, dividends, or other debts, or to insure the performance of contracts, and other deposits of a special nature; as distinguished from *sinking fund.* [18]

special devise: a gift, by will, of a specific parcel of real property. [32]

special district bond: see *bond, special district.*

special dividend: in addition to the regular corporation dividend, a further dividend in stock or money. synonymous with *extra dividend.*

special drawing rights (SDRs): the amount by which each country is permitted to have its international checking account with the International Monetary Fund go negative before the nation must ask for additional loans. SDRs were established at the Rio de Janeiro conference of 1967.

special endorsement: an endorsement that transfers title to a negotiable instrument to a party specified in the endorsement. [59]

special fund: any fund that must be devoted to some special use in accordance with specific regulations and restrictions. Generally, the term applies to all funds other than the general fund.

special guardian: a guardian appointed by a court for a particular purpose connected with the affairs of a minor or an incompetent person; sometimes a guardian ad litem is known as a special guardian. see *guardian ad litem.* [37]

special indorsement: see *special endorsement.*

special interest account: the term used by commercial banks to describe a savings account. Some states do not permit a commercial bank to accept savings accounts. However, deposits may be accepted on which interest is paid and under the same interest-bearing rates as a savings bank, but another name, such as "special interest accounts," must be used.

special issues: securities issued by the U.S. Treasury for investment of reserves of government trust funds and for certain payments to veterans.

specialist: a member of an exchange who has two functions: to maintain an orderly market, insofar as is reasonably practicable, in the stocks in which he or she is registered by an exchange as a specialist; and to act as a broker's broker.

specialist block purchase: purchase by the specialist for his or her own account of a large block of stock outside the regular market on the exchange. Such purchases may be made only when the sale of the block could not be made in the regular market within a reasonable time and at reasonable prices, and when the purchase by the specialist would aid him or her in maintaining a fair and orderly market. [20]

specialist block sale: opposite of "specialist block purchase." Under exceptional circumstances, the specialist may sell a block of stock outside the regular market on the exchange for his or her own account at a price above the prevailing market. The price is negotiated between the specialist and the broker for the buyer. [20]

special lien: see *particular lien.*

special lien bond: see *bond, special lien.*

special offering: occasionally a large block of stock that becomes available for sale requires special handling because of its size and the market in that particular issue. A notice is printed on the ticker tape announcing that the stock will be offered for sale on the exchange floor at a fixed price. Member firms may buy this stock for customers directly from the seller's broker during trading hours. The price is usually based on the last transaction in the regular auction market. Only the seller pays a commission on a special offering. Special offerings must be approved by the SEC.

special partner: a partner in a financial organization whose liability is limited to the interest he or she has in the company and is not active in the management. see *active partner, general partner, limited partnership, silent partner.*

special power of appointment: see *limited power of appointment, power of appointment.*

special-purpose computer: a computer that is designed to handle a restricted class of problems.

special-purpose funds: mutual funds that invest exclusively in securities from one industry. see *investment company.*

special security: effective September 1981, banks and savings and loan associations are able to take the deposits resulting from their new tax-exempt savings certificates and reinvest the money in securities offered by the Federal National Mortgage Association. see *All-Saver certificates.*

special situation: usually describes a venture capital type of investment, but may also refer to a conservative but relatively unknown investment or to heavy commitments in investments which, in the opinion of the management, are temporarily undervalued by the market. [30]

specialty (specialized) fund: investment company concentrating its holdings in specific industry groups (insurance, oil, aviation stocks, etc.). [30]

specialty stock: a security from a particular industry or grouping.

special warranty deed: see *deed, special warranty.*

specie: money in coin.

specifications: as used in foreign exchange, the conditions and terms used with bills of exchange drawn under letters of credit.

specific devise: a gift, by will, of a specific parcel of real property. [37]

specific legacy: a gift, by will, of a specific article of personal property, such as a watch. [32]

specific performance: the actual accomplishment of a contract by the party bound to fulfill it. An action to compel the performance of a contract according to its terms—that is, to do the thing contracted for, usually brought where the payment of money damages would not adequately compensate the aggrieved party. [37]

specific subsidy: the per unit subsidy on a commodity.

specific tax: the per unit tax on a commodity.

speculation: the employment of funds by a speculator. Safety of principal is a factor secondary to increasing capital. see *letter stock;* cf. *defensive investment, digested securities.*

speculative position: an open position held by a trader that is unhedged.

speculative purchasing: buying items when prices appear lowest, with the expectation that there will be a future price increase, making possible a profit.

speculator: one who is willing to assume a relatively large risk in the hope of gain. His or her principal concern is to increase capital rather than dividend income. Speculators may buy and sell the same day, or may invest in enterprises they do not expect to be profitable for years.

spendable earnings: net earnings after deductions for taxes. Often referred to as take-home pay, or the amount available for spending.

spendthrift provision: a provision in a trust instrument which limits the right of the beneficiary to dispose of his interest, as by assignment, and the right of his creditors to reach it, as by attachment. [32]

spillover trust: type of trust which by its terms is merged with or added to another trust or estate upon the occurrence of a certain event. see *pourover.* [37]

spinoff: with respect to federal income taxes, a transfer by a firm of a portion of its assets to a newly formed organization in exchange for the latter's capital stock, which is thereupon distributed as a property dividend to the stockholders of the initial corporation.

split: the division of the outstanding shares of a corporation into a larger number of shares. A 3-for-1 split by a company with 1 million shares outstanding would result in 3 million shares outstanding. Each holder of 100 shares before the 3-for-1 split would have 300 shares. Of course his or her proportionate equity in the company would remain the same, since 100 parts of 1 million is the equivalent of 300 parts of 3 million. Ordinarily, a split must be voted by directors and approved by shareholders. Such action by a corporation does not alter the total contributed capital but merely increases the number of shares issued and outstanding and the par value per share. cf. *stock split-down.*

split close: variations in price; for example, the Dow Jones shows a higher closing price for the industrial averages, but a lower closing price for the utility average.

split commission: sharing a commission with someone else who has assisted in procuring the business for the broker, agent, or counselor. see *give-up.*

split funding: a program which combines the purchase of mutual fund shares with the purchase of life insurance contracts or other products. [23]

split investment company: a closed-end investment firm issuing two types of capital stock. The first (income shares) receives dividends from investments; the second (capital shares) receives dividends from the appreciation of investments. synonymous with "dual-purpose fund."

split order: a large order that is separated into smaller units that are sold over a period of time. When purchasing or selling a security or commodity, a very large transaction could cause substantial price fluctuation which splitting may prevent.

split-rate account: a passbook savings account that pays increasing rate of interest, up to regulatory maximums, for increasing account balances. [59]

split stock: new outstanding securities of a corporation resulting from a stock split.

split-up: the issuance of two or more stock shares replacing each outstanding share, used for financial and tax purposes. This increase, although lowering the value per share, does not alter the total liability of the issuing firm for the outstanding capital stock. see *split*.

Sp. Off.: see *special offering*.

sponsorship: the banking institution holding an interest in the selling price of a specific securities issue.

spot commodity: see *cash commodity*.

spot delivery: immediate delivery.

spot delivery month: the nearest delivery month among all those traded at any point in time. The actual contract month represented by the spot delivery month is constantly changing throughout the calendar year as each contract month reaches its last trading day.

spot exchange transaction: a purchase or sale of foreign currency for ready delivery. In practice, market usage normally prescribes settlement within two working days. For purposes of the International Monetary Fund's Articles of Agreement, the term excludes transactions in banknotes or coins. [42]

spot market: a market where commodities are sold for cash and quickly delivered. see *fixing the price*.

spot price: the price at which the spot commodity is selling. [11]

SPP: see *stock purchase plan*.

spread
(1) *finance:* two prices given instead of one.
(2) *finance:* the difference between two prices.
(3) *investments:* two different options, a put (price below the prevailing market), and a call (price above the prevailing market), with both options pertaining to the same stock and expiring on the same day. Thus the trader is guaranteed a sale not lower than the put price if the market drops and a buy at a price not higher than the call price if the market increases. see also *butterfly spread, straddle*.
(4) *investments:* the differences between the bid and asked prices of securities.

sprinkling trusts: trusts in which the income or principal is distributed among the members of a designated class in amounts and proportions as may be determined in the discretion of the trustee. synonymous with "spraying trusts." [37]

SPS: see *second preferred stocks*.

spurt: any short, but considerable climb in prices.

squeeze
(1) *finance:* when interest rates are high and money is difficult to borrow.
(2) *investments:* results when people who have sold stocks short in a climbing market are obligated to buy back their securities at a loss in

order to fulfill their short-selling contract obligations. see *short covering, short sale.*

SS

(1) see *selling short.*
(2) see *senior securities.*
(3) see *short sale.*
(4) see *shrinking stocks.*
(5) see *Social Security.*

SSD: see *stock split-down.*

ST

(1) see *sales tax.*
(2) see *stock transfer.*

stabilization policy: the efforts of government to use fiscal and monetary means to eliminate inflation, unemployment, or both. see *wage stabilization.*

stable money: currency that remains constant in terms of the items and services it can purchase.

stag: an individual speculator who rapidly buys and then sells shares for profit, having had no intention of retaining the securities for any length of time. cf. *digested securities.*

stagflation: inflation coexisting with economic stagnation. Prices increase during a period of minimal capital investment in equipment, research and development, and so on.

Staggers Rail Act of 1980: gives the railroads greater freedom to set freight-hauling rates and greater authority to enter into long-term agreements with their customers, the freight shippers. It also makes it easier for railroads to eliminate unprofitable routes, although they will remain subject to control by the Interstate Commerce Commission.

stagnation: conditions of minimal growth rate, or growth increasing at a rate lower than expected.

stake: slang, a rather substantial amount of money.

stale check: any check dated 90 days prior to presentation for payment.

stamped bond: see *bond, stamped.*

stamped notes: paper money issued with revenue stamps on it to add to the value. [27]

stamped security: a stock that has been stamped to show any alteration made on it since it was first released—for example, a change in the date of maturity.

stamp tax: a government tax collected through the sale of stamps that are affixed to certain products (e.g., liquor, tobacco, stock certificates, or title deeds). see *transfer tax.*

Standard & Poor's 500-Composite-Stock Index: an index of stock prices composed of 425 industrials, 50 utilities, and 25 railroads. cf. *Dow Jones averages.*

standard cost: the predetermined cost of performing an operation or producing a product when labor, materials, and equipment are utilized efficiently under reasonable and normal conditions. [49]

Standard Industrial Classification System (SIC): a numerical system developed by the U.S. Bureau of the Budget to classify establishments by type of activity for purposes of facilitating the collection, tabulation, presentation, and analysis of data relating to such establishments and for promoting uniformity within U.S. agencies. cf. *Dictionary of Occupational Titles.*

standard of living: the level of material affluence of a nation as measured by per capita output. see *per capita output.*

standard payment: a customer's exact contract payment amount. see *nonstandard payment.* [55]

standard stocks: securities of established and well-known firms.

standby commitment: commitment for a limited period made, for a fee, as security for a construction lender by an investor who stands ready to make or purchase the committed loan at above-market terms in the event that a takeout commitment cannot be obtained on market terms. [22]

standing order: an authority given by the customer for the bank to regularly pay funds, usually a fixed dollar amount, from his or her demand deposit account.

standstill agreement: an arrangement between a debtor and a creditor under which exist new limits and conditions for the loan. Typically, a postponement of obligation payment is the result. cf. *novation.*

star notes: U.S. replacement notes. Also the name given to some interest-bearing notes issued in 1837 by the Treasury of Texas. [27]

state bank: a bank that is organized according to the laws of a state and is chartered by the state in which it is located to operate as a banking business. The various states have different laws governing the operation of banks.

state banking department: the organization in each state which supervises the operations and affairs of state banking institutions. The chief officer of this department is designated superintendent of banks or commissioner of banks or is given some comparable title. [39]

state bank notes: an American term referring to issues by banks which are subject to the laws in the state, as opposed to federal laws. [27]

state bond: see *bond, state.*

stated capital: the sum of capital amounts contributed by stockholders.

statement

(1) *banking:* a record prepared by a bank for a depositor listing all checks drawn and deposits made together with the new balance after each posting.

(2) *computers:* an instruction to perform some sequence of operations.

(3) *finance:* a summary of transactions between a creditor and his or her debts or a presentation of names and amounts of accounts to show a financial condition (e.g., an IRS statement).

statement clerk: an employee in the bookkeeping department of a bank. This title has two different meanings as applied to the duties of the clerk. In some banks the statement clerk posts the statements for depositors' checking accounts under the dual system. In other banks this title is used in describing an employee who is responsible for verification of all paid checks listed on a depositor's statement to see that the statement is complete before it is mailed to the depositor. [10]

statement of changes in financial position: a report summarizing the flow of funds within an organization during a designated period of time. The statement should disclose all important aspects of the organization's financing and investing activities regardless of whether cash or other elements of working capital are directly affected. [43]

statement of condition: a detailed listing of a bank's resources, liabilities, and capital accounts showing its conditions on a given date. On requests (calls) by supervisory authorities several times a year, banks are required to submit sworn statements of condition. In general accounting, this type of financial report is known as a balance sheet. [50]

statement of loan: a statement itemizing all details of a loan transaction which must be given to the borrower at the time the loan is negotiated. [55]

statement of operations: a summary of the financial operations during a given period showing the sources of income and its allocation to the payment of operating expenses, dividends to holders of savings accounts, and allocations to reserves for the protection of savers. [51]

statement of policy: a guide issued by the SEC to assist issuers, underwriters, dealers, and salespersons in complying with statutory disclosure standards as applied to sales literature, reports to shareholders, and other communications "addressed to or intended for distribution to prospective investors." [30]

state notes: issued by an American state, now forbidden. [27]

station

(1) *general:* a worker's assigned post or place of activity.

(2) *computers:* one of the input or output points of a system that uses communication facilities.

(3) *investments:* the place where a specialist on an exchange transacts orders.

statism: any indication of increased government intervention in a nation's economic activity, with primary focus on movement toward greater control over major industries. see *controlled economy.*

statistical accounting: the application of probability theory and statistical sampling approaches to the evolution of prime accounting information and/or verification, authentication, and audit of accounting data prepared by other means.

statute of frauds: a law that requires certain contracts, such as agreements of sale, to be in writing in order to be enforceable. [62]

statute of limitations: see *limitations of actions (statutes of).*

statutes of distribution: laws, rules, or statutes governing the distribution of personal property under intestacy. [37]

statutory exemptions: specified articles of personal property and a specified amount of cash left by a decedent which are set apart for his or her immediate family and which may not be subjected to the claims of creditors. [37]

statutory fee: the administrative cost of closing a loan. [78]

statutory investment: an investment which a trustee is specifically authorized to make under the terms of the statutes of the state having jurisdiction of the trust. [37]

statutory warranty deed: a warranty deed form prescribed by state statutes. [62]

steady: showing that market prices are barely moving in any direction.

stepped costs: costs that climb by increments with increased volumes of activity.

sterling: the currency of Great Britain. The unit is the pound sterling. May also represent bills of exchange that are drawn in terms of British currency. Sterling silver is silver of at least 222 parts out of 240 of pure silver, and no more than 18 parts of an alloy.

Stg.: see *sterling.*

Stk.: see *stock.*

Stk. Ex.: see *stock exchanges.*

stock: the legal capital of a corporation divided into shares. see *assented securities, authorized stock, blue chip, callable, capital stock, common stock, convertible, cumulative preferred (stock), deferred stock, float, growth stock, guaranteed stock, inactive stock (bond), issue, listed securities (stocks), nonassessable stock, noncumulative, no-par-value stock, ordinary stock, outstanding, over the counter, paid-up stock, participating preferred, par value, penny stocks, preferred stock, prior preferred (stock), redeemable stock, treasury stock, unissued stock, unlisted, voting right (stock), watered stock.*

stock ahead: describing a situation when an investor who has entered an order to buy or sell a stock at a certain price sees transactions at that price reported on the ticker tape before his or her own order has been executed. This may have occurred because other buy and sell orders at the same price came in to a trading specialist earlier and had priority.

stock-appreciation rights (SARs): privileges that can be attached to a nonqualified option. With an SAR, an executive can ignore the option and take a bonus equal to the value of the stock's appreciation over a span of time. An SEC rule permits an SAR bonus to be paid in cash, rather than in company shares. The SAR can be acted on at any time during the 10-year term of the attached nonqualified stock option.

stock association: a savings association organized as a capital stock corporation, with investors providing operating capital by purchasing an ownership interest in the institution, represented by shares of stock. Their stock holdings entitle them to virtually the same rights as stockholders in any other corporation, including a share of the profits. Stock associations operate in 23 states. [59]

stock-bonus trust: a trust established by a corporation to enable its employees to receive benefits in the form of the corporation's own stock as a reward for meritorious service or as a means of sharing in the profits of the enterprise. [37]

stock borrowed: securities borrowed by one broker from another to result in delivery. These stocks are subject to going interest and premium rates. see *short sale.*

stockbroker: an individual who acts as a middleman between buyers and sellers of stock. cf. *specialist.*

stock certificate: written evidence of ownership of a company's shares, indicating the number of shares registered in the name of the owner, the corporation issuing the capital stock, and whether the stock is a par value or a non-par-value stock.

Stock Clearing Corporation: the New

York Stock Exchange's clearing-house. Major responsibilities include the clearing and settling of money balances between members, the clearing of purchases and sales transaction, and the delivery of stock.

stock company: a company in which stockholders contribute all the capital, pay all the losses, and share in the profits. [12]

stock dividend: a portion of the net earnings of a corporation payable (in shares of fractional shares of designated stock of a given corporation) to the stockholders of record of the corporation. It is paid in securities rather than cash, and it may be additional shares of the issuing company or shares of another company held by the corporation.

stock exchanges: organizations that provide a market for the trading of bonds and stocks. Regulations for the admission of securities for trading on the stock exchanges are very stringent.

stockholder: the legal owner of at least one share of security in a corporation.

stockholder of record: a stockholder whose name is registered on the books of the issuing corporation. see *voting right (stock)*. [20]

stockholders annual report: report compiled annually for stockholders showing financial position and progress during the fiscal year. [18]

stock-in-trade

(1) *general:* equipment used to carry on a trade or business; by extension, the usual activity of a trade or business.

(2) *investments:* quantity of securities held.

stock jobbing: irresponsible or dishonest manipulation of the price of securities.

stock market: the buying and selling of stock for the purpose of profit for both buyers and sellers of the security. see *market.*

stock option: an arrangement for compensating top management, in addition to salary, with an opportunity to buy a certain amount of company stock, often under the market price. see *Tax Reform Act of 1976.*

stock power: a power of attorney permitting a person other than the owner of stock to legally transfer the title of ownership to a third party. Stock powers are usually given when stock is pledged as collateral to loans.

stock purchase plan: a company plan for the purchase of stock by employees, with or without a contribution from the employer at terms usually below the market price.

stock registrar: a bank, financial institution, or person permitted to serve in a fiduciary position, to certify that a corporation's issued shares have not exceeded the approved amount.

stock split: see *split.*

stock split-down: the reverse of stock split; the total number of shares outstanding is lowered without reducing the total value of the issue, by issuing a new stock share to replace each of two or more shares presently in circulation. The motivation is to increase the market price of a stock. synonymous with *reverse stock split.*

stock transfer: the act of canceling a stock certificate submitted for transfer, issuing a new certificate in the name of the designated transferee, and recording the change in ownership on the records of a corporation's stock transfer book. see *stock-transfer tax.*

stock-transfer agent: the agent of a corporation appointed for the purpose of effecting transfers of stock from one stockholder to another by the actual cancellation of the surrendered certificates and the issuance of new certificates in the name of the new stockholder. [37]

stock-transfer tax: a tax levied by some states on the transfer of securities from one owner to another, either when purchased or given as a gift. see *stock transfer.*

stock trust certificate: issued in exchange for stock of competing firms entering the trust form of combination, deposited with trustees, who issue in exchange trust certificates under the deposit agreement, and who control the firm's activities by reason of their power. synonymous with "trust certificate."

stock turnover: see *turnover.*

stock watering: see *watered stock.*

stock yield: the rate of return on a stock based upon its market value as of a particular date and the dividend being currently paid by the company. [37]

stone broke: slang, penniless.

stop limit order: a stop order that becomes a limit order after the specified stop price has been reached. see *limited order, stop order.* [20]

stop loss: a guarantee from one company (the reinsurer) to another (the reinsured) that losses over and above an agreed upon amount will be paid by the reinsuring company.

stop order: an order to buy at a price above or sell at a price below the current market. Stop buy orders are generally used to limit loss or to protect unrealized profits on a short sale. Stop sell orders are generally used to protect unrealized profits or to limit loss on a holding. A stop order becomes a market order when the stock sells at or beyond the specified price and thus may not necessarily be executed at that price. [20]

stop payment: the order given to a bank by a depositor who wishes to prevent payment on a check he or she has issued. The depositor requests the bank to stop payment of the item in writing, or telephones the instructions and confirms them in writing.

stopped at: a price for a security that is often guaranteed to a purchaser or a seller by the specialist in it.

stop price: the price at which a customer's stop order to his broker becomes a market order.

straddle

(1) *investments:* the purchase or sale of an equivalent number of puts and calls on a given underlying stock with the same exercise price and expiration date. [5]

(2) *investments:* an option allowing the trader to buy or sell securities at an agreed-upon price within a given period. see also *butterfly spread, spread.*

straight amortization plan: an amortization plan that provides for the payment of a fixed amount of principal at specified intervals, with interest payable on the remaining balance of the loan. [44]

straight bankruptcy: a proceeding by which an individual files for release from his debts after a court arranges for his creditors to divide whatever assets he has. [76]

straight bill of lading: a bill of lading that cannot be negotiated, identifying the individual who is to receive goods.

straight investment: a preferred stock or bond, limited in interest or dividend rate, that is bought because of its income return and not for expectation of any rise in value. see *investment.*

straight lease: a lease describing regular rental payments (e.g., monthly, quarterly). Also referred to as a "flat lease."

straight life: see *ordinary life.*

straight-line depreciation: the simplest method of depreciation. Amortization of capital cost in uniform periodic amounts over the anticipated life of the asset.

straight loan: a loan to an individual or other legal entity; the basis for granting credit is the debtor's general ability to pay, unsupported by any form of collateral security.

straight paper: a term covering all unsecured notes, bills of exchange, and acceptances.

straight serial bond: see *bond, straight serial.*

straight-term mortgage loan: a mortgage loan granted for a fixed term of years, the entire loan becoming due at the end of that time. [44]

strap: a stock option contract made up of two calls and one put. see *strip.*

strategic resource monopoly: an organization having a monopoly by virtue of controlling a vital input to a production process (e.g., DeBeers of South Africa owns most of the world's diamond mines).

strategics: slang, for investments made in precious metals, including, for example, chromium, manganese, germanium, titanium, nickel, and cobalt.

straw: untrue, valueless, or financially irresponsible; a "straw bid" is one whose maker is unable to fulfill the requirements for acquisition.

straw man: a person who purchases property for another without identifying the valid buyer. The result is that the "straw man" maintains a naked title on the property and is a dummy buyer.

Street: the New York financial community; the lower Manhattan (i.e., Wall Street) area.

street broker: an over-the-counter broker, as distinguished from a broker who is a member of an exchange.

street name: any stock certificate in the name of a broker who trades in securities and is a member of an exchange is said to be in "street name." This stock is never considered to be part of the broker's personal wealth.

street orders: form of order used by the representative of one carrier to secure tickets of another carrier's issue, settlement of which is made directly or through accounting office. [18]

stretch the float: keeping cash in a high-interest account as long as possible before using it to pay bills.

strict foreclosure: a legal proceeding in which the association brings court action against the borrower and the court sets a date by which the borrower must redeem his or her debt in full, or the title will pass automatically to the association without public sale. [59]

strike from the list: occurs when a stock exchange prevents, by canceling, any transactions in that particular stock. The stock is suspended. see *delist.*

striking price: see *exercise price.*

stringency: a money market condition in which it is hard to obtain credit, accompanied by an increase in the rates of interest.

string of coconuts: slang, money, especially a large number of bills.

strip: a stock option contract made up of two puts and one call. see *strap.*

strong market: a greater demand for purchasing than there is for selling.

structural inflation: increasing prices are caused by an uneven upward demand or cost pressures in a key industry, even when total demand remains in balance with total supply for the economy as a whole.

stuck (with): slang, having bought a poor or worthless good or service; overcharged.

Student Loan Marketing Association: a government-sponsored private corporation created to increase the flow of funds into student loans by facilitating the purchase of student loans in the secondary market; commonly called "Sallie Mae."

Sub.: see *subordination.*

subchapter M: the sections of the Internal Revenue Code which provide special tax treatment for organizations known as "regulated investment companies." [30]

subject bid: a bid that is negotiable, rather than firm.

subject to check: any payable-on-demand check where the customer need not inform the bank of his desire to withdraw funds. All commercial checking accounts are subject to check.

subject to redemption: stocks that can be called (redeemed) with advance notice to the shareholders.

subject to sale: when property has been offered for sale, a "subject to sale" stipulation provides for the automatic withdrawal of the offer if the property is sold before the party to whom the stipulation was made has accepted the offer.

sublease: the letting of premises to a third party with the original tenant retaining an interest in the property. All or part of the leased property may be subleased. If the tenant gives up his or her entire interest, the transaction becomes an assignment of lease. synonymous with *underlease.*

submission: mortgage banker's offering of mortgages for purchase by an investor. [22]

submittal notice: a broker's notification to a property owner stating that the owner's property has been offered for sale; offering price and prospect's name and address are included.

submortgage: the result of a pledge by a lender of a mortgage in his or her possession as collateral to obtain a loan for himself or herself.

subordinated debenture: a special debenture whose bearer has a chance for payment lower than that for other creditors. As it holds a higher yield, it is considered a risky bond.

subordinated interest: an interest in property that is inferior to another interest (e.g., a second mortgage that is inferior to the first mortgage). cf. *equal dignity.*

subordination: acknowledgment by a creditor in writing that the debt due him from a specified debtor shall have a status inferior or subordinate to the debt which the debtor owes another creditor. [44]

subordination agreement: where more than one legal entity has an interest or claim upon the assets of a prospective borrower, a bank may require that the other interested parties sign subordination agreements before a loan will be granted. The subordination agreement is an agreement in which another interested party grants the bank a priority claim or preference to the assets of the borrower ahead of any claim that he or she may have. [10]

subpoena: a process by a court requiring the attendance of a witness, usually at a trial. Failure to comply can result in a penalty. In addition to trials, a subpoena can compel a witness to appear at proceedings of a grand jury and at other investigations.

subrogation: substitution of one person for another, either as a creditor or the owner of any lawful right, in order that the substituted individual succeed to the rights, remedies, or proceeds of the claim.

subscriber: one who agrees in writing to purchase a certain offering—for example, a certain number of shares of designated stock of a given corporation or a certain number of bonds of a given stipulated face value.

subscribing witness: one who sees a document signed or hears the signature acknowledged by the signer and who signs his own name to the document, such as the subscribing wit-

ness to a will; to be distinguished from an *attesting witness*. [37]

subscription: an agreement to purchase a security; a solicitation of subscribers.

subscription rights: a privilege to the stockholders of a corporation to purchase proportionate amounts of a new issue of securities, at an established price, usually below the current market price; also, the negotiable certificate evidencing such privilege. [3]

subsidiary: any organization more than 50 percent of whose voting stock is owned by another firm.

subsidiary account: one of group of related accounts which support in detail the debit and credit summaries recorded in a control account. An example is the individual property taxpayers' accounts for taxes receivable in the general ledger. see also *control account, subsidiary ledger*. [49]

subsidiary ledger: individual records of mortgage loan accounts, savings accounts, loans in process, and other accounts whose total appear in the general ledger. [59]

subsistence theory of wages: an economic theory of the late eighteenth and early nineteenth centuries claiming that wages per employee tend to equal what the worker needs to maintain himself and his family. see *standard of living*.

substandard: describing conditions making a risk less desirable than normal for its class.

substituted trustee: a trustee appointed by the court (not named or provided for in the trust instrument) to serve in the place of the original trustee or of a prior trustee; to be dis-

tinguished from a *successor trustee.*
[32]

substitution: see *subrogation.*

Substitution Account: a plan of the International Monetary Fund that would allow dollar holders to exchange them for assets denominated in a basket of currencies known as special drawing rights (SDRs). The objective of the plan is to reduce the $500 billion to $1 trillion floating around the world, and thus cut the gyrations of the international financial markets. see *special drawing rights.*

subtenant: a tenant who leases a premises from another tenant; a sublessee. see *sublease.*

Suby.: see *subsidiary.*

succession

(1) *general:* following another in an office, estate, and so on.

(2) *law:* the transfer of all the rights and obligations of a deceased person to those who are entitled to inherit.

succession tax: a tax on the privilege of receiving property, either by descent or by will. It is not a burden on property.

successive beneficiaries

(1) beneficiaries who receive one after another by succession. Thus, under a will in which property is left to A for life, then to B for life, and then to C outright, B and C are successive beneficiaries.

(2) the inheritance of property by descent or transmission to the next in a succession—as from parent to child and so on down the direct line. [37]

successor trustee: a trustee following the original or a prior trustee the appointment of whom is provided for in the trust instrument; to be distinguished from a *substituted trustee.*
[32]

sucre: monetary unit of Equador.

suit: any proceeding at law for the purpose of obtaining a legal decision.

summons: a court writ directing the sheriff to notify the defendant that the plaintiff claims to have a cause of action against the defendant, who is expected to appear in court. A summons does not strictly compel the defendant to appear but merely puts him on notice that if he fails to appear, judgment is taken by default and the action will be decided against him.

sumptuary laws: laws that attempt to minimize the consumption of items believed to be harmful to individuals or society in general.

sunrise industries: high-risk ventures in advanced technology with promising potential for growth and export.

sunset: termination or the end of a time period.

superintendent of banking: see *state banking department.*

superseded suretyship rider: a continuity of coverage clause in the form of a rider attached to a new fidelity bond, taking the place of another bond and agreeing to pay losses that would be recoverable under the first bond except that the discovery period has expired. Losses caused by dishonest employees frequently have been found to have occurred at various times stretching over a period of years. This may involve a chain of several bonds, each one superseding a prior obligation. These losses will be covered if the chain of bonds is unbroken and each has included the superseded suretyship rider. [54]

supervised lender: according to the Veterans Administration classification, any lender subject to examination and supervision by a state or federal agency. [59]

supervisory merger: a move in the banking industry, where an institution in serious danger is forced to merge with a stronger one. To encourage this movement, loans are provided by the government-managed Federal Savings and Loan Insurance Corporation.

supplemental agreement: an amendment to an agreement setting forth additional terms to the agreement. [37]

supply and demand: economic forces that influence changes in business performance and strategy.

supply price: the lowest price needed to produce a specified output. It is the lowest price a seller will accept for the act of supplying a given quantity of a commodity.

supply-side economics: a concept that shifts the emphasis from aggregate demand economics (which Keynes considered the most important economic variable) to investment and production. It lays great stress on the repressive role of taxes, and it leads logically to a strong endorsement of tax cuts designed to encourage investment.

supporting the market: placing purchasing orders at or somewhat below the prevailing market level for the purpose of maintaining and balancing existing prices and to encourage a price rise.

Sur.: see *surplus.*

surcharge: an added charge to a tax or other cost or account.

surety
(1) *finance:* a bond, guaranty, or other security that protects a person, corporation, or other legal entity in cases of another's default in the payment of a given obligation, improper performance of a given contract, malfeasance of office, and so on.
(2) *law:* an individual who agrees, usually in writing, to be responsible for the performance of another on a contract, or for a certain debt or debts of another individual.

surety bond: see *bond, surety.*

sur mortgage: a document that demands that a person who has defaulted on mortgage payments show cause why the mortgage should not foreclose.

surplus
(1) *general:* anything remaining or left over.
(2) *banking:* the surplus account is a part of the capital structure of a bank, and is carried in the general ledger. Before a bank can open for business as a national bank, it must have a beginning surplus equal to 20 percent of the paid-in capital stock. A state bank must conform to whatever the laws of the state require as pertaining to surplus. After a bank has opened, the surplus account is made up of all past earnings less the dividends declared and paid from the profits. National banks are required to carry a minimum of 10 percent of each previous six months' earnings to their surplus account before the Comptroller of the Currency will approve the payment of a dividend. State laws deal with surplus require-

ments in various ways. The surplus is a part of the net worth or ownership of the bank, and in case of liquidation, any remaining portion of surplus after all creditors have been satisfied will be divided in the same related percent as the capital stock held by the stockholders. [10]

(3) *finance:* excess of assets over the total liabilities and capital.

surplus value: in Marxian philosophy, the profit derived from the amount above labor costs.

surrender of lease: a mutual agreement between landlord and tenant to terminate all aspects of a lease before its normal expiration date.

surrender value (cash surrender value): designating the amount of the total life insurance in force that will be paid to the policyholder after a certain stipulated number of premiums have been paid, if the policyholder elects to surrender the policy and receive such proportionate part. The cash surrender value of a policy is also the amount used to determine how much will be loaned against the policy.

surtax: the extra tax applied to corporations when their net taxable income has exceeded a certain amount. For example, a surtax is demanded at the rate of 26 percent for all corporate income over $25,000. see *Tax Reform Act of 1969.*

survivorship account: an account in the names of two or more persons, each signature alone being sufficient authority for the withdrawal of funds, the balance in the account belonging to the survivor or survivors on the death of the other or others. see *alternate account, joint account.* [50]

suspended trading: a binding stock exchange decision to cease trading resulting from an unusual occurrence, such as an unexpected jump in buy or sell orders on all or several securities. Sometimes, suspended trading may be brought about by equipment failure or other unexpected emergencies.

suspense account: an account in the general ledger used to hold over unposted items so that the business day can be closed in a state of balance.

suspense fund: a fund established to account separately for certain receipts pending the distribution or disposal thereof. [49]

suspension

(1) *general:* disciplinary layoff of a worker without pay.

(2) *banking:* a temporary closing of a bank.

(3) *investments:* a decision made by a stock exchange board of directors prohibiting a securities firm or broker from conducting business for a period. see *under the rule.*

swag: slang, stolen items or money.

swap

(1) *general:* to exchange or barter.

(2) *banking:* an arrangement between the central banks of two countries for standby credit to facilitate the exchange of each other's currencies. see *credit, swap network;* see also *bond swap.*

(3) *computers:* to write the main storage aspects of a job to auxiliary storage and read the image of another job into main storage.

(4) *investments:* a process by which portfolios are adjusted to lengthen or shorten maturities or

raise or lower coupon rates to wring out the last bit of revenue.

swap fund: a fund into which many investors put their own investments and receive a share in the pooled investment portfolio. The purpose of this exchange of investments is to obtain a diversified portfolio without selling stock and paying capital gains taxes.

swap network: to finance U.S. interventions in the foreign exchange market, a series of short-term reciprocal credit lines between foreign banks under which the Federal Reserve System exchanges dollars for the currencies of other nations within the group, thereby allowing the Fed to buy dollars in the foreign exchange market. see *swap*.

sweat equity: equity created by the labor of a purchaser or borrower that increases the value of the property. [62]

sweetening a loan: slang, to add more securities on deposit to margin a loan following the drop in security values so as to maintain the margin or to improve the condition of the margin.

swimming market: a healthy, active market.

swindle: slang, a deceptive business activity.

swindle sheet: slang, an account ledger organized by a businessman itemizing expenses in order that he will be reimbursed by his company.

swindling: the selling of worthless shares through misrepresentation.

swing: the price movement of a security, either up or down.

swingers: financial managers with considerable business transactions.

switch: a term to show the sale of an already existing long position and the simultaneous purchase of another position, or vice versa.

switching: selling one security and buying another. see *switch (contingent) order*.

switching and processing center (SPC): a facility that would link point-of-sale transaction terminals to depository and credit-granting institutions in order to accomplish instantaneous authorizations and funds transfers. [36]

switch (contingent) order: an order for the purchase (sale) of one stock and the sale (purchase) of another stock at a stipulated price difference. [20]

syli: monetary unit of Guinea.

symbol

(1) *general:* the single capital letter or combination of letters acquired by a corporation when it is to be listed on an exchange: International Business Machines is IBM; American Telephone and Telegraph is T.

(2) *computers:* a representation of something by reason of relationship, association, or convention.

(3) *investments:* the letters used to identify traded securities on a ticker tape, exchange board, or newspaper listing.

syndicate

(1) *general:* the association of two or more individuals, established to carry out a business activity. Members share in all profits or losses, in proportion to their contribution to the resources of the syndicate. cf. *joint venture, partnership*.

(2) *finance:* a group of investment bankers and securities dealers who, by agreement among themselves,

have joined together for the purpose of distributing a new issue of securities for a corporation.

syndicated loan: a loan in which a number of banks around the world participate.

synthetic fixed-rate loan: a new concept for the financial community; for borrowers, these loans would provide the security of fixed interest costs, and for lenders, it would have all the advantages of floating rates.

system

(1) *computers:* a collection of operations and procedures by which an activity is carried on.

(2) *systems:* an assembly of methods, procedures, or techniques united by regulated interaction to form an organized whole. see *systems theory.*

systems analysis: the analysis of any business activity to determine precisely what must be accomplished and how to accomplish it. see *operations research.*

systems theory: an analysis that stresses the necessity for maintaining the basic elements of input-process-output and for adapting to the larger environment that sustains the organization.

T: see *testator.*

TA

(1) see *tangible assets.*

(2) see *tax abatement.*

tab: slang, an unpaid bill.

tables, annual investment accumulation: shows amounts to be invested yearly at a given rate of interest which will accumulate to $1000 in a given number of years. [12]

tables, discount: tables showing the present value of a unit of money due at the end of various periods of time, or the present value of one unit per period for various periods of time at various rates. [12]

tables, interest: tables showing the amount to which a unit principal sum, or a unit periodic payment, will accumulate at the end of various periods of time, at various interest rates. [12]

tabulating equipment

(1) machines and equipment that use punched cards.

(2) synonymous with *electronic accounting machine.*

tacking: a process of adding a junior claim to a senior one in order to create some gain. Tacking is used in a mortgage, as when a third mortgage holder adds the first mortgage and tacks them to assume a superior position over the second mortgage holder. cf. *equal dignity.*

Taft-Hartley Act: the Labor-Management Relations Act of 1947, amending the Wagner-Connery Act of 1935. Major provisions are: (a) the closed shop is forbidden; (b) the government is authorized to seek an injunction preventing any work stoppage for 80 days when a strike threatens the nation's welfare and health; (c) unions cannot use union monies in connection with national elections (see also *Hatch Act*); (d) officers of unions must swear that they are not members of the Communist Party before the union can be certified (amended by the Landrum-Griffin Act); (e) unions must file financial reports with the U.S. Department of Labor along with a membership list; and (f) the states are permitted to pass right-to-work laws. Certain unfair labor practices are also identified.

T. Agt.: see *transfer agent.*

taha: monetary unit of Bangladesh.

take

(1) *law:* to lay hold of, seize, or have in possession. see *seisin (seizin).*

(2) *slang:* any profit from a business activity, usually one of a suspicious nature.

take a bath: to have a substantial financial loss.

take a flier: purchasing securities without thought, planning, and/or advice, with the expectation of making a large profit. Of course, a significant loss may also occur.

485

take on a line: purchasing a significant quantity of stock of one or more corporations over a set time period, in anticipation of climbing prices. cf. *put out a line.*

takeout loan: permanent loan on real property which takes out the interim, construction lender. [22]

takeover: the acquisition of an on-going organization by another through the purchase of the firm and/or exchange of capital stock. cf. *consolidation, merger.*

take-up

(1) paying for stock, originally bought on margin, in cash.

(2) an underwriters' term showing that they will handle specific securities for direct sale.

tala: monetary unit of Samoa.

tale: used in contracts detailing payment of metallic monies, where there is a request "by tale," that is, by count, as contrasted with payment based on weight.

talon

(1) *general:* a special coupon (e.g., a voucher stub).

(2) *finance:* that part of a debt instrument remaining on an unmatured bond after the interest coupons that were formerly attached have been presented.

tangible assets: physical and material (perceptible to touch) assets, as distinguished from intangible assets, which are imperceptible to touch. Examples of tangible assets are cash, land, and buildings.

tangible property: property in physical form. It can be touched, such as a house or land.

tap: slang, to ask a person or a lending organization for money.

tape price: the last sale of a stock as shown on the ticker tape.

tap out: slang, to lose one's money.

target company: a firm selected by another company as being attractive for takeover or acquisition.

tariff

(1) *finance:* any list of prices, charges, duties, and so on.

(2) *government:* a schedule of taxes on items imported or exported. In the United States the imposition of tariffs is made on imported goods only.

tariff war: a form of competition between nations as shown by tariff discrimination of various forms. see *retaliatory duty.*

taw: slang, sufficient funds to fully finance a business venture.

tax: a charge levied by government against the income of an individual, corporation, or other profit-making center of activity.

tax abatement: a decrease or rebate of a tax or burden improperly made. At times a tax abatement may reflect only an acknowledgment of a changed situation.

taxable estate: as defined by a state, the gross estate of a citizen or resident less allowable administrative and funeral expenses; indebtedness; taxes; losses; transfer for public, charitable, and religious uses; transfer to a surviving spouse; and a specific exemption. see *marital deduction.*

taxable income: the amount of income remaining after all permitted deductions and exemptions have been subtracted; thus the income that is subject to taxation.

taxable value: an assessed value utilized for taxing property, items, or income.

tax act of 1981: see *Economic Recovery Tax Act of 1981.*

Tax Adjustment Act of 1966: federal legislation; restored excise tax rates on transportation equipment and telephone service to rates in effect prior to January 1966. Introduced graduated withholding on personal tax collections.

tax anticipation note: any short-term, interest-bearing obligation created to be bought by businesses with monies assembled as a reserve in order to pay taxes. These notes are sold by government agencies to increase revenue.

tax avoidance: taking advantage of deductions and other provisions of tax law to reduce one's taxes. see *tax shelter;* cf. *tax dodge.*

tax base: the commodity, income, or service on which a tax is levied; the part of the value of an item that can be taxed.

tax-based income policy (TIP): a surcharge placed on the corporate income of a firm's tax if it grants its employees wage increases in excess of some government-set standard. Likewise, by holding their average wage increases below the standard, companies become eligible for a government tax reduction.

tax certificate: a certificate issued by a governmental unit as evidence of the conditional transfer of title to tax delinquent property from the original owner to the holder of the certificate. If the owner does not pay the amount of the tax arrearage and other charges required by law during the specified period of redemption, the holder can foreclose to obtain title. Also called, in some jurisdictions, tax lien certificate, or tax sale certificate. see also *tax deed.* [49]

tax cost: the figure used as the starting point under which gain or loss on a sale or exchange of property is determined. In the usual case, this gain or loss is simply the difference between the amount that a taxpayer paid for property (adjusted for depreciation) and the amount received when the taxpayer sells it. [37]

tax deed: a deed issued to the buyer of property that is sold because of nonpayment of taxes.

tax dodge: an activity (e.g., moving out of the country) that constitutes an illegal attempt to avoid paying taxes. see *tax exile (expatriate).*

tax evasion: unlawful attempts to avoid payment of a tax (e.g., not properly reporting all earned income).

tax-exempt bond: see *bond, tax-exempt.*

tax exemption: a right, secured by law, permitting freedom from a charge of taxes (e.g., on income that constitutes primary support of a child).

tax exile (expatriate): an individual choosing to leave his country rather than pay taxes.

tax foreclosure: the taking of property because of unpaid taxes.

tax haven: a nation offering low tax rates and other incentives for corporations of other countries. see *flight of capital.*

tax incidence: the business and/or persons on whom a tax finally comes to rest. see *nexus.*

tax lease: a long-term lease issued to

the buyer of tax-delinquent property when the law prevents an outright sale.

tax lien: a lien by the government against real property for unpaid taxes.

tax liens receivable: legal claims against property which have been exercised because of nonpayment of delinquent taxes, interest, and penalties. The account includes delinquent taxes, interest, and penalties receivable up to the date the lien becomes effective and the cost of holding the sale. [49]

tax limit: a legislative decision that limits the tax ceiling that can be imposed by an appropriate authority.

taxpayer

(1) *general:* a small building or store.

(2) *finance:* an owner of property who pays taxes.

(3) *government:* any person who payes taxes.

tax penalty: forfeiture of a sum because of nonpayment of taxes. [62]

tax policy: the policy whereby a government structures the tax rates. see entries under *tax.*

tax rate: the amount of tax applied per unit of tax base, expressed as a percentage; a tax of $5 on a base of $100, for example, represents a tax rate of 5 percent.

tax rate limit: the maximum rate at which a governmental unit may levy a tax. The limit may apply to taxes raised for a particular purpose, or to taxes imposed for all purposes, and may apply to a single government, to a class of governments, or to all governmental units operating in a particular area. Overall tax rate limits usually restrict levies for all purposes and of all governments, state and local, having jurisdiction in a given area. [49]

tax receivership: the office or function of a receiver appointed by a court or under a statute upon default of taxes. [62]

Tax Reduction Act of 1975: federal legislation; provided for 10 percent rebate on 1974 taxes up to maximum of $200 for individuals. Provided tax cuts retroactive to January 1975 for both individuals and corporations. For individuals it was in the form of increased standard deductions, a $30 exemption credit, and an earned income credit for low-income families. Reduced corporate income tax and increased investment surtax exemption. Increased investment tax credit to 10 percent.

Tax Reduction and Simplification Act of 1977: legislation signed by President Carter for a $34 billion tax cut, giving credit to industry to create jobs and attempting to simplify tax-filing procedures.

Tax Reform Act of 1969: federal legislation removing major benefits from controlled corporations. Multiple surtax exemptions and multiple accumulated earnings credits were withdrawn by 1975, and the incentives for establishing additional corporations within a controlled group ceased at the end of 1974. The law provided for the accumulation of capital losses to the three preceding years prior to the loss of revenue for a corporation, with no change in the future five-year advance provision for capital losses. Restrictions are given on employee benefit plans. see *Tax Reform Act of 1976.*

Tax Reform Act of 1976: Significant aspects as follows:

(a) *Income Taxes* (effective for years after December 31, 1975, except where otherwise noted).

capital gains: the holding period to qualify for long-term capital gains was increased from six to nine months in 1977 and to 12 months in 1978 and thereafter. The six-month holding period continues to apply to commodity futures contacts traded on a commodity exchange.

capital losses: the amount of an individual's ordinary income against which capital losses can be deducted was increased from $1000 to $2000 in 1977 and to $3000 in 1978 and later years.

interest expense deduction: individuals were formerly limited to a deduction for investment interest expense in the amount of $25,000 in excess of investment income; this limitation was reduced to $10,000 for debts incurred after September 11, 1975. Prepaid interest expense of cash basis taxpayers must be prorated and deducted over the period of the loan instead of being deductible in the year of payment of the interest.

stock options: the profit element of stock purchased on the exercise of qualified stock options issued to employees after May 20, 1976, is to be treated as ordinary income at the time of exercise rather than as capital gain.

maximum tax on earned income: the 50 percent maximum tax on earned income computation now requires earned income to be reduced by 100 percent of the so-called tax preference items (one half of long-term capital gains, the excess of accelerated depreciation over straight line depreciation, etc.) Formerly, the reduction was limited to the excess of preference items over $30,000. The law has been liberalized to include pension and annuity income as earned income.

minimum tax on preference items: the minimum tax rate is increased from 10 to 15 percent, and the exemption will be reduced to the greater of $10,000 or half the regular taxes. The earlier ruling allowed a $30,000 exemption plus all regular taxes. Additional items were designated as preference items (e.g., itemized deductions other than medical or casualty deductions in excess of 60 percent of adjusted gross income). The carry-over of regular taxes not previously used as an exemption was repealed.

minimum tax on preference items (corporations): the rate is increased from 10 to 15 percent, and the exemption is the greater of $10,000 or the full amount of regular taxes paid. The carry-over for taxes can no longer be used.

net operating loss carry-overs: businesses can carry losses back three years and forward seven years instead of three and five. In addition, companies may elect to skip the application of the loss back to the prior three years and only carry it forward.

buying and selling loss corporations: generally, net operating losses carry-overs of an acquired corporation will not be available if there is no continuity of ownership by the former stockholders of the loss corporation. Provisions are made for reductions in the loss where former owners have a partial continuing interest.

home sales: for taxpayers over the age of 65, exemption was raised from $20,000 to $35,000.

business use of home: a deduction is allowed only if an office at home is the taxpayer's principal and exclusive place of business or is a place where he or she meets patients, clients, or customers.

loss of rental of vacation home: the loss on the rental of a vacation home is not deductible if the taxpayer uses the vacation home for more than two weeks a year or more than 10 percent of the annual rental time.

sick pay: the sick pay exclusion of $100 a week was repealed. Substituted was a very limited exclusion for low-paid individuals under 65 years of age, who are permanently and totally disabled.

writers of options (puts and calls): losses for options from a closing transaction are treated as a short-term capital loss rather than as an ordinary loss. (Similar treatment is given to gains.)

tax shelters: individuals, partnerships, and corporations cannot deduct losses attributable to costs financed through loans made without any obligation to pay them or where the taxpayer's risk is limited by guarantees or repurchased agreements with the exception of real estate investments.

(b) *Estate and Gift Taxes*

exemptions: after 1976 the $60,000 estate tax exemption and the $30,000 exemption for lifetime gifts were eliminated. In their stead is a unified tax credit of $30,000 in 1977, rising to $47,000 by 1981. That is equivalent to an exemption of $120,666 in 1977 and $175,625 in 1981. The $3000 per donee annual exemption ($6000 for a joint gift) continues to exist.

marital deduction: the marital deduction is increased to the greater of $250,000 or half of the adjusted gross estate.

rates: the estate and gift tax rates were combined into a single schedule of 30 to 70 percent. This replaced the scheme in which gift tax rates were three-fourths of the estate tax rates.

inherited basis of property: heirs cannot get an accelerated basis for inherited property so that the increment in value can no longer escape income tax. One very big exception is that the increment in value to December 31, 1976, escapes income tax because for someone who dies after December 31, 1976, an heir's basis becomes the value on December 31, 1976.

tax roll: an official statement describing property taxed, including the names of the taxpayers and the amount of their tax.

tax sale: sale of property in default because of nonpayment of taxes. see *scavenger sale.*

tax-saving retirement plan: see *Keogh plan.*

tax search: a determination by searching official records to determine whether there are any unpaid property taxes.

tax selling: reducing or offsetting the tax liability on capital gains by selling off stocks that show a loss. It is sometimes done to realize profits.

tax service contract: an agreement between a title company and an association under which the title company is responsible for notifying the lender of all tax and improvement lien payments as they come due. [59]

tax sharing: see *revenue sharing, shared revenue.*

tax shelter: the term applied to a means of legal avoidance of paying a portion of one's income taxes by careful interpretation of tax regulations and adjustment of one's finances to take advantage of IRS rulings. The Tax Reform Act of 1976 placed new restrictions on tax shelters.

tax shield: the amount of depreciation charged against income, thus protecting that amount from tax; a depreciation deduction of $10,000 produces a tax shield of $3600 when the tax rate is 36 percent.

tax title: title to property acquired by purchasing land that was sold as the result of unpaid taxes.

tax waiver: a written consent of the state tax department permitting the withdrawal of property belonging to the estate of a decedent by the executor or administrator, in order to permit the assembling of assets and to permit distribution. [37]

Taylorism: the work of Frederick W. Taylor (1856–1915), who outlined the concepts of scientific management and work efficiency.

TC
(1) see *tax certificate.*
(2) see *time certificates of deposit.*

TD
(1) see *time deposit (open account).*
(2) *Department of the Treasury, U.S.*

T&E: see *travel and entertainment credit card.*

Technical Corrections Act of 1979: passed in April 1980, creates a possible refund opportunity for holders of "section 1244" stock.

technical position: a term applied to the various internal factors affecting the market; opposed to external forces, such as earnings, dividends, and general economic conditions. Some internal factors are the size of the short-term interest, whether the market has had a sustained advance or decline without interruption, and the amount of credit in use in the market.

technical research: analysis of the market and stocks based on supply and demand. The technician studies price movements, volume, and trends and patterns which are revealed by charting these factors and attempts to assess the possible effect of current market action on future supply and demand for securities and individual issues. see *fundamental research.* [20]

Tee.: see *trustee.*

teller: an employee of a bank who is assigned the duty of waiting on depositors and customers of the bank. The teller's principal responsibility is to handle cash for the depositor and the bank and to serve the depositor or the customer as far as his or her duties will permit. The teller is the "personal" contact between the customer and the bank. see also *head* *teller, loan teller, paying teller, receiving teller.* [10]

teller proof: a system of individual teller control whereby the teller balances and settles his own cash position daily. If the teller is using a bank teller's machine, this proof is very simple, because the machine will carry totals for cash received and cash paid out. Otherwise, the teller will maintain his own cash settlement sheet, listing all cash taken in and all checks cashed. Teller proof consists of using the teller's starting cash total, adding his cash received, and subtracting his cash paid out, to arrive at his cash on hand. The cash counted must agree with this cash ending total for proof. [10]

teller's check: a check drawn by a bank on another (drawee) bank and signed by a teller or tellers of the drawer bank. Tellers' checks are used in payment of withdrawal orders and, in lieu of savings bank money orders, are sometimes sold to depositors in exchange for cash. [39]

teller's stamp: a rubber stamp, usually showing the teller's number or initials and the bank's name or transit number, which the teller uses to identify deposits, cashed checks, or other posting media that he or she handles. [10]

teller terminal: an input-output unit of a computer system that replaces the teller's window posting machine in a computerized association. [59]

temporary administrator: an individual or a trust institution appointed by a court to take over and safeguard an estate during a suit over an alleged will, or over the right of appointment of an executor or administrator, or during the period that probate is delayed for any reason, such as difficulty in finding or citing missing heirs. [32]

temporary bond: see *bond, temporary.*

temporary loans: short-term obligations representing amounts borrowed for short periods of time and usually evidenced by notes payable or warrants payable. They may be unsecured, or secured by specific revenues to be collected. see *tax anticipation note.* [49]

tenancy: the holding of real property by any form of title. [37]

tenancy at sufferance: a tenancy in which the tenant comes into possession of real property under a lawful title or interest and continues to hold the property even after his title or interest has terminated. [37]

tenancy at will: that estate which may be terminated by either the lessor or the lessee at any time. [62]

tenancy by the entirety: tenancy by a husband and wife in such a manner that, except in concert with the other, neither husband nor wife has a disposable interest in the property during the lifetime of the other. Upon the death of either, the property goes to the survivor. To be distinguished from *joint tenancy* and *tenancy in common.* [37]

tenancy for years: a tenancy for a definite period of time—for example, a year or 99 years. It cannot be terminated by either party alone except at the expiration of the time agreed upon. [32]

tenancy in common: ownership of property by two or more persons, each holding a separate interest. No right of survivorship exists. see *undi-vided right.*

tenancy in common account

(1)   a savings account that is owned by two or more persons, each of whom has a separate interest; when one owner dies, his shares passes to his heirs, not to the remaining owner(s). [59]

(2)   also refers to a type of checking account, often requiring that both parties sign checks, notes, and so on; in other words, one individual cannot act independently of the other.

(3)   can refer to stock certificates that are issued to "tenants in common."

tenant: one who holds or possesses real property. [37]

tenant in dower: a wife who has survived her husband and in most states receives one-third of his inherited estate for the remainder of her life.

tender

(1)   *investments:* a corporation's offer of securities by asking for bids for them, at prices above a minimum.

(2)   *law:* the offering of money in satisfaction of a debt by producing the money and stating to the creditor a desire to pay.

tender offer

(1)   a bid by an outsider to purchase some or all of a firm's outstanding shares, usually for the purpose of obtaining effective control.

(2)   an offer by a company to purchase its own shares or other types of securities such as bonds or debentures. [43]

ten-forty: a U.S. bond that is redeemable after 10 years, and due and payable after 40 years.

tenor: the period between the formation of a debt and the date of expected payment.

ten-spot: slang, a $10 bill.

ten-year trust: see *Clifford trust.*

term: the prescribed time a person has to make an installment or other payments as identified in a loan or credit contract.

term bond: see *bond, term.*

term bonds payable: a liability account which records the face value of general obligation term bonds issued and outstanding. [49]

terminable bond: see *bond, terminable.*

terminal: a device connected to a computer system, used for the input and/or output of data. Technically, a terminal may be as simple as a telephone; as complex as a small computer. [36]

terminal market: a market (i.e., a commodity market) that deals in futures.

term life insurance: life insurance protection during a certain number of years, but usually expiring without policy cash value if the insured survives the stated period. see *extended term insurance, family income rider.*

term loan: usually a long-term loan running up to 10 years. Such loans are generally made by the larger commercial banks and insurance companies to large, well-established business enterprises for capital expenditures such as plant improvements and purchases of equipment.

term mortgage: a mortgage with a fixed time period, usually less than five years, in which only interest is paid. Following termination of the mortgage, the total principal is demanded.

terms: the details, specifications, and conditions of a loan.

territorial bond: see *bond, insular.*

testament: the declaration of an individual's intentions for the disposition he or she wishes to be made of property following death. synonymous with *will.*

testamentary account: a category of savings accounts recognized by the Federal Savings and Loan Insurance Corporation as separately insurable, and including funds owned by an individual and invested in a revocable trust account, tentative or Totten trust account, payable-on-death account, or similar account evidencing an intention that on his or her death the funds shall belong to a specified member of the owner's family. see *Totten trust.* [59]

testamentary disposition: the disposition of property by deed, will, or otherwise in such a manner that it shall not take effect unless or until the grantor dies. [37]

testamentary guardian: a guardian of a minor or an incompetent person named in the decedent's will. [37]

testamentary trust: a trust established through a will. The trustee (an individual or a bank) is named in the will to receive designated property from the executor of an estate and holds it in trust for the benefit of named beneficiaries.

testate: having completed and left an acceptable will.

testator: a deceased male who left a will setting forth the disposition of his wealth (total assets).

testatrix: a deceased female who left a will setting forth the disposition of her wealth (total assets).

THA: see *Taft-Hartley Act.*

thin corporation: a corporation owing a large number of debts relative to its equity position.

thin market: a market in which there are comparatively few bids to buy or offers to sell or both. The phrase may apply to a single security or to the entire stock market. In a thin market, price fluctuations between transactions are usually larger than they are when the market is liquid. A thin market in a particular stock may reflect lack of interest or a lack of demand for stock.

third-generation computer: a computer utilizing tiny circuits and components to replace vacuum tubes, increase accuracy, and speed up the processing of work.

third market: listed stocks not traded on a securities exchange; over-the counter trading in listed securities.

third mortgage: a mortgage that is junior to both the first and second mortgages.

third-party check: a check which is given by one party to another, the recipient of which offers it to still another (third) party. [55]

third-party credit transfers: automatic deposits, or credits, to a checking, savings, or NOW account from a third party. Examples include payroll credits, Social Security payments or other federal recurring retirement benefits. cf. *third-party debit transfers.* see *electronic fund transfers.*

third-party debit transfers: automatic withdrawals, or debits, from a checking, savings or NOW account and payable to a third party (e.g., periodic deductions for insurance premium payments). cf. *third-party credit* *transfers.* see *electronic fund transfers.*

third-party payment service: a payment plan whereby a financial institution transfers a depositor's funds to a third party or to the account of the third party upon the negotiable or nonnegotiable order of the depositor. A checking account is one type of third-party payment service. [59]

third-party transaction: a three-way business activity involving a buyer, a seller, and a source of consumer credit.

third-party transfer: a nonnegotiable order to a savings association, issued by an account holder, to pay a specified sum of money to a third party. [59]

thou: slang, $1000.

threshold companies: companies on the threshold of corporate maturity in that they are not yet managed by professionals but are run intuitively by a handful of entrepreneurs. This concept was developed by Donald Clifford, Jr.

thrift account: synonymous with *savings account* or *special interest account.* see *savings account, special interest account, thrifts.*

thrift institution: the general term for mutual savings banks, savings and loan associations, and credit unions. see *thrifts.* [1]

thrifts: there are two types of thrifts, the savings banks and savings and loan industries. Today they are both engaged in basically the same business—taking in consumer deposits and reinvesting them in mortgages. Together they hold almost $800 billion (1981) in assets, more than any financial industry except commercial banks, whose assets amount to $1.5 trillion (1981). Savings banks, which theoretically are owned by their depositors, were established by philanthropists to promote savings among the poor. The founders gave ultimate power to self-perpetuating boards of trustees. Thus, unlike depositors in S&Ls, savings bank depositors do not have the right to elect their trustees. Several savings banks are trying to convert to federal from state charters. Under federal rules, their depositors would gain voting rights within their respective organizations. Savings and loans originally were formed by community members to finance housing, not to promote savings. Initially, they existed for limited periods, long enough for each member to buy a home. The members chipped in to raise enough money to finance home construction. Lots were drawn to determine which member would be the first to get a house. The modern version of the savings and loan association got its start in the early 1930s. The industry boomed after World War II, when 11 million returning veterans needed housing.

through bill of lading: a bill of lading covering items moving from the origin point to a final location, even if they are moved from one carrier to another.

TI: see *taxable income.*

ticker: the instrument that prints prices and volume of security transactions in cities and towns throughout the United States and Canada within minutes of each trade on any listed exchange.

tickler: an index for maturity dates of notes, bonds, acceptances, and so on, serving as a reminder to banks and financial institutions that these instruments will at some future time period be approaching maturity.

tied loan: a foreign loan limiting the borrower to spending the proceeds only in the nation making the loan. cf. *counterpart monies.*

tight credit: see *tight money.*

tight money: high interest rates demanded in the borrowing of money. synonymous with "tight credit."

till money: funds kept at a front desk or register, as distinguished from monies held in a bank.

time adjusted rate of return: the rate of interest at which the existing value of anticipated cash inflows from a particular project equals the present value of expected cash outflow of the same activity.

time-and-a-half pay: compensation at the rate of one and one-half times the worker's regular pay. The Fair Labor Standards Act of 1938 made this rate mandatory for work performed beyond 40 hours a week by workers employed by firms engaged in interstate commerce.

time bargain: struck when a seller and a purchaser of securities consent to exchange a specific stock at a stated price at a stated future time.

time certificates of deposit: a time deposit evidenced by a negotiable or nonnegotiable instrument specifying an amount and a maturity. Savings bonds and savings certificates are merely forms of nonnegotiable time certificates of deposits. [69]

time deposit (open account): funds deposited under agreement. They bear interest from the date of deposit, although the agreement usually re-quires that such funds remain on deposit for at least 30 days. The agreement stipulates a fixed maturity date or number of days after which payment will be made, or it is stipulated that payment will be made after a given period following notice by the depositor of intention to withdraw. see *Regulation Q.*

time draft: a draft payable a specified number of days (30, 60, or 90 days, for example) after its date of issuance or acceptance. [10]

time loan: a loan made for a specified period. The maturity date generally is 30, 60, 90, or 120 days after the date of the loan. Interest is usually collected in advance, at the time the loan is made, as a "discount."

time money: funds loaned out for a specified time period.

time open accounts: a time deposit evidenced by a written contract specifying a maturity but leaving open the amount involved. [69]

time order: an order that becomes a market or limited price order at a specified time. [20]

time-sharing: a method of using a computing system that allows a number of users to execute programs on the same hardware and to interact with the programs during execution.

time warrant: a negotiable obligation of a governmental unit having a term shorter than bonds and frequently tendered to individuals and firms in exchange for contractual services, capital acquisitions, or equipment purchases. [49]

time warrants payable: the amount of time warrants outstanding and unpaid. [49]

timing of notes: the function of calculating and marking the maturity date on notes and other evidences of debt. Also the number of days that a loan must run until maturity for interest calculations. [10]

TIP: see *tax-based income policy.*

tips

(1) *finance:* monies offered to encourage or ensure promptness; monies given for services rendered (e.g., 15 percent of a restaurant bill constitutes the waiter's tip).

(2) *investments:* supposedly "inside" information on corporation affairs; a subjective recommendation to buy or sell a particular stock.

tipster sheet: an unofficial list of stocks that are recommended to customers.

title: proper and rightful ownership.

title company: see *title guaranty company.*

title deed: a legal document indicating proof of an individual's ownership of a piece of land.

title defect: a fact or circumstance that challenges property ownership. see *cloud on title.*

title guaranty company: a business firm created to examine real estate files (i.e., to conduct title searches) to determine the legal status of the property and to find any evidence of encumbrances, faults, or other title defects. Once a search has been completed and the property found sound, the company receives a fee from the property purchaser who needed to determine that his or her title was clear and good. The property purchaser receives an abstract of the prepared title, and the title is verified by an attorney of the company who gives an opinion but does not guarantee the accuracy of the title. The company agrees to indemnify the owner against any loss that may be experienced resulting from a subsequent defect. A title guaranty policy is evidence of the title insurance, with costs based on the value of the property and the risk involved as determined by the condition of the title. see also *title insurance.*

title guaranty policy: title insurance furnished by the owner, provided as an alternative for an abstract of title. synonymous with *Torrens certificate.* see also *title guaranty company.* [62]

title insurance: an insurance contract from a title guaranty company presented to owners of property, indemnifying them against having a defective or unsalable title while they possess the property. This contract is considered to be a true indemnity for loss actually sustained by reason of the defects or encumbrances against which the insurer agrees to indemnify. Title insurance includes a thorough examination of the evidences of title by the insurer. see *title guaranty company.*

title insurance company: see *title guaranty company.*

title search: see *search, title guaranty company, title insurance.*

title theory: a system in which the mortgagee has legal title to the mortgaged property and the mortgagor has equitable title. [62]

Title VII: see *Civil Rights Act of 1964, Title VII.*

TL

(1) see *time loan.*

(2) see *trading limit.*

TLI: see *term life insurance.*

TM: see *third market.*

TN: see *transferable notice.*

To.: see *turnover.*

TO: see *treasury obligations.*

token money: an object, usually coins, whose value as money is greater than the market value of the materials of which it is composed.

tombstone: an advertisement placed by an underwriting syndicate outlining a public sale. A listing of the syndicate members is given.

top credit: ready credit.

topping out: a term employed to denote loss of upside energy at the top after a long price run-up.

Torrens certificate: a document, issued by the proper public authority called a "registrar" acting under the provision of the Torrens law, indicating in whom title resides. [62]

tort: a wrongful act committed by a person against another person or his or her property.

tortfeasor: a person committing a tort.

total assets: all money, machinery, other equipment, real estate, and credits owned by a business.

total cost: the sum of a firm's total fixed costs and total variable costs.

total debt: all long-term obligations of the government and its agencies and all interest-bearing short-term credit obligations. Long-term obligations are those repayable more than one year after issue.

total debt to tangible net worth: obtained by dividing total current plus long-term debts by tangible net worth. When this relationship exceeds 100 percent, the equity of creditors in the assets of the business exceeds that of owners. [4]

total fixed costs: the costs that do not change with an organization's output (e.g., payments on rent, property taxes).

total of payments: the total of all installments scheduled to be made in the repayment of a loan or sales contract; face of note; the sum of the amount financed and the finance charges. [55]

total reserves: member bank deposits with Federal Reserve Banks plus member bank vault cash. The sum of required and excess reserves. [72]

total revenue: total receipts of a company. It is equal to the price per unit times the number of units sold.

total variable costs: costs that change directly with the firm's output, increasing as output rises over the total range of production (i.e., labor, fuel).

Totten trust: a trust created by the deposit of one's own money in his own name as trustee for another. Title is vested in the record owner (trustee), who during his life holds it on a revocable trust for the named beneficiary. At the death of the depositor, a presumption arises that an absolute trust was created as to the balance on hand at the death of the depositor. see *testamentary account.* [37]

touch: asking for a loan of a sum of money from an acquaintance or friend.

tough buck: slang, wages earned from a difficult or hard job.

TPS: see *trigger-price system.*

TPT: see *third-party transaction.*

Tr.: see *trust.*

TR

(1) see *tax rate.*

(2) see *trust receipt.*

TRA: see *Tax Reform Act of 1969, Tax Reform Act of 1976.*

trace

(1) *general:* the record of a series of events.

(2) *banking:* to record a policyholder's record of premium payment.

trade acceptance: a bill of exchange that is drawn by the seller of goods or materials at the time of the purchase and which is accepted by the purchaser. [10]

trade deficit: a negative trade balance.

trade discount: a deduction from the agreed price, usually expressed as a percentage or a series of percentages, that is used in commerce to encourage prompt payment of bills. Trade discount should not be entered in the books of account, nor should it be considered to be a type of earnings.

Trade Expansion Act of 1962: federal legislation permitting the president to negotiate additional tariff reductions, eliminate or reduce tariffs on items of the European Common Market, reduce tariffs on the basis of reciprocal trade agreements, and grant technical and financial assistance to employers whose business is adversely affected by tariff reductions.

trade house: a firm that buys and sells futures and actuals for the accounts of customers as well as for its own account. [11]

trademark: a distinctive identification of a manufactured product or of a service taking the form of a name, logo, motto, and so on; a trademarked brand has legal protection and only the owner can use the mark. Organizations that file an application at the U.S. Patent Office and use the brand for five years may be granted a trademark. A firm may lose a trademark that has become generic. Generic names are those which consumers use to identify the product, rather than to specify a particular brand (e.g., escalator, aspirin, and nylon).

trade name: the name under which an organization conducts business, or by which the business or its goods and services are identified. It may or may not be registered as a trademark.

trader

(1) *general:* anyone who is engaged in trade or commerce.

(2) *investments:* one who buys and sells for his or her own account for short-term profit. [20]

trade reference: a person or firm to which a seller is referred for credit data on a potential customer.

trading difference: a difference of a fraction of a point in the charged price for securities bought and sold in an odd-lot transaction, which is in excess of the price at which the security would be traded in traditional round lots.

trading floor: see *floor.*

trading limit

(1) the price limit above or below which trading in commodities is not allowed during a given day.

(2) as specified by the Commodity Exchange Act, the number of contracts a person may legally retain.

trading post: one of many trading locations on the floor of stock exchanges at which stocks assigned to that location are bought and sold. see *floor, specialist.*

trading range: the amount that futures prices can fluctuate during one trading session; essentially, the price distance between limit up and limit down.

traditio: delivery and transfer of possession of property by an owner.

transaction: any agreement between two or more parties, establishing a legal obligation.

transfer

(1) *general:* the shifting of an employee from one job to another within the same organization.

(2) *computers:* to move information from one storage device to another or from one part of memory to another.

(3) *investments:* see *stock transfer.*

transferable notice: a written announcement issued by a seller signifying his intention of making delivery in fulfillment of a futures contract. The recipient of the notice may make a sale of the futures contract and transfer the notice within a specified time to another party, on some exchanges directly, and on others through the clearing association. The last recipient takes delivery of the commodity tendered. Notices on some exchanges are not transferable. [2]

transfer agent: a transfer agent keeps a record of the name of each registered shareowner, his or her address, and the number of shares owned; it is the agent's responsibility to see that certificates presented to the office for transfer are properly canceled and that new certificates are issued correctly in the name of the transferee. [20]

transfer costs: the costs that a department accepts for items supplied by other departments. see *transfer price.*

transferee: the person or corporation to which property has been transferred. [37]

transfer in contemplation of death: a transfer of property by gift made in apprehension of death arising from some existing bodily condition or impending peril and not the general expectation of eventual decease commonly held by all persons. [37]

transfer of title: the change of property title from one person to another. synonymous with *voluntary alienation.*

transfer of value: a banking concept that offers the consumer a variety of ways to pay for what he or she wants without cash.

transferor: the person or corporation which conveys or transfers property. [37]

transfer payment: in government statistics, money transactions among people, government, and business for which no services are performed; there is no addition to the national product.

transfer price: the price charged by one segment of an organization for a product or service it supplies to another part of the same firm. see *transfer costs.*

transfers (mail, wire, cable): *mail transfer* is the remittance of money by a bank to be paid to a party in another town or city. The instruction to pay such funds is transmitted by regular mail, hence the term "mail transfer." *Wire transfer* is used to designate a transfer of funds from one point to another by wire or telegraph. *Cable transfer* is used to designate a transfer of funds to a city or town located outside the United States by cable. Commissions or fees are charged for all types of transfers. When transfers are made by wire or cable, the cost of transmitting the instructions to pay by wire or cable is charged to the remitter in addition to the commission. [10]

transfer tax: a tax imposed by the federal or some state governments when a security is sold or transferred from one person to another. The tax is paid by the seller. There is no tax on transfers of bonds. The transfer tax is usually collected as a stamp tax.

transfer voucher: a voucher authorizing transfers of cash or other resources between funds. [49]

transit department: a department of a bank whose function is the processing of all out-of-city items. The transit department writes all transit letters, both cash letters and remittance letters and forwards these letters to the Federal Reserve Bank, correspondent banks, and other banks for collection and payment. [10]

transit items: cash items payable outside the town or city of the bank receiving them for credit to customers' accounts. [50]

transit letter: a letter or form of deposit slip on which a bank lists and describes transit items. [50]

translation (of foreign currencies):   the expression of an amount denominated in one currency in terms of another currency by use of an exchange rate between the two currencies. [43]

Transmatic: the trade name of a

franchised, preauthorized payment system for savings associations. [59]

transmittal letter: a letter accompanying a shipment of securities, documents, or other property usually containing a brief description of the securities, documents, or property being forwarded and an explanation of the transaction. [37]

travel and entertainment credit card (T&E card):   a credit card issued for use primarily for the purchase of meals, lodging, and transportation. Major American cards are American Express, Carte Blanche, and Diner's Club.

travel department: a department in a bank established to render service to the bank's customers in any matter relative to travel or foreign transactions. In the larger coastal banks, all foreign transactions are handled by the foreign department of the bank. In interior banks, the travel department deals directly with their coastal bank correspondents in handling foreign transactions. The travel department will arrange accommodations for domestic or foreign travel, plan vacation trips, and handle foreign transactions for its customers. [10]

traveler's checks: a form of check especially designed for travelers, including persons on vacation and business trips. These checks are usually preprinted in denominations of $10, $20, $50, and $100, and can be cashed and used to purchase goods and services in places of business that accept them.

traveler's letter of credit: a letter of credit is issued by a bank to a customer preparing for an extended trip. The customer pays for the letter of credit, which is issued for a specified period of time in the amount purchased. The bank furnishes a list of correspondent banks or its own foreign branches at which drafts drawn against the letter of credit will be honored. see *guaranteed letter of credit, letter of indication.*

Tr. Co.: see *trust company.*

Treas.

(1) treasurer.

(2) treasury.

treasurer's check: see *cashier's check.*

treasureship: the functions of management holding responsibility for the custody and investment of money, the granting of credit and collection of accounts, capital provision, maintenance of a market for the firm's securities, and so on.

Treasury bill: a U.S. government short-term security sold to the public each week, maturing in 91 to 182 days.

Treasury bond: see *bond, Treasury.*

treasury cash holdings: currency and coin held by the Treasury. [40]

Treasury certificates: U.S. government short-term securities, sold to the public and maturing in one year.

Treasury currency outstanding: currency such as U.S. notes and silver certificates, and coin in the hands of the public for which the Treasury is responsible. [40]

Treasury note: a U.S. government long-term security, sold to the public and having a maturity of one to five years.

Treasury obligations: see *bond, Treasury; Treasury bill; Treasury certificates; Treasury note.*

treasury securities: interest-bearing obligations of the U.S. government issued by the Treasury as a means of borrowing money to meet government expenditures not covered by tax revenues. Marketable Treasury securities fall into three categories: bills, notes, and bonds. The Federal Reserve System holds more than $100 billion of these obligations, acquired through open market operations. [1]

treasury stock: the title to previously issued stock of a corporation that has been reacquired by that corporation by purchase, gift, donation, inheritance, or other means. The value of such stock should be considered to be a deduction from the value of outstanding stock of similar type rather than as an asset of the issuing corporation.

trend: the direction that prices are taking.

Trf.: transfer.

trial balance: a list of the balances of the accounts in a ledger kept by double entry with the debit and credit balances shown in separate columns. If these are equal or their net balance agrees with a controlling account, the ledger from which the figures are taken is said to be "in balance." [49]

triangular trade: trade between three countries, in which an attempt is made to create a favorable balance for each.

trickle down: the process by which federal funds flowing into the national economy stimulate growth through being distributed into organizations, as opposed to stimulating growth by direct payments (e.g., welfare).

trigger-price system: a federal system

for identifying all cut-rate steel "dumped" in the United States. It sets minimum prices below which imported steel cannot be sold in this country without "triggering" an investigation by the Treasury Department. If the agency determines that the steel has been sold at unfairly low prices, bonds and ultimately antidumping duties can be imposed on the products.

triple (bottom) top: the point, high or low, reached by the market or a particular security, duplicating a level attained on two earlier occasions. To the market specialist, the three levels establish a triple top (bottom) and show that a major wall of price support (overhead resistance) has been established.

trough: the lowest point of economic activity.

TRSA: see *Tax Reduction and Simplification Act of 1977.*

true cost banking: an efficient way of providing money to borrowers, a policy requiring consumers and corporations to pay higher borrowing costs. see *Depository Institutions Deregulation and Monetary Control Act.*

true interest: see *pure interest.*

truncation: a banking industry term for check safekeeping. The electronic sorting out of charges and transmitting them back to the issuer banks, which send payment back the same way.

trust

(1) *general:* a fiduciary relationship between persons: one holds property for the benefit and use of another.

(2) *investments:* a combination of corporations, usually in the same industry; stockholders relinquish their stock to a board of trustees, who then issue certificates and dividends. The purposes of creating a trust include controlling costs of production, increasing profits, and reducing competition. see *monopoly.*

trust, corporate: the name applied to the division of a bank that handles the trust and agency business of corporations.

trust, personal: that branch of a trust company whose function is connected with the handling of trusts for individuals. Some of the functions performed are those of executorship of estates, administration of trust funds, investment services, and guardianships. Detailed records are maintained and statements mailed to beneficiaries of every transaction affecting a trust. [10]

trust account: a general term to cover all types of accounts in a trust department, including estates, guardianships, and agencies as well as trusts proper. [37]

trust administrator: a person in the employment of a trust institution who handles trust accounts in the sense of having direct contacts and dealings with trust customers and beneficiaries. [37]

trust agreement (trust instrument): an agreement between an employer and a trustee used in connection with a pension plan. It defines the trustee's powers and duties, and tells how the funds of the pension plan shall be invested and how payments shall be made to those who benefit under the plan. A trust agreement is usually used in connection with self-administered pension plans and individual policy pension plans.

trust authority: the legal right of a corporation to engage in trust business. [32]

trust business: a trust company, or a trust department of a bank, which settles estates, administers trusts, and performs agency functions for individuals, corporations, governments, associations, and public or educational or related institutions is said to engage in the trust business. [10]

trust by order of court: a trust created by an order of a court of competent jurisdiction. [37]

trust certificate: see *stock trust certificate.*

trust charges: the charges made by a trust institution for its trust and agency services. see *commission, fee.* [32]

trust committee: a committee of directors or officers or both of a trust institution charged with general or specific duties relating to its trust business. [37]

trust company: an institution, usually state supervised, that engages in the trust business, and usually in all commercial banking activities.

trust costs: the costs to a trust institution of rendering trust and agency services; opposed to trust charges, which are the costs to trust institution customers or beneficiaries for obtaining trust and agency services. [32]

trust deed: see *deed, trust.*

trust department: the department of a bank that provides trust and agency services. The trust department by regulation must have books and as-

sets separate from those of commercial banking activities. [25]

trustee: a person to whom the title to property has been conveyed for the benefit of another.

trustee deed: see *deed, trustee.*

trusteed fund: any accumulation of capital held in trust for retirement, religious, educational, research, profit-sharing, or other purposes. [22]

trusteed pension plan: a pension plan in which the corporation's contributions to the plan are placed in a trust for investment and reinvestment, as distinguished from a plan in which the benefits are secured by life insurance. [37]

trustee in bankruptcy: the individual appointed by a court or by creditors to carry out the responsibilities of trust in a bankruptcy proceeding.

trusteeship: the status of a carrier's property while in the charge of trustees appointed under Section 77 of the Bankruptcy Act, approved March 3, 1933. A reorganization proceeding under trustees differs from a receivership equity proceeding chiefly in the fact that the former may be instituted by a railroad as well as by creditors and must follow a detailed prescribed procedure in regard to the presentation, consideration, and adoption of plans of reorganization, involving participation by the Interstate Commerce Commission as well as by the court. [18]

trust estate: an estate held in trust by one individual for the welfare of another.

trust for support: a trust which provides that the trustee shall pay or apply only so much of the income or principal as in its judgment is necessary for the support, including education, of the beneficiary. [37]

trust function: the fiduciary capacity in which an individual or a trust institution may act, such as executor, administrator, guardian, or trustee. [37]

trust fund: the funds held by a trustee for the benefit of another person.

trust funds, federal: trust funds established to account for receipts that are held in trust by the government for use in carrying out specific purposes and programs in accordance with a trust agreement or a statute.

trust indenture: an instrument in writing that contains a description of all property originally placed in the trust, the agreement with respect to the duties of the trustee in administering the property, the rights of all beneficiaries named, along with their proportionate shares in the trust, the duration of the trusteeship, the distribution of income from the trust principal to the life tenants, and the distribution of the trust property to the remaindermen at the termination of the trust.

trust institution: a trust company, state bank, national bank, or other corporation engaged in the trust business under authority of law. A corporation is a trust institution if any of its department is engaged in trust business, although other departments may be engaged otherwise. [37]

trust instrument: any writing will, trust agreement, declaration of trust, deed of trust, or order of court under which a trust is created. [37]

trust instrument committee: a committee of directors or officers (or both) of a trust institution charged with specific duties relating to trust investments; duties other than those relating to investments may be imposed by the board of directors. [37]

trust inter vivos: synonymous with *living trust* and *voluntary trust.*

trust investments: the property in which trust funds are invested; a broad term that includes all kinds of property, not securities alone. [37]

trust officer: the administrative officer of a trust company, or of the trust department of a bank. He is responsible for the proper administration of trusts, the investment of trust funds, and the administration of agencies for trust clients. [10]

trustor: an individual who establishes a trust. synonymous with *settlor.*

trust or commission clause: a clause extending the coverage of the insurance contract to the insured's interest in a legal liability for property belonging to others and held by the insured in trust, on commission, on storage, for repairs, or otherwise held. [53]

trust powers: as the term is used in the Federal Reserve Act, authority to engage in the trust business; to be distinguished from the powers of a trustee. [37]

trust receipt: a receipt in the form of an agreement by which the party signing the receipt promises to hold the property received, in the name of the bank delivering the property. It further agrees that the property shall be maintained in a form that can be readily identified. If the property is further fabricated in a manufacturing process, it must be properly identified on the trust receipt. Trust receipts are used mostly to permit importers to obtain possession of merchandise for resale. Arrangements for this type of financing are usually completed before the issuance of letters of credit. The trust receipt is used as collateral security for the advance of funds by the bank to meet the acceptances arising out of the letter of credit. Under the terms of the agreement, the importer is required to pay to the bank proceeds from the sale of merchandise as soon as they are received. The importer is also required to keep the merchandise insured, and the bank may take possession of the merchandise at any time without due process of law. Federal Reserve Banks do not recognize trust receipts as good collateral, and the legal status of the trust receipt has not been clearly defined by the courts. [10]

trust relationship: when an individual or other legal entity takes over legal title to certain property to hold it in trust for another individual or other legal entity as specified in the trust indenture, a trust or fiduciary relationship is established. The legal entity taking possession of the property is the trustee; the legal entity who will benefit from the relationship is the beneficiary. The beneficiary has an equitable title to the property, and may bring suit in courts of equity to maintain his or her rights as set forth in the trust agreement, and to prevent mishandling of the property by the trustee. [10]

trust under agreement: a trust evidenced by an agreement between the settlor and the trustee. synonymous with *trust inter vivos* or *living trust.* [32]

trust under decree: a trust evidenced by a decree of a court of equity. [37]

trust under deed: a trust evidenced by a deed of conveyance, as distinguished from an agreement; originally confined to real property but now frequently applied to personal property as well. [37]

trust under will: a trust created by a valid will, to become operative only on the death of the testator; opposed to a living trust and the same as testamentary trust. [37]

Truth in Lending Act of 1968: officially, the Consumer Credit Protection Act of 1968, it requires most categories of lenders to disclose the true annual interest rate on virtually all types of loans and credit sales as well as the total dollar cost and other terms of a loan. see *Fair Credit Billing Act, right of rescission.*

TS

(1) see *tax shelter.*

(2) see *treasury stock.*

tub, in the: slang, in bankruptcy.

tughrik: monetary unit of Mongolia.

turkey

(1) *general:* any poor or unprofitable venture.

(2) *finance:* any investment that initially appeared attractive but suddenly became unattractive.

(3) *investments:* a stock that suddenly, without reason, drops in value.

turn: a description of the full cycle in the buying and selling of a security or a commodity.

Turnkey program: any one of several U.S. Department of Housing and Urban Development programs for public housing whereby, under contract to a local housing authority, a private developer builds public housing with private loan funds and, upon completion of the project, turns over to the housing authority the keys to the property. [59]

turnover

(1) *general:* the rate at which workers move into and out of employment, usually expressed as the number of accessions and separations during a fixed period for every 100 employees. The Bureau of Labor Statistics computes turnover rates by industry on a monthly basis.

(2) *investments:* the volume of business in a security or the entire market. If turnover on the exchange is reported at 15 million shares on a particular day, this means that 15,000,000 shares changed hands. Odd-lot turnover is tabulated separately and ordinarily is not included in reported volume.

turnover ratio: a measure of capital activity, or another factor of business (e.g., where the portfolio of securities is altered, or turned over, within one year). see *operating profit ratio.*

turnover tax: a form of sales tax employed in the Soviet Union.

tutor: under civil law, a person legally appointed to care for the person and the property of a minor; the equivalent of a guardian. [37]

twenty percent rule: where a customer wishing to borrow funds from a bank must maintain an average deposit balance equal to at least twenty percent of the proposed borrowing.

twisting: the practice of inducing a policyholder to allow to lapse or cancel a policy for the purpose of replacing it with another, to the detriment of the policyholder. This practice is both unethical and illegal.

two bits: slang, a quarter, 25 cents.

two-case note: a $2 bill.

two-dollar brokers: members on the floor of the exchange who execute orders for other brokers having more business at that time than they can handle themselves, or for firms who do not have their exchange members on the floor. The term recalls the time when these independent brokers received $2 per hundred shares for executing such orders. see *give-up.*

twofer: see *neutral spread.*

two-name paper: a short-term negotiable instrument wherein two people guarantee payment.

tycoon: an extremely wealthy and potentially influential business person.

UCC: see *Uniform Commercial Code.*
UCCC: see *Uniform Consumer Credit Code.*
ultimate beneficiary: a beneficiary of a trust who is entitled to receive the principal of the trust property in final distribution; also called principal beneficiary; opposed to *immediate beneficiary* and *income beneficiary.* [37]
ultimo: the month prior to the existing one.
ultra vires: "beyond power" (Latin). Acts of a corporation are ultra vires when they exceed the power or capability of the corporation as granted by the state in its charter.
unadjusted rate of return: an expression of the utility of a given project as the ratio of the increase in future average annual net income to the initial increase in needed investment.
unallotted balance of appropriation: an appropriation balance available for allotment. [49]
unamortized bond discount: the portion of the original bond discount that has not been charged off against earnings.
unamortized discounts on bonds sold: that portion of the excess of the face value of bonds over the amount received from their sale which remains to be written off periodically over the life of the bonds. [49]

unamortized discounts on investments (credit): that portion of the excess of the face value of securities over the amount paid for them which has not yet been written off. [49]
unamortized premiums on bonds sold: an account which represents that portion of the excess of bond proceeds over par value and which remains to be amortized over the remaining life of such bonds. [49]
unamortized premiums on investments: that portion of the excess of the amount paid for securities over their face value which has not yet been amortized. [49]
unappropriated profits: that portion of a firm's profit which has not been paid out in dividends or allocated for any special purpose.
unassented securities: those stocks or bonds which a corporation wishes to alter but which have not been approved of for change by the stockholders.
unauthorized growth: capital investment that grows at different rates in different areas of an economy.
unauthorized investment: a trust investment that is not authorized by the trust instrument; to be distinguished from a *nonlegal investment.* [37]
unbilled accounts receivable: an account that designates the estimated amount of accounts receivable for

services or commodities sold but not billed. For example, if a utility bills its customer bimonthly but prepares monthly financial statements, the amount of services rendered or commodities sold during the first month of the bimonthly period would be reflected in the balance sheet under this account title.

uncalled capital: that portion of the issued share capital of a corporation which has not yet been called up.

unclaimed balances: the balances of the accounts for funds on deposit that have remained inactive for a period designated by the bank. Eventually these unclaimed balances are handed over to the U.S. Comptroller of the Currency.

uncollected cash items: checks in the process of collection for which payment has not yet been received from the banks on which the checks are drawn. [40]

uncollected funds: a portion of a deposit balance that has not yet been collected by the depository bank. That is, sufficient time has not elapsed to permit checks drawn on other banks to have been returned for nonpayment. see *float.*

uncontrollable expense: an expense not under the direct control of the authority who will ultimately be charged with it. For example, the foreman has no control over the amount of rent, taxes, or depreciation charged to his department. Generally speaking, uncontrollable expenses are fixed. see *fixed cost or expense.* [38]

uncovered money: irredeemable paper money; money only partially, or not at all, supported by a specie reserve.

uncover the stops: depressing the price of a security to a point where many stop orders are created. synonymous with *gather in the stops.*

undercharge: to charge less than the legal amount.

underdeveloped country: a nation in which per capita real income is proportionately low when contrasted with the per capita real income of nations where industry flourishes. see also *less developed country;* cf. *mature economy.*

underlease: a tenant's lease of property to a third party; a sublease.

underlying bond: see *bond, underlying.*

underlying company: synonymous with *subsidiary.*

underlying mortgage: a mortgage senior to a larger one (e.g., a building first mortgage of $100,000 that has a prior claim over a second one of $200,000). cf. *equal dignity.*

underlying stock: the stock subject to purchase upon exercise of the option. [15]

under the rule: an action of selling or buying by stock exchange officers to complete a transaction entered into by a delinquent member of the exchange, who is charged with any difference in price that occurs.

underwrite: the designing, preparing, bringing forth, and guaranteeing the sale of a new issue of stock. see *investment banker, syndicate.*

underwriter

(1) *general:* an individual or organization that assumes a risk for a fee.

(2) *investments:* an individual or party that agrees to underwrite a securities issue. cf. *letter stock.*

undesignated city: a city not designated by the Federal Reserve System as one of its reserve cities.

undigested securities: securities that are issued beyond the need for or ability of the public to absorb them. see *overissue;* cf. *float, oversubscribed.*

undistributed profit: the profit of a partnership, syndicate, or joint venture prior to division among the individuals concerned.

undivided interests: see *joint tenancy, tenancy by the entirety, tenancy in common.*

undivided profits: undistributed earnings available for dividends and for the writing off of bad debts or special losses. [50]

undivided right: a part owner's right that cannot be excluded from the other owner's rights. This right exists in tenancy in common and in joint tenancy.

undue influence: the influence that one person exerts over another person to the point where the latter is prevented from exercising his own free will. [37]

unearned discount: interest received but not yet earned.

unearned income: income that has been collected in advance of the performance of a contract; income derived from investment dividends, property rentals, and other sources not involving the individual's personal efforts. cf. *earned income.*

unearned increment: the increase in the value of property that can be attributed to changing social or economic conditions beyond the control of the title holder, as distinguished from an increase in value that can be attributed to the improvements made or additions made by the labor or investment of the title holder.

unearned interest: interest on a loan that has already been collected but has not yet been earned because the principal has not been outstanding long enough. [59]

unemployment compensation: a system of insuring workers against hardship during periods of unemployment. The Unemployment Insurance Act of 1935, as part of the Social Security program, is administered by the states individually, allowing for variations in rates, duration of payments, and eligibility. Costs are borne by the employers, who get allowances in the form of tax credits.

unencumbered property: real estate free and clear of any mortgages, liens, or debts of any type. see *perfect title.*

unexpired cost: any asset.

unfunded debt: any short-term or floating debt; any indebtedness not covered by a bond.

unfunded insurance trust: an insurance trust in which the premiums on the policies are to be paid by the insured or by some third person and not by the trustee; to be distinguished from a funded insurance trust. [37]

unified bond: see *bond, consolidated.*

uniform acts: a series of acts drafted by the National Conference of Commissioners on Uniform State Laws and suggested for passage in the various states with a view toward making the laws in the states uniform as to the particular subjects covered. [37]

uniform cash flows: cash flows that are the same for every year.

Uniform Commercial Code: a set of statutes purporting to provide some consistency among states' commercial laws. It includes uniform laws dealing with bills of lading, negotiable instruments, sales, stock transfers, trust receipts, and warehouse receipts.

Uniform Consumer Credit Code (UCCC): a consumer protection act which contains one uniform set of regulations for all major credit grantors.

Uniform Negotiable Instrument Act: see *negotiable instrument.*

uninsurable title: property that a title insurance company will not insure.

union rate: the minimum hourly wage rate, accepted by a union for a specific type of activity and employed in negotiations.

unissued stock: part of the authorized capital stock of a corporation that is not issued or outstanding. It is not part of the corporation's capital stock and receives no dividends, although it must be shown on the firm's balance sheet even though it is neither an asset nor a liability. see *when issued.*

unit bank: a single independent bank that conducts all its operations at one office. [50]

unit banking: a term used to refer to the type of banking in which an individual bank is separate and distinct from every other bank with regard to operation, management, and control. [50]

United States: see entries under *U.S.*

unit of trading: the lowest amount established by a stock exchange in which the market in a specific security may be made. see *odd lot, round lot.*

unit savings plan: a plan whereby savings deposits and withdrawals are posted by machine to the depositor's

passbook, the bank's ledger card, and the auditor's detailed audit tape, all in original printing in one simultaneous operation. The ledger card is posted at the teller's window by the teller in the same machine operation that posts the entry in the depositor's passbook. The entry must be identical, because of the simultaneous machine printing. This assures complete protection to the depositor (who can "audit" his or her account at the window), the bank teller, and the bank. see also *dual savings plan, no-ticket savings plan.* [10]

unit system: an accounting system in which the records of the customer and the association are posted simultaneously. [59]

unit teller: an employee of a bank who is charged with the duties of both a paying and receiving teller. This teller may receive deposits or pay out funds to depositors. His cash balance at the end of the business day will be the net of his cash received, less his cash paid out. see *paying teller, receiving teller.* [10]

unit teller system: an arrangement for the convenience of customers who wish to make deposits and withdrawals at the same time. When this system is in use, the bank representative at each window is responsible for handling both receiving and paying operations. [50]

unit trust

(1) corporate and municipal bonds; a mix of corporate issues and closed-end trusts, some designed for investors in a single state.

(2) a British term for mutual investment; a mutual fund.

(3) an inflexible investment. A trust managers buys a stated portfolio of

securities and deposits them with a trustee. After the deposit date, no new securities are added, and with rare exceptions, none are sold. As a result, the return, or yield, is fixed and predictable.

unlawful: see *illegal.*

unlimited accounts: large or reputable businesses that are eligible for any amount of credit.

unlimited mortgage: any open-end mortgage; a mortgage not limited to a fixed amount.

unlimited tax bond: see *bond, unlimited tax.*

unliquidated encumbrances: encumbrances outstanding. see also *encumbrance.* [49]

unlisted: a security not listed on a stock exchange; an over-the-counter stock. see *discontinuous market.*

unlisted trading privileges: on some exchanges a stock may be traded at the request of a member without any prior application by the company itself. The company has no agreement to conform with standards of the exchange. Companies admitted to unlisted trading privileges prior to enactment of the Securities Exchange Act of 1934 are not subject to the rules and regulations under that act. Today, admission of a stock to unlisted trading privileges requires SEC approval of an application filed by the exchange. The information in the application must be made available by the exchange to the public. No unlisted stocks are traded on the New York Stock Exchange. see *listed securities (stocks).* [20]

unloading

(1) *finance:* selling goods at a relatively low price.

(2) *investments:* the sale of stocks and commodities to avoid a loss during a period of a falling market. cf. *profit taking.*

(3) synonymous with *dumping.*

unpaid balance: on a credit purchase, the difference between the purchase price and the down payment or the value of a trade-in. With a cash loan, it is the difference between the total loan and the amount that is still owed.

unpaid dividend: a dividend declared but not yet distributed.

Unpd.: unpaid.

unrealized profits: paper profits that are not made actual until the firm's securities have been sold.

unregistered stock: a security that is not tradable and not easily converted into a cash position. It is usually sold in private transactions that are exempt from the SEC registration requirements, often at a discounted price. synonymous with *letter stock.*

unseasoned securities: the opposite of seasoned securities. see *seasoned security.* [67]

unsecured bond: see *bond, unsecured.*

unsecured debt: a debt for which no collateral has been pledged.

unsecured loan: a loan made by a bank based on credit information about the borrower and his or her ability to repay the obligation. The loan is not secured by collateral but is made on the signature of the borrower. A person's spouse may be asked to sign such a note. see *comaker, debenture.*

unsecured note: a loan granted on the basis of a borrower's credit worthiness and signature; not secured by collateral. [78]

unstable market: a market in which forces of disequilibrium are reinforced so that movements away from equilibrium are not reversible.

UOT: see *unit of trading.*

up: slang, any potential buyer.

UP: see *unrealized profits.*

up tick: a transaction made at a price higher than the preceding transaction. Also called a plus tick. A stock may be sold short only on an up tick, (i.e., a transaction at the same price as the preceding trade but higher than the preceding different price).

urbank: first proposed by Professor Charles Haar, in 1968, as an urban development bank controlled by a federal agency to assist communities to build needed facilities. The urbank would be a federally financed institution, making long-term loans at favorable interest rates to employers willing to return to or upgrade plants in cities.

US
(1)   see *underlying stock.*
(2)   United States.
(3)   see *unregistered stock.*

use: as a noun, the beneficial ownership of property the legal title to which is in another; the forerunner of the present-day trust. [32]

used mortgage: synonymous with *assumable mortgage.*

U. S. government deposits: all deposits in reporting member banks held for the account of the U.S. government or one of its departments or bureaus. [40]

U.S. rule: a method traditionally employed in first-mortgage real estate financing where payments are applied first to accrued interest and then to the reduction of principal. [41]

U.S. Savings Bond: see *Bond, U.S. Savings.*

usuance
(1)   *general:* employment.
(2)   *finance:* interest or income.
(3)   *finance:* the period allowed for payment of a foreign obligation.

usufructuary right: a right to appropriate use and pleasure from property owned by another.

usurious: describing a contract when made for a loan of money at a rate of interest in excess of that authorized by the statute.

usury: the rate of interest paid for the use of another's money, or for credit extended, which exceeds the legal limit allowed for that type of transaction by the state whose laws govern the legality of the transaction. see *legal interest.*

utility (1) *general:* the capability or power of an item to satisfy a need as determined by the satisfaction that one receives from consuming something.
(2) *finance:* a publicly owned facility, such as an electric power plant.

utter: to put out or pass off, to "utter a check" is to give it to another in payment of an obligation.

Uw.: see *underwriter.*

V: five.

VA: see *Veterans Administration.*

Val.: see *value.*

valeurs: French for "securities."

valid: that which is sufficient to satisfy the requirement of the law; a fact.

validation: proof or confirmation; an instrument or other evidence to confirm or give legal support to a claim or contract (e.g., factual data from an experiment).

valorization: governmental action leading to the establishment of a price or value for an item or service.

valuation: the fixing of value to anything. synonymous with "appraising."

valuation reserves

(1) *finance:* reserves established to provide for a drop in the existing value of the assets to which they pertain. see *appraisal.*

(2) *finance:* reserves established to provide for a reasonably probable failure to achieve full value.

value: the worth of property, goods, services, and so on; purchasing power. see *book value.*

value, book: the amount at which an asset is carried on personal, partnership, or corporation books and which may or may not represent market value; except under unusual circumstances, computed as historical cost less reserves for accrued depreciation. [6]

value, capitalized: a value indication produced by discounting anticipated future income at the going rate; "an indication of value by the net income capitalization approach." [6]

value, face: the state worth, in terms of money, of formal, written evidences of indebtedness. synonymous with *par value.* [6]

value added: that part of the value of produced goods developed in a company. It is determined by subtracting from sales the costs of materials and supplies, energy costs, contract work, and so on, and it includes labor expenses, administrative and sales costs, and other operating profits.

value-added tax (VAT): a government tax on the value added; a tax on the selling price of manufactured items less the cost of the materials and expenses used in their production.

value asset: *per common share,* a company's net resources (after deduction of all liabilities, preferred stocks' liquidating value, and accrued dividends, if any), divided by the number of common shares outstanding; *per preferred share* (another way of showing asset coverage), a company's net resources (after deduction of all liabilities, any prior preferred stocks' liquidating value, and accrued dividends, if any), divided by the number of preferred shares outstanding. [3]

value compensated: describing a purchase or sale of foreign exchange to be executed by cable; the purchaser reimburses the seller for the earlier value of the data of actual payment abroad of the foreign currency, theoretically resulting in no loss of interest to either party.

value date: the date on which a bank deposit becomes effective. The date is fixed based on the time required to collect a payment on the item deposited from another bank. see *collection.*

VA mortgage: mortgage made in conformity with requirements of the Servicemen's Readjustment Act, and guaranteed to an amount specified in the act by the Veterans Administration. [22]

variable: a quantity that may assume a succession of values, which need not be distinct. [57]

variable annuity: an annuity contract providing lifetime retirement payments that vary in amount with the results of investment in a separate account portfolio.

variable cost: a cost that is uniform per unit but changes in total in direct proportion to changes in the related total activity or volume.

variable interest plus (VIP): an innovative certificate of deposit. First attempted by Western Savings Bank, the second largest in Philadelphia; under the plan, the interest rate on the six-month certificate would be tied to the prevailing rate at the weekly auction of six-month Treasury bills. The primary motivation behind this new variable-interest-rate certificate was to stop the flow of funds out of the bank and into higher-yielding instruments, particularly money-market mutual funds. Under terms of the VIP, a depositor also could borrow as much as $9900 against the certificate at an interest rate of 1 percent above the weekly rate being earned. Bank regulators stopped this proposal in 1981.

variable life insurance: a relatively new form of coverage; the death benefit is based on the performance of the stock market, or more specifically, on the performance of stocks in the insurer's portfolio. The better the market performs over the life of the policy (i.e., a lifetime), the more cash the benefit will receive. If the market should collapse, a specified minimum death benefit will be paid nonetheless. A variable life insurance policy costs a little less than a standard whole life policy that pays dividends on its investments, but somewhat more than one that pays no dividends.

variable rate: offered by many major lenders, monthly bank payments that are tied to prevailing rates. The advantage is to the buyer when rates slide, and to the seller when they soar.

variable rate account: a passbook savings account that pays extra earnings if the customer leaves a specified amount on deposit for a specified term. [59]

variable-rate mortgage: a type of mortgage, initially available in California, and now authorized nationally, which permits the interest charges on the loan to rise or fall automatically in accordance with a predetermined index, for instance, an index of banks' cost-of-funds.

The interest rate can fluctuate every six months, but cannot be raised by more than $2\frac{1}{2}$ percentage points over the life of the mortgage. In addition, banks must offer customers a choice between variable-rate and conventional mortgages. see also *flexible mortgage, renegotiable-rate mortgage, Wachovia adjustable mortgage.*

variation margin: additional margin needed on commodities resulting from variations in price.

VAT: see *value-added tax.*

vault: a large room or rooms in a bank or financial institution, where the cash on hand is stored, and safe deposit boxes are located.

vault cash: that portion of the cash on hand which is not required for immediate use and is left in the vault of the bank as an immediate reserve. The remainder of the cash on hand is carried in the cash busses and cash tills under the custodianship of the tellers. [10]

VC: see *venture capital.*

VCF: see *venture capital funds.*

VD: see *volume discount.*

veil of money theory: the idea that money is neutral and does not reflect a nation's true economic condition but is merely a cosmetic for other social and financial forces and activity. cf. *savings and investment theory.*

velocity: the rate at which money is spent on goods and services within a given period (usually measured as the ratio of GNP to the money stock). Greater velocity means that a given quantity of money is used for greater dollar volume of transactions. [1]

velocity of circulation: the rate at which money supply is spent for a stated time period, usually one year.

velvet: slang, an unearned income or profit.

vend: any offer to sell something.

vendee: the party who purchases or agrees to purchase property owned by another.

vendor: a manufacturer, wholesaler, or importer from whom goods are purchased.

vendor's lien: an unpaid seller's right to take possession of property until the purchase price has been recovered. see *general lien.*

venture: a business activity or undertaking involving some or considerable risk.

venture capital
(1) *finance:* funds invested in enterprises that do not usually have access to conventional sources of capital (banks, stock market, etc.).
(2) *investments:* funds available from the issue of new stock.
(3) *investments:* reinvested monies from stockholders.

venture capital funds: mutual funds invested in securities of firms that are little known and often not yet registered with the SEC.

venue: the place or county where a suit is brought. [76]

vest: as a verb, to confer an immediate, fixed right of immediate or future possession and enjoyment of property. [37]

vested estate: an interest in property holding present and future rights, but with the existing interest able to be transferred.

vested interest: an immediate, fixed interest in real or personal property although the right of possession and enjoyment may be postponed until some future date or until the happening of some event; to be distinguished from a *contingent interest.* [37]

vested remainder: a fixed interest in real property, with the right of possession and enjoyment postponed until the termination of the prior estate; to be distinguished from a *contingent remainder.* [37]

vested renewals: future commissions for business placed to become due to a soliciting agent or general agency if the business remains in force. [12]

vested rights: provisions in a pension program ensuring that if a worker leaves the firm for any reason, he or she can retain the pension rights acquired while employed by the company offering the plan. see *fully vested.*

vesting: the right of an employee under a retirement plan to retain part or all of the annuities purchased by the employer's contributions on his or her behalf; or, in some plans, the right to receive a cash payment of equivalent value on termination of employment after certain qualifying conditions have been met. see *contingent interest.*

Veterans Administration: established as an independent agency on July 21, 1930, to coordinate and consolidate federal agencies concerned with the administration of laws providing benefits for veterans. The VA helps veterans purchase homes. see *VA mortgage.* [33]

Veterans Administration Mortgage Guarantees: home mortgage guarantees issued by the VA under the Servicemen's Readjustment Act, to eligible applicants for any of the following purposes: (1) the purchase or construction of an owner-occupied home by the veteran; (2) the construction of a farm residence on land owned by a veteran; (3) the repair, alteration, or improvement of an owner-occupied farm or home by the veteran. Interest is set by the Veterans Administration. [66]

VI: see *vested interest.*

VIP: see *variable interest plus.*

virtuous cycle: a concept describing the kinds of actions some bankers think governments should take to minimize the impact of currency fluctuations. The virtuous cycle approach produces a series of of sound economic policies to set off a chain of events in which improved economic performance produces sound currencies, which, in turn, further improves economic performance.

visible supply: usually refers to supplies of a commodity in licensed warehouses. [11]

visible trade: that portion of commerce between nations that is shown by records of transactions involving the exchange of tangible items.

V loans: pursuant to Regulation V of the Federal Reserve System, defense production loans guaranteed by the Board of Governors.

void: that which has no legal effect.

voidable contract: an agreement that can be rescinded by either of the parties in the event of fraud, incompetence, or other sufficient cause.

volatility: a measure of a stock's tendency to move up and down in price, based on its daily price history over the latest 12 months. Stocks with higher volatilities tend to exhibit greater price fluctuation than those with lower volatility values. A volatility of 20 percent would indicate the stock has, over the last 12 months of trading activity, fluctuated about 20 percent above and below the average price for that period. [68]

volume: the total number of securities traded during a stated period of time. synonymous with *turnover.*

volume discount: institutional organizations that invest heavily are often given a commission discount when the order is significant, that is, $500,000 or more.

volume of trading (or sales): represents a simple addition of successive futures transactions. It is the total of the sales (or of the purchases), and not of the sum of both. [11]

voluntary alienation: transfer of title when the property assumes a new owner.

voluntary association: a group of individuals, joined together for a common economical, social, religious, political, professional, or similar purpose, who have not incorporated or otherwise regularized their group under state statutes. [59]

voluntary association account: a savings account held by a nonincorporated group, such as a women's club, baseball team, church, civic group, or charity; otherwise, generally similar to the corporation account. [59]

voluntary bankruptcy: see *bankruptcy.*

voluntary conveyance or deed: the instrument of transfer of an owner's title to property to the lien holder. Usually such conveyance serves to bypass a legal situation of a court judgment showing insufficient security to satisfy a debt, and occurs without transfer of a valuable consideration. see *particular lien.*

voluntary plan: a type of accumulation plan for investment on a regular basis but without any total time period or ultimate investment amount specified. The sales charge is applicable individually to each purchase made. [23]

voluntary trust: established by a deed of transfer of certain property made voluntarily by an individual or other legal entity to a trustee for a specified purpose.

vostro account: "your account"; used by a depository bank to describe an account maintained with it by a bank in a foreign country. cf. *nostro account.*

voting right (stock): the stockholder's right to vote his or her stock in the affairs of the company. Most common shares have one vote each. Preferred stock usually carries the right to vote when preferred dividends are in default for a specified period. The right to vote is usually delegated by proxy of the stockholder to another person. [20]

voting trust: an agreement whereby stockholders turn over their voting rights to a small group of people, who are called voting trustees.

voucher: a written statement that bears witness or vouches for something (e.g., a voucher showing that services have been rendered or goods bought).

voucher check: a form of check to which is attached another form termed a voucher. The voucher portion of the check is used to describe or otherwise designate the purpose for which the check is drawn. When a voucher check is received from a buyer by a seller, the seller detaches the voucher from the check before presenting the check for payment. The voucher is then used as the posting medium to credit the accounts receivable ledger, thereby showing payment received from the buyer. Many businesses use copies of voucher checks as their record of invoices paid.

vouchers payable: liabilities for goods and services evidenced by vouchers which have been pre-audited and approved for payment but have not been paid. [49]

voucher payment plan: a method of construction loan payouts in which the contractor or borrower completes lender forms requesting each payout when a particular, prespecified stage of construction is reached. [59]

voucher system: a system which calls for the preparation of vouchers for transactions involving payments and for the recording of such vouchers in a special book of original entry known as a voucher register, in the order in which payment is approved. [49]

VR: see *vested rights*.

VRM: see *variable-rate mortgage*.

VT: see *voting trust*.

Vtg.: *voting*.

WA: see *Williams Act.*

Wachovia adjustable mortgage: a recent approach in mortgage lending, developed by this North Carolina bank. It works this way: a customer buys a home with a 30-year adjustable mortgage. The initial mortgage rate is tied to money market and local market rates. The interest rate is adjusted every quarter in line with bill rates. The monthly payment stays the same for five years, but the new rate determines how much will go for interest and how much for principal. Every five years the monthly payment is adjusted—up or down by up to 25 percent—so the loan will be paid off on time. After 25 years the monthly payment can be adjusted by more than 25 percent if there is a danger the loan will not be paid off on time. If after 30 years the loan has not been paid off, the borrower may refinance. see *renegotiable-rate mortgage; variable-rate mortgage.*

wad: slang, a roll of paper money.

wage: compensation of employees receiving a stated sum per piece, hour, day, or any other unit or period. Usually it is all compensation paid, including salaries. cf. *earnings, payroll, rate variance.*

wage and salary administration: a well-defined approach for establishing wages and salaries according to an organization's rule and policies, in line with the practice of other companies in the same industry and/or area of work.

wage assignment: an agreement permitting a lender to collect a certain portion of a borrower's salary from his or her employer if payment is not made as specified in the credit contract. [78]

wage earner plan: formally called adjustment of debt of an individual with regular income plan; a plan whereby a debtor arranges to make periodic payments to a trustee of the bankruptcy court. The trustee disburses the money to the creditors. [76]

wage freeze: a limit, usually imposed by a government, on salary increases.

wage stabilization: a governmental program to keep wages for a particular industry or location from rapidly increasing beyond existing levels. see *inflationary spiral, stabilization policy.*

Wagner-Connery Act: federal legislation that guarantees the right of workers to organize and bargain collectively for a contract and declares specific employer actions to be unfair labor practices. see *bargaining unit;* see also *Baby Wagner Acts,* which interfere with guaranteed rights. The law created the National Labor Relations Board to administer its functions.

waiting period

(1) *general:* the time between filing a claim for unemployment benefits or workmen's compensation and the beginning of such benefit payments.

(2) *investments:* the time, usually 20 days, that must pass between the application for listing a new security from the SEC and the date when the securities can be offered to the public.

waiver: the voluntary relinquishment of a right in a piece of property or to a claim against another's property that would be legally enforceable if the person waiving so elected.

waiver of citation: a document executed by an interested party in an accounting proceeding by which he relinquishes his right to the formal issue and service of a citation. [37]

waiver of premium: nearly all life insurance companies will add to their contracts, upon payment of a small additional premium, a clause providing that if the insured becomes totally and permanently disabled, his or her insurance policy will be continued in full force and the company will exempt the insured from paying further premiums during disability.

waiver of protest: a statement, signed by the endorser of a note, indicating that he or she will remain liable even if he or she is not notified that the note has not been paid when due.

Wall Street: popular name for the New York City business and financial district.

Wall Street Journal: one of America's leading newspapers, noted for its coverage of financial, corporate, and market news.

wanted for cash: a term appearing on the ticker tape showing that an individual is interested in purchasing a given quantity of shares designated and will pay for them the same day.

war babies (brides): securities of corporations involved in manufacturing materials for the U.S. Department of Defense.

ward: the infant or incompetent person who is the beneficiary of an estate of a deceased person. The ward is under the care of a guardian who is appointed by a court of law to administer the affairs of the ward with the sanction of the court having such jurisdiction, until some time as the court finds that the ward has reached majority or has become fully competent to handle his own affairs. [10]

warehouse, bonded: see *warehouse, state bonded; warehouse, U.S. Customs bonded.*

warehouse, captive: see *warehouse, private.*

warehouse, commodity: a warehouse storing commodity goods (cotton, wool, tobacco, and other grown items). see also *go-down.*

warehouse, company: see *warehouse, private.*

warehouse, private: a warehouse operated by an owner, which hold his goods. synonymous with "captive warehouse" and "company warehouse."

warehouse, public: a warehouse that is rented out by the owner as a facility for the storing of goods.

warehouse, state bonded: a public warehouse, under government supervision, that has been licensed by a state prior to operation. Merchandise is stored there without the payment of duties or taxes until it is withdrawn from the warehouse.

warehouse, U.S. Customs bonded: a federal warehouse where goods remain until duty has been collected from the importer. Goods under bond are also kept here.

warehouse, U.S. Internal Revenue: a public warehouse; the owner of goods has posted a bond guaranteeing payment of internal revenue tax on U.S.-produced items.

warehouse customs bond: see *bond, warehouse customs.*

warehouse receipt: an instrument listing the goods or commodities deposited in a warehouse. It is a receipt for the commodities listed, and for which the warehouse is the bailee. Warehouse receipts may be either non-negotiable or negotiable.

warehouse stock: goods held in quantity in a warehouse for reasons of economy.

warehousing: hypothecation of mortgage to a commercial bank as security for repayment of short-term loans. [22]

Warr.: see *warrant.*

warrant

(1) *investments:* a certificate giving the holder the right to purchase securities at a stipulated price within a specified time limit or at any time. Sometimes offered with securities as an inducement to buy. [20]

(2) *law:* a written order in the name of the state and signed by a magistrate directing an officer to make an arrest.

warrants payable: the amount of warrants outstanding and unpaid. [49]

warranty

(1) *banking:* a statement in a poli-cy of the existence of a fact or a condition of the subject of insurance which, if found to be untrue by misrepresentation, will void the policy.

(2) *law:* a statement, either written, expressed, or implied, that a certain statement identified in a contract is presently true or will be true.

warranty, implied: a warranty assumed to be a part of the insurance contract even though not expressly included. In connection with products liability insurance, the warranty is assumed to be made by one who sells a product that is fit for the purpose for which it is sold. [53]

warranty deed: see *deed, general warranty.*

wash sale: a false transaction of security or commodity sales that are purchased and sold by the same individual so as to create the impression of activity and/or volume of the item.

wasting assets: assets whose value is depleted and will eventually be exhausted by the continued operations of an extractive business (oil wells, mining claims, etc.). see *depletion allowance.*

wasting trust: a trust of property that is gradually being consumed.

watch filing: a procedure by which losses on small risks are referred to the underwriter for his or her attention.

watered stock: corporate stock issued by a corporation for property at an overvaluation, or stock released for which the corporation receives nothing in payment.

WD

(1) see *deed, general warranty.*

(2) see *withdrawal.*

weak holdings: stocks retained on

margin by speculators who will use any reason to sell them.

weak market: a situation characterized by a greater demand for selling than there is for purchasing.

wealth: an economic term designating the value of one's total possessions and rights in property. cf. *national wealth.*

wealth effect: see *Pigou effect concept.*

wealth tax: an annual tax on a person's assets above a stated minimum, even those assets which do not yield any income.

Webb-Pomerene Act of 1918: federal legislation exempting exporters' associations from the antitrust regulations.

weed off: slang, to take money from a roll of bank notes.

weekend arbitrage: a now defunct maneuver by which banks lowered their reserve requirements by borrowing clearing house funds overseas on Friday which they did not have to cover until Monday.

wellhead tax: a government proposal to tax domestic oil as it leaves the well; the amount of the tax is the difference between its current controlled price and the world market price imposed by the OPEC cartel.

went to the wall: any bankrupt or failing corporation or individual.

wheeler-dealer: slang, a scheming, clever person.

when issued: a short form of "when, as, and if issued." The term indicates a conditional transaction in a security authorized for issuance but not yet actually issued. All when-issued transactions are on a conditional basis, to be settled if and when the actu-al security is issued and the exchange or National Association of Securities Dealers rules that the transactions are to be settled. [20]

whipsawed: to have experienced a substantial loss at both ends of a securities transaction.

white elephant: property that is so costly to maintain that it is virtually impossible to operate it at a profit; also property with respect to which a loss is certain.

white knight: in order to encourage a successful company takeover by another firm, a friendly suitor is brought in to put down another bidder. cf. *gray knight.*

whole coverage: any type of insurance that provides for payment from all losses without any deductions.

whole life insurance: see *ordinary life.*

wholesale price index: a measure compiled by the U.S. Bureau of Labor Statistics, showing the average change in the price of approximately 2200 commodities at the primary market level (usually the level at which the commodity is first sold commercially in substantial volume), compared to the average level in selected base years.

Whous.: warehouse.

WI: see *when issued.*

wide opening: a securities situation characterized by a considerable difference in the bid and asked prices at the beginning of the market day.

widow-and-orphan stock: a high-income, noncyclical stock with security but which is in other ways unrewarding—that is, a slow market mover.

widow's allowance: the allowance of personal property made by the court or by statute to a widow for her immediate requirements after her husband's death. [37]

widow's exemption: the amount allowed as a deduction in computing the state inheritance tax on the widow's share of her husband's estate. [37]

wildcat bank: one of the unsound banks chartered by the states during the hectic banking years between 1816 and 1863. Most of these banks failed.

will: a document in which an individual (the testator or testatrix) having full mental faculties sets forth his or her desires and bequests regarding the disposition of his total wealth after his death. cf. *nuncupative will.*

Williams Act: federal legislation of 1968, requiring that tender offers be made to all securities holders at the same price. see *Saturday night special.*

Wilmington Plan: a plan initiated by the Wilmington Savings Funds Society, a mutual savings bank, providing individual customers with a free checking account, a savings account and an agreement to permit the savings account to serve as security for an automatic short-term advance if the checking account is overdrawn. Direct payroll deposit, automatic bill paying, a cash-dispensing machine, and a percentage credit to the customer on purchases via direct debit from the customer's checking account are also available. [36]

windfall profit: an unexpected profit arising from causes not controlled by the recipient.

windfall profits tax: federal legislation passed in 1980; a tax designed to di-

vert from the oil industry to the government a share of profits attributable to the president's decision to phase out price controls, earmarking the money for a variety of energy-producing and energy-saving programs. The Crude Oil Windfall Profits Tax act increased the dividend exclusion to $200 for single taxpayers and $400 for married taxpayers filing separately, and broadened exclusion to cover interest. But neither change was effective for 1980 returns. The act also increased the renewable-source energy credit to $4000 from $2200. The act repealed "carry-over basis" rules for heirs who sell inherited property.

winding up: the process of liquidating a company.

wiped out

(1) *general:* the failing of a business.

(2) *investments:* when all available margin and cash are exhausted.

(3) *investments:* a considerable, irreversible investment loss.

wire-fate item: check or other item sent for collection or in transit letters to out-of-town banks, accompanied by instructions to notify the sending bank by wire as to whether the item is paid or not paid. This enables the sending bank to ascertain quickly whether or not the item is paid. [10]

wire house: a member firm of an exchange maintaining a communications network either linking its own branch offices to offices of correspondent firms, or linking some combination of such offices. [20]

wire transfer: an order to pay or to credit money transmitted by telegraph or cable. [50]

with all faults: without a guarantee, usually in real estate transactions; of the absence of imperfections; as is.

withdrawal: the manner in which funds on deposit in savings accounts may be paid out by the bank. The depositor must present his passbook and sign either a withdrawal slip or the ledger card (no-ticket savings plan) before the bank can pay out funds against the deposit account. The signature on the withdrawal slip or signed on the proper line of the ledger card should always agree with the signature on file in the bank to insure that the right person is receiving the withdrawn funds. [10]

withdrawal form: a source document and authorization for withdrawals from a savings account used by the customers and kept by the association for its records. [59]

withdrawal plan: arrangement provided by certain open-end companies by which an investor can receive monthly or quarterly payments in a designated amount that may be more or less than actual investment income. [30]

withdrawal ratio: withdrawals expressed as a percentage of gross savings for a given period. [59]

withdrawal value: the amount credited to the savings account of a member, less deductions as shown on the records of the savings association. [59]

with full recourse: in lending, a term in a written agreement that gives the buyer in a sale or other transaction the right to full reimbursement from the seller for any losses resulting from the loans or other items purchased. [59]

withholding tax: federal, state, or city taxes withheld by employers from the salaries of employees and paid directly to the taxing agency.

without dividend: see *ex-dividend.*

without recourse

(1) *finance:* a term used in endorsing a negotiable instrument where the endorser of a note is no longer responsible, should the obligation not be paid. see *qualified endorsement.*

(2) *law:* an agreement that the purchaser accepts all risks in the transaction, and gives up all rights to any recourse. see also *caveat emptor.*

with partial recourse: in lending, a term in a written agreement that gives the buyer in a sale or other transaction the right to reimbursement for an agreed-upon portion of any losses resulting from the loans or other items purchased. [59]

with recourse

(1) *finance:* a term used in endorsing a negotiable instrument where the endorser of a note continues to be responsible, should the obligation not be paid.

(2) *law:* an agreement that if the seller is unable to meet his or her obligations, the purchaser has the right to endorse a claim against the seller for sustained damages.

wolf: an experienced and often crafty speculator.

won: monetary unit of Korea.

working asset: those assets invested in securities that can be expected to fluctuate more or less with common stock prices generally. Corrections may be made to eliminate an investment company's holdings of cash and high-grade senior securities and to give weight to holdings of junior issues. [3]

working capital: the excess of current assets over current liabilities representing the capital immediately available for the continued operation of a business.

working control: theoretically, ownership of 51 percent of a company's voting stock is necessary to exercise control. In practice—and this is particularly true in the case of a large corporation—effective (i.e., working) control sometimes can be exerted through ownership, individually or by a group acting in concert, of less than 50 percent of the stock.

working fund: the amount of money made available to a teller for the handling of routine transactions. [59]

work in process: the cost of partially completed products manufactured or processed, such as a partially completed printing job. Sometimes referred to as "work in progress." [49]

workmen's compensation: a system for compensating workers injured or disabled on the job. Workmen's compensation programs are established by state law and differ widely. Typically, benefits are paid under private insurance policies, but awards are determined by state boards. see *average weekly benefit.*

work simplification: a reorganization of methods, equipment, resources, and working conditions to minimize worker fatigue and increase worker efficiency and output.

World Bank: see *International Bank for Reconstruction and Development.*

worth: the total value of something, including an investment in a business. see *net worth.*

WP: see *windfall profit.*

WPA: see *Webb-Pomerene Act of 1918.*

WPT: see *windfall profits tax.*

WR: see *warehouse receipt.*

wraparound: see *wraparound mortgages.*

wraparound annuities: tax-deferral schemes allowing an individual to shelter current interest income on a bank savings certificate or shares in a mutual fund in a tax-deferred annuity administered by an insurance company. The Internal Revenue Service has protested this technique.

wraparound mortgages: involves two lenders, a mortgage originator and a wraparound lender. Rather than providing an entirely new mortgage at current market rates to a home buyer, the wraparound lender agrees to continue to pay the monthly installments on the existing mortgage on the home to be bought, at the original contract interest rate of the mortgage, and also to make any additional payments needed to meet the purchase price of the home. As a result, the terms of the original mortgage continue to be satisfied, the seller is compensated for the sale of his or her investment, and the home buyer is able to purchase a home and share in the benefits of the below-market rate paid by the wraparound lender on a portion of the money financed.

writ: a written instrument, under a state's seal, issued from a court directing an officer of the court to do some act, or enjoining an individual to do or refrain from doing some act.

write-down: the book value to which an asset has been reduced to adjust for the capital that has been lost on the decline of the asset's value.

write-off: an asset that has been determined to be uncollectible and therefore has been charged off as a loss. Sometimes it is the debt itself. cf. *written-down value.*

writer: the seller of an option contract. [5]

write-up: an increase in an asset's book value not resulting from added costs or an adjustment of an asset account to correspond to an appraisal value.

writ of execution: a court order issued to an officer of law commanding him or her to take certain action. [76]

written-down value: an accounting term for the valuation or cost of any asset minus the written-off depreciation.

Ws.: warrants, see *warrant.*

WS

  (1) see *Wall Street.*

  (2) see *watered stock.*

WSJ: see *Wall Street Journal.*

WT: see *wellhead tax.*

X: see *no protest.*

X-C: see *ex-coupon.*

X-Ch.: see *exchange.*

X-CL: excess current liabilities.

X-D: see *ex-dividend.*

X-Dis.: see *ex-distribution.*

X-Div.: see *ex-dividend.*

X-I: see *ex-interest.*

X-In.: see *ex-interest.*

X loan: loan made under a law other than a small loan law. [55]

Xmas Club account: see *Christmas Club account.*

X-R: see *ex-rights.*

X-Rts.: see *ex-rights.*

X-Warr.: see *ex-warrants.*

XX: without securities or warrants.

Yankee bond market: issues floated in the United States, in dollars, by reign governments and corporations.

yard: slang, a $100 bill, or $100.

yellow-back: slang, a bank note, specifically a gold certificate.

yen: monetary unit of Japan.

yield

(1) *general:* the profit or income created through an investment in property.

(2) *finance:* to give up possession; to pay.

(3) *government:* the net return of a tax.

(4) *investments:* the rate of return received from one's investment in a specific security or a specific piece of property; most commonly expressed in terms that designate the annual rate of return on the investment. Also known as *return*. see *ROI*.

yield spread: the difference in yields on varying stocks. A concept utilized by portfolio managers.

yield to maturity: the rate of return on an investment when it is retained until maturity, given as a percentage.

Y loan: loan made under a law other than a small loan or X loan law. [55]

young adult account: a limited amount of revolving credit which some retail establishments make available to young adults, primarily to give them direct experience in money management. [41]

yo-yo stocks: highly volatile securities; these stocks are high-priced specialty issues that fluctuate greatly in price.

Yr.: year

YS: see *yield spread*.

yuan: monetary unit of China.

YYS: see *yo-yo stocks*.

Z

zaire: monetary unit of Congo (Kinshasa) and Zaire.

ZBB: see *zero-base(d) budgeting.*

zero-balance account: an arrangement, agreed to in advance by a drawee bank, under which a customer issues checks on an account even though funds do not exist in that account to cover the items. When the checks are physically presented to the drawee and posted, creating a minus balance, the bank contacts the customer, reports the overdraft figure, and transfers funds from another account to eliminate it, thus restoring the account to a zero balance. Commonly used by corporations that have many disbursing points and by many agencies of government.

zero-base(d) budgeting (ZBB)

(1) *general:* a financial management technique to redirect funds from lower-priority current programs to higher ones, to pinpoint opportunities for improved efficiency and ef-fectiveness, to reduce budgets while raising operating performance, and to improve profitability. see also *planning-programming-budgeting.*

(2) *government:* the approach of justifying the budget and its program for each year or two, instead of studying funding increases or decreases in the programs separately as the need arises.

zero-coupon bond: see *bond, zero-coupon.*

zero floor limit: see *floor limit.*

zero-minus (plus) tick: any sale that takes place at the same price of the pervious sale, but at a price that is lower (higher) than the earlier, different price. see *up tick.*

zero-plus tick: see *up tick.*

zero proof: a mechanical method of posting records in a manner serving to prove that the previous balance on each line of posting was made correctly.

zloty: monetary unit of Poland.

APPENDIXES

Appendix A: General Banking—Finance Statistics

Federal Reserve Bank Interest Rates
(percent)

Effective Date	Range (or Level), All Federal Reserve Banks	Federal Reserve Bank of New York	Effective Date	Range (or Level), All Federal Reserve Banks	Federal Reserve Bank of New York
In effect December 31, 1970	$5\frac{1}{2}$	$5\frac{1}{2}$	1975—January 6	$7\frac{1}{4}$–$7\frac{3}{4}$	$7\frac{3}{4}$
			10	$7\frac{1}{4}$–$7\frac{3}{4}$	$7\frac{1}{4}$
1971—January 8	$5\frac{1}{4}$–$5\frac{1}{2}$	$5\frac{1}{4}$	24	$7\frac{1}{4}$	$7\frac{1}{4}$
15	$5\frac{1}{4}$	$5\frac{1}{4}$	February 5	$6\frac{3}{4}$–$7\frac{1}{4}$	$6\frac{3}{4}$
19	5–$5\frac{1}{4}$	$5\frac{1}{4}$	7	$6\frac{3}{4}$	$6\frac{3}{4}$
22	5–$5\frac{1}{4}$	5	March 10	$6\frac{1}{4}$–$6\frac{3}{4}$	$6\frac{1}{4}$
29	5	5	14	$6\frac{1}{4}$	$6\frac{1}{4}$
February 13	$4\frac{3}{4}$–5	5	May 16	6–$6\frac{1}{4}$	6
19	$4\frac{3}{4}$	$4\frac{3}{4}$	23	6	6
July 16	$4\frac{3}{4}$–5	5			
23	5	5	1976—January 19	$5\frac{1}{2}$–6	$5\frac{1}{2}$
November 11	$4\frac{3}{4}$–5	5	23	$5\frac{1}{2}$	$5\frac{1}{2}$
19	$4\frac{3}{4}$	$4\frac{3}{4}$	November 22	$5\frac{1}{4}$–$5\frac{1}{2}$	$5\frac{1}{4}$
December 13	$4\frac{1}{2}$–$4\frac{3}{4}$	$4\frac{3}{4}$	26	$5\frac{1}{4}$	$5\frac{1}{4}$
17	$4\frac{1}{4}$–$4\frac{3}{4}$	$4\frac{1}{2}$			
24	$4\frac{1}{2}$	$4\frac{1}{2}$	1977—August 30	$5\frac{1}{4}$–$5\frac{3}{4}$	$5\frac{1}{4}$
			31	$5\frac{1}{4}$–$5\frac{3}{4}$	$5\frac{3}{4}$
1973—January 15	5	5	September 2	$5\frac{3}{4}$	$5\frac{3}{4}$
February 26	5–$5\frac{1}{2}$	$5\frac{1}{2}$	October 25	6	6
March 2	$5\frac{1}{2}$	$5\frac{1}{2}$			
April 23	$5\frac{1}{2}$–$5\frac{3}{4}$	$5\frac{1}{2}$	1978—January 9	6–$6\frac{1}{2}$	$6\frac{1}{2}$
May 4	$5\frac{3}{4}$	$5\frac{3}{4}$	20	$6\frac{1}{2}$	$6\frac{1}{2}$
11	$5\frac{3}{4}$–6	6	May 11	$6\frac{1}{2}$–7	7
18	6	6	12	7	7
June 11	6–$6\frac{1}{2}$	$6\frac{1}{2}$	July 3	7–$7\frac{1}{4}$	$7\frac{1}{4}$
15	$6\frac{1}{2}$	$6\frac{1}{2}$	10	$7\frac{1}{4}$	$7\frac{1}{4}$
July 2	7	7	August 21	$7\frac{3}{4}$	$7\frac{3}{4}$
August 14	7–$7\frac{1}{2}$	$7\frac{1}{2}$	September 22	8	8
23	$7\frac{1}{2}$	$7\frac{1}{2}$	October 16	8–$8\frac{1}{2}$	$8\frac{1}{2}$
			20	$8\frac{1}{2}$	$8\frac{1}{2}$
1974—April 25	$7\frac{1}{2}$–8	8	November 1	$8\frac{1}{2}$–$9\frac{1}{2}$	$9\frac{1}{2}$
30	8	8	3	$9\frac{1}{2}$	$9\frac{1}{2}$
December 9	$7\frac{3}{4}$–8	$7\frac{3}{4}$			
16	$7\frac{3}{4}$	$7\frac{3}{4}$	In effect June 30, 1979	$9\frac{1}{2}$	$9\frac{1}{2}$

Source: Federal Reserve Bulletin.

The 50 Largest Trust Operations

1980 Rank	Company	Market Value of Trust Assets[1]		Trust Department Revenues		
		1980 ($ millions)	Percent increase over 1979	Total ($ thousands)	Percent Change from 1979	Percent of Total Operating Revenues
1	J.P. Morgan	36,119	18.9	147,627	15.3	2.9
2	Citicorp	26,317	3.4	109,310	23.9	0.8
3	Manufacturers Hanover	18,285	7.8	64,138	14.4	1.2
4	Bankers Trust	17,686	22.3	63,368	3.7	1.7
5	Mellon National	12,634	2.5	28,250	15.6	1.8
6	Harris Bankcorp	12,499	7.4	38,837	14.5	5.4
7	Chase Manhattan	11,198	19.2	73,690	17.7	0.9
8	Provident National	10,440	40.3	26,376	29.7	8.9
9	U.S. Trust	9,650	0.4	52,304	6.5	23.4
10	First Chicago	9,594	9.8	44,211	22.2	1.3
11	Continental Illinois	9,455	23.7	44,809	19.7	1.0
12	BankAmerica	9,269	31.6	60,520	11.1	0.5
13	Wells Fargo	9,175	28.3	28,928	11.0	1.1
14	Northern Trust	9,147	17.3	48,844	16.5	7.9
15	Chemical New York	9,094	10.9	49,811	13.0	1.2
16	Western Bancorp	8,656	3.9	44,190	15.2	1.3
17	Wilmington Trust	8,439	25.4	12,315	20.0	8.4
18	Crocker National	8,295	38.6	31,359	28.6	1.6
19	First Bank System	8,279	10.9	33,182	15.4	2.5
20	First National Boston	7,830	26.0	40,577	18.5	1.7
21	National Detroit	6,669	-10.5	27,874	12.6	2.7
22	Bank of New York	6,643	17.9	71,383	38.3	6.5
23	AmeriTrust	6,180	17.5	27,003	14.7	4.8
24	Fiduciary Trust Co. of N.Y.	5,794	20.4	16,151	-1.4	67.3
25	Capital Guardian Trust	5,647	25.5	N.A.	N.A.	N.A.
26	First International Bancshares	5,318	38.0	18,766	16.2	1.4
27	First Union Bancorp.	5,202	16.4	16,610	12.4	4.0
28	Northwest Bancorporation	5,081	12.6	26,915	10.4	1.8
29	Girard	4,800	14.3	21,155	14.0	4.7
30	Security Pacific	4,243	7.4	32,452	8.1	1.0
31	Republic of Texas	4,215	12.6	20,140	14.4	1.6
32	American Natl. (Chicago)	4,149	44.3	10,622	12.4	4.0
33	National City Corp.	4,117	17.4	14,548	12.5	2.8
34	First City Bancorp.	4,108	37.9	13,756	24.8	1.3
35	Irving Bank Corp.	3,510	7.5	24,863	6.0	1.4
36	State Street Boston Corp.	3,467	32.6	28,716	30.8	9.0
37	Boatmen's Bancshares	3,298	20.6	6,264	12.4	3.4
38	Citizens &Southern Ga.	3,246	16.8	9,728	4.9	2.1
39	DETROITBANK	3,212	7.7	15,428	20.3	2.9
40	First Wisconsin Corp.	3,166	13.3	13,375	18.6	2.6

Continued

1980 Rank	Company	Market Value of Trust Assets[1]		Trust Department Revenues		
		1980 ($ millions)	Percent increase over 1979	Total ($ thousands)	Percent Change from 1979	Percent of Total Operating Revenues
41	First Pennsylvania	3,158	1.9	16,603	13.1	2.2
42	Marine Midland	3,106	11.8	18,885	3.8	1.0
43	Trust Co. of Georgia	3,093	7.6	15,795	13.4	4.7
44	Mercantile Bancorp	3,093	16.0	10,899	11.3	2.3
45	Wachovia Corp.	3,083	0.7	17,791	13.1	3.2
46	Tex. Commerce Bancshares	2,940	52.4	13,602	11.9	1.3
47	Mercantile Bankshares	2,909	12.6	15,127	16.3	10.6
48	Pittsburg Natl. Corp.	2,876	12.0	17,737	9.0	2.8
49	American Fletcher Corp.	2,823	9.3	7,705	21.1	2.6
50	Hartford National	2,822	18.8	14,656	18.3	6.0

N.A., not available
[1]Includes accounts over which the bank exercises investment discretion.
Source: Forbes.

Financial Saving by Households
(billions of dollars)

Item	1972	1973	1974	1975	1976	1977	1978	1979
Demand deposits and currency	13.7	13.9	7.2	3.9	14.9	22.6	18.2	13.7
Savings accounts	74.5	63.8	55.9	84.0	109.3	109.2	105.2	79.6
Mutual savings banks	10.2	4.7	3.1	11.2	13.0	11.1	8.6	3.2
Commercial banks	29.0	35.3	34.1	24.6	40.2	40.2	44.1	35.0
Savings and loan associations	32.0	20.8	15.6	42.8	50.1	50.0	46.2	38.2
Credit unions	3.3	2.9	3.0	5.5	6.0	7.8	6.4	3.2
Life insurance reserves	6.9	7.6	6.7	8.7	8.4	11.6	12.0	12.2
Pension fund reserves	22.6	25.4	29.6	34.9	44.2	53.7	65.8	67.7
Direct market instruments	1.3	19.4	33.0	29.1	14.6	9.1	29.6	78.0
U.S. government securities	-0.4	18.8	19.4	16.8	9.5	15.7	27.0	47.3
State and local obligations	2.3	5.3	8.3	6.2	2.5	2.6	3.3	*
Corporate and foreign bonds	5.0	2.0	5.1	8.4	5.8	-3.3	-1.4	9.3
Money market fund shares	—	—	2.4	1.3	*	0.2	6.9	34.4
Investment company shares	-0.5	-1.2	-0.7	-0.1	-1.0	-0.9	-1.0	-2.1
Other corporate stock	-5.1	-5.5	-1.5	-3.5	-2.2	-5.2	-5.2	-10.9
Other financial assets	4.3	13.2	-5.6	-6.7	-3.7	12.7	17.3	3.0
Net acquisition of financial assets	123.1	143.4	126.8	153.8	187.7	219.1	248.3	254.3
Less: Net increase in liabilities	70.8	76.7	51.1	52.2	97.3	145.3	166.4	167.6
Net financial saving	52.3	66.7	75.7	101.6	90.4	73.8	81.9	86.7
Memoranda								
Disposable personal income	801.3	901.7	984.6	1,086.7	1,184.5	1,305.1	1,458.4	1,624.3
Personal saving	49.4	70.3	71.7	83.6	68.6	65.0	72.0	73.8
Saving as per cent of disposable personal income	6.2	7.8	7.3	7.7	5.8	5.0	4.9	4.5

*Less than $50 million.

Note: Household sector includes personal trusts and nonprofit organizations as well as persons who are members of households. Data for other U.S. government securities include issues of federally sponsored credit agencies. Pension fund reserves refer to private pension, government employees retirement funds and the Railroad Retirement Fund, but exclude Social Security and other OASI programs. Other financial assets include mortgages, commercial paper, net investment in noncorporate business, security credit advances, and miscellaneous assets.

Source: FRB and U.S. Department of Commerce.

Holdings of Federally Underwritten Mortgage Debt by Main Types of Financial Institutions

End of Year	Millions of Dollars					Percentage Distribution				
	Total	Mutual Savings Banks	Commercial Banks	Savings and Loan Associations	Life Insurance Companies	Total	Mutual Savings Banks	Commercial Banks	Savings and Loan Associations	Life Insurance Companies
1960	51,449	16,060	8,710	10,746	15,933	100.0	31.2	16.9	20.9	31.0
1961	53,451	17,312	8,602	11,319	16,218	100.0	32.4	16.1	21.2	30.3
1962	56,256	19,025	9,174	11,486	16,571	100.0	33.8	16.3	20.4	29.5
1963	59,954	21,174	9,967	11,656	17,157	100.0	35.3	16.6	19.4	28.6
1964	62,931	23,408	10,057	11,579	17,887	100.0	37.2	16.0	18.4	28.4
1965	65,486	25,199	10,390	11,543	18,354	100.0	38.5	15.9	17.6	28.0
1966	66,099	25,971	10,150	11,426	18,552	100.0	39.3	15.4	17.3	28.1
1967	67,699	26,869	10,405	12,142	18,283	100.0	39.7	15.4	17.9	27.0
1968	69,820	27,602	10,633	13,670	17,915	100.0	39.5	15.2	19.6	25.7
1969	71,626	28,028	10,622	15,560	17,416	100.0	39.1	14.8	21.7	24.3
1970	74,089	28,095	10,509	18,672	16,813	100.0	37.9	14.2	25.2	22.7
1971	79,459	28,216	11,290	24,298	15,655	100.0	35.5	14.2	30.6	19.7
1972	83,649	28,635	11,518	28,874	14,622	100.0	34.2	13.8	34.5	17.5
1973	83,331	28,452	11,531	29,738	13,610	100.0	34.1	13.8	35.7	16.3
1974	80,510	27,511	10,393	29,884	12,722	100.0	34.2	12.9	37.1	15.8
1975	78,614	26,818	9,383	30,590	11,823	100.0	34.1	11.9	38.9	15.0
1976	77,745	26,913	8,644	31,331	10,857	100.0	34.6	11.1	40.3	14.0
1977	74,611	26,120	8,401	30,151	9,939	100.0	35.0	11.3	40.4	13.3
1978	72,285	26,027	7,944	29,041	9,273	100.0	36.0	11.0	40.2	12.8
1979p	70,133	25,206	7,543	28,595	8,789	100.0	35.9	10.8	40.8	12.5

p, preliminary.

Note: Federally underwritten mortgage debt refers to VA-guaranteed and FHS-insured loans.

Source: ACLI, FRB, HUD, and NAMSB.

Number of Banks, Offices, and Ownership Units by State

State	December 1970 Number of Offices[1]	December 1970 Number of Banks	December 1970 Number of[2] Ownership Units	December 1979 Number of Offices[1]	December 1979 Number of Banks	December 1979 Number of[2] Ownership Units
Alabama	544	272	272	894	317	249
Alaska	73	11	11	122	12	11
Arizona	335	12	11	532	27	27
Arkansas	415	250	249	656	261	257
California	3,185	152	147	4,376	257	254
Colorado	289	270	237	509	410	318
Connecticut	497	61	59	659	65	60
Delaware	105	18	18	167	20	20
District of Columbia	117	14	14	157	17	17
Florida	533	500	361	1,544	585	325
Georgia	737	441	429	1,268	439	408
Hawaii	150	10	10	187	12	12
Idaho	180	24	24	263	27	26
Illinois	1,206	1,108	1,106	1,744	1,288	1,286
Indiana	1,039	407	407	1,492	406	406
Iowa	984	666	644	1,196	657	589
Kansas	670	601	601	895	617	612
Kentucky	671	343	342	1,047	343	342
Louisiana	624	231	231	1,031	262	260
Maine	269	43	33	341	41	25
Maryland	636	115	111	1,012	102	89
Massachusetts	906	162	141	1,087	149	100
Michigan	1,534	331	331	2,376	372	245
Minnesota	740	729	613	991	762	627
Mississippi	530	182	182	852	183	183
Missouri	764	671	637	1,142	727	516
Montana	145	140	108	193	165	125
Nebrasks	483	441	437	727	461	456
Nevada	94	8	7	144	9	9
New Hampshire	137	74	69	227	79	66
New Jersey	1,229	217	206	1,733	176	147
New Mexico	196	66	57	325	87	64
New York	2,752	311	273	3,738	302	259
North Carolina	1,217	98	97	1,807	83	82
North Dakota	240	169	141	298	175	144
Ohio	1,820	516	468	2,521	408	331
Oklahoma	494	434	434	745	496	494
Oregon	386	49	49	630	80	77
Pennsylvania	2,198	471	471	2,864	378	376
Rhode Island	184	13	13	248	17	17
South Carolina	520	102	102	776	85	85
South Dakota	259	161	149	313	155	142

Continued

State	December 1970			December 1979		
	Number of Offices[1]	Number of Banks	Number of[2] Ownership Units	Number of Offices[1]	Number of Banks	Number of[2] Ownership Units
Tennessee	796	308	300	1,349	352	308
Texas	1,267	1,191	1,181	1,661	1,427	1,169
Utah	187	48	47	349	76	61
Vermont	128	43	43	189	30	30
Virginia	1,058	233	187	1,613	234	189
Washington	649	91	87	994	110	109
West Virginia	205	200	200	294	235	234
Wisconsin	881	608	542	1,147	636	513
Wyoming	72	70	65	97	94	69
Total	35,330	13,686	12,954	51,522	14,708	12,820

[1]Includes limited facilities.

[2]Number of banks not owned by holding companies plus number of holding companies operating within the state. Thus, holding companies with multistate operations are counted as ownership units in all states in which they operate. Banks owned by holding companies are not counted as ownership units.

Banks that Have Retail EFT Machines Ordered or Installed by State, March 1979

State	Number of Banks						Number of Machines					
	Cash Dispensers		Automated Tellers		Point of Sale Terminals		Cash Dispensers		Automated Tellers		Point of Sale Terminals	
	Order	Install	Order	Install	Order	Install	Order	Install	Order	Install	Order	Install
Alabama	0	7	12	32	0	0	0	19	38	95	0	0
Alaska	0	0	0	3	0	0	0	0	0	12	0	0
Arizona	0	0	4	4	0	0	0	0	140	53	0	0
Arkansas	1	2	12	43	0	0	0	2	32	91	0	0
California	1	2	43	43	2	3	1	7	511	242	1,801	4,311
Colorado	2	1	27	75	0	0	3	1	115	133	0	0
Connecticut	0	6	9	21	0	0	0	13	67	163	0	0
Delaware	0	1	1	4	4	3	0	9	10	85	59	146
District of Columbia	0	0	5	8	0	0	0	3	129	68	0	0
Florida	6	12	61	107	3	9	9	13	138	277	8	46
Georgia	1	2	20	41	2	2	1	4	59	198	12	438
Hawaii	0	0	2	2	0	0	0	0	6	24	0	0
Idaho	0	0	2	2	0	0	0	0	22	19	0	0
Illinois	2	14	46	123	1	4	4	14	109	273	6	1,027
Indiana	2	8	39	51	0	0	2	14	112	173	0	0
Iowa	0	4	16	54	2	13	0	5	60	117	4	105
Kansas	1	12	18	66	1	3	1	9	59	116	10	90
Kentucky	1	1	26	64	1	1	1	2	78	205	20	61
Louisiana	0	6	23	60	0	0	0	8	71	212	0	0
Maine	0	0	0	5	0	0	0	0	0	8	0	0
Maryland	0	0	9	9	3	4	0	0	100	156	17	171
Massachusetts	1	2	21	28	2	2	1	6	108	89	503	338
Michigan	0	6	41	59	1	1	3	52	177	229	11	36
Minnesota	4	18	27	103	0	6	4	18	34	151	0	30
Mississippi	0	5	8	19	2	1	0	14	31	47	56	21
Missouri	4	6	31	63	0	0	5	6	46	95	0	0

Montana	0	3	4	25	0	0	0	0	3	4	27	0	0
Nebraska	0	3	11	20	3	10	0	0	3	23	33	8	76
Nevada	0	0	1	2	0	0	0	0	0	2	24	0	0
New Hampshire	0	2	3	5	0	1	0	0	3	16	11	0	5
New Jersey	1	3	13	21	3	4	4	0	6	89	109	443	1,091
New Mexico	0	1	4	8	1	0	0	0	1	20	25	42	0
New York	1	4	15	20	10	15	6	0	50	340	575	1,177	1,065
North Carolina	0	2	9	12	0	0	0	0	4	101	118	0	0
North Dakota	0	0	2	11	0	5	0	0	0	2	13	0	18
Ohio	2	13	31	92	0	5	2	0	16	274	493	0	797
Oklahoma	2	3	19	58	2	13	2	0	3	61	150	16	84
Oregon	0	0	5	4	0	0	0	0	0	123	80	0	0
Pennsylvania	2	5	20	35	0	2	26	0	6	143	245	0	30
Rhode Island	0	0	3	1	0	0	0	0	0	65	12	0	0
South Carolina	0	0	10	3	0	0	0	0	0	127	70	0	0
South Dakota	0	1	2	7	0	0	0	0	1	10	19	0	0
Tennessee	0	5	27	59	0	2	0	0	5	72	181	0	104
Texas	7	24	57	110	0	1	8	0	24	136	131	0	10
Utah	1	0	7	5	1	0	1	0	0	52	33	1	0
Vermont	0	0	4	2	0	0	0	0	0	34	12	0	0
Virginia	1	4	8	24	1	1	1	0	4	50	139	83	322
Washington	0	1	13	8	0	0	0	0	34	76	181	0	0
West Virginia	0	9	1	15	0	0	0	0	9	1	18	0	0
Wisconsin	1	1	22	70	1	3	1	0	1	32	149	15	15
Wyoming	0	2	8	17	0	0	0	0	2	18	19	0	0
Puerto Rico	0	1	1	2	0	0	0	0	1	4	17	0	0
Total	44	202	803	1,725	46	114	86		395	4,127	6,215	4,292	10,437

Source: FDIC Survey, March 1979.

Mortgage Participation Certificates

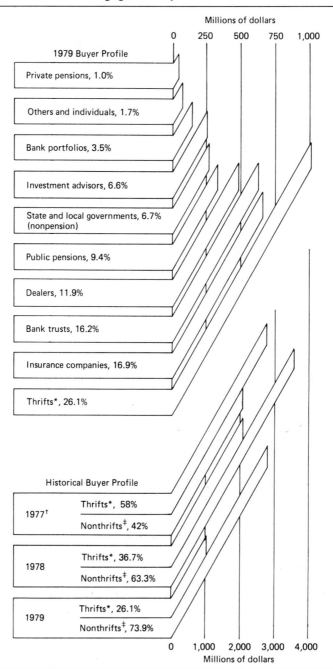

*Includes credit unions, savings and loans, and savings banks.
†In 1976, thrift institutions accounted for as much as 95% of total sales in any given month.
‡Includes banks, pension funds, insurance companies, investment advisors, state and local governments, and others.
Source: Federal Home Loan Mortgage Corporation.

Growth of Automated Clearinghouse and Preauthorized Payments

Date	Number of Operating ACHs	Membership		Participating Companies	Monthly volume (millions)	
		Banks	Thrifts		Private	Government
March 1974	2	—	—	—	—	0
September 1974	4	1,369	N.A.	N.A.	0.04	0
March 1975	6	2,165	N.A.	582	0.10	0.1
September 1975	13	4,184	N.A.	831	0.20	0.1
March 1976	19	5,883	161	1,566	0.30	0.7
September 1976	26	7,907	554	2,199	0.50	3.1
March 1977	27	8,994	804	3,528	0.60	5.2
September 1977	32	9,036	1,259	4,402	1.00	6.4
March 1978	32	9,379	1,422	4,864	1.50	7.5
September 1978	32	9,474	2,004	5,597	1.80	7.8
March 1979	32	9,722	2,169	6,803	2.40	9.2
September 1979	32	9,976	2,384	8,363	2.90	9.7

N.A. not available.
Source: National Automated Clearing House Association.

Canada's Leaders in Corporate Finance

Position			1979		1978	
1978	1979		$ Value (millions)	No. of Issues	$ Value (Millions)	No. of Issues
1	1	Wood Gundy	1,383.5	53	1,895.2	56
2	2	Dominion Securities	816.9	26	548.7	21
4	3	McLeod Young Weir	473.6	24	439.6	28
7	4	Salomon Brothers[1]	472.9	10	258.7	4
3	5	A. E. Ames	359.7	21	450.6	20
8	8	Merrill Lynch Royal Securities	274.4	17	239.8	14
6	7	Pitfield Mackay Ross	216.6	14	323.9	16
5	8	Greenshields	212.7	15	405.8	25
10	9	Nesbitt Thomson	178.8	14	199.2	14
15	10	Morgan Stanley[1]	97.9	5	44.5	3
13	11	Richardson Securities	94.8	15	111.9	18
9	12	Burns Fry	90.8	8	214.9	7
	13	Credit Suisse First Boston[2]	78.4	8	10.8	2
19	14	Orion Bank[1]	69.9	5	17.6	2
	15	Swiss Bank Corp	66.7	8	15.8	2
14	16	Levesque Beaubien	66.6	7	55.7	7
16	17	Midland Doherty	66.4	11	41.2	10
20	18	Pemberton Securities	61.9	20	17.5	3
	19	Walwyn Stodgell Cochran Murray	57.9	21	16.3	7
	20	Morgan Stanley Canada	56.6	2	10.0	1

[1]U.S. or European firm.
[2]Formerly Credit Suisse White Weld.
Source: Financial Post of Canada.

Canada's Top Brokers
(thousands of dollars)

Rank (by Capital) Dealer, Year-End	Total Capital Employed		Gross revenues (includes interest income)	After-Tax Net Earnings
	Latest Year	Previous Year		
1. Wood Gundy (December 31, 1979)	32,272	28,933	142,790	1,697
2. Merrill Lynch Royal Securities (Dec. 31, 1979)	26,209	17,616	98,185	5,693
3. Burns Fry (May 31, 1980)	26,117	16,613	91,659	5,360
4. Dominion Securities (March 31, 1980)	23,848	15,855	92,859	5,623
5. Pitfield Mackay Ross (January 31, 1980)	20,334	15,279	78,736	7,255
6. Midland Doherty (March 31, 1980)	20,318	12,535	120,196	8,005
7. Richardson Securities of Canada (December 31, 1979)	18,530	1 3,280	N.A.	N.A.
8. A.E. Ames (March 31, 1980)	18,068	15,920	N.A.	N.A.
9. McLeod Young Weir (December 31, 1979)	16,380	11,180	N.A.	N.A.
10. Nesbitt Thomson (March 31, 1980)	15,692	10,102	74,075	4,720
11. Walwyn Stodgell Cochran Murray (March 31, 1980)	12,435	7,735	73,458	4,078
12. Greenshields (March 31, 1980)	11,556	9,574	72,790	2,900

N.A. not available.
Source: Financial Post of Canada.

Appendix B: Statistics on Banks

Annual Scoreboard of 200 Banks, 1980

Bank	Deposits Assets, 12/31/80 ($ mil.)	Deposits Total, 12/31/80 ($ mil.)	Deposits Chg. from 1979 (%)	Deposits Time/demand (%)	Deposits Foreign (%)	Loans Total O/S 12/31/80 ($ mil.)	Loans Chg. from 1979 (%)	Loans Loan Loss Prov. 1980 ($ mil.)	Loans Chg. from 1979 (%)	Loans Net Charge-offs as % of loans	Loans Fed. Funds Borrowed (%)	Loans Net Oper. Income 1980 ($ mil.)	Loans Chg. from 1979 (%)	Perf. Return on Avg. Assets, 1980	Perf. Leverage, 1980	Perf. Return on Com. Equity, 1980	Perf. Net Interest Income, 1980	Perf. Chg. from 1979 (%)	Perf. Oper. Income as % of Net Int. Income	Perf. 5-year Growth EPS (%)
1 Citicorp (New York)	114,920	71,771	2	86/14	72	72,269	12	298.0	27	0.4(e)	11(e)	507.0	-7	0.47	28.7	13.6	2,622	1	19.3	8.9
2 BankAmerica (San Francisco)	111,617	88,426	4	79/21	46	64,693	10	241.5	7	0.3	8	645.0	7	0.62	28.3	17.5	2,979	8	21.7	16.6
3 Chase Manhattan (New York)	76,190	56,846	17	74/26	54	47,267	17	189.5	27	0.3	11	364.7	17	0.49	32.0	15.8	1,728	10	21.1	23.1
4 Manufacturers Hanover (New York)	55,522	41,745	9	67/33	50	33,044	21	77.8	-27	0.2	7	230.2	9	0.48	29.2	14.0	1,181	10	19.5	8.9
5 Morgan (J.P.) (New York)	51,991	35,594	18	70/30	52	26,489	17	42.1	41	0.1	17	367.7	28	0.77	23.2	17.8	995	18	36.9	12.8
6 Continental Illinois (Chicago)	42,089	27,314	14	81/19	50	27,367	16	96.0	37	0.2	38(d)	224.1	15	0.57	27.4	15.5	838	24	26.8	10.6
7 Chemical New York	41,342	30,067	4	68/32	43	23,852	10	63.0	5	0.2	12	175.2	23	0.44	33.8	14.7	1,018	19	17.2	10.9
8 Bankers Trust New York	34,202	23,816	6	68/32	48	17,581	9	90.0	89	0.4	17	214.0	87	0.64	34.9	22.3	764	26	28.0	25.1
9 Western Bancorp. (Los Angeles)	32,110	24,864	5	65/35	9	18,549	6	113.4	11	0.5	11	233.4	9	0.78	23.0	17.9	1,300	10	18.0	25.1
10 First Chicago	28,699	21,361	1	83/17	55	17,308	8	112.0	33	0.6	18	66.5	-42	0.23	23.9	5.5	437	-6	15.2	-4.2
11 Security Pacific (Los Angeles)	27,794	21,169	15	71/29	16	19,331	13	78.7	1	0.4	9	181.9	11	0.69	24.0	16.6	936	7	19.4	22.3

	23,638	2	74/26	14	16,829	9	71.9	13	0.4	12	121.7	-7	0.55	25.3	14.0	725	-1	16.8	16.8
12 Wells Fargo (San Francisco)	23,638	2	74/26	14	16,829	9	71.9	13	0.4	12	121.7	-7	0.55	25.3	14.0	725	-1	16.8	16.8
13 Crocker National (San Francisco)	19,063	19	72/28	24	12,993	16	72.1	19	0.5	8	95.1	6	0.55	25.0	13.8(g)	703	10	13.5	16.2
14 Irving Bank (New York)	18,090	5	58/42	40	8,707	17	51.0	48	0.3	15	85.8	24	0.52	30.6	15.8	474	19	18.1	14.8
15 Marine Midland Banks (Buffalo)	17,480	13	74/26	43	9,758	7	62.8	39	0.6	12	58.4	37	0.35	26.5	9.3	452	24	12.9	35.7
16 Mellon National (Pittsburgh)	16,157	15	75/25	29	8,152	16	28.5	2	0.4	16	114.2	13	0.78	17.0	13.3	392	7	29.2	13.5
17 First National Boston	15,949	21	80/20	52	8,848	20	48.0	-2	0.4	32	103.1	21	0.67	22.3	15.0	511	20	20.2	20.6
18 Northwest Bancorp. (Minneapolis)	14,395	15	72/28	5	7,832	2	25.8	26	0.3	7(d)	116.7	6	0.90	17.2	15.4	458	12	25.5	14.2
19 First International Bancshares (Dallas)	13,781	12	68/32	21	7,104	18	34.0	35	0.3	13	122.0	20	1.01	18.6	18.8	424	21	28.8	17.0
20 First Bank System (Minneapolis)	13,475	9	70/30	5	7,368	6	28.7	29	0.3	17	111.6	8	0.91	16.5	15.0	420	12	26.6	13.8
21 Republic of Texas (Dallas)	11,867	10	70/30	26	6,190	12	28.9	73	0.4	16	88.1	21	0.81	20.1	16.2(g)	320	19	27.5	18.4

Continued

Bank	Assets, 12/31/80 ($ mil.)	Deposits				Loans						Net Oper. In-come, 1980 ($ mil.)	Chg. from 1979 (%)	Performance						
		Total, 12/31/80 ($ mil.)	Chg. from 1979 (%)	Time/demand (%)	For-eign (%)	Total O/S, 12/31/80 ($ mil.)	Chg. from 1979 (%)	Loan Loss Prov. 1980 ($ mil.)	Chg. from 1979 (%)	Net Charge-offs as % of loans	Fed. Funds Bor-rowed (%)			Return on Avg. Assets 1980	Lever-age 1980	Return on Com. Equity, 1980	Net Interest In-come, 1980	Chg. from 1979 (%)	Oper. Income as % of Net Int. Income	5-year Growth EPS (%)
22 Texas Commerce Bancshares (Houston)	11,287	8,631	19	61/39	16	5,838	16	24.2	37	0.2	9	103.0	25	1.10	17.5	19.4	362	25	28.5	19.6
23 First City Bancorp. of Texas (Houston)	11,275	8,722	14	65/35	18	5,444	19	28.1	23	0.4	13(d)	90.4	28	0.98	18.4	18.0	353	26	25.6	18.5
24 National Detroit	10,869	7,804	13	70/30	18	5,313	15	18.1	29	0.4	17	80.0	-3	0.80	15.8	12.7	321	2	24.9	12.4(h)
25 Bank of New York	10,423	8,319	21	72/28	32	5,745	32	16.8	-32	0.2(b)	19	50.5	15	0.50	26.2	13.1	268	14	18.8	8.2
26 Seafirst (Seattle)	9,588	7,239	9	70/30	10	6,636	14	23.1	30	0.3	9	69.8	7	0.80	18.8	15.1	351	13	19.9	18.0
27 European American Bancorp (New York)	7,771	5,981	-6	62/38	41	4,555	3	32.0	61	0.7	12	30.1	44	0.40	24.9	10.0	221	23	13.6	35.3
28 NCNB (Charlotte, N.C.)	7,176	5,060	13	68/32	25	3,299	26	21.2	15	0.4	15	47.7	7	0.74	20.2	15.0	196	1	24.3	22.3
29 Union Bank (Los Angeles)	7,004	4,999	-3	54/46	9	3,947	3	10.0	16	0.3	22	32.5	-11	0.51	20.9	10.7	244	7	13.3	N.A.
30 Harris Bankcorp (Chicago)	6,905	4,795	5	68/32	23	3,560	6	8.0	14	0.2	17	33.0	-7	0.50	19.7	9.8	158	5	21.0	0.1
31 Republic New York	6,447	4,394	34	90/10	36	2,590	54	28.5	22	0.8	5(d)	74.0	119	1.21	29.1	35.1	167	74	44.3	28.2
32 Pittsburgh National	6,225	4,176	7	72/28	5	3,174	10	12.2	9	0.2	25	55.6	13	0.97	17.0	16.5	187	11	29.8	13.4

#	Bank																			
33	Philadelphia National	6,210	4,172	3	58/42	21	3,266	2	15.9	0	0.5	12	40.8	-10	0.68	18.6	12.7	212	7	19.2	11.4
34	Southeast Banking (Miami)	5,854	4,397	15	61/39	4	2,548	8	18.0	33	0.6	13	47.9	30	0.88	19.3	16.9	239	25	20.0	29.5
35	Northern Trust (Chicago)	5,849	4,163	6	65/35	30	2,884	20	4.0	-20	0.1	28	33.1	9	0.59	19.8	11.7	146	13	22.7	5.5
36	Michigan National (Bloomfield Hills)	5,757	4,710	4	76/24	0	3,810	3	21.8	51	0.5	2	40.7	-8	0.74	17.6	13.1	232	3	17.6	12.0
37	Valley National Bank of Arizona (Phoenix)	5,733	4,785	10	67/33	1	3,691	8	19.0	0	0.4	1	53.2	12	1.01	18.4	18.6	255	11	20.9	24.2
38	National Bank of North America (New York)	5,693	4,455	23	73/27	32	3,398	10	23.5	68	0.7	15	15.4	-10	0.23	18.1	4.2	168	17	9.2	2.2
39	Detroitbank	5,668	3,977	13	77/23	2	2,674	2	5.0	-10	0.2	32	39.1	-17	0.76	16.4	12.4	159	-6	24.5	10.6
40	Wachovia (Winston-Salem)	5,654	4,030	5	63/37	11	2,937	10	8.1	21	0.2	9	54.3	16	1.01	15.5	15.7	208	15	26.0	12.9
41	AmeriTrust (Cleveland)	5,602	3,936	5	73/27	6	3,206	-2	15.6	37	0.7	24	58.4	2	1.07	10.4	11.2	212	3	27.6	8.5
42	First Pennsylvania (Philadelphia)	5,497	3,619	-32	72/28	30	3,490	-17	78.4	101	1.9	28	-73.6	NM	1.13	22.2	-25.1	159	-7	N.M.	N.A.

Continued

Bank	Assets, 12/31/80 ($ mil.)	Deposits				Loans						Net Oper. Income 1980 ($ mil.)	Chg. from 1979 (%)	Performance					Oper. Income as % of Net Int. Income	5-year Growth EPS (%)
		Total, 12/31/80 ($ mil.)	Chg. from 1979 (%)	Time/demand (%)	Foreign (%)	Total O/S 12/31/80 ($ mil.)	Chg. from 1979 (%)	Loan Loss Prov. 1980 ($ mil.)	Chg. from 1979 (%)	Net Charge-offs as % of loans	Fed. Funds Borrowed (%)			Return on Avg. Assets, 1980	Lever-age, 1980	Return on Com. Equity, 1980	Net Interest In-come, 1980	Chg. from 1979 (%)		
43 National City (Cleveland)	5,490	3,425	3	70/30	13	2,212	-1	7.9	111	0.4	37	52.0	-3	1.04	14.4	14.9	173	6	30.0	8.8
44 Mercantile Texas (Dallas)	5,460	3,907	17	59/41	5	3,234	23	17.2	63	0.3	20	49.7	23	1.01	18.9	19.1	189	25	26.3	18.8
45 Rainier Bancorp. (Seattle)	5,222	3,833	8	71/29	16	3,424	3	14.1	3	0.4	9	39.4	3	0.82	17.0	13.9	214	6	18.4	12.8
46 BancOhio (Columbus)	5,002	3,917	3	70/30	0	2,761	2	23.4	90	0.8	18	18.7	-42	0.38	16.9	6.5	167	-9	11.2	0.2
47 U.S. Bancorp (Portland)	4,879	3,681	5	70/30	2	3,358	14	13.7	72	0.3	1	58.2	11	1.28	13.1	16.8	230	14	25.3	16.6
48 Manufacturers National (Detroit)	4,769	3,724	3	73/27	2	2,940	4	13.1	64	0.4	22	27.1	-19	0.59	18.6	10.9	154	0	17.6	9.5
49 Mercantile Bancorp. (St. Louis)	4,646	3,071	4	63/37	7	2,144	0	11.4	-7	0.4	23	37.8	16	0.91	17.5	15.8	132	7	28.6	10.9
50 First Wisconsin (Milwaukee)	4,524	3,245	-12	65/35	10	2,708	-2	7.0	39	0.3	34	29.4	27	0.63	23.1	14.6	133	11	22.1	23.3
51 Barnett Banks of Florida (Jacksonville)	4,431	3,573	15	59/41	0	2,083	14	13.9	55	0.6	-1	38.0	18	0.96	17.0	16.3	201	19	18.9	30.3
52 Girard (Philadelphia)	4,386	3,183	-2	56/44	20	2,610	7	13.2	14	0.4	21	35.0	11	0.86	17.5	15.0	151	11	23.2	20.7
53 Citizens & Southern Natl. Bank (Atlanta)	4,341	3,295	2	48/52	8	2,372	10	14.0	-46	0.8	20	37.2	52	0.87	18.2	15.8	177	13	21.0	16.7

54 First Union Bancorp. (St. Louis)	4,271	8	58/42	6	2,125	7	9.0	69	0.5	21	32.3	14	0.88	16.0	14.0	132	18	24.5	10.9
55 Southwest Bancshares (Houston)	4,158	19	58/42	8	2,031	16	10.4	46	0.4	9	30.9	23	0.88	16.4	14.4	137	25	22.5	14.8
56 Maryland National (Baltimore)	4,063	9	67/33	6	2,561	9	13.5	-5	0.4	15	32.0	24	0.86	17.0	14.6	166	15	19.3	11.5
57 Bank of Tokyo Trust (New York)	3,947	14	87/13	41	1,993	7	0.8	-64	0.0	6	11.7	-10	0.30(a)	21.0(a)	6.2(a)	37(f)	-5	31.8(f)	N.A.
58 First Natl. State Bancorp. (Newark)	3,919	26	64/36	5	2,168	28	4.5	-28	0.2	6	20.9	14	0.69	18.5	12.8	106	7	19.8	11.2
59 BanCal Tri-State (San Francisco)	3,852	7	68/32	22	1,918	-1	5.0	-31	0.2	39	17.9	-12	0.50	20.4	10.2	117	-1	15.3	51.1
60 California First Bank (San Francisco)	3,621	10	70/30	4	2,459	14	7.2	-4	0.2	2	17.8	-13	0.54	23.8	12.8	130	2	13.7	16.7
61 First Security (Salt Lake City)	3,601	5	69/31	0	2,192	1	4.9	-42	0.2	-3	41.1	10	1.23	13.2	16.2	168	6	24.4	13.6
62 Centran (Cleveland)	3,565	3	65/35	13	1,451	-1	6.3	38	0.5	45	26.0	5	0.76	18.7	14.2	102	-2	25.4	12.3
63 Shawmut (Boston)	3,456	12	55/45	6	1,788	9	8.5	20	0.5	22	17.4	6	0.55	19.9	10.9	120	13	14.5	55.9

Continued

Bank	Deposits					Loans							Performance						
	Assets, 12/31/80 ($ mil.)	Total, 12/31/80 ($ mil.)	Chg. from 1979 (%)	Time/ demand (%)	Foreign (%)	Total O/S 12/31/80 ($ mil.)	Chg. from 1979 (%)	Loan Loss Prov. 1980 ($ mil.)	Net Charge-offs as % of loans	Fed. Funds Borrowed (%)	Net Oper. Income 1980 ($ mil.)	Chg. from 1979 (%)	Return on Avg. Assets, 1980	Lever-age, 1980	Return on Com. Equity, 1980	Net Interest Income, 1980	Chg. from 1979 (%)	Oper. Income as % of Net Int. Income	5-year Growth EPS (%)
64 United Virginia Bankshares (Richmond)	3,454	2,673	7	66/34	1	2,376	11	12.8	0.4	8	34.2	15	1.04	16.6	17.3	167	11	20.5	25.8
65 Industrial National (Providence)	3,452	2,478	17	82/18	14	2,094	6	14.9	0.6	20	28.2	13	0.86	19.3	16.6	121	9	23.4	19.4
66 Lincoln First Banks (Rochester)	3,435	2,502	4	70/30	1	2,088	28	11.7	0.6	15	20.8	-2	0.59	18.9	11.1	131	6	15.9	16.6
67 Society (Cleveland)	3,431	2,603	9	74/26	1	1,682	-10	7.6	0.5	22	28.6	2	0.89	15.1	13.3	128	5	22.3	12.3
68 Midlantic Banks (West Orange, N.J.)	3,404	2,628	15	63/37	5	1,882	-36	6.4	0.3	10	28.8	16	0.81	17.6	14.2	140	12	20.6	36.0
69 Texas American Bancshares (Fort Worth)	3,371	2,554	13	60/40	0	1,814	46	9.0	0.4	15	30.2	22	1.04	14.8	15.3	126	21	24.0	16.8
70 Fidelcor (Philadelphia)	3,316	2,451	13	61/39	21	1,749	11	16.3	0.6	19(d)	14.2	93	0.50	18.9	9.5	108	13	13.2	-6.5
71 Sun Banks of Florida (Orlando)	3,312	2,863	14	61/39	0	1,609	12	7.1	0.4	0	29.8	28	0.90	18.3	16.4	148	24	20.1	41.8
72 First Union (Charlotte, N.C.)	3,283	2,270	3	64/36	24	1,910	13	6.7	0.2	23(d)	28.2	17	0.86	19.7	17.0	127	9	22.2	34.3
73 Fidelity Union Bancorp. (Newark)	3,259	2,559	41	62/38	1	1,707	29	5.7	0.4	3(d)	23.4	4	0.88	13.5	12.0	71	18	32.9	7.9

#	Bank																			
74	BayBanks (Boston)	3,207	2,717	12	68/32	0	1,706	5	8.3	19	0.3	-2(d)	26.5	17	0.91	16.3	14.9	154	14	17.2	19.6
75	CBT (Hartford)	3,175	2,331	11	53/47	8	1,762	7	8.7	13	0.4	19	21.4	20	0.75	20.2	15.3	123	16	17.4	20.9
76	Riggs National Bank of Washington, D.C.	3,149	2,501	15	59/41	28	1,539	14	7.3	25	0.5	15	24.3	12	0.90	16.2	14.5	113	15	21.6	13.1
77	First Atlanta	3,147	2,292	10	41/59	3	1,586	4	18.5	10	1.0	16	24.0	30	0.82	17.7	14.6	144	19	16.7	22.4
78	Trust Co. of Georgia (Atlanta)	3,112	2,196	12	40/60	0	1,454	5	14.2	15	0.5	9	37.7	36	1.30	16.7	21.8	160	22	23.5	72.0
79	State Street Boston	3,009	1,902	16	53/47	3	1,154	0	7.8	0	0.5	40	24.2	51	0.90	20.0	18.0	102	15	23.8	36.0
80	First Tennessee National (Memphis)	2,916	2,267	6	64/36	0	1,529	4	10.4	41	0.7	8	23.7	8	0.88	15.9	13.9	121	8	19.7	30.9
81	New England Merchants (Boston)	2,890	2,221	7	66/34	12	1,552	11	6.7	-12	0.2	36	21.4	23	0.71	23.5	16.8	103	15	20.7	22.4
82	Equimark (Pittsburgh)	2,863	2,087	2	74/26	4	1,517	2	4.5	94	0.2	21	9.6	13	0.27	28.0	7.6	76	6	12.6	-1.5
83	Allied Bancshares (Houston)	2,855	2,469	29	59/41	0	1,744	31	11.7	44	0.3	-7	37.3	29	1.51	15.3	23.1	134	35	27.8	22.7
84	Huntington Bancshares (Columbus)	2,831	2,133	10	68/32	2	1,567	13	6.9	18	0.4	11	22.8	5	0.89	16.0	14.3	109	8	20.9	21.3

Continued

Bank	Assets, 12/31/80 ($ mil.)	Deposits				Loans						Performance								
		Total, 12/31/80 ($ mil.)	Chg. from 1979 (%)	Time/ demand (%)	For- eign (%)	Total O/S 12/31/80 ($ mil.)	Chg. from 1979 (%)	Loan Loss Prov. 1980 ($ mil.)	Chg. from 1979 (%)	Net Charge- offs as % of loans	Fed. Funds Bor- rowed (%)	Net Oper. In- come, 1980 ($ mil.)	Chg. from 1979 (%)	Return on Avg. Assets, 1980	Lever- age, 1980	Return on Com. Equity, 1980	Net Interest In- come, 1980	Chg. from 1979 (%)	Oper. Income as % of Net Int. Income	5-year Growth EPS (%)
85 Banc One (Columbus)	2,824	2,321	9	70/30	0	1,630	6	9.8	12	0.6	5	33.4	10	1.27	13.3	16.9	131	9	25.5	15.3
86 Commerce Bancshares (Kansas City, Mo.)	2,765	2,235	4	61/39	0	1,452	-2	7.8	16	0.7	3(d)	25.0	7	0.95	12.7	12.1	123	9	20.3	12.1
87 Hartford National	2,753	2,209	6	43/57	1	1,385	7	3.3	-37	0.2	24	13.8	40	0.58	25.5	14.9	83	12	16.6	40.7
88 Provident National (Philadelphia)	2,752	1,944	7	64/36	9	1,549	2	5.2	4	0.3	18	30.9	31	1.24	12.1	15.1(g)	98	11	31.5	31.6
89 United Banks of Colorado (Denver)	2,740	2,076	12	55/45	0	1,562	15	6.4	-14	0.4	18	24.2	19	1.02	16.8	17.2	121	17	19.9	15.9
90 Alabama Bancorp. (Birmingham)	2,739	2,138	1	60/40	0	1,600	4	10.9	29	0.6	9	28.3	13	1.07	14.0	15.1	126	13	22.5	11.3
91 American Security (Washington, D.C.)	2,714	2,156	17	72/28	26	1,492	9	4.7	9	0.3	13	24.4	12	1.01	15.0	15.2	88	21	27.8	10.7
92 Lloyds Bank of California (Los Angeles)	2,709	2,344	9	71/29	0	1,872	12	7.3	0	0.3	-1	14.8	-1	0.58	19.7	11.4	102	-5	14.6	32.4
93 Virginia National Bankshares (Norfolk)	2,704	2,172	4	64/36	0	1,518	0	8.4	-12	0.5	-2	23.4	10	0.93	16.7	15.5	130	7	17.9	15.3

#	Bank																				
94	American Fletcher (Indianapolis)	2,657	1,773	-2	69/31	9	1,418	-5	4.6	-33	0.3(e)	30(d)	19.1	0	0.73	17.1	12.5	77	-5	24.7	16.1
95	Banco Popular de Puerto Rico (San Juan)	2,630	2,061	1	68/32	0	988	1	12.1	0	1.0	30	24.1	34	0.95(c)	21.7(c)	20.6(c)	130	18	18.5	29.2
96	United Jersey Banks (Princeton)	2,628	2,066	6	59/41	0	1,476	-3	7.5	-2	0.4	6	14.9	14	0.61	21.0	12.9	99	9	15.0	14.0
97	American National Bank & Trust (Chicago)	2,535	1,969	4	60/40	25	1,164	7	3.4	123	0.3	18	22.4	9	0.95	17.6	16.7	93	25	24.2	N.A.
98	Key Banks (Albany)	2,527	2,097	29	63/37	0	1,334	20	4.6	21	0.5	8	16.5	2	0.83	14.2	11.8	93	7	17.7	7.7
99	Dominion Bankshares (Roanoke)	2,526	2,010	7	71/29	0	1,460	0	5.1	-35	0.3	-1(d)	22.2	2	0.95	16.2	15.3	107	2	20.8	12.1
100	First National Bancorp. (Denver)	2,499	1,957	1	47/53	0	1,420	2	9.8	-30	0.6	10	21.0	30	0.89	16.8	15.1	120	16	17.4	16.9
101	Florida Natl. Banks of Florida (Jacksonville)	2,468	1,963	13	55/45	0	985	9	3.0	-5	0.1	-5	16.6	2	0.78	11.6	9.1	89	16	18.6	19.8(h)
102	Marshall & Ilsley (Milwaukee)	2,446	1,772	2	64/36	1	1,302	-4	2.7	18	0.2	15	20.1	4	0.87	15.9	13.9	88	5	22.9	12.9

Continued

Bank	Assets, 12/31/80 ($ mil.)	Deposits Total, 12/31/80 ($ mil.)	Deposits Chg. from 1979 (%)	Deposits Time/demand (%)	Deposits Foreign (%)	Loans Total O/S, 12/31/80 ($ mil.)	Loans Chg. from 1979 (%)	Loan Loss Prov. 1980 ($ mil.)	Loans Chg. from 1979 (%)	Net Charge-offs as % of loans	Fed. Funds Borrowed (%)	Net Oper. Income, 1980 ($ mil.)	Chg. from 1979 (%)	Return on Avg. Assets, 1980	Leverage, 1980	Return on Com. Equity, 1980	Net Interest Income, 1980	Chg. from 1979 (%)	Oper. Income as % of Net Int. Income	5-year Growth EPS (%)
103 Financial General Bankshares (Washington, D.C.)	2,427	2,054	5	58/42	0	1308	3	3.2	-24	0.2	-8	16.5	5	0.72	17.4	12.5	123	11	13.5	22.9
104 Bank of Virginia (Richmond)	2,403	1,723	7	73/27	1	1,550	-6	13.6	12	0.8	7(d)	13.2	-12	0.54	16.8	9.0	18	1	11.2	9.9
105 First American Bank (Kalamazoo)	2,400	2,119	40	74/26	0	1,411	34	4.4	33	0.4	-4	16.6	4	0.97	14.7	14.1	84	13	19.6	15.3
106 Indiana National (Indianapolis)	2,378	1,709	14	58/42	1	1,272	8	8.4	38	0.6	20	17.2	42	0.79	17.6	13.9	100	12	17.1	17.0
107 Flagship Banks (Miami)	2,374	1,944	25	55/45	0	1,124	19	3.9	-14	0.1	-2	22.5	20	1.12	14.8	16.7	104	16	21.6	61.9
108 First Maryland Bancorp (Baltimore)	2,358	1,701	9	63/37	17	1,466	11	7.3	17	0.4	6	20.8	10	0.94	17.3	16.3	99	14	20.9	16.2
109 Bancorp Hawaii (Honolulu)	2,343	2,026	15	69/31	13	1500	18	5.3	-3	0.1	0	25.5	20	1.19	17.3	20.5	103	10	24.8	19.3
110 First & Merchants (Richmond)	2,301	1,780	3	63/37	2	1,386	1	5.0	-12	0.3	15	16.5	9	0.74	17.8	13.1	93	7	17.8	13.5
111 United Bank Corp. of New York	2,274	1,808	10	67/33	0	1,075	9	2.8	6	0.3	2	28.2	16	1.32	10.8	14.2	113	11	25.1	8.2

#	Bank																			
112	First Oklahoma Bancorp. (Oklahoma City)	2,273	1,504	25	59/41	2	1,147	28	3.8	21	0.3	12	24.6	21	1.31	12.3	16.1	76	27	32.3	28.5
113	Merchants National (Indianapolis)	2,272	1,572	26	75/25	17	1,074	6	10.1	37	0.7	29	14.3	13	0.73	18.9	13.8	75	17	19.1	15.9
114	Central Bancorp. (Cincinnati)	2,264	1,757	5	63/37	0	1,275	8	5.3	75	0.4	13	18.5	-14	0.88	14.1	12.4	89	1	20.8	9.1
115	First Kentucky National (Louisville)	2,167	1,559	3	61/39	3	1,192	0	7.6	3	0.6	15	21.2	6	1.08	13.2	14.3	84	7	25.1	13.9
116	Cullen/Frost Bankers (San Antonio)	2,139	1,706	14	63/37	14	1,034	10	7.0	51	0.5	0	15.8	28	0.85	16.9	14.4	75	20	21.0	22.9
117	Tennessee Valley Bancorp (Nashville)	2,139	1,647	2	72/28	4	1,142	-2	12.6	58	0.9	9(d)	8.1	4	0.35	22.1	7.8	67	7	12.1	-2.3
118	U.S. Trust (New York)	2,074	1,624	12	42/58	17	812	-1	4.0	42	0.5	53(d)	11.2	32	0.65	17.1	11.1	50	17	22.2	4.8
119	Boatsmen's Bancshares (St. Louis)	2,073	1,429	3	52/48	0	865	-3	5.0	4	0.5	9	15.6	20	0.93	17.0	15.8	67	16	23.3	13.1
120	Central Bancshares of the South (Birmingham)	2,067	1,578	10	70/30	0	937	-7	10.2	38	1.0	18	17.1	-6	0.92	14.4	13.2	83	4	20.5	15.4

Continued

Bank	Deposits					Loans								Performance						
	Assets, 12/31/80 ($ mil.)	Total, 12/31/80 ($ mil.)	Chg. from 1979 (%)	Time/ demand (%)	For-eign (%)	Total O/S 12/31/80 ($ mil.)	Chg. from 1979 (%)	Loan Loss Prov. 1980 ($ mil.)	Chg. from 1979 (%)	Net Charge-offs as % of loans	Fed. Funds Bor-rowed (%)	Net Oper. In-come, 1980 ($ mil.)	Chg. from 1979 (%)	Return on Avg. Assets, 1980 (%)	Lever-age, 1980	Return on Com. Equity, 1980	Net Interest In-come, 1980	Chg. from 1979 (%)	Oper. Income as % of Net Int. Income	5-year Growth EPS (%)
121 Equitable Bancorp. (Baltimore)	2,066	1,747	-1	65/35	0	1,306	-7	12.2	110	0.9	2	9.6	-32	0.49	15.4	7.5	89	-1	10.8	6.3
122 First Florida Banks (Tampa)	2,055	1,655	12	58/42	0	891	9	3.4	12	0.2	-6	16.8	27	0.91	21.2	19.3	73	17	23.1	30.1
123 First National Charter (Kansas City, Mo.)	2,035	1,508	10	63/37	0	943	16	5.8	60	0.5	-2	17.0	12	0.91	13.2	12.0	73	18	23.4	10.6
124 Arizona Bank (Phoenix)	2,031	1,752	8	70/30	0	1,220	8	2.9	-15	0.3	11	15.9	11	0.84	21.2	17.9	84	8	18.9	21.3
125 Schroeder (J. Henry) (New York)	2,029	1,615	27	87/13	65	1,011	28	5.1	41	0.3	8	7.3	55	0.40	20.0	8.0	40	35	18.3	N.A.
126 First United Bancorp. (Fort Worth)	2,018	1,647	15	62/38	2	1,127	17	6.3	36	0.4	10	19.3	20	1.04	16.2	16.8	80	22	24.2	19.1
127 Citizens Fidelity (Louisville)	1,993	1,430	8	54/46	1	1,159	11	7.6	25	0.4	21	17.9	17	1.08	15.2	16.5	73	15	24.5	16.0
128 First Alabama Bancshares (Birmingham)	1,973	1,616	7	64/36	0	1,099	1	8.5	16	0.8	-4	25.5	14	1.40	12.2	17.1	99	11	25.6	15.3
129 Marine (Milwaukee)	1,971	1,534	11	70/30	1	1,150	9	3.9	76	0.4	8	11.7	3	0.68	17.8	12.1	66	8	17.7	11.0
130 United Missouri Bancshares (Kansas City)	1,953	1,401	10	57/43	0	689	-5	2.8	-3	0.3	-8	19.1	29	1.05	15.6	16.3	75	16	25.5	18.1

Rank / Bank																			
131 Old Kent Financial (Grand Rapids)	1,951	1,633	12	78/22	3	994	2	2.4	-29	0.2	6	20.0	2	1.06	13.7	14.5	75	5	26.6	13.5
132 Sumitomo Bank of Calif. (San Francisco)	1,949	1,720	14	75/25	1	1,476	21	2.4	-11	0.0	2	10.6	5	0.62	23.8	14.7	61	10	17.3	8.7
133 National Central Financial (Lancaster, Pa.)	1,938	1,475	8	78/22	0	1,249	9	6.5	27	0.3	16(d)	16.9	5	0.95	15.0	14.3	74	9	22.7	13.5
134 American B&T Co. of Pa. (Reading)	1,930	1,687	7	79/21	0	1,312	5	9.0	8	0.5	2	19.5	6	1.05	15.1	15.8	86	10	22.7	15.0
135 First National Cincinnati	1,912	1,336	5	57/43	0	791	0	3.2	19	0.2	-2	23.2	2	1.42	10.6	15.1	75	9	30.9	12.6
136 Central Fidelity (Richmond)	1,909	1,490	4	72/28	0	970	-1	4.6	-33	0.5	-2	15.8	3	0.87	16.7	14.5	83	1	19.0	16.6
137 Idaho First National Bank (Boise)	1,899	1,560	11	69/31	0	1,038	6	4.6	83	0.4	2	21.0	10	1.25	13.4	16.8	82	12	25.7	13.8
138 Atlantic Bancorp. (Jacksonville)	1,897	1,583	5	58/42	0	908	1	4.9	-7	0.5	-2	17.2	11	0.95	13.5	12.7	87	8	19.7	39.3

Continued

Bank	Assets, 12/31/80 ($ mil.)	Deposits				Loans							Performance						
		Total, 12/31/80 ($ mil.)	Chg. from 1979 (%)	Time/ demand (%)	For- eign (%)	Total O/S 12/31/80 ($ mil.)	Chg. from 1979 (%)	Loan Loss Prov. 1980 ($ mil.)	Net Charge- offs as % of loans	Fed. Funds Bor- rowed (%)	Net Oper. In- come 1980 ($ mil.)	Chg. from 1979 (%)	Return on Avg. Assets, 1980	Lever- age, 1980	Return on Com. Equity, 1980	Net Interest In- come, 1980	Chg. from 1979 (%)	Oper. Income as % of Net Int. Income	5-year Growth EPS (%)
139 Continential Bank (Norristown, Pa.)	1,893	1,594	14	70/30	0	1,289	11	11.0	0.5	5	20.9	15	1.22	14.5	17.7	89	13	23.4	13.8
140 Third National (Nashville)	1,885	1,477	3	66/34	1	1,091	7	8.0	0.7	4	13.7	19	0.77	17.2	13.2	75	10	18.2	29.4
141 First American (Nashville)	1,885	1,539	3	63/37	0	974	-4	10.8	1.2	0	14.8	20	0.80	16.6	13.2	78	16	19.0	34.6
142 Southern Bancorp. of Ala. (Birmingham)	1,861	1,376	-7	62/38	0	1,049	-3	10.7	0.7	7	18.4	11	1.01	15.8	15.9	82	4	22.4	10.8
143 First Empire State (Buffalo)	1,856	1,486	-2	75/25	1	1,301	2	9.3	0.7	9	9.9	14	0.55	17.8	9.9	68(f)	4	14.6	22.2
144 First Hawaiian (Honolulu)	1,856	1,592	10	64/36	0	1,234	13	4.4	0.3(a)	0(a)	17.0	13	0.91(a)	18.4(a)	16.8(a)	86	14	19.6	13.4
145 Northwestern Financial (N. Wilksboro, N.C.)	1,790	1,497	7	70/30	0	1,072	-4	5.4	0.6	3	13.6	16	0.79	16.7	13.2	82	5	16.7	20.9
146 Whitney Holding (New Orleans)	1,744	1,420	5	48/52	0	898	1	8.4	0.9	15	25.3	23	1.48	11.2	16.5	80	26	31.8	12.4
147 Liberty National (Oklahoma City)	1,740	1,250	14	52/48	1	691	18	4.8	0.1	20	11.6	27	0.74	24.1	17.8	49	21	23.7	17.4
148 Old Stone (Providence)	1,734	1,438	21	92/8	0	1,325	17	2.2	0.1	-3(d)	11.4	7	0.75	19.9	14.9	43	-2	26.3	17.5

149 Hospital Trust (Providence)	1,720	2	74/26	0	997	1	7.9	75	0.8	16	11.9	18	0.76	18.7	14.1	58	17	20.5	20.1
150 Deposit Guaranty (Jackson, Miss.)	1,669	4	60/40	0	793	-1	5.0	73	0.7	15	14.5	13	0.96	16.3	15.7	61	16	23.8	15.0
151 Zions Utah Bancorp. (Salt Lake City)	1,652	5	72/28	3	1,036	7	5.2	19	0.4	10	17.7	23	1.11	16.9	18.9	67	15	26.5	20.6
152 Union Commerce (Cleveland)	1,624	2	70/30	8	956	4	4.3	-75	0.3	15	5.7	NM	0.32	19.7	6.3	47	6	12.1	37.2
153 Industrial Valley B&T (Jenkintown, Pa.)	1,619	-7	70/30	0	803	10	2.4	24	0.3	18	9.8	-13	0.59	22.7	13.3	49	-1	20.0	3.3
154 South Carolina National (Columbia)	1,603	6	46/54	0	891	6	4.4	-2	0.5	8	18.2	5	1.21	12.4	15.0	90	9	20.1	20.1
155 First Virginia Banks (Falls Church)	1,570	7	72/28	0	967	4	4.7	63	0.4	-3(d)	15.4	9	1.00	15.9	16.0	75	8	20.5	15.6
156 City National (Beverly Hills)	1,549	16	57/43	0	782	15	2.0	-38	0.2	11	17.8	14	1.33	16.6	22.1	67	19	26.7	44.7
157 Wilmington Trust	1,494	6	62/38	0	583	9	2.3	20	0.2	28	11.0	-4	0.84	16.7	14.0	43	23	25.6	4.0

Continued

561

Bank	Deposits					Loans						Net Oper. Income, 1980 ($ mil.)	Chg. from 1979 (%)	Performance						
	Assets, 12/31/80 ($ mil.)	Total, 12/31/80 ($ mil.)	Chg. from 1979 (%)	Time/demand (%)	Foreign (%)	Total O/S, 12/31/80 ($ mil.)	Chg. from 1979 (%)	Loan Loss Prov. 1980 ($ mil.)	Chg. from 1979 (%)	Net Charge-offs as % of loans	Fed. Funds Borrowed (%)			Return on Avg. Assets, 1980	Leverage, 1980	Return on Com. Equity, 1980	Net Interest Income, 1980	Chg. from 1979 (%)	Oper. Income as % of Net Int. Income	5-year Growth EPS (%)
158 Affiliated Bankshares of Colorado (Boulder)	1,490	1,256	10	64/36	0	851	9	4.1	36	0.5	0	15.1	10	1.11	13.9	15.5	67	15	22.4	19.8
159 Peoples National Bank of Wash. (Seattle)	1,488	1,235	3	55/45	0	878	1	3.3	-3	0.3	-2	14.3	8	0.97	17.7	17.2	75	11	19.1	23.2
160 Suburban Bancorp. (Hyattsville, Md.)	1,481	1,264	2	61/39	0	853	-10	7.5	35	0.9	-4	17.1	5	1.22	12.7	15.5	84	9	20.4	11.2
161 Heritage Bancorp. (Cherry Hill, N.J.)	1,478	1,265	4	67/33	0	862	1	4.4	4	0.4	0	14.3	3	1.03	14.7	15.2	69	10	20.8	21.7
162 Winters National (Dayton)	1,461	1,093	10	64/36	2	735	3	4.1	6	0.5	11	10.1	-10	0.75	15.4	11.6	52	-2	19.4	10.3
163 Old National Bancorp. (Spokane)	1,461	1,095	7	69/31	0	823	5	3.2	8	0.3	10	8.7	9	0.62	19.8	12.3	61	8	14.3	11.0
164 Banks of Iowa (Cedar Rapids)	1,410	1,079	7	59/41	0	667	1	3.4	119	0.4	-1	13.8	19	1.06	14.5	15.5	58	27	23.7	19.9
165 First N. Mex. Bankshare (Albuquerque)	1,408	1,210	14	72/28	0	695	6	63.0	65	0.4	-9	12.8	5	1.00	14.9	15.0	55	12	23.5	12.0

166 Northern States Bancorp. (Detroit)	1,390	1,083	-10	71/29	4	889	-12	11.0	194	0.8	16	-5.1	NM	0.37	31.4	-11.7	45	-8	N.M.	N.A.
167 Orbanco Financial Services (Portland)	1,359	807	33	70/30	0	931	23	4.2	30	0.2	3	13.1	25	1.06	16.3	17.3	64	24	20.5	18.8
168 Union Trust Bancorp. (Baltimore)	1,353	949	5	58/42	2	874	3	8.5	19	0.7	9	7.2	-19	0.58	13.7	7.9	63	14	11.5	1.8
169 First Citizens B&T (Raleigh)	1,347	1,185	1	60/40	0	685	-8	2.5	-6	0.3	-7	11.2	-2	0.85	16.0	13.6(g)	70	6	16.0	28.5
170 Landmark Banking Corp. of Fla. (Ft. Lauderdale)	1,343	1,031	5	51/49	0	571	1	4.2	-4	0.4	18	13.1	35	1.03	17.6	18.2	65	18	20.0	22.1
171 Colorado National Bankshares (Denver)	1,317	974	5	58/42	0	749	7	4.2	30	0.5	7	15.1	10	1.29	15.1	19.4	56	10	26.8	29.3
172 Banco de Ponce (Ponce, P.R.)	1,314	1,096	2	73/27	0	600	-3	5.6	-10	1.0	9	9.1	13	0.73	19.2	14.0	54	9	17.0	34.2
173 First Capital (Jackson, Miss.)	1,299	1,064	6	61/39	0	683	-3	6.3	32	0.7	5	11.9	14	0.97	13.0	12.6	46	15	25.8	7.4
174 Mercantile Bankshares (Baltimore)	1,298	1,070	5	61/39	0	787	-3	3.8	4	0.4	0	16.1	12	1.25	10.9	13.6	67	10	24.3	13.0

Continued

Bank	Deposits					Loans						Performance								
	Assets, 12/31/80 ($ mil.)	Total, 12/31/80 ($ mil.)	Chg. from 1979 (%)	Time/ demand (%)	For- eign (%)	Total O/S, 12/31/80 ($ mil.)	Chg. from 1979 (%)	Loan Loss Prov. 1980 ($ mil.)	Chg. from 1979 (%)	Net Charge- offs as % of loans	Fed. Funds Bor- rowed (%)	Net Oper. In- come, 1980 ($ mil.)	Chg. from 1979 (%)	Return on Avg. Assets, 1980	Lever- age, 1980	Return on Com. Equity, 1980	Net Interest In- come, 1980	Chg. from 1979 (%)	Oper. Income as % of Net Int. Income	5-year Growth EPS (%)
175 Security New York State (Rochester)	1,292	1,073	5	77/23	0	736	-2	3.3	-11	0.5	5(d)	6.4	2	0.40	19.6	7.8	49	3	12.9	16.8
176 Colonial Bancorp (Waterbury, Conn.)	1,270	987	3	70/30	5	760	3	4.5	4	0.5	18	7.5	1	0.61	19.5	11.9	59	10	12.7	7.4
177 Fulton National (Atlanta)	1,268	855	6	46/54	2	629	11	3.3	42	0.4	6	10.1	42	0.80	20.9	16.8	65	6	15.5	40.3
178 National Bancshares Corp. of Texas (San Antonio)	1,260	1,062	15	58/42	0	622	15	3.2	52	0.3	-5	13.0	21	1.15	14.9	17.1	50	18	25.8	N.A.
179 LaSalle National Bank (Chicago)	1,252	881	13	71/29	3	666	14	1.7	-43	0.1	20	8.7	6	0.80	18.6	14.8	37	10	23.8	18.2
180 Horizon Bancorp (Morristown, N.J.)	1,231	973	21	67/33	1	730	14	2.6	-7	0.3	4	12.4	13	1.05	14.6	15.4	59	19	21.1	24.1
181 Northeast Bancorp (New Haven)	1,226	1,038	3	62/38	0	814	4	3.8	-5	0.4	3	12.6	5	1.08	13.8	14.9	63	8	20.2	13.6
182 First Commerce (New Orleans)	1,225	894	20	49/51	3	456	13	3.4	-32	0.6	14	14.9	76	1.39	16.8	23.2	53	26	28.2	148.3
183 Union National Bank of Pittsburgh	1,222	1,063	6	59/41	0	739	7	1.2	-50	0.1	3	15.9	1	1.40	9.5	13.3	68	5	23.5	18.4

Rank	Bank (Location)																			
184	New Jersey National (Trenton)	1,215	954	3	71/29	0	685	-5	0.7	-18	0.2	23	6.2	-12	0.49	18.6	9.2	41	-2	15.1	0.4
185	Toledo Trustcorp	1,209	931	13	70/30	0	689	13	2.5	48	0.3	12	16.0	2	1.42	10.4	14.8	51	11	31.3	10.3
186	General Bancshares (St. Louis)	1,201	1,030	3	71/29	0	715	-3	3.5	19	0.4	-5	10.4	2	0.89	17.0	15.1	47	9	22.3	28.0
187	Union Planters (Memphis)	1,198	838	10	62/38	1	555	5	0.8	-54	0.3	26	7.9	47	0.70	15.5	10.8	39	5	20.3	62.1
188	Banc-Oklahoma (Tulsa)	1,197	897	1	51/49	3	685	7	3.6	-10	0.4	12	7.3	26	0.69	16.2	11.1	43	15	17.2	2.6
189	Ellis Banking (Brandenton, Fla.)	1,186	1,044	2	69/31	0	602	5	1.4	47	0.1	-11	10.8	6	0.96	15.3	14.7	46	12	23.5	23.1
190	Fifth Third Bancorp (Cincinnati)	1,184	830	5	56/44	0	592	4	4.0	32	0.5	1	19.5	14	1.81	9.0	16.3	60	13	32.8	17.8
191	First Tulsa Bancorp.	1,154	899	2	46/54	2	584	10	2.3	-42	0.0	5	10.4	42	1.04	13.9	14.4	40	16	25.9	8.4
192	Century Banks (Ft. Lauderdale)	1,109	913	15	55/45	0	427	11	1.7	-13	0.2	4	10.8	25	1.09	11.8	12.8	45	15	23.7	26.5
193	Commonwealth National Bank (Harrisburg)	1,095	898	7	71/29	0	748	4	1.8	-2	0.3	8	6.4	-20	0.61	16.0	9.8	41	0	15.9	12.3

Continued

Bank	Assets, Total, 12/31/80 ($ mil.)	Deposits				Loans						Net Oper. In-come, 1980 ($ mil.)	Chg. from 1979 (%)	Performance							
		Total, 12/31/80 ($ mil.)	Chg. from 1979 (%)	Time/demand (%)	For-eign (%)	Total O/S, 12/31/80 ($ mil.)	Chg. from 1979 (%)	Loan Loss Prov. 1980 ($ mil.)	Chg. from 1979 (%)	Net Charge-offs as % of loans	Fed. Funds Bor-rowed (%)			Return on Avg. Assets, 1980	Lever-age, 1980	Return on Com. Equity, 1980	Net Interest In-come, 1980	Chg. from 1979 (%)	Oper. Income as % of Net Int. Income	5-year Growth EPS (%)
194 National Comm. Bank (Rutherford, N.J.)	1,091	881	-3	67/33	0	514	9	0.2	37	0.0	7	10.6	1	1.02	13.11	3.4	40	10	26.3	4.0
195 Exchange Bancorp. (Tampa)	1,078	883	6	60/40	0	551	8	2.5	15	0.3	-5	7.5	23	0.75	20.3	15.3	45	15	16.9	11.3
196 LITCO Bancorp. of New York (Garden City)	1,068	857	-1	62/38	0	470	0	3.9	39	0.8	11	5.1	-18	0.50	16.8	8.3	40	5	12.6	-2.7
197 Citizens & Southern (Charleston, S.C.)	1,067	849	13	41/59	0	555	9	3.8	25	0.5	2	12.9	25	1.34	13.9	18.6	61	18	21.2	20.3
198 Hibernia (New Orleans)	1,067	821	5	47/53	3	588	17	5.5	30	0.7	17	11.1	19	1.12	17.3	19.5	48	19	23.2	21.9
199 Multibank Financial (Boston)	1,052	908	6	64/36	0	633	3	3.5	-9	0.4	0	9.0	25	0.93	16.6	15.4	57	14	15.7	57.0
200 Citizens Commercial & Saving (Flint)	1,033	864	3	80/20	0	634	-2	4.1	24	0.7	7	5.6	-30	0.57	12.3	7.0	38	-10	14.9	8.9

(a) Year-end amounts. (b) Loans exclude direct lease financing. (c) Data are for banking operations only. (d) Includes other funds purchased and/or other funds sold. (e) Loans are net of unearned income only. (f) Total interest income is not adjusted for tax equivalents. (g) Includes preferred stock. (h) Earnings per share fully diluted. N.A. not available; N.M. not meaningful. Source: Standard & Poor's Compustat Services, Inc., and Business Week, April 13, 1981.

Population per Full-Service Bank Office, by State

State	Dec. 31, 1955	June 30, 1970	June 30, 1979	Net Change 1955–1979	Net Change 1970–1979	1980 Branching Category[1]
Alabama	10,951	6,486	4,303	−6,648	−2,183	L
Alaska	5,250	4,379	3,301	−1,949	−1,078	S
Arizona	9,500	5,470	4,861	−4,639	−609	S
Arkansas	6,984	4,668	3,417	−3,567	−1,251	L
California	9,523	6,403	5,464	−4,059	−939	S
Colorado	9,100	7,827	5,646	−3,454	−2,181	U
Connecticut	10,945	6,239	4,756	−6,189	−1,483	S
Delaware	5,735	5,426	3,527	−2,208	−1,899	S
District of Columbia	12,070	6,411	4,205	−7,865	−2,206	S
Florida	14,320	13,107	6,266	−8,054	−6,841	S
Georgia	7,825	6,365	4,137	−3,688	−2,228	L
Hawaii	7,738	5,346	5,479	−2,259	−133	S
Idaho	5,942	4,028	3,563	−2,379	−465	S
Illinois	10,077	9,378	6,637	−3,440	−2,741	U
Indiana	6,775	5,086	3,689	−3,086	−1,397	L
Iowa	3,222	2,888	2,491	−731	−397	L
Kansas	3,416	3,366	2,751	−665	−615	U
Kentucky	6,676	4,907	3,545	−3,131	−1,362	L
Louisiana	10,048	5,972	4,034	−6,014	−1,938	L
Maine	5,883	3,866	3,246	−2,637	−620	S
Maryland	8,575	6,306	4,237	−4,338	−2,069	S
Massachusetts	10,872	6,413	5,352	−5,520	−1,061	L
Michigan	9,204	5,904	4,094	−5,110	−1,810	L
Minnesota	4,650	5,162	4,207	−443	−955	L
Mississippi	7,231	4,263	2,902	−4,329	−1,361	L
Missouri	6,932	6,138	4,338	−2,594	−1,800	U
Montana	5,566	4,890	4,249	−1,317	−614	U
Nebraska	3,311	3,072	2,356	−955	−716	U
Nevada	6,714	5,491	4,979	−1,735	−512	S
New Hampshire	7,090	5,546	4,014	−3,076	−1,532	S
New Jersey	9,541	6,152	4,248	−5,293	−1,904	S
New Mexico	9,790	5,404	3,915	−5,875	−1,489	L
New York	10,349	6,785	4,902	−5,447	−1,883	S
North Carolina	7,956	4,336	3,157	−4,799	−1,179	S
North Dakota	3,612	2,584	2,266	−1,346	−318	U
Ohio	9,017	6,021	4,393	−4,624	−1,628	L
Oklahoma	5,696	5,265	4,039	−1,657	−1,226	U
Oregon	8,686	5,518	4,149	−4,537	−1,369	S
Pennsylvania	8,455	5,518	4,163	−4,292	−1,355	L
Rhode Island	10,342	5,365	3,807	−6,535	−1,558	S
South Dakota	9,821	5,150	3,915	−5,906	−1,235	S
South Carolina	3,036	2,572	2,244	−792	−328	S
Tennessee	7,812	5,030	3,328	−4,484	−1,702	L
Texas	9,170	9,022	8,224	−946	−798	U
Utah	8,302	5,884	4,142	−4,160	−1,742	S
Vermont	4,805	3,557	2,724	−2,081	−833	S
Virginia	7,274	4,539	3,285	−3,989	−1,254	S
Washington	8,383	5,428	4,391	−3,992	−1,037	S

Continued

State	Dec. 31, 1955	June 30, 1970	June 30, 1979	Net Change 1955–1979	Net Change 1970–1979	1980 Branching Category[1]
West Virginia	10,961	8,550	6,454	−4,507	−2,096	U
Wisconsin	5,266	5,083	4,362	−904	−721	L
Wyoming	5,778	4,616	4,787	−991	+171	U
United States (50 States and D.C.)	7,956	5,884	4,421	−3,535	−1,463	

[1]S, statewide branching; L, limited branching; U, unit banking.
Source: FDIC and Bureau of the Census.

Population per Depository Institution Office (Excluding Credit Unions), by State

State	1970	1979	Net Change 1970–1979
Alabama	5,415	3,377	−2,038
Alaska	3,885	2,762	−1,123
Arizona	4,415	3,427	−988
Arkansas	3,916	2,614	−1,302
California	5,044	3,368	−1,676
Colorado	5,300	3,426	−1,874
Connecticut	3,912	2,583	−1,329
Delawarel	4,455	2,812	−1,643
District of Columbia	4,229	2,553	−1,676
Florida	8,222	3,473	−4,749
Georgia	5,098	3,141	−1,957
Hawaii	3,756	2,990	−766
Idaho	3,444	2,891	−553
Illinois	6,677	4,153	−2,524
Indiana	4,087	2,952	−1,135
Iowa	2,611	2,000	−611
Kansas	2,766	2,138	−628
Kentucky	4,507	2,797	−1,260
Louisiana	4,834	3,088	−1,746
Maine	2,898	2,194	−704
Maryland	4,666	3,008	−1,658
Massachusetts	4,081	3,149	−932
Michigan	5,061	3,274	−1,787
Minnesota	4,462	3,269	−1,193
Mississippi	3,883	2,342	−1,541
Missouri	4,702	3,082	−1,620
Montana	4,311	3,316	−995
Nebraska	2,705	1,795	−910
Nevada	4,289	3,250	−1,039
New Hampshire	3,709	2,772	−937
New Jersey	4,304	2,721	−1,583
New Mexico	4,346	2,990	−1,356
New York	5,153	3,275	−1,878
North Carolina	3,499	2,572	−927
North Dakota	2,359	1,771	−588
Ohio	4,194	2,924	−1,270

Continued

State	1970	1979	Net Change 1970–1979
Oklahoma	4,513	3,210	−1,303
Oregon	4,278	2,668	−1,610
Pennsylvania	4,112	2,968	−1,144
Rhode Island	3,442	2,662	−780
South Carolina	4,146	2,983	−1,163
South Dakota	2,422	1,957	−465
Tennessee	4,401	2,767	−1,634
Texas	6,470	4,428	−2,042
Utah	4,995	3,216	−1,779
Vermont	3,156	2,231	−925
Virginia	3,935	2,570	−1,365
Washington	3,996	2,849	−1,147
West Virginia	7,421	5,174	−2,247
Wisconsin	4,232	3,024	−1,208
Wyoming	3,773	3,333	−440
United States	4,566	3,081	−1,485

Source: FDIC, Federal Home Loan Bank Board, National Association of Mutual Savings Banks, and Bureau of the Census.

Depository Institution Concentration Ratios by State, December 31, 1979

	Full Service Banks		Full Service Banks, FSLIC-Insured Savings and Loans, and Mutual Savings Banks	
	3 Firm	5 Firm	3 Firm	5 Firm
Alabama	38.4	54.0	29.5	41.5
Alaska	61.5	79.6	48.6	62.5
Arizona	85.2	94.6	58.3	74.6
Arkansas	13.1	18.3	10.2	14.4
California	57.6	73.7	34.1	43.7
Colorado	40.5	56.1	26.4	36.7
Connecticut	46.0	61.0	20.4	29.5
Delaware	73.4	91.7	57.6	80.9
District of Columbia	70.4	88.6	42.9	55.9
Florida	25.6	34.9	12.3	17.6
Georgia	40.3	47.7	26.9	35.3
Hawaii	79.2	91.4	61.3	73.4
Idaho	74.9	87.0	62.3	72.7
Illinois	32.8	38.5	22.6	27.3
Indiana	17.2	21.3	12.8	15.8
Iowa	17.3	24.2	13.0	18.1
Kansas	10.0	13.1	11.3	14.6
Kentucky	23.1	29.3	17.4	22.3
Louisiana	15.2	21.2	11.2	15.7
Maine	48.4	73.5	24.0	36.2
Maryland	44.9	62.2	27.5	38.1
Massachusetts	46.1	63.0	20.8	28.4
Michigan	35.0	47.4	25.7	37.1
Minnesota	52.5	56.2	41.5	48.3
Mississippi	27.5	34.3	22.9	29.1
Missouri	29.4	40.4	19.8	28.3
Montana	43.3	53.3	36.0	44.3
Nebraska	20.1	28.0	18.3	26.9
Nevada	83.5	96.2	54.8	71.2
New Hampshire	35.0	46.1	18.8	26.9
New Jersey	22.9	33.3	12.4	19.3
New Mexico	44.4	56.1	31.8	44.1
New York	37.2	55.0	23.4	34.7
North Carolina	50.8	66.0	33.5	43.5
North Dakota	39.1	47.6	28.2	41.8
Ohio	25.7	36.6	15.0	21.3
Oklahoma	19.0	26.9	15.2	22.8
Oregon	74.4	81.1	50.1	60.3
Pennsylvania	23.4	32.3	18.2	25.1
Rhode Island	87.3	93.7	59.0	74.6
South Carolina	44.5	62.3	23.8	33.5

Continued

	Full Service Banks		Full Service Banks, FSLIC-Insured Savings and Loans, and Mutual Savings Banks	
	3 Firm	5 Firm	3 Firm	5 Firm
South Dakota	43.7	50.5	36.5	42.4
Tennessee	27.9	39.7	21.3	30.4
Texas	24.7	35.9	18.7	27.1
Utah	61.6	75.0	43.7	58.5
Vermont	43.8	61.9	31.9	48.4
Virginia	33.0	50.2	23.7	36.1
Washington	62.3	75.9	39.6	49.0
West Virginia	8.6	12.2	7.5	10.8
Wisconsin	27.3	31.9	18.5	23.9
Wyoming	38.5	46.7	30.4	39.7

Source: FDIC.

Maximum Interest Rates Payable on Time and Savings Deposits at Federally Insured Institutions
(percent per annum)

Type and Maturity of Deposit	Commercial Banks				Savings and Loan Associations and Mutual Savings Banks			
	In Effect June 30, 1979		Previous Maximum		In Effect June 30, 1979		Previous Maximum	
	Percent	Effective Date	Percent	Effective Date	Percent	Effective Date	Percent	Effective Date
Savings	5	7/1/73	4½	1/21/70	5¼	(7)	5	(8)
Negotiable order of withdrawal accounts[1]	5	1/1/74	(9)	—	5	1/1/74	(9)	—
Money market time deposits of less than $100,000[2]	(10)	(10)	(10)	(10)	(10)	(10)	(10)	(10)
Time (multiple- and single-maturity unless otherwise indicated)[3]								
30 to 89 days								
Multiple-maturity	5	7/1/73	4¼	1/21/70				
Single-maturity	5	7/1/73	5	9/26/66	(9)	(9)	(9)	(9)
90 days to 1 year								
Multiple-maturity	5	7/1/73	5	7/20/66				
Single-maturity	5½	7/1/73	5	9/26/66	5¾	(7)	5¼	1/21/70
1 to 2 years[4]	6	7/1/73	5½	1/21/70	6½	(7)	5¾	1/21/70
2 to 2½ years[4]	6½	7/1/73	5¾	1/21/70	6¾	(7)	6	1/21/70
2½ to 4 years[4]	6½	7/1/73	5¾	1/21/70	6¾	(7)	6	1/21/70
4 to 6 years[5]	7¼	11/1/73	(11)	—	7½	11/1/73	(11)	—
6 to 8 years[5]	7½	12/23/74	7¼	11/1/73	7¾	12/23/74	7½	11/1/73
8 years or more[5]	7¾	6/1/78	(10)	—	8	6/1/78	(10)	—
Issued to governmental units (all maturities)	8	6/1/78	7¾	12/23/74	8	6/1/78	7¾	12/23/74
Individual retirement accounts and Keogh (H.R. 10) plans[6]	8	6/1/78	7¾	7/6/77	8	6/1/78	7¾	7/6/77

[1] For authorized states only. Federally insured commercial banks, savings and loan associations, cooperative banks, and mutual savings banks in Massachusetts and New Hampshire were first permitted to offer negotiable order of withdrawal (NOW) accounts on January 1, 1974. Authorization to issue NOW accounts was extended to similar institutions throughout New England on February 27, 1976 and in New York State on November 10, 1978.

[2] Must have a maturity of exactly 26 weeks and a minimum denomination of $10,000, and must be nonnegotiable.

[3] For exceptions with respect to certain foreign time deposits are the *Federal Reserve Bulletin* for October 1962 (at 1279), August 1965 (at 1094), and February 1968 (at 167).

[4] A minimum of $1,000 is required for savings and loan associations, except in areas where mutual savings banks permit lower minimum denominations. This restriction was removed for deposits maturing in less than one year, effective November 1, 1973.

[5] $1,000 minimum except for deposits representing funds contributed to an Individual Retirement Account (IRA) or a Keogh (H.R. 10) plan established pursuant to the Internal Revenue Code. The $1,000 minimum requirement was removed for such accounts in December 1975 and November 1976, respectively.

[6] Three-year minimum maturity.

[7] July 1, 1973 for mutual savings bank; July 6, 1973 for savings and loan associations.

[8] October 1, 1966 for mutual savings banks, January 21, 1970 for savings and loan associations.

[9] Commercial banks, savings and loan associations, and mutual savings banks were authorized to offer money market time deposits effective June 1, 1978. The ceiling rate for commercial banks is the discount rate on most recently issued six-month U.S. Treasury bills. Until March 15, 1979, the ceiling rate for savings and loan associations and mutual savings banks was one-quarter percentage point higher than the rate for commercial banks. Beginning March 15, 1979 the one-quarter percentage point interest differential is removed when the six-month Treasury bill rate is 9 percent or more. The full differential is in effect when the six-month bill rate is $8^3/_4$ percent or less. Thrift institutions may pay a maximum 9 percent when the six-month bill rate is between $8^1/_4$ and 9 percent. Also effective March 15, 1979, interest compounding was prohibited on money market time deposits at all offering institutions. For both commercial banks and thrift institutions, the maximum allowable rates in June were as follows; June 7, 9.425; June 14, 9.047; June 21, 8.873 (thrifts, 9.0); June 28, 8.903 (thrifts, 9.0).

[10] No separate account category.

[11] Between July 1, 1973 and October 1, 1973, there was no ceiling for certificates maturing in four years or more with minimum denominations of $1,000; however, the amount of such certificates that an institution could issue was limited to 5 percent of its total time and savings deposits. Sales in excess of that amount, as well as certificates of less than $1,000, were limited to the $6^1/_2$ percent ceiling on time deposits maturing in two and a half years or more.

Effective November 1, 1973, ceilings were reimposed on certificates maturing in four years or more with minimum denominations of $1,000. There is no limitation on the amount of these certificates that banks can issue.

Note: Maximum rates that can be paid by federally insured commercial banks, mutual savings banks, and savings and loan associations are established by the Board of Governors of the Federal Reserve System, the Board of Directors of the Federal Deposit Insurance Corporation, and the Federal Home Loan Bank Board under the provisions of 12 C.F.R. 217, 329, and 526, respectively. The maximum rates on time deposits in denominations of $100,000 or more were suspended in mid-1973.
Source: Federal Reserve Bulletin.

Appendix C: Commercial Banking

State Commercial Banking Concentration

State	1955 3 Firm	1955 5 Firm	1960 3 Firm	1960 5 Firm	1970 3 Firm	1970 5 Firm	1979 3 Firm	1979 5 Firm	1979 Branching Category[1]	Change 1955–1979 3 Firm	Change 1955–1979 5 Firm	Change 1970–1979 3 Firm	Change 1970–1979 5 Firm
Highly concentrated states													
1. Nevada	94.3	100.0	93.5	98.6	86.8	97.6	83.5	96.2	S	-10.8	-3.8	-3.3	-1.4
2. Arizona	90.4	95.6	95.8	98.3	90.6	96.9	85.2	94.5	S	-5.2	-1.1	-5.4	-2.4
3. Rhode Island	90.6	96.0	92.8	98.1	85.8	92.7	87.4	93.9	S	-3.5	-2.1	1.6	1.2
4. Delaware	73.4	84.4	79.8	92.3	74.2	91.5	73.5	91.7	S	-0.1	7.3	-0.7	0.2
5. Hawaii	93.0	98.7	89.2	97.2	76.5	88.9	79.2	91.4	S	-13.8	-7.3	2.7	2.5
6. District of Columbia	63.4	74.0	74.0	87.3	69.7	90.2	70.4	88.6	S	7.0	14.6	0.7	-1.6
7. Idaho	75.6	83.7	74.5	83.8	77.5	86.3	75.0	87.1	S	-0.6	3.4	-2.5	0.8
8. Oregon	89.1	91.1	86.7	88.8	83.6	86.3	74.3	81.1	S	-14.8	-10.0	-9.3	-5.2
9. Alaska	58.2	71.8	68.2	86.7	69.3	85.3	60.7	78.8	S	2.5	7.0	-8.6	-6.5
10. Washington	58.8	72.1	61.1	73.7	60.0	73.1	62.3	75.9	S	3.5	3.8	2.3	2.8
11. Utah	57.0	70.6	65.6	77.8	59.1	71.5	61.5	74.9	S	4.5	4.3	2.4	3.4
12. California	61.9	75.5	65.7	77.7	60.9	77.5	57.6	73.8	S	-4.3	-1.7	-3.3	-3.7
13. Maine	25.7	36.8	34.7	49.0	35.3	51.8	48.4	73.6	S	22.7	36.8	13.1	21.8
Moderately concentrated states													
14. North Carolina	33.1	42.5	46.8	56.9	51.0	66.8	50.9	66.1	S	17.8	23.6	-0.1	-0.7
15. Massachusetts	51.7	62.0	49.3	61.2	47.8	61.9	46.1	62.9	L	-5.6	0.9	-1.7	1.0
16. South Carolina	38.2	45.7	42.4	51.5	46.6	59.2	44.5	62.2	S	6.3	16.5	-2.1	3.0
17. Maryland	36.3	49.0	42.7	58.3	42.6	60.3	44.9	62.2	S	8.6	13.2	2.3	1.9
18. Vermont	20.8	30.0	25.6	35.2	37.5	49.5	43.8	62.0	S	23.0	32.0	6.3	12.5
19. Connecticut	39.6	48.7	42.7	56.5	45.8	59.8	46.0	61.1	S	6.4	12.4	0.2	1.3
20. New Mexico	45.1	56.0	43.0	54.0	45.5	52.1	44.5	57.2	L	-0.6	1.2	-1.0	5.1
21. Minnesota	56.6	60.6	58.6	63.7	53.7	57.3	52.5	56.1	U	-4.1	-4.5	-1.2	-1.2
22. Colorado	29.8	42.6	37.9	48.8	33.6	43.6	40.5	56.0	U	10.7	13.4	6.9	12.4
23. New York	39.9	54.5	40.0	55.4	40.7	56.2	37.2	55.1	S	-2.7	0.6	-3.5	-1.1
24. Alabama	34.4	43.9	31.2	40.6	23.2	31.3	38.5	54.1	L	4.1	10.2	15.3	22.8
25. Montana	50.3	58.5	48.9	57.6	48.4	58.0	43.3	53.4	U	-7.0	-5.1	-5.1	-4.6
26. South Dakota	37.2	41.0	37.5	43.0	42.4	46.6	43.7	50.5	S	6.5	9.5	1.3	3.9
27. Virginia	20.6	28.0	20.2	27.7	34.2	48.1	33.1	50.3	S	12.5	22.3	-1.1	2.2
28. Michigan	44.3	53.3	40.8	50.2	35.1	46.0	35.4	47.9	L	-8.9	-5.4	0.3	1.9
29. Georgia	48.8	57.5	48.6	56.9	41.9	49.5	40.3	47.8	L	-8.5	-9.7	-1.6	-1.7
30. North Dakota	48.1	53.9	46.6	54.2	39.7	49.3	39.1	47.6	U	-9.0	-6.3	-0.6	-1.7
31. Wyoming	37.7	45.7	35.1	44.3	28.1	37.1	38.6	46.7	U	0.9	1.0	10.5	9.6
32. New Hampshire	20.9	29.3	24.3	33.7	30.5	38.9	35.0	46.0	L	14.1	16.7	4.5	7.1

Least concentrated states

33. Missouri	31.2	40.9	26.6	35.8	22.1	28.8	29.4	40.4	U	−1.8	−0.5	7.3	11.6
34. Tennessee	29.3	43.8	28.7	40.9	26.6	39.9	27.9	39.7	L	−1.4	−4.1	1.3	−0.2
35. Illinois	38.1	45.3	35.5	42.2	32.0	38.3	32.8	38.5	U	−5.3	−6.8	0.8	0.2
36. Ohio	26.6	35.8	24.2	33.1	21.9	30.8	25.7	36.6	L	−0.9	0.8	3.8	5.8
37. Texas	19.0	25.7	21.1	27.9	14.7	21.0	24.7	35.9	U	5.7	10.2	10.0	14.9
38. Florida	20.6	27.9	17.9	23.2	15.7	21.3	25.6	34.9	L	5.0	7.0	9.9	13.6
39. Mississippi	21.1	25.2	24.9	29.0	28.6	33.7	27.6	34.4	L	6.5	9.2	−1.0	0.7
40. New Jersey	16.3	22.5	16.8	23.5	14.5	22.3	23.0	33.4	S	6.7	10.9	8.5	11.1
41. Pennsylvania	28.2	36.9	27.9	38.8	25.1	35.5	23.5	32.5	L	−4.7	−4.4	−1.6	−3.0
42. Wisconsin	30.4	34.1	31.4	33.8	27.2	31.3	27.3	31.8	L	−3.1	−2.3	0.1	0.5
43. Kentucky	26.9	34.7	27.6	34.1	24.7	32.4	23.1	29.4	L	−3.8	−5.3	−1.6	−3.0
44. Nebraska	33.6	41.0	31.6	41.4	24.7	33.9	20.5	28.4	U	−13.1	−12.6	−4.2	−5.5
45. Oklahoma	36.7	45.0	32.6	42.2	21.4	30.6	19.6	27.4	U	−17.1	−17.6	−1.8	−3.2
46. Iowa	13.9	19.6	14.2	19.8	11.9	16.9	17.3	24.2	L	3.4	4.6	5.4	7.3
47. Indiana	21.9	28.1	23.8	29.4	22.7	27.2	17.2	21.0	L	−4.7	−6.8	−5.5	−5.9
48. Louisiana	32.1	43.1	29.3	38.7	21.3	28.2	15.2	21.2	L	−16.9	−21.9	−6.1	−7.0
49. Arkansas	17.4	24.7	17.3	23.4	14.4	19.7	13.1	18.3	L	−4.3	−6.4	−1.3	−1.4
50. Kansas	16.5	20.6	14.3	18.7	11.7	15.7	10.0	13.2	U	−6.5	−7.4	−1.7	−2.5
51. West Virginia	20.6	26.7	17.3	22.7	13.2	17.9	8.7	12.3	U	−11.9	−14.4	−4.5	−5.6
Average (unweighted) for all states	42.1	50.5	43.3	52.1	41.0	50.7	41.8	53.0		−0.3	2.5	0.7	2.2

S, statewide branching; L, limited branching; U, unit banking.
Source: The Bank Holding Company Movement to 1978: A Compendium (Board of Governors of the Federal Reserve System, 1978), pp. 247–249; and Consolidated Summary of Condition 1979.

1979 Profile of Commercial Banking

SIC Code: 602	
Number of banks[1]	14,741
Number of branches[1]	34,857
Number of offices[1]	49,598
Employment (thousands)	1,360
Assets ($ billions)	1,409
Loans ($ billions)	876
In investments ($ billions)	285
Demand deposits ($ billions)	411
Time deposits ($ billions)	667

1978 year – end data
Source: Board of Govenors, of the Federal
Reserve System.

Commercial Banking: Trends and Projections
(billions of current dollars, except as noted)

	1974	1975	1976	1977	1978	Percent change, 1977–1978	1979[1]	Percent change, 1979–1978	1980[1]	Percent change 1979–1980
Assets	919	965	1,031	1,166	1,269	9	1,409	11	1,536	9
Loans	549	546	595	680	762	12	876	15	972	11
Investments	195	230	251	259	269	4	285	6	308	8
Demand deposits	316	324	337	383	399	4	411	3	419	2
Time deposits	432	463	501	556	612	10	667	9	720	8
Employment (thousands)	1,160	1,226	1,255	1,321	1,320[2]	—	1,360	3	1,401	3

[1]Estimates by Industry and Trade Administration (BDBD).
[2]New definition.
Source: Board of Governors of the Federal Reserve System and Bureau of Labor Statistics, Industry and Trade Administration (BDBD).

300 Largest Commercial Banks in the United States by State

Rank 6/30/79	Deposits 6/30/79	Rank 6/30/79	Deposits 6/30/79
Alabama		88 Sumitomo Bank of California, San Francisco	$1,413,796,628
108 First National Bank, Birmingham	$1,206,745,000	144 City National Bank, Beverly Hills	904,874,000
132 Birmingham Trust National Bank	1,006,519,587	205 Barclays Bank of California, San Francisco	595,900,981
213 Central Bank of Alabama NA, Decatur	570,774,000	215 Central Bank Oakland	564,390,000
265 Merchants National Bank, Mobile	469,676,488	223 Golden State Sanwa Bank, San Francisco	542,193,861
273 Central Bank of Birmingham	456,486,228	224 Manufacturers Bank, Los Angeles	540,458,391
276 First Alabama Bank of Montgomery NA	453,964,033	232 Chartered Bank of London, San Francisco	518,107,457
280 First National Bank, Mobile	450,359,138	236 Hibernia Bank, San Francisco	515,751,000
Alaska		248 Bank of the West, San Jose	501,848,000
244 National Bank of Alaska, Anchorage	506,482,000	249 San Diego Trust & Savings Bank	501,563,000
Arizona		260 Imperial Bank, Los Angeles	481,300,000
28 Valley National Bank, Phoenix	3,868,575,000	275 California Canadian Bank, San Francisco	454,233,373
46 First National Bank, Phoenix	2,692,886,000	**Colorado**	
81 Arizona Bank, Phoenix	1,502,972,018	114 United Bank of Denver NA	1,147,271,351
262 United Bank of Arizona, Phoenix	478,316,039	116 First National Bank, Denver	1,138,911,000
Arkansas		202 Colorado National Bank, Denver	599,804,000
295 Worthen Bank & Trust Co. NA, Little Rock	426,839,000	210 Central Bank of Denver	577,821,567
California		**Connecticut**	
1 Bank of America NT &SA, San Francisco	79,053,992,000	59 Hartford National Bank & Trust Co.	1,981,386,000
20 Security Pacific National Bank, Los Angeles	16,247,414,877	64 Connecticut Bank & Trust Co., Hartford	1,864,400,042
11 Wells Fargo Bank NA, San Francisco	15,099,624,000	142 Union Trust Co., New Haven	911,163,958
13 Crocker National Bank, San Francisco	11,631,645,000	148 Colonial Bank, Waterbury	885,460,928
15 United California Bank, Los Angeles	10,292,802,000	204 State National Bank, Bridgeport	596,233,408
26 Union Bank, Los Angeles	4,232,998,000	207 Connecticut National Bank, Bridgeport	584,329,025
48 California First Bank of San Francisco	2,640,997,000	227 Citytrust, Bridgeport	529,735,000
51 Bank of California NA, San Francisco	2,255,525,000	**Delaware**	
60 Lloyds Bank California, Los Angeles	1,974,288,547	149 Wilmington Trust Co.	883,017,403
		212 Bank of Delaware, Wilmington	573,901,589
		289 Delaware Trust Co., Wilmington	433,954,000

Continued

Rank 6/30/79	Deposits 6/30/79	Rank 6/30/79	Deposits 6/30/79
297 Farmers Bank of the State of Delaware, Dover	$426,129,000	34 Northern Trust Co., Chicago	$3,409,684,000
District of Columbia		71 American National Bank & Trust Co., Chicago	1,678,673,339
53 Riggs National Bank	2,132,962,450	167 LaSalle National Bank, Chicago	752,709,000
70 American Security Bank NA	1,687,282,040	241 Central National Bank, Chicago	507,662,000
181 National Bank of Washington	685,324,167	**Indiana**	
245 Union First National Bank	504,965,027	72 American Fletcher National Bank & Trust Co., Indianapolis	1,647,084,000
291 National Savings & Trust Co.	430,707,418		
Florida		90 Indiana National Bank, Indianapolis	1,409,169,227
79 Southeast First National Bank, Miami	1,550,244,242	109 Merchants National Bank & Trust Co., Indianapolis	1,189,917,719
198 Sun First National Bank, Orlando	608,589,000	251 Lincoln National Bank & Trust Co., Fort Wayne	499,054,581
238 Flagship National Bank, Miami	512,075,000	**Iowa**	
277 Landmark First National Bank, Ft. Lauderdale	453,326,594	197 Iowa-Des Moines National Bank	615,784,000
286 First National Bank of Florida, Tampa	436,569,000	**Kansas**	
Georgia		231 Fourth National Bank & Trust Co., Wichita	519,820,000
41 Citizens & Southern National Bank, Atlanta	3,108,162,000	**Kentucky**	
67 First National Bank, Atlanta	1,751,121,000	99 First National Bank, Louisville	1,314,596,968
110 Trust Company Bank, Atlanta	1,189,655,000	111 Citizens Fidelity Bank & Trust Co., Louisville	1,181,911,586
179 Fulton National Bank, Atlanta	693,193,000	184 Liberty National Bank & Trust Co., Louisville	665,564,848
Hawaii		258 First Security National Bank & Trust Co., Lexington	484,682,836
77 Bank of Hawaii, Honolulu	1,570,658,000		
103 First Hawaiian Bank, Honolulu	1,267,937,000	**Louisiana**	
Idaho		97 Whitney National Bank, New Orleans	1,329,203,001
96 Idaho First National Bank, Boise	1,332,446,194	173 Hibernia National Bank, New Orleans	715,025,000
137 First Security Bank of Idaho NA, Boise	953,999,676	186 First National Bank of Commerce, New Orleans	661,777,000
294 Bank of Idaho NA, Boise	427,632,101	247 Louisiana National Bank, Baton Rouge	501,954,370
Illinois		250 First National Bank, Shreveport	499,136,632
7 Continental Illinois National Bank & Trust Co., Chicago	21,067,943,000	271 Commercial National Bank, Shreveport	457,857,691
9 First National Bank, Chicago	17,453,024,000		
24 Harris Trust & Savings Bank, Chicago	4,418,493,499		

Continued

Rank 6/30/79	Deposits 6/30/79	Rank 6/30/79	Deposits 6/30/79
272 American Bank & Trust Co., Baton Rouge	$457,569,178	281 First National Bank & Trust Co., Kalamazoo	$449,140,000
		285 Community National Bank, Pontiac	436,874,697
Maryland			
50 Maryland National Bank, Baltimore	2,256,748,456	**Minnesota**	
73 Equitable Trust Co., Baltimore	1,635,945,000	52 Northwestern National Bank, Minneapolis	2,201,552,000
83 First National Bank, Baltimore	1,483,019,000	68 First National Bank, Minneapolis	1,725,716,000
115 Suburban Trust Co., Hyattsville	1,139,107,480	86 First National Bank, St. Paul	1,434,567,000
151 Union Trust Co., Baltimore	874,078,000	**Mississippi**	
243 Citizens Bank & Trust Co., Riverdale	506,542,522	120 Deposit Guaranty National Bank, Jackson	1,104,053,000
Massachusetts		136 First National Bank, Jackson	966,891,000
16 First National Bank, Boston	8,294,611,000		
82 New England Merchants National Bank, Boston	1,489,991,736	**Missouri**	
89 Shawmut Bank of Boston NA	1,411,546,000	74 Mercantile Trust Co., NA, St. Louis	1,628,322,000
113 State Street Bank & Trust Co., Boston	1,154,885,000	76 First National Bank, St. Louis	1,585,458,000
256 Worcester County National Bank, Worcester	488,869,000	182 Commerce Bank of Kansas City NA	681,778,000
300 BayBank Norfolk County Trust Co., Dedham	423,247,664	208 First National Bank, Kansas City	580,950,000
Michigan		214 Boatmen's National Bank, St. Louis	566,348,000
18 National Bank of Detroit	6,942,000,000	229 United Missouri Bank of Kansas City NA	523,703,000
38 Manufacturers National Bank, Detroit	3,227,059,000	**Nebraska**	
42 Detroit Bank & Trust	3,081,813,000	234 Omaha National Bank	516,266,000
87 Michigan National Bank, Detroit	1,432,448,000	**Nevada**	
91 Michigan National Bank, Lansing	1,396,149,000	112 First National Bank of Nevada, Reno	1,176,952,000
130 Old Kent Bank & Trust Co., Grand Rapids	1,029,915,000	192 Valley Bank, Las Vegas	630,159,756
145 City National Bank, Detroit	895,230,000	**New Jersey**	
146 Bank of the Commonwealth, Detroit	893,128,760	85 First National State Bank, Newark	1,437,292,000
153 Citizens Commercial & Savings Bank, Flint	866,895,079	121 United Jersey Bank, Hackensack	1,102,931,000
178 Genesee Merchants Bank & Trust Co., Flint	696,789,493	123 Midlantic National Bank, Newark	1,087,872,000
217 Security Bank & Trust Co., Southgate	563,514,722	154 New Jersey National Bank, Trenton	865,525,000
270 Union Bank & Trust Co., NA, Grand Rapids	459,322,000	156 National Community Bank, Rutherford	849,932,159

Continued

581

Rank 6/30/79	Deposits 6/30/79	Rank 6/30/79	Deposits 6/30/79
159 First Peoples Bank of N.J., Haddon Twp.	$835,716,242	20 Bank of New York	$6,169,441,300
164 Fidelity Union Trust Co., Newark	792,022,000	30 National Bank of North America, New York	3,663,426,000
166 New Jersey Bank NA, West Paterson	752,976,807	43 European American Bank & Trust Co., New York	3,011,204,000
174 Garden State National Bank, Paramus	714,713,000	45 Bank of Tokyo Trust Co., New York	2,729,239,383
188 First National Bank, Totowa	659,483,546	47 Republic National Bank, New York	2,641,390,239
189 National State Bank, Elizabeth	659,025,102	49 Lincoln First Bank NA, Rochester	2,323,225,000
190 Heritage Bank NA, Cherry Hill	648,899,000	63 Citibank (New York State) NA, Buffalo	1,911,794,000
201 First Jersey National Bank, Jersey City	602,299,000	93 Manufacturers & Traders Trust Co., Buffalo	1,365,648,915
226 First National Bank of South Jersey, Pleasantville	537,212,000	95 United States Trust Co., New York	1,333,121,769
228 Bank of New Jersey, Camden	529,403,000	105 J. Henry Schroder Bank & Trust Co., New York	1,241,112,000
235 Central Jersey Bank & Trust Co., Freehold	516,153,167	106 Bank Leumi Trust Co., New York	1,220,085,988
261 American National Bank & Trust, Morristown	479,515,000	155 National Commercial Bank & Trust Co., Albany	862,496,054
269 Trust Co., of New Jersey, Jersey City	462,981,000	183 State Bank of Albany	681,695,850
279 Citizens First National Bank, Ridgewood	450,382,000	185 Long Island Trust Co., Garden City	663,000,000
282 Colonial First National Bank, Red Bank	447,634,417	193 Industrial Bank of Japan Trust Co., New York	627,627,929
296 United Counties Trust Co., Elizabeth	426,562,452	194 Fuji Bank & Trust Co., New York	624,786,989
New Mexico		199 Oneida National Bank & Trust Co., of Central N.Y., Utica	608,300,138
191 Albuquerque National Bank	640,005,023	216 UBAF Arab American Bank, New York	564,258,452
299 First National Bank, Albuquerque	424,088,157	220 Liberty National Bank & Trust Co., Buffalo	552,726,047
New York		221 Security Trust Co., of Rochester	550,049,516
2 Citibank NA, New York	62,806,898,000	254 Brown Brothers Harriman & Co., New York	492,879,041
3 Chase Manhattan Bank NA, New York	48,436,793,000	257 Key Bank of Central N.Y., Syracuse	487,254,005
4 Manufacturers Hanover Trust Co., New York	35,335,181,000	274 Barclays Bank of New York	455,777,000
5 Morgan Guaranty Trust Co., New York	30,743,525,000	293 Empire National Bank, Middletown	428,285,000
6 Chemical Bank, New York	25,216,478,000	North Carolina	
8 Bankers Trust Co., New York	18,319,424,000	27 North Carolina National Bank, Charlotte	3,899,716,00
12 Marine Midland Bank, Buffalo	11,847,554,000	33 Wachovia Bank & Trust Co. NA, Winston-Salem	3,464,567,096
14 Irving Trust Co., New York	10,570,223,000		

Continued

Rank 6/30/79	Deposits 6/30/79	Rank 6/30/79	Deposits 6/30/79
62 First Union National Bank, Charlotte	$1,915,130,000	**Pennsylvania**	
94 Northwestern Bank, North Wilkesboro	1,339,311,294	17 Mellon Bank NA, Pittsburgh	$8,140,934,000
		21 First Pennsylvania Bank NA, Philadelphia	5,315,837,000
122 First Citizens Bank & Trust Co., Raleigh	1,098,611,000	29 Philaldelphia National Bank	3,678,930,000
253 Branch Banking & Trust Co., Wilson	498,030,896	37 Pittsburgh National Bank	3,262,177,481
		44 Girard Bank, Philadelphia	2,877,130,000
Ohio		54 Fidelity Bank, Philadelphia	2,112,165,000
31 BancOhio National Bank, Columbus	3,475,739,000	61 Equibank NA, Pittsburgh	1,959,645,000
40 Cleveland Trust Co.	3,186,902,000	78 Provident National Bank, Philadelphia	1,566,557,000
56 National City Bank, Cleveland	2,100,210,000	84 American Bank & Trust Co., Reading	1,455,303,000
65 Central National Bank, Cleveland	1,860,529,000	92 Industrial Valley Bank & Trust Co., Philadelphia	1,379,498,000
107 Society National Bank, Cleveland	1,215,400,774	101 Continental Bank, Norristown	1,290,726,000
128 Huntington National Bank, Columbus	1,056,155,563	102 National Central Bank, Lancaster	1,289,312,000
138 First National Bank, Cincinnati	939,227,007	139 Union National Bank, Pittsburgh	933,630,515
140 Union Commerce Bank, Cleveland	932,343,000	163 Commonwealth National Bank, Harrisburg	795,340,680
143 City National Bank & Trust Co., Columbus	904,894,020	170 First National Bank, Allentown	733,710,000
150 Central Trust Co. NA, Cincinnati	877,762,000	196 Northeastern Bank of Pennsylvania, Mt. Pocono	618,905,000
165 Winters National Bank & Trust Co., Dayton	757,885,000	209 Central Penn National Bank, Philadelphia	577,978,000
169 First National Bank, Akron	735,593,921	230 Southeast National Bank of Pennsylvania, Chester	520,937,432
172 Fifth Third Bank, Cincinnati	722,071,000	242 First Eastern Bank NA, Wilkes-Barre	507,523,909
200 Toledo Trust Co.	605,045,423	246 United Penn Bank, Wilkes-Barre	502,518,000
267 Provident Bank, Cincinnati	467,900,000	252 First Valley Bank, Lansford	498,078,936
290 Ohio Citizens Trust Co., Toledo	433,462,508	264 Dauphin Deposit Bank & Trust Co., Harrisburg	472,424,668
Oklahoma		278 Merchants National Bank, Allentown	450,544,972
119 First National Bank & Trust Co., Oklahoma City	1,110,499,363	283 Pennsylvania Bank & Trust Co., Warren	447,186,000
160 Liberty National Bank & Trust Co., Oklahoma City	825,077,179	**Puerto Rico**	
171 Bank of Oklahoma NA, Tulsa	726,598,000	66 Banco Popular de Puerto Rico, San Juan	1,846,607,613
177 First National Bank & Trust Co., Tulsa	707,597,000	133 Banco de Ponce	1,001,071,784
Oregon		**Rhode Island**	
35 First National Bank of Oregon, Portland	3,383,622,000	58 Industrial National Bank of Rhode Island, Providence	1,983.000,000
39 United States National Bank of Oregon, Portland	3,213,670,000	124 Old Stone Bank, Providence	1,075,706,000
225 Oregon Bank, Portland	539,737,586		

Continued

Rank 6/30/79	Deposits 6/30/79	Rank 6/30/79	Deposits 6/30/79
125 Rhode Island Hospital Trust National Bank, Providence	$1,070,684,000	162 Frost National Bank, San Antonio	$796,971,646
		203 Austin National Bank	597,965,000
South Carolina		219 First International Bank in Houston NA	558,292,000
127 South Carolina National Bank, Columbia	1,061,473,000	222 National Bank of Commerce, San Antonio	548,656,000
175 Citizens & Southern National Bank, Charleston	713,780,974	255 First National Bank of Midland	489,385,306
187 Bankers Trust of South Carolina, Columbia	659,512,355	266 Capital National Bank Austin	468,607,845
195 First National Bank of South Carolina, Columbia	619,570,000	268 Capital National Bank, Houston	467,483,000
		284 El Paso National Bank	441,670,840
South Dakota		288 First National Bank, Amarillo	434,345,721
263 National Bank of South Dakota, Sioux Falls	474,572,000	298 First City Bank of Dallas	425,461,000
Tennessee		**Utah**	
118 First Tennessee Bank NA, Memphis	1,118,552,000	98 First Security Bank of Utah NA, Ogden	1,320,707,000
126 First American National Bank, Nashville	1,063,209,000	131 Zions First National Bank, Salt Lake City	1,012,192,000
129 Commerce Union Bank, Nashville	1,051,132,141	211 Walk Bank & Trust Co., Salt Lake City	574,659,360
135 Third National Bank, Nashville	975,164,000	**Virginia**	
180 Union Planters National Bank, Memphis	688,871,621	57 Virginia National Bank, Norfolk	2,031,083,000
240 National Bank of Commerce, Memphis	508,581,096	75 First & Merchants National Bank, Richmond	1,606,408,199
259 American National Bank & Trust Co. Chattanooga	484,045,719	80 Bank of Virginia, Richmond	1,517,423,694
		152 First National Exchange Bank, Roanoke	872,557,223
Texas		158 United Virginia Bank, Richmond	840,897,000
22 Republic National Bank, Dallas	5,262,419,000	176 First American Bank of Virginia, McLean	711,098,392
23 First National Bank, Dallas	5,109,481,000	218 First Virginia Bank, Falls Church	561,921,097
25 First City National Bank, Houston	4,271,676,000	233 United Virginia Bank/ National, Vienna	517,870,000
32 Texas Commerce Bank NA, Houston	3,470,980,000	237 Fidelity American Bank NA, Lynchburg	514,586,000
69 Mercantile National Bank, Dallas	1,700,925,000	**Washington**	
104 Bank of the Southwest NA, Houston	1,259,945,000	19 Seattle-First National Bank	6,305,774,000
134 Fort Worth National Bank	976,915,472	36 Rainier National Bank, Seattle	3,295,000,053
147 First National Bank, Fort Worth	890,805,420	100 Pacific National Bank of Washington, Seattle	1,304,952,870
157 Allied Bank of Texas, Houston	842,643,016	117 Peoples National Bank, Seattle	1,128,733,172
161 Houston National Bank	801,604,000		

Continued

Rank 6/30/79	Deposits 6/30/79	Rank 6/30/79	Deposits 6/30/79
141 Old National Bank, Spokane	$925,782,000	168 M&I Marshall & Illsley Bank, Milwaukee	$738,237,000
206 Puget Sound National Bank, Tacoma	585,039,455	239 Marine National Exchange Bank, Milwaukee	509,654,000
287 Seattle Trust & Savings Bank	434,440,888	292 First Bank NA, La Crosse	429,880,000
Wisconsin			
55 First Wisconsin National Bank, Milwaukee	2,104,835,000		

Source: American Banker. Used with permission of the publisher.

Appendix D: Mutual Savings Banks

100 Largest Mutual Savings Banks in the United States

Rank 6/30/79	Total Deposits 6/30/79	6/30/78	Rank 6/30/78	Gain in Rank	Interest Rate[1]% 6/30/79	6/30/78
1 Philadelphia Saving Fund Society, Pa.	5,708,945,865	5,087,592,754	1		5.000–9.000	5.250–8.000
2 Bowery Savings Bank, New York	4,706,053,116	4,588,031,219	2		5.000–9.000	5.250–8.000
3 Dime Savings Bank of New York, Brooklyn	4,182,053,060	4,081,985,308	3		5.000–9.000	5.250–8.000
4 New York Bank for Savings	3,353,387,000	3,286,165,361	4		5.000–9.000	5.250–8.000
5 Emigrant Savings Bank, New York	3,005,890,196	2,395,842,047	6	+1	5.000–9.000	5.250–8.000
6 Dollar Savings Bank, Bronx, New York	2,508,046,995	2,435,651,081	5		5.000–9.000	5.250–8.000
7 Howard Savings Bank, Newark, N.J.	2,336,116,011	2,113,025,000	8	+1	5.000–9.000	5.250–8.000
8 Buffalo Savings Bank, N.Y.	2,243,842,702	2,029,575,964	9	+1	5.250–9.000	5.250–8.000
9 Dry Dock Savings Bank, New York	2,229,854,302	2,204,469,997	7		5.000–9.000	5.250–8.000
10 Manhattan Savings Bank, New York	2,160,704,280	2,019,404,261	10		5.250–9.000	5.250–8.000
11 Western Saving Fund Society of Philadelphia	2,099,938,802	2,008,593,249	11		5.250–9.000	5.250–8.000
12 Williamsburgh Savings Bank, Brooklyn, N.Y.	2,024,754,559	1,978,434,816	13	+1	5.000–9.000	5.250–8.000
13 Greenwich Savings Bank, New York	1,983,845,497	1,997,062,053	12		5.250–9.000	5.250–8.000
14 Lincoln Savings Bank of Brooklyn, N.Y.	1,903,117,416	1,887,934,200	14		5.250–9.000	5.250–8.000
15 Washington Mutual Savings Bank, Seattle	1,837,152,245	1,714,597,185	16	+1	5.000–9.000	5.250–8.000
16 Erie Savings Bank, Buffalo, N.Y.	1,835,585,569	1,682,005,793	18	+2	5.000–8.903	5.250–8.000
17 Metropolitan Savings Bank, Brooklyn, N.Y.	1,825,021,275	1,693,493,649	17		5.000–9.000	5.250–8.000
18 Peoples Savings Bank— Bridgeport, Conn.	1,735,378,038	1,581,072,991	19	+1	5.000–9.000	5.000–8.000
19 Seamen's Bank for Savings, New York	1,688,536,018	1,724,030,083	15		5.000–9.000	5.250–8.000
20 Greater New York Savings Bank, Brooklyn	1,582,647,377	1,490,383,914	22	+2	5.000–9.000	5.250–8.000
21 Anchor Savings Bank, Brooklyn, N.Y.	1,561,976,968	1,517,735,528	20		5.000–9.000	5.250–8.000
22 East River Savings Bank, New York	1,506,092,769	1,496,181,652	21		5.000–9.000	5.250–8.000
23 Franklin Savings Bank of New York	1,432,923,797	1,443,781,000	23		5.250–9.000	5.250–8.000

Continued

Rank 6/30/79	Total Deposits		Rank 6/30/78	Gain in Rank	Interest Rate[1] %	
	6/30/79	6/30/78			6/30/79	6/30/78
24 Society for Savings, Hartford, Conn.	1,430,438,450	1,392,307,265	24		5.000–9.000	5.250–8.000
25 Brooklyn Savings Bank, N.Y.	1,400,501,815	1,318,965,596	26	+1	5.000–9.000	5.250–8.000
26 Beneficial Mutual Savings Bank, Philadelphia	1,398,512,324	1,259,219,055	27	+1	5.250–8.000	5.250–7.646
27 Jamaica Savings Bank, New York	1,356,929,459	1,335,974,763	25		5.250–8.903	5.250–8.000
28 Union Dime Savings Bank, New York	1,206,922,000	1,204,890,276	28		5.000–9.000	5.250–8.000
29 Germantown Savings Bank, Bala Cynwyd, Pa.	1,153,702,916	1,071,877,059	30	+1	5.250–9.000	5.250–8.000
30 Albany Savings Bank, N.Y.	1,135,293,491	800,108,827	44	+14	5.00–9.000	5.250–8.000
31 Dollar Savings Bank, Pittsburgh, Pa.	1,120,579,784	1,116,340,897	29		5.250–9.000	5.250–7.750
32 Community Savings Bank, Rochester, N.Y.	1,070,854,580	1,019,215,915	31		5.250–9.000	5.250–8.000
33 Hudson City Savings Bank, Jersey City, N.J.	1,039,592,051	863,108,892	40	+7	5.250–9.000	5.250–7.640
34 Green Point Savings Bank, Brooklyn, N.Y.	1,014,093,665	964,913,721	32		5.250–9.000	5.250–8.000
35 Long Island Savings Bank, Queens, N.Y.	1,001,891,002	961,141,860	33		5.000–9.000	5.250–8.000
36 Schenectady Savings, Bank, N.Y.	958,657,626	847,714,125	41	+5	5.000–9.000	5.250–7.750
37 Independence Savings Bank, Brooklyn, N.Y.	953,197,100	896,741,137	36		5.250–9.000	5.250–8.000
38 Provident Institution for Savings, Boston	934,982,922	9 56,842,593	34[2]		5.000–9.000	5.000–7.750
39 Ridgewood Savings Bank, Brooklyn, N.Y.	928,395,238	888,743,039	37		5.250–9.000	5.250–8.000
40 Boston Five Cents Savings Bank, Mass.	896,124,505	913,766,171	35		5.000–9.000	5.000–8.000
41 East New York Savings Bank, Brooklyn, N.Y.	892,570,955	884,787,178	38[3]		5.250–9.000	5.250–8.000
42 Farmers & Mechanics Savings Bank, Minneapolis, Minn.	870,081,904	872,652,928	39		5.000–9.000	5.250–8.000
43 Western New York Savings Bank, Buffalo	846,032,238	778,430,711	45	+2	5.250–9.000	5.250–8.000
44 United Mutual Savings Bank, New York	827,002,878	817,179,732	43		5.000–9.000	5.250–8.000
45 Central Savings Bank in the City of New York	825,953,704	820,329,482	42		5.000–9.000	5.250–8.000
46 Savings Bank of Baltimore, Md.	824,257,744	733,710,807	50	+4	5.250–9.000	5.250–7.750

Continued

Rank 6/30/79	Total Deposits		Rank 6/30/78	Gain in Rank	Interest Rate[1]%	
	6/30/79	6/30/78			6/30/79	6/30/78
47 Rochester Savings Bank, N.Y.	797,087,277	729,403,192	51	+4	5.000–9.000	5.250–8.000
48 Onondaga Savings Bank, Syracuse, N.Y.	780,178,613	763,039,407	46		5.000–9.000	5.250–8.000
49 Harlem Savings Bank, New York	764,549,000	747,693,473	47		5.000–9.000	5.250–8.000
50 Peoples Westchester Savings Bank, Tarrytown, N.Y.	759,251,677	696,564,599	53	+3	5.250–9.000	5.250–8.000
51 Syracuse Savings Bank, N.Y.	739,606,830	708,424,804	52	+1	5.250–9.000	5.250–7.750
51 Charlestown Savings Bank, Boston	735,701,226	733,991,109	49		5.000–9.000	5.000–8.000
53 Roosevelt Savings Bank, Brooklyn, N.Y.	716,241,906	666,078,148	56	+3	5.000–9.000	5.250–8.000
54 Eastern Savings Bank, Scarsdale, N.Y.	706,205,249	740,558,939	48		5.250–9.000	5.250–8.000
55 Queens County Savings Bank, Queens, N.Y.	693,761,926	676,324,269	55		5.250–9.000	5.250–8.000
56 Connecticut Savings Bank, New Haven	693,093,096	631,238,991	60	+4	5.000–9.000	5.250–8.000
57 New Haven Savings Bank, Conn.	681,261,362	615,846,613	61	+4	5.000–9.000	5.000–8.000
58 Wilmington Savings Fund Society, Del.	676,789,870	650,673,636	58		5.250–9.000	5.250–7.750
59 Empire Savings Bank, New York	652,896,756	656,044,418	57		5.250–9.000	5.250–8.000
60 Hamburg Savings Bank, Brooklyn, N.Y.	646,510,218	640,877,785	59		5.250–9.000	5.250–8.000
61 Mooris County Savings Bank, Morristown, N.J.	637,517,233	576,510,644	64	+3	5.250–9.000	5.250–7.750
62 Provident Savings Bank, Jersey City, N.J.	615,627,150	577,320,596	63	+1	5.250–8.870	5.250–6.500
63 Suffolk Franklin Savings Bank, Boston	590,638,137	599,517,177	62		5.000–9.000	5.000–8.000
64 Richmond Hill Savings, Bank, Queens, N.Y.	563,850,569	528,983,640	68	+4	5.250–9.000	5.250–8.000
65 Citizens Savings Bank, Providence, R.I.	560,633,262	531,302,243	67	+2	4.500–8.000	4.500–7.750
66 Provident Savings Bank, Baltimore, Md.	557,615,566	540,742,266	65		5.250–9.000	5.250–7.750
67 Fidelity Mutual Savings Bank, Spokane, Wash.	551,345,396	533,141,511	66		5.250–9.000	5.250–8.000
68 Roslyn Savings Bank, N.Y.	550,513,098	498,660,365	71	+3	5.250–9.000	5.250–8.000
69 Banking Center, Waterbury, Conn.	527,603,479	497,926,715	72	+3	5.000–9.000	5.000–8.000
70 North Side Savings Bank, Bronx, N.Y.	522,587,741	515,123,105	70		5.000–9.000	5.250–8.000

Continued

Rank 6/30/79	Total Deposits		Rank 6/30/78	Gain in Rank	Interest Rate[1] %	
	6/30/79	6/30/78			6/30/79	6/30/78
71 Dime Savings Bank of Williamsburg, Brooklyn, N.Y.	500,851,328	481,664,108	73	+2	5.250–9.000	5.250–8.000
72 Mutual Bank for Savings, Newton, Mass.	500,191,078	474,452,346	74	+2	5.000–9.000	5.000–8.000
73 Binghamton Savings Bank, N.Y.	496,646,109	461,858,763	75	+2	5.250–9.000	5.250–8.000
74 Springfield Institution for Savings, Mass.	492,870,239	515,851,693	69		5.000–8.000	5.000–8.000
75 United States Savings Bank, Newark, N.J.	492,061,217	447,393,138	77	+2	5.250–9.000	5.250–8.000
76 American Savings Bank, New York	464,852,181	453,220,821	76		5.250–9.000	5.250–8.000
77 Staten Island Savings Bank, New York	461,322,000	418,880,022	80	+3	5.000–9.000	5.250–8.000
78 Savings Bank of Utica, N.Y.	459,134,270	431,345,526	78		4.750–9.000	4.750–7.750
79 Poughkeepsie Savings Bank, N.Y.	444,592,934	403,081,493	82	+3	5.250–9.000	5.250–8.000
80 Monroe Savings Bank, Rochester, N.Y.	438,061,718	422,957,002	79		5.250–9.000	5.250–8.000
81 Mechanics & Farmers Savings Bank, Bridgeport, Conn.	436,212,522	394,853,755	86	+5	5.000–9.000	5.000–8.000
82 Bloomfield Savings Bank, N.J.	430,218,488	398,212,005	85	+3	5.250–9.000	5.250–8.000
83 Orange Savings Bank, Livingston, N.J.	427,123,671	369,165,719	91	+8	5.000–9.000	5.250–6.750
84 Worcester County Institution for Savings, Worcester, Mass.	418,665,008	386,154,617	88	+4	5.000–9.000	5.000–8.000
85 Permanent Savings Bank, Niagara Falls, N.Y.	410,791,464	389,180,956	87	+2	5.250–9.000	5.250–8.000
86 Eastchester Savings Bank, Mt. Vernon, N.Y.	410,015,560	400,155,508	84		5.250–9.000	5.250–8.000
87 Lincoln Mutual Savings Bank, Spokane, Wash.	409,467,312	414,041,052	81		5.250–9.000	5.250–8.000
88 South Boston Savings Bank, Mass.	405,213,909	339,299,611	98	+10	5.250–9.000	5.000–8.000
89 Maine Savings Bank, Portland	402,879,193	362,072,567	94	+5	5.000–9.000	5.000–8.000
90 Union Warren Savings Bank, Boston	400,223,161	400,223,726	83		5.000–9.000	5.000–8.000
91 Home Savings Bank, White Plains, N.Y.	397,554,423	382,746,842	89		5.250–9.000	5.250–8.000
92 American Savings Bank, New Britain, Conn.	390,597,232	348,435,975	95	+3	5.000–9.000	5.000–8.000
93 Amoskeag Savings Bank, Manchester, N.H.	385,471,580	364,387,003	93		5.000–9.000	5.000–8.000
94 Home Savings Bank, Boston	374,031,508	369,509,390	90		4.750–9.000	4.750–8.000

Continued

Rank 6/30/79	Total Deposits		Rank 6/30/78	Gain in Rank	Interest Rate[1] %	
	6/30/79	6/30/78			6/30/79	6/30/78
95 Cambridge Savings Bank, Mass.	372,507,148	365,794,966	92		5.000–9.000	5.000–7.750
96 Mechanics Savings Bank, Hartford, Conn.	369,067,053	346,538,484	96		5.000–9.000	5.000–8.000
97 New Brunswick Savings Bank, N.J.	357,691,341	326,245,664	100	+3	5.250–9.000	5.250–8.000
98 Burlington Savings Bank, Vt.	353,326,165	341,062,796	97		5.250–9.000	5.250–8.000
99 Perth Amboy Savings Institution, N.J.	352,076,700	325,708,791	101	+2	5.250–7.000	5.250–7.000
100 Peoples Savings Bank, Worcester, Mass.	335,065,193	320,782,231	102	+2	5.250–9.000	5.000–8.000

[1]Range of rates is for all new accounts under $100,000, including interest-bearing NOW accounts and six-month money market certificates. In the case of MMCs, the rate used is the offering rate in effect on June 30.

[2]Based on revised data. Rank that bank would have had if revised data had been available.

[3]Revised data.

Source: American Banker. Used with permission of the publisher.

Savings Bank Life Insurance in Force, Selected Years
(millions of dollars)

Year	Total	Massachusetts Total	Massachusetts Ordinary	Massachusetts Group	New York Total	New York Ordinary	New York Group	Connecticut Total	Connecticut Ordinary	Connecticut Group
1908	0.1	0.1	0.1	—	—	—	—	—	—	—
1918	9.8	9.8	7.2	2.6	—	—	—	—	—	—
1928	57.8	57.8	46.3	11.5	—	—	—	—	—	—
1939	179.0	173.1	162.3	10.9	5.8	5.8	—	—	—	—
1942	252.7	222.8	210.3	12.5	28.8	28.2	0.6	1.2	1.2	—
1945	331.0	264.1	247.6	16.4	61.1	56.8	4.3	5.9	4.8	1.1
1950	579.8	392.6	360.7	31.9	172.9	158.9	14.0	14.4	12.5	1.9
1955	859.8	543.8	496.7	47.1	284.2	244.6	39.6	31.7	22.7	9.0
1960	1,248.7	738.5	669.8	68.7	448.6	391.9	56.7	61.6	37.9	23.7
1965	2,058.1	1,072.0	947.5	124.4	894.1	785.2	108.8	92.1	54.2	37.9
1970	4,019.7	1,512.3	1,300.9	211.4	2,380.8	1,521.0	859.8	126.6	71.7	54.9
1971	4,545.3	1,634.3	1,394.4	239.9	2,777.5	1,657.3	1,120.2	133.5	76.6	56.9
1972	5,257.8	1,764.3	1,490.7	273.6	3,352.6	1,953.7	1,398.9	140.9	82.5	58.4
1973	6,046.9	1,893.9	1,583.9	310.0	4,001.4	2,291.3	1,710.1	151.6	87.9	63.7
1974	6,923.5	2,029.5	1,679.6	349.9	4,736.8	2,654.1	2,082.7	157.2	91.8	65.4
1975	7,631.6	2,156.4	1,756.7	399.7	5,288.5	3,041.0	2,247.5	186.7	94.5	92.2
1976	8,396.0	2,264.0	1,848.9	415.1	5,913.8	3,444.8	2,469.0	218.2	97.4	120.8
1977	9,442.0	2,371.9	1,924.5	447.4	6,824.0	3,813.4	3,010.6	246.1	99.9	146.2
1978	10,574.5	2,535.9	2,031.9	504.0	7,713.5	4,145.0	3,568.5	325.1	110.0	215.1
1979	11,558.3	2,712.5	2,176.0	536.5	8,448.7	4,459.8	3,989.0	397.1	121.2	275.9

Note: Data are as of October 31 for Massachusetts and December 31 for New York and Connecticut. Data exclude amounts of reinsurance under various programs. Additions of these amounts bring total savings bank life insurance in force to $12.4 billion.

Source: Commissioner of Banks, Commonwealth of Massachusetts; Savings Bank Life Insurance, Massachusetts; Savings Banks Life Insurance Fund, New York; and The Savings Bank Life Insurance Company, Connecticut.

Savings and Time Deposits of Mutual Savings Banks by State

| State | Deposits Outstanding Dec. 31, 1979 | Percentage Deposit Change | | | |
| | | Excluding Interest | | Including Interest | |
		1979	1978	1979	1978
New York	75,895	−7.2	−1.5	−0.3	4.8
City	53,790	−9.2	−2.6	−2.4	3.6
Upstate	22,105	−1.9	1.5	5.2	7.9
Massachusetts	20,466	−4.6	−1.5	1.7	4.7
Boston	4,841	−10.0	−2.6	−3.4	3.6
Outside Boston	15,625	−2.9	−1.1	3.3	5.1
Connecticut	12,642	−2.4	2.9	4.3	9.2
Pennsylvania	11,939	−0.6	2.0	5.7	8.0
New Jersey	8,041	0.3	3.2	7.4	9.6
Washington	3,832	−3.9	−0.8	2.4	5.8
Maine	2,337	0.8	2.1	7.6	8.3
New Hampshire	2,301	−1.8	2.3	4.9	8.5
Rhode Island	1,572	−0.6	−1.1	5.3	5.6
Maryland	1,513	2.7	2.0	9.5	7.9
Vermont	767	−3.2	2.2	4.1	9.2
All other states	2,597	−3.2	−3.2	2.1	2.2
Total	143,903	−4.9	−0.4	1.8	5.8

Source: National Association of Mutual Savings Banks.

Deposits, Number of Accounts, and Average Size of Accounts in Mutual Savings Banks by State, December 31, 1979

| State | Deposits (millions of dollars) | | | | | Number of Accounts (thousands) | | Average Size of Accounts (dollars) | |
| | | Regular Deposits | | | | | | | |
	Total	Total	Savings	Time	Other	Total	Regular	Total	Regular
New York	77,022	76,012	31,580	44,432	1,010	17,185	14,588	4,482	5,211
Massachusetts	20,508	20,462	9,874	10,588	45	5,990	5,623	3,423	3,639
Connecticut	12,851	12,695	5,347	7,349	156	3,891	3,316	3,303	3,828
Pennsylvania	12,159	11,939	4,511	7,428	220	2,958	2,514	4,110	4,749
New Jersey	8,324	8,019	3,329	4,690	306	2,233	1,584	3,728	5,061
Washington	3,862	3,832	1,455	2,378	30	821	806	4,706	4,753
Maine	2,360	2,337	1,116	1,222	22	756	618	3,121	3,784
New Hampshire	2,316	2,311	1,043	1,268	5	688	635	3,366	3,641
Rhode Island	1,576	1,572	710	862	4	450	404	3,500	3,891
Maryland	1,570	1,513	868	645	57	508	406	3,090	3,728
Minnesota	852	843	314	529	9	198	176	4,306	4,783
Delaware	847	817	399	418	30	261	204	3,252	3,997
Vermont	794	780	291	489	14	257	195	3,092	3,989
Oregon	417	407	131	276	10	94	86	4,421	4,729
Indiana	241	223	72	151	18	70	48	3,447	4,637
Alaska	230	230	53	177	—	27	26	8,557	8,844
Wisconsin	78	77	31	46	1	24	20	3,294	3,824
Total	146,066	144,070	61,123	82,947	1,936	36,410	31,250	4,010	4,610

Note: Regular deposits include savings and time deposits. Savings deposits refer to all ordinary passbook or statement type savings accounts and interest-bearing NOW accounts. Time deposits consist of certicates, special notice accounts, term, and other time deposits. "Other" deposits include all school, club, checking, non-interest-bearing NOW accounts, and certain other accounts. Deposit data exclude mortgagors' escrow accounts.

Source: NAMSB.

594

Assets and Liabilities of Mutual Savings Banks by State, December 31, 1979
(millions of dollars)

Item	Total	New York	Mass.	Conn.	Pa.	N.J.	Wash.	Me.	N.H.	R.I.	Md.	All Other States
ASSETS												
Cash and due from banks	3,156	1,083	438	269	327	592	65	70	69	40	83	120
U.S. Treasury and federal agency obligations	7,658	3,606	1,599	411	561	146	158	153	156	171	196	
State and local obligations	2,930	1,847	68	165	685	93	4	8	6	4	5	45
Mortgage investments	110,729	57,997	15,695	10,517	7,687	6,341	3,522	1,880	1,863	1,256	1,045	2,926
Mortgage loans	98,908	50,265	14,377	10,181	6,799	5,267	3,426	1,804	1,767	1,190	1,024	2,810
Mortgage-backed securities	11,820	7,732	1,319	336	888	1,074	96	76	96	67	21	116
Corporate bonds	16,922	10,746	1,503	511	2,713	734	145	91	72	43	93	271
Other bonds, notes and debentures	3,584	2,359	497	242	295	97	16	13	16	17	10	21
Corporate stock	4,760	2,258	944	739	270	122	19	117	137	41	27	86
Other loans	9,253	3,746	1,638	1,201	631	472	445	248	266	132	247	227
Guaranteed education loans	1,274	735	157	142	91	94	7	16	11	10	5	6
Consumer installment loans	1,622	245	432	349	—	88	91	84	108	39	130	56
Home improvements loans	884	370	159	140	5	39	43	23	30	15	40	21
Federal funds	3,076	1,461	496	297	390	179	97	42	36	15	13	50
Passbook loans	1,340	559	315	176	40	64	27	41	42	31	10	34
All other loans	1,058	376	80	98	105	8	179	42	40	21	49	61
Bank premises owned	1,573	727	245	137	76	111	89	38	46	35	14	54

Continued

Item	Total	New York	Mass.	Conn.	Pa.	N.J.	Wash.	Me.	N.H.	R.I.	Md.	All Other States
Other real estate	304	139	42	73	3	16	14	2	3	2	*	10
Other assets	2,535	1,484	213	198	217	116	85	25	24	38	78	57
Total Assets	163,405	85,993	22,884	14,462	13,465	9,195	4,548	2,652	2,655	1,763	1,774	4,013
LIABILITIES												
Regular deposits	144,070	76,012	20,462	12,695	11,939	8,019	3,832	2,337	2,311	1,572	1,513	3,377
Savings	61,123	31,580	9,874	5,347	4,511	3,329	1,455	1,116	1,043	710	868	1,291
Time	82,947	44,432	10,588	7,349	7,428	4,690	2,378	1,222	1,268	862	645	2,085
School and club	199	86	22	14	46	15	1	2	3	3	2	5
Other deposits	1,737	925	23	142	173	290	28	20	2	1	55	77
Total deposits	146,006	77,022	20,508	12,851	12,159	8,324	3,862	2,360	2,316	1,576	1,570	3,458
Borrowings and mortgage warehousing	3,653	1,978	139	299	367	157	321	57	70	13	21	232
Other liabilities	2,220	1,163	398	186	127	127	51	24	35	28	32	50
Total Liabilities	151,879	80,163	21,045	13,337	12,652	8,608	4,234	2,440	2,421	1,617	1,623	3,740
Capital notes and debentures	385	158	—	42	94	52	5	1	4	4	—	26
Other general reserves	11,141	5,672	1,839	1,084	719	536	310	212	230	142	151	247
Total General Reserve Accounts	11,525	5,830	1,839	1,125	813	587	314	212	234	146	151	273
Total Liabilities and General Reserve Accounts	163,405	85,993	22,884	14,462	13,465	9,195	4,548	2,652	2,655	1,763	1,774	4,013
MEMORANDA Cash and investments:												
Maturing within one year	9,578	3,751	1,644	833	1,147	969	263	192	183	101	205	290
Maturing within five years	16,126	7,002	2,824	1,163	1,880	1,302	390	305	301	218	310	432

Total mortgage loans	99,675	50,774	14,455	10,235	6,867	5,283	3,428	1,806	1,773	1,198	1,039	2,817
Residential	83,081	41,754	12,296	8,987	5,402	4,592	2,856	1,544	1,502	958	960	2,231
FHA	13,816	10,241	1,166	287	866	693	107	81	66	55	80	172
VA	11,390	6,966	1,476	293	1,185	681	79	273	155	56	121	103
Conventional	57,875	24,546	9,654	8,408	3,350	3,218	2,669	1,189	1,280	846	759	1,956
Nonresidential	16,549	9,013	2,148	1,241	1,465	691	571	261	269	240	79	571
Farm	45	9	11	6	*	1	1	2	—	—	—	15
Total corporate stock	4,760	2,258	945	739	270	122	19	117	137	41	27	86
Preferred	1,823	1,301	102	111	93	79	11	26	16	3	24	56
Common	2,937	956	843	627	176	43	8	91	121	38	3	3
Number of banks	463	112	163	65	9	20	10	29	26	6	3	20

* Less than $500,000.

Note: Data for cash and investments maturing within one year and five years include cash, federal funds, securities and open market paper. Consumer installment loan data for New York include checking overdrafts and other loans. Breakdown of mortgage loans shown in memoranda item are gross of valuation reserves. See note to the following table.

Source: NAMSB.

Total Deposits, Including Interest, in Mutual Savings Banks by State, Selected Year-End Dates
(millions of dollars)

End of year	Total	New York	Mass.	Conn.	Pa.	N.J.	Wash.	Me.	N.H.	R.I.	Md.	All other States
1945	15,332	8,292	2,856	1,115	932	408	158	203	240	241	349	538
1950	20,025	11,662	3,312	1,335	1,076	599	200	238	278	268	402	655
1955	28,182	16,544	4,484	1,841	1,497	1,010	290	315	395	376	490	940
1960	36,343	21,436	5,793	2,516	2,090	1,347	382	415	543	506	561	753
1965	52,443	30,392	8,449	3,680	3,195	2,032	625	617	843	807	716	1,086
1966	55,006	32,104	8,694	3,830	3,240	2,164	699	6 57	888	851	735	1,144
1967	60,121	35,478	9,259	4,162	3,431	2,375	799	710	958	923	770	1,256
1968	64,507	38,031	9,809	4,487	3,547	2,547	1,109	769	1,038	1,020	808	1,344
1969	67,086	39,009	10,480	4,843	3,703	2,651	1,194	836	1,086	1,045	823	1,414
1970	71,580	40,921	11,271	5,313	4,242	3,043	1,288	924	1,037	1,111	882	1,547
1971	81,440	46,271	12,673	6,094	4,971	3,622	1,538	1,057	1,178	1,255	977	1,806
1972	91,613	51,718	14,072	6,880	5,802	4,239	1,801	1,201	1,340	1,420	1,047	2,092
1973	96,496	54,024	14,712	7,419	6,209	4,555	1,947	1,307	1,449	1,565	1,107	2,203
1974	98,701	55,130	14,991	7,797	6,615	4,777	2,144	1,397	1,478	1,035	1,006	2,330
1975	109,873	60,704	16,500	8,810	7,743	5,492	2,480	1,589	1,645	1,190	1,098	2,623
1976	122,877	67,308	17,989	10,043	9,101	6,251	3,180	1,792	1,824	1,313	1,192	2,885
1977	134,017	72,812	19,258	11,207	10,469	7,030	3,438	2,020	2,025	1,418	1,294	3,046
1978	142,701	76,948	20,161	12,265	11,317	7,741	3,637	2,191	2,198	1,496	1,398	3,350
1979	146,006	77,022	20,508	12,851	12,159	8,324	3,862	2,360	2,316	1,576	1,570	3,458

Source: NAMSB.

Appendix E: Savings and Loan Associations

Savings and Loans—Sales and Profits, 1980

Company	Sales				Profits				Margins		Return on common equity, 12 months ending 12/31	Price-earnings ratio, 2/20	12 months' earnings per share
	4th quarter, 1980 ($ mil.)	Change from 1979 (%)	12 months, 1980 ($ mil.)	Change from 1979 (%)	4th quarter, 1980 ($ mil.)	Change from 1979 (%)	12 months, 1980 ($ mil.)	Change from 1979 (%)	4th quarter, 1980 (%)	4th quarter, 1979 (%)			
Ahmanson (H.F.)	366.8	13	1371.1	13	16.3	−44	48.1	−59	4.5	9.0	5.8	9	2.07
First Charter Financial	246.0	4	955.1	13	15.7	−30	39.2	−57	6.4	9.4	5.0	11	1.32
Great Western Financial	266.1	12	997.2	14	12.2	−49	39.2	−58	4.6	10.0	6.2	9	1.74
Imperial Corp. of America	187.6	15	713.7	22	11.3	−47	40.7	−45	6.0	13.2	8.4	8	2.86
Industry Composite	1066.4	11	4037.1	15	55.5	−43	167.1	−55	5.2	10.1	6.1	9	1.86

Source: Standard & Poor's Compustat Services, Inc.

100 Largest Savings and Loan Associations in the United States

Rank 6/30/79	Total Deposits ($ millions)		Rank 6/30/78 Gain	Interest Rate[1]%	
	6/30/79	6/30/78			12/31/78
1 Home S&L Ass'n. Los Angeles	8,860,870	8,072,869	1	5.250–9.000	5.250–8.000
2 Great Western S&L Ass'n, Beverly Hills, Calif.	7,178,966	6,382,245	2	5.250–9.000	5.250–8.000
3 American S&L Ass'n, Beverly Hills, Calif.	6,835,662	5,893,832	3	5.250–9.000	5.250–8.000
4 California Federal S&L Ass'n, Los Angeles	4,328,705	3,858,817	4	5.250–9.000	5.250–8.000
5 Glendale Federal S&L Ass'n, Calif.	3,118,796	2,827,419	5	5.250–9.000	5.250–8.000
6 Gibraltar S&L Ass'n, Beverly Hills, Calif.	3,012,560	2,474,850	6	5.250–9,000	5.250–8.000
7 First Federal S&L Ass'n, Detroit	2,695,942	2,416,088	7	5.250–9.000	5.250–8.000
8 Imperial S&L Ass'n, San Francisco	2,544,542	2,415,336	8	5.250–9.000	5.250–8.000
9 Home Federal S&L Ass'n, San Diego, Calif.	2,502,777	2,183,959	9	5.250–9.000	5.250–8.000
10 Standard Federal S&L Ass'n, Troy, Mich.	2,374,987	2,083,090	10	5.250–9.000	5.250–8.000
11 World S&L Ass'n, Oakland, Calif.	2,253,155	1,865,358	14 +3	5.250–9.000	5.250–8.000
12 Citizens S&L Ass'n, San Francisco	2,129,174	2,009,069	11	5.250–9.000	5.250–8.000
13 First, Federal S&L Ass'n, Chicago	2,113,400	1,939,161	12	5.250–9.000	5.250–8.000
14 Allstate S&L Ass'n, Los Angeles	2,075,236	1,899,546	13	5.250–9.000	5.250–8.000
15 First Federal S&L Ass'n, Miami, Fla.	2,043,048	1,823,276	15	5.250–9.000	5.250–8.000
16 Coast Federal S&L Ass'n, Los Angeles	1,955,174	1,739,228	16	5.250–9.000	5.250–8.000
17 Gibraltar Savings Ass'n, Houston, Tex.	1,895,917	1,654,392	18 +1	5.250–9.000	5.250–8.000
18 Talman Federal S&L Ass'n, Chicago	1,779,046	1,614,212	19 +1	5.250–9.000	5.250–8.000
19 Twin City Federal S&L Ass'n, Minneapolis, Minn.	1,773,266	1,676,427	17	5.250–9.000	5.250–8.000
20 Farm & Home Savings Ass'n, Nevada, Mo.	1,762,406	1,577,681	20	5.250–9.000	5.250–8.000
21 First Federal S&L Ass'n of Broward Cty., Ft. Lauderdale, Fla.	1,725,658	1,524,097	21	5.250–9.000	5.250–8.000
22 Fidelity S&L Ass'n, San Francisco	1,681,282	1,243,790	27 +5	5.250–9.000	5.250–8.000
23 West Side Federal S&L Ass'n, New York	1,604,173	1,411,128	22	5.250–9.000	5.250–8.000

Continued

Rank 6/30/79	Total Deposits ($ millions)		Rank 6/30/78	Gain	Interest Rate[1]%	12/31/78
	6/30/79	6/30/78				
24 San Diego Federal S&L Ass'n, Calif.	1,522,905	1,260,905	25	+1	5.250–9.000	5.250–8.000
25 Bell Federal S&L Ass'n, Chicago	1,507,026	1,296,388	23		5,250–9,000	5.250–8.000
26 Dade Federal S&L Ass'n Miami, Fla.	1,449,482	1,270,412	24		5.250–9.000	5.250–8.000
27 Northern California S&L Ass'n, Palo Alto	1,408,556	1,234,037	28	+1	5.250–9.000	5.250–8.000
28 American S&L Ass'n of Florida, Miami Beach	1,328,001	1,066,954	37	+9	5.250–9.000	5.250–8.000
29 Florida Federal S&L Ass'n, St. Petersburg	1,325,530	1,245,613	26		5.250–9.000	5.250–8.000
30 Community Federal S&L Ass'n, St. Louis, Mo.	1,325,063	1,189,701	29		5.250–9.000	5.250–8.000
31 City Federal S&L Ass'n, Elizabeth, N.J.	1,321,461	1,141,984	32	+1	5.250–9.000	5.250–8.000
32 Western S&L Ass'n, Phoenix, Ariz.	1,281,538	1,125,897	33	+1	5.250–9.000	5.250–8.000
33 Santa Barbara S&L Ass'n, Cal.	1,275,843	1,117,155	34	+1	5.250–8.000	5.250–8.000
34 First Texas Savings Ass'n, Dallas	1,274,578	504,607	126	+92	5.250–9.000	5.250–8.000
35 Georgia Federal S&L Ass'n, Atlanta	1,232,395	1,157,575	31		5.250–9.000	5.250–8.000
36 Pacific First Federal S&L Ass'n, Tacoma, Wash.	1,224,143	1,177,296	30		5.250–8.000	5.250–8.000
37 Broadview S&L Co., Cleveland, Ohio	1,212,905	1,107,110	35		5.250–9.000	5.250–8.000
38 Midwest Federal S&L Ass'n, Minneapolis, Minn.	1,182,166	1,102,015	36		5.250–9.000	5.250–8.000
39 Fidelity Federal S&L Ass'n, Glendale, Calif.	1,112,535	712,018	70	+31	5.250–9.000	5.250–8.000
40 St. Paul Federal S&L Ass'n, Chicago	1,109,259	952,853	41	+1	5.250–9.000	5.250–7.750
41 Astoria Federal S&L Ass'n, Queens, N.Y.	1,096,979	932,357	43	+2	5.250–9.000	5.250–8.000
42 County Federal S&L Ass'n Rockville Centre, N.Y.	1,094,707	1,006,644	38		5.250–9.000	5.250–7.750
43 Coral Gables Federal S&L Ass'n, Fla.	1,094,355	952,748	42		5.250–9.000	5.250–8.000
44 Capitol Federal S&L Ass'n, Topeka, Kan.	1,076,879	993,772	39		5.250–9.000	5.250–8.000
45 Freedom Federal S&L Ass'n, Tampa, Fla.	1,046,519	894,162	45		5.250–7.750	5.250–7.750
46 Dallas Federal S&L Ass'n, Tex.	1,042,677	959,074	40		N.A.	5.250–8.000
47 Chase Federal S&L Ass'n, Miami, Fla.	1,040,517	867,781	49	+2	5.250–9.000	5.250–8.000

Rank 6/30/79	Total Deposits ($ millions)		Rank 6/30/78	Gain	Interest Rate[1]%	12/31/78
	6/30/79	6/30/78				
48 First Federal S&L Ass'n Phoenix, Ariz.	1,005,245	887,513	46		5.250–9.000	5,000–8.000
49 Guarantee S&L Ass'n, Fresno, Calif.	989,819	855,643	53	+4	5.250–9.000	5.250–8.000
50 Biscayne Federal S&L Ass'n, Miami, Fla.	979,236	698,970	71	+21	5.250–9.000	5.250–8.000
51 Equitable S&L Ass'n, Portland, Ore.	976,769	896,735	44		5,250–9,000	N.A.
52 Atlantic Federal S&L Ass'n, Ft. Lauderdale, Fla.	967,832	882,173	48		5.250–9.000	5.250–8.000
53 Cardinal Federal S&L Ass'n Cleveland, Ohio	952,144	852,036	54	+1	5.250–9.000	5.250–8.000
54 Western Federal S&L Ass'n, Denver, Colo.	951,802	867,218	50		5.250–9.000	5.250–8.000
55 Financial Federal S&L Ass'n, Miami Beach, Fla.	945,179	810,207	58	+3	5.250–9.000	5.250–8.000
56 Loyola Federal S&L Ass'n, Baltimore, Md.	939,185	858,691	52		5.250–9.000	5.250–8.000
57 Hollywood Federal S&L Ass'n, Fla.	937,198	866,087	51		5.250–9.000	N.A.
58 Commercial Federal S&L Ass'n, Omaha, Neb.	918,528	807,952	60	+2	5.250–9.000	5.250–8.000
59 United Savings Ass'n, Houston Tex.	914,041	774,698	63	+4	5.250–9.000	5.250–8.000
60 First Rederal S&L Ass'n, Rochester, N.Y.	892,925	886,630	47		5.000–9.000	5.250–6.750
61 Minnesota Federal S&L Ass'n, St. Paul	891,933	840,434	55		5.250–9.000	5.250–8.000
62 Suffolk County Federal S&L Ass'n, Centereach, N.Y.	885,789	811,752	57		5.,000–9.000	5.250–8.000
63 Fulton Federal S&L Ass'n, Atlanta, Ga.	872,358	809,604	59		4.000–9.000	5.250–8.000
64 Downey S&L Ass'n, Santa Ana, Calif.	868,841	745,474	65	+1	5.250–8.000	5.250–8.000
65 North West Federal S&L Ass'n, Chicago	856,674	726,313	67	+2	5.250–9.000	5.250–8.000
66 Decatur Federal S&L Ass'n, Ga.	829,314	752,424	64		5,250–9,000	N.A.
67 American S&L Ass'n, Salt Lake City, Utah	824,212	650,208	82	+15	5.250–9.000	5.250–8.000
68 First Savings Ass'n, of Wisconsin, Milwaukee	823,269	805,932	62		5.250–9.000	5.250–8.000
69 Perpetual Federal S&L Ass'n, Washington, D.C.	822,716	806,043	61		5.250–9.000	5.250–7.750
70 Benjamin Franklin Federal S&L Ass'n, Portland, Ore.	821,110	813,196	56		5.250–8.000	N.A.
71 Washington Federal, S&L Ass'n, Miami Beach Fla.	813,162	717,745	68		5.250–9.000	5.250–8.000

Continued

Rank 6/30/79	Total Deposits ($ millions)		Rank 6/30/78	Gain	Interest Rate¹ %	
	6/30/79	6/30/78				12/31/78
72 Carteret S&L Ass'n, Newark, N.J.	793,499	675,105	77	+5	5.250–9.000	5.250–8.000
73 United First Federal S&L Ass'n, Sarasota, Fla.	789,476	689,634	74	+1	5.250–9.000	5.250–8.000
74 Central Federal S&L Ass'n, San Diego, Calif.	787,808	677,653	76	+2	5,520–9,000	5.250–8.000
75 Honolulu Federal S&L Ass'n, Hawaii	779,941	647,014	83	+8	5.250–9.000	5.250–8.000
76 Gem City Savings Ass'n, Dayton, Ohio	777,837	736,157	66		5.250–9.000	5.250–8.000
77 Security S&L Ass'n, Milwaukee, Wis.	777,049	610,983	91	+14	5.250–9.000	5.250–8.000
78 Far West Federal S&L Ass'n, Portland, Ore.	774,400	715,460	59		5.250–9.000	N.A.
79 Clearwater Federal S&L Ass'n, Fla.	768,955	625,243	88	+9	5.250–9.000	N.A.
80 San Francisco Federal S&L Ass'n, Calif.	763,647	692,180	73		5.250–9.000	5.250–8.000
81 Houston First Savings Ass'n, Tex.	757,980	645,612	84	+3	5.250–9.000	N.A.
82 Leader Federal S&L Ass'n, Memphis, Tenn.	757,097	694,601	72		5.250–9.000	5.250–8.000
83 First Federal S&L Ass'n, Clearwater, Fla.	753,914	638,756	85	+2	5.250–9.000	5.250–8.000
84 Home Federal S&L Ass'n, St. Petersburg, Fla.	753,427	662,551	80		5.250–9.000	5.250–8.000
85 Valley Federal S&L Ass'n, Van Nuys, Calif.	740,528	596,270	96	+11	5.250–9.000	5.250–8.000
86 Baltimore Federal S&L Ass'n, Md.	733,757	687,964	75		5.250–9.000	5.250–8.000
87 Sooner Federal S&L Ass'n, Tulsa, Okla.	727,000	666,046	79		5.250–9.000	5.250–8.000
88 Third Federal S&L Ass'n, Cleveland, Ohio	726,930	669,816	78		5.250–9.000	5.250–7.750
89 Bay View Federal S&L Ass'n, San Mateo, Calif.	724,366	652,619	81		5.250–9.000	N.A.
90 Suburban S&L Ass'n, Wayne, N.J.	716,851	586,470	99	+9	5.250–9.000	5.250–7.750
91 Detroit & Northern S&L Ass'n, Hancock, Mich.	704,778	622,872	89		5.250–9.000	5.250–8.000
92 Columbia S&L Ass'n, Denver, Colo.	703,534	625,940	87		5.250–9.000	5.250–7.750
93 Empire Savings Building & Loan Ass'n, Denver, Colo.	685,453	562,387	103	+10	5.250–9.000	5.250–8.000
94 Cleveland Federal S&L Ass'n of Cuyahoga County, Ohio	684,519	604,237	93		5.250–9.000	5.250–8.000
95 Buckeye Federal S&L Ass'n, Columbus, Ohio	681,609	619,325	90		5.250–9.000	5.250–8.000

Continued

Rank 6/30/79	Total Deposits ($ millions)		Rank 6/30/78	Gain	Interest Rate[1] %	
	6/30/79	6/30/78				12/31/78
96 Franklin Society Federal S&L Ass'n, New York	678,979	610,596	92		5.000–9.000	5.250–8.000
97 State S&L Ass'n, Stockton, Calif.	674,235	528,340	121	+24	5.250–9.000	5.250–8.000
98 Home Federal S&L Ass'n, Chicago	666,059	629,518	86		5.250–9.00	5.250–8.000
99 San Antonio Savings Ass'n, Tex.	665,065	598,879	95		5.250–9.000	5.250–8.000
100 First Federal S&L Ass'n, Lincoln, Neb.	659,464	549,372	110	+10	5.000–9.000	5.250–8.000

N.A., not available.

[1] Range of interest rates is for all new accounts under $100,000, including interest-bearing NOW accounts and six-month money market certificates. In the case of MMCs, the rate used is the offering rate in effect on June 30.

Source: American Banker. Used with permission of the publisher.

Population per Savings and Loan Office by State

States	May 31, 1970	September 30, 1979	Net Change 1970–1979
Alabama	32,800	15,704	−17,096
Alaska	43,286	21,368	−21,918
Arizona	22,756	11,611	−11,145
Arkansas	24,342	11,122	−13,220
California	23,690	8,776	−14,914
Colorado	16,370	8,717	−7,653
Connecticut	37,900	18,006	−19,894
Delware	60,889	36,375	−24,514
District of Columbia	12,410	6,495	−5,915
Florida	22,048	7,792	−14,256
Georgia	25,631	13,054	−12,577
Hawaii	12,622	6,583	−6,039
Idaho	23,767	15,339	−8,428
Illinois	23,194	11,096	−12,098
Indiana	21,118	15,042	−6,076
Iowa	27,163	10,147	−17,016
Kansas	15,510	9,591	−5,919
Kentucky	23,341	13,359	−10,082
Louisiana	25,313	13,174	−12,139
Maine	33,133	24,932	−8,201
Maryland	22,947	12,164	−10,783
Massachusetts	49,470	44,721	−4,749
Michigan	35,246	16,353	−18,893
Minnesota	33,096	14,764	−18,332
Mississippi	43,471	12,145	−31,326
Missouri	20,077	10,650	−9,427
Montana	36,526	15,115	−21,411
Nebraska	22,500	7,531	−14,969
Nevada	19,560	9,360	−10,200
New Hampshire	38,684	28,613	−10,071
New Jersey	16,372	9,448	−6,924
New Mexico	22,109	12,663	−9,446
New York	44,708	27,361	−17,347
North Carolina	18,093	13,876	−4,217
North Dakota	26,870	8,111	−18,759
Ohio	13,822	8,746	−5,076
Oklahoma	31,593	15,632	−15,961
Oregon	19,551	7,897	−11,654
Pennsylvania	18,439	12,480	−5,959
Puerto Rico			
Rhode Island	39,583	30,967	−8,616
South Carolina	21,238	12,530	−8,708
South Dakota	41,625	15,311	−26,314

Continued

States	May 31, 1970	September 30, 1979	Net Change 1970–1979
Tennessee	35,054	16,404	−18,650
Texas	22,855	9,591	−13,264
Utah	32,094	14,389	−17,705
Vermont	55,625	41,083	−14,542
Virginia	29,437	11,811	−17,626
Washington	20,811	11,090	−9,721
West Virginia	56,258	26,083	−30,175
Wisconsin	25,686	9,916	−15,770
Wyoming	20,750	10,976	−9,774
United States	24,011	11,849	−12,162

Source: Federal Home Loan Bank Board and Bureau of the Census.

Appendix F: Bank Holding Companies

	Banks	Offices	Domestic Deposits (in millions)	Total Deposits (in millions)	Assets (in millions)
Alabama					
Alabama Bancorporation					
Birmingham	17	97	$ 2,108	$ 2,108	$ 2,671
Central Bancshares of the South, Inc.					
Birmingham	12	80	1,435	1,435	1,759
First Alabama Bancshares, Inc.					
Montgomery	17	93	1,515	1,515	1,829
First Bancgroup-Alabama, Inc.					
Mobile	6	39	656	656	752
Southern Bancorporation of Alabama					
Birmingham	14	82	1,473	1,473	1,847
Arizona					
Patagonia Corporation					
Tucson	1	1	426	426	556
Arkansas					
First Arkansas Bankstock Corporation					
Little Rock	4	28	613	613	819
California					
BankAmerica Corporation					
San Francisco	1	1,096	43,021	84,985	108,389
Central Banking System, Inc.					
Oakland	2	60	682	682	786
Crocker National Corporation					
San Francisco	1	368	9,975	12,517	16,139
Independent Bankshares Corporation					
San Rafael	5	31	435	435	484
Security Pacific Corporation					
Los Angeles	1	575	14,052	18,457	24,923
Wells Fargo & Company					
San Francisco	1	373	13,508	16,131	20,593
Western Bancorporation					
Los Angeles	21	842	21,600	23,631	29,687
Colorado					
Affilitated Bankshares of Colorado, Inc.					
Boulder	18	18	1,139	1,139	1,343
Colorado National Bankshares, Inc.					
Denver	12	12	926	926	1,183
The First National Bancorporation, Inc.					
Denver	12	12	1,920	1,920	2,499
United Banks of Colorado, Inc.					
Denver	19	19	1,320	1,329	2,371
Connecticut					
CBT Corporation					
Hartford	2	84	1,958	2,103	2,764
Colonial Bancorp, Inc.					
Waterbury	1	65	931	958	1,260

Continued

	Banks	Offices	Domestic Deposits (in millions)	Total Deposits (in millions)	Assets (in millions)
First Connecticut Bancorp, Inc. Hartford	3	33	$ 404	$ 404	503
FirstBancorp, Inc. New Haven	3	45	570	572	665
Hartford National Corporation Hartford	1	64	1,818	2,092	2,591
Northeast Bancorp, Inc. New Haven	2	55	1,006	1,009	1,172
Florida					
American Bancshares, Incorporated North Miami	8	11	289	189	336
Atlantic Bancorporation Jacksonville	16	62	1,511	1,511	1,806
Barnett Banks of Florida, Inc. Jacksonville	30	116	3,102	3,102	3,663
City National Bank Corporation Miami	1	4	373	373	418
Exchange Bancorporation, Inc. Tampa	10	25	829	829	1,019
Flagship Banks, Inc. Miami Beach	23	62	1,555	1,555	1,847
Florida Commercial Banks, Inc. Miami	7	15	479	479	534
Gulfstream Banks, Inc. Boca Raton	3	12	432	432	503
Landmark Banking Corporation of Florida Fort Lauderdale	5	28	985	985	1,285
National Banking Corporation of Florida, Inc. Miami	1	3	78	78	93
Pan American Bancshares, Inc. Miami	6	24	635	635	768
Southeast Banking Corporation Miami	25	71	3,715	3,828	5,028
Sun Banks of Florida, Inc. Orlando	20	104	2,553	2,553	2,872
Georgia					
The Citizens & Southern National Bank Citizens & Southern Holding Company Savannah	9	127	2,999	3,240	4,060
First Atlanta Corporation Atlanta	3	71	1,968	2,079	3,000
Illinois					
Continental Illinois Corporation Chicago	1	1	12,519	23,751	35,790
First Chicago Corporation Chicago	1	1	9,033	21,170	30,181

Continued

	Banks	Offices	Domestic Deposits (in millions)	Total Deposits (in millions)	Assets (in millions)
Indiana					
American Fletcher Corporation Indianapolis	1	60	$ 1,665	$ 1,803	$ 2,730
Indiana National Corporation Indianapolis	1	54	1,501	1,502	2,130
Money Management Corporation Merrillville	1	12	252	252	296
Iowa					
Banks of Iowa, Inc. Cedar Rapids	8	23	1,009	1,009	1,222
Brenton Banks, Inc. Des Moines	17	41	577	577	646
Hawkeye Bancorporation Des Moines	22	54	788	788	929
Kentucky					
First Kentucky National Corporation Louisville	2	52	1,438	1,520	2,089
Louisiana					
Hibernia Corporation New Orleans	1	15	737	782	968
Maine					
Canal Corporation Portland	2	33	198	198	245
Depositors Corporation Augusta	4	59	424	424	505
Maryland					
Equitable Bancorporation Baltimore	3	123	1,762	1,762	2,039
First Maryland Bancorp Baltimore	1	103	1,349	1,563	2,088
Maryland National Corporation Baltimore	1	149	2,517	2,709	3,732
Mercantile Bankshares Corporation Baltimore	9	65	882	882	1,098
Suburban Bancorporation Hyattsville	3	72	1,233	1,233	1,404
Union Trust Bancorp Baltimore	1	82	911	911	1,299
Massachusetts					
BayBanks, Inc. Boston	11	184	2,438	2,438	2,849
First National Boston Corporation Boston	7	76	4,241	8,968	13,760
Multibank Financial Corp. Quincy	8	83	855	855	993
New England Merchants Company, Inc. Boston	3	29	1,620	1,906	2,451

Continued

	Banks	Offices	Domestic Deposits (in millions)	Total Deposits (in millions)	Assets (in millions)
Shawmut Corporation Boston	8	113	$ 2,156	$ 2,238	$ 3,142
State Street Boston Corporation Boston	3	35	1,597	1,635	2,598
Michigan					
American National Holding Company Kalamazoo	7	36	344	344	410
DETROITBANK Corporation Detroit	8	123	3,474	3,527	5,067
Michigan National Corporation Bloomfield Hills	24	312	4,545	4,545	5,399
National Detroit Corporation Detroit	9	150	5,777	6,896	9,506
Northern States Bancorporation, Inc. Detroit	7	62	1,154	1,208	1,584
Minnesota					
First Bank System, Inc. Minneapolis	91	117	8,632	8,983	12,118
Mid America Bancorporation, Inc. Excelsior	7	7	168	168	188
Northwest Bancorporation Minneapolis	85	142	8,931	9,573	12,416
Missouri					
Boatmen's Bancshares, Inc. St. Louis	14	30	1,388	1,388	1,879
Commerce Bancshares, Inc. Kansas City	36	71	2,143	2,143	2,653
First National Charter Corporation Kansas City	21	40	1,377	1,377	1,918
First Union Bancorporation St. Louis	18	47	2,450	2,652	3,898
General Bancshares Corporation St. Louis	12	32	1,011	1,011	1,172
Mark Twain Bancshares, Inc. St. Louis	6	11	395	395	472
Mercantile Bancorporation Inc. St. Louis	29	54	2,668	2,941	4,327
United Missouri Bancshares, Inc. Kansas City	20	44	1,279	1,279	1,755
Nebraska					
Commerce Group, Inc. Lincoln	1	1	302	302	449
Omaha National Corporation Omaha	1	3	600	600	904
New Hampshire					
First Bancorp of N.H., Inc. Manchester	6	20	299	299	368

Continued

	Banks	Offices	Domestic Deposits (in millions)	Total Deposits (in millions)	Assets (in millions)
First Financial Group of New Hampshire, Inc.					
Manchester	2	7	$ 169	$ 169	$ 205
Indian Head Banks Inc.					
Nashua	8	35	401	401	474
New Jersey					
Bancshares of New Jersey					
Moorestown	3	51	895	895	1,020
First National State Bancorporation					
Newark	6	102	2,258	2,419	3,110
Heritage Bancorporation					
Cherry Hill	2	81	1,177	1,177	1,369
Horizon Bancorp					
Morristown	3	51	708	712	923
Midlantic Banks Inc.					
West Orange	6	114	2,230	2,280	2,280
New Jersey National Corporation					
Trenton	1	47	877	922	1,257
United Jersey Banks					
Princeton	9	115	1,944	1,946	2,525
New Mexico					
Bank Securities, Inc.					
Alamogordo	8	31	360	360	417
New York					
The Bank of New York Company, Inc.					
New York	1	150	4,703	6,870	8,994
Bankers Trust New York Corporation					
New York	6	206	11,664	22,437	30,953
The Chase Manhattan Corporation					
New York	1	217	22,386	49,355	64,708
Chemical New York Corporation					
New York	1	265	16,436	29,023	39,375
Citicorp					
New York	2	351	17,515	70,290	106,370
Irving Bank Corporation					
New York	15	137	8,439	13,525	16,702
Key Banks Inc.					
Albany	6	130	1,629	1,629	1,957
Lincoln First Banks Inc.					
Rochester	1	139	2,399	2,406	3,180
LITCO Bancorporation of New York, Inc.					
Garden City	2	47	866	866	1,092
Manufacturers Hanover Corporation					
New York	4	236	20,747	38,156	47,675
Marine Midland Banks, Inc.					
Buffalo	1	294	7,670	12,537	15,728
Security New York State Corporation					
Rochester	8	68	1,025	1,025	1,256
Sterling Bancorp					
New York	1	8	378	388	552

Continued

613

	Banks	Offices	Domestic Deposits (in millions)	Total Deposits (in millions)	Assets (in millions)
United Bank Corporation of New York Albany	4	120	$ 1,637	$ 1,637	$ 2,007
North Carolina					
First Union Corporation Charlotte	1	177	2,025	2,204	3,121
NCNB Corporation Charlotte	1	172	3,518	4,497	6,365
Northwestern Financial Corporation North Wilkesboro	1	178	1,410	1,410	1,699
United Carolina Bancshares Corporation Whiteville	2	83	584	584	665
The Wachovia Corporation Winston-Salem	1	187	3,405	3,825	5,096
Ohio					
Baldwin-United Corporation Cincinnati	12	12	993	993	2,071
BANC ONE CORPORATION Columbus	19	114	2,045	2,121	2,524
BancOhio Corporation Columbus	2	240	3,805	3,805	5,005
Huntington Bancshares Incorporated Columbus	1	101	1,879	1,942	2,553
Society Corporation Cleveland	13	119	2,359	2,378	3,019
Winters National Corporation Dayton	2	51	979	994	1,227
Pennsylvania					
Equimark Corporation Pittsburgh	1	89	1,869	2,053	2,661
Fidelcor, Inc. Rosemont	1	73	1,744	2,163	2,837
First Pennsylvania Corporation Philadelphia	1	68	3,319	5,296	8,987
Mellon National Corporation Pittsburgh	1	107	6,871	9,820	13,508
Pittsburgh National Corporation Pittsburgh	1	108	3,783	3,914	5,563
Rhode Island					
Industrial National Corporation Providence	1	46	1,739	2,119	3,225
South Carolina					
The Citizens & Southern Corporation Columbia	1	85	750	750	962
South Dakota					
Dacotah Bank Holding Co. Aberdeen	5	11	141	141	152

Continued

	Banks	Offices	Domestic Deposits (in millions)	Total Deposits (in millions)	Assets (in millions)
Tennessee					
First Amtenn Corporation					
Nashville	8	59	$ 1,492	$ 1,501	$ 1,832
First Tennessee National Corporation					
Memphis	13	105	2,139	2,139	2,700
Memphis Trust Company					
Memphis	1	13	220	220	268
National Commerce Bancorporation					
Memphis	1	21	567	567	701
Tennessee National Bancshares, Inc.					
Maryville	4	16	128	128	144
Tennessee Valley Bancorp, Inc.					
Nashville	12	70	1,498	1,608	1,999
Third National Corporation					
Nashville	8	60	1,400	1,500	1,823
Texas					
Allied Bancshares, Inc.					
Houston	20	20	1,896	1,896	2,260
Cullen/Frost Bankers, Inc.					
San Antonio	7	7	1,503	1,503	1,868
First Bancorp, Inc.					
Corsicana	10	10	271	271	310
First City Bancorporation of Texas, Inc.					
Houston	40	40	6,680	7,597	9,505
First International Bancshares, Inc.					
Dallas	32	32	6,411	8,921	11,504
First United Bancorporation, Inc.					
Fort Worth	9	9	1,419	1,437	1,757
Republic of Texas Corporation					
Dallas	19	19	5,201	7,647	10,798
Texas American Bancshares Inc.					
Fort Worth	12	12	2,254	2,254	2,929
United States National Bancshares, Inc.					
Galveston	2	2	153	153	170
Utah					
First Security Corporation					
Salt Lake City	13	153	2,583	2,583	3,426
Virginia					
Bank of Virginia Company					
Richmond	5	133	1,590	1,612	2,318
Central Fidelity Banks, Inc.					
Richmond	6	133	1,427	1,427	1,752
Dominion Bankshares Corporation					
Roanoke	10	115	1,634	1,634	2,013
First & Merchants Corporation					
Richmond	1	98	1,642	1,734	2,297
First Virginia Banks, Inc.					
Falls Church	20	166	1,296	1,296	1,458
Jefferson Bankshares, Inc.					
Charlottesville	5	59	560	560	640

Continued

	Banks	Offices	Domestic Deposits (in millions)	Total Deposits (in millions)	Assets (in millions)
United Virginia Bankshares Incorporated Richmond	1	160	$ 2,462	$ 2,496	$ 3,216
Valley of Virginia Bankshares, Inc. Harrisonburg	5	24	249	249	311
Virginia National Bankshares, Inc. Norfolk	1	154	2,076	2,079	2,521
Washington					
Old National Bancorporation Spokane	2	81	1,027	1,027	1,277
Rainier Bancorporation Seattle	1	123	2,923	3,460	4,496
Seafirst Corporation Seattle	1	171	6,100	6,700	8,400
Wisconsin					
Affiliated Bank Corporation Madison	5	5	271	271	314
Associated Banc-Corp. Green Bay	6	12	413	413	533
Central Wisconsin Bankshares, Inc. Wausau	6	9	255	255	316
Citizens Bancorporation Sheboygan	6	13	366	366	440
First Holding Company, Inc. Waukesha	6	11	315	315	372
First National Corporation Appleton	9	12	347	347	415
First Wisconsin Corporation Milwaukee	19	44	3,217	3,673	5,107
Heritage Wisconsin Corporation Milwaukee	7	18	371	371	488
M & S Bancorp Janesville	3	4	115	115	160
The Marine Corporation Milwaukee	17	30	1,345	1,381	1,716
Marshall & Ilsley Corporation Milwaukee	20	32	1,403	1,432	2,013
Security Financial Services, Inc. Sheboygan	3	3	196	196	237
United Banks of Wisconsin, Inc. Madison	4	6	150	150	171
United Bankshares, Inc. Green Bay	3	6	161	161	191
Valley Bancorporation Appleton	17	27	507	507	597
Wyoming					
Wyoming Bancorporation Cheyenne	18	18	432	432	504
Totals	1,450	15,066	$484,029	$719,009	$960,680

Source: Association of Bank Holding Companies.

The Top 25 U.S. Bank Holding Companies

Rank 1980	Rank 1979	Bank Holding Company	Total Assets December 31, 1980	Percent Change from 1979
1	2	Citicorp	$114,900,000,000	+ 8
2	1	BankAmerica	111,600,000,000	+ 3
3	3	Chase Manhattan	75,300,000,000	+18
4	4	Manufacturers Hanover	55,100,000,000	+16
5	5	J.P. Morgan & Company	52,000,000,000	+20
6	7	Continental Illinois	42,100,000,000	+18
7	6	Chemical New York	41,300,000,000	+ 5
8	8	Bankers Trust New York	34,200,000,000	+10
9	10	Western Bancorp.	32,100,000,000	+ 8
10	9	First Chicago	28,700,000,000	− 5
11	11	Security Pacific	28,000,000,000	+13
12	12	Wells Fargo	23,600,000,000	+15
13	14	Crocker National	19,100,000,000	+19
14	13	Irving Trust	18,100,000,000	+10
15	15	Marine Midland Banks	17,500,000,000	+12
16	17	Mellon National	16,200,000,000	+19
17	16	First National Boston	15,900,000,000	+15
18	18	Northwest Bancorp.	14,400,000,000	+16
19	20	First International Bancshares, Dallas	13,800,000,000	+20
20	19	First Bank Systems, Minneapolis	13,500,000,000	+12
21	21	Republic of Texas	11,900,000,000	+ 9
22	24	Texas Commerce Bancshares	11,300,000,000	+22
23	22	First City Bancorp., Houston	11,300,000,000	+19
24	23	National Detroit	10,900,000,000	+15
25	26	Bank of New York	10,400,000,000	+16

Source: The New York Times, January 26, 1981.

Offices and Deposits of Banks Affiliated with Bank Holding Companies by Year

	1956	1970	1971	1975	1977	1978	1979[1]
Number of companies	53	121	1,567	1,821	2,027	2,222	2,432
Banks	428	895	2,420	3,674	3,903	4,101	4,390
Branches	783	3,260	10,832	18,382	20,340	21,513	22,770
Total offices	1,211	4,155	13,252	22,056	24,243	25,614	27,160
Offices as a percentage of all bank offices	5.7	11.8	36.1	49.4	50.9	51.8	52.7
Domestic deposits ($ billions)	14.8	78.0	297.0	527.5	624.3	691.0	725.0
Domestic deposits as a percentage of all bank deposits	7.5	16.2	55.1	67.1	66.5	66.8	67.1

[1]Estimated.
Source: Association of Bank Holding Companies.

Ratings of Bank Holding Company Debt

	Ratings		
	Moody's	S&P's	PW
BankAmerica Corporation	Aaa	AAA	94
Bankers Trust New York Corporation	Aa	NR	70
Boatmans Bancshares, Inc.	A	A	NR
Centran Corporation	A	NR	NR
Charter New York Corporation	Aa	NR	74
Chase Manhattan Corporation	Aaa	NR	79
Chemical New York Corporation	Aaa	NR	77
Citicorp	Aaa	AAA	89
Continental Illinois Corporation	Aaa	AAA	87
Crocker National Corporation	Aa	NR	77
Dominion Bankshares	A	A+	NR
First Banc Group of Ohio	Aa	NR	NR
First Bank System	Aaa	AAA	90
First Chicago Corporation	Aaa	AAA	82
First International Bancshares, Inc.	Aa	AAA	89
First Maryland Bancorp	A	A+	NR
First National Boston Corporation	Aaa	AAA	89
First National State Bancorporation	A	A-	NR
First Security Corporation	Aa	NR	NR
First United Bancorporation	A	A	NR
Girard Company	A	A-	70
Harris Bankcorp, Inc.	Aaa	AAA	87
Industrial National Corporation	A	A	NR
Manufacturers Hanover Corporation	Aaa	AAA	86
Maryland National Corporation	A	A+	NR
Mellon National Corporation	Aaa	AAA	93
Mercantile Bancorporation	Aa	NR	NR
Midlantic Banks, Inc.	A	A-	NR
J.P. Morgan & Company, Inc.	Aaa	AAA	95
New England Merchants Company, Inc.	A	NR	NR
Northwest Bancorporation	Aaa	AAA	90
Ranier Bancorporation	A	NR	NR
Republic New York Corporation	A	AA	78
Republic of Texas Corporation	A	AA	79
Seafirst Corporation	Aa	AA	85
Security Pacific Corporation	Aa	AA	83
Shawmut Corporation	A	NR	NR
Southeast Banking Corporation	Baa	BBB+	NR
Southwest Bancshares, Inc.	A	A+	NR
State Street Boston, Inc.	Baa	BBB	NR
Sun Banks of Florida, Inc.	A	NR	NR
Texas Commerce Bancshares, Inc.	Aa	AAA	89
United Bank Corporation of New York	Aa	AA	NR
U.S. Bancorp	Aa	AA+	88
Virginia National Bankshares, Inc.	A	A	NR
Wells Fargo & Company	Aa	AA	83
Western Bancorporation	NR	AA	84

Note: PW ratings provided by Paine, Webber, Jackson & Curtis, Inc.
Source: American Banker. Used with permission of the publisher.

Appendix G: Finance Companies

Credit Provided by Finance Companies to Business
(millions of dollars, end of period)

Period	Retail Automotive (Commercial Vehicles)	Wholesale Automotive	Retail Paper on Business, Industrial, and Farm Equipment	Loans on Commercial Accounts Receivable	Factored Commercial Accounts Receivable	All Other Business Credit	Total
				Accounts Receivable Outstanding			
1973	5,429	6,387	8,458	2,891	1,961	7,198	32,324
1974	6,387	7,876	9,567	3,301	1,768	8,234	37,133
1975	7,099	7,412	10,890	3,539	1,876	8,483	39,299
1976	8,951	8,733	12,291	3,795	2,033	8,916	44,719
1977	11,985	11,966	14,441	3,901	2,253	10,507	55,053
1978	14,562	12,744	16,759	4,294	2,536	12,453	63,348

Source: Federal Reserve Bulletin and Annual Statistical Digest.

Balance Sheet of Finance Companies
(billions of dollars, end of period)

Account	1973	1974	1975	1976	1977	1978
Assets						
Accounts receivable, gross						
Consumer	34.5	36.1	36.0	38.6	44.0	52.6
Business	32.3	37.2	39.3	44.7	55.2	63.3
Total	67.7	73.3	75.3	83.4	99.2	116.0
Less: Reserves for unearned income and losses	8.4	9.0	9.4	10.5	12.7	15.6
Accounts receivable, net	59.3	64.2	65.9	72.9	86.5	100.4
Cash and bank deposits	2.6	3.0	2.9	2.6	2.6	3.5
Securities	0.8	0.4	1.0	1.1	0.9	1.3
All other	10.6	12.0	11.8	12.6	14.3	17.3
Total assets	73.2	79.6	81.6	89.2	104.3	122.4
Liabilities						
Bank loans	7.2	9.7	8.0	6.3	5.9	6.5
Commercial paper	19.7	20.7	22.2	23.7	29.6	34.5
Debt						
Short-term, n.e.c.	4.6	4.9	4.5	5.4	6.2	8.1
Long-term, n.e.c.	24.6	26.5	27.6	32.3	36.0	43.6
Other	5.6	5.5	6.8	8.1	11.5	12.6
Capital, surplus, and undivided profits	11.5	12.4	12.5	13.4	15.1	17.2
Total liabilities and capital	73.2	79.6	81.6	89.2	104.3	122.4

Source: Federal Reserve Bulletin and Annual Statistical Digest.

Nonbank Financial Companies—Sales and Profits, 1980

Company	Sales 4th quarter, 1980 ($ mil.)	Sales Change from: 1979 (%)	Sales 12 months, 1980 ($ mil.)	Sales Change from: 1979 (%)	Profits 4th quarter, 1980, ($ mil.)	Profits Change from 1979 (%)	Profits 12 months, 1980 ($ mil.)	Profits Change from 1979 (%)	MARGINS 4th quarter, 1980 %	MARGINS 4th quarter, 1979 (%)	Return on common equity, 12 months ending 12/31	Price-earnings ratio 2/20	12 months' earnings per share
Aetna Life & Casualty	3287.2	15	13317.9	16	133.8	-3	508.3	-9	4.1	4.8	16.9	5	6.30
American Express	1451.0	17	5504.0	18	92.4	12	376.0	9	6.4	6.7	21.9	8	5.27
American General	616.1	25	2291.7	22	52.1	12	167.4	1	8.4	9.5	15.8	6	6.56
Bache Group	176.2	36	674.5	50	12.2	245	35.7	211	6.9	2.7	24.0	6	3.49
Beneficial	337.3	24	1323.2	35	27.0	97	94.0	-7	8.0	5.1	9.3	6	3.45
CNA Financial	768.4	6	2966.4	11	31.0	-44	140.5	-22	4.0	7.6	17.1	5	2.71
Chubb—	335.9	2	1291.9	8	28.3	-4	105.4	8	8.4	8.9	18.1	5	8.53
Connecticut General Insurance	1419.9	7	5279.4	4	104.6	15	316.7	17	7.4	6.8	16.1	6	7.66
Continental Corp.	891.6	8	3419.0	5	26.4	-66	192.5	-33	3.0	9.4	9.6	6	3.74
Crum & Forster	516.0	12	1931.8	11	29.0	10	141.6	0	5.6	5.7	18.8	5	5.04
Donaldson, Lufkin & Jenrette	149.1	50	485.1	47	2.7	151	8.7	133	1.8	1.1	14.1	8	0.97
Federal National Mortgage Assn.	1319.7	18	5072.0	21	0.7	-98	14.2	-91	0.1	3.3	1.0	44	0.24
Gulf United	178.5	12	674.5	27	20.5	-1	78.5	21	11.5	13.1	16.5	7	2.76
Hall (Frenk B.)	88.1	26	309.6	16	5.0	-9	28.0	1	5.7	7.9	22.1	9	2.74
Heller (Walter E.) International	198.6	11	747.9	22	11.4	2	43.0	7	5.8	6.2	13.6	6	3.61
Hutton (E.F.) Group	313.0	42	1125.0	50	23.3	110	82.6	122	7.4	5.0	41.5	4	6.16
INA	1387.5	15	5254.6	15	71.8	12	278.6	14	5.2	5.3	17.2	5	7.11
James (Fred S.)	54.6	19	205.1	16	4.3	-19	20.7	-4	7.9	11.7	32.1	10	2.33
Kemper	359.7	8	1459.7	17	21.0	-11	83.1	0	5.8	7.1	17.2	5	6.57
Lincoln National	705.4	10	2692.9	10	39.5	3	156.6	-2	5.6	6.0	12.8	5	7.22

Marsh & McLennan	185.2	40	677.3	28	23.0	38	100.7	22	12.4	12.6	24.6	10	3.12
Merrill Lynch	853.4	44	3022.5	47	52.3	76	203.3	71	6.1	5.0	24.0	5	5.51
NLT	178.8	-5	748.2	1	35.1	-2	132.9	0	19.6	19.0	11.0	8	3.84
Paine Webber	268.4	59	995.6	75	10.2	46	-3.7	N.M.	3.8	4.1	-7.9	N.M.	-0.85
SAFECO	337.0	9	1317.3	9	20.0	-49	107.4	-22	5.9	12.6	13.7	6	5.58
St. Paul	496.1	3	1868.3	5	43.8	9	150.9	-1	8.8	8.3	15.4	5	7.20
Shearson Loeb Rhoades	257.7	75	861.6	109	29.0	144	85.7	179	11.3	8.1	62.8	4	6.26
Transamerica	1090.2	1	4384.9	8	58.4	6	245.0	2	5.4	5.1	17.8	5	3.75
Travelers	2190.8	16	8790.0	11	97.3	-9	365.6	-6	4.4	5.7	15.1	4	8.63
U.S. Fidelity & Guaranty	573.4	0	2252.9	5	45.5	-30	228.5	0	7.9	11.3	19.3	5	8.18
U.S. Leasing International	54.1	26	197.7	29	4.5	24	15.6	5	8.4	8.5	13.6	10	2.65
Witter (Dean) Reynolds Org.	206.8	36	761.1	40	15.7	238	47.1	272	7.6	3.0	24.9	4	4.64
Industry Composite	21245.6	15	81903.6	16	1172.0	-2	4551.2	0	5.5	6.5	15.9	7	4.91

N.M., not meaningful.
Source: Standard & Poor's Compustat Services, Inc.

100 Largest Finance Companies in the United States
(thousands of dollars)

Rank 12/31/78	Total Capital Funds 12/31/78	Total Capital Funds 12/31/77	Rank, 12/31/77	Gain in Rank	Capital and Surplus, 12/31/78	Receivables Net, 12/31/78	Total Assets, 12/31/78	Net Income, 1978	Deferred Income, 12/31/78	Receivables Acquired, 1978	Bank Credit, 12/31/78
1 General Motors Acceptance Corp., New York	3,680,447	3,162,743	1		2,005,804	25,622,660	26,903,364	299,690	1,977,798	66,621,155	5,559,263
2 Ford Motor Credit Co., Dearborn, Mich.	2,297,400	2,055,300	2		1246,500	14,077,300	14,683,700	120,100	1,065,900	27,785,200	3,059,000
3 Household Finance Corp., Chicago	1,347,978	1,274,516	3		1,153,066	3,136,519	4,496,388	153,182	782,740	3,758,895	554,900
4 C.I.T. Financial Corp., New York	1,215,157	1,079,384	4		884,504	4,057,823	5,087,043	86,464	812,225	7,345,240	1,051,810
5 Sears Roebuck Acceptance Corp., Wilmington, Del.	1,118,032	1,011,731	5		993,032	5,125,100	5,128,054	106,301	N.A.	N.A.	3,276,880
6 General Electric Credit Corp., New York	1,002,144	924,763	7	+1	676,593	5,965,281	6,658,755	77,345	973,339	7,150,528	1,432,000
7 Beneficial Corp., Wilmington, Del.	986,538	935,074	6		886,538	2,741,346	3,882,650	98,300	571,211	3,328,000	489,106
8 Commercial Credit Co., Baltimore, Md.	925,546	838,026	9	+1	640,926	4,216,611	5,117,694	48,139	645,768	9,532,685	1,349,287
9 Chrysler Financial Corp., Troy, Mich.	902,202	854,597	8		648,269	3,670,493	4,577,109	48,456	239,888	9,516,100	2,173,500
10 Avco Financial Services, Inc., Newport Beach, Calif.	865,800	609,008	11	+1	599,133	2,398,262	3,839,782	84,208	397,852	2,490,513	935,104
11 Associates Corp. of North America, New York	742,106	614,101	10		422,565	2,627,205	3,051,550	36,456	509,993	4,011,443	969,800
12 Montgomery Ward Credit Corp., Wilmington, Del.	662,957	581,695	12		492,957	3,094,361	3,304,503	51,262	0	3,392,200	1,368,000

13	International Harvester Credit Corp., Chicago	624,476	546,757	13		458,476	3,217,779	55,219	272,597	4,685,923	1,424,000
14	Walter E. Heller International Corp., Chicago	527,234	510,623	14		285,388	3,471,127	34,857	56,922	15,042,715	1,219,561
15	ITT Financial Corp., St. Louis, Mo.	404,547	318,590	16	+1	256,869	1,745,401	33,012	309,422	2,489,749	427,026
16	J.C. Penney Financial Corp., Wilmington, Del.	399,409	356,378	15		374,409	2,427,123	43,031	0	4,730,232	1,061,565
17	Westinghouse Credit Corp., Pittsburgh, Pa.	329,867	272,767	17		199,867	1,656,916	21,100	125,524	1,756,826	654,300
18	John Deere Credit Co., Reno, Nev.	304,052	203,427	21	+3	209,052	1,228,405	25,625	212,192	1,468,072	576,000
19	American Express Credit Corp., Wilmington, Del.	267,711	219,480	19		166,711	1,412,928	29,231	24,847	11,159,750	703,500
20	Borg-Warner Acceptance Corp., Chicago	264,700	211,087	20		122,800	1,231,200	15,300	133,200	1,325,600	444,000
21	Transamerica Financial Corp., Los Angeles	259,820	226,276	18		170,320	1,034,485	30,044	72,461	1,031,189	94,000
22	FinanceAmerica Corp., Allentown, Pa.	216,534	161,433	25	+3	111,755	1,024,310	8,782	208,137	1,571,531	20,600
23	Allis-Chalmers Credit Corp., West Allis, Wis.	200,121	189,759	22		121,641	783,111	12,002	90,255	1,435,047	368,200
24	Clark Equipment Credit Corp., Buchanan, Mich.	184,217	139,066	32	+8	103,792	734,403	13,826	77,184	1,599,110	189,650
25	American Credit Corp., Charlotte, N.C.	182,600	167,357	23		120,131	844,510	16,631	94,275	1,985,699	232,800
26	Dial Corp., Des Moines, Iowa	169,319	148,148	28	+2	88,318	610,923	13,710	140,888	790,095	69,640
27	Fruehauf Finance Co., Detroit, Mich.	164,956	152,044	27		164,956	631,643	12,687	154,411	390,103	301,400
28	J.I. Case Credit Corp., Racine, Wis.	162,486	154,334	26		102,886	746,141	12,052	58,945	1,004,140	333,380

Continued

625

Rank 12/31/78	Total Capital Funds 12/31/78	Total Capital Funds 12/31/77	Rank, 12/31/77	Gain in Rank	Capital and Surplus, 12/31/78	Receivables Net, 12/31/78	Total Assets, 12/31/78	Net Income, 1978	Deferred Income, 12/31/78	Receivables Acquired, 1978	Bank Credit, 12/31/78
29 Allstate Financial Corp., Wilmington, Del.	160,915	108,557	42	+13	115,915	727,747	743,964	7,358	66,962	612,168	522,500
30 Sperry Rand Financial Corp., New York	154,526	143,878	30		144,026	633,317	701,688	13,492	55,775	1,561,268	546,250
31 Aetna Business Credit, Inc., East Hartford, Conn.	154,411	124,546	35	+4	80,461	544,345	637,164	9,542	5,400	1,885,815	324,500
32 Gambles Credit Corp., Reno, Nev.	152,836	119,503	39	+7	79,771	362,892	430,742	6,573	0	N.A.	132,865
33 Mack Financial Corp., Allentown, Pa.	152,016	166,917	24		80,282	711,657	751,326	11,732	74,688	1,348,065	338,068
34 Credithrift Financial, Inc., Evansville, Ind.	151,983	145,708	29		94,530	787,368	927,759	13,539	183,097	978,116	166,600
35 Honeywell Finance, Inc., Minneapolis, Minn.	148,024	141,600	31		108,024	504,125	536,160	11,437	0	813,819	371,000
36 Mobil Oil Credit Corp., Kansas City, Mo.	146,345	121,318	27	+1	146,345	810,162	826,359	10,027	9,701	8,605,713	407,250
37 Security Pacific Finance Corp., Pasadena. Calif.	145,846	19,659	100	+63	88,067	459,022	579,276	4,685	92,167	533,464	0
38 General Finance Corp., Evanston, Ill.	143,732	130,197	33		98,264	501,026	534,448	9,823	88,961	629,064	218,650
39 Massey Ferguson Credit Corp., Des Moines, Iowa	123,584	97,054	44	+5	76,094	446,235	469,572	9,000	88,653	371,503	340,500
40 American Investment Co., St. Louis, Mo.	119,092	123,308	36		79,192	390,728	564,828	4,746	86,778	397,237	207,000
41 Capital Financial Services, Inc., Columbus, Ohio	114,041	110,961	40		80,034	380,351	425,734	6,570	96,797	437,081	108,240
42 Aristar, Inc., Wilmington,Del.	110,620	110,768	41		80,007	262,352	350,008	6,612	46,482	362,892	184,100
43 White Motor Credit Corp., Wilmington, Del.	103,198	97,343	43		91,298	386,863	414,140	6,955	44,698	560,186	202,228

44	Macy Credit Corp., Garden City, N.Y.	92,852	78,316	49	+5	77,852	436,969	439,858	7,036	0	1,317,979	223,500
45	Commercial Alliance Corp., New York	92,194	69,725	52	+7	49,215	309,824	333,792	9,203	85,701	375,837	261,100
46	Gulf Oil Financial Corp., Houston, Tex.	89,895	81,202	45		51,145	377,890	414,834	10,568	0	4,646,444	329,000
47	Southwestern Investment Co., Amarillo, Tex.	87,663	77,772	50	+3	58,305	180,305	514,239	6,153	36,655	231,169	79,650
48	Goodyear Financial Corp., Wilmington, Del.	87,449	80,525	47		62,449	406,408	428,582	6,924	0	N.A.	698,260
49	James Talcott, Inc., New York	84,483	125,387	34		56,622	197,533	394,965	627	20,339	888,569	240,000
50	USLIFE Credit Corp., Schaumburg, Ill.	84,142	80,802	46		57,112	165,890	190,818	6,028	27,748	231,804	46,500
51	Midland-Guardian Co., Cincinnati, Ohio	81,561	74,611	51		41,060	184,349	260,923	2,900	61,421	153,550	120,100
52	First Pa. Financial Services, Inc., Philadelphia	74,399	64,832	53	+1	39,149	187,470	216,690	5,201	35,854	289,055	104,100
53	A.J. Armstrong Co., Inc., New York	73,685	55,679	59	+6	41,685	225,509	235,784	4,317	0	2,248,000	175,955
54	Budget Capitol Corp., Los Angeles	73,340	37,168	72	+18	31,382	37,328	90,592	5,766	0	28,544	21,550
55	Carter Hawley Credit Corp., Los Angeles	73,054	48,860	64	+9	63,054	259,696	260,559	4,194	0	1,240,977	304,000
56	Liberty Loan Corp., St. Louis, Mo.	68,805	57,012	58	+2	37,251	214,546	257,904	7,037	55,709	232,288	81,002
57	May Department Stores Credit Co., Wilmington, Del.	68,381	59,993	55		68,381	336,586	336,592	8,388	14,016	80,700	0
58	Northwest Acceptance Corp., Portland, Ore.	67,697	38,067	68	+10	36,922	250,777	272,120	4,003	45,719	253,230	123,000
59	Cessna Finance Corp., Wichita, Kan.	64,987	62,213	54		44,987	233,753	249,288	2,774	0	501,220	70,000

Continued

Rank 12/31/78	Total Capital Funds 12/31/78	Total Capital Funds 12/31/77	Rank, 12/31/77	Gain in Rank	Capital and Surplus, 12/31/78	Receivables Net, 12/31/78	Total Assets, 12/31/78	Net Income, 1978	Deferred Income, 12/31/78	Receivables Acquired, 1978	Bank Credit, 12/31/78
60 UT Credit Corp., Hartford, Conn.	63,806	34,009	76	+16	38,806	105,205	308,519	5,797	44,498	1,328	500,000
61 Paccar Financial Corp., Bellevue, Wash.	62,659	45,115	66	+5	33,659	271,539	276,522	3,544	28,659	518,441	157,000
62 Ritter Financial Corp., Wyncote, Pa.	60,441	58,500	56		27,478	146,543	158,302	3,766	25,017	212,651	0
63 Government Employees Financial Corp., Denver, Col.	59,252	57,420	57		34,654	199,571	223,552	3,349	36,284	238,267	91,500
64 Amoco Credit Corp., Chicago	58,586	53,225	61		58,585	262,277	284,151	5,360	0	703,874	178,000
65 USI Credit Corp., New York	57,405	53,290	56		50,105	129,164	159,712	3,451	26,660	117,476	53,000
66 Appliance Buyers Credit Corp., Benton Harbor, Mich.	57,198	52,317	62		42,198	193,314	214,995	4,881	3,479	651,015	155,400
67 Allied Stores Credit Corp., Boise, Idaho	57,028	55,247	60		27,028	95,329	95,572	1,781	2,355	237,597	330,250
68 Postal Finance Co., Sioux City, Iowa	53,334	46,930	65		33,499	205,682	237,123	3,329	52,256	278,043	61,200
69 Singer Credit Corp., New York	49,554	48,709	65		29,554	76,415	81,318	995	554	N.A.	N.A.
70 FMC Finance Corp., Chicago	47,252	29,218	82	+12	22,252	184,859	186,859	3,034	32,982	225,959	0
71 TranSouth Financial Corp., Florence, S.C.	45,438	43,414	67		25,268	164,641	192,414	3,614	13,020	203,120	17,075
72 Associated Dry Goods Credit Corp., New York	44,419	32,303	78	+6	44,419	123,963	124,612	2,116	0	590,000	156,950
73 Standard Financial Corp., New York	38,980	37,323	70		36,918	24,005	125,459	2,872	354	51,007	33,300
74 International T & T Credit Corp., East Meadow, N.Y.	38,554	26,413	86	+12	38,554	221,183	224,651	3,141	0	141,210	250,000

75	BVA Credit Corp., Richmond, Va.	38,027	37,488	69		26,027	116,115	179,122	1,439	13,646	552,866	0
76	Union Oil Credit Corp., Los Angeles	37,542	36,188	73		27,542	47,287	78,447	1,354	0	581,400	225,000
77	Genesco Financial Corp., Nashville, Tenn.	37,502	35,791	74		28,502	126,845	145,015	N.A.	N.A.	N.A.	N.A.
78	Firstmark Financial Corp., Indianapolis, In.	37,267	37,254	71		28,794	157,492	211,996	4,168	20,380	139,830	16,750
79	Sunoco Credit Corp., Wilmington, Del.	34,192	32,029	79		34,192	150,845	151,428	2,163	0	N.A.	0
80	Freedom Financial Services Corp., Oak Brook, Ill.	33,448	33,892	77		29,848	118,222	122,665	898	22,380	168,653	50,000
81	Sunamerica Financial Corp., Cleveland, Ohio	32,410	23,826	90	+9	20,700	116,065	133,047	2,189	16,680	163,323	100,000
82	Kentucky Finance Co., Inc., Lexington	32,119	30,166	80		18,544	94,348	103,484	2,478	19,302	160,510	47,350
83	Koehring Finance Corp., Milwaukee, Wis.	31,453	28,891	83		19,353	120,658	125,821	2,014	701	199,272	92,340
84	Congress Factors Corp., New York	30,888	22,114	92	+8	17,388	128,634	134,853	2,217	301	0	21,000
85	Ingersoll Rand Financial Corp., Woodcliff Lake, N.J.	30,663	18,239	102	+17	30,663	157,851	164,478	2,424	21,456	203,634	236,000
86	CBT Financial Corp., Hartford, Conn.	30,645	29,394	81		30,645	185,327	194,349	1,917	0	N.A.	142,000
87	Fidelity Acceptance Corp., Minneapolis, Minn.	30,074	25,819	87		21,897	59,157	70,910	1,283	15,987	81,925	31,000
88	Nationwide Consumer Services, Inc., Columbus, Ohio	28,957	26,730	85		15,657	109,197	117,742	552	18,806	111,775	76,050
89	Gulf Finance Corp., of Mississippi, Atlanta, Ga.	28,665	28,064	84		14,150	110,688	122,081	2,477	37,369	155,488	38,425
90	Signal Financial Corp., Pittsburgh, Pa.	28,142	24,240	88		15,077	82,446	90,100	1,163	16,394	98,982	7,000

Continued

Rank 12/31/78	Total Capital Funds 12/31/78	Total Capital Funds 12/31/77	Rank, 12/31/77	Gain in Rank	Capital and Surplus, 12/31/78	Receivables Net, 12/31/78	Total Assets, 12/31/78	Net Income, 1978	Deferred Income, 12/31/78	Receivables Acquired, 1978	Bank Credit, 12/31/78
91 Public Loan Co., Inc., Binghamton, N.Y.	25,547	24,168	89		23,922	63,801	84,418	1,007	12,413	N.A.	75,725
92 Carrier Distribution Credit Corp., Syracuse, N.Y.	24,398	12,460	114	+22	14,398	70,682	76,018	1,938	149	200,026	180,000
93 Transway Finance Co., Savannah, Ga.	22,719	21,946	93		8,719	86,370	90,016	1,473	19,495	104,160	54,000
94 Commercial Securities Co., Inc., Baton Rouge, La.	22,698	21,015	97	+3	17,293	30,765	60,033	1,953	8,829	45,501	27,760
95 Oxford Finance Companies, Inc., Philadelphia	22,630	22,881	91		18,243	43,082	47,300	220	2,091	N.A.	N.A.
96 Allied Finance Co., Dallas, Tex.	22,599	21,668	94		13,948	49,103	106,428	2,502	9,343	75,845	36,215
97 Rosenthal & Rosenthal, Inc. New York	22,100	19,900	98	+1	13,700	114,700	129,600	N.A.	0	738,400	64,900
98 Foothill Group Inc., Los Angeles	21,935	7,713	139	+41	11,935	96,980	102,562	2,111	11,989	500,000	40,000
99 Federated Acceptance Corp., Cincinnati, Ohio	21,851	21,400	96		21,851	131,813	131,946	469	0	500,000	342,500
100 American Standard Credit, Inc., Peoria, Ill.	20,951	12,700	111	+11	12,851	87,032	89,858	1,451	260	57,372	60,000

N.A., not available.
Source: *American Banker.* Used with permission of the publisher.

Appendix H: Stocks, Bonds, and Commodities

The 25 Most Active Stocks Listed on the New York Stock Exchange for 1980

Issue	Sales (hds)	Last	Chg.
IBM	1340631	$67\frac{7}{8}$	$+ 3\frac{1}{2}$
Texaco	1269704	48	$+19\frac{1}{8}$
Mobil	1038817	$80\frac{3}{4}$	$+25\frac{3}{4}$
AT&T	937967	$47\frac{7}{8}$	$- 4\frac{1}{4}$
Gulf Oil	880394	$43\frac{1}{2}$	$+ 8\frac{1}{8}$
Sony Corp	845414	$15\frac{1}{2}$	$+ 7\frac{1}{8}$
Exxon Corp	802474	$80\frac{5}{8}$	$+25\frac{1}{2}$
Gen Motors	738832	45	$- 5$
Sears, R	732382	$15\frac{1}{4}$	$- 2\frac{3}{4}$
Occid Pete	722883	$34\frac{5}{8}$	$+ 7\frac{1}{2}$
Phillips Pete	650793	$58\frac{3}{4}$	$+10\frac{3}{4}$
Citicorp	649754	$24\frac{1}{4}$	$+ \frac{1}{2}$
Boeing s	637028	$44\frac{1}{8}$	$+10\frac{3}{8}$
LTV	550228	$20\frac{1}{4}$	$+12\frac{1}{4}$
K mart	540655	$17\frac{7}{8}$	$- 5\frac{7}{8}$
Eastman K	540146	$69\frac{3}{4}$	$+21\frac{5}{8}$
Dow Chem	525690	$32\frac{1}{8}$	
Amer Cyan	502217	$32\frac{5}{8}$	$- 1\frac{3}{8}$
Benguet CIB	481814	$8\frac{1}{4}$	$+ 2\frac{1}{4}$
Int'l T&T	476548	30	$+ 4\frac{1}{2}$
Gen Electric	471231	$61\frac{1}{4}$	$+10\frac{5}{8}$
Colgate Pal	456711	$14\frac{5}{8}$	$+ \frac{1}{4}$
Fed Natl Mtg	456589	$11\frac{7}{8}$	$- 4\frac{1}{4}$
Amer Home	455851	$28\frac{1}{8}$	$+ \frac{7}{8}$
Tesoro	454474	$21\frac{1}{2}$	$+ 2\frac{3}{8}$

Market Diary

	1980	1979	1978
Advances	1283	1351	951
Declines	967	842	1240
Unchanged	17	21	34
Total issues	2267	2214	2225

Source: New York Times.

Money Market Mutual Funds

(funds with assets of $100 million or more that are available to individuals; for the period ended December 30, 1980)

Fund	Assets ($ million)	Average Maturity (days)	7-Day Average Yield (%)	30-Day Average Yield (%)
Alliance Capital Reserves	694.5	21	17.6	16.1
American General	120.0	21	17.7	16.8
American Liquid	205.5	22	17.3	16.2
Capital Preservation	780.3	6	15.1	14.4
Cash Equivalent Fund	1,417.7	27	17.5	15.3
Cash Management Trust	339.8	22	17.4	17.7
Cash Reserve Management	3,241.2	40	19.8	18.1
Columbia Daily Income	360.7	27	17.0	15.7
Current Interest	591.2	25	16.0	14.3
Daily Cash Accumulation	2,374.8	22	18.1	16.6
Daily Income	556.8	24	17.0	16.1
Delaware Cash Reserves	657.4	22	17.5	16.4
Dreyfus Liquid Assets	3,868.0	19	15.9	15.1
Eaton & Howard	132.5	25	17.5	16.9
FedFund	544.8	17	15.1	14.8
Fidelity Cash Reserves	1,018.0	18	16.4	15.0
Fidelity Daily Income	2,681.2	19	15.5	14.3
Fidelity M.M.T. Domestic	187.8	12	15.2	14.3
Financial Daily Income	121.8	17	18.2	17.3
First Investors Cash Management	223.5	19	18.2	16.7
First Variable Rate	429.4	*6	13.8	13.8
Franklin Money Fund	300.3	21	17.6	16.7
Fund/Government Investors	396.1	15	14.1	13.4
Government Investors Trust	115.3	*5	15.7	15.3
Gradison Cash Reserves	309.9	23	16.7	15.5
I.D.S. Cash Management	433.7	29	16.8	15.5
INA Cash Fund	245.0	25	16.1	14.9
Intercapital Liquid Assets	4,157.4	24	16.2	14.9
John Hancock Cash Management	145.3	19	18.4	17.0
Kemper Money Market	997.5	28	17.9	15.6
Legg Mason Cash Reserve	114.0	27	17.0	14.9
Liquid Capital Income	1,057.3	20	17.8	16.7
Lord Abbett Cash Reserve	197.2	25	16.4	13.0
Mass. Cash Management	379.4	38	16.3	15.0
Merrill Lynch Government	151.0	16	15.4	15.4
Merrill Lynch Ready Assets	11,279.4	27	18.0	16.4
Merrill Lynch Institutional	676.3	23	16.1	14.7
Midwest Income	126.5	20	16.1	15.7
Money Market Management	271.5	27	16.8	14.9
Moneymart Assets	1,778.0	23	17.2	16.2
Mutual of Omaha	129.4	31	17.7	16.2
National Liquid Reserves	1,539.3	16	16.8	15.3
N.E.L. Cash Management	285.0	26	16.7	15.0
NRTA-AARP U.S. Government MM Trust	306.9	30	17.4	16.6
Oppenheimer Money Market	753.6	20	17.6	16.5
Paine Webber Cashfund	2,493.4	26	15.9	14.9
Putnam Daily Dividend	171.7	26	17.1	16.7
Reserve Fund	2,059.7	10	17.9	17.1
Rowe Price Prime Reserve	1,3807.7	14	19.2	17.5
Scudder Cash Investment	650.4	15	17.6	16.3
Shearson Daily Dividend	2,367.9	18	17.2	16.0
SteinRoe Cash Reserves	390.9	17	18.3	16.5
T-Fund	209.8	8	15.8	16.0
TempFund	2,162.2	24	16.3	13.2
Union Cash Management	363.1	13	17.8	17.1
United Cash Management	165.7	16	17.3	16.0
Vanguard Money Market Trust	400.5	27	16.1	15.3
Webster Cash Reserve	601.4	22	16.1	15.6
Donoghue's Money Fund Average		23	16.6	15.6

*Average term to next rate adjustment date.
Yields represent annualized total return to shareholders for past 7- and 30-day periods.
Past returns are not necessarily indicative of future yields.
Source: Donoghue's Money Fund Report of Holliston, Mass.

A Year's Action in Commodities

	1/2/80	High	Low	12/31/80
Cattle (lb.)	0.6795	0.7512	0.5850	0.6515
Cocoa (metric ton)	2,987.00	3,401.00	1,870.00	2,050.00
Corn (bu.)	2.8925	3.96	2.565	3.78
Coffee (lb.)	1.822	2.03	1.021	1.268
Copper (lb.)	1.080	1.431	0.7705	0.8375
Cotton (lb.)	0.7450	0.9777	0.7160	0.9512
Gold (troy oz.)	562.50	875.00	453.00	591.30
Heating oil (gal.)	0.8700	0.9736	0.7170	0.9690
Hogs (lb.)	0.4155	0.5345	0.2715	0.4775
Lumber (1,000 bd. ft.)	212.00	218.00	146.50	161.40
Orange juice (lb.)	0.9525	1.011	0.7675	0.7740
Platinum (troy oz.)	780.00	1,085.00	465.00	578.00
Pork bellies (lb.)	0.4670	0.7450	0.2730	0.5557
Silver (troy oz.)	39.50	50.35	10.20	15.69
Soybeans (bu.)	6.41	9.56	5.695	7.885
Sugar (lb.)	0.1665	0.4480	0.1510	0.3058
Wheat (bu.)	4.535	5.445	3.805	5.01
U.S. T-bills	88.68	93.97	82.90	87.86
U.S. T-bonds	80.04	95.27	63.08	71.12
GNMA certs.	77.25	91.16	65.18	71.11
Gt. Brit. pounds	2.2300	2.4485	2.0650	2.4185
W. Ger. marks	0.59170	0.61350	0.49350	0.5143
Japan yen	0.004334	0.004964	0.003847	0.005025
Swiss francs	0.64630	0.72100	0.54300	0.5697
Chi. Bd. of Trade Seat	200,000	330,000	141,000	282,000
Chi. Merc. Ex. Seat	230,000	380,000	225,000	320,000
Intl. Mon. Mkt. Seat	125,000	280,000	105,000	225,000
Comex Seat	122,000	350,000	102,500	265,000
Cotton Exch. Seat	35,000	95,000	35,000	80,000
N.Y. Fut. Exch. Seat	20,000	40,000	20,000	27,000

Source: Barron's.

Highs and Lows of Dow Jones 65 Stocks Composite Average

	Highs			Lows		
1980	Nov.	28	388.87	Mar.	27	271.73
1979	Aug.	15	315.05	Feb.	28	274.27
1978	Sept.	8	315.26	Mar.	6	260.66
1977	Jan.	3	324.86	Oct.	25	274.31
1976	Dec.	31	325.49	Jan.	2	264.50
1975	July	15	268.20	Jan.	2	205.32
1974	Mar.	13	282.51	Oct.	3	184.24
1973	Jan.	3	334.08	Dec.	5	247.67
1972	Dec.	11	338.54	Oct.	16	302.13
1971	Apr.	28	318.44	Jan.	4	270.18
1970	Dec.	30	273.21	May	26	208.66
1969	Feb.	7	346.23	Dec.	17	252.99
1968	Nov.	29	353.09	Mar.	25	290.09
1967	Aug.	4	337.32	Jan.	3	282.69
1966	Feb.	11	352.40	Oct.	7	261.27
1965	Dec.	31	340.88	June	28	290.37
1964	Nov.	20	314.15	Jan.	2	269.09
1963	Dec.	18	269.08	Jan.	2	228.67
1962	Jan.	3	245.80	Jan.	3	204.77
1961	Nov.	15	251.43	Oct.	25	189.84
1960	Jan.	5	222.62	Feb.	9	200.09
1959	Aug.	3	224.35	Jan.	2	147.41
1958	Dec.	31	202.43	June	26	187.41
1957	July	12	179.87	Oct.	22	142.49
1956	Aug.	2	184.11	Jan.	23	164.29
1955	Dec.	6	174.21	Jan.	17	144.39
1954	Dec.	31	150.22	Jan.	11	106.03
1953	Mar.	17	113.96	Sept.	14	98.24
1952	Dec.	30	113.56	Feb.	20	96.05

Source: Barron's.

Appendix I: Organization

Afars and Issas, French Territory of the: Monday–Saturday 7:15–11
Afghanistan, Republic of: *summer:* Saturday–Wednesday 8–5; *winter:*
    Saturday–Wednesday 9–4
Algeria, Democratic and Popular Republic of: Monday–Friday 8:30–11:30, 1:30–5:30;
    Saturday 8:30–11:30
Andorra: Monday–Friday 9–1
Antiqua, State of: Monday–Thursday 8–12; Friday 8–12, 3–5
Argentina (Argentine Republic): Monday–Friday 12–4
Australia, Commonwealth of: Monday–Thursday 10–3; Friday 10–5
Austria, Republic of: Monday–Wednesday, Friday 8–12:30, 1:30–3; Thursday 1:30–5:30
Azores: Monday–Friday 9–12, 2–3:30
Bahamas, Commonwealth of the: Monday–Thursday 9–3; Friday 9–5
Bahrain, State of: Saturday–Wednesday 7:30–12; Thursday 7:30–11
Bangladesh, People's Republic of: Monday–Thursday, Saturday 10–5; Friday 10–12
Barbados: Monday–Thursday 8–12; Friday 8–12, 3–6
Belgium, Kingdom of: Monday–Friday 9–1, 2:30–3:30
Belize, Colony of: Monday, Tuesday, Thursday, Friday 9–3; Wednesday 9–12; Saturday
    9–11
Benin, People's Republic of: Monday–Friday 7:30–11, 2:30–4
Bermuda, Colony of: Monday–Thursday 9:30–3; Friday 9–3, 4:30–5:30
Bolivia, Republic of: Monday–Friday 9–12, 2–4
Botswana, Republic of: Monday–Friday 8:30–1; Saturday 8:30–11
Brazil, Federal Republic of: Monday–Friday 9:30–4:30
Brunei, State of: Monday–Friday 9–5, Saturday 9–12
Bulgaria, People's Republic of: Monday–Friday 8–5
Burma, Socialist Republic of the Union of: Monday–Friday 10–2; Saturday 10–12
Burundi, Republic of: Monday–Friday 8–11:30
Cameroon, United Republic of: Monday–Friday 7:30–12, 2:30–6
Canada, Dominion of: Monday–Friday 10–3
Cape Verde, Republic of: Monday–Friday 8–12
Cayman Islands: Monday–Thursday 8:30–1; Friday 8:30–1
Central African Republic: Monday–Saturday 7–1
Chad, Republic of: Monday–Saturday 7–11:30
Channel Islands (United Kingdom): Monday–Friday 9:30-3:30; one evening per week
    4:30–6
Chile, Republic of: Monday–Friday 9–5
China, People's Republic of: Monday–Saturday 8:30–12, 3–6
China, Republic of (Taiwan): Monday–Friday 9–3; Saturday 9–12
Columbia, Republic of: Monday–Friday 9:30–3
Congo, People's Republic of the: Monday–Saturday 6:20–1
Costa Rica, Republic of: Monday–Friday 8–11, 1–3; Saturday 8–11
Cuba, Republic of: Monday–Friday 8–5; Saturday 8–12
Cyprus, Republic of: Monday–Saturday 8:30–12:30
Czechoslovakia (Czechoslovak Socialist Republic): Monday–Friday 8–4:30
Denmark, Kingdom of: Monday–Wednesday, Friday 9–3; Thursday 9–5
Dominican Republic: Monday–Friday 8–1; Saturday 9–11:30
Ecuador, Republic of: Monday–Friday 9–1:30
Egypt, Arab Republic of: Monday–Thursday, Saturday 8:30–12:30; Sunday 10–12

Continued

El Salvador, Republic of: Monday–Friday 8:30–11:30, 2:30–5:30

England (United Kingdom): Monday–Friday 9:30–3:30

Equatorial Guinea, Republic of: Monday–Saturday 8–1

Ethiopia: Monday–Friday 9–1, 3–5; Saturday 9–1

Fiji, Dominion of: Monday–Thursday 10–3; Friday 10–4

Finland, Republic of: Monday–Friday 9:15–4:15

France (French Republic): *Paris:* Monday–Friday 9–12, 1:30–4:30; *provinces:* Tuesday–Saturday 9–12, 2–4

French Guiana, Department of: Monday–Friday 7:15–11:30, 2:45–4:30

French Polynesia, Territory of: Monday–Friday 8–3:30

Gabon (Gabonese Republic): Monday–Friday 7:30–11:30, 2:45–4:30

Gambia, Republic of the: Monday–Friday 8–1; Saturday 8–11

Germany, Democratic Republic of (East): Monday–Friday 9–4

Germany, Federal Republic of (West): Monday–Wednesday, Friday 9–1, 3–4; Thursday 9–1, 3–5:30

Ghana, Republic of: Monday–Thursday 8:30–2; Friday 8:30–3

Gibraltar, Colony of: Monday–Thursday 9–3:30; Friday 9–3:30, 4:40–6

Greece (Hellenic Republic): Monday–Saturday 8–1

Grenada, State of: Monday–Thursday 8–12; Friday 8–12, 3–6

Guadeloupe, Department of: Monday–Friday 9–12, 2–5:30

Guam: Monday–Thursday 10–3; Friday 10–6

Guatemala, Republic of: Monday–Thursday 8:30–2; Friday 8:30–2:30

Guinea, Republic of: Monday–Thursday, Saturday 7:30–3; Friday 7:30–1

Guinea-Bissau, Republic of: Monday–Friday 8–12, 3–5; Saturday 8–11; banks closed last day of each month

Guyana, Cooperative Republic of: Monday–Friday 8–11:30

Haiti, Republic of: Monday–Friday 9–1:30; May 1–September 30: Friday 9–1

Honduras, Republic of: Monday–Friday, 9–3; Saturday 9–12

Hong Kong, Colony of: Monday–Friday 9–3; Saturday 9–12:30

Hungary (Hungarian People's Republic): Monday–Friday 9–1; Saturday 9–11

Iceland, Republic of: *Monday–*Friday 9:30–3:30

India, Republic of: Monday–Friday 10–2; Saturday 10–12

Indonesia, Republic of: *national:* Monday–Friday 8:30–11; Saturday 8:30–10; *foreign:* Monday–Friday 8–5; Saturday 8–12:30

Iran, Empire of: *Summer:* Saturday–Wednesday 7:15–1; Thursday 7:15–11:30; *Winter:* Saturday–Wednesday 8–1, 4–7

Iraq, Republic of: *summer:* Saturday–Wednesday 7–2; Thursday 7–12; *winter:* Saturday–Wednesday 10–3:30; Thursday 8:30–1:30

Ireland, Republic of: Monday–Wednesday, Friday 10–12:30, 1:30–3; Thursday 10–12:30, 1:30–5

Israel, State of: Monday–Thursday 8:30–12:30; Friday 8:30–12

Italy (Italian Republic): Monday–Friday 7:30–12, 2:30–6

Jamaica: Monday–Thursday 9–2; Friday 9–12, 2:30–5

Japan: Monday–Friday 9–3; Saturday 9–12

Jordan, Hashemite Kingdom of: Saturday–Thursday 8–2

Kenya, Republic of: Monday–Thursday 9–1; Saturday 9–11

Korea, Republic of (South): *November–*February: Monday–Friday 9:30–4:30; Saturday 9:30–1:30; *March–October:* Monday–Friday 9–4; Saturday 9–1

Continued

Kuwait, State of: Saturday–Wednesday 8–1; Thursday 8–1

Laos, People's Democratic Republic of: Monday–Friday 8–12, 2–5

Lebanon, Republic of: Monday–Saturday 8–12

Lesotho, Kingdom of: Monday–Friday 8:30–1; Saturday 8:30–11

Liberia, Republic of: Monday–Thursday 8–12; Friday 8–2

Libya (Libyan Arab Republic): Saturday–Thursday 9–2

Liechtenstein, Principality of: Monday–Friday 8–12, 1:30–4:30

Luxembourg, Grand Duchy of: Monday–Friday 8–12, 2–5

Madeira: Monday–Friday 9–12, 2–2:30

Malagasy Republic: Monday–Friday 8–12, 2–4

Malawi, Republic of: Monday–Friday 8–11:30; Saturday 8–10:30

Malaysia: *Christian:* Monday–Friday 10–2:30; Saturday 9:30–11:30; *Moslem:* Saturday–Wednesday 10–3; Thursday 9:30–11:30

Mali, Republic of: Monday–Friday 7:30–12, 3–5:30; Saturday 7:30–12:30

Malta, Republic of: Monday–Friday 8:30–12:30; Saturday 8:30–12

Martinique, Department of: Monday–Friday 8–12, 2:30–4

Mauritania, Islamic Republic of: Monday–Saturday 8–12, 3–6

Mauritius: Monday–Friday 10–2; Saturday 10–11:30

Mexico (United Mexican States): Monday–Friday 9–2

Monaco, Principality of: Monday–Friday 9–12, 2–4

Mongolia (Mongolian People's Republic): Monday–Friday 9–3

Morocco, Kingdom of: Monday–Friday 8:15–11:30, 2:15–4:30; *summer:* Monday–Friday 8–11:30, 3:30–5:15; *Ramadan:* Monday–Friday 9:30–2

Mozambique, People's Republic of: Monday–Friday 8–11

Namibia: Monday, Tuesday, Thursday, Friday 8:30–3:30; Wednesday 8:30–1; Saturday 8:30–11

Nauru, Republic of: Monday–Friday 9–12, 2–5

Nepal, Kingdom of: Sunday–Thursday 10–3; Friday 10–12

Netherlands, Kingdom of the: Monday–Friday 8–12, 1:30–4

New Zealand, Dominion of: Monday–Friday 10–4

Nicaragua, Republic of: Monday–Friday 8:30–12, 2–4; Saturday 8:30–11:30

Niger, Republic of: Monday–Friday 8–11:30, 4–5

Nigeria, Republic of: Monday 8–3; Tuesday–Friday 8–1:30

Northern Ireland: Monday–Friday 9:30–3:30; one day per week 4:30–6

Norway: Monday, Wednesday, Friday 8:15–4:45; Tuesday, Thursday 8:15–5

Oman, Sultanate of: Saturday–Wednesday 8–12; Thursday 8–11:30

Pakistan, Islamic Republic of: Monday–Thursday 9–1; Friday–Saturday 9–10:30

Panama, Republic of: Monday–Friday 8:30–1; Saturday 8–12

Panama Canal Zone: Monday–Friday 8:30–1

Papua New Guinea: Monday–Friday 9–2; Saturday 8:30–10

Paraguay, Republic of: *Summer:* Monday–Friday 7:30–11; *Winter:* Monday–Friday 7–10:30

Peru, Republic of: *January–March:* Monday–Friday 8:30–11:30; *April–December:* Monday–Friday 9:15 –12:45

Philippines, Republic of the: Monday–Friday 8–3

Poland (Polish People's Republic): Monday–Saturday 8:30–12:30; banks close on Saturday 12 times each year

Portugal (Portuguese Republic): Monday–Friday 9:30–12, 2–3:30

Puerto Rico, Commonwealth of: Monday–Friday 9–2:30

Continued

Qatar, State of: Saturday–Wednesday 8–1, 4–7; *Ramadan:* shorter hours
Romania, Socialist Republic of: Monday–Friday 8–11; Saturday 8–10
Rwanda, Republic of: Monday–Friday 9–12, 2–5; Saturday 9–12
St. Christopher-Nevis-Anguilla, State of: Monday–Wednesday 8–12; Friday 8–12, 3–5
St. Pierre and Miquelon, Territory of: Monday–Friday 8:30–12, 1:30–5
Saudi Arabia, Kingdom of: Saturday–Wednesday 8:30–12
Scotland (United Kingdom): Monday–Wednesday 9:30–3:30; Thursday 9:30–3:30, 4:40–6;
    Friday 9:30–12:30
Senegal, Republic of: Monday–Friday 8–12, 2:30–6
Seychelles, Colony of the: Monday–Friday 8:30–12:30
Sierra Leone, Republic of: Monday–Friday 8–1; Saturday 8–11
Singapore, Republic of: Monday–Friday 10–3; Saturday 9:30–11:30
Somalia (Somali Democratic Republic): Saturday–Thursday 7–11:30
South Africa, Republic of: Monday, Tuesday, Thursday, Friday 8:30–3:30; Wednesday
    8:30–1; Saturday 8:30–11
Southern Rhodesia, Colony of: Monday, Tuesday, Thursday, Friday 8:30–1; Wednesday
    8:30–12; Saturday 8:30–11
Soviet Union (Union of Soviet Socialist Republics): Monday–Friday 9–2
Spain (Spanish State): Monday–Friday 8–3; Saturday 8–12; each region has special
    holidays during which businesses and banks close
Sri Lanka, Republic of: Monday 9–1; Tuesday–Friday 9–1:30
Sudan, Democratic Republic of the: Saturday–Thursday 8:30–12
Surinam: Monday–Friday 7:30–12:30; Saturday 7:30–12
Swaziland, Kingdom of: Monday–Friday 8:30–1; Saturday 8:30–11
Sweden, Kingdom of: Monday–Friday 9:30–3, 4:30–6
Switzerland (Swiss Confederation): Monday–Friday 8–12, 2–5
Syria (Syrian Arab Republic): Saturday–Thursday 8:30–2:30
Tanzania, United Republic of: Monday–Friday 8:30–12:30; Saturday 8:30–11
Thailand, Kingdom of: Monday–Friday 8:30–3
Togo, Republic of: Monday–Friday 7:30–12, 2:30–6
Tonga, Kingdom of: no banks
Trinidad and Tobago: Monday–Thursday 8–12:30; Friday 8–12, 3:30–5:30
Tunisia, Republic of: *October–May:* Monday–Friday 8–11, 2–4: *June 1–15:*
    Monday–Friday 8–12, 3–4:30; *June 15–September 15:* Monday–Friday 7:30–11;
    September 15–30: Monday–Friday 8–11, 3–4:30
Turkey, Republic of: Monday–Friday 9–5
Uganda, Republic of: Monday–Friday 8:30–12:30, 2–3:30; Saturday 8–11:30
United Arab Emirates: Saturday–Thursday 7–1
United States: see individual states in the next table
Upper Volta, Republic of: Monday–Friday 8–12
Uruguay, Oriental Republic of: Monday–Friday 1–5
USSR: Monday–Saturday 9–6
Vatican City, State of: Monday–Friday 8:30–1:30
Venezuela, Republic of: Monday–Friday 9–11:30
Virgin Islands, U.S. (Virgin Islands of the United States): Monday–Thursday 9–2:30;
    Friday 9–2:30, 4–6
Wales (United Kingdom): Monday–Friday 9:30–3:30; one day per week 4:30–6
Western Samoa, The Independent State of: Monday–Friday 9:30–3

Continued

Yemen (Yemen Arab Republic): Saturday–Wednesday 8–2; Thursday 8–1
Yemen, People's Democratic Republic of: Saturday–Thursday 7:30–2
Yugoslavia, Socialist Federal Republic of: Monday–Friday 7–3
Zaire, Republic of: Monday–Friday 8–12
Zambia, Republic of: Monday–Wednesday, Friday 8:15–12:45; Thursday 8:15–12;
    Saturday 8:15–11

Banking Hours by State[1]

Alabama: Monday–Thursday 9–1, 3–6; Friday 9–6, Saturday 9–12 (some)
Alaska: Monday–Friday 10–3
Arizona: Monday–Thursday 9–4; Friday 9–6
Arkansas: Monday–Thursday 9–3; Friday 9–6; Saturday 9–12
California: Monday–Friday 9–4; Saturday 9–12 (some)
Colorado: Monday–Friday 9–4; Saturday 9–12 (some)
Connecticut: Monday–Friday 8–5, 10–4; Saturday 9–1 (some)
Delaware: Monday–Thursday 9–3; Friday 9–6; banks remain open on Lincoln's Birthday,
    Washington's Birthday, Columbus Day, and Veterans Day
District of Columbia: Monday–Friday 9–2:30, 9–3
Florida: Monday–Friday 9–4, Saturday (some)
Georgia: Monday–Friday 9:30–4; Saturday (some)
Hawaii: Monday–Friday 10–3
Idaho: Monday–Thursday 9–5; Friday 9–6; Saturday (some)
Illinois: Monday–Friday 9–3; Saturday (some)
Indiana: Monday–Thursday 9–3:30; Friday 9–6
Iowa: Monday–Friday 9–3:30; Saturday (some)
Kansas: Monday–Friday 9–6; Saturday 9–12
Kentucky: Monday–Friday 9–2; Saturday (some)
Louisiana: Monday–Friday 10–3
Maine: Monday–Friday 9–3
Maryland: Monday–Friday 9–2, 10–5; Saturday (some)
Massachusetts: Monday–Friday 10–3; Saturday (some)
Michigan: Monday–Friday 9:30–3:30; Saturday 9–12
Minnesota: Monday–Friday 9–3; Monday or Friday open to 9 p.m.; Saturday 9–12
Mississippi: Monday–Friday 9–2; Saturday (some)
Missouri: Monday–Thursday 9–4:30; Friday 9–6; Saturday (some)
Montana: Monday–Thursday 9–2, Friday 9–6; Saturday 9–12
Nebraska: Monday–Friday 9–4; Saturday 9–12
Nevada: Monday –Friday 10–3:30; banks also close on December 24
New Hampshire: Monday–Friday 8–5; Saturday (some)
New Jersey: Monday–Friday 9–2, 10–2; Friday 9–8 (some); Saturday 9–12 (some)
New Mexico: Monday–Friday 9–3, 10–3; Friday 10–4:30 (some), Saturday (some)
New York: Monday–Friday 9–3; Saturday 9–12 (some)
North Carolina: Monday–Thursday 9–3; Friday 9–5; banks that not open on Saturdays
    open three hours after 3 p.m. Friday
North Dakota: Monday–Friday 9–3; Saturday (some)
Ohio: Monday–Friday 9–5; Saturday (some); bank closing optional on Martin Luther King
    Day
Oklahoma: Monday–Friday 9–3
Oregon: Monday–Thursday 10–5; Friday 10–6; Saturday (some)
Pennsylvania: Monday–Friday 9–3, 10–2; Saturday 9–12 (some) bank closing optional on
    Columbus Day; some banks closed on December 26
Rhode Island: Monday–Friday 9–2:30; Saturday (some); optional holiday on Washington's
    Birthday
South Carolina: Monday–Friday 9–1, 3–5: Saturday (some); optional bank holiday on
    Confederate Memorial Day and Labor Day
South Dakota: Monday–Friday 9–4; Saturday (some); optional closing on December 24

Continued

Tennessee: Monday–Friday 9–2, 8–3; banks may be closed on Wednesdays or Thursdays
Texas: Monday–Friday 9–3; Saturday (some); banks also close on December 24
Utah: Monday–Friday 10–3: Saturday 9–12; on Lincoln's Birthday and Arbor Day, banks
  operating a 5-day week stay open
Vermont: Monday–Friday 9–3; Saturday (some)
Virginia: Monday–Friday 9–2, 4–6; Saturday 9–12; banks closed on December 24
Washington: Monday–Friday 10–3; Saturday (some)
West Virginia: Monday–Friday 9–2, 9–3; Saturday 9–12
Wisconsin: Monday–Thursday 8:30–4:30; Friday and Saturday 8:30–12 (some)
Wyoming: Monday–Friday 9–3; Saturday (some)

[1]Many banks now have Sunday hours as well.

Bank Holidays in the States

	January	February	March	April	May	June	July	August	September	October	November	December
Alabama	1, 21	18		13, 28	30	2	4		1	13	4, 11, 27	25
Alaska	1	12, 18	28		30		4		1	13	4, 11, 27	25
Arizona	1	12, 18			30		4		1	13	4, 11, 27	25
Arkansas	1, 19	19			30		4				4, 11, 27	25
California	1	12, 18		13	30		4		1, 9	13	4, 11, 27	25
Colorado	1	12, 18			30		4	4	1	13	4, 11, 27	25
Connecticut	1	12, 18		4	30		4		1	13	4, 11, 27	25
Delaware	1	18		4	30		4				4, 11, 27	25
District of Columbia	1, 15	18			30		4				4, 11, 27	25
Florida	1, 19	18		4, 26	30	2	4		1	13	4, 11, 27	25
Georgia	1, 19	18		26	30	2	4		1	13	4, 11, 27	25
Hawaii	1	12, 18	24	4	30		4	18	1	13	4, 11, 27	25
Idaho	1	18			30		4		1	13	4, 11, 27	25
Illinois	1	12, 18			30		4		1	13	4, 11, 27	25
Indiana	1	12, 18		4	30		4		1	13	4, 11, 27	25
Iowa	1	12, 18			30		4		1		4, 11, 27	25
Kansas	1	12, 18			30		4		1		4, 11, 27	25
Kentucky	1, 19	12, 18		4	30	2	4		1		4, 11, 27	25
Louisiana	1, 19	18		4	30		4		1		4, 11, 27	25
Maine	1	12, 18		21	30		4		1	13	4, 11, 27	25
Maryland	1, 15	12, 18		4	30		4		1	13	4, 11, 27	25
Massachusetts	1	18	17	21	30	17	4		1	13	4, 11, 27	25
Michigan	1	12, 18		4	30		4		1	13	4, 11, 27	25
Minnesota	1	18			30		4		1	13	4, 11, 27	25
Mississippi	1, 21	18		28	30	2	4		1	13	4, 11, 27	25
Missouri	1	12, 18			8, 30		4		1	13	4, 11, 27	25
Montana	1	12, 18			30		4		1	13	4, 11, 27	25
Nebraska	1	12, 18		22	30		4		1	13	4, 11, 27	25
Nevada	1	18			30		4		1		4, 11, 27	25

Continued

	January	February	March	April	May	June	July	August	September	October	November	December
New Hampshire	1	18		28	30		4		1	13	4, 11, 27	25
New Jersey	1	12, 18		4	30		4		1	13	4, 11, 27	25
New Mexico	1	12, 18			30		4		1		4, 11, 27	25
New York	1	12, 18			30		4		1	13	4, 11, 27	25
North Carolina	1, 19	18		11	10, 30		4		1	13	4, 11, 27	25
North Dakota	1	18		4	30		4		1		4, 11, 27	25
Ohio	1	18			30		4		1	13	4, 11, 27	25
Oklahoma	1	18			30		4		1	13	4, 11, 27	25
Oregon	1	4, 18			30		4		1		4, 11, 27	25
Pennsylvania	1	12, 18			30	14	4		1	13	4, 11, 27	25
Rhode Island	1	18			30		4	11	1	13	4, 11, 27	25
South Carolina	1, 19	18			10, 30		4		1		4, 11, 27	25
South Dakota	1	18			30		4		1	13	4, 11, 27	25
Tennessee	1	18		4	30		4		1	13	4, 11, 27	25
Texas	1, 19	18	2		30		4	27	1	13	4, 11, 27	25
Utah	1	12, 18		25	30		4		1	13	4, 11, 27	25
Vermont	1	12, 18	4		30		4		1	13	4, 11, 27	25
Virginia	1, 21	18			30		4		1	13	4, 11, 27	25
Washington	1	12, 18		4	30		4		1	13	4, 11, 27	25
West Virginia	1	12, 18			30		4		1	13	4, 11, 27	25
Wisconsin	1	18			30		4		1	13	4, 11, 27	25
Wyoming	1	18			30		4		1	13	4, 11, 27	25
Puerto Rico	1	18			30		4		1		4, 11, 27	25

Source: Banker's Diary and Guide.

Alabama
Mr. Kenneth R. McCartha
Acting Superintendent of Banks
64 North Union Street, Room 651
Montgomery, Alabama 36130
Telephone: (205) 832-6256

Alaska
Hon. Julius J. Brecht
Director of Banking and Securities
Pouch D
Juneau, Alaska 99801
Telephone: (907) 465-2521

Arizona
Hon. Walter C. Madsen
Superintendent of Banks
Commerce Building, Room 101
1601 W. Jefferson Street
Phoenix, Arizona 85007
Telephone: (602) 271-4421

Arkansas
Hon. Beverly J. Lambert, Jr.
State Bank Commissioner
1 Capitol Mall, 4B-210
Little Rock, Arkansas 72201
Telephone: (501) 371-1117

California
Mr. Morton R. Michaels
Acting Superintendent of Banks
235 Montgomery Street, Suite 750
San Francisco, California 94104

Colorado
Hon. Harry Bloom
State Bank Commissioner
State Office Building, Room 325
Denver, Colorado 80203
Telephone: (303) 839-3131

Connecticut
Hon. David H. Neiditz
Bank Commissioner
State Office Building, Room 239
Hartford, Connecticut 06115
Telephone: (203) 566-7580

Delaware
Hon. John E. Malarkey
State Bank Commissioner
15 The Green
Kirk Building
Dover, Delaware 19901
Telephone: (302) 678-4235

Florida
Hon. Gerald A. Lewis
Comptroller of Florida
State Capitol Building
Tallahassee, Florida 32304
Telephone: (904) 488-0370

Georgia
Hon. Edward D. Dunn
Commissioner of Banking and Finance
148 International Blvd., N.E., Suite 640
Atlanta, Georgia 30303
Telephone: (404) 656-2050

Hawaii
Hon. Tany S. Hong
Director of Regulatory Agencies
P.O. Box 541
Honolulu, Hawaii 96809
Telephone: (808) 548-7505

Idaho
Hon. Tom. D. McEldowney
Director of Finance
Statehouse Mall
Boise, Idaho 83720
Telephone: (208) 384-3313

Illinois
Hon. William C. Harris
Commissioner of Banks and Trust
  Companies
Reisch Building, Room 400
117-119 South Fifth Street
Springfield, Illinois 62701
Telephone: (217) 782-7966

Indiana
Hon. James E. Faris
Director, Department of Financial
  Institutions
State Office Buildings, Room 1024
Indianapolis, Indiana 46204
Telephone: (317) 633-4365

Iowa
Hon. Thomas H. Huston
Superintendent of Banking
418 Sixth Avenue, Room 530
Des Moines, Iowa 50309
Telephone: (515) 281-4014

Continued

Kansas
Hon. Roy P. Britton
State Bank Commissioner
818 Kansas Avenue, Suite 600
Topeka, Kansas 66612
Telephone: (913) 296-2266

Kentucky
Hon. John L. Williams, Jr.
Commissioner of Banking and Securities
911 Leawood Drive
Frankfort, Kentucky 40601
Telephone: (502) 564-3390

Louisiana
Hon. Frank D. Lassiter
Commissioner of Financial Institutions
P.O. Box 44095—Capital Station
Baton Rouge, Louisiana 70804
Telephone: (504) 925-4661

Maine
Hon. Donald De Matteis
Superintendent, Bureau of Banking
State Office Building
Augusta, Maine 04333
Telephone: (207) 289-3231

Maryland
Hon. W. H. Holden Gibbs
Bank Commissioner
1 North Charles Street, Room 2005
Baltimore, Maryland 21201
Telephone: (301) 383-2480

Massachusetts
Hon. Gerald T. Mulligan
Commissioner of Banks
100 Cambridge Street
Boston, Massachusetts 02202
Telephone: (617) 727-3120

Michigan
Hon. Richard J. Francis
Commissioner, Financial Institutions
  Bureau
P.O. Box 30224
Lansing, Michigan 48909
Telephone: (517) 373-3460

Minnesota
Hon. Michael J. Pint
Commissioner of Banks
Metro Square Building, 5th Floor
7th and Robert Streets
St. Paul, Minnesota 55101
Telephone: (612) 296-2715

Mississippi
Hon. James H. Means
State Comptroller, Department of Bank
  Supervision
P.O. Box 731
Jackson, Mississippi 39205
Telephone: (601) 354-6106

Missouri
Hon. Earl L. Manning
Acting Commissioner of Finance
P.O. Box 716
Jefferson City, Missouri 65101
Telephone: (314) 751-3397

Montana
Hon. Kent Kleinkopf
Director, Department of Business
  Regulation
805 North Main Street
Helena, Montana 59601
Telephone: (406) 449-3163

Nebraska
Hon. Paul Amen
Director of Banking and Finance
301 Centennial Mall, South
Lincoln, Nebraska 68509
Telephone: (402) 471-2171

Nevada
Hon. Joseph O. Sevigny
Superintendent of Banks
406 East Second Street
Carson City, Nevada 89710
Telephone: (702) 855-4260

New Hampshire
Hon. A. Roland Roberge
Bank Commissioner
97 North Main Street
Concord, New Hampshire 03301
Telephone: (603) 221-3561

Continued

New Jersey
Hon. Angelo Bianchi
Commissioner of Banking
36 West State Street
Trenton, New Jersey 08625
Telephone: (609) 292-3420

New Mexico
Hon. Arthur L. Ortiz
Director, Financial Institutions Division
Commerce and Industry Department
Lew Wallace Building
Santa Fe, New Mexico 87503
Telephone: (505) 827-2217

New York
Hon. Muriel F. Siebert
Superintendent of Banks
2 World Trade Center, 32nd Floor
New York, New York 10047
Telephone: (212) 488-2310

North Carolina
Hon. James S. Currie
Commissioner of Banks
P.O. Box 951
Raleigh, North Carolina 27602
Telephone: (919) 733-3016

North Dakota
Hon. Leroy Gilbertson
Commissioner of Banking and Financial
  Institutions
State Capitol, Room 1301
Bismarck, North Dakota 58505
Telephone: (701) 224-2253

Ohio
Hon. Frederick E. Mills
Superintendent of Banks
Borden Building, 14th Floor
180 East Broad Street
Columbus, Ohio 43215
Telephone: (614) 466-2932

Oklahoma
Hon. Robert Y. Empie
Bank Commissioner
Malco Building
4100 N. Lincoln Blvd.
Oklahoma City, Oklahoma 73105
Telephone: (405) 521-2783

Oregon
Hon. John B. Olin
Superintendent of Banks, Department of
  Commerce
Busick Building
Salem, Oregon 97310
Telephone: (503) 378-4140

Pennsylvania
Hon. Ben McEnteer
Secretary of Banking
P.O. Box 2155
Harrisburg, Pennsylvania 17120
Telephone: (717) 787-6992

Rhode Island
Hon. Peter A. Nevola
Bank Commissioner
100 North Main Street
Providence, Rhode Island 02903
Telephone: (401) 277-2405

South Carolina
Hon. Robert C. Cleveland
Commissioner of Banking
1026 Sumter Street, Room 217
Columbia, South Carolina 29201
Telephone: (803) 758-2186

South Dakota
Hon. Walter E. Wintrode
Director of Banking and Finance
State Capitol Building
Pierre, South Dakota 57501
Telephone: (605) 773-3421

Tennessee
Hon. Thomas C. Mottern
Commissioner of Banking
Capitol Hill Building, Suite 460
311 7th Avenue, North
Nashville, Tennessee 37219
Telephone: (615) 741-2236

Texas
Hon. Robert E. Stewart
Banking Commissioner
2601 North Lamar
Austin, Texas 78705
Telephone: (512) 475-4451

Continued

State Banking Authorities (continued)

Utah
Hon. M. D. Borthick
Commissioner of Financial Institutions
10 West Broadway, Suite 331
Salt Lake City, Utah 84101
Telephone: (801) 533-5461

Vermont
Hon. Stewart Ledbetter
Commissioner of Banking and Insurance
State Office Building
Montpelier, Vermont 05602
Telephone: (802) 828-3301

Virginia
Hon. Sidney A. Bailey
Commissioner of Financial Institutions
701 East Byrd Street, Suite 1600
Richmond, Virginia 23261
Telephone: (804) 786-3657

Washington
Hon. M. D. Edwards
Supervisor of Banking
General Administration Building, Room
  219
Olympia, Washington 98504
Telephone: (206) 753-6520

West Virginia
Mr. W. Lovell Higgins
Acting Commissioner of Banking
State Office Building 6, Room B-406
1900 Washington Street, East
Charleston, West Virginia 25305
Telephone: (304) 348-2294

Wisconsin
Hon. Erich Mildenberg
Commissioner of Banking
30 West Mifflin Street, Room 401
Madison, Wisconsin 53703
Telephone: (608) 266-1621

Wyoming
Hon. Dwight D. Bonham
State Examiner
819 W. Pershing Boulevard
Cheyenne, Wyoming 82002
Telephone: (307) 777-7797

Guam
Hon. Manuel A. Chaco
Director of Revenue and Taxation
Government of Guam
P.O. Box 2796
Agana, Guam 96910

Puerto Rico
Hon. Julio Cesar Perez
Secretary of the Treasury
Commonwealth of Puerto Rico
P.O. Box 4515
San Juan, Puerto Rico 00905
Telephone: (809) 722-3048

Virgin Islands
Hon. Henry A. Millen
Lieutenant Governor
Chairman of the Banking Board
Government House, Charlotte Amalie
St. Thomas, Virgin Islands 00801
Telephone: (809) 774-2991

Geographic Restrictions on Branch Banking in the States

Statewide Branch Banking Prevalent	Limited Branch Banking Prevalent	Unit Banking Prevalent
Alaska	Alabama	Colorado
Arizona	Arkansas	Illinois
California	Florida	Kansas
Connecticut	Georgia	Minnesota
Delaware	Indiana	Missouri
Hawaii	Iowa	Montana
Idaho	Kentucky	Nebraska
Maine	Louisiana	North Dakota
Maryland	Massachusetts	Oklahoma
Nevada	Michigan	Texas
New Jersey	Mississippi	West Virginia
New York	New Hampshire	Wyoming
North Carolina	New Mexico	
Oregon	Ohio	
Rhode Island	Pennsylvania	
South Carolina	Tennessee	
South Dakota	Virginia	
Utah	Wisconsin	
Vermont		
Washington		

Note: This classification is made for the purpose of discussing changes in the banking structure, and is based on the type of banking seemingly prevalent in each state and not necessarily on the current status of legal provisions. The classification of some states in this list depends on the interpretation of the key words "prevalent," "limited," "severely limited," and "prohibited," and this classification may differ in respect to a few states from similar classification made for other purposes.

State	Branching Statutes
Alabama	There are sixty-seven counties located within the state and approximately fifty-eight of those counties are authorized to have some form of branching. Almost every county has a different branch banking bill: some permit branches to be established anywhere, subject to approval by the state superintendent; some permit branches to be established only in those cities having population above a specified number.
Alaska	Statewide branching.
Arizona	Statewide branching.
Arkansas	The supervisory banking authority may approve the establishment of a branch in the following locations: (1) within the corporate limits of the city or town in which such establishing bank's main office is located, provided that it is not closer than 300 feet to another bank's principal office; but a bank that relocates its main office may continue to use its former main office for a branch office as long as its use as a banking facility is uninterrupted; (2) within any incorporated city or town having a population of 250 or more in the county of the establishing bank's

Continued

State	Branching Statutes
	principal office, provided that there is no legally chartered bank then having its principal office in such city or town; and (3) within any planned community development having a population of 250 or more in the county of the establishing bank's principal office.
	Any bank may, at its option, operate any presently existing branch office, teller's window, or other banking facility that is separate from the main office of the bank, heretofore legally established under any prior law and in operation as a full service branch on the effective date of the governing act.
California	Statewide branching.
Colorado	Branching is prohibited; one facility is permitted within 3,000 feet of the main office.
Connecticut	Statewide branching; home office protection.
Delaware	Statewide branching.
Florida	Any bank may establish up to two branches per calendar year within the limits of the county in which its main office is located and, in addition, may establish branches by merger with other banks located within the county in which the bank's main office is located, effective January 1, 1977.
Georgia	The state commissioner may approve bank offices or facilities in the same county in which the principal office is located or in counties in which a branch bank is located, the number of facilities being determined by the following schedule based on county population:

County Population	Additional Offices or Facilities
0–20,000	2
20,001–40,000	3
40,001–60,000	4
60,001–80,000	5
80,001–100,000	6
100,001–120,000	7
over 120,000	Not limited

"Branch banks" are defined as one designated office or facility located in a county other than that of the principal office, where the county population exceeds 250,000 and the branch bank was established prior to January 1, 1971. No future branch may be established.

Any bank located in any county of the state having a population of 400,000 or more may establish branch banks within any adjacent county having a population of 400,000 or more.

Facilities located within 200 yards of an existing office are not considered bank offices or facilities subject to population limitation.

State	Branching Statutes
Hawaii	Statewide branching, except for a four-branch limitation per zone in Honolulu.
Idaho	Statewide branching.
Illinois	Branching is prohibited; one facility is permitted within 1,500 feet and another within 3,500 yards of the main banking premises.
Indiana	In counties having less than 500,000 inhabitants or in counties having three or more cities of second class, a bank may branch in any city or

Continued

	town within the county, provided there is no bank in such city or town. In all counties having an excess of 500,000 inhabitants and not having three or more cities of second class, any bank may branch in any city or town within the county limits.
Iowa	Branching is specifically prohibited. However, banks may operate up to four full-service facilities within the municipal corporation or urban complex in which the principal office is located if the municipal corporation or urban complex has a population of over 200,000; three such facilities if the population is over 100,000 but less than 200,000; and two such facilities if the population is less than 100,000.
	Full-service office facilities are also permitted outside the municipal corporation or urban complex in which the principal office is located, provided that they are in the same county or in a contiguous county.
Kansas	Branching is prohibited; one or more banks may operate one attached auxiliary teller facility and not more than three detached auxiliary banking service facilities. Such facilities must be located within the city or township in which the bank's designated place of business is located and more than 50 feet from any other non-participating bank or facility thereof. Any bank electing to establish the maximum number of detached facilities shall establish and maintain at least one within 2,600 feet of its principal place of business.
Kentucky	A bank may establish a branch within the city or county in which its principal office is located, except that a branch may not be established in a city in which there is an existing bank, nor within an unincorporated area in a radius of one mile of an existing bank.
Louisiana	Any bank having capital of $100,000 or more may open a branch in parishes where there are no state banks; not more than one branch is permitted in any parish other than the parish of domicile.
Maine	Statewide branching.
Maryland	Statewide branching.
Massachusetts	Branches may be established in the same city as a bank's principal office and in other towns in the same county having no or inadequate banking facilities.
	Banks may branch across county lines to locations within 15 miles of the county boundary, de novo or by merger, subject to a limitation of only one application per year for a branch outside the bank's home county.
Michigan	Any bank may establish a branch within a village or city in the county in which its principal office is located or in an adjacent county, within 25 miles of the principal office; no branch may be established in a city or village in which a bank or branch thereof is in operation.
Minnesota	Branching is prohibited; facilities are permitted.
Mississippi	A bank may establish a branch bank within a radius of 100 miles of its principal office, except that no bank shall establish more than fifteen branch banks, and no branch banks are permitted in a town or city of less than 3,100 population according to the last preceding federal census where such town or city has one or more banks in operation. All parent banks permitted to establish branch banks shall have a paid-in,

Continued

unimpaired capital (exclusive of reserves and undivided profits) of not less than $100,000, and such minimum required capital shall be increased for each branch bank established by an amount not less than the minimum required capital for a unit bank in the municipality in which the branch bank shall be established.

A bank may establish a branch office within the corporate limits of the city where the bank is domiciled when the population is not less than 10,000; within the limits of the county wherein such bank is domiciled; and within the limits of any county adjacent to the county within which such banks are domiciled, provided that no branch office shall be established in any town or city of less than 3,500 population where such town or city has one or more banks or branch banks in operation.

A bank may establish a drive-in teller's window apart from the main building of such bank, a branch bank thereof, or a branch office thereof, within or adjacent to the corporate limits of the municipality in which the bank, branch bank, or branch office is located, without regard to the size or population of such municipality. In order to offer services other than paying and receiving at such a drive-in-window, a bank must apply to the state comptroller, who shall have the authority to grant any additional services that are needed.

Missouri   Branching is prohibited; facilities are permitted. All banks are authorized to maintain two separate facilities within the same city, town, village, or unincorporated community as the main banking house and within the same county as the main banking house. The facility may not be located closer than 400 feet to the main banking house of another existing banking institution unless the facility is located closer to the main banking house of the banking institution operating the facility than it is to the competing institution's main banking office, or unless the affected banking institution's consent is in writing.

Montana   Branching is prohibited; a facility is permitted, provided that it is located within 1,000 feet of a bank's principal office and is not closer than 200 feet to a facility of another bank, nor closer than 300 feet to another bank's principal office.

Nebraska   Branching is prohibited; a bank may maintain an attached auxiliary teller office and establish and maintain two detached auxiliary teller offices within the city in which the bank is located. Any bank that establishes two detached offices must locate one such office within 3 miles of its designated principal place of business. No detached office shall be located within 300 feet of another bank and 50 feet of another auxiliary teller office.

Nevada   Statewide branching.

New Hampshire   A bank may establish a branch within the town in which its principal office is located, or within a contiguous town or noncontiguous town within a radius of 15 miles of the principal office; branches are not permitted in a contiguous town, however, if there is an operating bank that was in existence on October 1, 1963 in such town, or in a noncontiguous town if there is an operating bank that was in existence on October 1, 1963, within a radius of 10 miles of the proposed branch location.

Continued

State	Branching Statutes
New Jersey	A bank may establish a branch office in the same municipality in which it maintains its principal office. It may also establish a full branch or minibranch office in any municipality except one which has a population less than 10,000 and in which another banking institution maintains its principal office. However, if the other institution is a member of a multibank holding company, the prohibition does not apply. A bank may establish a manned or unmanned communication terminal branch without the above restrictions. It may also establish one auxiliary office (facility) to the main office or any branch office. Such auxiliary office may perform limited activities, as prescribed in the law.
New Mexico	A bank may establish a branch within the county in which its principal office is located, and in an adjoining county or within a 100-mile radius, provided that another bank is not in operation in such county.
New York	A bank may establish one or more branch offices at any location in the state, provided that no branch may be established in a city or village (except for the city or village in which its principal office is located) with a population of 50,000 or less within which is located the principal office of another bank.
North Carolina	Statewide branching.
North Dakota	Branching is prohibited. A bank may establish paying and receiving stations within the county in which its home office is located or in any adjoining county with a 35-mile radius, provided that no such station may be established in any city or town with an established banking institution located therein.

Every bank under the supervision of the state banking board and any national bank doing business in the state may, upon compliance, maintain and operate separate and apart from its banking house one facility for drive-in and walk-in service, in addition to such service at its main banking house and at its paying and receiving station, if any. |
Ohio	A bank may establish a branch countywide in the county of its main office or in a contiguous county, commencing in 1979. Statewide branching will be permitted in 1989.
Oklahoma	Branching is prohibited; a bank is permitted one facility within 1,000 feet of its principal office.
Oregon	Statewide branching is permitted, except that a branch is not permitted in any city of less than 50,000 population where the principal office of another bank is located.
Pennsylvania	A bank may establish a branch only in the same county in which its principal office is located or in a contiguous county.
Rhode Island	Statewide branching.
South Carolina	Statewide branching.
South Dakota	De novo branch offices shall not be granted after July 1, 1969; however, branch banks may be established by a bank consolidating or merging with or purchasing the assets of another bank, with certain limitations.
Tennessee	A bank may establish a branch with the county in which its principal office is located.
Texas	Branching is prohibited; facilities are permitted.
Utah	A bank and its branches must be located within the corporate limits of a

Continued

State	Branching Statutes
	city or town or within unincorporated areas of a county in which a first-class city (100,000 population or more) is located; except, in such first-class cities or within such unincorporated areas, no branches may be established in any city or town in which the principal office of another bank is located, unless the bank seeking to establish a branch takes over the existing bank, and no branch may be established outside the corporate limits of a city or town in such close proximity to an established bank or branch as to interfere unreasonably with the business thereof.
Vermont	Statewide branching.
Virginia	Branches may be established within the town, city, or county limits in which a bank's principal office is located; in cities contiguous to the county or city in which the principal office is located; 15 miles from the boundary of the city or county where its main office is located, regardless of what jurisdiction. Banks can acquire branches by merger where the merging banks have been in existence for five or more years. A bank's main office, for branching purposes, is fixed by the establishment of its first branch after June 30, 1978. Banks that have merged may branch from the former main offices of the merged banks, if the former office was a main office for six years before the merger took place and the former main office was in a city of 25,000 or more, or in a county of 100,000 or more (according to the last census).
Washington	Statewide branching is permitted to banks having paid-in capital of not less than $500,000; a bank having capital of not less than $200,000 may establish a branch within the county in which its principal office is located; except through acquisition, no bank may establish a branch in any city or town outside the city or town within which its principal place of business is located in which another bank or branch is located.
West Virginia	Branching is prohibited.
Wisconsin	A bank may establish a branch in municipalities in which its principal office is not located, provided that no bank or branch is located within 3 miles of the proposed branch site; the proposed branch shall be located in the same county as the bank's principal office or in a contiguous county so long as the branch is within 25 miles of the bank's principal office.
Wyoming	No statute; there are no branch banks in the state.

Note: The term "principal office" signifies a bank's main office or legally established place of business.

The term "branch" signifies a banking office at which a relatively full range of banking services are permitted, particularly the authority to make loans.

The term "facility" signifies a banking office at which a restricted range of banking services are authorized; usually, these services are limited to accepting deposits, cashing checks, and receiving loan payments. The drive-in or off-premises teller window is a typical facility. The type of services offered and location of facilities in relationship to a bank's principal office or the principal office of another bank vary among those states authorizing facilities. Facilities as a rule are permitted in states allowing the full-service branch.

In addition to statutes referring to branch and facility location, state codes have varying capital requirements relating to the establishment of new offices.

Source: A Profile of State-Chartered Banking, Conference of State Bank Supervisors. Used with permission of the publisher.

Directory of Professional and Trade Associations, Federal Government Regulatory Agencies, and Special-Purpose Governmental Units
(names, addresses, and telephone numbers of interest to bankers and financial specialists)

American Bankers Association
1120 Connecticut Avenue, N.W.
Washington, D.C. 20036
(202) 467-4000

American Conference of Real Estate Investment Trusts
608 13th Street, N.W.
Washington, D.C. 20005
(202) 347-9464

American Institute of Financial Brokers
121 West Wacker Drive
Chicago, Illinois 60601
(312) 346-6080

American Recovery Association, Inc.
P.O. Box 52076
New Orleans, Louisiana 70152
(504) 367-0711

The American Safe Deposit Association
330 West Main Street
Greenwood, Indiana 46142
(317) 888-1118

American Savings and Loan League, Inc.
1435 G Street, N.W.
Suite 1019
Washington, D.C. 20005

American Stock Exchange
86 Trinity Place
New York, New York 10006
(212) 938-2388

Associated Credit Bureaus, Inc.
6767 Southwest Freeway
Houston, Texas 77036
(713) 774-8701

Association of Bank Holding Companies
730 15th Street, N.W.
Washington, D.C. 20005
(202) 393-1158

Association of Bank Travel Bureaus
915 South Clinton Street
Fort Wayne, Indiana 46802
(219) 461-7726

Association of Publicly Traded Investment Funds
767 Fifth Avenue, Room 4302
New York, New York 10022
(212) 754-9350

Association of Reserve City Bankers
135 South LaSalle Street, Room 2110
Chicago, Illinois 60603
(312) 782-7545

Bank Administration Institute
303 South Northwest Highway
Park Ridge, Illinois 60668
(312) 693-7300

Bank Marketing Association
309 West Washington Street
Chicago, Illinois 60606
(312) 782-1442

Bank Stationers Association
P.O. Box 3080
Falls Church, Virginia 22209
(703) 827-0162

Bankers Association for Foreign Trade
1101 16th Street, N.W., Suite 501
Washington, D.C. 20036
(202) 833-3060

Conference of State Bank Supervisors
1015 18th Street, N.W., Suite 606
Washington, D.C. 20036
(202) 296-2840

Consumer Bankers Association
1725 K Street, N.W.
Washington, D.C. 20006
(202) 466-2590

Consumer Credit Insurance Association
307 North Michigan Avenue
Chicago, Illinois 60601
(312) 726-9895

Council of Mutual Savings Institutions
507 Fifth Avenue
New York, New York 10017
(212) 867-2776

Continued

Credit Union Executives Society
6320 Monona Drive, Suite 300
Madison, Wisconsin 53716
(608) 221-4237

Credit Union National Association
P.O. Box 431
Madison, Wisconsin 53701
(608) 241-1211

Credit Women—International
20F Railway Exchange Building
St. Louis, Missouri 63101
(314) 621-9510

Dealer Bank Association
1800 K Street, N.W., Suite 1014
Washington, D.C. 20006
(202) 857-0100

Electronic Funds Transfer Association
1312 18th Street, N.W.
Washington, D.C. 20036
(202) 466-3880

The Electronic Money Council
1775 K Street, N.W., Suite 215
Washington, D.C. 20006
(202) 296-8920

Export-Import Bank of the United States
811 Vermont Avenue, N.W.
Washington, D.C. 20571
(202) 566-2117

Farm Credit Administration
490 L'Enfant Plaza East, S.W.
Washington, D.C. 20578
(202) 755-2130

Farmers Home Administration
U.S. Department of Agriculture
14th Street and Independence Avenue,
    S.W.
Washington, D.C. 20250
(202) 447-4323

Federal Deposit Insurance Corporation
550 17th Street, N.W.
Washington, D.C. 20429
(202) 393-8400

Federal Home Loan Bank Board
1700 G Street, N.W.
Washington, D.C. 20552
(202) 377-6000

Federal Home Loan Mortgage Corporation
1776 G Street, N.W.
P. O. Box 37248
Washington, D.C. 20013
(202) 789-4700

Federal Housing Administration
Department of Housing and Urban
    Development
451 7th Street, S.W.
Washington, D.C. 20410
(202) 755-5111

Federal National Mortgage Association
3900 Wisconsin Avenue, N.W.
Washington, D.C. 20016
(202) 537-7000

Federal Reserve System
Board of Governors of the Federal
    Reserve System
20th Street and Constitution Avenue, N.W.
Washington, D.C. 20551
(202) 452-3000

Federal Savings and Loan Insurance Corporation
Federal Home Loan Bank Board
1700 G Street, N.W.
Washington, D.C. 20552
(202) 377-6000

Federal Trade Commission
Pennsylvania Avenue at 6th Street, N.W.
Washington, D.C. 20580
(202) 523-3625

Financial Analysts Federation
1633 Broadway, 14th Floor
New York, New York 10019
(212) 957-2860

Financial Executives Institute
633 Third Avenue
New York, New York 10017
(212) 953-0500

Financial Managers Society for Savings Institutions, Inc.
111 East Wacker Drive
Chicago, Illinois 60601
(312) 644-3100

Continued

Government National Mortgage Association
Department of Housing and Urban Development
451 7th Street, S.W.
Washington, D.C. 20410
(202) 755-5111

Independent Bankers Association of America
P.O. Box 267
Sauk Centre, Minnesota 56378
(612) 352-6546

Interbank Card Association
888 Seventh Avenue
New York, New York 10019
(212) 974-5700

International Association of Credit Card Investigators
Box 813
Novato, California 94947
(415) 897-8800

International Association of Financial Planners
2150 Parklake Drive, N.E., Suite 260
Atlanta, Georgia 30345
(404) 934-0533

International Consumer Credit Association
243 North Lindbergh
St. Louis, Missouri 63131
(314) 991-3030

Investment Company Institute
1775 K Street, N.W.
Washington, D.C. 20006
(202) 293-7700

Mortgage Bankers Association of America
1125 15th Street, N.W.
Washington, D.C. 20005
(202) 785-8333

Municipal Finance Officers Association of the United States and Canada
180 N. Michigan Avenue
Chicago, Illinois 60601
(312) 977-9700

Municipal Treasurers Association of the United States and Canada
1301 Aviation Boulevard
Redondo Beach, California 90278
(213) 374-7178

National Association of Bank Servicers
50 West Broad Street, Suite 1331
Columbus, Ohio 43215
(614) 461-4011

National Association of Bank Women, Inc.
111 East Wacker Drive
Chicago, Illinois 60601
(312) 565-4100

National Association of Consumer Credit Administrators
Lew Wallace Building
Santa Fe, New Mexico 87503
(505) 827-2217

National Association of County Treasurers and Finance Officers
1735 New York Avenue, N.W.
Washington, D.C. 20006
(202) 785-9577

National Association of Credit Management
475 Park Avenue South
New York, New York 10016
(212) 725-1700

National Association of Estate Planning Council
2017 Walnut Street
Philadelphia, Pennsylvania 19103
(215) 569-3650

National Association of Federal Credit Unions
1111 North 19th Street, Suite 700
Arlington, Virginia 22209
Mail: P.O. Box 3769
Washington, D.C. 20007
(202) 522-4770

National Association of Installment Companies, Inc.
38 West 32nd Street
New York, New York 10001
(212) 239-6520

Continued

National Association of Mutual Savings Banks
200 Park Avenue
New York, New York 10017
(212) 973-5432

National Association of Real Estate Investment Trusts
1101 17th Street, N.W.
Washington, D.C. 20036
(202) 785-8717

National Association of Securities Dealers
1735 K Street, N.W.
Washington, D.C. 20006
(202) 833-7200

National Association of Small Business Investment Companies
618 Washington Building, N.W.
Washington, D.C. 20005
(202) 638-3411

National Association of State Credit Union Supervisors
1001 Connecticut Avenue, N.W., Suite 800
Washington, D.C. 20036
(202) 452-1530

National Association of State Savings and Loan Supervisors
1001 Connecticut Avenue, N.W.
Washington, D.C. 20036
(202) 452-1523

National Automated Clearing House Association
1120 Connecticut Avenue, N.W.
Washington, D.C. 20036
(202) 467-4016

National Savings and Loan League
1101 15th Street, N.W.
Washington, D.C. 20005
(202) 331-0270

New York Clearing House Association
100 Broad Street
New York, New York 10004
(212) 943-2200

New York Stock Exchange
11 Wall Street
New York, New York 10005
(212) 623-3000

Office of the Comptroller of the Currency
490 L'Enfant Plaza East, S.W.
Washington, D.C. 20219
(202) 566-2000

Robert Morris Associates
National Association of Bank Loan and Credit Officers
Philadelphia National Bank Building
Philadelphia, Pennsylvania 19107
(215) 665-2850

Savings Institutions Marketing Society of America
111 East Wacker Drive
Chicago, Illinois 60601
(312) 938-2570

Securities and Exchange Commission
500 North Capital Street
Washington, D.C. 20549
(202) 272-2000

Securities Industry Association
20 Broad Street
New York, New York 10005
(212) 425-2700

Small Business Administration
1441 L Street, N.W.
Washington, D.C. 20416
(202) 653-6395

Society of Financial Examiners
1406 Third National Building
Dayton, Ohio 45402
(513) 223-0419

The Stock Transfer Association, Inc.
c/o Manufacturers Hanover Trust Company
Four New York Plaza
New York, New York 10015
(212) 623-3162

United Mortgage Bankers of America
210 West St. George Avenue
Linden, New Jersey 07036

Continued

United States League of Savings Associations
111 East Wacker Drive
Chicago, Illinois 60601
(312) 644-3100

Visa
P.O. Box 8999
San Francisco, California 94128
(415) 573-1012

Bad-Check Laws in the States

State	Misdemeanor	Felony	Penalties	Evidence Rules
Alabama	All amounts		Check of $500 or more—fine of not less than $500 nor more than $5,000 or imprisonment up to 3 years, or both. Check under $500—fine depends on amount and offense. Convicted defendant pays court costs.	Nonpayment within 10 days in prima facie evidence of intent to defraud and knowledge of insufficient funds.
Alaska	$500 or less	Greater than $500	Issuing check for $50 or more, up to $500—maximum of $5,000 or imprisonment up to 1 year, or both. Issuing check under $50—maximum fine of $1,000 or imprisonment up to 90 days, or both. Issuing check for $25,000 or more—maximum fine of $50,000 or imprisonment up to 10 years, or both. Issuing check for $500 or more, up to $25,000—maximum fine of $50,000 or imprisonment up to 5 years, or both.	Uttering or delivering without funds or credit is prima facie evidence of intent to defraud unless maker has paid within 2 days after default.
Arizona	Under $25	$25 or over, or no account	Up to 6 months in jail or fine up to $300, or both. Up to 5 years in state prison or up to 1 year in county jail or fine up to $500, or both if between $25 and $100; if over $100 or if no account, up to 5 years in state prison.	State need not show that specific false representations extrinsic to check itself were made.
Arkansas	$100 or less	One or more checks totaling over $100	1st offense—fine of not less than $200 nor more than $500 or imprisonment up to 30 days, or both; 2nd offense—fine of not less than $50 nor more than $1,000 or imprisonment up to 60 days, or both; 3rd and subsequent offenses—fine of not less than $100 nor more than $2,000 or imprisonment up to 1 year, or both. Fine not exceeding $100,000 or imprisonment not exceeding 10 years, or both.	Making, drawing, uttering, or delivering is prima facie evidence of intent.
California	Discretion of court	Any amount	Up to one year in county jail, or up to 14 years in the state prison. Where amount is less than $100 and is first offense, up to one year in county jail.	Making, drawing, uttering, or delivering with intent to defraud and knowledge of insufficient funds is the crime. Notice of protest is presumptive evidence of knowledge of insufficiency of funds, but intent to defraud must be affirmatively proved by the prosecution.

Continued

661

State	Misdemeanor	Felony	Penalties	Evidence Rules
Colorado	From $50 up to $200	$200 or more or conviction involving 2 or more bad checks within 30 days totaling $200	Imprisonment in county jail for not less than 3 months nor more than 12 months or fine of not less than $250 nor more than $1,000, or both. Imprisonment in state penitentiary for not less than 1 year nor more than 5 years or fine of not less than $1,000 nor more than $15,000, or both. If twice previously convicted—imprisonment in state penitentiary for not less than 1 year and not more than 10 years or fine of not less than $2,000 nor more than $30,000, or both.	Except as to a postdated check, nonpayment is presumptive evidence of intent. Full satisfaction of check within 15 days after dishonor is a defense. Person instituting prosecution who fails to cooperate in the full prosecution of alleged offender may be liable for costs of prosecution.
Connecticut	All amounts		Up to $1,000 fine or 1 year in jail, or both.	Issuer is presumed to know that check would not be paid if no payment made within 8 days after receiving notice of dishonor.
Delaware	All amounts		Check under $100—fine not exceeding $500 or up to 1 year in jail, or both. Check for $100 and over fine and or imprisonment at discretion of court; person issuing check must make restitution.	Nonpayment within 10 days is prima facie evidence of knowledge of insufficient funds.
District of Columbia	Under $100	$100 or more	Up to 3 years in jail and $3,000 fine, or both.	Making, drawing, uttering, or delivering is prima facie evidence of intent to defraud and knowledge of insufficient funds if maker has not paid amount due within 5 days after draft has not been paid.
Florida	Under $50	$50 or over	Up to $300 or 6 months in jail. Up to 5 years in jail or $1,000 fine.	Refusal of drawee to pay is prima facie evidence of intent.
Georgia	All amounts	Except if check drawn on bank of another state	Up to $1,000 fine or 1 year on public works, or both, or 6 to 12 months with State Board of Correction.	Drawing, uttering, or delivery is prima facie evidence of knowledge of insufficient funds if maker has not paid amount due within 10 days after notice by certified mail.
Hawaii	All amounts		Up to 1 year in jail or $1,000 fine, or both.	Insufficient funds or credit is prima facie evidence of intent provided check not paid within 5 days.
Idaho	All amounts		Fine or imprisonment, or both, as follows: if under $25 and 1st offense—$300 and 6 months; 2nd offense—$1,000 and 1 year; 3rd offense, or if amount in excess of $25—$5,000 and 3 years.	Making, drawing, uttering, or delivering is prima facie evidence of intent.
Illinois	All amounts		Up to $500 fine or 1 year in jail, or both.	Failure to have sufficient funds is prima facie evidence of intent.
Indiana	All amounts		Up to $5,000 fine or up to 1 year in jail, or both.	Failure to have sufficient funds in or an account with the drawee institution constitutes prima facie evidence that drawer knew it would not be paid.

State	Amount	Penalty	
Iowa	Under $20	Up to $100 fine or 30 days in jail.	Nonpayment is prima facie evidence of intent providing makers shall not have paid the amount due within 10 days.
	Over $20, or no account	Up to 7 years in penitentiary, or 1 year in jail or up to $500 fine, or both.	
Kansas	Under $50	Up to $2,500 fine or up to 1 year in jail, or both.	No payment 7 days after notice.
	Over $50	Up to $5,000 fine or 1 to 5 years in jail, or both.	
Kentucky	Under $20	Up to $100 fine or 90 days in jail, or both.	Making or delivering is prima facie evidence of intent. Withdrawal to prevent payment is crime.
	Over $20	1 to 2 years in penitentiary.	
Louisiana	Under $100	Imprisonment for not more than 6 months or fine of not more than $500, or both. 3rd or more such conviction—fine of not more than $1,000 or imprisonment for not more than 2 years, or both.	Refusal of bank to pay prima facie evidence of lack of funds at time of issuing check.
	Over $100	Check for $100 or more and less than $500—imprisonment for not more than 2 years or fine of not more than $2,000, or both. Check for $500 or more—imprisonment for not more than 10 years or fine of not more than $3,000, or both. In addition, court may order restitution of bad check plus attorney's fees.	
Maine	All amounts	Up to $1,000 fine or 11 months in jail, or both.	Nonpayment within 5 days after notice is prima facie evidence of intent.
Maryland	Under $500	Maximum fine of $100 or imprisonment up to 18 months, or both.	When a check is drawn on an account having funds insufficient to cover it, the drawer is presumed to know of the insufficiency.
	Over $500	Maximum fine of $1,000 or imprisonment up to 15 years, or both.	
Massachusetts	Up to $100	Up to $300 fine or 1 year in jail.	Nonpayment within 2 days after notice is prima facie evidence of intent.
	Over $100	Up to $600 fine and up to 2 years in jail, or up to 5 years in penitentiary.	
Michigan	$50 or less	Up to $250 fine or 6 months in jail.	Nonpayment within 5 days is prima facie evidence of intent.
	Over $50	Up to $500 fine or 1 year in jail.	
Minnesota	All amounts	Up to $100 fine or 90 days in jail, or both.	Nonpayment within 5 days is prima facie evidence of intent.
Mississippi	Under $100	Fine of not less than $25 nor more than $500 or imprisonment in the county jail for not less than 5 days nor more than 5 months, or both; 2nd offense—fine of not less than $50 nor more than $1,000 or imprisonment of not less than 30 days nor more than 1 year; 3rd offense—imprisonment in state penitentiary for a term of not less than 1 year nor more than 5 years.	Insufficient funds when check was issued is prima facie evidence of intent.
	Over $100	Fine of not less than $100 nor more than $1,000 or imprisonment for a term of not more than 3 years, or both.	

Continued

State	Misdemeanor	Felony	Penalties	Evidence Rules
Missouri	$100 or under		Up to $500 fine or 6 months in jail, or both.	Nonpayment of check and costs within 10 days after notice is prima facie evidence of intent.
Montana	NSF under $25	$100 or over	Up to $1,000 fine or 1 year in jail, or both. Up to $300 fine or 6 months in jail, or both.	Nonpayment within 5 days after notice is prima facie evidence of intent.
	NSF over $25, or no account		Up to $5,000 fine or 5 years in penitentiary, or both.	
Nebraska	Under $300	Over $300	Obtaining property worth: More than $1,000—Class III felony. More than $300—Class IV felony. More than $75—Class I misdemeanor; 2nd offense—Class IV felony. Less than $75—Class II misdemeanor; 2nd offense—Class IV felony. Issuing or passing a check of any amount—Class II misdemeanor.	Nonpayment within 5 days after notice of dishonor is prima facie evidence of intent.
Nevada	Up to $100	Over $100	Up to 6 months in county jail or $500 fine, or both. State prison term of 1 to 10 years or $5,000 fine, or both.	Nonpayment within 10 days after notice is prima facie evidence of intent to defraud and knowledge of insufficient funds.
New Hampshire	Larceny or attempted larceny		Up to $200 fine or up to 1 year in jail, or both.	Making and drawing is prima facie evidence of intent, provided check not paid within 10 days.
New Jersey	$200 or more		Up to $1,000 fine or up to 1 year in jail, or both.	Making and drawing is prima facie evidence of intent.
New Mexico	More than $1, less than $25	$25 or over	Up to $100 fine or 30 days in jail, or both.	Prima facie evidence of intent from fact that the maker had no account at the bank the check was drawn on or that the maker failed to pay check and cost within 10 days of notice.
New York	All amounts—Class B misdemeanor		1 to 3 years in jail or up to $1,000, or both. Up to 3 months in jail, or up to $500, or up to double the amount of the drawer's gain from the commission of the offense.	Nonpayment is prima facie evidence of intent. Notice of Protest Certificate or officer of bank under oath to prove nonpayment. Full payment within 10 days after dishonor is an affirmative defense.
North Carolina	All amounts		Fine of $50 to $500 or up to 6 months in jail. If check is less than $50—$50 fine or up to 30 days in jail; over 3 convictions—up to 1 year in jail. If check drawn on nonexistent account—fine not to exceed $1,000 or imprisonment for not more than 2 years, or both. If check drawn on account closed by drawer prior to time check drawn—fine not to exceed $400 or imprisonment for not more than 5 months, or both.	No presumption.

664

State	Amount	Penalty	Intent/Presumption
North Dakota	All amounts	Fine of $25 to $250 or up to 3 months in county jail, or both. If no account—fine up to $500 and 1 year in jail.	No presumption.
Ohio	Under $60	Fine of $50 to $200 or up to 6 months in jail, or both.	Refusal of payment by bank is prima facie evidence of intent.
	Over $60	Fine of $50 to $200 or 1 to 7 years in jail, or both.	
	$20 or less	Up to 1 year imprisonment or up to $1,000 fine, or both.	Refusal of payment by bank is prima facie evidence of intent provided not paid within 5 days after presentation.
	More than $20 or one of a series of checks whose total exceeds $20	1 to 10 years imprisonment or up to $5,000 fine.	
Oregon	Up to $75	Up to $1,000 fine or up to 1 year in jail, or both.	Refusal of drawee to pay within 10 days is prima facie evidence of intent. Notice of protest is proof of presumptive intent.
	Over $75	Imprisonment for not more than 5 years.	
Pennsylvania	Over $200	Up to $1,000 fine or up to 2 years in penitentiary, or both.	Making is prima facie evidence of intent if not paid within 10 days after notice.
Rhode Island	Not exceeding $100	Up to $500 fine or up to 1 year imprisonment, or both.	As against maker or drawer the making, drawing, uttering, or delivering is prima facie evidence of intent to defraud unless paid within 15 days.
South Carolina	Over $100	Up to $1,000 fine or up to 1 year imprisonment, or both.	If not paid within 7 days after notice, prima facie evidence of intent.
		Up to $1,000 fine or up to 30 days in jail, or both.	
South Dakota	All amounts	1st offense—fine of not more than $100 or imprisonment for not more than 30 days, or both. 2nd offense—fine of not more than $300 nor less than $100 and imprisonment of not more than 6 months or less than 30 days. 3rd and subsequent offenses—fine of not more than $500 nor less than $300 and imprisonment for not more than 1 year nor less than 6 months.	Making, drawing, uttering, and delivering is prima facie evidence of intent.
	Agent or officer of business issues check, or checks totaling $1,000 or more within 30 days	Up to 3 years and not more than $1,000 fine.	
Tennessee	All amounts	Check not over $100—not over 11 months 29 days in jail or not over $500 fine, or both. Check more than $100—3 to 10 years in penitentiary.	Nonpayment is prima facie evidence of intent. Nonpayment within 5 days after written notice from bank in state. Out-of-state, no notice required.

Continued

State	Misdemeanor	Felony	Penalties	Evidence Rules
Texas	1st offense under $50 2nd offense under $50 3rd offense or over $50		Up to 2 years in county jail or up to $1,000 fine, or both. 30 days to 2 years in jail and up to $2,000 fine. 2 to 10 years.	Nonpayment within 10 days after notice is prima facie evidence of intent and knowledge.
Utah	Under $100; over $100 but not more than $250	From $250 to $1,000	Up to $299 fine or up to 6 months in jail, or both. Up to $5,000 fine or up to 5 years in jail, or both. Up to $10,000 fine or up to 15 years in jail, or both.	Making, drawing, uttering, or delivering check is prima facie evidence of intent. Presumption of knowledge if issuer had no account with drawee at time of issue.
Vermont	No criminal liability	Under "false token" statute use of check to defraud subject to penalty of 10 years plus $1,000 fine	Provision for civil arrest.	Refusal of drawee to pay within 8 days is prima facie evidence of knowledge of insufficient funds at time of making.
Virginia	$5 or less	$5 or over	Fine of $5 to $100 or 10 days to 12 months in jail, or both. 1 to 5 years in the penitentiary or fine and jail, or 1 to 10 years in penitentiary in discretion of court.	Nonpayment within 5 days is prima facie evidence of intent.
Washington	All amounts—gross misdemeanor		Up to 1 year in jail or up to $1,000 fine, or both.	Giving of check is prima facie evidence of intent.
West Virginia	Under $200	$200 or over	$5 to $100 fine or 5 to 60 days in jail, or both. Up to $500 fine and 1 to 5 years in penitentiary.	Making check is prima facie evidence of intent. If paid before trial or examination by justice of the peace, no presumption of knowledge shall arise.
Wisconsin	All amounts		Up to $1,000 fine or 1 year in jail.	Nonpayment within 5 days after notice is prima facie evidence of intent. Issuer liable for costs and expenses of collection.
Wyoming	All amounts		1st offense under $50—up to $500 fine or up to 6 months in jail, or both. 2nd offense under $50—up to $1,000 fine or up to 6 months in jail, or both. Over $50—up to $1,000 fine or up to 1 year in jail, or both.	Nonpayment within 5 days after notice is prima facie evidence of intent.

Source: National Association of Credit Management.

Appendix J: Computational Tables and Foreign Exchanges

Foreign Exchange

Country	Currency	Consisting of:
Abu Dhabi	Dinar	1,000 fils
Aden	Dinar	1,000 fils
Afghanistan	Afghani	100 puls
Albania	Lek	100 qintar
Algeria	Dinar	100 centimes
Andorra	Peseta	100 centimos
Angola	Kwanza	100 centavos
Antigua	Dollar	100 cents
Argentina	Peso	100 centavos
Australia	Dollar	100 cents
Austria	Schilling	100 groschen
Azores	Escudo	100 cents
Bahamas	Dollar	100 cents
Bahrain	Dinar	1,000 fils
Balearic Island	Peseta	100 centimos
Bangladesh	Taka	100 paise
Barbados	Dollar	100 cents
Belgium	Franc	100 centimes
Belize	Pound	100 pence
Benin	Franc	100 centimes
Bermuda	Pound	100 pence
Bhutan	Ngultrum	100 chetrum
Bolivia	Peso	100 centavos
Botswana	Pula	100 cents
Brazil	Cruzeiro	100 centavos
British Honduras	Dollar	100 cents
Brunei	Dollar	100 cents
Bulgaria	Lev	100 stotinki
Burma	Kyat	100 pyas
Burundi	Franc	100 centimes
Cambodia	Riel	100 sen
Cameroons	Franc	100 centimes
Canada	Dollar	100 cents
Canary Islands	Peseta	100 centimos
Cape Verde Islands	Escudo	100 centavos
Central African Empire	Franc	100 centimes
Chad	Franc	100 centimes
Chile	Peso	100 centavos
China	Yuan	10,000 jen min piao
Columbia	Peso	100 centavos
Comoros	Franc	100 centimes
Congo (Kinshasa)	Zaire	100 makutu
Congo (Brazzaville)	Franc	100 centimes
Costa Rica	Colon	100 centimos
Cuba	Peso	100 centavos
Cyprus	Pound	1,000 mils
Czechoslovakia	Koruna	100 hellers

Continued

Country	Currency	Consisting of:
Dahomey	Franc	100 centimes
Denmark	Krona	100 ore
Djibouti	Franc	100 centimes
Dominica	Dollar	100 cents
Dominican Republic	Peso	100 centavos
Dubai	Gulf Riyal	100 dirhams
Ecuador	Sucre	100 centavos
Egypt	Pound	100 piasters = 1,000 milliemes
El Salvador	Colon	100 centavos
Equatorial Guinea	Ekuwele	100 centimos
Ethiopia	Dollar	100 cents
Fiji Islands	Pound	100 pence
Finland	Markka	100 pennis
France	Franc	100 centimes
French Somaliland	Franc	100 centimes
Gabon	Franc	100 centimes
Gambia	Dalasi	100 bututs
Germany	Deutsche mark	100 pfennig
Ghana	Cedi	100 pesewas
Gibraltar	Pound	100 pence
Grand Cayman Island	Pound	100 pence
Greece	Drachma	100 lepta
Grenada	Dollar	100 cents
Guadeloupe	Franc	100 centimes
Guam	U.S. dollar	100 cents
Guatemala	Quetzal	100 centavos
Guiana, French	Franc	100 centimes
Guinea	Syli	100 centimes
Guinea-Bissau	Escudo	100 centavos
Guyana	Dollar	100 cents
Haiti	Gourde	100 centimes
Honduras (Republic)	Lempira	100 centavos
Hong Kong	Dollar	100 cents
Hungary	Forint	100 fillers
Iceland	Krona	100 aurar
India	Rupee	100 paise
Indonesia	Rupiah	100 sen
Iran	Rial	100 dinars
Iraq	Dinar	1,000 fils
Ireland (Republic)	Pound	100 pence
Israel	Shekel	100 new agorot
Italy	Lira	100 centesimi
Ivory Coast	Franc	100 centimes
Jamaica	Dollar	100 cents
Japan	Yen	100 sen
Jordan	Dinar	1,000 fils
Kampuchea	Riel	100 sen
Kenya	Shilling	100 cents

Continued

Country	Currency	Consisting of:
Kiribati	Dollar	100 cents
Korea (North)	Won	100 chon
Korea (South)	Won	100 chon
Kuwait	Dinar	1,000 fils
Laos	Kip	100 at
Lebanon	Pound	100 piasters
Lesotho	Rand	100 cents
Liberia	U.S. dollar	100 cents
Libya	Dinar	1,000 fils
Liechtenstein	Franc, franken	100 centimes
Luxembourg	Franc	100 centimes
Macao	Pataca	100 avos
Madagascar	Franc	100 centimes
Madeira	Escudo	100 centavos
Malagasy	Franc	100 centimes
Malawi	Kwacha	100 tambala
Malaysia	Ringgit	100 sen
Maldives	Rupee	100 cents
Mali	Franc	100 centimes
Malta	Pound	100 pence
Marshall Islands	U.S. dollar	100 cents
Martinique	Franc	100 centimes
Mauritania	Ouguiya	5 khoums
Mauritius	Rupee	100 cents
Mexico	Peso	100 centavos
Monaco	Franc	100 centimes
Mongolia	Tughrik	100 mongos
Montserrat	Dollar	100 cents
Morocco	Dirham	100 Moroccan francs
Mozambique	Escudo	100 centavos
Nauru	Dollar	100 cents
Nepal	Rupee	100 pice
Netherland Antilles	Guilder	100 cents
Netherlands	Guilder	100 cents
Nevis	Dollar	100 cents
New Caledonia	Franc	100 centimes
New Guinea	Dollar	100 cents
New Hebrides Islands	Franc	100 centimes
New Zealand	Dollar	100 cents
Nicaragua	Cordoba	100 centavos
Niger	Franc	100 centimes
Nigeria	Naira	100 kobo
Norway	Krone	100 ore
Oceania (French)	Franc	100 centimes
Oman	Rial	100 dinars
Pakistan	Rupee	100 paisa
Panama	Balboa	100 centesimos
Papua	Kina	100 cents

Continued

Country	Currency	Consisting of:
Paraguay	Guarani	100 centimos
Peru	Sol	100 centavos
Philippines	Peso	100 centavos
Poland	Zloty	100 grosze
Portugal	Escudo	100 centavos
Portuguese East Africa	Escudo	100 centavos
Portuguese Guinea	Escudo	100 centavos
Puerto Rico	U.S. dollar	100 cents
Qatar	Gulf Riyal	100 dirhams
Réunion Island	Franc	100 centimes
Romania	Leu	100 bani
Rwanda	Franc	100 centimes
Ryukyu Islands	U.S. dollar	100 cents
St. Kitts	Dollar	100 cents
St. Lucia	Dollar	100 cents
St. Vincent	Dollar	100 cents
Samoa	Tala	100 sene
San Marino	Lira	100 centesimi
San Tome and Principe	Dobra	100 cents
Somoa (British)	Dollar	100 cents
Saudi Arabia	Riyal	20 gurshes = 100 halalah
Senegal	Franc	100 centimes
Seychelles	Rupee	100 cents
Sierra Leone	Leone	100 cents
Singapore	Dollar	100 cents
Solomon Islands	Dollar	100 cents
Somalia	So. schilling	100 centesimi
South Africa (Republic)	Rand	100 cents
South West Africa (Namibia)	Rand	100 cents
South Yemen	Dinar	1,000 fils
Spain	Peseta	100 centimos
Sri Lanka	Rupee	100 paise
Sudan	Pound	100 piasters = 1,000 milliemes
Suriname	Guilder	100 cents
Swaziland	Lilangeni	100 cents
Sweden	Krona	100 ore
Switzerland	Franc	100 centimes
Syria	Pound	100 piasters
Tahiti	Franc	100 centimes
Taiwan	Dollar	100 cents
Tanzania	Shilling	100 cents
Thailand	Baht	100 satang
Timor	Escudo	100 centavos
Togo	Franc	100 centimes
Tonga Islands	Pa'anga	100 cents
Trinidad and Tobago	Dollar	100 cents
Tunisia	Dinar	1,000 milliemes
Turkey	Lira	100 centesimi

Continued

Country	Currency	Consisting of:
Tuvalu	Dollar	100 cents
Uganda	Shilling	100 cents
United Arab Emirates	Dirham	100 francs
United Kingdom	Pound	100 pence
Upper Volta	Franc	100 centimes
Uruguay	Peso	100 centesimos
USA	Dollar	100 cents
USSR	Ruble	100 kopecks
Vatican City	Lira	100 centesimi
Venezuela	Bolivar	100 centimos
Viet-Nam	Dong	100 cents
Virgin Islands (U.S.)	U.S. dollar	100 cents
Yemen	Rial	100 dinars
Yugoslavia	Dinar	100 paras
Zaire	Zaire	100 makutu
Zambia	Kwacha	100 newee
Zimbabwe	Dollar	100 cents

Compound Interest Table
(interest compounded semiannually)

Year	1%	2%	3%	4%	4 1/2%	5%	6%	7%	8%	10%
1	1.0100	1.0201	1.0302	1.0404	1.0455	1.0506	1.0609	1.0712	1.0816	1.1025
2	1.0201	1.0406	1.0613	1.0824	1.0930	1.1028	1.1255	1.1475	1.1692	1.2155
3	1.0303	1.0615	1.0934	1.1261	1.1438	1.1596	1.1940	1.2292	1.2646	1.3400
4	1.0407	1.0828	1.1264	1.1715	1.1948	1.2184	1.2667	1.3168	1.3678	1.4773
5	1.0511	1.1045	1.1605	1.2188	1.2481	1.2800	1.3439	1.4105	1.4794	1.6287
6	1.0616	1.1267	1.1956	1.2681	1.3004	1.3448	1.4257	1.5110	1.6002	1.7957
7	1.0723	1.1494	1.2317	1.3193	1.3643	1.4129	1.5125	1.6186	1.7307	1.9747
8	1.0830	1.1725	1.2689	1.3726	1.4264	1.4845	1.6047	1.7339	1.8720	2.1827
9	1.0949	1.1961	1.3073	1.4281	1.4913	1.5596	1.7024	1.8574	2.0247	2.4064
10	1.1059	1.2201	1.3463	1.4858	1.5592	1.6385	1.8061	1.9897	2.1899	2.6530
11	1.1170	1.2446	1.3875	1.5458	1.6301	1.7234	1.9161	2.1315	2.3687	2.9250
12	1.1281	1.2696	1.4295	1.6082	1.7044	1.8086	2.0326	2.2833	2.5619	3.2248
13	1.1394	1.2952	1.4727	1.6732	1.7820	1.9001	2.1564	2.4459	2.7710	3.5553
14	1.1508	1.3212	1.5172	1.7408	1.8631	1.9963	2.2878	2.6201	2.9971	3.9198
15	1.1623	1.3478	1.5630	1.8111	1.9479	2.0933	2.4271	2.8068	3.2417	4.3216
16	1.1740	1.3748	1.6103	1.8843	2.0365	2.2027	2.5749	3.0067	3.5062	4.7645
17	1.1857	1.4025	1.6589	1.9604	2.1272	2.3142	2.7317	3.2208	3.7923	5.2429
18	1.1976	1.4307	1.7091	2.0396	2.2240	2.4313	2.8981	3.4502	4.1018	5.7883
19	1.2096	1.4594	1.7607	2.1220	2.3252	2.5544	3.0746	3.6960	4.4365	6.3816
20	1.2218	1.4888	1.8140	2.2078	2.4310	2.6837	3.2618	3.9592	4.7985	7.0362
21	1.2341	1.5187	1.8686	2.2970	2.5415	2.8196	3.4605	4.2412	5.1900	7.7574
22	1.2465	1.5492	1.9253	2.3898	2.6572	2.9624	3.6712	4.5433	5.6136	8.5525
23	1.2590	1.5804	1.9835	2.4863	2.7781	3.1123	3.8948	4.8669	6.0716	9.4292
24	1.2716	1.6121	2.0434	2.5868	2.9045	3.2699	4.1320	5.2136	6.5670	10.3957
25	1.2843	1.6445	2.1052	2.6913	3.0367	3.4354	4.3836	5.5849	7.1030	11.4612

Continued

673

				Interest (dollars) at:						
Year	1%	2%	3%	4%	41/2%	5%	6%	7%	8%	10%
26	1.2973	1.6776	2.1688	2.8006	3.1749	3.6094	4.6506	5.9827	7.6826	12.6359
27	1.3103	1.7113	2.2344	2.9131	3.3193	3.7921	4.9338	6.4088	8.3094	13.9311
28	1.3235	1.7457	2.3019	3.0318	3.4703	3.9841	5.2343	6.8653	8.9875	15.3591
29	1.3367	1.7808	2.3715	3.1543	3.6282	4.1858	5.5531	7.3543	9.7208	16.9334
30	1.3501	1.8166	2.4432	3.2818	3.7933	4.3977	5.8913	7.8781	10.5143	18.6691
31	1.3637	1.8430	2.5170	3.4144	3.9660	4.6203	6.2500	8.4391	11.3742	20.5827
32	1.3773	1.8800	2.5931	3.5523	4.1465	4.8542	6.6307	9.0402	12.3024	22.6924
33	1.3911	1.9176	2.6715	3.6958	4.3351	5.0990	7.0345	9.6841	13.3062	25.0184
34	1.4051	1.9562	2.7522	3.8451	4.5324	5.3581	7.4629	10.3738	14.3920	27.5828
35	1.4192	1.9955	2.8354	4.0005	4.7387	5.6294	7.9174	11.1126	15.5644	30.4081
36	1.4334	2.0356	2.9211	4.1621	4.9543	5.9144	8.3996	11.9041	16.8367	33.5249
37	1.4478	2.0765	3.0094	4.3302	5.1798	6.2138	8.9111	12.7620	18.2105	36.9612
38	1.4623	2.1183	3.1004	4.5052	5.4146	6.5284	9.4538	13.6709	19.6965	40.7497
39	1.4770	2.1608	3.1941	4.6872	5.6610	6.8589	10.0295	14.6446	21.3038	44.9266
40	1.4918	2.2043	3.2907	4.8766	5.9288	7.2061	10.6403	15.6877	23.0422	49.5316
41	1.5067	2.2486	3.3901	5.0736	6.1986	7.5709	11.2883	16.8050	24.9224	54.6086
42	1.5218	2.2938	3.4926	5.2785	6.4807	7.9542	11.9758	18.0020	26.9561	60.2059
43	1.5371	2.3399	3.5982	5.4928	6.7756	8.3569	12.7051	19.2842	29.1857	66.3771
44	1.5545	2.3869	3.7070	5.7147	7.0840	8.7800	13.8832	20.6577	31.5348	73.1807
45	1.5701	2.4349	3.8191	5.9456	7.4062	9.2245	14.7287	22.1290	34.1080	80.6817
46	1.5858	2.4838	3.9345	6.1858	7.7430	9.6915	15.6257	23.7052	36.8813	88.9516
47	1.6017	2.5338	4.0432	6.4357	8.0954	10.1822	16.5773	25.3936	39.8908	98.0692
48	1.6178	2.5847	4.1655	6.6957	8.4638	10.6967	17.5868	27.2022	43.1459	107.1213
49	1.6330	2.6367	4.2914	6.9662	8.8490	11.2383	18.6597	29.1397	46.666	118.1012
50	1.6494	2.6897	4.4211	7.2477	9.2516	11.8072	19.7941	31.2141	50.4746	130.2066

Bond Interest Table
(interest on $1000 from 1 day to 6 months)

Exclude day of delivery, and to the interest for the full month or months add the interest for the remaining days. Calculate 30 days to the month and 360 days to the year.

Interest (dollars) at:

Day	3½%	3¾%	4%	4¼%	4½%	4¾%	5%	6%	7%
1	0.0972	0.1041	0.1111	0.1180	0.125	0.1319	0.1389	0.1667	0.1944
2	0.1944	0.2083	0.2222	0.2361	0.250	0.2638	0.2778	0.3333	0.3889
3	0.2916	0.3125	0.3333	0.3541	0.375	0.3958	0.4167	0.5000	0.5833
4	0.3889	0.4166	0.4444	0.4722	0.500	0.5277	0.5556	0.6667	0.7778
5	0.4861	0.5208	0.5555	0.5903	0.625	0.6597	0.6944	0.8333	0.9722
6	0.5833	0.6250	0.6667	0.7083	0.750	0.7916	0.8333	1.0000	1.1667
7	0.6805	0.7291	0.7778	0.8264	0.875	0.9236	0.9722	1.1667	1.3611
8	0.7778	0.8333	0.8889	0.9444	1.000	1.0555	1.1111	1.3333	1.5556
9	0.8750	0.9375	1.0000	1.0625	1.125	1.1875	1.2500	1.5000	1.7500
10	0.9722	1.0416	1.1111	1.1805	1.250	1.3194	1.3889	1.6667	1.9444
11	1.0694	1.1458	1.2222	1.2986	1.375	1.4513	1.5278	1.8333	2.1389
12	1.1667	1.2500	1.3333	1.4166	1.500	1.5833	1.6667	2.0000	2.3333
13	1.2639	1.3541	1.4444	1.5347	1.625	1.7152	1.8055	2.1667	2.5278
14	1.3611	1.4583	1.5555	1.6527	1.750	1.8472	1.9444	2.3333	2.7222
15	1.4583	1.5625	1.6667	1.7708	1.875	1.9791	2.0833	2.5000	2.9167
16	1.5555	1.6666	1.7778	1.8888	2.000	2.1111	2.2222	2.6667	3.1111
17	1.6528	1.7708	1.8889	2.0069	2.125	2.2430	2.3611	2.8333	3.3056
18	1.7500	1.8750	2.0000	2.1250	2.250	2.3750	2.5000	3.0000	3.5000
19	1.8472	1.9791	2.1111	2.2430	2.375	2.5069	2.6389	3.1667	3.6944
20	1.9444	2.0833	2.2222	2.3610	2.500	2.6388	2.7778	3.3333	3.8889
21	2.0417	2.1875	2.3333	2.4791	2.625	2.77G8	2.9167	3.5000	4.0833
22	2.1389	2.2916	2.4444	2.5972	2.750	2.9027	3.0555	3.6668	4.2778

Continued

675

Interest (dollars) at:

	3½%	3¾%	4%	4¼%	4½%	4¾%	5%	6%	7%
23	2.2361	2.3958	2.5555	2.7153	2.875	3.0347	3.1944	3.8333	4.4722
24	2.3333	2.5000	2.6667	2.8333	3.000	3.1666	3.3333	4.0000	4.6667
25	2.4305	2.6041	2.7778	2.9514	3.125	3.2986	3.4722	4.1667	4.8611
26	2.5278	2.7083	2.8889	3.0694	3.250	3.4305	3.6111	4.3333	5.0556
27	2.6250	2.8125	3.0000	3.1875	3.375	3.5625	3.7500	4.5000	5.2500
28	2.7222	2.9166	3.1111	3.3055	3.500	3.6944	3.8889	4.6667	5.4444
29	2.8194	3.0208	3.2222	3.4236	3.625	3.8263	4.0278	4.8333	5.6389
30	2.9167	3.1250	3.3333	3.5416	3.750	3.9583	4.1667	5.0000	5.8333
Month									
1	2.9167	3.1250	3.3333	3.5416	3.750	3.9583	4.1667	5.0000	5.8333
2	5.8333	6.2500	6.6667	7.0833	7.500	7.9166	8.333	10.0000	11.6667
3	8.7500	9.3750	10.0000	10.6250	11.250	11.8749	12.5000	15.0000	17.5000
4	11.6667	12.5000	13.3333	14.1666	15.000	15.8332	16.6667	20.0000	23.3333
5	14.5833	15.6250	16.6667	17.7083	18.750	19.7915	20.8333	25.0000	29.1667

Tax-Free vs. Taxable Bonds

Tax-Exempt Yields	Individual Income Brackets (thousands of dollars)																								Corporate Tax Equivalent Yields	
	Not Over $2, 20%	$2 to $4, 22%	$4 to $6, 26%	$6 to $8, 30%	$8 to $10, 34%	$10 to $12, 38%	$12 to $14, 43%	$14 to $16, 47%	$16 to $18, 50%	$18 to $20, 53%	$20 to $22, 56%	$22 to $26, 59%	$26 to $32, 62%	$32 to $38, 65%	$38 to $44, 69%	$44 to $50, 72%	$50 to $60, 75%	$60 to $70, 78%	$70 to $80, 81%	$80 to $90, 84%	$90 to $100, 87%	$100 to $150, 89%	$150 to $200, 90%	Over $200, 91%	A	B
0.75	0.94	0.96	1.01	1.07	1.14	1.21	1.32	1.41	1.50	1.60	1.70	1.83	1.97	2.14	2.42	2.68	3.00	3.41	3.95	4.69	5.77	6.82	7.50	8.33	1.56	0.96
1.00	1.25	1.28	1.35	1.43	1.52	1.61	1.75	1.89	2.00	2.13	2.27	2.44	2.63	2.86	3.23	3.57	4.00	4.55	5.26	6.25	7.69	9.09	10.00	11.11	2.08	1.28
1.10	1.37	1.41	1.49	1.57	1.67	1.77	1.93	2.08	2.20	2.34	2.50	2.68	2.89	3.14	3.55	3.93	4.40	5.00	5.79	6.87	8.46	10.00	11.00	12.22	2.29	1.41
1.25	1.56	1.60	1.69	1.79	1.89	2.02	2.19	2.36	2.50	2.66	2.84	3.05	3.29	3.57	4.03	4.46	5.00	5.68	6.58	7.81	9.62	11.36	12.50	13.89	2.60	1.60
1.40	1.75	1.79	1.89	2.00	2.12	2.26	2.46	2.64	2.80	2.98	3.18	3.41	3.68	4.00	4.52	5.00	5.60	6.36	7.37	8.75	10.77	12.73	14.00	15.56	2.92	1.79
1.50	1.87	1.92	2.03	2.14	2.27	2.42	2.63	2.83	3.00	3.19	3.41	3.66	3.95	4.29	4.84	5.36	6.00	6.82	7.89	9.37	11.54	13.64	15.00	16.67	3.12	1.92
1.60	2.00	2.05	2.16	2.29	2.42	2.58	2.81	3.02	3.20	3.40	3.64	3.90	4.21	4.57	5.16	5.71	6.40	7.27	8.42	10.00	12.31	14.55	16.00	17.78	3.33	2.05
1.75	2.19	2.24	2.36	2.50	2.65	2.82	3.07	3.30	3.50	3.72	3.98	4.27	4.61	5.00	5.65	6.25	7.00	7.95	9.21	10.94	13.46	15.91	17.50	19.44	3.65	2.24
1.80	2.25	2.31	2.43	2.57	2.73	2.90	3.16	3.40	3.60	3.83	4.09	4.39	4.74	5.14	5.81	6.43	7.20	8.18	9.47	11.25	13.85	16.36	18.00	20.00	3.75	2.31
1.90	2.38	2.44	2.57	2.71	2.88	3.06	3.33	3.58	3.80	4.04	4.32	4.63	5.00	5.43	6.13	6.79	7.60	8.64	10.00	11.87	14.62	17.27	19.00	21.11	3.96	2.44
2.00	2.50	2.56	2.70	2.86	3.03	3.23	3.51	3.77	4.00	4.26	4.55	4.88	5.26	5.71	6.45	7.14	8.00	9.09	10.53	12.50	15.38	18.18	20.00	22.22	4.17	2.56
2.10	2.62	2.69	2.84	3.00	3.18	3.39	3.68	3.96	4.20	4.47	4.77	5.12	5.53	6.00	6.77	7.50	8.40	9.55	11.05	13.12	16.15	19.09	21.00	23.33	4.37	2.69
2.25	2.81	2.88	3.04	3.21	3.41	3.63	3.95	4.25	4.50	4.79	5.11	5.49	5.92	6.43	7.26	8.04	9.00	10.23	11.84	14.06	17.31	20.45	22.50	25.00	4.69	2.88
2.40	3.00	3.08	3.24	3.43	3.64	3.87	4.21	4.53	4.80	5.11	5.45	5.85	6.32	6.86	7.74	8.57	9.60	10.91	12.63	15.00	18.46	21.82	24.00	26.67	5.00	3.08
2.50	3.12	3.21	3.38	3.57	3.79	4.03	4.39	4.72	5.00	5.32	5.68	6.10	6.58	7.14	8.06	8.93	10.00	11.36	13.16	15.62	19.23	22.73	25.00	27.78	5.21	3.21
2.60	3.25	3.33	3.51	3.71	3.94	4.19	4.56	4.91	5.20	5.53	5.91	6.34	6.84	7.43	8.39	9.29	10.40	11.82	13.68	16.25	20.00	23.64	26.00	28.89	5.42	3.33
2.75	3.44	3.53	3.72	3.93	4.17	4.44	4.82	5.19	5.50	5.85	6.25	6.71	7.24	7.86	8.87	9.82	11.00	12.50	14.47	17.19	21.15	25.00	27.50	30.56	5.73	3.53
2.80	3.50	3.59	3.78	4.00	4.24	4.52	4.91	5.28	5.60	5.96	6.36	6.83	7.37	8.00	9.03	10.00	11.20	12.73	14.74	17.50	21.54	25.45	28.00	31.11	5.83	3.59
2.90	3.62	3.72	3.92	4.14	4.39	4.68	5.09	5.47	5.80	6.17	6.59	7.07	7.63	8.29	9.35	10.36	11.60	13.18	15.26	18.12	22.31	26.36	29.00	32.22	6.04	3.72
3.00	3.75	3.85	4.05	4.29	4.55	4.84	5.26	5.66	6.00	6.38	6.82	7.32	7.89	8.57	9.68	10.71	12.00	13.64	15.79	18.75	23.08	27.27	30.00	33.33	6.25	3.85
3.10	3.87	3.97	4.19	4.43	4.70	5.00	5.44	5.85	6.20	6.60	7.05	7.56	8.16	8.86	10.00	11.07	12.40	14.09	16.32	19.37	23.85	28.18	31.00	34.44	6.46	3.97
3.25	4.06	4.17	4.39	4.64	4.92	5.24	5.70	6.13	6.50	6.91	7.39	7.93	8.55	9.29	10.48	11.61	13.00	14.77	17.11	20.31	25.00	29.55	32.50	36.11	6.77	4.17
3.50	4.37	4.49	4.73	5.00	5.30	5.65	6.14	6.60	7.00	7.45	7.95	8.54	9.21	10.00	11.29	12.50	14.00	15.91	18.42	21.87	26.92	31.82	35.00	38.89	7.29	4.49
3.75	4.69	4.81	5.07	5.36	5.68	6.05	6.58	7.08	7.50	7.98	8.52	9.15	9.87	10.71	12.10	13.39	15.00	17.05	19.74	23.44	28.85	34.09	37.50	41.67	7.81	4.81
4.00	5.00	5.13	5.41	5.71	6.06	6.45	7.02	7.55	8.00	8.51	9.09	9.76	10.53	11.43	12.90	14.29	16.00	18.18	21.05	25.00	30.77	36.36	40.00	44.44	8.33	5.13
4.25	5.31	5.45	5.74	6.07	6.44	6.85	7.46	8.02	8.50	9.04	9.66	10.37	11.18	12.14	13.71	15.18	17.00	19.32	22.37	26.56	32.69	38.64	42.50	47.22	8.85	5.45

Continued

677

Individual Income Brackets (thousands of dollars)

Tax-Exempt Yields	Not Over $2, 20%	$2 to $4, 22%	$4 to $6, 26%	$6 to $8, 30%	$8 to $10, 34%	$10 to $12, 38%	$12 to $14, 43%	$14 to $16, 47%	$16 to $18, 50%	$18 to $20, 53%	$20 to $22, 56%	$22 to $26, 59%	$26 to $32, 62%	$32 to $38, 65%	$38 to $44, 69%	$44 to $50, 72%	$50 to $60, 75%	$60 to $70, 78%	$70 to $80, 81%	$80 to $90, 84%	$90 to $100, 87%	$100 to $150, 89%	$150 to $200, 90%	Over $200, 91%	Corporate Tax Equivalent Yields A	B
4.50	5.62	5.77	6.08	6.43	6.82	7.26	7.89	8.49	9.00	9.57	10.23	10.98	11.84	12.86	14.52	16.07	18.00	20.45	23.68	28.12	34.62	40.91	45.00	50.00	9.37	5.77
4.75	5.94	6.09	6.42	6.79	7.20	7.66	8.33	8.96	9.50	10.11	10.80	11.59	12.50	13.57	15.32	16.96	19.00	21.59	25.00	29.69	36.54	43.18	47.50	52.78	9.90	6.09
5.00	6.25	6.41	6.76	7.14	7.58	8.06	8.77	9.43	10.00	10.64	11.36	12.20	13.16	14.29	16.13	17.86	20.00	22.73	26.32	31.25	38.46	45.45	50.00	55.56	10.42	6.41

Note: Interest from state and municipal bonds is exempt from federal income taxes. Taxable income is currently subject to tax rates ranging from 20 to 91 percent, as specified in the Internal Revenue Code of 1954. This table gives the approximate yields which taxable bonds must earn in various income brackets to produce, after tax, yields equal to those on tax free bonds yielding 0.75 to 5.00 percent.

This table is computed on the theory that the taxpayer's highest bracket tax rate is applicable to the entire amount of any increase or decrease in his taxable income resulting from a switching from taxable to tax-free bonds, or vice versa.

Figures at top of columns are the taxable income brackets and the tax rates applying to such brackets.

The rates shown are applicable to taxpayers filing single returns. To find the taxable equivalent yield for taxpayers filing joint returns, divide the entire taxable income by 2, and use the income bracket column applicable to the amount thus obtained.

Tax exempt bonds vs. taxable dividends: To make approximate comparison of taxfree yields with dividend income, an individual entitled to the 4 percent dividends received credit should use the bracket rate column which is 4 percentage points (or the one closest thereto) below his top bracket. On joint returns follow the instructions in the paragraph above and then reduce by 4 percentage points to find the appropriate column.

Maximum tax: For taxable years beginning after December 31, 1953, the total tax cannot exceed 87 percent of the net income for the taxable year. For persons using the alternative capital gains tax, the tax ceiling is 87 percent of their ordinary taxable income plus 25 percent of their net long-term gain.

Bond yield equivalent to banks and other corporations: The income tax on banks and other corporations having taxable income in excess of $25,000 is 52 percent, of which 30 percent is the normal tax and 22% the surtax. Figures in Column A are taxable equivalent yields to corporations subject to the 52 percent rate. Corporations having taxable income of $25,000 or less are subject to a normal tax of 30 percent. For taxpayers in this position, approximate taxable bond equivalent yield comparisons may be made by using the column shown for the $6,000 to $8,000 income bracket and the Tax-Exempt Bond Yield column.

Partially tax-exempt governments vs. fully tax-exempt bonds: When held by banks and other corporations having income in excess of $25,000, partially tax-exempt U.S. government bonds are exempt from the normal tax (30 percent), but are subject to the surtax of 22 percent. Column B shows the yields of partially tax-exempt Governments which are equivalent after such 22 percent tax to yields of fully tax-exempt bonds.

Source: The Bond Buyer.

Simple Interest Table
(showing at different rates the interest on $1 from 1 month to 1 year, and on $100 from 1 day to 1 year)

		3%	4%	5%	6%	7%	8%
$1.00	1 month	0.002	0.003	0.004	0.005	0.005	0.006
	2 months	0.005	0.007	0.008	0.010	0.011	0.013
	3 months	0.008	0.011	0.013	0.015	0.017	0.020
	6 months	0.015	0.020	0.025	0.030	0.035	0.040
	12 months	0.030	0.040	0.050	0.060	0.070	0.080
$100.00	1 day	0.008	0.011	0.013	0.016	0.019	0.022
	2 days	0.016	0.022	0.027	0.032	0.038	0.044
	3 days	0.025	0.034	0.041	0.050	0.058	0.067
	4 days	0.033	0.045	0.053	0.066	0.077	0.089
	5 days	0.041	0.056	0.069	0.082	0.097	0.111
	6 days	0.049	0.067	0.083	0.110	0.116	0.133
	1 month	0.250	0.334	0.416	0.500	0.583	0.667
	2 months	0.500	0.667	0.832	1.000	1.166	1.333
	3 months	0.750	1.000	1.250	1.500	1.750	2.000
	6 months	1.500	2.000	2.500	3.000	3.500	4.000
	12 months	3.000	4.000	5.000	6.000	7.000	8.000

Number of Years in Which a Given Amount Will Double
at Various Rates of Interest

Rate	At Simple Interest	At Compound Interest		
		Compounded Yearly	Compunded Semi-annually	Compounded Quarterly
1	100	69.660	69.487	69.237
1½	66.66	46.556	46.382	46.297
2	50.00	35.003	34.830	34.743
2½	40.00	28.071	27.889	27.748
3	33.33	23.450	23.278	23.191
3½	28.57	20.149	19.977	19.980
4	25.00	17.673	17.501	17.415
4½	22.22	15.747	15.576	15.490
5	20.00	14.207	14.035	13.949
5½	18.18	12.942	12.775	12.689
6	16.67	11.896	11.725	11.639
6½	15.38	11.007	10.836	10.750
7	14.29	10.245	10.074	9.966
7½	13.38	9.584	9.414	9.328
8	12.50	9.006	8.837	8.751
8½	11.76	8.497	8.327	8.241
9	11.11	8.043	7.874	7.788
9½	10.52	7.638	7.468	7.383
10	10.00	7.273	7.103	7.018
12	8.34	6.116	5.948	5.862

Income Table

Purchase Price	1%	1½%	2%	2½%	3%	3½%	4%	4½%
10	10	15	20	25	30	35	40	45
15	6.66	10	13.33	16.66	20	23.33	26.66	30
20	5	7.50	10	12.50	15	17.50	20	22.50
22	4.54	6.81	9.09	11.36	13.36	15.90	18.18	20.45
24	4.16	6.25	8.33	10.41	12.50	14.58	16.66	18.75
26	3.84	5.76	7.69	9.61	11.53	13.46	15.38	17.30
28	3.57	5.35	7.14	8.92	10.71	12.50	14.28	16.07
30	3.33	5	6.66	8.33	10	11.66	13.33	15
32	3.12	4.68	6.25	7.81	9.37	10.93	12.50	14.06
34	2.94	4.41	5.88	7.35	8.82	10.29	11.76	13.23
36	2.77	4.16	5.55	6.94	8.33	9.72	11.11	12.50
38	2.63	3.94	5.26	6.57	7.89	9.21	10.52	11.84
40	2.50	3.75	5	6.25	7.50	8.75	10	11.25
42	2.38	3.57	4.76	5.95	7.14	8.33	9.52	10.71
44	2.27	3.40	4.54	5.68	6.81	7.95	9.09	10.22
46	2.17	3.26	4.34	5.43	6.52	7.60	8.69	9.78
48	2.08	3.12	4.16	5.20	6.25	7.29	8.33	9.37
50	2	3	4	5	6	7	8	9
51	1.96	2.94	3.92	4.90	5.88	6.86	7.84	8.82
52	1.92	2.88	3.84	4.80	5.76	6.73	7.60	8.65
53	1.88	2.83	3.77	4.71	5.66	6.60	7.54	8.49
54	1.85	2.77	3.70	4.62	5.55	6.48	7.40	8.33
55	1.81	2.72	3.63	4.54	5.45	6.36	7.27	8.18
56	1.78	2.67	3.57	4.46	5.35	6.23	7.14	8.03
57	1.75	2.63	3.50	4.38	5.26	6.14	7.01	7.89
58	1.72	2.58	3.44	4.31	5.17	6.03	6.89	7.75
59	1.69	2.54	3.38	4.23	5.08	5.93	6.77	7.62
60	1.66	2.50	3.33	4.16	5	5.83	6.66	7.50
61	1.63	2.45	3.27	4.09	4.91	5.73	6.55	7.37
62	1.61	2.41	3.22	4.03	4.83	5.64	6.45	7.25
63	1.58	2.38	3.17	3.96	4.76	5.55	6.34	7.14
64	1.56	2.34	3.12	3.90	4.68	5.46	6.25	7.03
65	1.53	2.30	3.07	3.84	4.61	5.38	6.15	6.92
66	1.51	2.27	3.03	3.78	4.54	5.30	6.06	6.81
67	1.49	2.23	2.98	3.73	4.47	5.22	5.97	6.71
68	1.47	2.20	2.94	3.67	4.41	5.14	5.88	6.61
69	1.44	2.17	2.89	3.62	4.34	5.07	5.79	6.52
70	1.42	2.14	2.85	3.57	4.28	5	5.71	6.42
71	1.40	2.11	2.81	3.52	4.22	4.92	5.63	6.33
72	1.38	2.08	2.77	3.47	4.16	4.86	5.55	6.25
73	1.36	2.05	2.73	3.42	4.10	4.79	5.47	6.16
74	1.35	2.02	2.70	3.37	4.05	4.72	5.40	6.08
75	1.33	2	2.66	3.33	4	4.66	5.33	6
76	1.31	1.97	2.63	3.28	3.94	4.60	5.26	5.92
77	1.29	1.94	2.59	3.24	3.89	4.54	5.19	5.84
78	1.28	1.92	2.56	3.20	3.84	4.48	5.12	5.76

Continued

Purchase Price	1%	1½%	2%	2½%	3%	3½%	4%	4½%
79	1.26	1.89	2.53	3.16	3.79	4.43	5.06	5.69
80	1.25	1.87	2.50	3.12	3.75	4.37	5	5.62
81	1.23	1.85	2.46	3.08	3.70	4.32	4.93	5.55
82	1.21	1.82	2.43	3.04	3.65	4.26	4.87	5.48
83	1.20	1.80	2.40	3.01	3.61	4.21	4.81	5.42
84	1.19	1.78	2.38	2.97	3.57	4.16	4.76	5.35
85	1.17	1.76	2.35	2.94	3.52	4.11	4.70	5.29
86	1.16	1.74	2.32	2.90	3.48	4.06	4.65	5.23
87	1.14	1.72	2.29	2.87	3.44	4.02	4.59	5.17
88	1.13	1.70	2.27	2.84	3.40	3.97	4.54	5.11
89	1.12	1.68	2.24	2.80	3.37	3.93	4.49	5.05
90	1.11	1.66	2.22	2.77	3.33	3.88	4.44	5
91	1.09	1.64	2.19	2.74	3.29	3.84	4.39	4.94
92	1.08	1.63	2.17	2.71	3.26	3.80	4.34	4.89
93	1.07	1.61	2.15	2.68	3.22	3.76	4.30	4.83
94	1.06	1.59	2.12	2.65	3.19	3.72	4.25	4.78
95	1.05	1.57	2.10	2.63	3.15	3.68	4.21	4.73
96	1.04	1.56	2.08	2.60	3.10	3.64	4.16	4.68
97	1.03	1.54	2.06	2.57	3.09	3.60	4.12	4.63
98	1.02	1.53	2.04	2.55	3.06	3.57	4.08	4.59
99	1.01	1.51	2.02	2.52	3.03	3.53	4.04	4.54
100	1	1.50	2	2.50	3	3.50	4	4.50
101	0.99	1.48	1.98	2.47	2.97	3.46	3.96	4.45
102	0.98	1.47	1.96	2.45	2.94	3.43	3.92	4.41
103	0.97	1.45	1.94	2.42	2.91	3.39	3.88	4.36
104	0.96	1.44	1.92	2.40	2.88	3.36	3.84	4.32
105	0.95	1.42	1.90	2.38	2.85	3.33	3.80	4.28
106	0.94	1.41	1.88	2.35	2.83	3.30	3.77	4.24
107	0.93	1.40	1.86	2.33	2.80	3.27	3.73	4.20
108	0.92	1.38	1.845	2.31	2.77	3.24	3.70	4.16
109	0.91	1.37	1.83	2.29	2.75	3.21	3.66	4.12
110	0.90	1.36	1.81	2.27	2.72	3.18	3.63	4.09
111	0.90	1.35	1.80	2.25	2.70	3.15	3.60	4.05
112	0.89	1.33	1.78	2.23	2.67	3.12	3.57	4.01
113	0.88	1.32	1.77	2.21	2.65	3.09	3.54	3.98
114	0.87	1.31	1.75	2.19	2.63	3.07	3.50	3.94
115	0.86	1.30	1.73	2.17	2.60	3.04	3.47	3.91
116	0.86	1.29	1.72	2.15	2.58	3.01	3.44	3.87
117	0.85	1.28	1.70	2.13	2.56	2.99	3.41	3.84
118	0.84	1.27	1.69	2.11	2.54	2.96	3.38	3.81
119	0.84	1.26	1.68	2.10	2.52	2.94	3.36	3.78
120	0.83	1.25	1.66	2.08	2.50	2.91	3.33	3.75
121	0.82	1.23	1.65	2.06	2.47	2.89	3.30	3.71
122	0.81	1.22	1.63	2.04	2.45	2.86	3.27	3.68
123	0.81	1.21	1.62	2.03	2.43	2.84	3.25	3.65
124	0.80	1.20	1.60	2.01	2.41	2.82	3.22	3.62
125	0.80	1.20	1.60	2	2.40	2.80	3.20	3.60

Continued

Purchase Price	1%	1½%	2%	2½%	3%	3½%	4%	4½%
130	0.76	1.15	1.53	1.92	2.30	2.69	3.08	3.46
135	0.74	1.11	1.48	1.85	2.22	2.59	2.96	3.33
140	0.71	1.07	1.42	1.78	2.14	2.50	2.85	3.21
145	0.68	1.03	1.37	1.72	2.06	2.41	2.75	3.10
150	0.66	1	1.33	1.66	2	2.33	2.66	3
155	0.64	0.96	1.29	1.61	1.93	2.25	2.58	2.90
160	0.62	0.93	1.25	1.56	1.87	2.18	2.50	2.81
165	0.60	0.90	1.21	1.51	1.81	2.12	2.42	2.72
170	0.58	0.88	1.17	1.47	1.76	2.95	2.35	2.64
175	0.57	0.85	1.14	1.42	1.71	2	2.28	2.57
180	0.55	0.83	1.11	1.38	1.66	1.94	2.22	2.50
185	0.54	0.81	1.08	1.35	1.62	1.89	2.16	2.43
190	0.52	0.78	1.05	1.31	1.57	1.84	2.10	2.36
195	0.51	0.76	1.02	1.28	1.53	1.79	2.05	2.30
200	0.50	0.75	1	1.25	1.50	1.75	2	2.25
210	0.47	0.71	0.95	1.19	1.42	1.66	1.90	2.14
220	0.45	0.68	0.90	1.13	1.36	1.59	1.81	2.04
225	0.44	0.66	0.88	1.11	1.33	1.55	1.77	2
230	0.43	0.65	0.86	1.08	1.30	1.52	1.73	1.97
240	0.41	0.62	0.83	1.04	1.25	1.45	1.66	1.87
250	0.40	0.60	0.80	1	1.20	1.40	1.60	1.80
275	0.36	0.54	0.72	0.90	1.09	1.27	1.45	1.63
300	0.33	0.50	0.66	0.83	1	1.16	1.33	1.50

Purchase Price	5%	5½%	6%	6½%	7%	7³⁄₁₀%	7½%	8%
10	50	55	60	65	70	73	75	80
15	33.33	36.66	40	43.33	46.66	48.66	50	53.33
20	25	27.50	30	32.50	35	36.50	37.50	40
22	22.72	25	27.27	29.54	31.81	33.18	34.09	36.36
24	20.83	22.91	25	27.08	29.16	30.41	31.25	33.33
26	19.23	21.15	23.07	25	26.92	28.07	28.84	30.76
28	17.85	19.64	21.42	23.21	25	26.07	26.78	28.57
30	16.66	18.33	20	21.66	23.33	24.33	25	26.66
32	15.62	17.18	18.75	20.31	21.87	22.81	23.43	25
34	14.70	16.17	17.64	19.11	20.58	21.47	22.05	23.52
36	13.88	15.27	16.66	18.05	19.44	20.27	20.83	22.22
38	13.15	14.47	15.78	17.10	18.42	19.21	19.73	21.05
40	12.50	13.75	15	16.25	17.50	18.25	18.75	20
42	11.90	13.09	14.28	15.47	16.66	17.38	17.85	19.04
44	11.36	12.50	13.63	14.77	15.90	16.59	17.04	18.18
46	10.86	11.95	14.04	14.13	15.21	15.86	16.30	17.39
48	10.41	11.45	12.50	13.54	14.58	15.20	15.62	16.66
50	10	11	12	13	14	14.60	15	16
51	9.80	10.78	11.76	12.74	13.72	14.31	14.70	15.68
52	9.61	10.57	11.53	12.50	13.46	14.03	14.42	15.38

Continued

Purchase Price	5%	5½%	6%	6½%	7%	7³⁄₁₀%	7½%	8%
53	9.43	10.37	11.32	12.26	13.20	13.77	14.15	15.09
54	9.25	10.18	11.11	12.03	12.96	13.51	13.88	14.81
55	9.09	10	10.90	11.81	12.72	13.27	13.63	14.54
56	8.92	9.82	10.70	11.60	12.50	13.03	13.39	14.28
57	8.77	9.64	10.52	11.40	12.27	12.80	13.15	14.03
58	8.62	9.48	10.34	11.20	12.06	12.58	12.93	13.79
59	8.47	9.32	10.16	11.01	11.86	12.37	12.71	13.55
60	8.33	9.16	10	10.83	11.66	12.16	12.50	13.33
61	8.19	9.01	9.83	10.65	11.47	11.95	12.39	13.11
62	8.06	8.87	9.67	10.48	11.29	11.77	12.09	12.90
63	7.93	8.73	9.52	10.31	11.11	11.58	11.90	12.69
64	7.81	8.59	9.37	10.15	10.93	11.40	11.68	12.50
65	7.69	8.46	9.23	10	10.76	11.23	11.53	12.30
66	7.57	8.33	9.09	9.84	10.60	11.06	11.36	12.12
67	7.46	8.20	8.95	9.70	10.44	10.89	11.19	11.94
68	7.35	8.08	8.82	9.55	10.29	10.73	11.02	11.76
69	7.24	7.97	8.69	9.42	10.14	10.57	10.86	11.59
70	7.14	7.85	8.57	9.28	10	10.42	10.71	11.43
71	7.04	7.74	8.45	9.15	9.85	10.28	10.56	11.26
72	6.94	7.63	8.33	9.02	9.72	10.13	10.41	11.11
73	6.84	7.53	8.21	8.90	9.58	10	10.27	10.95
74	6.75	7.43	8.10	8.78	9.45	9.86	10.13	10.80
75	6.66	7.33	8	8.66	9.33	9.73	10	10.66
76	6.57	7.23	7.89	8.55	9.21	9.60	9.86	10.52
77	6.49	7.14	7.79	8.44	9.09	9.48	9.74	10.38
78	6.41	7.05	7.69	8.33	8.97	9.35	9.61	10.25
79	6.32	6.96	7.59	8.22	8.86	9.24	9.49	10.12
80	6.25	6.87	7.50	8.12	8.75	9.12	9.37	10
81	6.17	6.79	7.40	8.02	8.64	9.01	9.25	9.87
82	6.09	6.70	7.31	7.92	8.53	8.90	9.14	9.75
83	6.02	6.62	7.22	7.83	8.43	8.79	9.03	9.63
84	5.95	6.54	7.14	7.73	8.33	8.69	8.92	9.52
85	5.88	6.47	7.05	7.64	8.23	8.58	8.82	9.41
86	5.81	6.39	6.97	7.55	8.13	8.48	8.72	9.30
87	5.74	6.32	6.89	7.47	8.04	8.39	8.62	9.19
88	5.68	6.25	6.81	7.38	7.94	8.29	8.52	9.09
89	5.61	6.17	6.74	7.30	7.86	8.20	8.42	8.98
90	5.55	6.11	6.66	7.22	7.77	8.11	8.33	8.88
91	5.49	6.04	6.59	7.14	7.69	8.02	8.24	8.79
92	5.43	5.97	6.52	7.06	7.60	7.93	8.15	8.69
93	5.37	5.91	6.45	6.98	7.52	7.84	8.06	8.60
94	5.31	5.85	6.38	6.91	7.44	7.76	7.97	8.51
95	5.26	5.78	6.31	6.84	7.36	7.68	7.89	8.42
96	5.20	5.72	6.25	6.77	7.29	7.60	7.81	8.33
97	5.15	5.67	6.18	6.69	7.21	7.52	7.73	8.24
98	5.10	5.61	6.12	6.63	7.14	7.45	7.65	8.16
99	5.05	5.55	6.06	6.56	7.07	7.37	7.57	8.08
100	5	5.50	6	6.50	7	7.30	7.50	8

Continued

Purchase Price	5%	5½%	6%	6½%	7%	7³⁄₁₀%	7½%	8%
101	4.95	5.44	5.94	6.43	6.93	7.22	7.42	7.92
102	4.90	5.39	5.88	6.37	6.86	7.15	7.35	7.84
103	4.85	5.33	5.82	6.31	6.79	7.08	7.28	7.76
104	4.80	5.28	5.76	6.25	6.72	7.01	7.21	7.69
105	4.76	5.23	5.71	6.19	6.66	6.95	7.14	7.61
106	4.71	5.18	5.66	6.13	6.60	6.88	7.07	7.54
107	4.67	5.14	5.60	6.07	6.54	6.82	7	7.47
108	4.62	5.09	5.55	6.01	6.48	6.75	6.94	7.40
109	4.58	5.04	5.50	5.96	6.42	6.69	6.88	7.33
110	4.54	5	5.45	5.90	6.36	6.63	6.81	7.27
111	4.50	4.95	5.40	5.85	6.30	6.57	6.75	7.20
112	4.46	4.90	5.35	5.80	6.25	6.51	6.69	7.14
113	4.42	4.86	5.30	5.75	6.19	6.46	6.63	7.07
114	4.38	4.82	5.26	5.70	6.14	6.40	6.57	7.01
115	4.35	4.78	5.21	5.65	6.08	6.34	6.52	6.95
116	4.31	4.74	5.17	5.60	6.03	6.29	6.46	6.89
117	4.27	4.70	5.12	5.55	5.98	6.23	6.41	6.83
118	4.23	4.66	5.08	5.50	5.93	6.18	6.35	6.77
119	4.20	4.62	5.04	5.46	5.88	6.13	6.30	6.72
120	4.16	4.58	5	5.41	5.83	6.08	6.25	6.66
121	4.13	4.54	4.95	5.37	5.78	6.03	6.19	6.61
122	4.09	4.50	4.91	5.32	5.73	5.98	6.14	6.55
123	4.06	4.47	4.87	5.28	5.69	5.93	6.09	6.50
124	4.03	4.43	4.83	5.24	5.65	5.88	6.04	6.45
125	4	4.40	4.80	5.20	5.60	5.80	6	6.40
130	3.84	4.23	4.61	5	5.38	5.61	5.76	6.15
135	3.70	4.07	4.44	4.81	5.18	5.33	5.55	5.92
140	3.57	3.92	4.28	4.64	5	5.21	5.35	5.71
145	3.44	3.79	4.13	4.48	4.82	5.03	5.17	5.51
150	3.33	3.66	4	4.33	4.66	4.86	5	5.33
155	3.22	3.54	3.87	4.19	4.51	4.70	4.83	5.16
160	3.12	3.43	3.75	4.06	4.37	4.56	4.68	5
165	3.03	3.33	3.63	3.93	4.24	4.42	4.54	4.84
170	2.94	3.23	3.52	3.82	4.11	4.29	4.41	4.70
175	2.85	3.14	3.42	3.71	4	4.17	4.23	4.57
180	2.77	3.95	3.33	3.61	3.88	4.05	4.16	4.44
185	2.70	2.97	3.24	3.51	3.78	3.94	4.05	4.32
190	2.63	2.89	3.15	3.42	3.68	3.84	3.94	4.21
195	2.56	2.82	3.07	3.33	3.58	3.79	3.84	4.10
200	2.50	2.75	3	3.25	3.50	3.65	3.75	4
210	2.38	2.61	2.85	3.09	3.33	3.47	3.57	3.80
220	2.27	2.50	2.72	2.95	3.18	3.31	3.40	3.63
225	2.22	2.44	2.66	2.88	3.11	3.24	3.33	3.55
230	2.17	2.39	2.60	2.82	3.04	3.17	3.26	3.47
240	2.08	2.29	2.50	2.70	2.91	3.04	3.12	3.33
250	2	2.20	2.40	2.60	2.80	2.92	3	3.20
275	1.81	2	2.18	2.36	2.54	2.65	2.72	2.90
300	1.66	1.83	2	2.16	2.33	2.40	2.50	2.66

Purchase Price	8½%	9%	9½%	10%	11%	12%	15%	20%
10	85	90	95	100	110	120	150	200
15	56.66	60	63.33	66.66	73.13	80	100	133.33
20	42.50	45	47.50	50	55	60	75	100
22	38.63	40.90	43.18	45.45	50	54.54	68.18	90.90
24	35.41	37.50	39.58	41.66	45.83	50	62.50	83.33
26	32.69	34.61	36.53	38.46	42.30	46.15	57.69	76.92
28	30.35	32.14	33.92	35.71	39.28	42.85	53.57	71.42
30	28.33	30	31.66	33.33	36.66	40	50	66.66
32	26.56	28.12	29.68	31.25	34.37	37.50	46.87	62.50
34	25	26.47	27.94	29.41	32.35	35.29	44.11	58.82
36	23.61	25	26.38	27.77	30.55	33.33	41.66	55.55
38	22.36	23.68	25	26.31	28.94	31.57	39.47	52.63
40	21.25	22.50	23.75	25	27.50	30	37.50	50
42	20.23	21.42	22.61	23.80	26.19	28.57	35.71	47.61
44	19.31	20.45	21.59	22.72	25	27.27	34.09	45.45
46	18.47	19.56	20.65	21.73	23.91	26.08	32.60	43.47
48	17.70	18.75	19.79	20.83	22.91	25	31.25	41.66
50	17	18	19	20	22	24	30	40
51	16.66	17.64	18.62	19.60	21.56	23.52	29.41	39.21
52	16.34	17.30	18.26	19.23	21.15	23.07	28.84	38.46
53	16.03	16.98	17.92	18.86	20.75	22.64	28.30	37.73
54	15.74	16.66	17.59	18.51	20.37	22.22	27.77	37.03
55	15.45	16.36	17.27	18.18	20	21.81	27.27	36.36
56	15.17	16.07	16.96	17.85	19.64	21.42	26.78	35.71
57	14.91	15.78	16.66	17.54	19.29	21.05	26.31	35.08
58	14.65	15.51	16.37	17.24	18.96	20.68	25.86	34.48
59	14.40	15.25	16.10	16.94	18.64	20.33	25.42	33.80
60	14.16	15	15.83	16.66	18.33	20	25	33.33
61	13.93	14.75	15.57	16.39	18.03	19.67	24.59	32.78
62	13.70	14.51	15.32	16.12	17.73	19.35	24.19	32.25
63	13.49	14.28	15.07	15.87	17.46	19.04	23.80	31.74
64	13.28	14.06	14.84	15.62	17.18	18.75	23.43	31.28
65	13.07	13.84	14.61	15.38	16.92	18.46	23.07	30.76
66	12.87	13.63	14.39	15.15	16.66	18.18	22.72	30.30
67	12.68	13.43	14.17	14.92	16.41	17.91	22.38	29.85
68	12.50	13.23	13.97	14.70	16.17	17.64	22.05	29.41
69	12.31	13.04	13.76	14.49	15.94	17.39	21.73	28.98
70	12.14	12.85	13.57	14.28	15.71	17.14	21.42	28.57
71	11.97	12.67	13.38	14.08	15.49	16.90	21.12	28.16
72	11.80	12.50	13.19	13.89	15.28	16.66	20.83	27.77
73	11.63	12.32	13.01	13.69	15.06	16.43	20.54	27.39
74	11.49	12.16	12.83	13.51	14.86	16.21	20.27	27.02
75	11.33	12	12.66	13.33	14.66	16	20	26.66
76	11.18	11.84	12.50	13.15	14.47	15.78	19.73	26.31
77	11.03	11.68	12.33	12.98	14.27	15.58	19.48	25.97
78	10.89	11.53	12.17	12.82	14.10	15.38	19.23	25.64
79	10.75	11.39	12.02	12.65	13.92	15.18	18.98	25.31

Continued

Purchase Price	8½%	9%	9½%	10%	11%	12%	15%	20%
80	10.62	11.25	11.87	12.50	13.75	15	18.75	25
81	10.49	11.11	11.72	12.34	13.58	14.81	18.51	24.69
82	10.36	10.97	11.58	12.19	13.41	14.63	18.29	24.39
83	10.24	10.84	11.45	12.04	13.25	14.45	18.04	24.09
84	10.11	10.71	11.30	11.90	13.09	14.28	17.85	23.80
85	10	10.58	11.17	11.76	12.94	14.11	17.64	23.52
86	9.98	10.46	11.04	11.62	12.79	13.95	17.44	23.25
87	9.77	10.34	10.91	11.49	12.64	13.79	17.24	22.98
88	9.65	10.22	10.79	11.36	12.50	13.63	17.04	22.72
89	9.55	10.11	10.67	11.23	12.35	13.48	16.85	22.47
90	9.44	10	10.55	11.11	12.22	13.33	16.66	22.22
91	9.34	9.89	10.44	10.98	12.08	13.18	16.48	21.97
92	9.23	9.78	10.32	10.86	11.95	13.04	16.30	21.73
94	9.04	9.57	10.10	10.63	11.70	12.76	15.95	21.27
95	8.94	9.47	10	10.52	11.57	12.63	15.78	21.05
96	8.85	9.37	9.89	10.41	11.46	12.50	15.72	20.83
97	8.76	9.27	9.79	10.30	11.34	12.37	15.46	20.61
98	8.67	9.18	9.69	10.20	11.22	12.24	15.30	20.40
99	8.58	9.09	9.59	10.10	11.11	12.12	15.15	20.20
100	8.50	9	9.50	10	11	12	15	20
101	8.41	8.91	9.40	9.90	10.89	11.88	14.85	19.80
102	8.33	8.82	9.31	9.80	10.78	11.76	14.709	19.60
103	8.25	8.73	9.22	9.70	10.67	11.65	14.56	19.41
104	8.17	8.65	9.13	9.61	10.57	11.53	14.42	19.23
105	8.09	8.57	9.04	9.52	10.47	11.42	14.28	19.04
106	8.01	8.49	8.96	9.43	10.37	11.32	14.15	18.86
107	7.94	8.41	8.87	9.34	10.28	11.21	14.01	18.69
108	7.87	8.33	8.79	9.25	10.18	11.11	13.88	18.51
109	7.79	8.25	8.71	9.17	10.09	11	13.76	18.34
110	7.72	8.18	8.63	9.09	10	10.90	13.63	18.18
111	7.65	8.10	8.55	9	9.90	10.81	13.51	18.01
112	7.58	8.03	8.48	8.92	9.81	10.71	13.39	17.85
113	7.52	7.96	8.40	8.84	9.73	10.61	13.27	17.69
114	7.45	7.89	8.33	8.77	9.64	10.52	13.15	17.54
115	7.39	7.82	8.26	8.69	9.56	10.43	13.04	17.39
116	7.32	7.75	8.18	8.61	9.48	10.34	12.93	17.24
117	7.26	7.69	8.11	8.54	9.40	10.25	12.83	17.09
118	7.20	7.62	8.05	8.47	9.32	10.16	12.71	16.94
119	7.14	7.56	7.98	8.40	9.24	10.08	12.60	16.80
120	7.08	7.50	7.91	8.33	9.16	10	12.50	16.66
121	7.02	7.43	7.85	8.26	9.09	9.91	12.39	16.52
122	6.96	7.37	7.78	8.19	9.01	9.83	12.29	16.39
123	6.91	7.31	7.72	8.13	8.94	9.76	12.19	16.26
124	6.85	7.66	7.85	8.06	8.87	9.67	12.09	16.12
125	6.80	7.20	7.60	8	8.80	9.60	12	16
130	6.53	6.92	7.30	7.69	8.46	9.23	11.53	15.38
135	6.29	6.66	7.03	7.40	8.14	8.88	11.11	14.81

Continued

Purchase Price	8½%	9%	9½%	10%	11%	12%	15%	20%
140	6.07	6.42	6.78	7.14	7.85	8.57	10.71	14.28
145	5.86	6.20	6.55	6.89	7.58	8.27	10.34	13.79
150	5.66	6	6.33	6.66	7.33	8	10	13.33
155	5.48	5.80	6.12	6.45	7.09	7.74	9.67	12.90
160	5.31	5.62	5.93	6.25	6.87	7.50	9.37	12.50
165	5.15	5.45	5.75	6.06	6.66	7.27	9.09	12.12
170	5	5.29	5.58	5.88	6.47	7.05	8.82	11.76
175	4.85	5.14	5.42	5.71	6.28	6.85	8.57	11.42
180	4.72	5	5.27	5.55	6.11	6.66	8.33	11.11
185	4.59	4.86	5.13	5.40	5.94	6.48	8.10	10.81
190	4.47	4.73	5	5.26	5.78	6.31	7.89	10.52
195	4.35	4.61	4.87	5.13	5.64	6.15	7.69	10.25
200	4.25	4.50	4.75	5	5.50	6	7.50	10
210	4.04	4.28	4.52	4.76	5.23	5.71	7.14	9.52
220	3.86	4.09	4.31	4.54	5	5.45	6.81	9.09
225	3.77	4	4.22	4.44	4.88	5.33	6.66	8.88
230	3.69	3.91	3.90	4.34	4.78	5.21	6.52	8.69
240	3.54	3.75	3.90	4.16	4.58	5	6.25	8.33
250	3.40	3.60	3.80	4	4.40	4.80	6	8
275	3.09	3.27	3.45	3.63	4	4.36	5.45	7.27
300	2.83	3	3.16	3.33	3.66	4	5	6.66

Appendix K: Dictionary References

[1] Federal Reserve System, Board of Governors: *Glossary.*

[2] The Association of Commodity Commission Merchants: *Trading in Commodity Futures.*

[3] Edison Electric Institute: *Glossary of Electric Utility Terms.*

[4] Dun & Bradstreet, Inc.: *How Does Your Business Compare with Others in Your Line?*

[5] American Stock Exchange, Inc.: *Introducing Puts.*

[6] Society of Residential Appraisers: *Real Estate Appraisal Terminology.*

[7] Federal Reserve Bank of New York: *The Story of Checks.*

[8] National Association of Mutual Savings Banks: *This is NAMSB.*

[9] U.S. Department of Commerce: *Selected U.S. Marketing Terms and Definitions.*

[10] National Cash Register Corp.: *Financial Terminology.*

[11] Commodity Research Publication Co.: *Understanding the Cocoa Market.*

[12] Mutual of Omaha: *Terms and Definitions.*

[13] American Marketing Association: *Report on Definitions—SBA Aids, No. 127.*

[14] National Association of Mutual Savings Banks: *Annual Report, 1980.*

[15] American Stock Exchange, Inc.: *The Versatile Option.*

[16] World Bank: *Development Finance Companies.*

[17] National Foreign Trade Council: *Revised American Foreign Trade Definitions.*

[18] Association of American Railroads: *Railway Statistics Manual.*

[19] American Insurance Association: *National Building Code.*

[20] The New York Stock Exchange, Inc.: *The Language of Investing.*

[21] U.S. Office of Management and Budget: *American National Dictionary for Information Processing.*

[22] Mortgage Bankers Association of America: *Mortgages for Retirement and Endowment Funds.*

[23] Investment Company Institute: *Mutual Fund Fact Book, 1979, "Glossary."*

[24] U.S. Postal Service: *Glossary of Postal Terms.*

[25] American Bankers Association: *Trust Fact Book.*

[26] Securities Industry Association: *A Profile of Investment Banking.*

[27] Beresiner, Y. A.: *Collector's Guide to Paper Money.* New York: Stein & Day, 1977.

[28] National Foundation for Consumer Credit: *Using Credit Intelligently.*

[29] New York State Bankers Association: *What Every Woman and Man Should Know about Consumer Banking.*

[30] Wisenberger Investment Companies Service: *Investment Companies, 1979.*

[31] Burroughs Corp.: *Glossary of Financial and Data-Processing Terms.*

[32] American Institute of Banking: *Trust Department Service.*

[33] American Bankers Association: *Bank Fact Book.*

[34] International Business Machines Corp.: *Data Processing Glossary.*

[35] Small Business Administration: *SBIC Financing for Small Business.*

[36] National Science Foundation: *Consequences of Electronic Funds Transfer.*

[37] American Bankers Association: *Glossary of Fiduciary Terms.*

[38] National Cash Register Corp.: *Industrial Accounting Terminology.*

[39] American Institute of Banking: *Savings Banking.*

[40] Federal Reserve System: *Terms.*

[41] International Consumer Credit Association: *How to Use Consumer Credit Wisely.*

Continued

Dictionary References (continued)

[42] International Monetary Fund: *Annual Report on Exchange Arrangements and Exchange Restrictions.*

[43] American Institute of Certified Public Accountants: *Glossary for Accounting Terms.*

[44] American Institute of Banking: *Home Mortgage Lending.*

[45] UNIVAC: *Glossary of Computer Terms.*

[46] Conference Board: *Economic Almanac.*

[47] U.S. Department of Commerce, National Bureau of Standards: *Units and Systems of Weight and Measures, Their Origin, Development, and Present Status.*

[48] American Marketing Association: *A Glossary of Marketing Terms.*

[49] Municipal Finance Officers Association: *Governmental Accounting and Financial Reporting Principles.*

[50] American Institute of Banking: *Principles of Bank Operation.*

[51] United States League of Savings Associations: *Savings and Loan Fact Book.*

[52] Municipal Finance Officers Association: *Public Employee Retirement Administration—Terminology.*

[53] Chamber of Commerce of the U.S.: *Dictionary of Insurance Terms.*

[54] The Hartford: *Glossary—Terms and Phrases Commonly Used in Property, Casualty, and Life Insurance.*

[55] Household Finance Corporation: *General Glossary.*

[56] Employers Insurance of Wausau: *A Dictionary of Insurance Terms.*

[57] Federal Reserve Bank of Atlanta: *Econometric Models.*

[58] American Council of Life Insurance: *Life Insurance Fact Book.*

[59] Institute of Financial Education: *Glossary of Savings Association Terminology.*

[60] U.S. Department of Labor: *Glossary of Currently Used Wage Terms.*

[61] U.S. Department of Commerce: *A Basic Guide to Exporting.*

[62] Realtors National Marketing Institute: *Real Estate Handbook.*

[63] Retail Merchant Association: *Glossary—The Display Manual.*

[64] Association of Bank Holding Companies: *Bank Holding Companies Today.*

[65] Federal Reserve Bank of New York: *Definitions.*

[66] Federal Home Loan Bank Board: *Types of Mortgages-Fact Sheet.*

[67] American Institute of Banking: *Investments.*

[68] Pacific Coast Stock Exchange: *Directory of Securities, Options Stock Analysis.*

[69] Federal Reserve Bank of Boston: *Pandora's Box—Glossary of Terms.*

[70] Tax Foundation, Inc.: *Glossary—Facts and Figures on Government Finance,* 20th edition, 1979.

[71] Federal Reserve Bank of Cleveland: "Terms," *Economic Review,* January 1967

[72] Federal Reserve Bank of St. Louis: "Definitions," *Review.*

[73] U.S. Department of Commerce: *Dictionary of Economical and Statistical Terms.*

[74] Federal Reserve Bank of Chicago: *Definitions.*

[75] Federal Reserve Bank of Philadelphia: *What Are Federal Funds?*

[76] Associated Credit Bureaus, Inc.: *Glossary.*

[77] American Institute of Certified Public Accountants: *Accounting Research and Terminology.*

[78] Federal Reserve Bank of New York: *Consumer Credit Terminology Handbook.*

[79] Federal Reserve Bank of St. Louis: *Review,* December 1980.

[80] Financial Accounting Standards Board: *FASB Discussion Memorandum.*